D1587592

The Letters of Sarah Harriet Burney

THE LETTERS OF

Sarah Harriet Burney

Edited by Lorna J. Clark

The University of Georgia Press *Athens and London*

Drawing of The Adam Doorway to
Dr. Burney's Apartments, Royal Hospital, Chelsea, by John
Claude Nattes, 1812. (Courtesy of Chelsea Library.)

Athens, Georgia 30602

Designed by Louise OFarrell
Set in 10/13 Janson by Integrated Composition Systems
Printed and bound by Braun-Brumfield, Inc.

The paper in this book meets the guidelines for permanence and
durability of the Committee on Production Guidelines for Book
Longevity of the Council on Library Resources.

Printed in the United States of America

01 00 99 98 97 C 5 4 3 2 1

Library of Congress Cataloging in Publication Data

Burney, Sarah Harriet, 1772–1844.
[Correspondence]
The letters of Sarah Harriet Burney / edited by Lorna J. Clark.
p. cm.
Includes bibliographical references and index.
ISBN 0-8203-1746-2 (alk. paper)
1. Burney, Sarah Harriet, 1772–1844—Correspondence.
2. Women novelists, English—19th century—Correspondence.
I. Clark, Lorna J. II. Title.
PR4279.B7Z48 1997
823'.7—dc20 94-49167
[B]

British Library Cataloging in Publication Data available

To W.H.D., H.A.L., M.M.I. Clark

In memoriam

Contents

Preface

Sarah Harriet Burney (1772–1844), British novelist and woman of letters, belonged to a talented family, noted for their achievements in the fields of music, painting, and literature. The father of a remarkable generation, Dr. Charles Burney was a professional musician who managed to win acceptance in fashionable London society through a distinguished reputation as a historian of music. One son, Charles, was a noted Greek scholar; another, James, accompanied Captain Cook on his last two voyages of discovery. Best known of this generation was, of course, the famous novelist, Frances Burney, who wrote the bestseller of 1778, *Evelina*, and who was thereafter lionized by literary circles in London. At her death, she left behind vivid accounts of a long and varied life, which soon established her reputation as one of England's great diarists.

The Burneys have attracted recent scholarly interest, partly on their own merits and partly for the amount of material available. The "scribbling habit" as well as the hoarding habit extended through several generations, so that Joyce Hemlow was able to list more than ten thousand letters from more than a thousand people in her *Catalogue of the Burney Family Correspondence* in 1971, making it one of the richest collections of eighteenth- and nineteenth-century material extant. Despite inroads made by teams of scholars in the last twenty years (added to the twenty-four projected volumes of journals and letters of Frances Burney are four for Charles Burney and one for his fragmentary memoirs), most of the vast riches of this archive remain untapped. Until this edition, there has been little work done on the youngest Burney.

Sarah Harriet Burney was herself a novelist whose literary achievements have been unjustly overlooked. She published five works of fiction between 1796 and 1839 that met with reasonable success; her most popular work, *Traits of Nature* (1812), sold out within three months. Burney was writing at a time when so many women writers flourished, about whom little is known. Her letters are useful in positioning her amidst this silent host; they document her relations with her publisher and her attitudes toward her fiction, her audience, and herself as a writer. They also offer a lively commentary on the contemporary literary scene, including many now forgotten women writers. The range and scope of her reading, as well as her awareness of current literary developments, were impressive; she was also remarkably percipient in recognizing the genius of Jane Austen, for whose work she was an immediate enthusiast.

Her letters offer a unique perspective on the family situation. The youngest child of the second marriage of Charles Burney, and the only daughter to remain unmarried, she had the unenviable task of caring for her father in his later years. In her letters is seen a darker side to the personality of Dr. Burney, which sharpens our image of this eighteenth-century patriarch, hitherto viewed almost exclusively through his own surviving papers or those of his devoted daughter Frances, who undertook to edit, censor, and destroy many of these after her father's death. Distortions have necessarily resulted from the overwhelming dominance of a single viewpoint; the voice of Sarah Harriet Burney should do much to correct this imbalance.

The letters of Sarah Harriet Burney, ninety percent of which are here published for the first time, are also of interest in their own right. She was adept at the art of letter writing and undertook to amuse and entertain her correspondents. A professional writer, she did perhaps her best writing in her letters, which reflect the quiet but heroic struggle of a single woman, relegated to the margins of society, for independence and self-respect. Displaying literary qualities and a lively sense of humor, they provide a fascinating insight into the literary, political, and social life of the day.

Acknowledgments

A work of these proportions would not have been possible without the help of many people. I would first of all like to thank my friend and mentor, Professor G. E. Bentley Jr., an unfailing source of inspiration and support. Several members of the faculty at the University of Toronto read an earlier version of this work and made valuable suggestions: Professors J. R. de J. Jackson, John D. Baird, Brian Corman, Desmond G. Neill, David W. Smith, and John Robson.

The Burney Room at McGill University offered a hospitable venue for research. I am indebted to Professor Lars Troide for kindly granting access to their archives and facilities and for his generous assistance and advice; to Professor Alvaro Ribeiro for his care in reading my manuscript and many useful comments; to Professor Slava Klima for answering queries; and to Dr. Stewart Cooke for help of various kinds. Ever present in spirit was Professor Joyce Hemlow, whose pioneering research continues to inspire generations of scholars and critics in Burney studies.

My research has put me in touch with a Burney fraternity that stretches around the world. Mr. Michael Kassler of Australia drew my attention to a published letter of Sarah Harriet Burney. Dr. Patricia Crown assisted with the notes on the artist, Edward Francesco Burney. Dr. Roger Lonsdale, biographer of Dr. Burney, offered his views on the subject. Two Burney descendants, John R. G. Comyn, Esq., and Mr. Michael Burney-Cumming, welcomed me hospitably into their homes and freely opened up their family archives; Mrs. John Comyn shared her considerable expertise in Burney genealogy.

Initially, I conducted an extensive search by mail for Sarah Harriet Burney letters. The many librarians, curators, dealers, and collectors who conscientiously replied are far too numerous to name, but their helpfulness was indeed appreciated. Especially generous with their enclosures or advice were Abbot Hall, Kendal, Cumbria; County Library of South Glamorgan; Dickens House Museum, London; Forbes Library, Northampton, Massachusetts; Indiana University Libraries; Lynn Museum, King's Lynn, Norfolk; Trinity College, Cambridge; and Winchester College. I am also indebted to the editors of the

Johnsonian News Letter, *Notes and Queries*, and *Country Life* for printing my query and to those who responded.

For specific problems, I drew on the knowledge of many individuals, among whom I would like to thank: Professor D. L. McDonald for information about Gaetano Polidori and the Rossetti family; Mr. Douglas Hewitt, editor of *Notes and Queries*, for identifying a quotation; Mr. Paul Stone for his recommendations of contemporary travel books; Professor Philip H. Highfill Jr., for his research on the musical Tibbs family; Mr. David Gilson for providing evidence of Sarah Harriet Burney's ownership of Jane Austen's novels; Professor J. R. de J. Jackson for suggesting a source; and Professor D. W. Smith for sharing his file on the de Choisieul family. The following individuals and institutions also provided valuable information on various subjects: Professor Betty T. Bennett; Mr. Robert Gittings; Dr. Sarah Lloyd; Mr. Jay Ellis Ransome; Bath Reference Library and Record Office; Music Library, British Library, London; Cornwall County Record Office; Douai Abbey, Upper Woolhampton, Reading; Gloucester County Library; Greater London Record Office; Guildhall Library, London; Hampshire Record Office; Rare Book and Special Collections Library, University of Illinois at Urbana-Champaign; Lewis Walpole Library, Farmington, Connecticut; London Borough of Lewisham; Museum of London; Norfolk Record Office; Public Record Office, London; Central Reference Library, Richmond; Royal Hospital Chelsea; Victoria and Albert Museum, London; Wellcome Institute for the History of Medicine, London; City of Westminster Archives.

In the course of my research, I have been given access to various libraries and collections and am grateful to the custodians and staff for their help. In North America, these include: McGill University Library, Montreal; National Library, Ottawa; John P. Robarts Research Library, Toronto; Columbia University Library, New York; Pierpont Morgan Library, New York; Fales Library, Elmer Holmes Bobst Library, New York University; Beinecke Rare Book and Manuscript Library, Yale University Library, particularly the James Marshall and Marie-Louise Osborn Collection; Sophia Smith Collection (Women's History Archive), Smith College, Northampton, Massachusetts; New York Public Library and the Henry W. and Albert A. Berg Collection located therein. As the Carl H. Pforzheimer Shelley and his Circle Collection of the New York Public Library was temporarily closed when I was there, I was unable to see their manuscripts, but I am grateful to the curator, Mr. Mihai H. Handrea, for arranging for a set of photographs instead, and to Mr. Richard Landon of the Thomas Fisher Rare Book Library, University of Toronto, for taking responsibility for these prints.

I also visited many archives and institutions in Great Britain and benefited from their facilities and resources. I would like to thank the staff of the British Library (Reading Room, Department of Manuscripts, and India Office Library and Records); Bodleian Library; National Libraries of Scotland and Wales; Dr. Williams's Library, London; Guildhall Library, London; Wellcome Institute for the History of Medicine, London; Public Record Office, Greater London Record Office and General Register Office, London; City of Westminster Archives, London; Society of Genealogists, London; Central Reference Library, Richmond; Bath Reference Library; Somerset Record Office; Cheltenham Public Library; Gloucester County Record Office; Cheshire Record Office.

I am grateful also to Mrs. B. J. Peters, the Archivist of Coutts and Co., who allowed me to examine the bank account of Sarah Harriet Burney; to Miss Robin Myers for permitting a search through the Registers of the Worshipful Company of Stationers; and to Lt.-Col. J. J. Kelly, O.B.E., the Curator of the Museum of the Royal Hospital Chelsea, who informed me about the history of the hospital and the records of the military staff.

For permission to publish the letters of Sarah Harriet Burney, grateful acknowledgment is made in the Manuscripts section that follows. Special thanks are due the late Dr. Lola L. Szladits, Curator of the Berg Collection, and Dr. Stephen R. Parks, Curator of the Osborn Collection, who were most generous with the wealth of Burney material collected in their archives, from which they have also given permission to quote. The Keeper of Manuscripts in the British Library has extended the same courtesy for all Burney letters and manuscripts, as has the Keeper of Western Manuscripts in the Bodleian Library for manuscripts of Burneys, Henry Crabb Robinson, and Robert Finch. The Archivist of the John Rylands University Library of Manchester has kindly allowed me to quote from the letters of Marianne Francis to Mrs. Thrale; and Mr. John Creasey, Librarian of Dr. Williams's Library, has permitted me to use extracts from the letters of Henry Crabb Robinson. The Trustees of Dr. Williams's Library, who allowed access to these manuscripts, are not responsible for the selection made, for which the editor waives any copyright.

For providing photographs and giving permission to reproduce them, I am grateful to the National Portrait Gallery, London; the Royal Borough of Kensington and Chelsea Libraries and Arts Service; Trustees of Dr. Williams's Library, London; Fotek, Bath; James Marshall and Marie Louise Osborn Collection, Beinecke Rare Book and Manuscript Library, Yale University; Henry E. Huntington Library and Art Gallery; Division of Special Collections and Archives, Margaret I. King Library, University of Kentucky Library; Department of Rare Books and Special Collections, McGill University Libraries.

Such a project would not have been feasible without generous financial support. Funding for my doctoral research was provided by the Social Sciences and Humanities Research Council of Canada (SSHRCC), the University of Toronto, Massey College, and Trinity College, Toronto. The Associates of the University of Toronto and the Trustees to the Theodora Bosanquet Bursary helped finance my research trips. Visiting fellowships at the Humanities Research Centre in Canberra, Australia, and LaTrobe University in Melbourne, Australia, provided me with time, space, and interested colleagues. Finally, a postdoctoral fellowship from the SSHRCC held at McGill University in Montreal has enabled me to prepare my manuscript for the press.

In the last stages of preparation, the computer expertise of Dr. R. S. Smith and the unsuspected proofreading abilities of my family were essential. Finally, I owe my greatest debt to Richard, William, Sarah, and Jenny, who have accorded Sarah Harriet Burney a room in our house and a place in our lives, while managing to keep me firmly entrenched in the land of the living.

Editor's Introduction

The Manuscripts

The bulk of the Sarah Harriet Burney letters that survive descended with the letters of other Burneys through the family in two lines, as outlined by Joyce Hemlow in her Introduction to *A Catalogue of the Burney Family Correspondence, 1749–1878*.[1] In her will, Mme d'Arblay divided the manuscripts in her possession, leaving those that had belonged to her father to her nephew, Charles Parr Burney, but the whole "of my own immense Mass" to her niece, Charlotte Barrett, stipulating that they should be passed on to Charlotte's son, Richard Barrett.[2]

The bulk of the letters of Charles Burney, together with those of his son, Charles Burney Jr., and grandson, Charles Parr Burney, were acquired by the collector, Dr. James Osborn, and are housed with the James Marshall and Marie-Louise Osborn Collection in the Beinecke Rare Book and Manuscript Library, Yale University. This collection includes 15 letters of Sarah Harriet Burney written from Chelsea Hospital, where she lived with her father for many years. Some are addressed to her half-brother, Charles; others are sent on business of her father's. There are also several letters signed by Dr. Burney but written in the hand of Sarah Harriet, acting as her father's amanuensis.[3]

A large part of the d'Arblay papers bequeathed to Mrs. Barrett, augmented by her own, as well as those of her mother, sister, brother, and daughter, were ultimately acquired by the Henry W. and Albert A. Berg Collection, New York Public Library, in 1941. The majority of the surviving letters of Sarah Harriet (107 of the total 183) are preserved there, which include 16 to Mme d'Arblay, 7 to Charlotte Broome and no less than 58 to Charlotte Barrett, Sarah Harriet's favorite niece and correspondent. The collection also includes 22 letters written to Anna Wilbraham (later Grosvenor), Sarah Harriet's former pupil, which were presumably returned to Mrs. Barrett after Mrs. Grosvenor's death in 1864.

A smaller portion of the Burney-d'Arblay-Barrett papers remained in the family until 1952, when they were sold to the British Museum, now the British Library. Among the 27 letters of Sarah Harriet preserved there is the only surviving record of her correspondence with her mother's family, in this case 11 letters to her mother's married sister, Martha (Allen) Young and her daughter. Another interesting feature of the Barrett Collection are the letters of Maria (Allen) Rishton, Sarah's half-sister, who wrote a long and colorful account of Sarah's departure from the family home in 1798, which includes copies of notes, the originals of which do not survive.

There still remain within the family two private collections, owned by the great-grandsons of the fifth and last Charles Burney. John R. G. Comyn, Esq. and Mr. Michael Burney-Cumming own one and two letters respectively, written by Sarah Harriet Burney to their ancestor, Charles Burney Jr. (1757–1817).

Of Sarah Harriet's letters that have survived outside the family, by far the greatest number are concentrated in Dr. Williams's Library, London, where the diaries, journals, and correspondence of Henry Crabb Robinson are kept.[4] Sarah Harriet met Robinson in Italy in 1829, and corresponded with him from March 1830 until the end of her life; in fact, Robinson's last letter arrived too late and was returned to him shortly after her death in 1844.[5] A few of Sarah Harriet's letters are also preserved in the Bodleian—one to the publisher, Henry Colburn, and three among the papers of Robert Finch, another of her Rome associates.

Stray letters have turned up in various places. In the Ayrton Collection of the British Library are two letters addressed to William Ayrton, the music critic and friend of James Burney. With other miscellaneous autographs in the Pierpont Morgan Library is a letter to her publisher, Henry Colburn. The Fales Library of New York University owns a letter to Caroline Anne Bowles, the provenance of which could not be explained. The New England Hospital Collection of the Women's History Archive at Smith College has a letter to Gaetano Polidori, grandfather to the Rossettis. One of two letters addressed to Elizabeth Carrick in the National Library of Wales was written by S. H. Burney. In an album of letters of "Eminent Women" collected by William Upcott of the London Institution is a letter to Sarah Harriet's doctor, John Ayrton Paris, preserved in the Carl H. Pforzheimer Shelley and His Circle Collection, New York Public Library.

All but one of these are new discoveries; recent acquisitions or items previously overlooked also came to light in collections already known to hold Burney letters,[6] which (added to a letter found in a published source)[7] brings to 15 the number of letters presented in this edition that were not listed in Hemlow's *Catalogue of the Burney Family Correspondence.*

Many of these new finds were the direct result of an extensive search for manuscripts undertaken in 1983–84, in which approximately 2,500 letters were sent to libraries and archives, book dealers, and private collectors in the United Kingdom, Ireland, Europe, the Commonwealth, and elsewhere in the world. Burney descendants were approached, auction records were searched, and advertisements were placed in specialist journals. The results were reassuring rather than dramatic. New Burney letters were discovered in thirty repositories that were not listed in the *Catalogue* of 1971 . However, no hidden cache of Sarah Harriet Burney letters came to light; the very modesty of the results after such an exhaustive search is in itself significant and should establish beyond a reasonable doubt the claims of this edition to completeness. All the letters of Sarah Harriet Burney known to have survived are here presented in their entirety for the first time.

Notes

1. The account given is drawn from Joyce Hemlow, "Introduction," *A Catalogue of the Burney Family Correspondence, 1749–1878,* comp. Joyce Hemlow et al. (New York: New York Public Library, 1971), x–xiii; see also Joyce Hemlow, "Introduction," *The Journals and Letters of Fanny Burney (Madame d'Arblay),* vol. 1, ed. Joyce Hemlow (Oxford: Clarendon Press, 1972), xxv–xxviii.

2. Mme d'Arblay's will, dated 6 Mar. 1839, proved 17 Feb. 1840, is transcribed in *JL,* 12: 976–81.

3. CB to FC, 13 Feb. [1793], CB to CB Jr., 13 May 1808, 6 Nov. 1809, CB to JCH, 4 Mar. 1808, 20 May 1808, 30 May 1808, Osborn; all will soon be published in the forthcoming edition of Charles Burney's letters.

4. Sixteen of the eighteen letters in Dr. Williams's Library have been published in Edith J. Morley, "Sarah Harriet Burney 1770–1844," *Modern Philology* 39 (Nov. 1941): 123–58.

5. HCR, 13–18 Feb. 1844, Diaries.

6. Namely, 3 in the Berg, 1 in the Osborn, 1 in the Bodleian, 1 in the Hyde, and 2 in the Burney-Cumming Collection.

7. Richard Clark, ed. *An Account of the National Anthem Entitled God Save the King!* (London: W. Wright, 1822), 53–54; L. 88.

Locations of the Correspondence of Sarah Harriet Burney

Berg	Henry W. and Albert A. Berg Collection, New York Public Library; Astor, Lenox and Tilden Foundations. 107 letters from, 3 letters to Sarah Harriet Burney.
Barrett	Barrett Collection of Burney Papers, Department of Manuscripts, British Library. 27 letters from, 6 letters to Sarah Harriet Burney.
Dr. Williams'	Dr. Williams's Library, London. 18 letters from Sarah Harriet Burney.
Osborn	James Marshall and Marie-Louise Osborn Collection, Beinecke Rare Book and Manuscript Library, Yale University. 15 letters from, 1 letter to Sarah Harriet Burney.
Bodleian	Department of Western Manuscripts, Bodleian Library, Oxford. 4 letters from Sarah Harriet Burney.
Ayrton	Ayrton Collection, Department of Manuscripts, British Library. 2 letters from Sarah Harriet Burney.
Burney-Cumming	Family Collection in the possession of Mr. Michael Burney-Cumming, Oundle, Peterborough, Northants. 2 letters from Sarah Harriet Burney.
Comyn	Family Collection in the possession of John R. G. Comyn, Esq. Herefordshire. 1 letter from, 2 letters to Sarah Harriet Burney.
Pierpont Morgan	Pierpont Morgan Library, New York. 1 letter from, 1 letter to Sarah Harriet Burney.
Fales	Fales Library, Elmer Holmes Bobst Library, New York University. 1 letter from Sarah Harriet Burney.
Hyde	Hyde Collection, Four Oaks Farm, Somerville, New Jersey. 1 letter from Sarah Harriet Burney.
National Library, Wales	Department of Manuscripts and Records, National Library of Wales, Aberystwyth. 1 letter from Sarah Harriet Burney.
Pforzheimer	Carl H. Pforzheimer Shelley and His Circle Collection, New York Public Library; Astor, Lenox and Tilden Foundations. 1 letter from Sarah Harriet Burney.
Sophia Smith	New England Hospital Collection, Sophia Smith Collection, Smith College, Northampton, Mass. 1 letter from Sarah Harriet Burney.
National Library, Scotland	Department of Manuscripts, National Library of Scotland, Edinburgh. 1 letter to Sarah Harriet Burney.
Northwestern	Northwestern University, Evanston, Illinois. 1 letter to Sarah Harriet Burney.

For permission to publish letters written by Sarah Harriet Burney, the editor wishes to make grateful acknowledgment to the curators or librarians of the institutions listed above, as well as to the owners of private collections, the Viscountess Eccles (Hyde Collection), John R. G. Comyn, Esq., and Mr. Michael Burney-Cumming.

Editorial Principles

This edition aims to present every letter or part of a letter written by Sarah Harriet Burney. The editor has worked from the manuscripts with very few exceptions (LL. 16, 20, 40, 106) where a photograph or photocopy serves as the basis of the text; L. 88 exists only in a printed source. While trying to remain as faithful as possible to the originals, one must acknowledge that some features will inevitably be lost when translated into print. The purpose of the exercise and the needs of the reader must be kept in mind.

The letters appear in chronological order, as closely as that can be determined. A standardized heading precedes each letter, giving the number, the name of the correspondent, and the place and date(s) of writing. Undated letters are placed conjecturally, with square brackets enclosing any part of the date that has been supplied. Where the basis for this choice is not immediately obvious (from the postmark or the endorsement), the evidence is given in a note.

A bibliographical description follows: each letter is classified; its location is given, as well as details of any previous publication. Where present, the address and postmarks are transcribed; additions to the manuscript of contemporary or known authority are described.

The text is transcribed as faithfully and accurately as possible. The date and place of writing, closings, and signatures are positioned as in the original. Where there is a salutation, it is placed flush left. Spacing is imitated where it appears to be significant, as in lists, lines of poetry, or dialogue. Indentation for paragraphing is standardized, however that may be indicated in the manuscript. Postscripts are given at the end of the letter in probable order of composition.

The casual and occasional nature of a letter has been kept in mind in presenting a fairly clean version of the text. A canceled word replaced by another is preserved within angle brackets, but overwritten or deleted letters, word fragments or punctuation are ignored, as are deleted words replaced by the same word, completely illegible cancellations, and inadvertent repetition. Insertions are silently incorporated into the text. Where a change in word order is indicated by numbering, the passage is revised accordingly. Words or letters obscured or lost because of damage are restored conjecturally inside square brackets. Suggested readings are occasionally supplied for passages whose meaning would otherwise be unclear; all editorial interventions are italicized and placed within square brackets. Editorial doubt is indicated by an italicized question mark.

Spelling, grammar, punctuation, and capitalization appear exactly as in the original, but some minor standardizations have unavoidably been introduced. The long "s" has been modernized; the raised superscript used for abbreviations is retained but without its underlying dot. Multiple underlinings are indicated by a double line. The length of dashes has been regularized; the use of a double line (=) to indicate a hyphen is transcribed as an ordinary hyphen. Newly created end-of-line hyphens are set as slanted hyphens. The placement of quotation marks is followed exactly, with one exception. Where the lineation of the printed text is not that of the manuscript, the marks at the beginning of each quoted line in the original have been removed.

As much as possible, the text of the letter is allowed to speak for itself; the editor does not intrude to point out errors or inconsistencies of spelling, grammar, or usage, and is sparing with the use of [*sic*]. Similarly, brief incursions into foreign languages are allowed to stand as they are, uncorrected and untranslated. Editorial silence also applies to other letters in the correspondence; unless otherwise indicated, the reader may assume that these no longer exist. Every effort has been made to identify the people, places, and events discussed in the letters, but where these efforts have been fruitless, the reader will be informed.

Editorial Symbols

[roman]	Words or letters supplied conjecturally	< >	Cancellations
italic	Editorial commentary	A.L.S.	Autograph Letter Signed
?	Editorial doubt	A.L.	Autograph Letter
		P.S.	Postscript

Abbreviations

Persons

AA	Alexander Charles Louis Piochard d'Arblay (1794–1837)
ABt	Arthur Charles Barrett (1816–80)
AY	Arthur Young (1741–1820)
CB	Charles Burney (1726–1814)
CB Jr.	Charles Burney Jr. (1757–1817)
CBF	Charlotte Ann (Burney) Francis (1761–1838)
CBFB	above, after 1 March 1798 Mrs. Broome
CF	Charlotte Francis (1786–1870)
CFBt	above, after 19 June 1807 Mrs. Barrett
CPB	Charles Parr Burney (1785–1864)
EBB	Esther (Burney) Burney (1749–1832)
FB	Frances Burney (1752–1840)
FBA	above, after 28 July 1793 Mme d'Arblay
FC	Frances Anne (Greville) Crewe (1748–1818)
FP	Frances Phillips (1782–1860)
FPR	above, after 13 July 1807 Mrs. Raper
HBt	Henry Barrett (c. 1756–1843)
HCR	Henry Crabb Robinson (1775–1867)
HLT	Hester Lynch (Salusbury) Thrale (1741–1821)
HLTP	above, after 23 July 1784 Mrs. Piozzi
HnBt	Henrietta Hester Barrett (1811–33)
JB	James Burney (1750–1821)
JBt	Julia Charlotte Barrett (1808–64)
JBtT	above, after 2 Aug. 1836 Mrs. Thomas
JCH	Johann Christian Hüttner (c. 1765–1847)
MAR	Maria (Allen) Rishton (1751–1820)
M. d'A	Alexandre-Jean-Baptiste Piochard d'Arblay (1754–1818)
MF	Marianne Francis (1790–1832)
SBP	Susanna Elizabeth (Burney) Phillips (1755–1800)
SHB	Sarah Harriet Burney (1772–1844)

Short Titles and Abbreviations

Alumni Cantab.	J. A. Venn, *Alumni Cantabrigienses: A Biographical List of All Known Students, Graduates and Holders of Office at the University of Cambridge, from the Earliest Times to 1900*, Pt. 2, 6 vols. (Cambridge: Cambridge University Press, 1940–54).
Alumni Oxon.	Joseph Foster, *Alumni Oxonienses: The Members of the University of Oxford, 1715–1886*, 4 vols. (Oxford: Oxford University Press, 1887–88).
"Appendix," *AR*	"Appendix to Chronicle," *Annual Register, or A View of the History, Politics, and Literature . . .* [1792–1844].
Bénézit	Emmanuel Bénézit, *Dictionnaire critique et documentaire des peintres, sculpteurs, dessinateurs et graveurs*, 3rd ed., 10 vols. (Paris: Librairie Gründ, 1976).
Bryan's	*Bryan's Dictionary of Painters and Engravers*, ed. George C. Williamson, 4th ed., 5 vols. (London: George Bell and Sons, 1903–5).
Burke	Sir John Bernard Burke, *A Genealogical and Heraldic Dictionary of the Peerage and Baronetage, the Privy Council, Knightage and Companionage*, ed. Ashworth P. Burke, 63rd ed. (London: Harrison & Sons, 1901).
Burke, *LG*	Sir John Bernard Burke, *A Genealogical and Heraldic History of the Landed Gentry of Great Britain*, ed. A. C. Fox-Davies, 12th ed. (London: Harrison & Sons, 1914).
Burke, *DLG*	John and Sir John Bernard Burke, *A Genealogical and Heraldic Dictionary of the Landed Gentry of Great Britain & Ireland*, 3 vols. (London: Henry Colburn, 1849).
Burke, *Commoners*	John Burke, *A Genealogical and Heraldic History of the Commoners of Great Britain and Ireland*, 4 vols. (London: Henry Colburn, 1833–38).
Burke, *Extinct*	John and Sir John Bernard Burke, *A Genealogical and Heraldic History of the Extinct and Dormant Baronetcies of England, Ireland, and Scotland*, 2nd ed. (London: John Russell Smith, 1844).
Catalogue	*A Catalogue of the Burney Family Correspondence, 1749–1878*, comp. Joyce Hemlow, with Jeanne M. Burgess and Althea Douglas (New York: New York Public Library, 1971).
CB, *Memoirs*	*Memoirs of Dr. Charles Burney, 1726–1769*, ed. Slava Klima, Garry Bowers, and Kerry S. Grant (Lincoln: University of Nebraska Press, 1988).
Cokayne	G. E. C[okayne], *Complete Baronetage*, 6 vols. (Exeter: William Pollard, 1900–1909).
Colburn papers	Papers of the Henry Colburn publishing firm (1806–35), Richard

	Bentley and Son Papers, Rare Book and Special Collections Library, University of Illinois at Urbana-Champaign.
Coutts ledgers	Bank account of Sarah Harriet Burney, 10 July 1801–18 Jan. 1845, Coutts & Co., London.
DL	*Diary and Letters of Madame d'Arblay (1778–1840)*, ed. Austin Dobson, 6 vols. (London: Macmillan, 1904–5).
DAB	*Dictionary of American Biography*, ed. Allen Johnson et al. (1928–36); rpt. in 11 vols. (New York: Charles Scribner's Sons, [1946?–58]).
Dean	Captain C. G. T. Dean, *The Royal Hospital Chelsea* (London: Hutchinson, 1950).
DNB	*The Dictionary of National Biography to 1901*, ed. Sir Leslie Stephen and Sir Sidney Lee, 22 vols. (1885–1901; rpt., London: Oxford University Press, 1963–64).
ED	*The Early Diary of Frances Burney, 1768–1778*, ed. Annie Raine Ellis, 2 vols. (London: G. Bell and Sons, 1913).
EJL	*The Early Journals and Letters of Fanny Burney*, ed. Lars E. Troide et al. (Oxford: Clarendon Press, 1988–).
Finch, Diaries	Robert Finch, Nov. 1829–May 1830, Diaries, Bodleian MS. Finch, e. 18–19.
Foster	Joseph Foster, *The Peerage, Baronetage and Knightage of the British Empire for 1880* (Westminster: Nichols and Sons, n.d.).
Gazley	John G. Gazley, *The Life of Arthur Young, 1741–1820* (Philadelphia: American Philosophical Society, 1973).
Gibbs	G. E. C[okayne], *The Complete Peerage of England Scotland Ireland Great Britain and the United Kingdom Extant Extinct or Dormant*, ed. the Hon. Vicary Gibbs et al., rev. ed., 13 vols. (London: St. Catherine Press, 1910–59).
GM	*The Gentleman's Magazine* (1731–1868).
GRO	General Register Office, St. Catherine's House, London.
HFB	Joyce Hemlow, *The History of Fanny Burney* (Oxford: Clarendon Press, 1958).
HCR, *Reminiscences*	*Diary, Reminiscences, and Correspondence of Henry Crabb Robinson*, ed. Thomas Sadler, 3 vols. (London: Macmillan, 1869).
HCR, Travel Journals, Diaries	Henry Crabb Robinson, 25 Nov. 1829–7 Oct. 1831, Travel Journals; 14 Oct. 1831–18 Feb. 1844, Diaries; Dr. Williams's Library, London.
Highfill	Philip H. Highfill Jr., Kalman A. Burnim, and Edward A. Langhans, *A Biographical Dictionary of Actors, Actresses, Musicians, Dancers, Managers & Other Stage Personnel in London, 1660–1800*, 16 vols. (Carbondale: Southern Illinois University Press, 1973–93).

Hodson	Major V. C. P. Hodson, *List of the Officers of the Bengal Army, 1758–1834*, Pt. 1 (London: Constable, 1927).
IGI	International Genealogical Index.
India Office Library	India Office Library and Records, British Library.
JL	*The Journals and Letters of Fanny Burney (Madame d'Arblay)*, ed. Joyce Hemlow et al., 12 vols. (Oxford: Clarendon Press, 1972–84).
Johnson	Edgar Johnson, *Sir Walter Scott: The Great Unknown*, 2 vols. (New York: Macmillan, 1970).
Lodge	Edmund Lodge, *The Peerage of the British Empire*, 6th ed. (London: Saunders and Otley, 1837).
London Stage	*The London Stage, 1660–1800*, ed. Emmett L. Avery et al., 5 pts. in 11 vols. (Carbondale: Southern Illinois University Press, 1960–68).
Lonsdale	Roger Lonsdale, *Dr. Charles Burney: A Literary Biography* (Oxford: Clarendon Press, 1965).
Manwaring	G. E. Manwaring, *My Friend the Admiral: The Life, Letters, and Journals of Rear-Admiral James Burney, F.R.S.* (London: George Routledge & Sons, 1931).
Marshall	John Marshall, *Royal Naval Biography*, 4 vols. in 8 (London: Longman, Hurst, Rees, Orme, and Brown, 1823–35); *Supplement*, pts. 1, 2, and 3 (London: Longman, Rees, Orme, Brown, and Green, 1827–29).
Memoirs	*Memoirs of Doctor Burney, Arranged from His Own Manuscripts, from Family Papers, and from Personal Recollections*, by his daughter, Madame d'Arblay, 3 vols. (London: Edward Moxon, 1832).
Morley	Edith J. Morley, "Sarah Harriet Burney, 1770–1844," *Modern Philology* 39 (Nov. 1941): 123–58.
Munk's Roll	William Munk, *The Roll of the Royal College of Physicians of London*, 2nd ed., 3 vols. (London: Printed by the College, 1878).
Misc. Lib.	Leigh and Sotheby, *A Catalogue of the Miscellaneous Library of the late Charles Burney . . . which will be sold by auction . . .* (9 June 1814).
Namier & Brooke	Sir Lewis Namier and John Brooke, *The House of Commons, 1754–1790*, 3 vols. (London: HMSO, 1964).
New Grove	*The New Grove Dictionary of Music and Musicians*, ed. Stanley Sadie, 20 vols. (London: Macmillan, 1980).
Nichols, *Anecdotes*	John Nichols, *Literary Anecdotes of the Eighteenth Century*, 9 vols. (London: Printed for the Author, 1812–15).
Nichols, *Illustrations*	John Nichols, *Illustrations of the Literary History of the Eighteenth Century*, 8 vols. (London: Printed for the Author, 1817–58).

Nobiliaire universel	Nicolas Viton de Saint-Allais, *Nobiliaire universel de France ou Recueil général des généalogies historiques des maisons nobles de ce royaume*, 21 vols. (Paris, 1872–77).
OED	*The Oxford English Dictionary, being a corrected re-issue . . . of A New English Dictionary on Historical Principles*, ed. Sir James A. H. Murray et al., 13 vols. (1933; rpt., Oxford: Clarendon Press, 1978).
Ormerod	George Ormerod, *The History of the County Palatine and City of Chester*, 2nd ed., ed. Thomas Helsby, 3 vols. (London: George Routledge, 1882).
P.C.C.	Prerogative Court of Canterbury.
PRO	Public Record Office, Chancery Lane, London.
Scholes	Percy A. Scholes, *The Great Dr. Burney: His Life His Travels His Works His Family and His Friends*, 2 vols. (London: Oxford University Press, 1948).
Scots Peerage	*The Scots Peerage*, ed. Sir James Balfour Paul, 9 vols. (Edinburgh: David Douglas, 1904–14).
Shaw	William A. Shaw, *The Knights of England*, 2 vols. (London: Central Chancery of the Orders of Knighthood, 1906).
Stenton	Michael Stenton, *Who's Who of British Members of Parliament*, vol. 1 (Hassocks, Sussex: Harvester Press, 1976).
Survey of London	*The Survey of London* (London: London County Council, 1900–).
Thième-Becker	Ulrich Thième, Felix Becker et al., *Allgemeines Lexikon der bildenden Künstler von der Antike bis zur Gegenwart*, 37 vols. (Leipzig: Verlag von Wilhelm Engelmann and Verlag von E. A. Seemann, 1907–50).
Thorne	R. G. Thorne, *The House of Commons 1790–1820*, 5 vols. (London: History of Parliament Trust, 1986).
Times	*The Times* (1792–1844).
Walpole	*The Yale Edition of Horace Walpole's Correspondence*, ed. W. S. Lewis et al., 48 vols. (New Haven: Yale University Press, 1937–83).
Westminsters	*The Record of Old Westminsters: A Biographical List of all those who are known to have been educated at Westminster School from the earliest times to 1927*, comp. G. F. Russell Barker and Alan H. Stenning, 2 vols. (London: Chiswick Press, 1928).
"Worcester Mem."	"Memoranda of the Burney Family, 1603–1845," TS, Osborn Collection, Yale University.
Young	*The Autobiography of Arthur Young with Selections from his Correspondence*, ed. M. Betham-Edwards (London: Smith, Elder, 1898).

Biographical Notes on the Burney Family

These biographical notes on the Burney family abridge, supplement, and revise those provided in *The Journals and Letters of Fanny Burney*, ed. Joyce Hemlow, vol. 1 (Oxford: Clarendon Press, 1972), lxix–lxxv, and *The Early Journals and Letters of Fanny Burney*, ed. Lars E. Troide, vol. 1 (Oxford: Clarendon Press, 1988), xlii–xlvi.

CHARLES BURNEY (1726–1814), Mus. D. (1769), F.R.S. (1773), appointed organist at the Royal Hospital, Chelsea (18 Dec. 1783). For his biography see Percy A. Scholes, *The Great Dr. Burney* (1948) and Roger Lonsdale, *Dr. Charles Burney* (1965). His fragmentary memoirs have been edited by Slava Klima, Garry Bowers, and Kerry S. Grant, as *Memoirs of Dr. Charles Burney* (1988). The first volume of *The Letters of Dr. Charles Burney*, ed. Alvaro Ribeiro, SJ (Oxford: Clarendon Press, 1991–) has appeared.

CHARLES BURNEY married (1) on 25 June 1749 Esther Sleepe (1725–62).
The surviving children of the marriage were:

1. ESTHER BURNEY (1749–1832), who married 20 Sept. 1770 her cousin Charles Rousseau Burney (1747–1819), harpsichordist and music teacher (see below).
   Their children were:
   1. Hannah Maria or "Marianne" (1772–1856), who married 30 Oct. 1800 Antoine Bourdois de Bréviande (c. 1761–1806).
   2. Richard Allen (1773–1836), B.A. Oxford (1799), M.A. (1807); Rector of Rimpton, Somerset (1802); Master of St. Mary Magdalen Hospital, Winchester (1804); Curate of Brightswell, Berkshire (1815–31). He married on 10 Oct. 1811 Elizabeth Layton Williams (1786–1862).
      Their children were:
      1. Henry (1814–93)

   2. Clara (1818–59)
   3. Cecilia Mary (1823–39)
   4. Emma (1826–post 1901)
3. Charles Crisp (1774–91).
4. Frances or "Fanny" (1776–1828).
5. Sophia Elizabeth (1777–1856).
6. Henry (d. inf. 1781).
7. Cecilia Charlotte Esther (1788–1821).
8. Amelia Maria (1792–1868).

2. JAMES BURNEY (1750–1821), 2nd Lieutenant, R.N. (1772), Commander (1780), Captain (1782), retired on half-pay (1785), Rear-Admiral (1821); F.R.S. (1815). For his biography, see G. E. Manwaring, *My Friend the Admiral* (1931). He married on 6 Sept. 1785 Sarah Payne (1759–1832), daughter of Thomas Payne (1719–99), the bookseller.
Their children were:
   1. Catherine (1786–93).
   2. Martin Charles (1788–1852), a solicitor. He married on 18 April 1816 Rebecca Norton (c. 1799–1868).
   3. Sarah (1796–post Dec. 1868) who married 14 April 1821 her (illegitimate) cousin John Payne (c. 1796–1880).

3. FRANCES BURNEY (1752–1840), novelist and journalist, for whose life, see Joyce Hemlow, *The History of Fanny Burney* (1958), and Margaret Anne Doody, *Frances Burney* (1988). Her journals and letters have been edited by Joyce Hemlow et al. in *The Journals and Letters of Fanny Burney (Madame d'Arblay)* (1972–84) and by Lars Troide et al. in the ongoing *The Early Journals and Letters of Fanny Burney* (1988–). On 28 July 1793, she married Alexandre-Jean-Baptiste Piochard d'Arblay (1754–1818), comte d'Arblay (1815).
Their only child was:
   1. Alexander Charles Louis Piochard d'Arblay (1794–1837), B.A. (Cambridge) 1818, M.A. 1821; perpetual curate of Camden Town (1824–37); Minister of Chapel of St. Etheldreda, Ely Place, Holburn (1836).

4. SUSANNA ELIZABETH BURNEY (1755–1800), married 10 Jan. 1782 Molesworth Phillips (1755–1832), 2nd Lieutenant, Royal Marines (1776), Lieutenant-Colonel (1798).
Their children were:

1. Frances (1782–1860), who married 13 July 1807 Charles Chamier Raper (1777–1842) of the War Office.
   Their only child was:
   1. Catherine Minette (1808–82)
2. Charles Norbury (1785–1814), B.A. Trinity College, Dublin (1806).
3. John William James (1791–1832).

5. CHARLES BURNEY JR. (1757–1817), M.A. Aberdeen (1781); F.R.S. (1802), D.D. Lambeth (1812). Schoolmaster, classical scholar and divine. He kept a school at Hammersmith (1786–93) and later at Greenwich (1793–1813). He married 24 June 1783 Sarah Rose, or "Rosette" (1759–1821), daughter of Dr. William Rose (1719–86).
   Their only child was:
   1. Charles Parr (1785–1864), B.A. Oxford (1808), D.D. (1822); he succeeded his father at the Greenwich School (1813–34) and later became Archdeacon of St. Albans (1840). He married 24 Dec. 1810 Frances Bentley Young (c. 1792–1878).
      Their children were:
      1. Frances Anne (1812–60)
      2. Rosetta d'Arblay (1814–1910)
      3. Charles Edward (1815–1907)
      4. Edward Kaye (1817–80)
      5. Susan Sabrina (1818–74)
      6. Ellen Hodgson (1820–1911)

6. CHARLOTTE ANN BURNEY (1761–1838), who married (1) 11 Feb. 1786 Clement Francis (c. 1744–92) of Aylsham, Norfolk, a surgeon, and medical officer in the East India Company (1778–85).
   The children of this marriage were:
   1. Charlotte (1786–1870), Sarah's favourite correspondent, who married 19 June 1807 Henry Barrett (c. 1756–1843).
      The Barrett children were:
      1. Julia Charlotte (1808–64), who married (1) Aug. 1836 James Thomas (d. 6 Jan. 1840), of the Madras Civil Service.
         Their children were:
         1. Henrietta Anne (b. 8 June 1837)
         2. James Cambridge (b. 3 Feb. 1839)

         Julia married (2) 5 Nov. 1842 Charles Maitland (c. 1815–66).
         The only child of this marriage was:

1. Julia Caroline (1843–90)
2. Henrietta Hester (1811–33), died in Italy.
3. Richard Arthur Francis or "Dick" (1812–81), B.A. Cambridge (1835), M.A. (1838), Fellow of King's College (1834–59); Rector of Stower Provost with Todbere, Dorset (1858–81).
4. Henry John Richard (1814–29).
5. Arthur Charles (1816–80), B.A. Cambridge (1838), M.A. (1841); private tutor at Cambridge, schoolmaster, author. He married 5 April 1849 Hannah Poole (fl. 1828–54) and had five sons.

2. Marianne (1790–1832).
3. Clement Robert (1792–1829), B.A. Cambridge (1817), M.A. (1820); Fellow of Caius College (1820–29); Dean (1821–22); Bursar (1827–28); died of tuberculosis.

CHARLOTTE ANN married (2) 1 March 1798 Ralph Broome (1742–1805) formerly of India, author of *Simkin's Letters* (1789).
The only child of this marriage was:
1. Ralph or "Dolph" (1801–17).

CHARLES BURNEY married (2) on 2 Oct. 1767 Elizabeth née Allen (1728–96), widow of Stephen Allen (1725–63), merchant of King's Lynn, Norfolk.
The surviving children of this second marriage were:

1. RICHARD THOMAS BURNEY (1768–1808), who was in India by 1787 and became Headmaster of the Orphan School at Kidderpore (1795–1808). He married in Calcutta on 9 Nov. 1787 Jane Ross (1772–1842) and had a large family; see Walter K. Firminger, "Madame D'Arblay and Calcutta," *Bengal Past and Present*, 9 (July-Dec. 1914), 244–49.
The children of this marriage who came back to England were:
   1. Richard (1790–1845), joined East India Company (1807); on furlough in England (1817–22), took B.A. Cambridge (1822), M.A. (1839); returned to India, Captain, Bengal Army (1824), resigned (1825); he came back to England in 1838 and lived with his sister Jane Caroline at Cunningham Place, St. John's Wood, London. He endowed the Burney Prize at Cambridge.
   2. Henry (1792–1845), joined East India Company (1807), Lieutenant-Colonel, Bengal Army (1834); Political Agent to Siamese States (1825) and Resident to Court of Ava, Burma (1829). See Daniel G. E. Hall, *Henry Burney: A Political Biography* (1974). He married on 30 June 1818 Janet Bannerman (c. 1797–1865).

The surviving children of this marriage were:

1. Henry Bannerman (b. 30 June 1819); B.A. Oxford (1841)
2. Janet Phillips (1820–63)
3. Susan Allen (1823–95)
4. Charles James (1833–51)
5. Richard Thomas (b. 2 May 1835)
6. Frederick William (1837–57)
7. Alexander d'Arblay Burney (1839–81)
8. Robert Payne (1843–64)

3. James Christian (1797–post 1828), joined East India Company (1819), Lieutenant, Bengal Army (1823), retired (1826).
4. John (1799–1837), joined East India Company (1819), Lieutenant, Bengal Army (1823), retired (1828).
5. Jane Caroline (1802–71), who returned to England in 1817 with her brother, Richard, and was chaperoned by Esther Burney. She went back to India, but eventually returned to England, and after 1838, lived with her brother, Richard, at Cunningham Place. She would ultimately inherit Sarah Harriet Burney's property.
6. Sarah Ross (1808–91), who returned to England in 1817 with her brother, Richard, but seems to have gone back to India.

2. SARAH HARRIET BURNEY (1772–1844), novelist.

Elizabeth (Allen) Burney's children by her first marriage were:

1. MARIA ALLEN (1751–1820), who married 16 May 1772 Martin Folkes Rishton (c. 1747–1820).

2. STEPHEN ALLEN (1755–1847), matriculated at Cambridge (1771); he married at Gretna Green on 28 Oct. 1772 Susanna Sharpin (1755–1816). Vicar of Dereham (1789–1800), of St. Margaret's, King's Lynn (c. 1797–1847), Rector of Haslingfield, Cambs. (1800–47).

   The children of this marriage included:

   1. Stephen (c. 1775–1855).
   2. Elizabeth Mary (1779–1801).
   3. Mary Susanna (1780–post 1843).
   4. Susanna (1785–1820).
   5. Sarah (1790–post 1843).
   6. William Maxey (1792–1865) curate of Wimbotsham and of Fordham, Norfolk. He married Lucy Elizabeth Bell (c. 1791–1841).

3. ELIZABETH or "Bessie" ALLEN (1761–c. 1826), who married (1) on 12 Oct. 1777 Samuel Meeke (fl. 1777–1802) and (2) post 1802 a second husband.

RICHARD BURNEY (1723–92), of Barborne Lodge, Worcester, elder brother of CHARLES BURNEY, married c. 1745 Elizabeth Humphries (c. 1720–71). *Their surviving children were:*

1. Charles Rousseau (1747–1819), harpsichordist and music teacher, who married 20 Sept. 1770 his first cousin, Esther Burney (above).
2. Ann or "Nancy" (1749–1819), married on 27 Jan. 1781 the Rev. John Hawkins (d. 19 June 1804), Rector of Hinton Ampner, Hants. (1789), of Halstead, Essex (1791), and Master of Magdalen Hospital, near Winchester (c. 1796).
3. Richard Gustavus (1751–90), music and dancing master.
4. James Adolphus (1753–98).
5. Elizabeth Warren, or "Blue" (1755–1832).
6. Rebecca (1758–1835), who married 24 March 1788 William Sandford (1759–1823), a surgeon.
7. Edward Francesco, or "Inny" (1760–1848), an artist.
8. Thomas Frederick (1765–85).

General Introduction

The Life

Sarah Harriet Burney was born on 29 August 1772 and baptized (as Sarah Harriotte) on 25 September in the Chapel of St. Nicholas, King's Lynn, Norfolk.[1] She was the youngest child of the second marriage, in 1767, of Charles Burney with Elizabeth Allen, widow of a merchant of King's Lynn. With a brother, Richard Thomas, four years her senior, she had numerous half-brothers and half-sisters much older than she. Two of the three children from her mother's first marriage married in the year of her birth. A generation also separated Sarah Harriet from the older members of Dr. Burney's first family of six. In fact, she was born in the same year as her niece, the eldest child of Dr. Burney's daughter, Esther. Approximately ten years separated Sarah from the youngest of these half-siblings, Charlotte Burney, to whom she was closest in affection: "I loved her warmly & fondly,—perhaps, the best of any of my family."[2]

It seems likely that Sarah Harriet spent her earliest years in King's Lynn, judging from passing references in the journal of the young Fanny Burney[3] and the letters of Maria Rishton.[4] In 1775, however, she seems to have joined her father's household in London, as Fanny reported, "Little Sally is come Home, & is one of the most innocent, artless, *queer* little things you ever saw, & all together, she is a very sweet, & very engaging Child."[5] The impression she made at this time was not altogether favorable, one of her father's friends describing her as a "little thing buried under a great perriwig, that turned out to be Queerness."[6] Sarah Harriet was never noted for her beauty, her one redeeming feature being luxuriant hair. She herself would later believe that "I was better looking as an old woman, than I had ever been as a young one. . . . I never had any bloom. My nose was often red; my teeth were early injured,—and except fine hair, I had not a single beauty to lose" (L. 164).

The family household she joined in St. Martin's Street was a lively one. These are the years, documented in the *Early Journals and Letters of Fanny Burney*, of musical evenings attended by various celebrities and the lionization (after the publication of *Evelina* in 1778) of Fanny Burney among the literati, some of whom paid visits to the house. The young Sarah seems to have had no formal education until 1781 when she accompanied her elder brother Richard to Switzerland. There she was placed under the care of Marie-Anne-Louise Cuénod at Vevey, and probably returned with her brother in 1783.[7] This formative experience appears to have influenced her considerably, although her half-sister Fanny's remark in 1786 that "she has been so much of her time abroad that she forgot her English, and has not yet recovered it sufficiently,"[8] is surely hyperbole. Queen Charlotte would ask after Sarah in 1787 as "*the little Swiss Girl.*"[9] In 1793, when pleased with the surrounding countryside, Sarah searches back through her memory for a comparison: "This place is by far the most beautiful of any I ever saw in England, & I was too young to remember any more beautiful even in Switzerland" (L. 3). All her life she retained a fluency in the French language and a sympathy with the culture; she moved with ease among the émigrés at Lymington (L. 68), and expressed a preference for French society: "I am never happy without some dear little french liaison" (L. 31).

In the decade of the 1780s, Dr. Burney was at the peak of his professional career and highly regarded as a teacher of music. His literary reputation was established by the publication of *A General History of Music* (1776–89) and his acceptance into London society indicated by his election to The Club (1784). His appointment as Organist at Chelsea Hospital when he was fifty-seven (in 1783) would ease his later years, and in July 1787, he moved into an apartment there with his wife and youngest daughter, Sarah.[10]

Sarah Harriet figures only briefly in the surviving letters of her busy father at this time, for instance, when she "Grumbles, & scolds sorely at the early & late hours wch business & other engagem^{ts} oblige me to keep."[11] A "giddy, thoughtless, wild 14,"[12] she is described as a young girl of robust health & spirits: "Sally never was stouter or more riotous than at present."[13] Dr. Burney remarks humorously that "she is fat, ragged and saucy,"[14] and asks to bring "The Snip" along to visit her famous half-sister Fanny at Court.[15]

As the youngest daughter and the only one left at home after 1786, the year that Charlotte married and Fanny was appointed to the Queen's household, Sarah Harriet would often accompany her mother on outings with family and friends.[16] Many of her earliest letters (from 1792 to 1796) are addressed to her mother's sister, Mrs. Arthur Young, or to Mary Young, her daughter. While this may be the chance preservation of time, it may well be that her connection to this family was closer before her mother's death in 1796.

It is clear from Charles Burney's letters that Mrs. Burney was an invalid for years before she died and that "for some time past she [*Sarah*] has been as closely confined as a monthly Nurse."[17] Sarah Harriet was at her post when the end came and was not included in Mrs. Burney's last considerate injunctions to spare her husband's sleep should she die during the night.[18] What is omitted in Sarah Harriet's letters can be as important as what is there; there is little mention of the many hours spent in the sickrooms of her aging parents, which give the ring of authority to her remark, "Nothing leaves a sadder gap than the loss of one whom we have watched over, and nursed" (L. 164). After her mother's death, she was left alone with her father and became "a more steady & prudent house-keeper than I ever expected, & moreover, a kind & good girl."[19]

In the letters of Mme d'Arblay, the death of Mrs. Burney was perceived as an advantage to Sarah Harriet, which would lead to the "general amelioration of manners." She believed that Sarah would soon "rise into a much fairer & smoother & more pleasing character from this change," and hoped that "the mischief done by her education" could be eradicated.[20] The "mischief" was thought to be the pernicious influence of her stepmother, Mrs. Burney, who had managed to spoil an inherently good nature. As Susan Phillips remarked, "I cannot find in my heart to form any genuine hopes of that poor Woman's Children."[21]

The strong resentment of the Burney children toward their stepmother has been amply discussed by Hemlow.[22] It is difficult to form an objective evaluation of the second Mrs. Burney, whose correspondence with her husband was destroyed and who is seen by posterity almost wholly through the hostile eyes of her stepchildren. Dr. Burney's affection for his wife, as shown by his inconsolable grief after her death, appears to have been genuine. He paid tribute to the "bosom friend & rational companion of 30 years, who had virtues, cultivation, & intellectual powers, sufficient to make home not only desirable, but preferable" to any other place.[23] Bereft of "the dearest part of myself,"[24] he confessed to feeling the loss even more deeply than that of his first wife.[25]

His own strong testimony to the success of the marriage is necessary to counteract Mme d'Arblay's unqualified assertions to the contrary. She believed that Dr. Burney's "unmixed adoration" was reserved for "*our* Mother" alone, and thought that "so much was previously gone of happiness in the [*second*] Union, that the tenderness of his pitying nature, not the penetrated affections of his heart, was all that seemed remaining."[26] She saw her stepmother's death in effect as a release for her father, which would allow "the affections long pent or restrained" to flow towards their natural objects, "his Children" (presumably those of his first marriage).[27] It seems that Mme d'Arblay could be an unreliable witness where her stepmother was concerned.

One must keep in mind this background of conflict between the first and second families before accepting too readily Fanny's opinion of Sarah Harriet, whose deficiencies in temper and manners she deplores, and whose "mingled flippancy & bluffness had lessened my regard.—"[28] In her criticisms of the inadequate companionship provided by her half-sister for her father,[29] one is tempted also to see some jealousy of an elder for a younger sibling. Ardently devoted to her father, an exclusive attachment which was loosened only at the age of forty-one, when she married the Chevalier d'Arblay, Fanny could not be expected to judge impartially the sister who was able to enjoy the happiness of caring for that beloved parent. Sarah Harriet's role was one from which Fanny herself was excluded by her marriage, but which, despite the success of that union, she may well have envied. In her predictions of "a change the most favourable in all respects from living only with so sweet a Nature as my dearest Father's,"[30] she was far indeed from understanding the domestic situation at Chelsea Hospital, which was hardly ideal, and which before long fell into crisis.

In March 1798, Maria (Allen) Rishton, fleeing an unhappy marriage, came to seek a respectable asylum with her stepfather. She came with high hopes, anticipating "all the Luxury of happiness,"[31] remembering, no doubt, the happy days of girlhood when a big family was collected under one roof. However, the atmosphere was very different from what she had expected, and "so unlike what I remember when I was a girl." The Doctor and his daughter passed days without speaking; Sarah "complaind bitterly of her Father's Severity and Coldness towards her . . . and that if he did address or Answer her it was with bitter raillery—or Harshness." On Dr. Burney's side, there was disapproval of Sarah's closeness to her half-brother, James, who spent much of his time at Chelsea, neglecting his wife and children. James ultimately separated from his wife and proposed to live in Chelsea and board with his father, who refused to "suffer any such impropriety or Countenance such proceedings." The day after receiving this answer (1 September 1798), James and Sarah left their respective homes to set up house together.

Mrs. Rishton was left alone at Chelsea over the weekend, dreading the unpleasant task of communicating the news to Dr. Burney. She recalled how "your dear Father very early after my living here told me all his <u>dread</u>ful Apprehensions about their uncommon Intimacy." She told Fanny that the suspicion of incest, first voiced by his late wife, "had taken strong hold of your Father—and agonised his Mind." Mrs. Rishton feared that Dr. Burney's interpretations of their actions "will be of the most allarming Nature—he has imbibed such dreadful Ideas of their Intimacy." Moreover, she predicted that "it will be represented in such dreadful Colours by Mrs Burney I dread to think of the Consequence."[32]

These few remarks of Mrs. Rishton (in a state of extreme emotional distress) have formed the basis for portraying James and Sarah's actions as a romantic "elopement," with the exciting possibility of incest, a view first suggested by Hemlow, and accepted without question by other scholars since.[33] One commentator uses the terms "ménage" and "liaison" quite openly, while conceding that "Sarah H. is not known to have borne James any children."[34] Another critic analyzes the motives of the "incestuous pair" to discover a classic Oedipean conflict, James competing and Sarah uniting symbolically with the father, and both expressing repressed anger in their "most shameful liaison."[35] Clearly, these charges cannot be ignored, and a thorough investigation must be made into their truth.

It is perhaps unfortunate that such a sensational incident (which would surely be the most intriguing phase of an otherwise unstartling existence) is not borne out by a sober consideration of the facts. All of the evidence (with the exception of the few remarks of Mrs. Rishton, quoted above) actually points in the other direction. However, it is worth examining in some detail this notorious escapade in Sarah Harriet's life, to lay any suspicions of irregularity to rest.

In the first place, the originator of the notion, the second Mrs. Charles Burney, does not appear to be the most credible witness. The journals and letters of the Burney children attest to the lengths she could go when feeling neglected (feigning illness or giving way to hysteria) in order to get attention.[36] Jealous of her children's preference for each other's company, she was capable of imagining dark plots and "cabals" against her and forming exaggerated suspicions of their motivation.[37] In the same letter in which Maria Rishton reports her mother's dire insinuations, she makes it clear that she did not believe them nor did her brother, Stephen Allen (his mother's staunch supporter). When Dr. Burney repeated Mrs. Burney's "Tale" of horror, "I endeavourd to Calm his Fears by urging how impossible it was that any thing but Brotherly Affection coud bring them to gether." James and Sarah, aware of the calumny, denied any "improper Attachment." Mrs. Rishton, the closest observer in the situation, was convinced of their innocence: "I trust their own hearts and Consciences acquit them of any harm."[38] She considers Sarah to be "an Unfortunate Girl who has plunged herself into difficulties—but not into guilt."

Moreover, it appears that Dr. Burney himself, on learning of their departure, did not in fact react as Mrs. Rishton had feared. By her account, he took the news of James and Sarah's departure quite calmly and "seems more Satisfied about the motives that have actuated them, than I coud have hoped."[39]

Even Mme d'Arblay, recipient of the first "dreadful tydings" and not prone to take things lightly, came to the same conclusion: "let me, nevertheless, hasten to try to relieve your precious mind from what my own mind is relieved, 'horrible thoughts—' I bless God those, at least, have passed away,—& ever for a moment to have been assailed by them makes all else *LIGHT*!"[40]

Not only words but actions confirm the absence of any such suspicion being current in the Burney family or in their social circle. Charlotte and Esther kept up social relations with James and Sarah, Esther in particular allowing her unmarried (and unportioned) daughters to visit, dine, and spend the night with Sarah and James,[41] an unlikely indulgence if she felt the association would taint their reputation in any way.

During the remainder of Sarah Harriet's life, there is no evidence whatsoever to suggest that any scandal was attached to her name. In fact, on leaving James, she was hired as governess by a woman described as "squeamishness so overstrained, that she makes me sick." The mother who "burnt Parisina, the property of a daughter nearly thirty years old" (L. 84) and ostracized a young married woman because "infamous stories were known of her previous to her marriage" (L. 79) would not be likely to employ as governess someone whose character was the least bit dubious.

Finally, there is the reaction of James's wife. Pained as she was by his desertion, and "fully persuaded they are together,"[42] she does not seem to have given vent to any injurious surmises. In fact, the only concern she is known to have expressed on the subject was about the extra expense of trying to maintain two households.[43] In a few years' time, she would welcome her husband back and keep up social relations with Sarah Harriet. There are references in both James's and Sarah's letters to visits, sometimes in James Street, sometimes at Chelsea;[44] prior to her marriage, James's daughter spent a week with her Aunt Sarah (L. 96); Mrs. Burney herself spent evenings out with her sister-in-law;[45] and at a crisis in Sarah Harriet's life after James's death, Mrs. Burney was "kind enough to offer me house-room for a few weeks" (L. 116). It seems unlikely that such attentions would have been shown had Mrs. Burney suspected Sarah Harriet of being her husband's mistress.

Sarah would later return to her father's home and watch over the last years of his life. It is difficult to believe that Dr. Burney, a stickler for propriety and protective of his daughters to the point of prudery, would receive and countenance one whom he thought guilty of such enormity. In fact, there is every reason to suppose that the crime of incest was not in his thoughts. He did not react with shock, horror, and outrage; although resentful of "this Unthinking Girls desertion"[46] and offended by his children's disobedience, he was initially conciliating. He wrote kindly to Sarah Harriet, offering her money and inviting her to visit him.[47] It was only when he learned that James and Sarah had tried to entice his servant away that he was enraged beyond the point of forgiveness. "This I own did mortify & chagrine me to the quick. Not content wth leaving me so suddenly at my time of life, but to try to seduce from me a most excellent & faithful servant"![48] His original "Mild resignation"[49] then hardened, and Sarah, who had rejected his clemency in proposing a visit, was herself refused when she requested one later. Mme d'Arblay noticed that her father "is more & more incensed, not less, upon this unhappy subject. I doubt, indeed, now, if any application for reconciliation would be received."[50] Dr. Burney expressed anger at being abandoned and the way in which he was abandoned; but if tempting away his servant was his children's worst offense, then clearly he did not seriously contemplate the more heinous sins of seduction, adultery, and incest.

It might be argued that without the notion of a romantic attachment to her half-brother, there would be insufficient motivation for Sarah Harriet to leave. But the unpleasant tension in which she and her father were living in the household, which "went from bad to Worse," might well have given her cause. Maria Rishton was made "so Wretchedly uncomfortable for some time at being a Witness of such constant Unhappiness"[51] that she declared, "I was never so happy as when I turnd my back of the College." She showed herself very unwilling to take on the post that Sarah had relinquished: "I hope your Father will fix on Some Part of his Family as his Housekeeper—if not I must request to have one of his Grandaughters to remain with me while I am at Chelsea for I cannot support the Idea of living alone there."[52] Before another year was out, Mrs. Rishton also escaped from Chelsea, although no replacement for Sarah had yet been found.[53]

Eventually, the post was filled by Dr. Burney's granddaughter, Fanny Phillips, who came to Chelsea as housekeeper when her mother died. After living with her grandfather for seven years, she would write a curious tale entitled *Laura Valcheret.* In it, several of the characters seem to be patterned on members of the Burney family. A middle-aged aunt who has, like Mme d'Arblay, married a French émigré, is full of good advice. A pious cousin who is a model of industry and prodigy of learning is reminiscent of Marianne Francis. The heroine is a young lady who lives alone with an elderly father, having lost her mother (like Fanny Phillips herself) at the age of sixteen. Conflict arises when she displeases her aged parent by failing to employ her time well and neglecting him for gayer society. In the chilling scenes that follow, she endures her father's unspoken disapproval and withdrawal of affection until her spirit of resistance is broken and she abases herself to win forgiveness. In this convincing and realistic portrayal of virtual emotional blackmail, one is tempted to see a reflection of life with Dr. Burney, of the tension in which Sarah lived and from which she fled in 1798. (Years later, Sarah Harriet would read her niece's work in manuscript, declare it to be "excellent" and report herself deeply moved by it [L. 72]).

While it may not be surprising that Sarah Harriet would leave her uncomfortable home in search of a better, it is difficult to ascertain the success of the experiment. Very few letters survive from the five-year period of her residence with James. The reports of Maria Rishton paint a picture of a rather unsettled existence under considerable financial constraint. On the night they left Chelsea, Sarah and James traveled to Bristol, but were soon back in London, lodging at 37 Fetter Lane, "where the Woman of the House emptied their Slops for them once or twice a day when Sally had deposited them in a tin pail she had bought that they Cookd their own dinners—and went to Market—and the Woman Washd for them."[54] By November, they were in Tottenham Court Road, "living in the most Grovling mean Style. Making their own Beds Cooking their Food—and have taken a dirty Lodging in a Suspicious House . . . Where they have found out that the Womans Daughter is a Common Prostitute who brings home a different Visitor every Night—and they dare not both leave their Apartments together lest they shou'd be rob'd."[55] Despite their poverty, however, Sarah was looking "fat and Well and appears quite happy" during this period.[56]

By 16 January 1799, James and Sarah were located at 21 John Street, Fitzroy Square,[57] but they left in the spring for Bristol, taking a "small house with a little garden to it, about a quarter of a mile out" of the city.[58] One can gauge Sarah Harriet's emotional state at the time by her enthusiasm for her surroundings: "I love and honour its various beauties to my very heart of hearts. No place I ever visited pleased me so much at the time, or has left more agreable recollections in my mind" (L. 28). Almost thirty years later, seeking a comparison for some lovely scenery in Italy, her mind traveled back to the countryside of Bristol Hotwells (L. 128). The time Sarah Harriet spent in the country with James and his son, Martin, may well have been one of the happiest of her life.

In two years' time, they were back in London,[59] and within another two years, Sarah Harriet had decided to leave her half-brother and seek employment. James, it seems, had proposed to have his daughter live with them, an arrangement that Sarah felt would be "cruel and odious" to Mrs. Burney: "I neither will deprive James of the satisfaction of having his child with him: nor will I take upon myself the odium that would attach to my character were I to undertake the charge of her to the exclusion of her mother" (L. 26). The cause was a noble one, but it is tempting to seek other possible reasons for the breakup of housekeeping.

It appears that Sarah suffered somewhat from the well-known hastiness of James's temper. A few months after she began living with him, she made an odd appeal to Mme d'Arblay, quaking so much at the "resentment" she had created "in my Brother's mind" that she lacked the "courage to persevere" in some plan, and ending piteously enough: "endeavour—O my dearest Sister, to forgive, & pity me" (L. 22). It is interesting to note that immediately after leaving James, she was struck by the quality of patience in her employer, the more remarkable in a man (L. 27). Years later, she would make a revealing comment on someone who was difficult to get along with, which may apply to James: "[*she*] is not like some, who whilst you live with them torment you by their odd tempers, but when you are divided leave so many kind recollections upon the mind that you forget whatever was amiss, and almost wonder how you could ever have been dissatisfied" (L. 118). Although it was she who ended the living arrangement with James, Sarah Harriet would remain on friendly terms with him until his death, which was "a loss . . . the most heart-piercing she has ever endured."[60]

The five years' sojourn with James seems to have been an emotional watershed of some kind. Consciousness of her role as a spinster, which is conspicuous in several of Sarah Harriet's letters, begins here. Declaring that "the men intend never to make a wife of me," she humorously predicts her own fate as that of all "old maiden Aunts"—to be "very cross, ugly, spiteful &c" (L. 24). She soon refers to herself in jest as a "mortal old maid" or "a craving spinster" (L. 31). A wry awareness of her lowly position in society is thereafter evident, as well as a wish to dissociate herself from the general species of those "who would have married if any body had asked them, but whose attractions were not sufficient to procure an offer. Of course they are not rich, else they would have been gladly snapt up, faults & all. But, when not touchy, and ill-tempered, they are not seldom eminently trivial, inquisitive, and empty-headed" (L. 175). By implication, Sarah Harriet would like to consider herself the exception to the rule.

The feeling of insecurity about her position may be economic in origin. Whatever the benefits of her home with James, financial security was not one of them. Maria Rishton had voiced this concern right at the outset, certain that her half-sister would insist on paying her own way, although she had very limited means.[61] This appears to have been the case, judging from Sarah's bank account at Coutts, which shows all of her investment income (approximately £100) going to James over a two-year period (1801–3). In addition, she sold out £340 in investments, giving the proceeds or transferring the stock itself to her half-brother. As her capital was reduced by almost one-third in five years, it is clear that such an arrangement could not last forever. Only after Sarah began working as a governess did the situation improve; in the course of her employment, she acquired new stock, building her investment holdings back up almost to their previous level.[62]

On 4 January 1804, Sarah Harriet writes from her new situation in the home of George Wilbraham, a Cheshire M.P. and head of an old county family. She draws a flattering picture of a calm and refined retirement, which seems to have come as somewhat of a relief. The family is sketched in precious terms; Mrs. Wilbraham, her "lady patroness," is "a most attractive and lovely woman," whose manners are "gentle, & elegant." Her two grown-up daughters are "the comforts and delights of my life." One "draws charmingly"; the other "is yet more accomplished as a musician." All are "sweet-tempered, sociable, chearful," and as for Mr. Wilbraham, "I love him—He is quite a dear" (L. 27). A marked change of tone is observable within months; a note of asperity appears in the description of her duties and the difficulty of imparting knowledge into "Miss's thimble-full of brains" (L. 29). The master of the house later cuts a much poorer figure, "sniggering and shaking his fat sides" (L. 32). Before too long, the delightful family has become "tolerably uninteresting to me" (L. 35). This pattern of high expectation and initial enthusiasm, followed by a rather sour disillusionment is frequently repeated, lending credence to the charge of "Capriciousness"[63] in Sarah Harriet's nature. Disappointment seems to be a major motif in her letters and, one suspects, in her life.

As she had left her father for James, and James for the Wilbrahams, so after a few years as a governess, Sarah Harriet wanted to return home, and sought a reconciliation with her father. Her half-sister, Esther, acted as mediator, conveying her sincere repentance of "her late rash & undutiful desertion" and her good intentions of "making him all the reparation in her power by her future cares & attention on this score."[64] By August 1807, she was reinstated in her old apartments (L. 36), where she would remain until Dr. Burney's death seven years later.

The task of caring for her aged father cannot have been an easy one. After a paralytic seizure in 1806, the eighty-year-old man "treated himself as an invalid" and withdrew into semiseclusion in his Chelsea apartments.[65] The tone of his letters at this period is often peevish and self-pitying.[66] His daughter noticed his growing self-absorption: "matters of sentiment fade prodigeously in his estimation now, and every thing is referred to convenience or interest" (L. 61). It is perhaps not purely coincidental that the description of a valetudinarian in Jane Austen's *Emma* was able to strike such a chord: "the dear old man's 'gentle selfishness.'[67]—Was there ever a happier expression?" (L. 84).

The restrictions on Sarah's life at this period are seen in the difficulty of obtaining an outing or holiday, and her corresponding surprise and delight if permission was unexpectedly or easily granted (L. 53). When invited out, she liked to be given a convincing reason, a plausible "excuse to plead to Daddy" (L. 64). She herself would turn down invitations, as a preferable alternative to placing herself in the demeaning position of asking a favor: "I have to ask leave, an odious thing to me . . . . Oh—if you did but know how I hate, face to face, asking for any thing! If my father was away, I could write—but to speak. . . ." (L. 55). She seems to have lived in some fear of her father, judging by the "great fright" she was in when she thought some gossip about her companions at a bathing-place might be repeated to him (L. 69). She believed also that he required flattery to be kept in humor,[68] and advised Charlotte, when returning a borrowed book to Dr. Burney, that "you must thank him as if he had sent you a dowry for Julia, and a title and estate for yourself" (L. 63).

When she was at home, she was fully occupied, acting as her father's amanuensis, taking his letters from dictation (and even conducting some of his correspondence herself, such as her letters to Mr. Hüttner), and transcribing his articles for the press. Dr. Burney found her "very useful,"[69] as "she reads & writes French as readily as English, and has, lately, seriously studied Italian, and writes a very good hand."[70] The volume of work she was expected to do is indicated by the amount of writing that could accumulate during even a fortnight's absence (L. 57) and by Dr. Burney's complaints of helplessness when she was away: "My daughter was out & I had no one to make a transcript of the article. . . . I have been writing to day till my right hand has forgotten its Cunning."[71]

Other duties as housekeeper would include the management of the household and servants, the payment of accounts, and "rigmaroles without end to look after." Sarah's least favorite task would seem to have been the "beastly debates to read in the evening paper" (L. 65), which, given Dr. Burney's vehemence on the subject of politics,[72] is perhaps not surprising. She also tried to keep her father cheerful, an effort which, for an infirm man in his eighties, did not always meet with success. In one of her letters, Sarah Harriet makes a desperate appeal to her half-brother Charles to come and help her "to rouse my poor father's spirits," after she has exhausted all her own powers of amusement (L. 74).

Heated exchanges and disagreeable scenes are described in her letters (L. 61) as well as his. The tension that sometimes existed between Sarah and her father is indicated by a curiously savage letter of Dr. Burney's showing a side of his personality never presented by Mme d'Arblay in her adulatory *Memoirs of Doctor Burney* (1832): "Miss did not appear; but has affected great care & tenderness with a pretended desire to be employed by me some way or other—till I c^{d} hold out no longer . . . Though she, in the spite & malignity of her heart, was very near giving birth to quarrel that c^{d} never be made up, & w^{d} have obliged me to turn her out of my house for ever. She feebly tried to defend herself; but I w^{d} not let her—& made her hold her tongue. Nothing has passed since till, at going to bed, I condescended to let her shake my index."[73]

It would seem that the hostility that Dr. Burney expressed toward Sarah Harriet when she left him to live with James never entirely disappeared, and that he never fully forgave his two undutiful children. This became clear after his death on 12 April 1814 when, in his will, he left Sarah Harriet considerably less than two of her half-sisters, and not even so much as one of her nieces. James, the eldest son, was virtually disinherited, and for the daughter who had cared for him in his old age, there was little enough, £1000.[74] Immediately invested, this sum brought Sarah's small annual income up to £85.[75]

It is clear that Sarah Harriet suffered under considerable financial constraint after losing her home with her father. She moved almost immediately to another apartment in the Chelsea Hospital, for which she had now to pay rent. Other expenses, for instance, for medical attention during a serious illness in 1816 and a convalescence at Malvern Wells, began to make inroads into her small capital. To offset these charges, she had recourse to her pen, anticipating with some shrewdness the profits she would realise by the sale of her fiction. She also gave lessons to supplement her income, although the ill health of her pupil, Miss Gell, led her to cancel the arrangement. This circumstance, which "rather deranged my Christmas accounts," taught her that "an income depending in any degree upon contingencies—upon the health either of others or of oneself—an income, in short, not secured from every species of uncertainty, ought, least of any, to be forestalled—And that, I trust, I shall hereafter never forget" (L. 89).

Apparently, she never did forget the tenuous nature of her hold upon gentility and the desirability of achieving financial independence. The precariousness of her income imposed a restraint upon her actions that would become habitual. She could not "go gallanting, and making merry, as if I were an independent gentlewoman. I expect, at least, I fear, little by little, to lose all my friends;—for I am too poor to go near them, and they think it is indifference;

whereas, it is prudence in the shape pen and ink" (L. 82). As in many people of restricted incomes, the closeness became a habit, and Sarah Harriet's anxiety about her expenditures sometimes appears to be exaggerated. More than once, her claims of being in dire financial straits or of spending beyond her income are not borne out by the entries in her bank account (e.g. L. 161).

The constraint upon her inclinations was also a fetter to her spirit, which prevented her from flouting social mores. She felt the inferiority of her position keenly when, fearing that one of her nieces would lose caste by an ill-advised marriage, she was unable to support her as she would have wished: "I am such a coward from my conscious insignificance." Although "ashamed" of her own lack of courage, she pleaded necessity, and furthermore believed it unlikely that she could wield any influence: "when you think of my known poverty—of the obligations which I am perpetually receiving in the way of invitations, without the ability to return one of them, some little excuse may be found for me" (L. 96).

Her position must have been all the more galling for a proud spirit, which reveals itself in several ways: her horror of falling into debt and insistence on returning even a small sum borrowed from a sister; her honorable fight to refund the unearned tuition to Mrs. Gell; and her rejection of the notion of depending on relatives (LL. 57, 89, 118). There is a quiet heroism and courage in her struggle, as an unprotected woman, for self-sufficiency and respect. Her letters avoid any hint of self-pity; some of the jarring elements (the harshness of her ridicule of "Goosecappy," the pettiness of her description of "poor Bone," or the triviality of her dabbling in mineralogy [L. 86]) may represent a brave attempt to keep up a good front and to extract amusement from unlikely materials.

Another feature of her position was undoubtedly loneliness. Soon after her father's death she tried the experiment of taking in a companion but lived to rue her choice and was glad to free herself of the intruder: "she has taught me the folly and hazard of accepting (for <u>any</u> remuneration) an inmate whose temper, understanding and habits are unknown; & she has taught me, moreover, how many millions of times better it is to have no companion at all, than to possess one from whom the heart recoils" (L. 86). However, the few female inhabitants at Chelsea Hospital, the wives or daughters of members of staff, she found for the most part uncongenial, certainly unstimulating: "There are no bookish people here—on the contrary, they seem to me to look with an evil eye on every reader of every production save a Newspaper" (L. 62). Most of her society during the last fifteen years spent in the College was in books, the "dear mute companion[s] of my life" (L. 61), and the record of her reading is tremendous.

There is a certain lack of continuity in the circle of friends who appear in Sarah Harriet Burney's letters. Relatively few names recur throughout the course of her life, compared with the number of people with whom she is intimate during one period of her existence and never mentions again. This applies to the passing show at the boardinghouses (for instance, Mrs. Stuart, Mrs. Jennings, Mrs. Jerdein) as well as to longtime associates (for instance, the charitable Mrs. Spicer). Her own family and the families of her employers appear to be the only ones with whom she maintained contact for any length of time. At some periods of her life, she seems to have been wholly dependent on the kindness of passing strangers.

In her occasional forays outside the walls of the Hospital during these years, she found a weapon against solitude. At the resorts where she took her vacations (Malvern, Cheltenham, and Brighton), she would arrange to board where she lodged. This gave her the prospect of some company at least, and she was often pleased with the result. However, after associating with a "pleasant, friendly little coterie" for several weeks, she found the homecoming even harder: "so little attraction has Chelsea and its present inhabitants, that I feel quite a distaste to the idea of sallying forth and making myself visible to the few Cats, male & female, now residing here" (L. 93).

Finally, it seems that Sarah Harriet reached the point where she could keep up the pretense no longer; suddenly the mask dropped to reveal her discontent: "I am, to begin, sick of Chelsea College. . . . this focus of inconvenience and dullness. I seem just to have discovered that it is neither town nor country; that the air is moist & relaxing; the society miserably confined" (L. 95). She was ready to seek another situation, mostly to achieve a "life of more sociability . . . than the solitary paradise which I now inhabit." Another advantage would, of course, be financial, "By saving house-rent, coals, &c, I should be able perhaps to put by £50 a year" (L. 93). In the battle to raise a bulwark against the accidents of time, her chief strategy was to try to live without expense and bank her salary; with the savings gathered, she would purchase low-return but safe investments. The goal was to acquire enough capital to yield a comfortable annual income, to "make me easy . . . the rest of my days" (L. 89).

Successful in her quest, Sarah Harriet began in April 1821 to act as a companion to a young lady called Gregor, who "from ill health, is entirely deprived of all the amusements of the gay world." Initially, everything looked rosy; she anticipated with pleasure her agreeable duties, "to talk, and read, and walk and draw with her" (L. 97). She was particularly struck with Mrs. Gregor, the aunt of her wealthy charge, a cultured woman. Sarah's reading at this time was a steady diet of travel books, particularly of classical tours in Italy. Living in a house surrounded by casts of the Elgin marbles and the sculpture of Canova also encouraged in her a taste for classical art and architecture.

Unfortunately for the pursuance of this scheme, Sarah Harriet suffered during the winter of 1821–22 from a liver complaint, perhaps exacerbated by grief for the death of her half-brother, James, on 17 November 1821.[76] Concluding her strength to be unequal to her duties, her employer let her go (very tactfully) during the summer of 1822. Mrs. Gregor proves the exception to the rule, and never descends from the elevated position in which she initially appears. Sarah Harriet seems genuinely to have admired her and to have been disappointed by the failure of her plan.

Almost immediately, however, another opportunity presented itself to her that quite dazzled the Burney family, and was considered "quite providential in her present situation." In September 1822, she was hired by Lord Crewe, an old family friend, to take charge of his two granddaughters. She would have the responsibility of overseeing their education, of hiring masters and a governess, and of presiding over the Crewe residence near Grosvenor Square. "In short no more trouble than if she were the mother of these young Ladies, with every earthly Comfort." Her salary was fixed at £300, making "the present prospects of poor dear Aunt Sarah better than any she has ever had."[77]

At first, all went well. Taking up her duties at Crewe Hall, Cheshire, in the middle of September, Sarah Harriet was reported "in high Spirits & Feather" throughout the winter;[78] in the spring, she returned to London with her pupils. However, cracks soon began to appear in the façade. The Crewe property in the West Indies diminished in value, and the family had to retrench. The town residence was given up, and Sarah Harriet returned with her charges to Lord Crewe's mansion in Cheshire,[79] which put her "in mind of being at a large Hotel, where . . . as in a Magic-Lanthorn, new people pass in review before me who stay for a night or two, and then are off." Some of her discomfiture was not uncommon in a situation of dependence; associating with those who were her superiors in rank, she was unlikely to be treated as an equal. She resented "some superfines, who never debase themselves by bestowing more than an unlooking look upon me. Do you know what I mean? One of those sort of looks you cast upon a fire-skreen or a hearth-broom, and are not sure you have ever cast at all" (L. 105).

However, there is some doubt as to the true cause of her resentment in this instance; the chief offender turns out to be "a dandy of the first water," a Mr. Sneyd, who was extremely handsome, though affected, and "clever & entertaining to a degree where & when he lists, and keeps his chosen neighbour at dinner in continual laughter: but the vulgar herd is never admitted to hear a word he says, and eyes he has none save for the purpose of seeing who he shall not see." Sarah Harriet appears to have suffered from his neglect, perhaps because she prided herself on these same qualities of intelligence and humor and felt capable of reciprocating the entertainment, if her claims to his attention were only recognized.

A susceptibility to male charm is a marked feature of Sarah Harriet Burney's letters during her time with the Crewe family. A clergyman, a widower in his thirties, arouses sufficient interest to merit several mentions, though not of equal praise. He first appears as "good-humoured Willoughby Crewe," who is diverted by some word-puzzles of Sarah Harriet's, which provide "a great deal of amusement" for an evening or two (L. 108). Later, however, his attention seems to have wandered to a younger (and perhaps prettier) inhabitant of the house; Sarah Harriet's remarks on both parties are scathing enough to suggest that she was stung by the defection (LL. 110, 111). One cannot help but wonder whether her resentment was rooted in jealousy, although (given that she was past fifty and had little beauty to boast of), her anger may have been caused by the injury to her amour-propre in being forced to recognize the limitations of her attractions.

It is possible that another affair of the heart occurred during this period, which may have been capped by a proposal of marriage. An enigmatic passage, which was later deleted from a letter of Mme d'Arblay's, states that Sarah Harriet "has finally denied Mr. J. Greville. I am really sorry. But she had no reasons very rational." In this case, the gentleman was twenty years her senior and uncle to her charges. The editor of Mme d'Arblay's letters relates this proposal to one that came from the same quarter a decade later (L. 149), that of being his companion and reader during the London season.[80] However, at the time of the first invitation (late 1824 or early 1825), just two years had elapsed of Sarah's engagement to the Crewes, a lucrative and responsible position that was understood to last until her charges reached the age of majority. Mme d'Arblay believed her situation would be "of *permanent* advantage" and that "*once begun*, it would be *ruinous* to renounce it."[81] It seems unlikely that a humble relation of the Crewe family should seek to entice her away to a less exalted post in his own household or that Mme d'Arblay would express such chagrin on learning that Sarah Harriet had declined to change positions. It is more plausible that "denied" was being used in its conventional sense, a refusal of a proposal of marriage, which might well occasion regret.

Deeper discontent appears in Sarah Harriet's situation a few years later (1828), but caused by a woman, not a man. The villain of the piece was the children's aunt, Mrs. Cunliffe, who apparently took an interest in the motherless heiresses, and chaperoned them in London. Sarah Harriet resented her interference and considered her a bad influence, fearing that her youngest pupil would become as "miserably affected" as Mrs. Cunliffe herself (L. 112). One of the "completely thoughtless, dashing women of ton," whose life consisted of nothing but "dress and dissipation," she took her fourteen-year-old niece out to the opera, the play, and on morning visits, activities of which Sarah Harriet strongly disapproved: "the whole style of the thing makes me sick" (L. 113). She also confessed herself ill-at-ease with Mrs. Cunliffe, whom she accused of "manoeuvring, and subtlety, and love of cabal" (L. 118).

Clearly the Crewe household could not hold the two of them, and the tension finally built to the point where Sarah Harriet declared that she would give up her duties during the London season and take charge of her younger pupil only in the country. The offer was accepted, but her salary, which depended on West Indian property much diminished in value, was to be reduced to £100. When Sarah proudly refused, she found herself free again (in March 1829) but somewhat disoriented, "all at sixes and sevens on this sudden change of pursuits, of persons, of places, and of occupations." After enjoying luxurious surroundings for seven years, she found that London looked "dirtier and more to be recoiled from now than it ever did before" (L. 118).

No annuity was settled on her by the Crewes, and her financial position was not greatly improved; her investments yielded £100 per year rather than £80.[82] This probably helped to make even more attractive the plan that now presented itself for her acceptance, to travel abroad in company with the Wilbrahams, who were planning to winter in Italy (L. 119) (where one could live much more cheaply than in England). In 1821, Sarah had considered the possibility of travel as one of the advantages of her position with the Gregors (L. 100), so the opportunity may have come as the fulfillment of a long-held desire.

Sarah Harriet did not, as it turned out, travel with the Wilbrahams but set out from London sometime after 22 July 1829 (when she withdrew £250 at Coutts). By her own account, years later:

> I left London in one of Emery's clumsy coaches, which set out from some office in Regent Street. . . . The main expence of the distance from London to Lausanne, amounted as well as I can remember, to £18. That includes every thing.—You pay nothing on the road,—beds, meals &c, &c, every thing is ordered & defrayed for you. . . . My further proceedings from Lausanne to Florence, & thence to Rome were carried on in much the same manner,—only with Italian drivers, with wretched Italian horses, and most tremendously hard seats! (L. 177)

She arrived in Rome shortly before 25 November 1829.[83]

In one of Sarah Harriet's tales, the heroine journeys alone by vetturino, from France to Rome. By chance, she encounters a male of her acquaintance on the road, who treats her with reserve. She accounts for her cool reception by his finding her in the somewhat compromising position of "*strolling* over the world, without attendants, without protectors, without, in short, any of the pomp and circumstance, that ought to accompany her."[84] Sarah may have felt some of this embarrassment about her own situation when she encountered in Florence a friend of her half-brother James, Henry Crabb Robinson.

She explained her solitary state by observing that "she had set out on this journey with a female friend, who had deserted her at Dover, not daring to cross the water in rough weather."[85] Who this "female friend" might be is not clear, and it seems possible that she was an imaginary one, a subterfuge that is in itself revealing. Sarah's half-sister certainly believed she had traveled out alone, a feat that required some courage and that she referred to with some admiration: "She Chaproned Herself Out, & I dare say will not care a pin about a Chaprone Home."[86] Sarah declined, however, to repeat the experiment on her return journey and confessed: "I am anxious to join some respectable party, & have not the courage to travel as I did before under the sole protection of a Voiturier" (L. 138). Although economical, this mode of travel seems to have appeared somewhat disreputable to Robinson, who sent the above description of her journey to a lady of his acquaintance: "it does little more than shew you how cheaply persons may travel whose circumstances and position in society require & enable them to travel as Miss Burney did." He hastened to assure his correspondent, however, that he by no means placed her in "that class."[87]

The eccentricity and independence for which Sarah was noted in her own family[88] shows nowhere in her life more clearly than during the time spent in Italy, where she was able to indulge her marked preference for male society. During several months that she spent in Rome, she belonged to a group of tourists who met at an inexpensive restaurant for dinner; these were friends of Crabb Robinson's, consisting for the most part of several young men whom he had met traveling. Robinson called her the "*pet*" of the party, and described several excursions they made to the sights of Rome.[89] These "pedestrian expeditions with all her 'Merry Men'" lasted until the wet weather set in. Sarah Harriet's delight was evident, in meeting with congenial companions "who seem to admire her as she deserves and to be always at her beck, for any frisks or excursions she chuses to make."[90] She was reported to be "wonderfully well & gay" during her first winter in Italy,[91] which was arguably the happiest period of her life.

Crabb Robinson would see her at least every other day and often daily.[92] A middle-aged man of independent though moderate means, he liked to associate with literary people, including Wordsworth, Coleridge, and Southey. He was also a friend of Charles Lamb, through whom he had met her half-brother, James, and his son, Martin.[93] Part of his interest in Miss Burney, at least initially, was as "a younger sister of Madame d'Arblay,"[94] and he was polite (though not enthusiastic) about her own literary ventures. He apparently considered her a pleasant companion, on whose cordial welcome he could depend, finding her always "the same cheerful and friendly person."[95] In Robinson's journal is reflected a very flattering image of Sarah Harriet Burney, attesting perhaps to "the charms of manner & conversation" which she could exert for an appreciative audience, which made her "so pleasing when pleased."[96]

Mme d'Arblay had criticized Sarah Harriet as a young woman for an unbecoming desire for attention: "She knows she is a very clever Girl, & she is neither well contented with others, nor happy in herself, but where this is evidently acknowledged."[97] There may have been some truth to the charge, and the qualities which she did have—intellectual curiosity, an informed mind, a rather sharp sense of humor—were far more likely to be acceptable in male company than in female. The majority of the women she encountered she considered to be "as full of prejudices as they are empty of general knowledge of the world" (L. 163); the few whose society she enjoyed, she valued for one quality above all, their intelligence. Men were by definition better company: "They may be vulgar, and they may be illiterate, but at all events, they can bring home some news from the Library,—and they know nothing about caps, & bonnets, & female bargains" (L. 175). Even as a young woman, she had scouted the supposedly female domain of fashion, in which she took no interest and for which (one may surmise) she had no aptitude; she preferred discoursing on political or literary subjects (LL. 1, 8).

The first winter in Rome, she was fortunate in finding companions to her own mind, but after a few months, the party broke up; Crabb Robinson and his young friends went to Naples, and Sarah Harriet left on 10 March 1830 for Florence.[98] There she stayed with the Wilbraham sisters in a house near the Uffizi, and when the weather grew warmer, at a villa outside the city (LL. 125–27). Toward the end of June, she joined her niece, Charlotte Barrett, with her two daughters at the Baths of Lucca (L. 128). The Italian countryside was alluring at first, but she soon tired of it; by the end of the summer, she was glad to return to Florence, having had "rurality enough, and to spare" (L. 130).

It is interesting to note that although Charlotte Barrett would remain in Italy for three years while Sarah Harriet was there, and for most of that time was at

Pisa, just fifty miles away, they made very little effort to see each other or coordinate their plans. In fact, after the first summer at the Baths of Lucca, they never stayed together again. Charlotte's frequent letters to her mother and husband made little mention of her Aunt Sarah, and that little was not always favorable. Signs of irritation appear, for instance, when Sarah Harriet recommended an unsuitable book (L. 139).[99] The Barrett girls were unwilling to be left with their great-aunt: "you w^{d} not approve of having A^{t} Sally with you."[100] Mrs. Barrett was disappointed when Sarah Harriet failed to help her find a lodging in Florence, but "bade me come to an Hotel & chuse."[101]

Preoccupied with nursing a consumptive daughter, Charlotte no doubt could have used some help in entertaining the invalid or in accompanying her other daughter on outings. This aunt-like role, however, was not filled by Sarah Harriet herself but by a newly-made acquaintance, Lady Caroline Morrison, who became "the kindest friend we have here";[102] she helped the Barretts to find suitable accommodation, invited Julia to the seaside, and chaperoned her in Rome. When Sarah Harriet, acting on a tip from the Wilbrahams, passed on some gossip about this valuable friend (L. 145), all communication between her and her favorite niece ceased for several years. Censure of Lady Caroline, who had done so much to help the Barretts in their hour of need, may have been particularly unwelcome from a source that had proven less than reliable.

Charlotte may have been alienated by a flaw in Sarah Harriet's nature, which had been noticed by others. In the words of her harshest critic, Mme d'Arblay, she had "an habit of exclusively consulting *just what she likes best*,—not what would be or prove best for others. She thinks, indeed, but little of any thing except with reference to herself, & that gives her an air, & will give her a character for inconstancy, that is in fact the mere result of seeking her own gratification, alike in meeting or avoiding her connexions."[103] There seems to have been an element of truth in what she says; very little consideration for the feelings of others is shown, for instance, in her sharp teasing of Charlotte on her engagement (L. 33), her philosophic dismissal of Anna Grosvenor's miscarriage (L. 144), or her letters of condolence, which have an odd tendency toward contemplating her own loss (LL. 45, 115). The most blatant example of selfishness occurs in the peculiar series of letters written 10–17 March 1822 (LL. 100–102) when she first courts, then accepts, and finally rejects an invitation from Charlotte Broome. While coolly announcing her acceptance of a subsequent but preferable offer of hospitality, Sarah requests yet another favor of her half-sister, to help repay the kindness of her hostess!

On Sarah Harriet's side, however, it might have been to her advantage to have joined Mrs. Barrett, given her extreme loneliness in Florence. She remained in the city for three years from September 1830, leading an increasingly isolated existence. At first, she attended some gatherings of the English colony there but found that they "deal in large, and dressy, and late, and tiresome parties: but not in friendly, unceremonious intercourse" (L. 138). The style of society "suit neither my taste nor my pocket" (L. 136). One wonders if she endured any snubs as did Crabb Robinson, when he attended a large party where nobody spoke to him but the host.[104] Sarah Harriet apparently felt out of place at gatherings with "heaps of folks with mines of wealth on their backs, and not a real cordial face amongst them," where she sat "eating ices in a circle with men and women who all seem to be made of ice too" (L. 133).

However, alternatives were not easy to find. First, she fell into "a little sociable set, where I can drink tea in my bonnet, and hear a little rational talk" (L. 133). This group of Swiss and French people probably congregated around her lodgings with a "Swiss Lady,"[105] but they fade out of her letters quite quickly. By the end of the first winter, Sarah Harriet confessed that it was "bad for me . . . to depend solely upon myself for amusement," and that "if I live another season here . . . I will not condemn myself to such complete solitude" (L. 136). In May 1831, therefore, she moved into Henry Crabb Robinson's former apartments with two elderly Italian ladies.[106] A few friends gathered at their home every evening, including the Florentine poet, Giuseppe Niccolini. At first Sarah Harriet took pleasure in attending these soirees, but before many months had passed, gave them up, finding the rapid conversation of an all-Italian party difficult to follow (they "tire me to death") (L. 142). For a while she had recourse to a family of Layards who lived opposite and whom she could visit without ceremony, to "chat and work with the wife, or play at chess and get well beaten by the husband" (L. 140). The Layards were kind to her, lending her books and introducing her to other people (L. 138), but they went to Rome in November 1832, leaving her only "two dicky-birds" for company, and an odd assortment of morning visitors, which included former servants of the Wilbrahams and "an old Venetian Abate." By the end of the third winter in Florence, she could no longer keep up the brave front: "I have spent . . . not the most unhappy, positively—but the most uninteresting and stupid winter that in the whole course of my long life I ever remember to have passed" (L. 146).

In fact, fairly early in Sarah Harriet's Italian period, she was overtaken by the discontent which seemed to dog her steps. During the first year of her residence in Florence, she professed herself "heartily ready to go back to England, if I knew how to manage it in safe and good company. . . . Italy is to me like the plums in a Grocer's shop to a new 'prentice boy;—it is very irresistable at first, but palls after a while" (L. 135). In almost every letter thereafter she expressed her desire to go home, a journey she feared to undertake alone. She had to wait almost three years until she was able to return under the protection of her niece and husband.[107]

On her return to England (in November 1833), Sarah Harriet settled at Bath, where a life of genteel retirement was within her means. By 26 March 1834, she was established in a ladies' boardinghouse on the outskirts, "in a wide handsome street, and open at one end to the hills & fields. . . . My bed room at the back of the house looks out upon fields, & distant Villas and Cottages, & is chearful & quiet" (L. 147). However, she found Bath society unintellectual and soon described herself as a "hermit" (L. 155). Still in search of congenial company, she had high hopes in May 1835 of a new living arrangement, that of sharing an apartment with a "gentle, rational, & friendly associate" (L. 152). The experiment was not a success; within three months, she had discovered that her associate was "illiterate, naturally common-place, is too high for a servant, & too dull & tiresome for a companion." She was relieved to move back into her former lodgings, "whose guests are so often shifting, there is at least a chance that some soul or other may arrive from whom a little agreeability may [*be*] extracted" (L. 153).

During the period of residence at Bath, she suffered from various illnesses and her life acquired a gentle monotony. Fearing cold weather and the night air, she generally kept to her room, and received very few visitors; at teatime she descended to the drawing room, and read alone until bedtime. She no longer took the trouble to return formal calls, and disdained to associate with her fellow-lodgers, spinsters and widows of narrow views and education, "persons who have never been beyond Clifton, or perhaps Weston super-mer," whose conversation was not worth listening to, even if she had not been hard of hearing (L. 163).

She was happier after her move to Cheltenham in June 1841, to "a very chearfully-situated" house on the Promenade (L. 170). Sarah Harriet liked the bustling activity of the town, and "all the Cockney doings" (L. 167). She enjoyed the passing show before her windows, like "an ever-shifting magic lanthorn" (L. 177). She also preferred having the company of gentlemen as well as ladies, resigning herself to her boardinghouse existence as the easiest way of staving off solitude: "I am too old now to live by myself. My eye-sight will not always hold out for a whole day's reading, & when evening comes, I want a little society without being at the trouble of going out for it" (L. 175). She seemed tolerably contented; Crabb Robinson, who saw her in 1841, thought that she had aged.[108]

During the last decade of Sarah Harriet's life, signs of age appear in her letters, which are shorter and sometimes disjointed. Errors of spelling and grammar increase, and lapses of memory occur. She rambles over her subjects, sometimes drifting into a vein of irrelevant reminiscence (L. 162) or descending to gossip "in true Old Maid character," about her ailments and physicians (L. 182). Some of her former asperity has mellowed, and terms of endearment are more plentiful; to old friends like Anna Grosvenor, she expresses warm affection and laments the distance that separates her from those she loves. Happily, the breach with Charlotte Barrett was healed, and they would take a holiday together shortly before her final illness. On her return, she bids "farewell" to her niece in a grateful letter that becomes vague and confused, and strikes a wistful chord at the end, "Oh that I could see you all, & be amongst you once more!! . . . I miss & regret you every hour" (L. 182). Characteristically, perhaps, this note of soft melancholy is not to be Sarah Harriet's last word; the latest letter that survives is full of acid strictures on two of her fellow boarders who have offended her by marrying (L. 183).

The long life drew to a close in the early weeks of 1844, and at the age of seventy-one, she died "suddenly and without pain" on 8 February.[109] It appears that no friends or family were present; the death certificate was signed by the hostess of the boardinghouse, and her will was witnessed by one of her fellow boarders.[110] It seems a fitting close to the life of Sarah Harriet that she should face her end alone.

The Writing

After reading what survives of a lifetime's worth of letters of Sarah Harriet Burney, one is still left with questions unanswered. The lack of closure is partly owing to the accidents of chance and time, which have preserved a tantalizing sample of her correspondence but by no means all. It is safe to assume that what remains represents a small proportion of the whole, considering the number of correspondents mentioned whose letters have been lost (as well as the replies to those letters), for instance her pupil and loyal friend, Harriet Crewe; her highly respected employer, Mrs. Gregor; her eldest half-sister, Esther Burney; her half-brother, Stephen Allen; and her vivacious nieces Sophia Burney and Sarah (Burney) Payne.

Moreover, the task of assessing her personality and her life is complicated by the fact that the letters that do survive are not self-revelatory. Unlike Frances Burney, who selected (or perhaps projected) an intimate audience who would sympathize fully with her joys, sorrows, triumphs, and trepidations, Sarah Harriet, it seems, had no boon companion, no other self to whom she could unburden herself, without disguise. The act of writing a letter was a public one, a social convention that (like formal visiting) she would conform to somewhat reluctantly, sometimes complain of, and often neglect. She performed it from a sense of duty, an obligation to maintain contact. The purpose of the exercise was a self-conscious, deliberate attempt to entertain her correspondent.

The letters of other members of the Burney family make very little reference to Sarah Harriet. It is hardly surprising that she was forgotten at the time of Esther's death and had the shock of learning of her half-sister's demise from the newspaper.[111] Even Charlotte Broome, her favorite half-sister, and Charlotte Barrett, her closest correspondent, mention her only rarely. In the inner circle, there were none with whom she was intimate. In a life that was often solitary, the most revealing feature is the distance of tone when writing to her nearest and dearest. The letters of Sarah Harriet Burney, even to those for whom she professes the warmest friendship, aim primarily to amuse.

As though she were conscious of the dangers of spinsterhood, Sarah Harriet fears, above all, the possibility of boring her correspondent. If she will not speak of herself, then she must discuss other people. When she is living a full or active life, as a young woman gadding about London, or as a governess in a mansion full of guests, this poses no problem. But many periods of her life were spent in virtual isolation, which afforded few opportunities for observation: "Lord love you! where am I, the old Hermitess of Henrietta Street, to find materials for a letter to a London gentleman, who goes gadding about from dawn to dewy eve, knows every body, hears every thing, and out of one evening's gossip (beg pardon for so denominating it) could furnish more matter for a full sheet of foolscap than I could scramble together in a twelvemonth" (L. 163). She seems genuinely chagrined when forced to confess that she is unable to compose an "amusing letter" because of a dearth of suitable subjects (L. 162).

To some degree, however, the emotional isolation of the writer represents a gain for the reader. Her letters, according to the biographer of Henry Crabb Robinson (who corresponded with several literary figures) are "among the liveliest and most amusing" of his correspondence.[112] There is much to suggest the self-conscious nature of the exercise, for instance the lengths she was willing to go in search of materials (anecdotes related even at thirdhand, items culled from newspapers). The manuscripts show great care in composition, judging from the number of minor changes made that improve subtly the nuance or rhythm of a sentence. Her concern with these details is in itself revealing. She enjoyed words, and enjoyed using them ("a'n't I very sublime in my terms?" [L. 58]). She also experimented with different styles, indulging in mock-romance (L. 112) or imitating the dialogue of a play (L. 25). There are numerous examples of careful phrasing and construction, using the devices of parallelism or repetition to impart a touch of humor: "the first thing in a morning it came across my imagination with a painful twinge; the last thing at night it sat heavy on my soul; and all day long it recurred to me with antipathy and disgust" (L. 151).

Aside from the question of style, there are other literary qualities in her letters. The incorporation of foreign phrases (although often misspelled or incorrect) indicates a certain level of culture, and the numerous quotations demonstrate extensive reading. By far the greatest number are taken from the plays of Shakespeare, but there is a good scattering as well from the poets of the eighteenth century, notably Pope, Johnson, Cowper, and Thomas Campbell. With most of her correspondents, Sarah Harriet engages in some form of literary discussion, and to some (notably her former pupil, Anna Wilbraham, and her niece, Charlotte Barrett), she recommends books in a schoolmarmish fashion. Her lifelong engagement with literature is evident in her letters as well as in her novels.

One is led naturally from the letters of Sarah Harriet Burney to a consideration of her fiction. She wrote five novels between 1796 and 1839 that were fairly successful in their day. Most are written in the genre of the domestic novel of manners and at times do recall the well-known works of her half-sister, a resemblance that led the reviewers to tax the younger Burney with a "*family likeness.*"[113]

Her first effort, *Clarentine* (1796), is a familiar mix of satire and romance; the central love interest is enlivened by an array of stock comic characters (a fop, a rake, a sentimental miss, an agreeable rattle, a brazen widow, and so forth). The second, *Geraldine Fauconberg* (1808), is an epistolary novel, whose fastidious hero almost spoils his own felicity. The story of cross-purposes unfolded in the letters of his sprightly sister is resolved by the brooding recluse of a Gothic subplot. The best-seller *Traits of Nature* (1812) evokes realistically contemporary society in which two hostile families eventually intermarry and reconcile. *Tales of Fancy* promises to range further afield: the first volume (1816) contains *The Shipwreck*, where a tale of Crusoe-like castaways borrows motifs from *The Tempest* and *Twelfth Night*, with the heroine, Viola, donning male attire. The second tale, *Country Neighbours* (1820), is set among the English gentry; the narrative purports to be the journal of a forty-year-old spinster, a clear-eyed critic of her own domestic circle into which is introduced a beautiful niece of foreign extraction; the tone is rather acerbic. Finally, *The Romance of Private Life* (1839) also consists of two tales; in *The Renunciation*, a young girl is kidnapped from England to a life of imposture abroad; she later renounces her supposed father and travels to Italy where she discovers her identity, her family, and an appropriate helpmate. The second tale, *The Hermitage*, develops into a melodrama involving a ruined country maiden and an unsolved murder.

In evaluating the fiction of Sarah Harriet Burney, one is struck by the prevalence of dysfunctional families. Even allowing for the advantages to the plot of an unprotected heroine, a remarkable number of parental figures are absent, unsatisfactory, or simply dead. Of seven heroines, three are orphans, one is motherless, one fatherless. Only one heroine enjoys a loving relationship with a nurturing mother (who dies); another maternal death within the novel's pages closes a pitiful career whose scandal has cast a shadow on her innocent daughter's fortunes. The one mother who is left alive at the novel's end faces what "was not a happy old age,"[114] embittered by the failure of matrimonial projects for her daughter and the consequences of mismanagement of her son. (Nor do the heroes fare much better; seven heroes can boast only three parents, all of them mothers, and only one of them good.)

The heroine's surviving fathers are not very admirable. One is absent for much of the action and functions mostly as a potential blocking device for a happy marriage. Another is a manipulative villain who in order to secure a fortune kidnaps a little girl who astonishingly turns out to be his own daughter. The most fully delineated is a revengeful tyrant who disowns the heroine; even when placated at the end, his "wholly unamiable" character has hardly been worth the effort, according to the narrator.[115] The most common paternal characteristic, which pervades the subplots as well, is implacable resentment; father figures evoke awe but rarely uncheckered warmth.

Female siblings or cousins can be allies but are sometimes driven by rivalry in the matrimonial market to malicious or petty acts. Brothers too are ambivalent figures; some have been spoiled by indulgence, the effect of an ill-judged parental favoritism (a recurring motif). Others are all too positive, with a frequent pattern being a forbidden romance with a childhood associate. In S. H. Burney's first novel, *Clarentine*, the fraternal relationship is split: a beautiful orphan inspires an unreciprocated passion in one cousin while herself cherishing a preference for another. Descriptions of the protective guardian have been identified boldly by some Burney scholars as "idealized portraits of J[*ames*] B[*urney*]."[116] Certainly, the situational resemblances are strong; a sailor by profession, Somerset is apparently involved with a woman his own age. However, lest this fictional romance be cited as actual proof of incest (as has been done),[117] it is worth remarking that the sense of warm fraternal regard is more convincingly portrayed than the supposed passion.

Even more suggestive from a biographical point of view is *Traits of Nature*, where for most of the novel, the heroine is denied her father's acceptance and exiled from home. When finally reinstated, she meets a cool reception and incurs his wrath for having neglected her musical studies. In a striking scene preceding the reconciliation, Adela attends a soiree where she converses with her admirer, the protector and friend of her childhood, now widowed with two children. Knowing that this friendship is fiercely frowned on by her family, she turns to meet the petrifying gaze of her estranged father, who will not acknowledge her in public.[118] Again, certain details are telling, especially the thankless and "harrassing" task of nursing the elderly man, an invalid of "unconquerable petulance" in the desperate hope that her attendance will arouse some affection.[119] The suffering inflicted by the father's stern rejection, which resonates throughout the novel, is difficult to disentangle from Burney's own experience and private fears. Since the éclaircissement with the lover is achieved long before the final curtain, the emotional thrust of the narrative is displaced onto a quest for paternal approval (grudgingly bestowed at the end).

It seems that for Sarah Harriet Burney, the patriarchal family, potentially a source of refuge and support, could become an instrument of oppression and tyranny. Her heroines are placed in a vulnerable position; most suffer from a sense of loss, dislocation, or isolation. Some experience a dark moment of despair at the nadir of their fortunes: "Once more she saw herself a lone being in creation . . . she was without kindred—without a home—without even a name she could legally appropriate—without other means of existence than such as depended upon the precarious favour of the public! It was a perspective that at once filled her with grief, terror, and self-compassion, and her tears long continued to flow with undiminished bitterness."[120] The feeling of abandonment may derive from a friendless condition but can also occur in the midst of a crowd. The tone is often gray, suffused with sadness until the somewhat adventitious resolution confers wealth and marriage on the principals. The reader is left with a sense of profound loneliness pervading the public and private writing of Sarah Harriet Burney.

Several incidents included in the novels also feature in the letters. Like her heroine, Agnes, Burney herself was removed from her English home at an early age and sent to the Continent to learn French; this may lend authenticity to her portrayal of a homesick child. Her travel experiences amidst the picturesque scenery of Wales and the art treasures of Italy are worked into her fiction. After 1803, when she took up her first position as governess, her descriptions of the mansions of the country gentry and the fashionable society of London are more convincing. Certain characters are familiar, such as the irascible but warm-hearted Julius, who (like Lionel in Mme d'Arblay's *Camilla*) may reflect the impetuosity of Charles Burney Jr.[121] A Mme d'Arzele who lives in rural seclusion with the Chevalier Valcour, a noble fugitive from revolutionary France, evokes the d'Arblays in name and situation. An unlikable female pedant who studies dead languages incurs some of the rancor and ambivalence aroused by Sarah Harriet's niece, Marianne Francis.

Other themes and attitudes are articulated alike in both letters and novels (especially in the words of a sprightly confidante, a foil to the more serious heroine). Favorite authors are cited; phrases or quotations, moral reflections on life and human nature are repeated. Her characters often share the author's aptitudes (for drawing and the modern languages) and antipathies (for needlework and harsh Italian voices). Sensitivity toward the stigma of spinsterhood is shown in the fiction by wry slurs on the state of "single blessedness";[122] more than one novel contains ridicule of the educational role adopted by "decayed gentlewomen."[123] Elsewhere, a middle-aged spinster receives a ludicrous proposal from a rustic squire in which nevertheless "there was much to tempt a spinster with a narrow income, in the prospect of becoming mistress of an affluent establishment, and wife to a man who, though tedious, was otherwise unexceptionable. . . . Besides it was something to wipe off the disgrace of Old Maidism." In the end, although her character does not act on the "mere motive of pecuniary prudence,"[124] the wistfulness remains; the telling incident occurs in the final pages of Burney's last work.

Literary tastes are also discussed within the context of the fiction. One extended dialogue inveighs against the excesses of sentimental novels that feature unrealistically perfect heroines and immoderately passionate heroes.[125] These remarks coincide with the distinction made in one of Burney's letters between "genuine, and really virtuous & good sentimentality" as opposed to "Nervous hippishness." She concludes unambiguously, "And Novel Romance makes me puke!—"(L. 59). Her own fiction, she felt, did not always live up to these standards, creating a gap between profession and practice of which she was painfully aware: "I never insert love but to oblige my readers: if I could give them humor and wit, however, I should make bold to skip the love, and think them well off into the bargain. But writing for the press, . . . cramps my genius, & makes me weigh my words, and write as you call it mawning" (L. 84).

This evaluation is perhaps unfairly harsh and may reflect the high quality of her models. Sarah Harriet Burney's literary activities were not restricted to writing alone; she was also an avid reader and critic, recording her judgments "with pen and ink in my little private reviews" (L. 55) (she also appears to have done some editing for the publisher Thomas Tegg).[126] Her letters attest to the range and scope of her reading and her awareness of current literary developments; she often read a work within weeks or even days of publication. Her instinct for quality in novels is remarkable. Of the writers in her day, she valued Maria Edgeworth as "the most useful" (L. 75) and appreciated the originality of James Fenimore Cooper. But her highest admiration was reserved for two of her contemporaries, Sir Walter Scott and Jane Austen. Her enjoyment of Scott as the "most spirit-stirring Author" (L. 111) is less unusual than her percipience in recognizing the genius of Austen, for whose work she was an immediate enthusiast.

Pride and Prejudice impressed her greatly even on first reading: "I could quite rave about it! How well you define one of its characterestics when you say of it, that it breaths a spirit of 'careless originality.'—It is charming.—Nothing was ever better conducted than the fable; nothing can be more piquant than its dialogues; more distinct than its characters" (L. 73). She later claimed to have read it as many times "as bumper toasts are given—three times three!" (L. 159). She also praised *Emma* highly, "which, even amidst languor and depression, forced from me a smile, & afforded me much amusement" (L. 83), and from which she could quote passages verbatim: "I have read no story book with such glee, since the days of 'Waverley' and 'Mannering,' and, by the same Author as 'Emma,' my prime favorite of all modern Novels 'Pride & Prejudice'" (L. 84). While she discusses only two of Austen's novels in her letters, Sarah Harriet also owned copies of *Sense and Sensibility* and *Mansfield Park*.[127] It is interesting to note that it was her publisher, Henry Colburn, who sent her one of these works (L. 83), perhaps sensing a kindred spirit.

Burney's appreciation of Austen is telling, but equally interesting is the fact that the favor was returned, at least that Austen formed part of her own audience. (Admittedly, Jane Austen's remarks on *Clarentine* are not wholly flattering; she was "surprised" to find it "does not bear a 3^{d} [*reading*] at all.")[128] But the astuteness of Sarah Harriet's critical perceptions does not appear to have given her confidence in her own ability. She was diffident about her work, and sensitive to the opinions of others, whose advice she solicited and often followed. Those whom she consulted included her nephew, Martin, and her nieces, Fanny Burney, Fanny Raper, and Charlotte Barrett, as well as two inhabitants of Chelsea Hospital, Mrs. Haggitt and young Emma Keate. Moreover, the changes she made on their suggestions were not insubstantial: for her third novel, they included the title, the opening scene, and the final resolution.

This lack of confidence may reflect a lack of encouragement. In a family that excelled in literary and other fields, Sarah Harriet probably suffered from comparison with her more famous half-sister. *Clarentine*, her first novel, was published within a few days of Mme d'Arblay's *Camilla*. Yet while Charles Burney zealously defended and promoted the latter as "his most ardent passion,"[129] he seems to have paid little attention to his youngest daughter's effort. When he does speak of it, he is rather apologetic: "Don't you find considerable merit in her novel, particularly in the conversations? The opening is embarrassed & incorrect; but she afterwards gets on very well."[130] James was no less patronizing, apparently, judging from the laughs he raised in the family by his witticism on *Geraldine Fauconberg* (L. 60).

When discussing her novels, Sarah invariably uses deprecating language. The first one is a "little work" (L. 13), the second a "poor bantling" (L. 38), and the last is diminished as a "little booky." She speaks disparagingly of her audience, "the common run of Novel readers," and claims to respect only those "who read better things habitually, [*who*] are the only satisfactory persons for a writer of fiction to have any dealings with" (L. 166). Her position as a published author she considers demeaning and refers to her literary pursuits with some embarrassment: "I live here amongst such a set of idle and heavy-bottomed old and young women, that, of a morning, my time is never my own. Our Street door opens with a latch; and people who know me intimately, think themselves priveleged to walk up stairs without ringing . . . . I am forced therefore to avoid as much as possible all ungenteel jobs; and as I reckon scribbling by trade <u>very</u> ungenteel, I never set too with comfort, till candles come, & visitors cease" (L. 82). (Her remark brings to mind the story of Jane Austen and the squeaking door which gave her timely warning of visitors, from whom she hid her literary employment).[131]

The only aspect of her work of which she speaks with unabashed enthusiasm is the money that she makes, anticipating with relish the profits of each publishing venture, which she sometimes depends on for living expenses.[132] Insisting that her literary activity is for the sake of gain ("I must scribble, <u>or I cannot live</u>" [L. 82]), she looks forward to the day when she will be freed from the necessity of "compulsory Authorship" (L. 89). When publishing her last work, she excuses herself by pleading impoverishment (L. 159). It is curious, however, that her bank account does not confirm any crisis in her finances, leading one to suspect an element of pose in her attitude. Moreover, Sarah Harriet did not stop writing when it was no longer financially necessary, and when she had no immediate plans to publish. In Italy, where she could live very cheaply, she composed a two-volume tale, which she read to family and friends, and whose completion she reported with satisfaction. An endeavor that concentrated her faculties probably provided a welcome occupation during the solitary winters in Florence. She experienced the same release at Chelsea Hospital, where, although her life was "dull, monotonous, and lonely" (L. 116), she was able to become absorbed into "a little ideal world of my own, and care nothing about the humdrum of surrounding realities" (L. 95).

The clue to her writing and to her reading may well be in the possibility of escape from a lonely life; in the exercise of the imagination, she could fill the emptiness of her existence. In her letters, taking an obvious pleasure in the use of language ("I like that word past expression" [L. 62]), she could transform the dullness of everyday reality into a moment of beauty: "I am sitting in such a snug corner of my exquisite bed room as you might almost envy even at Richmond. I see nothing but the tops of the trees and the western sky, though close to the window—and I have tea and bread and butter beside me, & drink a little, & write a little, & then drink again" (L. 60). It is the poignancy of that moment, crystallized and suspended in time, vividly evoking the past with all the immediacy of the present, that is shared by the reader of Sarah Harriet Burney.

Notes

1. Parish register, St. Nicholas, King's Lynn, Norfolk.
2. L. 162 below. All further references to the letters in this edition appear in the text.
3. *EJL*, 1: 265.
4. MAR to FB, 21 May [1774], Berg.
5. *EJL*, 2: 163.
6. Thomas Twining to CB, 6 Oct. 1777, BL Add. MS. 39929, ff. 143–46.
7. L. 3, n. 8.
8. *DL*, 3: 76.
9. *DL*, 3: 508.
10. Lonsdale, 283, 292–96, 335.
11. CB to CBF, 25 Feb. 1786, Barrett, Eg. 3700A, ff. 2–3v.
12. CB, 29 Aug. 1786, Poetical Notebook, Osborn.
13. CB to FB, 2 Oct. 1786, Osborn.
14. CB to "Rosette" Burney, 24 Oct. 1787, Burney-Cumming.
15. CB to FB, 4 Sept. 1786, Osborn.
16. E.g., *DL*, 1: 30.
17. CB to "Rosette" Burney, 9 Oct. 1795, Burney-Cumming.
18. *JL*, 3: 217–18.
19. CB to FBA, 2 Dec. 1796, Berg.
20. *JL*, 3: 250, 219, 352.
21. SBP to FB, 20 July–5 Oct. [17]89, Barrett, Eg. 3692, ff. 55–90v.
22. *HFB*, 35–40.
23. CB to Ralph Griffiths, 2 Nov. 1796, Bodleian, MS. Add. C. 89, ff. 1–2.
24. CB to [Dorothy Young], 7 Feb. 1797, Berg.

25. CB to [Dorothy Young], [c. 27–31 Oct. 1796], Osborn.
26. *JL*, 3: 218.
27. *JL*, 3: 212.
28. *JL*, 3: 219.
29. *JL*, 3: 239.
30. *JL*, 3: 212.
31. MAR to FBA, 9 Jan. 1797, Barrett, Eg. 3697, ff. 247–50v.
32. MAR to FBA, [3 Sept. 1798], Barrett, Eg. 3697, ff. 276–77v.
33. *HFB*, 281–85, cited in Lonsdale, 387; see also *EJL*, 1: 39, n. 13.
34. Winifred F. Courtney, "New Light on the Lambs and Burneys," *Charles Lamb Bulletin*, NS no. 57 (Jan. 1987): 19–27. Courtney does not give a source for her account of these events, but she is clearly following that of Hemlow, either in *HFB*, 281–85; or *JL*, 4: LL. 295–97 and nn.
35. Margaret Anne Doody, *Frances Burney: The Life in the Works* (New Brunswick, N.J.: Rutgers University Press, 1988), 277–81.
36. See e.g., SBP to FB, 20 July-5 Oct. [17]89, Barrett, Eg. 3692, ff. 55–90v.
37. *HFB*, 36–37; MAR to FB, 24 Sept. [1776], Berg.
38. MAR to FBA, [3 Sept. 1798], Barrett, Eg. 3697, ff. 276–77v.
39. MAR to FBA, 5 Sept. [1798], Barrett, Eg. 3697, ff. 278–79v.
40. *JL*, 4: 214.
41. *JL*, 4: 244, 247, 263, 279; LL. 24, 25, 26 below.
42. MAR to FBA, 19 [Oct. 1798], Barrett, Eg. 3697, ff. 282–83v.
43. MAR to FBA, 23 Oct. [1798], Barrett, Eg. 3697, ff. 284–85v.
44. See e.g. JB to FBA, 7 May 1816, Berg; L. 99 below.
45. Manwaring, 276.
46. MAR to FBA, 9 Oct. [1798], Barrett, Eg. 3697, ff. 280–81v.
47. MAR to FBA, 23 Oct. [1798], Barrett, Eg. 3697, ff. 284–85v.
48. CB and MAR to FBA, 26 Oct. 1798, Berg.
49. MAR to FBA, 9 Oct. [1798], Barrett, Eg. 3697, ff. 280–81v.
50. *JL*, 4: 306–7.
51. MAR to FBA, [3 Sept. 1798], Barrett, Eg. 3697, ff. 276–77v.
52. MAR to FBA, 5 Sept. [1798], Barrett, Eg. 3697, ff. 278–79v.
53. *JL*, 4: 329.
54. MAR to FBA, 30 Oct. [1798], Barrett, Eg. 3697, ff. 286–87v.
55. MAR to FBA, [Nov. 1798], Barrett, Eg. 3697, ff. 288–90v.
56. CB and MAR to FBA, 26 Oct. [17]98, Berg.
57. *JL*, 4: 245.
58. JB to FBA, [post 13 May 1799], Berg.
59. *JL*, 4: 479.
60. *JL*, 11: 340.
61. MAR to FBA, [3 Sept. 1798], Barrett, Eg. 3697, ff. 276–77v.
62. Coutts ledgers.
63. MAR to FBA, [30 Oct. 1798], Barrett, Eg. 3697, ff. 286–87v.
64. EBB to CB Jr., 1 Mar. 1806 [1807], Osborn.
65. Lonsdale, 460–61.

66. See e.g. CB to CPB, 9 Jan. 1808, Osborn; CB to Lady Manvers, 18 July 1809, Osborn.
67. The phrase occurs in the first chapter of Jane Austen's *Emma* (1816).
68. MAR to FBA, [3 Sept. 1798], Barrett, Eg. 3697, ff. 276–77v.
69. CB to FBA, 5 May 1810, Osborn.
70. CB to FBA, 12 Nov. 1808, Berg.
71. CB to Edmond Malone, 23 June [1808], Bodleian, MS. Malone 38, f. 161.
72. See e.g. CB to FC, 31 Oct. 1792, 2 Dec. 1792, Osborn.
73. CB to CB Jr., 7 June 1809, Osborn.
74. Charles Burney's will is transcribed in Scholes, 2: 262–72.
75. Coutts ledgers.
76. *JL*, 11: 294, n. 1; below L. 100, n. 3.
77. CFBt to CBFB, 14 Sept. [1822], CFBt to FPR, CFBt to MF, 22 Sept. [1822], Barrett, Eg. 3706D, ff. 42–48v.
78. *JL*, 11: 382–83, 387, 398.
79. *JL*, 11: 448.
80. *JL*, 12: 574 and n. 4.
81. *JL*, 11: 405, 466.
82. Coutts ledgers.
83. HCR, 25 Nov. 1829, Travel Journals.
84. [Sarah Harriet] Burney, "The Renunciation," *The Romance of Private Life* (London: Henry Colburn, 1839), 2: 95.
85. HCR, *Reminiscences*, 2: 452–53.
86. CBFB to CFBt, 4 Nov. 1831, Berg.
87. HCR to Miss Fenwick, 6 Mar. 1843, Dr. Williams'.
88. MAR to FBA, [24 Dec. 1796], Barrett, Eg. 3697, ff. 237–44v; *JL*, 3: 219.
89. HCR, *Reminiscences*, 2: 453–54; HCR, 7, 9, 12, 22, 29 Dec. 1829, Travel Journals.
90. CFBt to FBA, 28 Jan. 1830, Berg.
91. *JL*, 12: 740.
92. HCR, 25 Nov. 1829–10 Mar. 1830, passim, Travel Journals.
93. For his life, see Edith J. Morley, *The Life and Times of Henry Crabb Robinson* (London: J. M. Dent, [1935]).
94. HCR, *Reminiscences*, 2: 452.
95. HCR, 13 Nov. 1833, Diaries.
96. CFBt to FPR, 22 Sept. [1822], Barrett, Eg. 3706D, ff. 45–48v.
97. *JL*, 3: 352.
98. HCR, 10–13 Mar. 1830, Travel Journals.
99. CFBt to CBFB, 19 June [1832], Berg.
100. CFBt to JBt, 20[–22] Sept. [1832], Barrett, Eg. 3702A, ff. 202–3v.
101. CFBt to JBt, 19 Oct. [1832], Barrett, Eg. 3702A, ff. 211–12v.
102. CFBt to JBt, 14 Sept. [1832], Barrett, Eg. 3702A, ff. 200–201v.
103. *JL*, 3: 352.
104. HCR, 1 Jan. 1830, Travel Journals.
105. CFBt to HBt, 28–30 Apr. [1831], Berg.
106. HCR, 23 May 1831, Travel Journals.

107. *JL*, 12: 787, 807.
108. HCR, 21 Apr. 1841, Diaries.
109. HCR, 18 Feb. 1844, Diaries.
110. Death certificate, 8 Feb. 1844, GRO; will of Sarah Harriet Burney, PRO/PROB/10/6242, dated 21 Sept. 1842, proved 15 Feb. 1844.
111. CFBt to HBt, 6–7 Apr. [1832], Barrett, Eg. 3702A, ff. 70–77.
112. Morley, 128.
113. *Monthly Review*, 2nd ser. 21 (1796): 456.
114. [Sarah Harriet] Burney, *The Hermitage*, vol. 3 of *The Romance of Private Life* (London: Henry Colburn, 1839), 339.
115. [Sarah Harriet] Burney, *Traits of Nature* (London: Henry Colburn, 1812), 5: 335.
116. *JL*, 4: 288, n. 5.
117. Doody, 278–79.
118. Burney, *Traits of Nature*, 4: 165–66.
119. Burney, *Traits of Nature*, 5: 104.
120. [Sarah Harriet] Burney, *The Renunciation*, vols. 1 and 2 of *The Romance of Private Life*, 184.
121. *HFB*, 254.
122. See e.g., Burney, *Traits of Nature*, 3: 10.
123. See [Sarah Harriet Burney], *Geraldine Fauconberg* (London: G. Wilkie and J. Robinson, 1808), 2: 23; *Traits of Nature*, 2: 40–46.
124. Burney, *The Hermitage*, 3: 333–34, 336.
125. [Burney], *Geraldine Fauconberg*, 1: 150–53.
126. Judging from Tegg's edition of Henry Mackenzie's *The Man of Feeling* and a translation of Bernardin de Saint-Pierre's *Paul et Virginie*, edited by Miss Burney, and bound together as issued in copies still extant.
127. Sarah Harriet Burney's copy of the second edition of *Sense and Sensibility* is in the Fales Library, New York University; her copy of the first edition of *Mansfield Park* is in the Beinecke Rare Book and Manuscript Library, Yale University.
128. *Jane Austen's Letters to her Sister Cassandra and Others*, ed. R. W. Chapman (Oxford: Clarendon Press, 1932), 1: 180.
129. *JL*, 3: 239.
130. CB to FBA, 2 Dec. 1796, Berg.
131. John Halperin, *The Life of Jane Austen* (Baltimore, Md.: Johns Hopkins Press, 1984), 183.
132. Her earnings must have been a welcome supplement to an income that never exceeded £100 per annum; the sums she was offered (£100 per volume for *Tales of Fancy*) compared favorably to those earned by other women writers of the time. The popular Charlotte Smith was usually paid about £50 a volume, while the relatively unknown Jane Austen earned £110 for the copyright of *Pride and Prejudice*. At the upper end of the scale, however, the highly successful Maria Edgeworth could earn £2,000 for a single novel.

The Letters of Sarah Harriet Burney

1. To Mary Young

[Chelsea College], 4 December 1792
A.L.S., Barrett, Eg. 3700A, ff. 226–27v
Address: Miss Young / Arthur Young's Esqr / Bradfield Hall near / Bury St. Edmonds
Postmarks: [A]NDERSO[N]
B DE / 4 / 92

Dec^ber 4th 1792

My dear Miss Mary.[1]

This will be the <u>first</u> letter I have written since my return from Bradfield,[2] & I am so out of the habit of scribbling, I scarcely know how to begin.—Let me however thank you for your very obliging letter, & congratulate you upon your two Balls. I have not had any thing so agreable here, & have been but once or twice at most out of an evening. My greatest frolick, was with the Farquhars[3] to the new play house coven Garden. We went a very large party in two coaches, & filled the box ourselves—You have seen the house I beleive; it is very showy, but though the pillars do not appear the bulge in the boxes, & the quantity of gold & crimson give it a very heavy look.[4] I dined on Saturday with Mrs Robson,[5] & made an engagement to go with Charlotte[6] & her father to the new play of the Pirates on Thursday,[7] when I am likewise to sleep in town. I am promised another play by the Farquhars who are all longing to see Columbus:[8] I am quite a rake you will find. Tomorrow Papa[9] & I dine at Mrs Devismes to meet Mr Devisme from Portugal:[10] John[11] cut his hand so dreadfully at school, the surgeon was apprehensive he would lose the use of it, but it is better now, nay I believe quite well. I went about ten days ago to see Mr Eckardts manufactory with the Farquhars; he gave us tickets to go to Lord Dovers[12] for whom he has been fitting up two rooms. I never saw any thing so beautiful as the paintings, & ornaments are. We saw all the children at work, & while we were in their room, an engine was playing which changed the air in five minutes, & entirely carried off the smell of the paint, which might else be very prejudicial to them.[13] This contrivance keeps them all in health, & they really look quite fresh, & strong.—I have been hearing a great deal about fashions at a Milliners Kitty Farquhar[14] carried me to.—Short sleeves are to be worn this winter, with little muslin cufs like a shift sleeve, with wristbands & robbins. No white muslins, but for the youngest people, slight sattins, or sarsenets, made like round gowns, very long indeed behind, & trimmed at the bottom with deep fringes & tassell's.—I saw a fringe which was to cost nine shillings a yard!—It was handsome but no more worth the money than my nose is. The stays are all to be cut down, & worn as low, as of late they have been high.—Helmet bonnets are still much in fashion, but alas! plaids are quite out. I have not yet left off love ribbons,[15] & am obliged to new sleeve my black jacket so much has it been hacked.—I hate short sleeves in winter, but it will very soon become a singularity to wear long ones. I have had a beautiful blue silk handker[f] with a deep purple border given me to wear as a turban, which are not yet out of fashion, but while I am in black I cannot use it, & it will become like my plaid bonnet, too antiquated to be worn afterwards.

Rubbishly as all this is, perhaps you may like to hear it, & if not you can but run it over, & throw it into the fire.

The political alarm is now become so general, & so frightful that nothing else is thought or talked of.[16] Indeed, if the precautions now taking by goverment do not succeed every thing is to be dreaded, from the madness of the people. When we read [in] history of revolutions, civil wars, & [ass]assinations, how little did we suppose [the] same evils were preparing for ourselves, or dream that in our time events of such direful importance would ever take place. Cold, & indifferent as I have hitherto been concerning changes in goverment, I now am awakened to expectations of horrors, & tumults scarcely inferior to those that have passed in france.[17] The tower is doubly guarded, barracks are forming for the soldiers,[18] proclamations issued out, & torn down as soon as pasted up, & treason, & rebellion the wish, & the avowed purpose, of all the lower order of the people. The King goes tomorrow to the play! How anxious are we all to hear how he is receivd![19] And yet more how he will get to the house of Parliament![20]

Sarah Rawlinson was one week at the Latrobes,[21] one with us, & one with her uncle[22] to whom she is now returned.—We have heard no particulars, but when I see M[rs] Latrobe I shall enquire the cause of so sudden a removal. She did not let us know when she was going away, but as she is with her uncle, I hope he will endeavour to get her another place.—I had made her promise not to go till she had told us of it, but that she forgot.—

My best respects to M[rs] Young, & love to Bobbin.[23]

Arthur[24] looked very well, & very chearful.—He walked home with Blancherie[25] who drank tea here that evening.

I am dear Miss Mary

yours affectionately

S. H. Burney.

My father & Mother unite in love & compliments to Mrs Young, & yourself.

I have forgot what book M^rs^ Y means unless it was Paul & Virginia in English called Paul & Mary.[26]—I have seen nothing new, & have been reading the Memoirs of M^de^ de Maintenon in french[27] which are exceedingly entertaining. Gonzalve de Cordova is translated.[28]—

1. Mary Young (1766–1851), eldest daughter of Arthur Young (1741–1820), agriculturist and author. In 1765, he had married Martha Allen (1740–1815), younger sister of Charles Burney's second wife, Elizabeth (*DNB;* Gazley, 24; "Appendix," *AR*, 93 (1851): 333).

2. In June, Arthur Young had invited the Burneys to his estate at Bradfield, near Bury St. Edmunds, Suffolk, which he had inherited (through the generosity of his elder brother) in 1785. Charles Burney declined for himself and his wife, on the grounds of poor health and prior commitments, but sent his daughter, Sarah Harriet. She was there in late July when Young wrote appreciatively of her lively spirits: "She has an excellent understanding, and with that dash of originality that renders it interesting; I assure you that she enlivens us much" (Gazley, 1, 187–88; *JL*, 12: 991–92; Young, 127, 214–15; AY to CB, 31 July [1792], Osborn).

Her visit was enlivened by the arrival of the duc de Liancourt (1747–1827), fleeing from the Terror in France, for whom she acted as interpreter and who in return "seems to have conceived a real kindness for her" (*JL*, 1: 244). She was still there in October when her half-sister Frances joined them (*JL*, 1: 231–48; 12: 992–94).

3. Walter Farquhar (1738–1819), M.D. (1796), apothecary, physician, and family friend. Well respected in his profession, he was created a baronet in 1796, and soon after was appointed physician-in-ordinary to the Prince of Wales. In 1771 he had married Ann (Stephenson) Harvie (d. 1797), by whom he had a large family (*DNB;* Burke; Foster; *GM*, 67 (1797): Pt. 2, 806).

4. The Covent Garden theater was completely redesigned for the 1792–93 season. The refurbished playhouse was "neat, airy, and lofty, and has a proper degree of elegance" (*London Stage*, Pt. 5, Vol. 3, 1473–76; *GM*, 62, Pt. 2 (1792): 862).

5. Probably the wife of the bookseller, James Robson (1733–1806), formerly a Miss Perrot (d. 15 Nov. 1818), whom he had married before 1766. Robson was a friend of Thomas Payne, whose daughter had married Charles Burney's son, James; he also helped to publish some of Charles Burney's works (*DNB;* Ian Maxted, *The London Book Trades 1775–1800* (Folkestone, Kent: Dawson, 1977); *GM*, 76, Pt. 2 (1806): 783, 871–72; 88, Pt. 2 (1818): 476).

6. Charlotte Robson (d. 31 July 1839), the third of five daughters, was later to marry

on 14 July 1819 the Rev. Samuel Hartopp (c. 1764–1852), Vicar of Little Dalby and Rector of Cold Overton, Leics. (1788–1852) (*Alumni Cantab.*; *GM*, 89, Pt. 2 (1819): 87; NS 12 (1839): 321; NS 37 (1852): 208).

7. *The Pirates*, written by James Cobb, with music composed principally by Stephen Storace, opened on 21 November 1792 at the King's Theatre, Haymarket. It enjoyed an initial run of eleven nights and was performed thirty times in its first season. Apparently the music, costumes, scenery, and acting contributed more to its success than the plot (*London Stage*, Pt. 5, Vol. 3, 1501–52; *Times*, 21–22 Nov. 1792).

If Sarah did go to the theater on Thursday, 6 December 1792, she would have been disappointed, as George Farquhar's *The Inconstant* was playing instead. However, on Saturday, 8 December, *The Pirates* was on again (*Times*, 6–8 Dec. 1792).

8. *Columbus; or, A World Discovered*, a new play by Thomas Morton, was first performed at Covent Garden on Saturday, 1 December 1792 and repeated thirty times that season. Especially striking was a scene in which the Temple of the Sun was destroyed by an earthquake, to the accompaniment of thunder and lightning (*London Stage*, Pt. 5, Vol. 3, 1504–5; *Times*, 3 Dec. 1792).

9. Charles Burney (1726–1814), musician and author, Mus.D. (1769), F.R.S. (1773); in 1783, he had been appointed organist at the Royal Hospital, Chelsea (1783), where he lived with his second wife, Elizabeth (Allen) Allen (1728–96), and his two unmarried daughters, Frances and Sarah Harriet (*JL*, 1: lxix).

10. Probably Gerard de Visme (1726–97), younger brother to the diplomat, Louis de Visme (1720–76), who had helped Charles Burney during his visit to Munich (*DNB*; Lonsdale, 115). A merchant in the firm of Purry, Mellish, and De Visme, he had lived in Portugal for forty years where he amassed a large fortune. Recently returned to England for his health, he had dined in company with Charles Burney's friend, Edmond Malone, in August 1791, when he entertained the company with a description of the Lisbon earthquake of 1755 (Sir James Prior, *Life of Edmond Malone* (London: Smith & Elder, 1860), 409–12; Walpole, 11: 160, n. 2; 43: 145; Burke; Burke, *Commoners*, 4: 320–22; *Westminsters*; *GM*, 67, Pt. 2 (1797): 990). Both of these brothers were unmarried but Mrs. de Visme could be a sister-in-law or a niece.

11. Unidentified, but from the context, he might be related to the de Vismes.

12. Joseph Yorke (1724–92), created Baron Dover (1788), Minister at the Hague (1751–61), and Ambassador there (1761–80). He died on 2 December 1792 at his house in Hill Street, Mayfair (Gibbs; Namier & Brooke; *DNB*; *GM*, 62, Pt. 2 (1792): 1155–56; "Appendix," *AR*, 34 (1792): 60).

13. The Dutch artisan, Anthony George Eckhardt (d. 1809), best known for the portable table he invented in 1771, now in the Victoria and Albert Museum (Geoffrey Beard and Christopher Gilbert, eds., *Dictionary of English Furniture Makers, 1660–1840* (London: Furniture History Society, 1986)).

During the 1790s, he ran a factory with his brother, Francis Frederick, producing fine wallpaper "of exquisite design and workmanship," located in Whitelands House, just north of the Royal Hospital, Chelsea. One of the workrooms, where about forty girls were employed in painting, was ventilated by means of a special air-pump, perhaps of his own design (E. A. Entwisle, "18th Century London Paperstainers: The Eckhardt Brothers of Chelsea," *Connoisseur* 143 (Mar. 1959): 74–77).

14. Catherine Farquhar (c. 1772–1849), eldest daughter of Walter Farquhar (n. 3).

She was later to marry on 8 May 1802 as his second wife, Gilbert Mathison of Jamaica (Burke; *GM*, 71, Pt. 1 (1801): 285; 72, Pt. 1 (1802): 469; NS 32 (1849): 663).

15. A narrow gauze ribbon with satin stripes formerly worn in mourning (*OED*), in this case for SHB's brother-in-law, Clement Francis (c. 1744–92), who had married 11 February 1786 Charlotte Ann Burney (1761–1838). On 19 October 1792, he died suddenly at Aylsham, Norfolk, leaving his wife with a newborn baby (*JL*, 1: lxxii, 257).

16. Alarm swept England in November 1792 with "the threat of radical egalitarianism in league with French republicanism" (Albert Goodwin, *The Friends of Liberty* (London: Hutchinson, 1979), 264). Rumors of insurrection were rife, and on 1 December the King issued a proclamation calling out the militia and summoning Parliament (*Times*, 3 Dec. 1792). Sarah's political opinions may have been influenced by her father, whose letters of the time expressed horror at the revolution in France, fear lest its contagion spread to England, and opposition to any reform (see e.g., CB to FC, 31 Oct. 1792, 2 Dec. 1792, 25 Dec. 1792, Osborn).

17. Recent political developments in France to which SHB may be alluding were the capture of the Tuileries on 10 August 1792, the massacre of prisoners beginning 2 September, the abolition of the monarchy (21 September) and the declaration of the Republic, the November Edict of Fraternity, and the ongoing debate in the National Convention over the trial of the King.

18. The newspapers of the time were full of reports of emergency security measures taken by the government. On 3 December the *Times* announced that "Great preparations of defence are making at the Tower, which is fortifying on all sides." The unaccustomed activity attracted crowds of the curious and a public breakfast was given, followed by a Royal tour of inspection (*Times*, 4, 10 Dec. 1792). The purpose for the renovations was ominously clear, "to furnish Winter apartments for some persons who have made themselves very active in a deep laid scheme to overthrow the Constitution of this Country" (*Times*, 11 Dec. 1792).

19. When the Royal Family attended Covent Garden on 5 December 1792, their presence evoked a strong show of loyalty: "The People huzza'd, and joined with voice and heart in the call of 'God Save the King' which was four times repeated. The QUEEN looked particularly well" (*Times*, 6 Dec. 1792).

20. The King opened Parliament on 13 December 1792: "His Majesty's procession . . . occasioned a most immense concourse of spectators, who testified the loudest acclamations of Loyalty" (*Times*, 14 Dec. 1792).

21. Friends of the family since 1784 were two brothers: Christian Ignatius Latrobe (1758–1836), a Moravian minister and amateur musician, who married Hannah Sims of Yorkshire (*DNB; New Grove; GM*, NS 5 (1836): 674); Charles Joseph Latrobe, *Letters of Charles Joseph La Trobe*, ed. L. J. Blake (Melbourne, Australia: Government of Victoria, 1975), 1); and Benjamin Henry Latrobe (1764–1820), an architect, who married 27 February 1790 Lydia Sellon (d. 1793) and was to emigrate to America in 1795 (for his life and career, see Talbot Hamlin, *Benjamin Henry Latrobe* (New York: Oxford University Press, 1955)).

22. Sarah Rawlinson and her uncle have not been further traced.

23. "Bobbin," the pet name of Martha Ann Young (1783–97), youngest daughter of Arthur Young (Young, 110, n. 1).

24. Arthur Young (1769–1828), the only son, was a student at Trinity College, Cam-

bridge, from which he would take a B.A. in 1793, and be ordained shortly thereafter. He was to marry Jane Berry in 1799 and leave for Russia in 1805, residing there for the rest of his life (*Alumni Cantab.; GM*, 98, Pt. 1 (1828): 274; Gazley, passim).

25. Flammès-Claude-Catherine Pahin Champlain de Lablancherie (1752–1811), French man of letters, whom Frances Burney had met at Windsor on 7 July 1787 and "was not much charmé"; nevertheless, at his request, she wrote him a letter of introduction to her father. His frequent and voluble visits to the Burney family at Chelsea Hospital were not always welcome; he "comes here perpetually, & nearly wears us out with his visits," Fanny complained in December 1791 (FB to SBP, 1–31 July 1787, Berg; FB to CB, 8 July [17]87, Berg; *JL*, 1: 95, n. 2; 2: 9, 25).

26. The idyll of Bernardin de Saint-Pierre (1737–1814), *Paul et Virginie* (1788), had been translated into English [by Daniel Malthus] as *Paul and Mary. An Indian story*, 2 vols. (London: J. Dodsley, 1789).

27. Charles Burney owned a copy of [Laurent Angliviel de La Beaumelle (1726–73)], *Mémoires pour servir à l'histoire de Madame de Maintenon* (Amsterdam, 1755–56), a literary forgery, which was not discovered until 1865 (*Misc. Lib.*, 31; Charlotte Haldane, *Madame de Maintenon* (London: Constable, 1970), 283–86).

28. The novel of Jean-Pierre Claris de Florian (1755–94), *Gonzalve de Cordoue, ou Grenade reconquise* (1791), based on the life of Gonzalo Fernández de Córdoba (d. 1515), famed for his exploits in recapturing Granada from the Moors. It was translated into English as *Gonzalva of Cordova; or, Grenada reconquered* (1793).

---

2. To Martha (Allen) Young

[Chelsea College], 28 June 1793
A.L.S., Barrett, Eg. 3700A, ff. 213–14v
Address: Mrs Young / Arthur Young's Esqr / Bradfield Hall / near Bury / Suffolk
Postmarks: [AN]DERSON
D J[U] / 28 / 93

Friday June 28th
1793.

Dear Madam

My history compared to yours, is such a blank I am almost ashamed to bore you with it—One adventure (if I may so call it) I have now, however, to relate to you, which for its extreme childishness & folly, claims some title to singularity & notice.

It is now about a week since I dined by invitation at the Farquhars. There was a large party, & after dinner we all walked in different groups round the garden. Ann Farquhar[1] stuck by me so assiduously I began to wonder what she had got into her head, for in general we are by no means over attentive to each other. At last, I found what she was aiming at—she had formed a scheem to go to Mrs Williams's in Gower street,[2] & wanted me to accompany her on her reputable errand the following morning. I resisted her very kind invitation till I was tired of giving my reasons, & at length, upon condition she would allow me to decline any personal introduction to the fair Witch, agreed to go. As I have no idea of keeping such folly secret, I told the whole history to my father & mother at supper, & you may be sure they did not laugh at me a little. Determined not to see the woman myself, the morning came & we set out; but not as I expected on foot, but in the Farquhar's carriage,—with four other girls besides myself, & a gentleman who had slept there, & had begged them to set him down in their way. I soon found him perfectly acquainted with the motive of our expedition, which was openly talked of as a thing of course. "Pray," said I to Ann, when I saw how well she was attended, "Why was I pressed into the servise so much against my wishes? You have surely quite as many friends to keep you in countenance as you could possibly require?" To this question I could not obtain a satisfactory answer, on the contrary they all looked <&> at one another & laughed exceedingly—I wished myself a thousand miles off, & felt yet more uncomfortable when we alighted at Mademoiselle of Endor's.[3] That the girls should go, though nothing can be more silly, I do not much wonder at—but that they should order the coachman to the very door, keep it in waiting the whole time, & subject themselves to the footmans witty remarks, I own astonishes me, particularly as Ann, & I believe Kitty too, had been there once before. To make short of my story, rather than be supposed too poor to pay my half-crown, or too wise to do as they did, I had the absurdity to go up after them, listened patiently to the greatest lies I ever heard in my life, gulped down a promise of seven children!!! & came away so mad at my own stupidity I could have brained myself. Why is this woman suffered to sell her lies to every comer in so open & impudent a manner?

Do you not envy the Farquhars? They have been introduced to sweet Mrs Siddons[4] & have had her at their house in town. She shewed them on their first visit a bust of her brother,[5] done by herself in a sort of composition like bronze—They protest nothing was ever so like, & she began & finished it by memory. Till very lately she had made no attempt of the kind, but now in the country devotes a great deal of her time, to this very difficult art.

My mother still continues uncommonly well[6] & even dined in town last Tuesday, after making a number of morning v[isits] all over the town. Do you hear a[ny] thing of your M[rs] Hoole? Is she better?[7] She has not written to my Mother a great while. That nasty beast M[de] d'Eon whom my father calls a Jack whore, saving your presence has had a fencing bout at Ranelagh for her benefit[8]—This is the second time she has treated the public in this <year> way within three months—I hear that the first time, she fenced without a gown, in a pair of stays sans shoulder straps, shift sleeves visible, & a loose handkersheif unpined which was every moment falling off,—The audience burst into a roar of laughter, then grew ashamed, & ended by clapping her.

Adieu dear Madam—Love to Mary & Bobbin. O, pray do you reccolect where you bought my mothers dimity gown, & the name of the shop? If you do, send it, & my Mother will be much obliged.—I remain dear Madam, yours gratefully

S. H. B.

1. Anne Farquhar (c. 1774–1844), second daughter of Walter Farquhar, the physician. She was later to marry 1 June 1797 the Rev. James Hook (c. 1772–1828), Dean of Worcester (1825) (*DNB; GM*, 67, Pt. 1 (1797): 527; 98, Pt. 1 (1828): 369–70; NS 22 (1844): 445).

2. Mrs. Williams was a fortune teller who advertised herself as from "Bath and Bristol Hot Wells" (Walpole, 31: 280, n. 4).

3. I.e., a witch. Through a medium at Endor, King Saul sought to communicate with the spirit of the dead Samuel; see 1 Samuel 28.

4. The famous actress, Sarah Kemble (1755–1831), who had married William Siddons (c. 1744–1808) in 1773 (Highfill).

5. Probably the well-known actor and manager, John Philip Kemble (1757–1823). In the summer of 1793, Sarah Siddons was staying at the rectory cottage at Nuneham, practicing her hobby of sculpting (Highfill; Roger Manvell, *Sarah Siddons: Portrait of an Actress* (New York: G.P. Putnam's Sons, 1971), 174, 185, 298).

6. Mrs. Burney had continued feeble and unwell for some time after a "most terrific internal Hemorrhage" the previous summer (CB to Thomas Twining, [mid-Aug. 1792], Osborn; CB to FC, 27 Aug. 1792, 19 Sept. 1792, Osborn; *JL*, 1: 221–22; 2: 73).

7. Mrs. Young's second daughter, Elizabeth ("Bessy") (1768–94). She had acted as Charles Burney's amanuensis in 1791 before her marriage on 15 September of that year to the Rev. Samuel Hoole (c. 1758–1839). They lived at Abinger, Surrey, where she may have begun to show symptoms of the tuberculosis of which she was to die on 1 August 1794 (*Alumni Oxon.;* Gazley, 275, 332–34; Young, 250–52; *GM*, 61, Pt. 2 (1791): 873; 64, Pt. 2 (1794): 769; NS 11 (1839): 440; CB to FB, 8 Oct. 1791, Berg).

8. Charles-Geneviève-Louis-Auguste-André-Timothée d'Éon de Beaumont (1728–1810), who led a strange career as diplomat, soldier, and secret agent, and posed as a woman for the last three decades of his life. Living in England after 1785, he earned money by giving exhibitions of fencing, a sport in which he excelled, attired variously as a male or female. This resource was closed in 1796 by a wound from a broken foil,

and he ended his life in sickness and poverty. After his death on 21 May 1810, his body was examined by a surgeon and pronounced unmistakably male, ending years of speculation (*Times*, 25 May 1810; *GM*, 80, Pt. 1 (1810): 586–88; Pierre Pinsseau, *L'Etrange Destinée du Chevalier d'Éon (1728–1810)*, 2nd ed. (Paris: Raymond Clavreuil, 1945), 244–57).

---

3. To Mary Young

Clifton Hill, 2–4 August 1793
A.L.S., Barrett, Eg. 3700A, ff. 228–29v
Address: Miss Young / Arthur Young's Esqr / Bradfield Hall / near Bury / Suffolk
Postmarks: BRISTOL
A AU / 5 / 9[3]
7 / [?] P / P

Clifton Hill. August 2^{d}
1793

My dear Mary

The date of this letter will surprise you I believe not a little, & concern you too, when you hear that it is with my poor brother Charles,[1] & on his account that I am here, as a sort of assistant-nurse to Mrs Bicknel,[2] who, for above a month has been confined to the closest attention to him. I came down here only two days ago with James,[3] & I believe <when> shall return to town on Monday or Tuesday with Mrs Bicknell, & both my brothers.

Have you (though surely you must) yet heard, of Fanny's sudden, & most unexpected marriage?[4] Your mother, (I say once more) is a witch, for she foretold this match at Chelsea in the spring,[5] I think, or at least foretold their tumbling into love! When I shall overcome the incredible astonishment an event so little thought of, first excited, Heaven only knows!—But really now, I never shall look upon any thing as being improbable, or unlikely, & as Capt. Phillips[6] says, "shall make it a rule to lay aside all surprise, for the future."

This place is by far the most beautiful of any I ever saw in England,[7] & I was too young to remember any more beautiful even in Switzerland[8]—The walks are most extremely romantick & charming, & the weather just such as one would desire in a country so hilly as this—indeed there seems to have been no want of rain, for every thing looks very green & pleasant—Chelsea after such an excursion will I am affraid appear rather flat, & odious, & dishcloutish, yet less so however, than if I had come on a party of pleasure, for charming as the country is withoutdoors—within we are dull enough God knows.

August 4th

Tomorrow I hope & believe Charles will be able to leave Clifton, for never did poor man loath a place as he does this—besides it is incredible how much he is wanted at home: His wife is in town very ill, poor creature! in her old way.[9]

We have been Mrs Bicknell, James, & I to see Lord de Cliffords house about 6 miles from hence;[10] & the Point, a peice of rocky land from whence an arm of the sea is visible, & a view of the surrounding country, rich & beautiful beyond measure—The West India Fleet consisting of nine or ten large Merchantmen was lying at Anchor in full sight. At Lord de Cliffords they have a very good view of the sea (if the branch I speak of may be so called) from the house, into which however as the family was down, we were not allowed to enter—The grounds are very pleasantly laid out, & the situation so well chosen, that though even I have seen much larger & more splendid ones, I never yet saw one I had rather live in.

This is a very stupid letter my dear Mary, but remember, a sick mans room, is no scene for great vivacity, or spirit—And I merely write that you might not think I had quite given up all intention of ever doing it again.—

Adieu dear Mary—My next shall be more agreeable—At least I hope so,—Wish us well home with our poor Invalide, & believe me truely & affectionately

yours, S. H. Burney.

Best compliments to Mrs Young, & love to Bobbin.

Write soon pray dear girl

1. Charles Burney Jr. (1757–1817), classical scholar and divine, who was running a school at Hammersmith (*JL*, 1: lxxi; 3: 1, n. 4). He had been at Clifton since July, suffering from influenza (Hannah Maria Burney to FBA, 7 July 1791 [*pmk* 93], Barrett, Eg. 3697, ff. 1–2v).

2. Sabrina (formerly Sidney) Bicknell (c. 1759–1843), Charles Burney Jr.'s housekeeper. An orphan, she had been raised on Rousseauistic principles as a suitable wife by Thomas Day (1748–89) (*DNB; Memoirs of Richard Lovell Edgeworth, Esq.* (London: R. Hunter, 1820), 1: 214–18, 337–46; 2: 109–14; *JL*, 1: 70, n. 18; 5: 6–7, n. 2). The experiment failed and Day married someone else; Sabrina wed c. 1784 Day's friend John Bicknell (c. 1746–87) but was soon left a widow with two infant sons. CB Jr. employed her in his household and educated her sons; for her long association with the family,

see Roger Lonsdale, "Dr. Burney, 'Joel Collier,' and Sabrina," *Evidence in Literary Scholarship*, ed. René Wellek and Alvaro Ribeiro (Oxford: Clarendon Press, 1979), 281–308, esp. 304–7.

3. SHB's half-brother James Burney (1750–1821), who had gone to sea as a child, became Captain, R.N. (1782), retired on half-pay (1785), and would later be made Rear-Admiral (1821) (*JL*, 1: lxix). James and Sarah Harriet arrived at Clifton on 31 July (*JL*, 2: 181, n. 1).

4. At the age of forty-one, Frances Burney (1752–1840), novelist, married on 28 July 1793 Alexandre-Jean-Baptiste Piochard d'Arblay (1754–1818), an émigré whom she had met in January (*JL*, 1: lxx). For the story of their courtship and wedding, see *HFB*, 228–41; *JL*, 2: passim. James, who had been present at the wedding, brought the news to Clifton, whereupon Charles immediately wrote a letter of congratulations (*JL*, 2: 181, n. 1).

5. Mrs. Young had visited Chelsea in the spring and was present on 15 April when M. d'Arblay came to tea (*JL*, 2: 80).

6. Molesworth Phillips (1755–1832), Captain of the Royal Marines (1780), later Lt.-Col. (1798), who had accompanied Cook's last expedition. A friend of James, he had married on 10 January 1782 Susanna Elizabeth Burney (1755–1800). They lived at Mickleham, Surrey, where Fanny had met her future husband, and both attended the wedding (*JL*, 1: lxx; *HFB*, 228–29; *JL*, 2: ix–xix, 178).

7. The village of Clifton, built on a hill, was renowned for its picturesque beauty. For a description of its attractions, see [John Chilcott], *Chilcott's Descriptive History of Bristol*, 3rd ed. (Bristol: J. Chilcott, 1835), 284–87.

8. In 1781, the nine-year-old Sarah and her brother Richard Thomas (1768–1808) had been sent to Switzerland to further their education. Sarah studied with Marie-Anne-Louise Cuénod (1762–1848) of Corsier-sur-Vevey, and probably returned in 1783. All her life, she seems to have retained vivid memories of this formative experience, as well as a fluency in French (*JL*, 1: lxxiii, 214, n. 74; 2: 56, 58; William Holden Hutton, *Burford Papers* (London: Archibald Constable, 1905), 60; *Thraliana*, ed. Katharine C. Balderston, 2d ed. (Oxford: Clarendon Press, 1951), 1: 481–82; *The Letters of Samuel Johnson with Mrs. Thrale's Genuine Letters to Him*, ed. R. W. Chapman (Oxford: Clarendon Press, 1952), 3: 42).

9. Sarah ("Rosette") (1759–1821), daughter of Dr. William Rose (1719–86), schoolmaster, had married Charles Burney Jr. on 24 June 1783 (*JL*, 1: lxxi). A volatile personality, she apparently suffered from periodic bouts of depression, euphemistically referred to here as "her old way" (*JL*, 1: 81, n. 8; 7: 52, n. 7, 164, n. 5).

10. Charles Clifford (1759–1831), 6th Baron Clifford (1793), who had married 29 November 1786 Eleanor Mary (1756–1835), daughter of Henry, 8th Baron Arundell (Burke; Lodge). His seat, King's Weston, about four miles from Clifton, was designed by Sir John Vanbrugh c. 1710: "In its hey-day it excited the greatest admiration, for the setting was superbly chosen on rising ground, with a view over the Bristol Channel to the Welsh hills . . . to conform to the idea of landscape as a background to architecture" (Madeleine Bingham, *Masks and Façades* (London: George Allen & Unwin, 1974), 216–17). For a fuller description of the house, see Andor Gomme, Michael Jenner, and Bryan Little, *Bristol* (London: Lund Humphries, 1979), 107–14.

4. [To Martha (Allen) Young]

[Chelsea College], 7 October 1793
A.L.S., Barrett, Eg. 3700A, ff. 215–16v
Address: [Mrs. Youn]g / [Arthur You]ng's Esqr / [Bradf]ield Hall / [nea]r Bury / [S]uffolk.
Postmarks: ANDERSON

Monday 7th Oct^{ber} 1793.

My dear Madam

To a letter so earnest, & pressing as yours, I should think myself inexcusable were I not to send an imediate answer, & sorry am I to say; that answer can <alone> only be the same I have hitherto made[1]—The same reasons that induced me before to decline a Bradfield Journey still subsist, & allow me dear Madam, setting all modesty aside, to remind you, of how very little efficacy my presence ever was, towards preventing, or indeed any way checking, the scenes, you with justice so much dread.[2]—I flatter myself you think well enough of me, to believe, that were it in my power, by taking the step you wish, to lessen the discomfort you indure, nothing should retard my setting out—But tell me—<Should> Would you yourself, in similar circumstances, resolve to forfeit all tranquility by entering so unsettled a family, without the most distant prospect of being of use to others? I am sure & was so, from the first fortnight of my residence at Bradfield, that I may, ruin my own peace, & happiness, by being there, but unfortunately, have no chance of procuring either to you![3]

I have spoken with a sincerity you will I hope forgive—It is most painful to me to have nothing more satisfactory to say; yet, when you, & Mary, consider what the wretchedness of my last years visit was,[4] you will surely make allowances for my present reluctance—In your house, so little was the power I had of affording you any satisfaction by keeping off disturbances, that on the contrary, I was a mere wretched witness <to> of your sufferings[5]—equally powerless, & insignificant.—

My Mother has not it is true answered your last—But far from being insensible to its contents, she hopes one day to prove to you, the earnest attempt she made, to soften your situation, & to restore you to comfort![6]—What now however can she do, but bewail with me, yours & poor Mary's misery!

Give my kindest love to Mary, & tell her, (what I speak with the utmost sincerity,) that if there is one being upon earth, I feel for more than another, it is her![7] I am sure my Mother joins in the same pity & concern—

Farewell my dear Madam—Pray forgive this second refusal; & believe me with the heartiest good wishes for better times, your obliged & affectionate

S. H. Burney

1. This letter apparently conveys a second refusal to repeated invitations to Bradfield Hall. Mrs. Young's original offer, SHB's reply, and the reiteration are all missing. The young Fanny Burney also mentioned "pressing Invitations" to Bradfield, which she was glad to evade (*EJL*, 1: 273).

2. The Young marriage was an unhappy one, and the Burneys witnessed the discord: the "violent disputes & quarrels" that ultimately gave way to a "calm, easy contempt" (*EJL*, 1: 153–54). Mrs. Young's violent temper may well have been at fault, exacerbated perhaps by her husband's numerous flirtations (Gazley, 175, 635). Mr. Young reports "quarrels and irritations never subsiding" and accuses his wife of "the grossest falsehoods and the blackest malignity" (Young, 339, 429; see also 359, 365; *EJL*, 1: 131–33, 268, 273, 323–24; Gazley, 24–25, 60, 82, 94, 175, 200, and 634–36).

3. Sarah was not the only visitor to complain of conditions at Bradfield: "I do not enjoy paying him a visit, first because his table is the worst and dirtiest possible, and secondly on account of his wife, who looks exactly like a devil. She is hideously swarthy and looks thoroughly evil: it is rumoured that she beats her husband, and that he good-temperedly puts up with it. . . . She continually torments her children and her servants and is most frequently ill-tempered towards visitors" (Jean Marchand, ed., *A Frenchman in England 1784: Being the* Mélanges sur l'Angleterre *of François de la Rochefoucauld*, trans. S. C. Roberts (Cambridge: Cambridge University Press, 1933)).

4. For SHB's visit to Bradfield from July to November? 1792, see L. 1 above. Fanny, joining her there in early October, described the "tremendous appearance" of Mrs. Arthur Young in a rage, and gave "a specimen of the language she held all the time I stayed" (*JL*, 1: 232). Finding it unpleasant, she abridged her own stay, exclaiming, "I would not have spent a Week thus for the World!" (*JL*, 1: 242). It is hardly surprising then that Sarah Harriet, who spent many weeks in this "wretchedness," would be reluctant to return.

5. Fanny, too, had listened to Mrs. Young's complaints of her husband's ill-treatment, but found her sympathies unmoved: "her intemperate rage made her seem meriting all, & rendered her husband alone to be lamented" (*JL*, 1: 243).

6. With the loss of Mrs. Young's letter, the nature of its contents and the "attempt" made by Mrs. Burney (at reconciliation?) is open to conjecture. Mrs. Young had visited her sister in the spring (CB to AY, 12 May 1793, BL Add. MS. 35127, ff. 257–58).

7. The Burneys pitied Mary, the eldest daughter of the mismatch, witness to her parents' unhappiness, and temperamentally "the reverse of her exentric Parents: she is moderation personified,—in sense, manners, beauty & parts" (FB to SBP & Frederica Locke, May [1790], Berg). Ironically, equal concern was felt for Sarah Harriet, left alone at home with her mother, who shared the family traits of ill-temper and malignity (according to her stepchildren) (*HFB*, 35–40). Maria Rishton reported Sarah living "in a perpetual State of of [*sic*] Warfare" with her mother: "She was Violent and often took

up things too warmly—and Certainly my poor Mother did irritate and try her temper to the Utmost" (MAR to FBA, [24 Dec. 1796], Barrett, Eg. 3697, ff. 237–44v; see also *HFB*, 47; *JL*, 3: 212, 219, 225, 250, 352).

5. [To Frances (Burney) d'Arblay][1]

[Chelsea College], 19 October 1794
A.L., incomplete, Osborn

Octber 19th 1794.

My dear Sister

Look at the edges of this paper—Do you see? They are gilt! Well,—and that you could but behold the pen, the ink-bottle, in short, the desk I write upon! It is all mahogony—turns over like a square box fit for travelling—forms ocasionally a reading desk—is furnished with two quires of large gilt paper, six of small dito—a dozen new pens—a stick of red, and another of black sealing-wax—a number of note and other coloured wavers. Locks with a patent key &c, &c!—And besides, is MINE OWN! Now how to you think, (O, I forgot to tell you of some silver sand there is in it!) I came by it? Why, when I was at Bristol with Carlos[2] he shewed me this very treasure, and, to my utter amazement & unspeakable joy, said, he intended soon to buy a larger one (though this covers half our Pembroke table,)[3] and then would make me (poor little me) a present of that. Judge of little Scribble's rapture! Well, since then not a word of the matter have I ever heard, till some day last week happening to mention the promise to Papa, he advised me boldly to remind Charles of what he had said, and laughed prodigiously at his readiness to make promises he so quietly forgot.[4] Not daring however to stand the consequences of such a step face to face, I e'en wrote him as ridiculous a letter as I could, humbly representing to him the despair I was in &c, and This day to my inexpressible shame, pleasure, and gratitude, saw the dear creature enter with the desk in the exact order I have described to you! It was little Charles's Ninth Birthday,[5] to celebrate which the good little fellow brought me a lovely peice of plumb-cake!

O, and sweet Mr Farquhar—Not having been very well, I took your advice, drew up my little case, got Mama to copy it, and sent it him, upon which, like an Angel as he is, he immediately hastened to us, and I am to take some famous french medecine he and Mr North[6] are to contrive together for me according to my strength. He said, (what you know, I always thought) that while a bit of it remained, it would constantly take life again, and encrease till it overpowered the unhappy patient. Dear Sister how I thank you for your encouraging advice! I hope now, when the effect of this filth is over, to be as blooming, as mince, as lovely as the best of you!

M[r] F. at going said—"Tell M[rs] d'Arblay, it is a shame this good soul, (meaning my father, who true Scribbler-like appeared to him with a pen in his mouth) should wear himself to death with writing,[7] and <that> therefore she must supply his place to the world and begin as fast [*The letter is incomplete.*]

1. FBA is the most likely recipient because of the complimentary reference to her writing (it was Sarah's practice to pass these on) and the "advice" about her health, since the d'Arblays had recently visited Chelsea when such advice could have been given. Moreover, on 21 October, Fanny promises her half-sister a letter in "4 or 5 days" (*JL*, 3: 81, n. 1, 86).
2. Probably the previous summer. For SHB's stay at Clifton with her half-brother, see L. 3 above.
3. A table having two hinged flaps, which can be spread horizontally (*OED*).
4. For a strain of levity or carelessness in Charles's character, which might well lead him to promise more than he meant to perform, see *HFB*, 76, 254 and below L. 66.
5. Charles Parr Burney, the only child of CB Jr., was born at Chiswick on 19 October 1785; in 1794, he was attending his father's school at Greenwich. For an account of his later career as schoolmaster and clergyman, see *GM*, 3rd ser. 18 (1865): 106–8.
6. William North (c. 1745–1816), Surgeon's Deputy at The Royal Hospital, Chelsea (1779–1802), Surgeon's Mate (1802–9) (*GM*, 86, Pt. 2 (1816): 478; Dean, 312–13).
7. An indefatigable worker when absorbed in some literary venture, Charles Burney was then wholly preoccupied with his biography of the poet Metastasio, which would be published in 1796 (CB to FBA, 17–18 Nov. 1794, Berg).

---

6. To Charlotte (Burney) Francis

[Chelsea College], March 1796
A.L.S., Berg
Address: M[rs] Francis / N[o] 9 Downing Street / Westminster
Endorsed: Sister Sarah / March 1796

Brava, Brava! Keep it up! I applaud your spirit, & will very readily, gladly, & joyfully wait upon you if wind, weather, &—tempers,[1] permit. I am so great an advocate for your present system, that, rather than sit still I would willingly

"When I have danced off both my legs
"Go dance upon my stumps.[2]

Papa is out—I can therefore send you no answer from him, & to tell you he is better after telling you he is out, would be needless—The Lady much as she was when you saw her[3]—

Remember me to all enquiring friends little & great—Grand & mean; & believe me devotedly, & admiringly yours

S. H. Burney.

Wednesday Evening.
March the somethingth
1796.

1. SHB is probably referring to her mother, whose temper was remarked by children and stepchildren. Long after Mrs. Burney's death, Fanny commented, "Her Temper alone was in fault, not her heart or intentions. But for that impracticable Temper, I should always have loved her as I did at the first" (*JL*, 12: 783).

2. A parody of the lines from "The More Modern Ballad of Chevy Chace": "For when his legs were smitten off, / He fought upon his stumpes." This version appeared in vol. 1 of [Thomas Percy, ed.], *Reliques of Ancient English Poetry* (London: J. Dodsley, 1765), ll. 211–12. Charles Burney owned a copy of this edition (*Misc. Lib.*, 42).

3. "The Lady" refers to Mrs. Burney, who had been unwell for years (*HFB*, 36; *JL*, 1: 96 and n. 3). In March, Charles Burney wrote, "M[rs] Burney's hemorrhage has not broke out again since my last letter; but we have both dreadful & incessant coughs" (CB to Thomas Twining, 21 Mar. 1796, Osborn).

7. With Charles Burney to Frances (Burney) d'Arblay

[Chelsea College, 15] July 1796
A.L. CB with A.L.S. SHB, Berg
Address: M[rs] d'Arblay / Alexander d'Arblay's Esq[r] / Bookham near / Leatherhead / Surry.
Postmarks: F JY / 16 / 96
Annotated by FBA: Delicious partial praise of little New Born Camilla. (34)
·⁂·

[*The first 1½ pages consist of an A.L. CB to FBA on Friday [15] July 1796 (misdated 16) in praise of her newly published novel,* Camilla; or, a Picture of Youth.]

My vast dear Sister!

O why, instead of 5, not give us ten volumes, twenty,[1] of such dear delicious people?—I have devoured the whole,—and now feel so forlorn, so greived to have none for tomorrow, that I tremble lest some greivous melancholly malady should seize upon me!—One after another, and then almost all at once, I have loved nearly every soul among them so much, that to part with them is quite dreadful. Dear Sir Hugh![2]—But to me, if not most dear, at least most amusing Sir Sedley[3]—where did you pick up that delightful, ridiculous vast enchanting character?—and how could you be so cruell as to dismiss him to the Hebrides with such a stink, and never to let us hear of him again?—I missed him ineffably—I love him superlatively, and, at the last moment, must own, I hated him inexpressibly! Sweet little good Eugenia![4]—Shall I ever dare to grumble again at a red nose and a dwarfs height![5]—I wish, however, I had, like her, a little Latin and greek to make it go down rather more palateably. Of Camilla[6] herself what can I say sufficiently expressive of my rapturous fondness for her! She is all that could be put together to make a character perfectly bewitching—Her gaiety, her animation, her goodness of heart, her desperate sufferings—in all & each she is equally fascinating, equally interesting!—I really adore her—And her poor little 20.£.! so nobly given, and so detestably accepted!—Vile, vile Lionel![7]—How often did I long to hang him with my own hands in my own garters! In Dr Orkburne[8] I have found a spur to give nimbleness to my father by, whenever he keeps the dinner, supper or breakfast waiting, that never fails in its effect—I have but to "hollow Orkburne in his ear," and up he starts for the mere pleasure of shaking me.—I wish Henry had not married Lavinia,[9] for I found myself disposed very humbly to be at his service—I like him almost as well as his frank and honest-hearted old father. Edgar[10] there is no bearing to speak of in vulgar, common English, for besides his own peculiar merit, he bears, in my eyes, so strong a resemblance to the person in the world who I have always looked up to as possessing the highest and rarest of human characters, that my insipid praise would appear, even to myself, a species of profanation!—I am often very angry with Dr Marchmont,[11] much as he is to be respected—Did he imagine people were to deceive or to be faithless to Edgar because they had taken it into their heads to be so to him?—Miss Margland,[12] or any thing like Miss Margland may Heaven for ever keep out of my path.—But Sir Hugh—oh Sir Hugh, that I might to eternity live with such benign, such perfectly indulgent souls as his!—Master Clermont[13] I should like to put upon a bread and water allowance for ten years, and then to bind pprentice to some tavern-keeper in the city for life, with a white apron tied round him and a pair of blue & white half sleeves drawn on over his coat. Miss Indiana[14] is so mawkish, so like a thousand Misses even I could fancy I have seen, that, sick as I was of the heart-less doll, I could not help being diverted by her.—Mrs Arlbery is enchanting, and her first introduction at the Assize ball[15] one of the most striking parts I think of the book—Her cool—"How do you do?" to Sir Sedley after passing him over to her with such trouble is exquisite, and the poor man's involuntary consternation thereupon, I enjoyed with genuine good nature!—Enfin, with blessings and thanks that (tho' not for me singly in the world) you have <given it such> brought forth so unequalled a treat, I will conclude by proudly signing myself the most enchanted of readers & affectionate of Sisters

S. H. B.

A blister has cured my tooth-ache, which, severe as it was, is I hope quite gone.

[*The letter concludes with a 6-line P.S. above the address panel, CB to FBA, Saturday morning, [16 July 1796] (misdated 17).*]

1. The number of volumes (to be sold by subscription) had been an issue: Mme d'Arblay intended to write six, changed her mind to four, and ended up with five (*JL*, 3: 121, n. 18). Sarah Harriet's enthusiasm was not shared by all; the novel's excessive length, improbable characters, and faulty style drew criticism. For a summary of the reviews, see *JL*, 3: 205, n. 3.

2. Sir Hugh Tyrold, the heroine's well-intentioned but ineffectual uncle, generates many incidents in the novel with his ill-conceived schemes. The *British Critic* 8 (1796): 531, found "much originality" in his character.

3. Sir Sedley Clarendel, an affected fop whose undesired and unmeaning attentions compromise the heroine, solaces his wounded ego with a northern tour (Bk. 7, Ch. 7).

4. Eugenia Tyrold offers the reader a simple moral lesson; blessed with every beauty of mind and soul, she is physically deformed. Her triumph over her handicaps represents the transcendence of the spirit, and she is rewarded with a devoted (and handsome) husband. Acclaimed as an angel, she is dubbed "dear little Greek and Latin" by her irreverent brother, in reference to her learning (Bk. 6, Ch. 14).

5. Sarah Harriet was not considered very attractive, her one redeeming feature being luxuriant hair. The redness of her nose was remarked by others, and she was slight in build. Decidedly, in the words of her nephew, "she is no beauty" (CPB to Robert Finch, 13 Nov. 1829, Bodleian, MS. Finch d. 3, ff. 346–48v; Thomas Twining to CB, 6 Oct. 1777, BL Add. MS. 39929, ff. 143–46; MAR to FBA, 30 Oct. [1798], Barrett, Eg. 3697, ff. 286–87v).

6. The titular heroine is beautiful, virtuous, affectionate and merry—but unthinking, a quality that causes her much unhappiness before the novel's end. Of all Burney's unprotected heroines making their debuts, Camilla fares the worst and must learn prudence and foresight before she wins the hero's acceptance. Chastened and subdued, even harrowed, by the difficulties in which her unguided precipitance involves her, she resigns herself with relief into more capable hands. Her perilous career is meant to show the dangers with which the education of a female is fraught.

7. Early in the novel (Bk. 5, Ch. 8), Camilla donates her pocket money to her scapegrace brother, Lionel, a generous but unwise action with far-reaching consequences. Her penniless condition involves her in complex pecuniary and moral obligations that drive her to the brink of madness.

8. Dr. Orkborne, a comic pedant, is exasperatingly absentminded and proves impossible to rouse from abstruse rumination. Dr. Burney, often absorbed in his work, good-naturedly acknowledged the resemblance, which seems to have become a family joke (R. Brimley Johnson, *Fanny Burney and the Burneys* (London: Stanley Paul, 1926), 224).

9. Two subsidiary characters, Lavinia, the faultless elder sister, and Henry Westwyn, an upright but colorless young man, are paired off. Hemlow suggests that young Hal and his doting father are "vengeful shades of Owen Cambridge and his son George," a backward suitor of Frances Burney (*HFB*, 193, 253).

10. Edgar Mandlebert, an exacting hero who delays the heroine's felicity by a minute and critical investigation into her suitability as a wife, is not universally admired. His most outspoken critic within the novel condemns him as a coldhearted prig who lacks the generosity to act openly (Bk. 6, Ch. 12) and even doubts that "a man who piques himself on his perfections" would make a good husband (Bk. 5, Ch. 6). His suspicious scrutiny and reluctance to commit himself are culpable, and he must learn to trust.

11. Dr. Marchmont, Edgar's tutor, is able to cool the hero's ardor with his cynicism born of two unhappy marriages.

12. Miss Margland, the sour governess, has been warped by spinsterhood and dependence. Unmarried females of the Burney family took her example to heart, fearing the same fate. Sarah's niece, Fanny Burney, reportedly wrote that she was "just what I shall be myself twenty years hence and *I hate her accordingly*" (cited in Brimley Johnson, 224). Sarah herself apparently never forgot the lesson and remarked several years later that she strove for financial independence as "my only means of keeping out of Marglandism" (L. 82).

13. Clermont Lynmere, Camilla's cousin, is a conceited boor who has not been much improved by continental travel.

14. Clermont's sister, Indiana, is a perfect foil to Eugenia: with a flawless beauty that is only skin-deep, she has no other redeeming qualities.

15. Mrs. Arlbery, witty and worldly, makes her memorable entrance in Bk. 2, Ch. 2.

8. With Elizabeth (Allen) Burney to Mary Young

[Chelsea College, 10 October 1796]
A.L.S. SHB with A.L.S. Elizabeth (Allen) Burney, Barrett, Eg.3700A, ff. 230–31v
Address: [Bradfield] Hall / [near] Bury / Suffolk
Postmarks: A ANDERSON
7 o'Clock Ni[ght] / 10 OC 96 / [?]
E O / [?] / [?]

Monday morning.

My dear Miss Young

How in the world came it ever to enter your pericranium to apply to me, of all people, for instructions in the art of fashionable dress?—A more decided ignoramus upon that subject exists not within the bills of mortality; nor, in truth, one more likely to mislead you by wrong, and tasteless, tonless advice.—My own head, whenever I go out, which, upon an average, may be about once in six weeks, is decorated by my own lilly hands exactly, as by said lilly hands, it was decorated a twelvemonth ago!—A <half> muslin worked half handker^{f} put on turbanwise, with sometimes a bunch of roses, sometimes a white feather, and occasionally a row of beads—friz I treat with none, nor curling neither—nor do I observe that many do: ten to one, however, if I have observed right; so do not conceive me to be giving you an accurate account of what other people do—for, like a true egotist, I am myself <for> the only person I can really answer for, because, I suppose, I am the only one, who, with any interest, I have really attended to.—

The necklaces & earings which Bobbin I believe mentioned to you, are composed of very, very small beads of almost any colour, woven into braids that tie tight round the throat from which are suspended five or six rows, strung plain, which hang down low upon the neck, one below the other. The earings are likewise strung, & consist of six loops.—Mine are—do not start!—Green!—And two Ladies who saw me wear them, ill, as you may naturally suppose they became me, liked them so well as to order for themselves a set exactly similar—

One more little bit of fashion, which by chance I picked up, let me communicate for your further great improvement—The Ladies of ton are lengthening their waists every day, & they are now actually worn two inches longer than they were last spring!—I am glad of it, for it used to give me the cramp in my fingers to pin up my coats.

Adieu my dear Miss Young—I leave, for my mother to add a word, the remainder of the paper; & with best compliments to Mrs Young, remain very sincerely yours

S. H. Burney.

Bobbin not only promises to be, but is already, one of the finest girls that can be seen:[1]—when here last, she was very chearful, & seemed very happy.

[*The last 9 lines consist of an A.L.S. Elizabeth (Allen) Burney to Mary Young, dated Monday the 10th:*] "here I am still on this Planet a poor weary Being—waiting as patiently as I can, the Stroke of Mercy—." [*She was then in her last illness.*]

1. The thirteen-year-old Martha Ann Young was then at school in London (see below L. 12, n. 1). For her father's fond description, see Young, 279–80.

---

9. [To Martha (Allen) Young][1]

[Chelsea College], 20 October 1796
A.L.S., Barrett, Eg. 3700A, f. 217–v

Oct^ber^ 20th 1796.

My dear Madam

As a duty, however melancholy and dreadful, I think myself bound to announce to you the fatal event which has this morning taken place in our house. My poor Mother, after only a day and a half's dangerous illness—(or at least of such illness as foretold the approach of immediate dissolution) expired at half past eight o'clock—Her sufferings from Tuesday half past two, till then, (except at those intervals when she obtained sleep by means of opiates) were agonizing—but the last few minutes were calm & composed[2]—

You will excuse, I am sure dear Madam a longer letter at such a time, & believe me with gratitude & affection

Yours sincerely
S. H. Burney.

1. The most likely correspondent is Mrs. Arthur Young. See next letter.

2. After nursing her mother through her final illness, Sarah wrote to inform the family of her death on 20 October 1796, her father being overcome with grief. As the end neared, his wife had thanked him for his patience and kindness throughout her sufferings, and ordered that he not be disturbed during the night (CB to Christian Latrobe, 14 Nov. 1796, Osborn; *JL*, 3: 217–18).

It is difficult to establish with certainty how much SHB inherited from her mother. In the will of her maternal grandmother, proved 2 October 1776, she was bequeathed a one-third share of £666.13.4. Besides the reversion of £1,000, the two children of the second marriage would receive a house in King's Lynn, and the residue of the estate (to value at least £300) after Mrs. Burney's death, "well knowing the same will be in the power of the said Charles Burney her Husband and therefore earnestly requesting and not doubting that . . . if he Survives her confiding in his Honor and Integrity that he will leave the same to her Children by him in such Shares and manner as prudence Suggests" (will of Mary Allen, dated 4 Oct. 1775, proved 2 Oct. 1776, PRO/PROB/11/1024/410).

On 10 July 1801, SHB would open an account at Coutts with a deposit of £450 (Coutts ledgers). This may well have been her share in the sale of the house at King's Lynn, as a similar amount (£476) was also sent to her brother in India as his "moity" (CB to FBA, 28–30 July 1802, Osborn; Scholes, 2: 262). More problematic are the stocks she held at that time, £340 in Navy 5 percents and £250 in 4 percents; it is possible, however, that such an amount could accumulate over a twenty-five-year period from an original investment of £222, if the dividends were also reinvested. Certainly Maria Rishton, an informed observer, knew of no other source of income for SHB: "I believe you are mistaken in thinking she has inherited any thing from her Mother—her trifling Legacy was from my Grandmother" (MAR to FBA, 21 June [1814], Barrett, Eg. 3697, ff. 304–5v).

It is doubtful whether Charles Burney passed on all the property intended for the two children of his second marriage. In his own will, he mentions only the house in King's Lynn, reducing Richard's share in his estate accordingly, and leaving Sarah considerably less than her two half-sisters (see below L. 77, n. 2). Mme d'Arblay would later be startled to discover the amount of money brought into the marriage by the second Mrs. Burney and the terms of the grandmother's will, but loyally defended her father's apparent oversight as unintentional: "if my Father wrote word to Richard that his Mother had nothing but her blessing to leave to him, it must have been from being in the dark himself of the contrary; &, consequently, & most naturally, deeming himself the life-inheritor of whatever, during her own life, had been possessed by his Wife." She was anxious, however, to read the letters containing these revelations to Sarah Harriet (*JL*, 12: 788; see also LL. 1429, 1430, 1432; CB, *Memoirs*, 181–82).

10. To Martha (Allen) Young

Chelsea College, 28 October 1796
A.L.S., Barrett, Eg. 3700A, ff. 218–19v
Address: Mrs Young / Arthur Young's Esqr / Bradfield Hall / near Bury / Suffolk
Postmarks: D OC / 28 / 96

Chelsea Coll:
Octr 28th ——96

My dear Madam

Although I flatter myself that by this time you have received the letter which I dispatched from hence on Thursday sennight, yet, as that may not have happened, I beg leave to assure you that the neglect you very naturally (from the letter's missing) suppose us to have been guilty of, we do not deserve should be imputed to us—You being, Dear Madam, the first to whom on so melancholy an occasion we should think of writing: accordingly, on the day above mentioned, I sent a letter off, containing the sad intelligence, & fully directed to you as usual at Arthur Young's Esqr—Bradfield Hall, near Bury, Suffolk.—That this letter, (which my father was in the room when I wrote) should have miscarried,[1] is indeed one of the most unfortunate accidents that could have happened, & must have led you to conclude me at once inattentive & unpardonably unfeeling.

My father returned only last night from Charles' at Greenwich where he went the Saturday before:[2] your letter to him therefore could not be opened yesterday till it was too late to answer it; else you may certainly be assured, either he or I, would have written to exculpate ourselves by return of post.—

All of the family who were within reach of Chelsea, hastened to us on the first intelligence of the dreadful event[3]—And at the mournful ceremony of the funeral (which took place on Wednesday)[4] Charles, James, Mr Burney[5] & cousin Edward,[6] personally attended—whilst in the house with me, were my three sisters Fanny, Hester & Charlotte. Mrs Phillips, whose loss to my father at such a time as this is almost irreparable, is now on her road to Ireland.[7]

Long as my poor mother's end seemed to be approaching, it may be said at the last to have arrived with a sudden & almost unexpected rapidity, which added considerably to our shock.[8]—Till the day before her death, (Tuesday) neither Mr North himself I believe, nor any of those about her, were at all aware of her immediate danger—consequently therefore none of her own family, (nor indeed, at the moment,) any of my father's could be summoned in time to chear and support him upon the first dreadful intimation which I was obliged to give him of—All being over! My sister Burney who was the nearest to us was nursing one of her children ill with a sore throat[9]—[A]nd Charlotte was with all her [f]amily at Richmond.[10] However, as I tell you, they all hastened hither as early as it was well possible they could—and now are <vying> exerting themselves to the utmost to uphold & console my dearest father, whose spirits are extremely low indeed.[11]—He hopes you will excuse his writing immediately.—

I beg, my dearest Madam, that you will remember me very kindly to Miss Young, and accept the sincere excuses I have offered for what, in fact, deserves less to be excused than lamented.—

I remain, dear Madam, your obliged & affectionate neice.

S. H. Burney

1. Mrs. Young had apparently complained of neglect in not being informed of her sister's death. SHB may be referring to the letter of 20 October 1796 above, which shows no evidence of mailing.

2. Charles Burney stayed with his son and daughter-in-law from 22 to 27 October 1796, and was grateful for their attentions to him in his hour of grief: "Indeed you contrived to drive away gloom much more than I thought possible at that time, and much more than it has been driven away since" (CB to CB Jr., [15 Nov. 1796], Berg).

3. Charles Burney appreciated this rallying of his family at time of need, which he remarked on when writing to his friends: "I am not insensible to the kindness of my children on this distressing occasion; who not only participate, but try by every means in their power to alleviate my sorrows. I spent some of the most gloomy days under Charles' hospitable roof at Greenwich; & all my children & grand-children, in or near London, assembled on the melancholy day of interment: the males all attending the performance of the last sad Scene!" (CB to Ralph Griffiths, 2 Nov. 1796, Bodleian, MS. Add. C. 89, ff. 1–2).

4. The funeral took place on Wednesday, 27 October 1796; Mrs. Burney was interred in the old burial ground, Chelsea Hospital, where her gravestone still stands (*JL*, 3: 208, n. 1; 209, n. 2).

5. Charles Rousseau Burney (1747–1819), eldest son of CB's elder brother, Richard (1723–92), of Barborne Lodge, Worcester. A harpsichordist and music teacher, he had married on 20 September 1770 his cousin, Esther Burney (1749–1832) (*JL*, 1: lxix, lxxiv; *EJL*, 1: 139).

6. Fourth son of Richard Burney, Edward Francesco Burney (1760–1848), an artist of some talent, was living with his brother Charles Rousseau (*JL*, 1: lxxv; 4: 163, n. 4). His work is the subject of Patricia Dahlman Crown, "Edward F. Burney: an Historical Study in English Romantic Art" (Ph.D. diss., University of California at Los Angeles, 1977), and H. A. Hammelmann, "Edward Burney's Drawings," *Country Life*, 6 June 1968, 1504–6.

7. Susanna (Burney) Phillips was accompanying her husband back to his estate in Ireland; for her reluctance to go, and the sadness of the parting, see *JL*, 3: 200, n. 1; *HFB*, 277–78; *Memoirs*, 3: 219–22.

8. Charles Burney's letters of the time express the same idea: "The calamity w[ch] has befallen me; though it was so long expected, I found myself as unprepared for, as if the poor soul had died suddenly, while in perfect youth and beauty" (CB to Thomas Twining, 6 Dec. 1796, Berg).

9. Esther Burney was living at No. 2, Upper Titchfield Street, Portland Place with her family, which consisted of Hannah Maria or "Marianne" (1772–1856); Richard Allen (1773–1836); Frances or "Fanny" (1776–1828); Sophia Elizabeth (1777–1856); Cecilia Charlotte Esther (1788–1821); Amelia Maria (1792–1868) (*JL*, 1: lxix).

10. After her husband's death in October 1792, Mrs. Francis had returned to London and set up house in Downing Street, Westminster, from which she had recently moved (between May 1795 and October 1796) to Hill Street, Richmond, near her Aunt Beckey (*JL*, 3: 101, 146, 226). The three children of her first marriage were: Charlotte (1786–1870), Marianne (1790–1832), and Clement Robert (1792–1829) (*JL*, 1: lxxii–lxxiii).

11. Charles Burney was depressed for months by his wife's death; see Lonsdale, 382–86. In December, Burney wrote: "nothing but these domestic circumstances can fasten upon me—all else is so insipid & uninteresting, that I sit whole hours with my hands before me, without the least inclination or power to have recourse either to such business, or amusem[ts] as I used to fly to with the greatest eagerness" (CB to Thomas Twining, 6 Dec. 1796, Berg).

---

11. To Martha (Allen) Young

[Chelsea College], 12 November 1796
A.L.S., Barrett, Eg. 3700A, f. 220–v
Address: M[rs] Young / Bradfield Hall / near Bury / Suffolk
Postmarks: A ANDER[SON]
[*?*] NO / 12 / 96
[*?*] / 12 NO 96 / PENNY POST PAID

Saturday 12th Nov[r] ——96.

My dear Madam

The books you mention were all carefully put away at the time of their coming, and will be forthcoming whenever there is an opportunity of conveying them to M[r] Richardsons[1]—I do not remember, however, to have seen among them the Vol: of Swift which you speak of—It <u>may</u> be with them, tho', for it is so long since they were put up, I have forgot their complete number as well as titles. The Sugar bason, I had washed & put aside for you the very day you wrote. But now, my dear Madam, allow me to enquire on what occasion a draft for £3,,16,,0—on Langston & Co[2] was sent up to my poor mother—whether the money was to be received on <u>her</u> account or yours?—And, in short, how it came among her papers?—Its date is Octr 7th ——96.

With the books, & Sugar dish, I shall sent to Richd^ns a packet of letters (Mr Lofts,[3] I believe) addressed mostly to Miss Young—which were likewise found in my mothers bureau.

My father bids me say he shall write to you very soon—He is still extremely low & has not been quite well for some days—I flatter myself however that when he comes to go out a little, this languor will wear off.—

As soon as he is enough recovered to bear a little more chearfulness in the house, I shall be very happy, dear Madam, with your permission, to send, or call for Bobbin, who, you may be well assured will be as cordially received & as carefully attended to as in former times. I remain dear Madam with sincere affection your grateful S. H. Burney.

Kind remembrances to Miss Young & Arthur.

1. Probably William Richardson (c. 1736–1811), bookseller, who had a shop at 23 Cornhill (Maxted; Nichols, *Illustrations*, 8: 522).

2. The London banking firm of Langstons, Towgood and Amory were located at 29 Clement's Lane, Lombard Street (F. G. Hilton Price, *A Handbook of London Bankers*, rev. ed. (London: Leadenhall Press, 1890–91), 211).

3. Capell Lofft (1751–1824), a lawyer and miscellaneous writer, who lived at Troston Hall, Bury St. Edmunds, Suffolk, near the Youngs (*DNB;* "Appendix," *AR*, 66 (1824): 224; Gazley, 149).

12. To Martha (Allen) Young

[Chelsea College], 12 December 1796
A.L.S., Barrett, Eg. 3700A, ff. 221–22v
Address: Mrs Young / Bradfield Hall / near Bury St Edmonds / Suffolk
Postmarks: [Du]ke Street
F [D]E / 12 / 96

Decr 12th ——96.

Dear Madam

According to your directions, received on Saturday or Friday last, I made up a parcel, consisting of Mr Lofts letters, the Sugar-bason & the books; this was sent to No 57 Conduit Street, Bond Street as you desired, but refused house-room at the door, by two different women, who concurred in saying they knew nothing of any persons of the name of Young, & neither had, nor expected any such lodgers.—Afterwards happening to be in town, I called there myself to leave the little paper ornaments you wished to have purchased, & received the same unexpected rebuff—What shall I do next? That odious Campden House, (odious from its distance)[1] is such a way off, I find it impossible, without utter ruin, to send there as often as these little commissions require, in order to be made perfectly clear.—

Trophies are now become so common, that I thought you would prefer little Etruscan figures and groups—I have therefore purchased seven small ones at sixpence each, & one rather larger with more figures in it, at nine-pence; which in all, by dint of calculation, I have found out amounts to four & <nine> three-pence.

Mrs M——ke, tho' I did not see her, has of late been in town upon Law business, & so much taken up, it seemed impossible she could undertake any other employment. Now, however, she is at home again, and as dealing with principals is always the pleasantest, if you direct a letter of enquiry to her by the following address, it will reach her perfectly securely—

Mrs Bruce[2]
To be left at the Post Office
Till Called for
Bristol.

With regard to the rings,[3] I know not what makes James so slow in delivering them—He undertook the sole business, and I know received your measure some time ago—Probably you will have it sent, in the course of a few days.

I beg to be remembered to Miss Young, <& her brother>, and remain, Dear Madam, with great regard

Your affectionate neice & obliged Servant
S. H. Burney

1. Campden House, Kensington, was a twenty minutes' walk from Sarah's door. Built in the late sixteenth century, the mansion was greatly altered and used as a girls' boarding school from about 1751 to 1847. Believing the site to be healthy, Arthur Young had sent his daughter there before 22 February 1796; however, when Bobbin sickened in March of 1797, he removed her from what he was later to term "that region of constraint and death" (*Survey of London*, 37: 55–56; AY to CB, [22 Feb. 1796], Osborn; Young, 263–64).

2. Elizabeth "Bessie" Allen (1761–c. 1826), youngest daughter of Mrs. Burney's first marriage with Stephen Allen (1725–63) of King's Lynn, Norfolk, had eloped with Samuel Meeke, whom she married 12 October 1777 at Ypres (*JL*, 1: lxxiii–lxxiv). She had apparently left her husband, and was posing as a Mrs. Bruce, which may account for the shocked outrage in the few family references to her (e.g., MAR to FBA, 12 [Aug. 1793], Barrett, Eg. 3697, ff. 216–19v; see also *JL*, 3: 4, n. 12). She was left a widow in 1802 (CB to FBA, 28 July 1802, Osborn), and known as Mrs. Bruce to the end of her life, "after another marriage to a man who it seems married her for her money and deprived her of every comfort" (Cornelia Cambridge to CFBt, [Oct. 1826], Barrett, Eg. 3705, f. 65, cited in *JL*, 11: 447, n. 5). The assumption that by 1796 Bessie's first husband was dead and Bessie already remarried, and the supposition of a third spouse (as in *EJL*, 1: xlv, 22, n. 57; *JL*, 11: 447, n. 5), appear to be unwarranted.

3. Probably a mourning ring for Mrs. Young's sister (Sarah's mother) who had died 20 October 1796. See above L. 9.

---

13. To Martha (Allen) Young

[Chelsea College], 29 December 1796
A.L.S., Barrett, Eg. 3700A, ff. 223–24v
Address: Mrs Young / Bradfield Hall / near Bury St Edmunds / Suffolk
Postmarks: A ANDERSON
F DE / 30 / 96
7 oClock Nig[ht] / 30DE96 / [?]

29th Dec^r ——96

My dear Madam

I received the favour of your last letter this morning, and am fully sensible of your kindness in wishing to employ the very ingenious pen of Mr Loft in my behalf:[1] at the same time, dear Madam, allow me to say, that I feel so averse to being in any way accessory to giving such trumpery employment to any one, that I am fully determined to leave the little work to its fate;[2] and if it must sink to oblivion unless I help to support, quietly to let it sink—stink & die!—I have always laughed at & scouted the idea of authors who made interest with their friends either directly or indirectly to obtain a favourable mention in the Reviews—What then should I deserve in my turn, were I to consent to the same collusion?—So much therefore for that, & now for the Opera Shawls—

The cheapest that can be bought of any durability or warmth are from 18^{s} to a guinea—Others of a less price are only lined with Rabbit-skins which rub off upon every thing.

I am very glad the parcel so long delayed got down safe.

With best wishes for the perfect recovery of Miss Young & poor Bobbin,[3] I remain, dear Madam,

Your ever obliged & affectionate neice
S. H. Burney.

1. A neighbor to the Youngs, Capell Lofft contributed to the *Monthly Magazine* and other periodicals. Conjecturally, Mrs. Young wished to ask him to review SHB's novel favorably (see next note).

2. Sarah Harriet Burney's first novel, *Clarentine*, was brought out in three volumes by her father's friends and publishers, G. G. & J. Robinson of Paternoster Row. Advertised in the *Times* as "This day is published" on 7 July 1796, it appeared almost simultaneously with her half-sister's *Camilla* (*JL*, 3: 135, n. 1, 168, n. 1). While enthusiastically praising and zealously defending Mme d'Arblay's literary achievement, Charles Burney makes only slight mention of his youngest daughter's effort (CB to FBA, 2 Dec. 1796, Berg; see by contrast CB to FBA, 14 July 1796, Berg; CB to CB Jr., 3 Aug. [17]96, Bodleian, MS. Don. c. 56, ff. 87–88; Lonsdale, 379–80).

The idea of influencing reviews was not unprecedented, as her father had been active in promoting both his own work and that of his daughter Fanny (Lonsdale, 218–19; *JL*, 3: 205, n. 2, 368). *Clarentine* fared quite well, earning qualified praise from reviewers: the *Analytical Review* 24 (1796): 404, recommended it for "harmless amusement"; the *Monthly Review*, 2nd ser. 21 (1796): 452–56, found "much adroitness of composition, vivacity of dialogue, and morality of sentiment," while the *British Critic* 9 (1797): 137–41, saw promise in a first performance.

At least one of these was a friendly voice: the article in the *Monthly Review* was written by the son of the editor and publisher, Ralph Griffiths (1720–1803), a valued friend of Dr. Burney (Benjamin Christie Nangle, *The Monthly Review Second Series, 1790–1815* (Oxford: Clarendon Press, 1955), 5, 26, 103).

3. Bobbin may have been showing signs of consumption (see next letter), although Arthur Young was later to claim that she was "in good health" when taken to school in January 1797 (Young, 263).

14. To Martha (Allen) Young

[Chelsea College], 19 March [1797]
A.L.S., Barrett, Eg. 3700A, f. 225–v
Address: Mrs Young / Bradfield Hall near / Bury St Edmunds / Suffolk—
Postmarks: A ANDERS[ON]
7 oClock Night / 20MR97 / Penny Po[st]

Sunday eve: 19th March.

Dear Madam.

I sent a note to Mr Young requesting we might see Bobbin before she went back to school, & he wrote word <back> she should come to us tomorrow (Monday) when her visit to him was over. This morning, however, I received a short note from Bobbin to inform me that [*having*] not been quite well,[1] Dr Turton[2] had been sent for to see her, and given her a strict charge not to go out [for some] days. Consequently she remains I suppose with her [father[3] where] I shall make a point of calling to see her the first morning it is in my power.—I am not perfectly well myself, however,—full of cold, & a feel as if I had been bruized from head to foot—The fellow-sufferers I daily hear of & see, make me hope it is owing merely to these piercing easterly winds,[4] which when a warmer April sun shines upon us, will give way—My poor father coughs incessantly, & every night is feverish and really ill[5]—You, I hope, have escaped, as well as Miss Young, to whom I beg my kindest remembrances—And remain, dear Madam, gratefully & sincerely

Yours,

S. H. Burney.

1. This was the beginning of an illness from which she was never to recover. Martha Ann Young died of consumption on 14 July 1797 at the age of fourteen (see Young, 263–80; Gazley, 364–74, for a full account). Overpowering grief at the loss of his beloved child would change Arthur Young's life, turning his mind increasingly toward religion.

2. Bobbin's physician was the famous Dr. John Turton (1735–1806), M.D. (1767), F.R.C.P. (1768), who was appointed physician in ordinary to the Queen (1782) and to the King and Prince of Wales (1797). Having amassed a large fortune from his successful practice, he retired to a country estate in 1800 (Gazley, 365; *DNB;* Munk's Roll, 2: 284–85).

In Young's opinion, Dr. Turton "mistook her case entirely, not believing in a consumption, and by physic brought her so low that she declined hourly." The frantic father consulted five physicians in her case, none of whom agreed, a fact he would comment upon bitterly afterwards (Young, 264, 287).

3. Young, who spent most of the year in London as Secretary to the Board of Agriculture (1793), kept Bobbin in his lodgings in Jermyn Street until 12 April 1797 when he removed her to Bradfield. She died at Boston, Lincs, where she was taken for a change of air (Young, 264, 277–78).

4. For most of the preceding month, winds had come from the east, but changed to southerly after the nineteenth (*GM*, 67, Pt. 1 (1797): 266).

5. Charles Burney suffered from a cough that recurred in cold weather (*JL*, 3: 313; CB to FBA, 4 June [1797], King's Lynn Museum).

---

15. To Frances (Burney) d'Arblay

[Chelsea College, 24 June 1797]
A.L.S. fragment, Berg
Address: M^rs^ d'A[rblay] / Alexander [d'Arblay's] / B[ookham]
Postmarks: F JU / 24 / 97
Annotated by FBA: ⊗
Verso (the address page) was used by FBA for notes for a novel.

just now for a [fe]w [d]ays—[P]apa has been out so constantly lately, that he himself had the charity to ask her to come[1] & prevent my hanging myself.

Should not the Chancellor be asked whether <u>this</u> is legal weather?[2]

Kindest remembrances to dear M. d'Arblay—& darling Baby,[3] and believe me my dearest Sister your ever most affectionate

S. H. Burney

1. There is no indication in Dr. Burney's letters at the time as to who this visitor might be. However, he began to recover in the spring from the depression that followed the death of his wife. In early June, he wrote quite jauntily of the unwonted flurry of activity he was enjoying (CB to FBA, 4 June [1797], King's Lynn Museum).

2. Skies had been overcast and rainy during the preceding two weeks, and on 21 June, "The air [was] so chill, that the thermometer in the evening [was] at 44" (*GM*, 67, Pt. 2 (1797): 538).

3. Mme d'Arblay had given birth on 18 December 1794 to a son, Alexander Charles Louis Piochard d'Arblay, baptized 11 April 1795. The family was living in a rented cottage at Great Bookham, Surrey, but had spent Christmas of 1796 at Chelsea, a visit that gave Alexander fond memories of "Sally's singing, & dancing, & milk & water presents on her Knee" (*JL*, 3: 254). Their acquaintance was renewed when Sarah spent a day

with the d'Arblays in May (*JL*, 3: 92, n. 1, 311; *HFB*, 241; CB to [Dorothy Young], 7 Feb. 1797, Berg).

16. With Charles Burney to Frances (Burney) d'Arblay

[Chelsea College, 13 September 1797]
A.L.S. CB with A.L. SHB, Berg
Address: To / M^rs^ d'Arblay / Bookham / near Leatherhead / Surry.
Postmarks: ANDERSON
14 / 97
Endorsed: Sept. 13. 97
Annotated by FBA: ⁜ + / Written at 71. visit to Litchfield, / Garrick Dr james Dr JOHNSON *Pasted on over previous endorsement:* Dr Burney to Madame d'Arblay
Numbered: 5
[*The first 3½ pages consist of an A.L.S. CB to FBA, dated 13 September 1797, describing his visit to Lichfield.*]

My dearest Sister—I forgot to mention in my letter, that a few days after my return from Bookham,[1] I called in my way to town for your watch at Styels,[2] & have it now in the house—it shall certainly be sent by the first opportunity.—Are there any hopes of soon (if at all) procuring the gloves we talked of?—I am as bare-fingered a gentlewoman as you would desire to see—yet while in uncertainty respecting the bespoken ones, feel unwilling to buy any others. Adieu dearest of sisters—

1. Sarah had spent a week (c. 19–26 Aug. 1797) with the d'Arblays at Great Bookham, while her father visited Crewe Hall, Cheshire, for the month of August (*JL*, 3: 330, n. 2, 347, 352).

2. Possibly the firm of Richard Style, who was a member of the Clockmakers' Company in London, serving his apprenticeship from 1742–50, becoming a freeman in 1750, and a liveryman in 1766; he held a variety of offices within the company, culminating in 1790 when he served as master. He is listed as watchmaker in the London directories from 1782–96 at 3 Carey Lane, Foster Lane. No one of the name appears in the directories for 1797 or 1798, but in 1799, John Styles operates a watch and clockmaking business from 47 Fleet Lane (information kindly supplied by the Guildhall Library, London).

Captain James Burney. Artist unknown. (Courtesy of the National Portrait Gallery, London. Every effort has been made to contact the owner.)

17. [From James Burney or Sarah Harriet Burney][1] [To Maria (Allen) Rishton][2]

[Chelsea College, 1 September 1798][3]
L. Copy, in hand of MAR included in A.L.S. MAR to FBA, [1 September 1798], Barrett, Eg. 3697, f. 275–v
Published: JL, *4: 214–15, n. 5*
Endorsed: Sept 2[d] 98

Dear M[rs] R. Be So Kind to give the inclosed to my Father on his return.[4] And let me recommand to you to be so considerate as to let as little noise be made about our absence as possible—

1. This brief note, copied by Maria Rishton into a letter to Mme d'Arblay, announces the departure of Sarah Harriet and her half-brother James from their respective homes to live together. Enclosing a letter to Dr. Burney (presumably to account for this decision), the writer is more likely to be James, as SHB would leave a message for her father with her servant (see next letter).

2. Maria (Allen) Rishton (1751–1820), Sarah's half-sister, the eldest daughter of Mrs. Burney's first marriage. She had married secretly at Ypres on 16 May 1772 Martin Folkes Rishton (c. 1747–1820), despite the two families' opposition. Unhappy in her marriage with a man who was "austere, haughty, irascible, & impracticable" and who forced her to sever "all her early connexions," she had sought refuge with her stepfather at Chelsea Hospital (*JL*, 1: lxxiv; 4: 75; *HFB*, 41–42; *EJL*, 1: 222–27; MAR to FBA, 1796–98, Barrett).

Writing to Mme d'Arblay, Mrs. Rishton describes the situation as she found it: "I have been in town since Wednesday found Sally very low—and yesterday your dear Father told me James and his Wife were parted—to day After being out with Mrs Burney Shopping on my return Molly told me Sally was gone up to town—with James—but that never struck me and I was packing up some things when she came into my room with a packet of letters directed to me inclosing two for your Father one to Molly one to me the last I inclose mine—the one Molly has is to me dreadful As it seems to say she does not mean to return." She closes with a plea to Fanny to come and help her face this family crisis.

3. Although endorsed by FBA 2 September (a Sunday), both Maria Rishton's enclosing letter and this one were probably written on Saturday the first. The day Mrs. Rishton discovered Sarah's absence she had been out shopping, and "yesterday's" discussion with Dr. Burney took place on a Friday. Her servant delivered her letter to West Humble, bringing back a reply on Sunday, the day she did not go out for fear of meeting anyone. For the chronology of events, see MAR to FBA, [1 Sept. 1798], [3 Sept. 1798], Barrett, Eg. 3697, ff. 275–77v; *JL*, 4: 214–15.

4. Dr. Burney (she explains) was visiting his friend Lady Mary Duncan at Hampton Court and was not due back until Monday, 3 September 1798.

---

18. [To Mary More][1]

[Chelsea College, 1 September 1798][2]

L. Copy, in hand of MAR included in A.L. MAR to FBA, [3 September 1798], Barrett, Eg. 3697, ff. 276–77v

Address: M^rs^ D'Arblay / West Humble / near Dorking / Surry / Single Sheet

Postmarks: Charing / Cross

Endorsed: Septr 3^d^ 98

Dear Molly

I beg <you> that when your Master returns you will give him the inclosed letter—I trust Implicitly to your good will for taking as much Care of the things I leave behind me as you can[3]—I hope soon to reclaim them—mean while any thing except the linnen which may be of use to you, you are heartily Welcome to. Do not hear me more abused than you can help—I trust I am gone to be happy & Comfortable—it is no part of my Intention to be good-for-nothing and deserve abuse.[4] God bless you my good little Molly[.] Wherever I am, or may be, I shall always remain your grateful and Affectionate Friend

1. In her second missive, Maria Rishton transcribes the "letter from Miss" to "Molly," Mary More (fl. 1793–1819), Charles Burney's housekeeper (*JL*, 2: 79, n. 30).

2. Presumably written on the day of her departure, SHB's note entrusts a message for Dr. Burney to her servant's care. In her lengthy epistle, Mrs. Rishton expounds upon the family tensions she had observed. Sarah had "complaind bitterly of her Father's Severity and Coldness towards her—that they passd days without Speaking—and that if he did address or Answer her it was with bitter raillery—or Harshness." Dr. Burney was also cold towards James, who, he felt, neglected his wife and children to spend too much time with his half-sister; moreover, he had imbibed "dreadful Apprehensions about their uncommon Intimacy" from his late wife.

Matters came to a head when James separated from his wife, and wrote to his father (Thursday, 30 August 1798), proposing to lodge nearby and board with him; when the Doctor refused (Friday), James went home to pack, and he and SHB left Chelsea together the next day (MAR to FBA, [3 Sept. 1798], Barrett, Eg. 3697, ff. 276–77v).

3. Sarah had taken nothing with her, not even a change of linen; the family learned later the "distresses Sally had felt for Want of her Cloaths—for she did not take even a Night—and as I fancy they set out for Bristol the very Night they left Chelsea and travelld all Night she bought a Mans Cotten Cap and tied it under her Chin—and had bought a ready made gown" (MAR to FBA, 30 Oct. [1798], Barrett, Eg. 3697, ff. 286–87v).

4. James and Sarah's departure did shock the family, although apparently convinced their relations were innocent (see Introduction). Even if not incestuous, the living arrangement was open to misconstruction, and likely to "make the World very ill natured" (MAR to FBA, 9 Oct. [1798], Barrett, Eg. 3697, ff. 280–81v); it was also inconvenient to Dr. Burney, who resented being abandoned. During the ensuing weeks, the family discussed how to make contact, how to account for the situation to their friends, and how to replace Sarah at Chelsea. See MAR to FBA, [3 Sept. 1798], 5 Sept. [1798], 9 Oct. [1798], 19 [Oct. 1798], 23 Oct. [1798], 30 Oct. [1798], [Nov. 1798], Barrett, Eg. 3697, ff. 276–90v; *JL*, 4: 204–20.

19. [To Mary More][1]

[37 Fetter Lane], 22 October [1798]
L. Copy, in hand of MAR included in A.L.S. MAR to FBA, 23 October [1798], Barrett, Eg. 3697, ff. 284–85v
Address: Mrs Darblay / West Humble / near Darking / Surry. / Single Sheet.
Postmarks: 7 oClock Nig[ht] / 23 OC 98 / Penny Post [?]
C OC / 23 / 98
Endorsed: Oct. 23. ——98.

Oct 22^d^

I am much Concernd my dear Molly to hear that you have been ill and shall be very glad to see you if you can come any day after to Morrow (Tuesday) to No 37 Fetter Lane[2]—Capt Burney will meet you; you can bring my things best in a Coach, Which I will discharge; but as soon as you receive this, write me a line to fix the day and hour when you may be expected[3] and put your letter (with whatever others you may have for me) under a Cover directed for Capt Burney, at Tom's Coffee house Russel Street Covent Garden.[4]

Be so good as to return the Framed print which I borrowd of Mrs Keate—& a Manuscript Musick Book belonging to Miss Keate:[5] they are both I beleive in the Drawr where I kept my Cloak and Shawl.

God Bless you my dear Molly.

1. This is a reply to a (missing) letter from Molly [pre 19 October 1798]. Having learned that James and Sarah were in town, though ignorant of their address, Dr. Burney instructed his servant to write to Sarah Harriet, "to tell her she had a letter from the D^r^ to Miss Sally written six weeks ago—which she supposed was of great Consequence as it was to be deliverd into her own hands and that she had the keys of all her Drawers. to give Up her Things when she chose to send for them." This letter was forwarded to James through his wife (MAR to FBA, 19 [Oct. 1798], Barrett, Eg. 3697, ff. 282–83v).

2. After her visit to this lodging, Molly would report on their way of life: "she said she never Saw Sarah look so well or in such good Spirits—that at present they had a little Lodging near Kentish Town—where the Woman of the House emptied <u>their Slops for them</u> once or twice a day when Sally had deposited them in a tin pail she had bought that they Cookd their own dinners—and went to Market—and the Woman Washd for them—but they meant to get a Lodging nearer London . . . Molly says she never saw her Face so Clear from Humour and her Nose has not lookd so well for some years—

I suppose the Active life she leads, agrees with her—she rises every Morning at Eight" (MAR to FBA, 30 Oct. [1798], Barrett Eg. 3697, ff. 286–87v).

3. After consulting with her employer, Molly arranged to take Sarah's things to her on Thursday, 25 October at 3 P.M. Her reply, with Dr. Burney's letter to Sarah, was sent as directed on Tuesday, 23 October (MAR to FBA, 23 Oct. [1798], Barrett, Eg. 3697, ff. 284–85v).

4. Tom's Coffee House, 17 Russell Street, Covent Garden; originally owned by Thomas West (d. 1722), it flourished in the reign of Queen Anne and was still drawing the luminaries of London society fifty years later (including David Garrick, Samuel Johnson, and Arthur Murphy). A subscription club was formed and the premises enlarged in 1768; the coffeehouse business was to close in 1814 (Bryant Lillywhite, *London Coffee Houses* (London: George Allen and Unwin, 1963), 590–93).

5. Emma (née Browne) Keate (d. pre 1818), the daughter of Lyde Browne (d. 1787), a director of the Bank of England, by his wife, Margaret, daughter of Richard Barwell of Esher, Surrey (*DNB; GM*, 57, Pt. 2 (1787): 840; *Westminsters*, under Barwell Browne; and information supplied by Robert Gittings).

Emma Browne had married 13 November 1784 Thomas Keate (1745–1821), Surgeon to Chelsea Hospital (1790–1821), and recently appointed Surgeon-General to the Army (15 February 1798). Her eldest daughter was Emma Keate (fl. 1795–1842) (*DNB; JL*, 1: 143, n. 20; Dean, 311; parish register, St. George's, Hanover Square; will of Thomas Keate, dated 5 Jan. 1818, proved 18 July 1821, PRO/PROB 11/1646/411).

---

20. [To Charles Burney][1]

[37 Fetter Lane, 25 October 1798][2]

L. Copy, in hand of CB included in A.L. CB with A.L. MAR to FBA, 26 October [17]98, Berg

Address: Mrs Darblay / West Humble / Dorking / Surry

Postmarks: OC / 26 / 98

Endorsed: Oct. 26. ——98

Sir.

The reason wch you point out as the properest to be given in order to acc^t^ for my absence (namely making room for my Sister Phillips & her Fanny)[3] appears to me the best I can assign; and therefore I shall take advantage of your permission to make use of it. I shall be glad to do anything else in my power to prevent the Step I have taken from producing further inconvenience: you speak of my calling at Chelsea; but to meet you (at least for the present) w^d^ require more courage than I am mistress of.[4]—Your letter to me is much more lenient than I had any right to expect, & has increased my regret for a circumstance attending my departure w^ch^, if I had known how, I w^d^ most gladly have remedied before I left London.[5] I cannot think myself entitled, in consequence of any former promise, to the increase of income you mention, & therefore, wth many acknowledge^ts^, inclose the note[6] you were So good as to Send me.[7]

1. This was SHB's reply to her father's letter of c. 4–7 September 1798, in which he apparently suggested a plausible way of accounting for her absence from home, invited her to see him, and sent her £10. Mrs. Rishton expected Sarah "to melt I shoud hope at your Fathers Kindness" (MAR to FBA, 23 Oct. [1798], Barrett, Eg. 3697, ff. 284–85v).

2. Sarah wrote her reply during Molly's visit of 25 October (MAR to FBA, 30 Oct. [1798], Barrett, Eg. 3697, ff. 286–87v).

3. Susan (Burney) Phillips and her only daughter, Frances ("Fanny") (1782–1860) (*JL*, 1: lxxi). The line suggested to parry awkward questions about Sarah's whereabouts may have come naturally given the family's increasing anxiety about Susan's health, safety, and happiness in Ireland. Their efforts to persuade her husband to allow her to return would be intensified, now that Dr. Burney wanted her to take Sarah's place as his housekeeper and companion. This plan was to end tragically on 6 January 1800 when Susan died shortly after landing in England, en route to her father (*HFB*, 285–87; *JL*, 4, passim; letters of CB, Oct. 1798 to Jan. 1800 (listed in *Catalogue*)).

4. Although Sarah declined to visit her father at this time, she was later (in the spring of 1799) to propose it herself. The delay had angered Dr. Burney, who resisted her request for some time. She was finally received, according to FBA, "with the most petrifying coldness & sternness. Who can wonder? She burst into tears,—& they were both long silent. They then spoke only of common topics,—& in a very short time, he said he must prepare for an engagement & she retreated. What a wretched interview!" (*JL*, 4: 307, 279 and n. 2).

5. On leaving Chelsea, SHB and JB had set out almost immediately for Bristol (L. 18, n. 3).

6. Sarah refused the £10 Dr. Burney had sent her (n. 1). Maria Rishton observed that "she has such a high Spirit and dreads pecuniary Obligations so much" and wondered how she would manage living with James: "I cant think she will ever submit to keep his house without paying for her board—and she has not above twenty pounds a year of her own" (MAR to FBA, [3 Sept. 1798], Barrett, Eg. 3697, ff. 276–77v).

Sarah Harriet's bank account at Coutts shows that she would pay to James over a two-year period all the dividends on her stock holdings (totaling £1,146.8.4), a sum of £98.10s. In addition, she would sell £100 of Navy 5 percents on 13 May 1803, giving the proceeds to James; after they broke up house, he would continue to receive the dividends on her remaining £240 of Navy 5 percents, which never thereafter appeared in her account (Coutts ledgers).

7. After copying this letter into his own, Dr. Burney continues: "All this I was trying to gulp down & digest, & perhaps sh^d^ soon have succeeded, had not I learned . . . that

these 2 dutiful, affectionate, & considerate Children, had been trying to persuade Molly to quit my Service & live wth them! This I own did mortify & chagrine me to the quick." This last treasonable act enraged him, and hardened his heart against forgiveness: "It is so completely Jacobinical & selfish in both J. & herself, that I never can forget such a barbarous piece of egotism—merely because she, forsooth, does not like a strange Servant!" He ends by vowing never to think of, write to, or be reconciled with either of them again (CB to FBA, 26 Oct. 1798, Berg).

---

21. [To Hannah Maria Burney][1]

[21 John Street, 5 or 6 February 1799][2]
L. Copy, in hand of FBA included in A.L. FBA to SBP, 12 March 1799, Berg
Published: JL, *4: 248*
Address: Mrs. Phillips, / Belcotton, / Drogheda.
Annotated by SBP: about brother James & S.
Docketed by FBA: March ——99. *Numbered: 2 and 3*

Dear Marianne. My Brother James cannot come. He sends love to all. I have such a pain in my face[3]

1. Hannah Maria or "Marianne" Burney, Esther's eldest child, to whose (missing) invitation Sarah Harriet was replying: "Marianne wrote to Sally—saying that we [the d'Arblays] were but an hour come to the house & that her Mama, with her kind love, invited her & dear uncle J[ames] to dine with us the next day. She added many apologies that her Mama had not yet called, which she hoped Sally would excuse, from her colds, & the severe weather. Then put in *our* love to both, & finished" (*JL*, 4: 247).

2. The letter is conjecturally dated from the end of the d'Arblays' visit at Chelsea and removal to Esther's, which, according to Charles Burney, took place on Tuesday 5 February 1799 (CB to CB Jr., [5 Feb. 1799], Berg; *JL*, 4: 234–36, 243, 248). The invitation was sent immediately, and the reply must have been written that day or the next. Although FBA later remembers the day as a Thursday, her memory of events that took place the previous month may not be reliable. The date suggested by her editor "Thursday 1 Feb." (or alternatively the eighth) (*JL*, 4: 247, n. 12, 236, n. 1) cannot be correct in any case, as the first of February was a Friday in 1799.

3. That James and Sarah declined to see her disappointed Mme d'Arblay, who summarized the remainder of the letter: "& then an account of a swelled gum, & bad weather, which made her fear a fall without an arm. This was all. No reason, no excuse whatever from James! & no love, no message whatever from herself! nor a word of regret from either, nor a hint of hoping any other meeting?—" (FBA to SBP, 12 Mar. 1799, Berg).

While she attributed their reluctance to "conscious feelings" or fear of remonstrance, James explained that his refusal was due to resentment of the d'Arblays' attitude and behavior (*JL*, 4: 248, 305–6). Happily, cordial relations between brother and sister were restored by an exchange of letters in May (see below L. 23, n. 2).

22. [To Frances (Burney) d'Arblay]

[21 John Street, 19 April 1799][1]
L. Copy, in hand of FBA included in A.L. FBA with A.L. M. d'A to SBP, 8 May 1799, Berg
Published: JL, *4: 287–88*
Address: Mrs. Phillips, / Belcotton, / Drogheda.

20. April, 99.

Before you can have taken any step in the business I wrote to you about this morning,[2] again I trouble you, my dearest sister, (& implore your forgiveness for this apparent capriciousness,) to forget every word you have read. I sat down passionately & hastily, unawares of the resentment—such a step was likely to create in my Brother's mind.[3] He will do nothing towards preventing the effect of my first Letter himself—but he seems so much incensed at it, that I have not the courage to persevere in my plan.

You will hate me for thus trifling with you—but rather endeavour—O my dearest sister, to forgive, & pity me.

Friday night.

1. SHB's letter was written on a Friday night, which fell on 19 April 1799. As the original is missing, it is impossible to determine if the erroneous date of "20. April, 99" was hers or FBA's. For the address of their lodging, see L. 23, n. 4.

2. In her letter to Susan, FBA describes her astonishment at suddenly receiving this letter without any forerunner, and transcribes her reply:

> 21. April ——99—
>
> With the greatest amazement I have just received a few lines, referring to a Letter that has never reached me, & containing allusions to a plan which I cannot comprehend. Pray endeavour to trace if your Letter was put into the post. I shall make all the enquiries I can about it at Dorking. Write speedily, my dear Sally, with a firm reliance that I will either do, or omit to do, whatever you may wish that you think can conduce either to serve or console you,—if either

should in the smallest degree be in my power. My original disturbance is again renewed,—though not, indeed, so bitterly as while you seemed both Wholly to forget you had a Sister at West Hamble (FBA with M. d'A to SBP, 8 May 1799, Berg).

3. James seems to have been somewhat irascible, "always unwilling to take offence; yet always eager to resent it" (*EJL*, 1: 94). Immediately after leaving James, Sarah Harriet remarks that her employer is "very patient—tho'—a man.—" (L. 27).

23. [To Frances (Burney) d'Arblay]

[21 John Street], 23 April 1799
L.S. Copy, in hand of FBA included in A.L. FBA with A.L. M. d'A to SBP, 8 May 1799, Berg
Published: JL, *4: 289*
Address: Mrs. Phillips, / Belcotton, / Drogheda.

23^{d} April ——99—

The Letter, my dearest sister, concerning which you naturally express such surprise, fortunately never was delivered at the office;[1] which I did not discover till after the second was put in. I have since destroyed it, & am extremely concerned to have given you <such> so much unnecessary uneasiness, as well as most sincerely grateful for the kindness with which you assure me of your readiness to serve or advise me. The firm dependance I have upon this is a very great comfort & pleasure to me, & will encourage me, should any occasion present itself, sooner to apply to you than to any other human being.

My Brother desires his kind love, & will write before he leaves town,[2] which, with little Martin,[3] we now mean to do very soon.[4] Accept my repeated excuses for the perplexity I occasioned you, & believe me, my dearest sister, your ever most grateful

S. H. B.

1. The subject of the missing letter is now irrecoverable, but possibly it contained an appeal to Fanny to intercede with Dr. Burney on James's behalf. Sarah's first visit to her father since leaving his house had taken place before 20 April 1799 (*JL*, 4: 279, n. 2); Fanny was later to comment that, "I never thought that though Sally alone *applied* for pardon, Sally alone covetted it" (*JL*, 4: 400). James, however, declined to discuss "the subject of the unhappy breach between my Father and me," although confessing

that "though I have remained silent, it has not been with ease to myself," especially since "Sally's late application." Nevertheless, he concludes that "much unkindness and ill usage has passed on both sides . . . and any attempt at advance by me would be a disturbance to him, and useless to both" (JB to FBA, [post 13 May 1799], Berg).

Fanny, strongly attached to both her father and her brother, did not give up her desire to see them reconciled, and a year later forwarded a letter from James to Dr. Burney. Assuring him that "James heartily repented the rash—wild—& unjustifiable step he has taken," she tried to soften CB's displeasure by pointing out her brother's "contrition, his evident unhappiness & ill health, & his avowal that the *wish nearest his heart* is your forgiveness" (*JL*, 4: 399–400). Although eventually father and son were outwardly reconciled, it is doubtful whether Dr. Burney ever really forgave his eldest son, whom he virtually disinherited in his will (Scholes, 2: 262; *JL*, 7: 292, 325; MAR to FBA, 21 June [1814], Barrett, Eg. 3697, ff. 304–5v).

2. James did write a conciliatory letter on 12 May 1799, apologizing for his "hastiness," to which Fanny responded affectionately on the thirteenth (*JL*, 4: 305, 293–94). On the back, she answered SHB's second letter: "I wrote as kindly as I knew how, desiring to hear how she went on, how she employed herself, how she was settled, & every particular she could write that would remind me of her former confidence, with strong expressions of satisfaction in her promise to apply to me without reserve if I could ever in any manner be of the least utility or comfort to her" (*JL*, 4: 306).

3. James's only son, Martin Charles Burney (1788–1852), was about eleven (*JL*, 1: lxx).

4. James and Sarah led a somewhat itinerant life together, moving at least three times in eight months (see Introduction). By 16 Jan. 1799, they were located at 21 John Street, Fitzroy Square (*JL*, 4: 245), but would soon leave for Bristol, to try the waters for James's failing health (*JL*, 4: 401). They took a "small house with a little garden to it, about a quarter of a mile out of Bristol" (JB to FBA, [post 13 May 1799], Berg), apparently a beautiful spot. Within two years (by 18 March 1801), they were back in London, at No. 9 Charles Street, Soho Square (*JL*, 4: 479).

24. With James Burney to Charlotte Francis[1]

72 Margaret Street, [8 June 1802]
A.L.S. JB with A.L.S. SHB, Berg
Address: Miss Francis / Mrs Budd's / Richmond Green / Richmond / Surry
Postmarks: Two Penny / POST / Oxford St N E
2 o'Clock / 8 JU / 1802 [^ND]
4 o'Clock / JU 8 / 1802 EV

[*The first page consists of an A.L.S. JB to CF, asking her to send her mother's address, and inviting her to visit them at No. 72 Margaret Street, Cavendish Square.*]

What the devilaccio are you doing so long at Richmond?[2] Have you ever had the grace, you young hussey, to go and see dear good Aunt Beckey?[3]—I am an Aunt you know already—and I intend, when time shall serve, to be old—and the men intend never to make a wife of me—and so, some of these days, I shall be Aunt Beckey personified—Only that I shall be very cross, ugly, spiteful &c—And for this reason, I begin very devoutely to take the part of all old maiden Aunts—"A fellow feeling makes me wondrous kind."[4]—

Sophy[5] dined here yesterday, and was well & merry—

Adieu—I like you & love you, and am your

S: H: Burney

1. This is the first letter to Charlotte Francis, the eldest child of Charlotte Broome; the former would become Sarah Harriet's favorite niece and correspondent.

2. Judging from the address, the fifteen-year-old Charlotte was a pupil of Mrs. Sarah Budd who operated a Ladies' Boarding School at Richmond from c. 1790 to c. 1830. She is probably the Sarah Gulliver who married at Richmond 27 May 1783 Mr. Thomas Budd, apparently a musician. A daughter, Isabella, baptized 25 September 1787, may be the Miss Isabella Budd who ran from a different location "an establishment for young ladies of high respectability" from 1823. Both are listed in the directories until 1830; and thereafter Miss Budd alone is shown, with a boarding school on the Green, making her last appearance in the Rate Book of 1860 (Richmond directories, 1791–1838; Richmond Poor & Highway Rate Book, 1790–1870; 1841, 1851 Census, Richmond; John Evans, *Richmond and Its Vicinity* (Richmond: James Darrill, [1825]), 188, 192; and information supplied by Central Reference Library, Richmond).

3. Rebecca Burney (1724–1809), Charles Burney's spinster sister, who lived at Richmond (*JL*, 1: lxviii, 69, n. 8).

4. "A fellow-feeling makes one wond'rous kind," a line taken from "An Occasional

Prologue" spoken by David Garrick (1717–79), on the night of his last performance, 10 June 1776, printed in *The Poetical Works of David Garrick* (London, 1785; rpt., New York: Benjamin Blom, 1968), 2: 325–27.

5. Esther Burney's third daughter, Sophia, was noted for her gaiety, with "a Good humour & innocence that make her drollery & quaint fancies remarkably agreeable" (*JL*, 5: 20).

Esther and her family maintained contact with James and Sarah throughout, as "the only one of his tribe he seems now to see" (*JL*, 4: 263). Esther credited her own forbearance with preventing the social ostracism that might otherwise have resulted: "to have totally withdrawn myself from her [SHB], would have been (I thought) in a manner proclaiming it to everyone, & might have led to shutting the door against her being recieved in any Creditable Society.—The best consequences have certainly resulted from the Conduct I held towards her" (EBB to CB Jr., 1 Mar. 1806 [1807], Osborn).

25. To Charlotte Francis

[72 Margaret Street], 20 March 1803
A.L., Berg
Address: Miss Francis / at Ralph Broome's Esqr / Clifs End / Exmouth / Devon
Postmarks: BEAU[M]ONT / STREET
[?] / 20 / [?]

Sunday 20th March 1803.

My dearest Charlotte,

Why, the people think, at least those that I have seen, that your dear mother had only Hobson's choice;[1] i e, reunion with M^r B: for the sake of obtaining Ralph—or, no Ralph: and so, as it is the general opinion, that dirty pudding is better than no bread—she is universally allowed to have done a very wise thing in cheerfully adopting the only measure that remained to her exclusive of parting with her child.[2]—She will remember, I am sure, that as far as I thought myself justified in giving any opinion, I always voted for her doing that which promised to give the most ease to her feelings as a mother—and to set that meddling old gossip, the world, at defiance.[3] To do so in the present instance, can require no great exertion of mind—for what is there that she has done, which it was not almost her duty to do?—James and I, in the plenitude of our satisfaction, shook hands, & wished each other joy very cordially, when we learnt the turn her affairs had taken. My sister Burney, I have every reason to believe, participates in the same sentiments—and so must every rational body throughout the United Empire of England, Scotland, Ireland & Wales.

Now I'll tell you a pretty story.

Three evenings ago, just as we were sitting down to tea, comes a note addressed to Captain Burney, & conceived in the following terms—

D^r & Mrs Ward[4] present compliments to Captain and Miss, and if agreable, will do themselves the honour of picking a bone with them this evening, and taking a bed.—

Now Mrs Ward was a great crony of brother Jamie's in days of yore, being a daughter of Dr Ayrton's, and his very near neighbour in James Street.[5] She is now married to a Surgeon and 'Potecary', and settled in the country. Concluding, however, that she and her husband might be come to town on some business, and knowing that she was not upon very good terms with her brother,[6] we immediately settled it in our minds that she had sent us the above agreeable scroll, and were in momentary expectation of seeing them both stalk in. No bed had we for either of their little toes, however: but for the sake of old acquaintanceship, we determined to endeavour to procure them one. Accordingly, our maid was dispatched to the different lodging-houses in the neighbourhood, upon the hunt and to bring in a pint of brandy for the D^r after supper—and presently, comes a consequential rat-tat-tat-tarara at the door. I went out upon the landing-place, to receive the bumpkins, & tell lies about our concern at having no spare bed; when behold! Mrs Ward turned out to be—Cousin Sophy—and the D^r was metamorphosed into Amelia![7]—We did not even know she (Soph.) was in town, a hussy, till we saw her![8] So, you may conceive our astonishment, & the shouts that resounded through the house.—On hearing the errand our damsel had been gravely sent upon, her delight knew no bounds; and when the poor woman actually returned, she entreated we would have her in, to hear the result of her perigrination—

Enter Maid—

Captain.—Well, Ann,[9] what luck have you had?

Maid.—Why, Sir, I have been round to all the houses any ways likely to take in chance lodgers for a single night: but they none of 'em liked to be at the trouble of setting their rooms to rights just merely for so little a while.—

Captain.—So, then, you have'n't been able to get any bed?

Maid.—Yes, Sir, I believe that what I heard of at the last place I called at, will do. They've got a very nice room, and well aired bed, & every thing very comfortable, except only that they have but one clean sheet, & all their pillow-cases

are dirty. But if my mistress can send a sheet, & a couple of pillow-cases, I dare say the room will do charmingly.—
Captain.—Well, but our friends have disappointed us, & I don't think they will want the room: so you must go back & let them know as much as soon as you can.—
Sophy.—For fear they should be beginning to wash their sheet.—
And thus ended this saucy joke.

My sister will be very sorry to hear a piece of intelligence of a much more serious nature. Her old acquaintance and neighbour, poor Patty Payne[10] died last Tuesday of a Quinsey in her throat. Mrs J^ms^ Burney[11] was sent to so late, that she did not reach Liverpool till Thursday, two days after her poor sister expired.—She is not yet returned; and probably will not be able to undertake night-travelling till she has had a little time to recover the horrid shock she must have received.

I have not forgotten your enquiry concerning Smalt and Ultramarine: but I have yet had no opportunity of putting the question to Cousin Edward[12]—Not having once beheld an inch of him since you left town. You may depend upon correct copies of all his and Laurence's exhibition pictures.[13] What I have not time to finish, Martin shall do for you.

My brother Jamie—whom you may see smiling at you, as per margin—sends as many loves and kind remembrances to your mother and self, as his "South Sea Discoveries"[14] allow him time to utter. Adieu my dearest Charlotte. I must send this to Beaumont Street to be directed.[15] Have'n't sent [*seen*] F.P.[16] these thousand years.

1. I.e., no choice at all, named after stable owner Tobias Hobson (1544–1631), who always obliged his customers to take the horse nearest the door.

2. Charlotte's second marriage of 1 March 1798 to Ralph Broome (1742–1805), a union opposed by her family, proved to be unhappy (*HFB*, 279–81; *JL*, 4: 47, n. 4 and passim). One child was born, Ralph Broome Jr. (c. 4 July 1801) (*JL*, 5: 21, n. 8), whom Charlotte had left behind with his father when she visited the d'Arblays in France in the autumn of 1802. On her return from her two months' visit, she heard that her husband was threatening to leave England with their son, possibly for America: "I don't believe he will be <u>quite</u> so mad—for he is in such a dreadful state of Health. . . . He w^d^ have gone the <u>same</u> <u>road</u> if I had <u>not</u> declared my intention of claim^g^ my right to my Baby, for his nephew says he told him he intended it, before I left England" (CBFB to FBA, [23 Oct. 1802], Barrett, Eg. 3693, ff. 84–85v; *JL*, 5: 335, n. 5, 436–37).

Apparently, Charlotte sought access to her child although separated from her husband, a difficult situation that was currently being resolved by reunion. For Mr. Broome's strange behavior, and his deterioration in health of mind and body, see *JL*, 5: 20, n. 2, 435, n. 3; 6: 471, n. 11.

3. An interesting comment, as Sarah may feel she has done so in deciding to live with James.

4. Ann Ayrton, the daughter of Edmund Ayrton (see next note), had married 20 May 1802 Jabez Ward, M.D. (d. post 1808), formerly of Westminster Hospital and afterwards of Bridgnorth, Salop (W. Bruce Bannerman, ed., *The Registers of St. Helen's, Bishopsgate, London* (London, 1904), 217; *GM,* 72, Pt. 2 (1802): 684; family tree of the Ayrton family, BL Add. MS. 60381, vol. 24).

5. Edmund Ayrton (1734–1808), Mus.D. (1784), English organist and composer, was James Burney's neighbour at 24 James Street, James having inherited No. 26 from John Hayes in 1792 (*DNB; New Grove;* Manwaring, 201–2; *JL,* 1: 82, n. 10).

6. Mrs. Ward had several brothers, but SHB may be referring to the youngest, William Ayrton (1777–1858), a musician like his father, who apparently remained in the family home (*DNB; New Grove;* HCR, *Reminiscences,* 1: 192; *GM,* 78, Pt. 1 (1808): 470).

7. Two of Esther Burney's daughters, Sophia Elizabeth and Amelia Maria.

8. Sophy, employed by Lord Brownlow as a governess (see below L. 26), might be expected to be at Belton, Lincs., the family seat. She was initially reluctant to take up this livelihood, although urged by her mother to ease the financial burden at home; however, she was "happy and comfortable" when placed (CB to FBA, 28 July 1802, Osborn; *JL,* 4: 281–82, 287).

9. Ann, the servant of James and Sarah, has not been further traced.

10. Martha Payne (1757–1803), eldest daughter of Thomas Payne the bookseller (1719–99), by his wife, Elizabeth (née Taylor) (d. 1767), whom he had married 6 October 1750; Martha was the elder sister of James's wife, Sarah (see next note) (*DNB; EJL,* 2: 193 and n. 11; Nichols, *Anecdotes,* 6: 440; parish registers, Finchley, St. Martin in the Fields, St. James, Clerkenwell).

11. James's estranged wife, formerly Sarah Payne (1759–1832), whom he had married 6 September 1785 and separated from twice before (parish register, St. Martin in the Fields; *JL,* 1: lxix; MAR to FBA, [3 Sept. 1798], Barrett, Eg. 3697, ff. 276–77v).

12. Edward Burney, the artist, now living at New Lisle Street, Leicester Square (Algernon Graves, *The Royal Academy of Arts* (London, 1905–6; rpt., New York: Burt Franklin, 1972)).

13. Thomas Lawrence (1769–1830), the distinguished artist, Kt. (1815) (*DNB*). Several of his portraits appeared in the exhibition of the Royal Academy, which opened 2 May 1803 at Somerset Place, but particularly commended were those of Lady C. Campbell (No. 182), Lord Thurlow (No. 21) and the Rt. Hon. W. Windham (No. 105) (Graves; *Times,* 2 May 1803).

14. James Burney had been working for three years on a history of voyages in the Pacific, the first volume of which was soon to be published (see below L. 26, n. 14) (Manwaring, 214–16; *JL,* 5: 409, n. 2).

15. I.e., to Esther Burney, who had moved c. 21 June 1798 from 2 Upper Titchfield Street, Portland Place, to 43 Beaumont Street, Devonshire Place (*JL,* 4: 56, n. 2, 153, 161). Esther may have known that Charlotte was staying with her mother and half-brother at her stepfather's in Exmouth (*JL,* 5: 435, n. 2).

16. F.P. was Susan's daughter, Frances Phillips, who lived at Chelsea with Dr. Burney after her mother's untimely death.

26. To Charlotte Francis

[72 Margaret Street, 11 May 1803][1]
A.L.S., Berg
Address: Miss Francis / at Ralph Broome's Esqr / Exmouth / near Exeter / Devonshire
Postmarks: B MA / 12 / 803

My very dear, and very droll niece

Will you think this letter worth reading, when I begin by telling you I have not yet inhaled the balmy atmosphere of the Exhibition Room? Here is no classic-minded Charlotte Francis to tempt me thither; and I am mighty lall about going with Jemmy or Marty. Moreover, I have seen no one who has been there: but I am told, there is a chalk-drawing of Fanny Phollips [*Phillips*], by little Monsr Bouche,[2] Boud's[3] friend, in the model-room, and two highly-finished coloured designs by Cousin Edward, of which the subject is the Millenium age.[4] Dear Sophy drank tea here and shared my bed with me on Saturday night. She is well and merry, and wishes you would include her in the list of your correspondents. If you do (and I think the proposal is too pleasant to be sneezed at) direct to her under cover to the Right Honble Lord Brownlow Berkley Square, London.[5] She thinks that if you write upon thinnish paper, you may pop a letter to me within hers, and yet not make the frank too heavy.[6] What say you, my lass, to this saving scheme? When she writes to you, the same frank will serve both her & me: and at her house there are two very obliging Senators, father and son,[7] who never deny their good offices to her.

Does your dear mother happen to know any worthy soul in them there parts she abides in, who would like to give me a good fat salary as governess to her brats? I assure you I am in earnest. My sister Burney is on the look-out for me here in town, but as yet, has heard of nothing but a vile Hibernian family, that would require me to live among their bog-trotting countrymen all the year round. I have no relish for Paddy, <or> nor any of Paddy's ways and haunts—and so, I hope I shall not be established in his domains. The solution of this riddle is briefly as follows. James is miserable without his little girl,[8] and has proposed to me, (after putting her to school at Mrs Budds[9] for a few months to take off her rough edges) <having> to have her to live with us. The idea is, as far as relates to Mrs Burney, cruel and odious. I have therefore made up my mind, to shift my quarters. I neither will deprive James of the satisfaction of having his child with him: nor will I take upon myself the odium that would attach to my character were I to undertake the charge of her to the exclusion of her mother. These objections, duly weighed & considered, I have so sagaciously represented to Jamie, that I have brought him round to consent, in a chearful & friendly manner, to the plan I meditate. I am sure of your dear and kind mother's (I do love her) approbation when she considers my motives. So, be upon the seek for me, hussey of my heart.

Now for other chat.—Are you vulgar enough to know that in little country shops, when a pound of candles is asked for by a customer, and is weighed, if they are not exactly heavy enough, a smaller kind of candle, made on purpose, and called make-weights, is put into the scale to give it due preponderance. This premised, peruse the sequel.—Amelia went one morning with your sister Marianne[10] to call upon a Mrs Middleton.[11] There was a harp in the room. The ever-graceful Amelia seated herself at it in a classical attitude, and calling to the Lady of the house, said,—"How do I look at the harp, Mrs Middleton?"

"Very like a make-weight to a pound of candles, my dear"—answered the unsparing dame.

Clement[12] and Marianne performed their parts in the play that was acted at Lord Brownlow's to admiration. But what amused me most in Sophy's account of the eventful evening was, the dear Clemken's cordial manner to the whole noble family on his first introduction. He heartily shook hands with the boys[13] all round; and with the same good-humoured familiarity, went up with his extended hand to Lady Brownlow also. They were extremely delighted with him, and they were all the best friends in the world.—

The book (Jamie's book, I mean) will be completely printed, I hope, in a week from this day (Wednesday the 10th).[14] I will not let him forget to act the part you so much approve, that of a generous uncle. Let me hear from you soon, and pray bestow upon me a few more views.

Adieu my dear Charlotte.
How should you like such a pretty little husband?

Yours ever affectionately.
S: H: Burney

1. The letter is postmarked 12 May 1803; although the day of writing is specified as "Wednesday the 10th," the tenth actually fell on a Tuesday that year. Since an error in the date is more likely than the day of the week, the letter is dated to Wednesday, 11 May 1803.

2. [Jean-Pierre] Bouché (fl. 1794–1803), an artist best known for his portrait in 1797 of the Earl of St. Vincent in the National Portrait Gallery. A drawing of Fanny Phillips, Sarah's attractive niece, appears as No. 808 in the catalogue of the *Exhibition of the Royal Academy* (1803), but is attributed to J. Barry. The d'Arblays, or possibly the Bourdois,

apparently took this picture to France, where Fanny mentions her son's copying it in October [1804] (*JL*, 6: 492 and n. 2; Mary Pettman, ed., *National Portrait Gallery* (New York: St. Martin's Press, 1981), 499, 714).

3. "Boud" or "Bood" was the family's nickname for Lambert Antoine Bourdois de Bréviande (c. 1761–1806), a lifelong friend of M. d'Arblay; he had married Sarah Harriet's niece, "Marianne" Burney, on 30 October 1800 (*JL*, 3: 342, n. 10; 4: 420, 422, n. 1, 455, n. 2).

4. Edward Burney exhibited two pictures titled "The millenial age," Nos. 447 and 730 in the 1803 exhibition of the Royal Academy, according to the catalogue.

5. Brownlow Cust (1744–1807), 4th Bt. Brownlow (1770) was M.P. for Ilchester, Somerset (1768–74) and for Grantham, Lincs. (1774–76) and created 1st Baron Brownlow (20 May 1776). From his second marriage on 31 August 1775 to Frances (1756–1847), only child of Sir Henry Bankes, Alderman of London, he had eleven children (five daughters), currently ranging in age from four to twenty-three years (Burke; Lodge; Gibbs).

6. As a member of the House of Lords, Lord Brownlow would have the privilege of franking his mail, so that letters sent by him or addressed to him would pass through the Post Office free during and within forty days of a parliamentary session. By an Act of 1795, franked letters were limited to one ounce in weight. By franking letters for other people (particularly those with a second enclosure), Sophy's employer was abusing his privilege; however, such abuse was widespread. The practice is discussed in Howard Robinson, *The British Post Office* (Princeton: Princeton University Press, 1948), 114–19, 153, and passim.

7. Lord Brownlow's eldest son, John (1779–1853), would have franking privileges as M.P. for Clitheroe, Lancs. (1802–7). Later he would be advanced to the Viscountcy of Alford and Earldom of Brownlow (27 November 1815) (Burke; Lodge; Gibbs).

8. James's daughter, Sarah (1796–post Dec. 1868) (*JL*, 1: lxx), was six years old and by all accounts a very engaging child. The family had remarked that James's being deprived of his daughter would be a trial to him (MAR to FBA, [3 Sept. 1798], Barrett, Eg. 3697, ff. 276–77v; *JL*, 4: 307).

9. For Mrs. Budd's school at Richmond where Charlotte Broome had sent her daughter, see above L. 24, n. 2. It seems that James did follow suit, as young Sarah is mentioned with Mrs. Budd in a letter of 1810 (CFBt to HBt, 19 June [1810], Berg).

10. Marianne Francis, the younger daughter of Charlotte Broome, was then about thirteen.

11. Marianne's friend, Mrs. Middleton, may be the "Mother Mid . . . that great fat thing with a little cocked up hat" whom she mentioned in a letter to Charlotte in 1809, and whose husband had died not long before her letter of 12 September 1811—otherwise untraced (MF to CFBt, [1809], Barrett, Eg. 3704A, ff. 3–5v; MF & CBFB to CFBt & Ralph Broome Jr., 12 Sept. 1811, Berg).

12. Clement Francis, Charlotte's ten-year-old brother.

13. Lord Brownlow had six sons: John (1779–1853); Henry Cockayne (1780–1861); Richard (1785–1864); William (1787–1845); Peregrine Francis (1791–1873); Edward (1794–1878) (Burke; Lodge; Gibbs).

14. James Burney, *A Chronological History of the Discoveries in the South Sea or Pacific Ocean*, vol. 1 (London: G. and W. Nicol, 1803), was published in June (*A Monthly List of New Publications*, no. 12 (June 1803), 24). The *Monthly Review*, 2nd ser. 42 (1803),

414–23, praised the work which "successfully combines the attractions of novelty and antiquity. The geographical and nautical remarks are drawn up with clearness and brevity; and they are expressed in terms which render them intelligible to every class of readers." Under a slightly different title, the subsequent four volumes were to appear in 1806, 1813, 1816, and 1817.

---

27. To Charlotte Francis and Charlotte (Burney) (Francis) Broome

Delamere Lodge, 4 January 1804
A.L., Berg
Address: Miss Francis / No 7 South Parade / Bath
Postmarks: NO[RTHW]ICH
Endorsed: ansd *Numbered:* 52

January 4th 1804.
Delamere Lodge.[1]

Dear Sister—Dear Niece

Long looked for, come at last—Better late than never.—Your joint letter found a very kind reception when it did arrive; but to tell you how long I thought it was in coming, would be quite impossible. I have got it, however, at last—so I will magnanimously forbear all reproaches—and proceed to tell you all I think worth communicating respecting myself.

for I am in a family made up of goodness and <worthiness> kindness[.] My lady patroness,[2] who is a cotemporary of Mrs Crewe's,[3] and in her youth, rivaled her in beauty, is still a most attractive and lovely woman. Her manners are gentle, & elegant—when in spirits, she is irrisistably pleasant—and at all times, is interesting and loveable. She has two grown-up daughters, who are the comforts and delights of my life. The eldest[4] <is> draws charmingly, from busts, from nature, (living nature)—in water colours, and in chalks. She generously and zealously, upon all occasions, assists and encourages me in all my drawing attempts—and the improvement I have made under her kind tuition is, to myself, quite astonishing. The second sister, Miss Eliza,[5] is yet more accomplished as a musician, than Miss Emma is as a paintress. She is a scholar of Mr Cramer's,[6] and, as my sister Burney allows, one of his best scholars—She sings likewise with a great deal of taste, tho' but little voice. But what is of far

Maria née Wilbraham, engraved by Thomas Watson after Daniel Gardner. (Courtesy of the National Portrait Gallery, London.)

more consequence to those who are inmates with these young ladies, is, that they are sweet-tempered, sociable, chearful, & void of all pride or affectation. A particular friend, indeed a relation of Miss Eliza's, is now at Bath. Lady Mary Bennet, one of Lord Tankerville's daughters,[7] is the person I mean. Most likely you will see her in public—and I want to know your opinion of her. Miss Eliza would be delighted if you could send me any particulars respecting her; such as, whether she is much admired—whether she looks well, &c. They are great correspondants, and, within half a year, the same age. You will find out which is Lady Mary, by her being the prettiest and the least of the grown-up lady Bennets.[8]

Well now, my dear Charlotte, let me talk a little gusto & classics with you. Have you heard that I took courage, some time after my arrival here, to write to Cousin Edward, entreating him to purchase for my two dear Miss Wilbra-

Self-portrait by Edward F. Burney. (Courtesy of the National Portrait Gallery, London.)

ham's a couple of busts?—They had fixed upon Sapho for one, and Ethodea, the eldest daughter of Niobe,[9] for the other. Besides these, I wrote to him for some good etchings of cattle, some large coloured-paper to draw on, & two sorts of black chalk. We talked of nothing but Cousin Edward, plaister busts, etched cattle, & black chalk from the time of my applying to him, till the moment of their arrival. And when they did arrive, they were such loves, that we almost fell down & worshipped them!—Six such dear etchings, from Gilpin & Barret[10]—and two such adorable plaister loves!—And, will you believe that even I have drawn from them, & am said to have succeeded marvellously.—Oh, and another dear little bit of information I have to communicate. We have had here for a week, a young woman from Chester, whose father is an Etcher and Gilder, and who has brought her up to his business. She came to teach the ladies here to gild, & kind M^rs^ W—— proposed to me to learn with them. The gilding part of the business, however, did not, as Cecilia[11] used to say, amoose me: but she taught me to etch—and to engrave upon gilt glass; & when we meet, I shall delight to teach you; if you wish to learn. Cousin Edward just before I left town, had suffered me to beg, or rather to filch from him, a design he had lately finished in black, red & white chalk. I copied this for my first etching—and lovely it would have been, had not some abominable mistake in the strength of the aquafortis used to eat away the copper where it is cut, occasioned it to produce too pale an impression. Still, however, it is "not to be sneezed at."—On the left side of the plate, at the bottom of the figure, is engraved E. F. Burney del.—On the right side, S. H. Burney, sculp.—Altogether, it looks very scientific.

Pray, if you were in earnest when you proposed it, send me, by all means, your copy of Inny's design for the Pleasures of Hope[12]—I worship the very ground he treads on—the very paper he has touched, or that any copyist of his has touched.

I do, and always have doated, unsight, unseen, upon dear Dolf.[13]—My heart yearns (or my bowels rather, I should say) to behold him.—I congratulate you all upon his being such a love.—Poor Mr Wilbraham would do well, I think, to take a trip to Bath, for he is at this very time laid up with the gout.—I love him—He is quite a dear—and very patient tho'—a man.—

What think you? Martin Burney and I are in very friendly correspondance—And my father is almost one of my most faithful letter-writers—He is in spirits and tolerable health. The Post is going out—I have only time to add that I love you both very dearly indeed—and long, with my whole heart, to see you—
Yours ever

M^rs^ W—— has just given me one of Inny's Souvenirs[14] for a new years Gift.—

1. Sarah's wish to find employment as a governess had been fulfilled, and she writes from Delamere Lodge, near Nantwich, Cheshire, the seat of George Wilbraham (1741–1813). M.P. for Bodmin (1789–90), and High Sheriff of Cheshire (1791–92), he belonged to an old county family (B. E. Harris, ed., *A History of the County of Chester*, vol. 2 (London: Institute of Historical Research, 1979), 145; Namier & Brooke; *GM*, 83, Pt. 2 (1813): 700).

The change was beneficial financially; the drain on SHB's resources in payments to Capt. Burney was halted, and she now received the dividends on her remaining £806.8.4 in government securities, yielding £32.5s. a year. Her salary is unknown, but she was able to acquire £50 of stock the following winter, £100 a year later and a further £100 shortly after the termination of her employment (Coutts ledgers).

2. George Wilbraham's wife (m. 13 Oct. 1774), Maria (1755–1822), daughter of William Harvey (1714–63) of Rolls Park, near Chigwell, Essex, and his wife, Emma née Skinner (d. 1767). Maria's father, descended from "an opulent family in the county,"

represented it in Parliament 1747–63, and her mother was connected through marriage with the wealthy Grosvenor family (Burke, *LG; GM*, 37 (1767): 144; 44 (1774): 541; 92, Pt. 2 (1822): 285; parish register, Chigwell, Essex; Namier & Brooke).

3. Frances Anne (1748–1818), daughter of Fulke Greville (1716–1806), patron and friend of Charles Burney. She had married on 4 April 1766 John Crewe (1742–1829), M.P. (1765–1802), later created Baron Crewe (1806) (Burke; Namier & Brooke; Thorne; *JL*, 1: 2, n. 10).

4. Since the death of her elder sister, Maria (1775–94), Emma Wilbraham was the eldest daughter, at twenty-seven years. Born 8 November 1776, she was to die unmarried at Brighton 21 December 1855 (Ormerod, 2: 138; *GM*, NS 45 (1856): 211; death certificate, GRO).

5. Elizabeth Wilbraham, born 23 February 1783, was almost twenty-one; she was to outlive all her sisters and die a spinster at Chelsea, 23 May 1865 (Ormerod, 2: 138; *GM*, 3rd ser. 19 (1865), 121; death certificate, GRO).

6. Johann Baptist Cramer (1771–1858), noted pianist, composer, and publisher in London, who was in high demand as a teacher and charged the top fee of a guinea per lesson (*New Grove*).

7. Lady Mary Elizabeth Bennet (1785–1861), fourth daughter of Charles Bennet (1743–1822), 4th Earl of Tankerville (1767), who had married on 7 October 1771 Mrs. Wilbraham's cousin, Emma Colebrooke (1752–1836). Lady Mary would later marry as his second wife on 26 July 1831 Charles Miles Lambert (Middleton) Monck (1779–1867), 6th Bt. Middleton (1795) (Burke; Lodge; Gibbs).

8. Lady Mary Bennet had three unmarried sisters at the time: Anna (1774–1836), soon to marry 19 July 1804 the Hon. and Rev. William Beresford (1780–1830); Margaret Alicia Emma (1780–1813); and Augusta Sophia (1786–1809), who would marry William Fanning of Cork (Burke and Lodge under Tankerville, Decies; *Alumni Oxon.*).

9. Sappho, the Greek Lyric poet (fl. 600 B.C.) and Niobe (of Greek myth), whose numerous progeny were killed by the gods to punish her rash maternal boast.

10. Sawrey Gilpin (1733–1807), the talented animal painter, and George Barret (c. 1732–84), the landscape artist, who frequently collaborated (*DNB;* Ellis Waterhouse, *The Dictionary of British Eighteenth-Century Painters in Oils and Crayons* (Woodbridge, Suffolk: Antique Collectors' Club, 1981)). Sarah Harriet would undoubtedly have seen their celebrated work decorating the walls of a room at Norbury Park, Surrey, described in Christopher Hussey, "Italian Light on English Walls," *Country Life*, 17 February 1934, 161–64.

11. Esther Burney's fourth daughter, Cecilia, "all smiles, grace & enchantment" as a child, whose memorable remarks Sarah quotes elsewhere (L. 103) (*JL*, 1: 228).

12. "Inny," the family nickname for Cousin Edward (see below L. 105), who illustrated Thomas Campbell's popular poem, *The Pleasures of Hope* (1799), beginning with the fourth edition in 1800.

13. "Dolf" or "Dolph," the family nickname for Charlotte Broome's youngest son, Ralph, then two and a half (*JL*, 1: lxxiii).

14. Edward Burney also designed headpieces for memorandum books or pocket calendars from 1794 to 1829, which members of the family often received as presents. One of these was called, *Le Souvenir, a Pocket Remembrancer* (information on Edward Burney here and above n. 12 kindly supplied by Patricia Crown).

28. To Charlotte Francis

Delamere Lodge, [spring-summer 1804][1]
A.L., Berg
Address: Miss Francis / Granby Place / Clifton / Bristol / N° 2
Postmarks: [NORTHWICH]
Endorsed: ansd—

George Wilbraham's Esqr Delamere Lodge
near Northwich, Cheshire.

I will not venture to assert that this scrib,[2] tho' begun the very moment I had finished reading yours, will be concluded, sealed, directed and sent off in less than a month. However, the maggot happens to bite, and I happen to have time,—so I sit down to answer, the moment I have received it.—

Acquainted with Clifton! Lord help thee, child, dost thee not know I resided near a year with Bro: James & Martin in its vicinity?[3] I love and honour its various beauties to my very heart of hearts. No place I ever visited pleased me so much at the time, or has left more agreable recollections in my mind. I am glad thee hast taste enough to relish it properly.—As for the "Venus of the shell", she is another intimate acquaintance of mine, & deservedly enough, I think, a very first-rate favorite. During my late séjour with this family in town, I took unto myself a dear, slayer of-the-king's-English drawing-master[4]—A lovely black-&-yellow Italian, the main prop & comfort of my life! And he made me draw from your Venus, & from the one y'cleped the "crouching"[5] over & over again: and I fell deeply in love with both. By subscribing a shilling a week to Papara, the Plaisterman,[6] I got what busts or whole length figures I pleased. Were you ever at that queer old fish's shop?—Inny knows, & takes him off incomparably.—The Exhibition this year contained some admirable portraits—but no historical pictures of much merit, save one or two small ones of Westalls.[7]—

My visit into Cambridgeshire was perfect in its kind. I was at dear Haslingfield a month within two days. The party there consisted of my brother himself, Mrs Allen, their three daughters,[8] Mrs D. Young[9] (an angel in grain) My two darling boys from India,[10] and William Allen,[11] the youngest of my brother's sons.—Leaving all my wise faces, & sayings, behind me, & feeling in perfect health, & in excellent spirits, & loving every soul around me with all my heart & soul, I never spent so merry & happy a time. The only serious employment I chose to set about whilst there, was, occasionally, drawing. I went amply provided

The arrival of Raphael in Milton's *Paradise Lost*, drawing by Edward F. Burney. (Courtesy of the Henry E. Huntington Library and Art Gallery.)

with materials—and took five portraits, two of which were (I blush to be forced to confess it) speaking likenesses!—One was of dear Mrs Young, in chalks, the size of life, upon brown paper—the other was of the eldest of the India boys, as fine a creature as these green eyes of mine (mixed with streaks of orange-yellow) ever beheld. I wish you could see that same lad:—he is just <fourteen> thirteen—has an opene, noble, generous countenance—a figure the best proportioned & most graceful possible—and a character frank, ingenuous, manly, yet playful. He writes the finest hand you can imagine—is a good latin & french scholar—injenious, active & quick in all he does—and loves kissing as much as I love currant & raspberry tart!—C'est tout dire.—His brother is an arch, comic, good-natured darling, as fat & round as a roll of butter, & a perfect love-&-a-half. The girls, & I to-boot, played with them and William, at Trap-ball,[12] at marbles, at battledore & shuttlecock, at Pope Joan,[13] & at two or three games of romping per diem—and I left them with a stock of good-humour sufficient I hope to last me throughout the year—sweet!

My favorite passage in Il Paradiso Perduto is this—When our good old grand pa', Adam, and the Angel Gabriel are discoursing over the repast Eve had set before them, Milton, to put our minds at ease as to the ill consequences of such dawdling, kindly tells us—the meal consisting wholly of fruits

"No fear lest dinner cool!"[14]—

In "Paradise Regained," however, there is an address from the Devil to our Saviour worth its weight in gold—meeting him in the Wilderness, & affecting not to know him, he begins a conversation thus—

"Sir, by what ill chance &c[15]—

Now that Sir appears to me the very acme of burlesque—and sets me a shouting every time it comes into my head.—My two dear grown-ups, Miss Wilbraham, & Miss Eliza, who, as well as me, read both Paradises last winter, doat upon Sir as much as I do:—and whenever we prate over our fruit luncheons, apologise for it by saying—"No fear lest luncheon cool."—

[Now I will tell y]ou a [story]. I am Ass enough to be fond of [*The page is torn and part of the story missing.*] door, it flew out of the window, and, for aught I know, is now making love to Storace.[16] However that may be, I pined mainly for Billy's desertion, & used every means in my power to recall the wanderer back—He never came, though; and so I began to call reason to my aid, and to endeavour to reconcile myself to the jilting trick he had played me: but this morning, on entering the school-room, what should I behold upon my work-table near the window, but a new Billy Braham,[17] the gift of dear Mrs W——, who had sent I d'ont know how far to procure him for me?—Was it not a lovely little mark of kindness?—Billy sends his love to [y]ou.—

My best love to your dear Mother. I long to see you both again—When will the happy day arrive? Pray write soon to your ever affectio:

1. The letter may be dated conjecturally by a number of factors: SHB's position with the Wilbrahams in Cheshire, the ages of the two boys from India, the presence of Dorothy Young (who died early in 1805), and the mention of Westall's pictures in the Exhibition. As well, a drawing-master is introduced in this letter, who is named in L. 29 below (written on 26 Oct. 1804), as if in answer to a query of Charlotte's.

2. "Scrib" is an abbreviation of "scribble"; the only example given in the *OED* is from a letter of Dr. Burney's (7 May 1795).

3. For Sarah Harriet's one-year sojourn at Bristol with James and Martin, see above L. 23, n. 4.

4. Apparently, Andrea Tendi, who is named below, L. 29.

5. SHB had taken as her model two common types of Hellenistic sculpture: the crouching Venus and the goddess rising from the sea were represented in dozens of surviving statues (Dericksen Morgan Brinkerhoff, *Hellenistic Statues of Aphrodite* (New York: Garland, 1978), 35–37, 56–57).

6. Probably B. Papera (fl. 1790–1825), listed in the London directories alternately as a plaster figure-maker, sculptor, and modeler, who supplied busts to his customers from his shop at 16 Marylebone Street, Golden Square. His son, James Philip (fl. 1825–51), was better known, exhibiting at the Royal Academy (1829–30) and sending statues to the Great Exhibition in 1851 (London Directories 1790–1834; Rupert Gunnis, *Dictionary of British Sculptors, 1660–1851*, rev. ed. (London: Abbey Library, [1968])).

7. Richard Westall (1765–1836), historical painter and illustrator (*DNB*). To the 1804 Exhibition of the Royal Academy he contributed several works, but only one (according to the Catalogue) which could be called historical, "Henry the Third replying to the bishops," No. 23.

The reviewer in the *Times* was disappointed in the paintings, which consisted chiefly of portraits with comparatively few historical pictures, although "these are not of such a character as to lead us very deeply to regret that they constitute so inconsiderable a proportion of the whole collection" (*Times*, 28 Apr. 1804).

8. Sarah's half-brother, Stephen Allen (1755–1847), the son of Mrs. Burney's first marriage, was educated at Harrow and Cambridge (matric. 1771). Ordained as a priest in 1780, he was Vicar of St. Margaret, King's Lynn, Norfolk (c. 1797–1847) and Rector of Haslingfield, Cambs. (1800–47) (*JL*, 1: lxxiv; *GM*, NS 28 (1847): 102). Since c. April 1802 he had been residing in his living of Haslingfield (MAR to FBA, 12 Jan. 1803, Berg).

His wife, whom he had married at Gretna Green on 28 October 1772, was Susanna (1755–1816), daughter of Dr. Edward Sharpin of Norfolk (*EJL*, 1: 5, n. 14). Of their large family of twelve, there were three surviving daughters: Mary Susanna (1780–post 1843), Susanna (1785–1820), and Sarah (1790–post 1843) (parish register, East Dereham, Norfolk; memorial tablet in St. Margaret's Church, King's Lynn; will of Stephen Allen, dated 17 March 1843, proved 21 July 1847, PRO/PROB/11/2058/347).

9. Dorothy Young (c. 1721–1805), a close family friend from King's Lynn, Norfolk. She was living with Stephen Allen and his family at Haslingfield, where she was to die

on 31 January 1805, making Stephen her residuary legatee (*EJL*, 1: 20, n. 54; CB, *Memoirs*, 115–16 and n. 6; *HFB*, 7–8; *GM*, 75, Pt. 1 (1805): 187).

10. Children of Sarah's brother, Richard Thomas Burney (1768–1808), who had lived in India since 1787, and was headmaster of the Orphan School at Kidderpore by 1795. Having married Jane Ross (1772–1842) in Calcutta 9 November 1787, he had a large family (some fourteen children). His eldest two sons, Richard (1790–1845) and Henry (1792–1845), had been sent to England for their health and education and were maintained with the help of their grandfather, Charles Burney (*JL*, 1: lxxiii, 203, n. 50; Hodson; Walter K. Firminger, "Madame d'Arblay and Calcutta," *Bengal Past and Present* 9 (1914): 244–49; CB to FC, Jan. 1808, Osborn; CB to FBA, 12 Nov. 1808, Berg). See further, L. 76, n. 2.

There appears to be little evidence to support the supposition of scandal surrounding Richard's emigration to the East. The notion of "libidinous conduct, resultant victimization by blackmailing, debts, and early exile" (accepted as fact in *EJL*, 1: 183–84, n. 4) depends on an unproven assertion that his early career "may be reflected fairly realistically" in the character of one of Mme d'Arblay's novels (*JL*, 1: 203, n. 50) even though elsewhere the same character is said to have a different model: "historically, he is the young Charles Burney" (*HFB*, 254).

The fact that after his second wife's death, Charles Burney apparently destroyed Richard's letters along with many others is not necessarily indicative, but it does mean that any assertion about their contents is purely speculative (the notion of a "scrape" whose "details" have been "lost" (*JL*, 11: 185, n. 4)). One surviving comment may have a simple explanation. On hearing of Richard's marriage in India, Susan (Burney) Phillips remarked, "Heaven avert indeed greater Evils, for of all his transgressions I find this the least difficult to forgive—& yet it was a very faulty step, & very probable to be not only his own ruin but that of his poor Companion.—" (SBP, Journals, June 1789, Barrett, Eg. 3692, f. 43, cited in *JL*, 1: 203, n. 50).

The mystery of this "faulty step" is solved in an unpublished letter of Charles Burney, who fears prejudice may be shown towards his son Richard as one of "those who have married natives" (CB with SHB to CB Jr., [Dec. 1807], Burney-Cumming). Years later, one of the children of this Anglo-Indian match was indeed described as having a "Complection a little Indian" (*JL*, 11: 195).

11. William Maxey Allen (1792–1865), the youngest of Stephen Allen's sons, was twelve. He would later follow his father's calling, as curate of Wimbotsham and of Fordham, Norfolk (*JL*, 12: 789, n. 7; *GM*, 3rd ser. 19 (1865), 252).

12. Trap-ball: "A game in which a ball, placed upon one end (slightly hollowed) of a trap . . . is thrown into the air by the batsman striking the other end with his bat, with which he then hits the ball away" (*OED*).

13. Named after the legendary female Pope, "Pope Joan" was a card game, played with a pack from which the eight of diamonds was removed (*OED*).

14. This phrase occurs in Bk. 5, l. 396 of John Milton's *Paradise Lost* (London, 1667). God has sent the angel Raphael to warn Adam of Satan's presence, and Eve hospitably prepares for him a repast of the choicest fruits. The arrival of Raphael is one of the scenes illustrated by Edward Burney for Charles Whittingham's 1799 edition of the poem (Patricia Crown, *Drawings by E. F. Burney in the Huntington Collection* (San Marino, Calif.: Huntington Library, 1982), 34–35).

15. John Milton, *Paradise Regain'd* (London, 1671), Bk. 1, l. 321.

16. Anna Storace (1765–1817), the English soprano, whose union with John Abraham Fisher in 1783 proved to be unhappy.

17. Sarah's songbird was named after the English tenor John Braham (1774–1856), linked romantically from 1797 to 1816 with soprano Anna Storace (n. 16) (*New Grove*).

---

29. To Charlotte Francis

Delamere Lodge, 26 October 1804
A.L., Berg
Address: Miss Francis / Ralph Broom's Esqr / Park Street / Bath
Postmarks: NORTHWICH

Delamere Lodge
Octr 26th 1804

Dear, Merry Charlotte—Now I hope this will not come popping upon you at the very moment you are wiping pearly drops from your beauteous cheek—In that case, the epithet merry might be rather mal-a-propos. I think, however, from my experienced acquaintance with your character, the chances are all in my favour—And at all events, one of my epithets will save its bacon; for dear, very dear are you to me whether merry or sad. Poets and Philosophers are all fibbers, my good friend, when they tell us, absence is a cure for love.[1] I protest, I never idolized any of my kin and kind half so fervently as I do at this present juncture. So much for sentiments.—I hope yours will keep pace with mine.—

What a warbling must your house send forth! And what a mortal consumption of gravel, seeds and saffron must it occasion! Admire the wise economy of my nature.—I thought, the last time I sent for saffron, they gave me a very small bit for my penny—I make no doubt, it is owing to the abominable expenditure of it which your stock of screammers cause![2] I hate to have the markets raised in this manner—It is ruin to the middling ranks!

The name and place of abode of my tawney darling of a drawing Master, is Tendi,[3] N^{o} <41> 54. Lower Titchfield Street.—I will now tell you how my delicacy and my love of improvement accommodated matters between them with regard to drawing from naked (Pah!) plaister figures. I took a little flannel dicky (sometimes called, but vulgarly, a peticoat) and threw it over the object: then, with a pair of scissars, I cut away such parts as concealed what the laws of modesty allow to be shewn, i e, the face, hands, arms, feet, throat—and the rest all remained snug behind its woolen veil, which besides, made very pretty light drapery. You will see, when we meet, the agreeable effect produced by this injenious device.—

I heard a day or two since from Sophy at Belton—But pardon me, my dear Charlotte—I know I ought not to mention her name to you thus bluntly—I did it unawares. I am sorry, however, that there should be any coolness between you, and can never cease wishing that it might be in my power to reconcile two people who used to be such warm friends. Keep this part of my letter entirely to yourself. I am sure your dear mother would be vexed to hear that you could so far have forgotten yourself—since, to speak frankly, my dear girl, there is not one of our family that does not regard you as the aggressor in this business. Sophy I dare assert, would be glad to make the first advances towards a reconciliation had she the smallest hope of succeeding: but you have been so unaccountably violent and bitter, that she fears every step she might take, would be misconstrued, and might bring on new invectives.[4]

About a week ago, whilst very busy with my pupil[5] at morning lessons, a message was brought to us, desiring we w^d^ both go down to see a very curious sight in M^r^ W——'s Study. I begged we might be excused, disliking to do any thing that may dissipate my Miss's thimble-full of brains, when, after much trouble, I have succeede[d in] settling her to her business. However, a second and more pressing summons soon arrived—and I was compelled to relent. On entering the study, I found the whole family, to which were added Butler, Steward, & Housekeeper, assembled before an unlocked Cabinet, constructed within an outward wall, and fitted up with drawers, &c, to contain law-parchments and papers, such as leases, conveyances, &c, &c. A smell, at the same moment, assailed my nostrils, the most mouldy, damp, and even putrid, you can imagine. M^rs^ W—— with vexation and concern united, then told me, she had been remonstrating <u>five years</u> in order to get this cabinet opened and examined; that, at last, perceiving some substance, resembling a fungus, sprouting out at the lock, she had prevailed—And then she proceeded to display to me <u>such</u> a sight, as mortal eyes perhaps never beheld before!—The outside and inside of every drawer, and every paper within them, was closely incrusted with a sort of fungus or lichen, in some places full an inch thick—In all parts, tough leathery, and variously coloured with blue, green, and yellow—Not a single parchment could be opened, & not a letter upon any of them was discernable. While sighing and groaning in concert with the rest of the party over this dismal object, what think you was M^r^ W——'s employment? That of calmly selecting, from the heap before him, the largest, finest, and most flourishing bit of fungus, to wrap up in a letter, and carry to a botanical friend of his, who he thought would delight in so curious a production!—

Pray do not communicate the fungus history to Mr B——[6] Your dear mother must hear it, as I know she would like to assist me in wipping Mr W——'s brown bottom for his supiness first, and his ill-timed love of natural history afterwards.

Best love to Moll—Is she at home for good?[7] Will she write to me sometimes? I should be very glad—I am copying in chalks a groupe from one of Poussins seven Sacraments[8]—that of confirmation—And I have painted three miniatures, one from a large oil picture of Guido's representing a young Sybil[9]—Did'st ever hear of such a body?—

1. Miguel de Cervantes (1547–1616) called absence "that common cure of love" in *Don Quixote*, Pt. 1, Bk. 3, Ch. 10.

2. In her (missing) letter, Charlotte apparently spoke of her songbirds, perhaps in response to the story of the lost bird in L. 28.

3. Andrea Tendi (fl. 1790–1804) who had exhibited at the Royal Academy in 1793 and 1797 (Graves; Waterhouse).

4. On 1 June [1804], Sophia Burney had written to her cousin Charlotte, "Your long silence is petrifying, & cuts me to the soul." She seemed to fear that Charlotte had taken amiss the loss of a letter: "Too true alas! your best letter was lost, but is it me you blame?" Sophia apparently had written again on 10 October 1804 but did not receive a reply. SHB's intervention may have had some effect; in January 1805, Sophia would refer to her aunt's intercession when thanking Charlotte for an "entertaining letter" she had recently received (Sophia Elizabeth Burney to CF, 1 June [1804], 5 Jan. [1805], Berg).

5. Sarah's pupil (see below passim) was the third and youngest daughter of the Wilbraham family, Anna (1791–1864) (Ormerod, 2: 138; Burke, *LG; GM*, 3rd ser. 16 (1864): 814).

6. Mr. B[roome], Charlotte Francis's stepfather.

7. "Moll" is Marianne, Charlotte's younger sister, who had been staying with her grandfather Charles Burney earlier in the year, copying his letters and taking music lessons. After leaving Chelsea, she may have been on extended visits to family or friends, or attending school (CB to "Rosette" Burney, [24 Jan. 1804], Osborn).

8. Nicholas Poussin (1594–1665) painted the first series of *The Seven Sacraments* for Cassiano dal Pozzo c. 1638–40. "Confirmation" comes second in the series, the whole of which was purchased by the Duke of Rutland and exhibited at the Royal Academy in 1787 (Anthony Blunt, *The Paintings of Nicolas Poussin* (London: Phaidon, 1966), 73–76).

9. More than one work on this subject was painted by or attributed to the Bolognese painter, Guido Reni (1575–1642). A painting of *Sibyl* of 1635–36 was owned by George Nassau, 3rd Earl Cowper (1738–86); another was sold at Christie's on 14 May 1802. For these and other possible originals of Sarah's copy, see D. Stephen Pepper, *Guido Reni* (New York: New York University Press, 1984), 274, 301–2.

30. To Charlotte Francis

Delamere Lodge, 3 November [1805][1]
A.L., Berg
Address: Miss Francis / Mrs Broome's / Marlborough Street / Bath
Postmarks: NORTHWICH

Delamere Lodge
Novr 3^{d}—

Dear Me! You have been in Monmouthshire, & you have been jumbled upon a dicky,[2] & you have seen hills, & rivers, & lambs, & cottages, whilst poor I have only been through Flintshire, Merionethshire, Denbighshire, Caernarvonshire & Anglesea, & have only seen half a dozen magnificent Castles in lovely ruin, and a score or two of tremendous mountains, and two or three roaring Fleuves, & flocks of goats, and the Main Ocean, or the Irish Sea, (whichever you chuse to call it); and spent three days at a Baron's Castle (Lord Penryhn's),[3] and two days at a Baronet's Park (Sir Forster Cunliffe),[4] and paid two visits, one in the evening, and one a breakfast visit to the ladies at Llangollen, the celebrated lady Elinor <Ponsonby> Butler and Miss Ponsonby[5]—and had the misfortune to travel in a Sociable[6] with our own horses, and to stop whenever we liked it to make sketches (or scratches)—for we none of us shine in the art of landskape drawing—However my trees always afford me some satisfaction when I contemplate them—they precisely put me in mind of Uncle Sleep's[7] Sunday wig.—I therefore do not mean to attempt any mistaken plan of improvement in the art—No trees that were like trees could ever afford me half the amusement I derive from their present admirable representation of what used to cover & comfort Uncle Sleepe's sagacious noddle. Talking of noddles, we were very near seeing, once or twice, the sublime noddle of old sulky Snowden[8]—but warmth being prescribed to him after a severe fit of the mumps, he invariably wore a good thick, soft night-cap of impenetrable clouds. To the aforementioned catalogue of woes, I am truly concerned to be obliged to add that at Conway, where we slept and spent a whole day, just as we were sitting down before supper to write journals, the striking-up of a Harp reached my tingling ears! A Harp at Conway! Conceive the rapture it inspired—The shade of Gray flitted before me—I beheld, in my mind's eye, the Bard of former days

On a rock whose haughty brow
Frowns o'er old Conway's foaming flood[9]—

Pity me, my Charlotte—He was summoned to the landing place, and for a few dirty shillings condescended to play to us such ravishing sweet music, that my very soul took wing, & conveyed me to celestial abodes of Heroes, Poets, Bards, Druids, Monarchs!—I defied the cool blasts upon the stairs, and the whiffs that ascended from the kitchin, where they were dressing our supper, and popped myself down upon a step close beside him—He had been eating leeks, but I scorned to bestow a thought upon the nausea his vile effluvia occasioned.—Well—and then a pretty lad of a clerk offered his services to come and sing to us Welsh Songs—He was made thus And he sung words like these—Yang Yoss,

O yang oh yoss,—Oh
Yoss o yang, oh yang
oh yoss, oh yoss oh—
yang oh yoss—

To the tune of "The rising of the Lark".[10] I recommend them to Marianne to warble with a due quantum of nasal twang.—Grieve with me, however, when I seriously add, that the harper himself was really exquisite—He had officiated in that revered capacity in various noble families, but having seven brats & a wife at Conway, at last made up his mind to perform only to chance passengers, to take chance shillings, & eat his daily leek at the venerable place of his nativity.[11]—The morning after his friendly visit to our shillings, we prowled over Conway and its environs, and its Castle,[12]—and went upon the river—and were the most curious, busy & delighted people in the world or ten miles round it.—Were I not apprehensive of exciting the sympathetic <emotions> sorrows of your susceptible soul too powerfully, I would farther add, that our sojourn at Carnarvon, at Bethgellert, at Penryhn &c, &c, teemed with rapture—

Exulting, trembling, raging, fainting,
Possessed beyond the muses painting,[13]

We were "alive all o'er"[14] to the sublime beauties around us!

You ask me (pertly enough—pardon the expression) Whether I have read The Lay of the Last Minstrel[15]—Alas, only twice—And have, in addition, only the following Catalogue to subjoin of pleasing works which have come under my examination—

English—Thalaba.[16]

Cowper Walker on	
The revival of Italian	Italian,—Metastasio's Olympiade
Tragedy[17]—	Demofoonte, Giusepe riconosciuto,
Southey's Tour in	Gioas, La Clemenza di
Spain[18]—	Tito, Catone, Regolo,
Tommy Jones[19]	Ciro, Zenobia[20]—
	Tasso's Aminta[21]—
	Seven Canto's of Ariosto,[22]
French—None	Il Vero Amore,[23] an Italian novel—
	La bella pelegrina,[24] La Zingana[25]
	Merope, del Maffei,[26] &c, &c, &c, &c

If you wish to know how I came to poke my green eyes into so many Italian books, I have this reply at your service. There has been an Italian Master[27] here for above a month—and he brushed up for me the rusty odds an ends of his dulcet language which I had formerly picked up, & whilst he was here, & since his departure, I have done nothing but peep & pry into the works of his countrymen—And learn poetry by heart, such lines, for example, as these—

Perduto è tutto il tempo

Che in amor non si spende[28]—Our Italian master corresponds with us, & procures books for us, and is a love, with, as I mentioned to Sophy in a recent letter, only one fault, at least in my eyes—He is Married,[29] and be hanged to him!—Hold your tongue about my darling Sphinx—You are not worthy to hold a tallow candle to her Cook.—I have been copying a portrait she painted in town of Miss Eliza, which, if I keep in the same mind, you shall never "the fringed curtains of your eyes advance"[30] to look upon.—By the way, poke old Craigg's directions for miniature painting,[31] which I gave you last spring, into the fire—they are not worth a button. Beaurepaire[32] has set me right, and by her instructions I mean to abide for life—Above all, never spat indian ink into flesh, however mixed up and jumbled with other colours.—

I don't understand your taking another house at Bath—What do you all mean by it? To skip London? to cut us all? Do let me come at the bottom of this precious piece of business. Am I to be defrauded of my sister, and nieces, & nephews, in this shabby manner!—I shall hate you every one, if such is your intention. Remember, I have never seen Dolph, and though I have seen you others, I partly think I could bear to see you again.—Don't be a hundred years before you write again all particulars upon this subject.

There came here yesterday two Cupids, one of 60 or 70, the other some 50 years old, with musical bells—Says I to the young one who stood by doing nothing while the other toodled—"Don't you play, my friend?"—"No Ma'am—

I'm like the lady my father sold a set of bells to in Yorkshire—Her husband the squire, came in after she had bought 'em—Says he, Mrs Fox,[33] what's the use of your having them bells if you can't play upon em'—" —"Umph," says She "they do to look at"—and that was her answer Ma'am."—a very apropos answer to my enquiry, was it not?—

My kindest love to my sister—And to Moll & Dolf—

1. This letter is conjecturally dated 1805, because (judging from the address) it seems to have been written after Mr. Broome's death, which took place in February 1805, but before June 1806, when Mrs. Broome moved with her family to Exmouth, Devons. See *JL*, 5: 334, n. 4 and below L. 31. The mention of a Scott poem published in 1805 confirms this guess.

2. A donkey (*OED*).

3. Near Bangor, Caernarvonshire, Penrhyn Castle, the seat of Richard Pennant (c. 1737–1808), M.P. (1761–80, 1784–90), created Baron Penrhyn (1783) in the peerage of Ireland. He was known for extensive improvements to his estate, developing slate quarries and building roads through the mountains. The house was redesigned by Samuel Wyatt (1737–1807) from 1782 on (Gibbs; *DNB;* Namier & Brooke; John Martin Robinson, *The Wyatts* (Oxford: Oxford University Press, 1979), 137–40, 258). For a contemporary description of the "wild and barren" countryside and the celebrated quarries, see *The Journeys of Sir Richard Colt Hoare through Wales and England, 1793–1810*, ed. M. W. Thompson (Gloucester: Alan Sutton, 1983), 71, 258.

4. Sir Foster Cunliffe (1755–1834), 3rd Bt. (1778), whose paternal seat of Acton Park near Wrexham, Denbighshire, was altered in 1786–87 by the famous architect, James Wyatt (1746–1813), impressing Charles Burney on a visit in 1798 (Burke; Robinson, *The Wyatts*, 239; CB to Thomas Twining, 1 [Jan.] 1798, Folger).

5. Lady Eleanor Butler (1739–1829) and Sarah Ponsonby (1755–1831), the "ladies of Llangollen," whose romantic friendship led them to share a life of retirement for more than fifty years; see Elizabeth Mavor, *The Ladies of Llangollen* (London: Michael Joseph, 1971).

6. An open, four-wheeled carriage having two seats facing each other and a box seat for the driver (*OED*).

7. Probably James Sleepe (1716–94), the brother of CB's first wife, Esther née Sleepe (1725–62). Semiliterate and poor, he seems to have been viewed in a slightly comic but affectionate light by the younger generation of Burneys (*EJL*, 1: 172, n. 82; *JL*, 1: 68, n. 7; 11: 43, n. 17; 12: 762, n. 1).

8. The personification of Snowdon, the highest mountain in Wales, was probably suggested by Thomas Gray's poem, quoted below (l. 11).

9. Thomas Gray, "The Bard. A Pindaric Ode," first published in *Odes* (1757) by Horace Walpole at Strawberry Hill. The lines (15–16) open the first antistrophe, which introduces the last of the Welsh Bards.

10. A well-known Welsh folk song and a popular song for the harp, found in *The National Songs of Wales*, ed. E. T. Davies and Sidney Northcote (London: Boosey & Hawkes, 1959), 30–31.

11. Influenced by the popular myth that Welsh music descended directly from the ancient Druids, English tourists "expected to see venerable harpists everywhere." A contemporary traveler noted their presence at the inns, where they would play to the company during dinner (Prys Morgan, *The Eighteenth Century Renaissance* (Dyfed, Wales: Christopher Davies, 1981), 125–32; *Hoare*, 71).

12. Conway Castle was constructed between 1283 and 1287 by Edward I (1239–1307) to consolidate his victory over the Welsh. With the town walls, which extend almost a mile in circumference, it is considered "one of the outstanding achievements of medieval military architecture in all Europe" (A. J. Taylor, *Conway Castle and Town Walls* (1957; rpt., London: HMSO, 1966), 6).

Noted for its picturesque beauty, the site became famous through its association with Gray's poem (see Donald Moore, "The Discovery of the Welsh Landscape," *Wales in the Eighteenth Century*, ed. Donald Moore (Swansea: Christopher Davies, 1976), 143; Morgan, 120–21).

13. William Collins, "The Passions. An Ode for Music," *Odes on Several Descriptive and Allegoric Subjects* (1747), ll. 5–6.

14. Alexander Pope, *An Essay on Man*, 1: 197.

15. Walter Scott's poem, *The Lay of the Last Minstrel*, which came out in the first week of January 1805, was a spectacular success (Johnson, 1: 225).

16. Robert Southey, *Thalaba the Destroyer* (1801).

17. Joseph Cooper Walker, *An historical and critical essay on the revival of the drama in Italy* (1805), or possibly the same author's *Historical memoir on Italian tragedy* (1799).

18. Robert Southey, *Letters written during a short residence in Spain and Portugal* (1797).

19. Henry Fielding, *The history of Tom Jones, a foundling* (1749). Sarah Harriet owned her own copy (CB to FBA, 5 Feb. 1794, Berg).

20. Pietro Metastasio (1698–1782), Italian librettist and lyric poet, about whom Charles Burney had written his *Memoirs of the life and writings of the Abate Metastasio* (1796). Of his many works, SHB mentions reading his plays *L'Olimpiade* and *Demofoonte* (1733), the sacred dramas *Giuseppe riconosciuto* (1733) and *Gioas re di Giuda* (1735), as well as *La clemenza di Tito* (1734), *Catone in Utica* (1728), *Attilio Regolo* (1750), *Ciro riconosciuto* (1736), and *Zenobia* (1740).

21. Torquato Tasso (1544–95), *Aminta* (1573).

22. Ludovico Ariosto (1474–1533), probably his epic, *Orlando furioso*, published in a final, expanded version in 1532.

23. Possibly *Il balliano; ovvero, Il vero amore ne'cimenti è più forte* (1727), a play set at the court of Frederic II.

24. A novel by Pietro Chiari (1711–85), *La bella Pellegrina* (1759).

25. Possibly *La zingara* (1753), the intermezzo of Rinaldo di Capua (c. 1705–c. 1780), better known in the French adaptation of *La bohémienne* (1755). Charles Burney had met the composer on his Italian tour in 1770 (*New Grove;* Scholes, 1: 174–75, 179).

26. The tragedy of Scipione Maffèi (1675–1755), *La Merope* (1713).

27. Apparently Gaetano Polidori (1764–1853) (see below L. 172), father of John William Polidori (*DNB*) and grandfather to the Rossettis. A native of Italy, formerly secretary to Count Vittorio Alfieri, he moved to London in 1789 where he established himself as a teacher, poet, and translator (William Michael Rossetti, "Memoir of Dante Gabriel Rossetti," *Dante Gabriel Rossetti* (London: Ellis and Elvey, 1895), 1: 24–36).

28. The words of Dafne in Torquato Tasso's *Aminta*, first presented in 1573 (I, i, 121–22).

29. Polidori had married in February 1793 Anna Maria Pierce (or Pearce) (c. 1770–1853) (Rossetti, 1: 26, 30–31; *GM*, NS 39 (1853): 676).

30. "The fringed curtains of thine eye advance," William Shakespeare, *The Tempest*, I, ii, 411.

31. Probably William Marshall Craig (fl. 1788–1828), a notable miniature painter who worked in London as a drawing master from 1791 and was eventually appointed painter in water-colours to the Queen. He published several works on technique, including *An Essay on the Study of Nature in drawing Landscape* (1793) and *The Complete Instructor in Drawing* (1814) (*DNB;* Daphne Foskett, *A Dictionary of British Miniature Painters*, 2 vols. (London: Faber & Faber, 1972)).

32. A Mlle and Mme de Beaurepaire exhibited at the Royal Academy between 1804 and 1822 (Graves). It is unclear whether this was a mother or daughter, or the same person, who may be identical with the Louise Chacaré de Beaurepaire who married René Gaillard (c. 1719–90), the French engraver (Foskett; Bénézit; Thième-Becker). Basil S. Long identifies her simply as a "miniature painter and teacher of drawing" in his *British Miniaturists* (London: Holland Press, 1929).

33. Mrs. Fox of Yorkshire has not been identified.

31. To Charlotte Francis

Upper Seymour Street, [pre 10 June 1806][1]
A.L.S., Berg
Address: Miss Francis / M[rs] Broome's / Exmouth / Devonshire
Postmarks: A JU / 10 / 80[6]

Upper Seymour Street, N[o] 56.[2]

I have no objections in life to plucking my old crow[3] with you now, Miss, without any more loss of time. By your last letter, you were Ass enough (Heaven forgive me for calling any of my own kin and kind by so vile a name) to betray your <assinine> atrocious soul in two several instances. First, you shewed a stupid rigmarole letter of mine to M[r] Barnwell[4] and next you wisely or foolishly, I leave you to determine which, let me <u>know</u> you had done so. Now you certainly in the second point tripped more erroneously than in the first. I forgive your shewing the letter, if you thought it contained matter worthy of making a cat grin:[5] but I can, with all my natural sweetness, hardly forgive your <u>telling</u> me you had shewn it, and asking me to write again that you might shew that also.—I could not have written whilst you were at Bath,[6] under the influence of <that> such an idea, without feeling myself under the most uneasy constraint. You know I never have any thing but nonsense to chat to you about: but under the apprehension that Mr Barnwell was to see all I scribbled, I should have stopped short every two minutes, and have thought to myself—"No, I must not say that—he'll think it vulgar—I must not add this—he'll think it dirty—I must not put in the other—he'll think I am trying to be witty."—And so on—And at last I should have produced the dryest, dullest, d——'d morcel of fogramity[7] that ever mortal old maid raked from her withered brain.

There—Now I have plucked my Crow—And I am better—and you, I hope are wiser.—

Clement the Buck[8] I popped upon last Sunday at Brother James' door. I was going on to Chelsea—Clement the Buck was going there too: so I did him the honour to recline four and twenty pounds of my weight upon his arm, and to walk with him to the old College. In our way, I learnt that he had hopes, or some thoughts of going with one of Lady Paxton's's[9] tickets to the next Tuesdays Opera. I always prick up my ears at the mention of the word Opera. So says I—"Shall you sit in the Pit, or in Lady Paxton's box?"—"O in the Pit." says Clement the Buck. "Then," returns I—"We'll go together, my friend. I have only been to the Opera once this year, and never to the play, or to any other public place—And I mean to treat myself to hear Billington[10] in preference to any thing else."—"Well then" says Clement the Buck—"I'll call in Seymour Street on Tuesday morning to settle where we shall meet at night—And perhaps I may get a ticket for you too."—"O never mind" says I, "getting me no tickets—for I wants to go—and for this once I does'n't mind paying my own money."—Well, all this pretty little arrangement, how do you think it ended? Why Clement the Buck never came near me no more from that time to this—And my money now lies fretting great holes in my purse, and turning as yellow as gold for very madness.—Clement the Buck may depend upon getting a good dressing from me for this, the very first time he comes in my way;—if its thirty years hence, whether young or old, the little varlet shall know and feel what it is to disappoint a craving spinster.

Friend Barrett[11] brought me your letter yesterday, the very day he arrived in town. He says he has been much with you, and he admires you and likes you all extremely. "Ces demoiselles sont bien franches" dit-il—"Et nous avons disputé ensemble bien souvent, car je suis franc aussi, comme vous savez. Leur mere est la bonté, la douceur, l'aimabilité personifiée. J'aime beaucoup—mais beaucoup, toute cette interessante famille."—I hope you aime him a little, for he has always seemed to me a very good creature, for all he wears such enormous wiskers.

It was a real and a rich regale to me to hear that sweet Madame de Beaurepaire gained ground in all your good graces. I quite love her. A little friend of hers, who is now in town, Madame Herbster,[12] whom she always calls la petite follette, and I are trez liez ensemble. I am never happy without some dear little french liaison. A few nights ago, at Wolfl's Concert,[13] I had a party of amis françois about me, consisting of seven Gallic individuals. The more the merrier, say I. Clement the Buck says you have taken a likeness of one of the maids, which very much affronts her—Ha, ha, ha!—I should like to hear the damsel's comments. I trespassed in the same way upon one of our Betty Bucket's in the country, and the wry faces she made, amused me so excessively, that I fell into convulsions of laughter every time I saw her afterwards for above a month. I desire and insist that you write to me till your arm is ready to drop off when you get to your Heavenly little Exmouth Cottage. I long to hear some anecdotes of the horse pond and the swing.[14] If you should happen to plump souse into said horse pond, out of said swing don't mince the matter, never spoil a good story, as Captain Mirvan[15] says, but write me all how and about it.—O, and another thing. You are so plaguy modest, that you say never a word as to your improvement in the art of miniature painting.

Adieu, Charlotte of my heart—Pray write long windedly and often—Give my kindest love to your dear Mother—And tell Moll she must study less, and use more exercise[16]—or else settle speedily what she means to leave me in her will.

Carissima nipote addio.
Credete mi sempre vostra
amichevole, zia
Enrichetta Burney

1. Although the letter is postmarked 10 June, it would appear to have been written several days earlier, from the reference to "last Sunday" as the one preceding Billington's performance at a "Tuesday's opera." The only Tuesday on which the prima donna sang between 15 May and 10 June 1806 (according to advertisements in the *Times*) was Tuesday, 27 May (see n. 10).

2. Sarah Harriet writes from the town address of the Wilbrahams (Stenton).

3. William Shakespeare, *The Comedy of Errors*, III, i, 84.

4. John Thomas Barnewall (1773–1839), 15th Baron Trimlestown (1813), who had married in January 1793 Maria Theresa (d. 12 Oct. 1824), eldest daughter of Richard Kirwan (1733–1812) (*DNB*), of Cregg, Galway, Ireland. Mrs. Barnewall, a former pupil of Charles Burney and friend of the family, had renewed acquaintance with Charlotte Broome at Bath. The *New Bath Directory* for 1805 shows her living at 5 Upper Park Street (Burke; Gibbs; CB to "Rosette" Burney, 28 May 1804, Osborn; *ED*, 2: 267, 305, 313–17).

5. SHB may be recalling the expression "to grin like a Cheshire Cat," perhaps an allusion to the crest of a prominent Cheshire family or to a characteristic inn sign of that county (*Notes & Queries*, 1st ser., 5 (1852): 402; [T. W. Williams, ed.], *Lean's Collectanea*, vol. 1 (Bristol: J. W. Arrowsmith, 1902), 44).

6. Mrs Broome and her family had lived at Bath from 1803? until the summer of 1806 when they moved to Exmouth (*JL*, 5: 334, n. 4; letters of MF, 1806–7, John Rylands Library, listed in *Catalogue*).

7. An antiquated thing. It seems to have formed part of the family vocabulary, as the first instance given in the *OED* of the word "fogram" is from *The Early Diary of Frances Burney* (on 3 Feb. 1772), and of "fogramity" is from Mme d'Arblay's *Camilla* (1796). Charles Burney had apparently acquired the term from his patron, Fulke Greville (*Memoirs*, 1: 46; *EJL*, 1: 191, n. 26).

8. Clement Francis, Charlotte's brother, an adolescent of thirteen.

9. Anne Dawney (fl. 1793–1806), the daughter of Thomas Dawney, of Aylesbury, Bucks., had married pre 1793 William Paxton (c. 1744–1824) of Middleton Hall, Carmarthen, Wales. Formerly of the East India Company, Sir William Paxton was M.P. for the borough of Carmarthen (1803–6) and for the shire (1806–7), and was knighted in 1803. The Paxtons were friendly with Mrs. Broome (Thorne; Burke, *LG; GM*, 76, Pt. 2 (1806): 977; CBFB & CF to FBA, 23 Oct. [1802], Barrett, Eg. 3693, ff. 84–85v).

10. The great English soprano, Elizabeth Billington (1765–1818), who had returned from Europe to England in 1801, and was in high demand. She sang with John Braham in Mozart's *La Clemenza di Tito* at the King's Theatre on Tuesday, 27 May 1806 (*New Grove; Times*, 27 May 1806).

11. Henry Barrett (c. 1756–1843), who had seen Mrs. Broome and her daughters at Exmouth, lived on an inheritance of property in England and Jamaica (*JL*, 6: 570, n. 5; *JL*, 9: 140, n. 9; death certificate, Barrett, Eg. 3707, ff. 56–57v). He may have had French origins, as Charlotte Broome commented on the "French set" who were his associates, and Esther Burney reportedly "found it Difficult to understand his English" (CBFB to CF, 16 May [1807], Barrett Eg. 3700A, ff. 82–83v; see also Barrett family tree, Barrett, Eg. 3707, ff. 269–70v; death certificate, Barrett, Eg. 3707, ff. 56–57v).

12. A miniature painter by the name of Herbst exhibited two portraits at the Royal Academy in 1800, and in 1801 a Miss Herbst contributed one portrait as an Honorary Exhibitor (Graves).

13. Joseph Wölfl (1773–1812), the Austrian pianist and composer, had arrived in London in May 1805 and won immediate renown. During the previous two weeks he had been playing in several concerts, but Sarah may have attended "Mad. BARTOLOZZI and Mr. WOELFL's GRAND CONCERT" on Wednesday, 28 May 1806, at the King's Theatre, which featured a "New Grand Overture" and a "Grand Symphony," both his own compositions (*Times*, 26 May 1806).

14. The delights of Exmouth—the swing over the pond, scenic walks, and sea-bathing—are described by Marianne Francis to Mrs. Piozzi (MF, CBFB & CF to HLTP, 9 June [1806], John Rylands).

15. The boisterous sea captain in Fanny Burney's first and most famous novel, *Evelina* (1778), makes this remark when teasing Mme Duval about her ducking in the mud (vol. 1, L. 19).

16. "Moll" was Marianne Francis, Charlotte's sixteen-year-old sister, known in the

family as a "prodigy" of learning. A polyglot (fluent in French, Italian, German, and Spanish), she also studied the ancient languages of Latin, Greek, Hebrew, and Arabic. She understood geometry and algebra and played admirably on the piano (CB to FBA, 5 May 1810, Osborn; CB to FBA, 12 Nov. 1808, Berg; *JL*, 7: 31–32 and nn.; *HFB*, 327–28).

32. To Charlotte Francis

Delamere Lodge, 20 November [1806][1]
A.L., Berg
Address: Miss Francis / M[rs] Broome's / Exmouth / Devon
Postmarks: NORTHWICH

Delamere Lodge
November 20th

Dear Charlotte

I know you will not answer me these three months, and think myself a great fool for beginning a letter to you again so soon. You are the most tardy correspondent I ever had, except one, who though a dear creature, and a writer of incomparable letters, sent them so rarely, that I at last sent her to the D——l. —I hate to be tantalized in such a way.—It is like being condemned to eat green pease, one by one, with a <ear> tooth-pick, a method much recommended, for the economization of Human Pleasures, by Count Rumford.[2] Did you ever meet with the passage? If the goods of life are to be thus scantily doled out to me, I had rather philosophically make up my mind to do without them. Answer me therefore in reasonable time, or . . . . . .

So you are in correspondence with M[rs] Piozzi?[3] Enviable Mortal!—Do you know I am, at this present writing, stark staring mad for love [*of*] her. I have been reading her Journey through France and Italy,[4] and nothing that I ever luxuriously licked my lips over, ever delighted me half so much. The book is one huge mass of entertainment from begining to end—And written in such an unaffected spirit of Christian charity for the errors of mankind—breathing such candour, chearfulness, and good nature, that I quite adore her. She uses various quaint phrazes, very comical and expressive; but somewhat odd "somehow" (as she says) till one gets accustomed to her style.[5] The original poetry thinly scattered through the work, I do not admire.[6] But a woman cannot have every excellence of heart & genius. She has enough to satisfy a more fastidious spirit than mine. If you have not already sucked down à long traits, this charming book, read it without loss of time—if you have, read it again: and when you come to its conclusion, do as I have done ever since yesterday, that I unavoidably finished it—sit down and howl, that the world is not all made of such pleasant writing.

If the cold weather should take you by the nose before I see you, send to me; I have a muckinder[7] of yours in my d[ra]wer, lent to me three years ago (new and unhemmed) in John Street,[8] and hardly a bit the worse for my wear. It stares me in the face, with its fringed edges, every time I open the afore-said drawer. Shall I use it, and make it soft for you against you happen to have a "red and raw" nose?[9]—Horne Tooke is a dirty dog—He gives the derivation of such words![10]—There sits Mr Wilbraham two hours every morning in the library, sniggering and shaking his fat sides over such grave nastiness as is enough to make a modest soul like me blush or turn sick: and he always puts a little paper mark into the worst passages to shew them to me when I go down. Was ever any thing so impertinent and insulting! As if I loved dirt—"in good time, I trow!"—Piozzi[11]—Hem.—

I like poor dear Dolph's pathetic <lamentation> exclamation at sight of the two curly dogs playing together. I am glad you encouraged him to set aside his dignity, and go and play with them. I always take those little liberties with my own grandeur, when I can do it snugly, and get any good by it.

I have not even seen The Wild Irish Girl.[12] At first the title tickled my ear, and I wished much to read it. Not being able, however, to procure it, I began comforting myself with the reflection that very likely the title was the best part of the book—that it had a good clever catch-penny sound—and that probably Miss Owenson was a cunning nincumpoop. NB; Nin-cum-poop, sometimes erroneously spelt nincoompoop is derived from the Anglo-Saxon word, Ninny, a fool;—from the middle syllable of the Gothic <forms> verb to, incumber, or molest; and from the Greek verb to poop, or, as we vulgarly say in English, to f——t[.] Its full meaning, when all its component parts are properly understood, is, that a cumbersome ninny fool is only fit to poop at![13]—

We have a little French story in the house, called Elizabeth, much admired and praised: but "somehow," I have taken it into my head it is too good for my palate, <for> because Mrs W—— the strictest person in the world about Novels, put it into the hands of my Bone[14]—and my Bone yawned over it—and when I asked her how she liked it, said—"O very much—only there's hardly any love in it!"[15] Whip Novels without love!—

I have got an Invisible peticoat, and it shews my nether cheeks to great advantage—And when I get over a style, it curls up, and for five or ten minutes afterwards, keeps my legs <so> quite cool and airy.—Nothing at this season of the year can be more desirable[.] We have had some very grand folks here lately; Lord and Lady Cholmondely[16] who staid two days. They brought with them two young Ladies; one of them, Miss Seymour, is a celebrated beauty, and a very amiable creature: but during twenty years that she has lived in the world, nobody has been able to settle who is her Papa; some say it is the P—— of W——; others think it my lord Cholmondeley himself; in short, the matter is wholly in doubt.[17] The other young lady was a Miss Cholmondely, really, I believe, a little unlawful chip of his Lordship.[18] She is a pretty French-looking girl of sixteen; very lively & quick, and plays well upon the piano-forte: but her great merit is her style of singing; in my life I never heard a voice so soft, so flexible, so easy, so tender, and affecting. She sings Italian, English, French, and even Russian songs—and before she gets half through her air, she inclines <one> you to weep, you can hardly tell why: but not from any painful emotion, certainly. Do not repeat any part of this account in a letter to Chelsea, for yesterday, I wrote it all, nearly in the same words, to my father. It is not the less true, however, for that.—Adieu. Best love to my sister, & Moll.

1. The letter can be dated by the address, to Miss Francis at Exmouth, Devons. The only November Charlotte spent there as an unmarried woman was in 1806.

2. Sir Benjamin Thompson, Count von Rumford (1753–1814) (*DNB*), makes such a recommendation in the third of his *Essays, Political, Economical, and Philosophical* (1796–1812). After arguing that a much smaller quantity of food is sufficient for nutrition than is commonly believed, he suggests that reducing the size of the portions while increasing the time of mastication will actually enhance the gourmand's pleasure. However, his prime concern in "Of Food; and particularly of feeding the poor" is economical, not epicurean (see especially Chs. 1–2). Charles Burney owned a copy of this essay (*Misc. Lib.*, 49).

3. Hester Lynch Piozzi (formerly Thrale) (1741–1821), once a close friend of Frances Burney; the acquaintance with her, cultivated particularly by Marianne Francis, was begun in 1805 at Bath (*HFB*, 332–33). Soon after the family's move to Exmouth, a joint letter by Marianne, Charlotte, and their mother was written, as if in answer to (a missing) one of Mrs. Piozzi's, which began the correspondence. There was another collaborative effort on 18 August [1806]. Many subsequent letters from Marianne Francis to Mrs. Piozzi survive in the John Rylands Library (MF, CBFB & CF to HLTP, 9 June [1806], 18 Aug. [1806], John Rylands; letters of MF to HLTP, listed in *Catalogue*, 354–70).

4. Hester Lynch (Thrale) Piozzi, *Observations and Reflections made in the course of a journey through France, Italy, and Germany*, 2 vols. (London: A. Strahan and T. Cadell, 1789).

5. Her colloquial style and singularity of expression provoked criticism at the time

(James L. Clifford, *Hester Lynch Piozzi (Mrs. Thrale)*, 2nd ed. (Oxford: Clarendon Press, 1952), 343–46).

6. Poetical rhapsodies are often introduced into the work as having been left behind at an inn, for example:

> Let thy warm, thy wond'rous clime,
> Animate my artless rhyme,
> Whilst alternate round me rise
> Terror, pleasure, and surprise.
> (Piozzi, 2: 9–10)

7. A pocket-handkerchief (*OED*).

8. No. 5 John Street, Oxford Street, the home of Esther Burney and her family, to which she had moved (from 43 Beaumont Street) sometime between June 1803 and January 1804 (*JL*, 6: 469, 559; CB to "Rosette" Burney, [24 Jan. 1804], Osborn).

9. In the song which closes William Shakespeare's *Love's Labour's Lost*, "Marion's nose looks red and raw" (V, ii, 909).

10. John Horne Tooke (1736–1812) (*DNB*), political radical, whose philological work, *ΕΠΕΑ ΠΤΕΡΟΕΝΤΑ, or the Diversions of Purley*, was published in two parts 1786 and 1805. Sarah might be objecting to his chapter "Of Abstraction," where he gives the derivation of such words as "harlot," "wench," "trull," "punk," "drab," and "strumpet" ("prostitute" and "concubine" apparently "Need no explanation").

As Tooke's partisanship tinges many of his explanations, George Wilbraham's relish for the work may reflect his political bias, otherwise undeterminable from his brief parliamentary career (Namier & Brooke).

11. "In good time," a colloquial phrase in Piozzi's *Observations*, e.g., 2: 369.

12. Sydney Owenson, afterwards Lady Morgan (1783?–1859) (*DNB*), created a sensation with her novel, *The Wild Irish Girl*, published in 1806.

13. SHB's definition is reminiscent of Tooke's account of the word "numscull" (Tooke, *Diversions of Purley*, 2nd ed., vol. 2 (1805; rpt., Menston, England: Scolar Press, 1968), 305).

14. Probably SHB's pupil, Anna Wilbraham, as in "bone of my bones, and flesh of my flesh," Genesis 2:23.

15. Marie "Sophie" (née Risteau) Cottin (1770–1807), whose novel, *Élisabeth, ou les Exilés de Sibérie* (1806), is primarily concerned with filial devotion: a young girl undertakes a heroic journey to obtain the Tsar's pardon for her father. She is, however, united to her faithful lover at the end.

16. George James Cholmondeley (1749–1827), 4th Earl (1770), created Marquess of Cholmondeley (1815), who had married 25 April 1791 Georgiana Charlotte (1764–1838), daughter of Peregrine Bertie, 3rd Duke of Ancaster. Their principal residence was at Cholmondeley Castle, near Nantwich, Cheshire (Burke; Gibbs).

17. Georgina (or Georgiana) Augusta Frederica Seymour Elliott (1782–1813), the daughter of a former mistress of Lord Cholmondeley, Grace Dalrymple Elliott (c. 1758–1823) (*DNB*). The paternity of the child was doubtful, although attributed to the Prince of Wales; other possible contenders were George Selwyn, Charles Wyndham, and Lord Cholmondeley himself. He brought the girl up in his family and married her from his house on 21 September 1808 to William Charles Augustus Bentinck (1780–

1826), third son of the 3rd Duke of Portland (Walpole, 11: 255, n. 27; 33: 181, n. 9; Burke under Portland; *GM*, 78, Pt. 2 (1808): 850; 83, Pt. 2 (1813): 700; Thomas Raikes, *A Portion of the Journal kept by Thomas Raikes, esq. from 1831 to 1847*, rev. ed. (London: Longman, Brown, Green, Longmans & Roberts, 1858), 1: 479).

18. Purportedly an illegitimate daughter of the Earl by another mistress, Mme St. Alban (d. pre 1812), Henrietta Cholmondeley (d. 1815) would marry at Gretna Green in January 1812 John George Lambton (1792–1840), created Baron Durham (1828), Earl of Durham (1833). Having these two beautiful girls in the house apparently cast Lord Cholmondeley's legitimate daughter in the shade (Burke; Gibbs under Durham; *GM*, 82, Pt. 1 (1812): 188; Raikes, 1: 479; Walpole, 11: 87, n. 23, 109, n. 19, 245, n. 43).

---

33. To Charlotte Francis

[Upper Seymour Street, 6 May 1807]
A.L.S., Berg
Address: Miss Francis / Mrs Cooke's / Exmouth / Devonshire
Postmarks: A MA / 6 / 807

With a great coarse sheet of vulgar paper, and a great monster of a skewer of a pen as thick as the end of il mio naso, I sit down, in sober sadness, and hearty good will, to congratulate my dearest Charlotte upon having made precisely the choice, which, had I been at her elbow I should have done myself the honour and pleasure of prescribing to her.—Your Henry,[1] with all the love and duty befitting a discreet Nephew-elect, did me the favour of calling here early on Sunday morning, and was received (I blush to own it) all but a bras ouverts. He was always a decided favourite of mine; and as I am not one of those capricious mortals who quarrel with a man for becoming my relation, whom I approved of for my friend, I assure you I like him none the worse for having secured a good snug retreat in your heart. As I should think it heinous, whilst he is separated from the sovereign of his affections, to propose to him any thing frisky, I have prevailed upon him to accept a seat in a box taken by a very sweet creature (a friend of mine picked up when the last star fell from Heaven) to see Mrs Siddons next Thursday in the character of Isabella;[2] and given him leave to weep and sigh the whole evening. I thought it no bad scheme to accustom him to the sort of misery that play represents—for very likely, you, like poor Isabella, have another husband somewhere abroad, who may be popping forth un de ces beaux jours, crying out—

> Henry, avaunt! She's mine—And here I swear
> Nor Heaven, nor Earth, nor Hell, shall claim my fair![3]

Your madre, la mia carissima sorella, dined, con la nostre carissima nipote, Francesca Phillipsa, at Chelsea last Sunday, and I had the pleasure of finding my little figure popped and perked in between them.—La madre looks thin, but clear, and rosy, and affectionate; and I love her much. I have not seen her since: but we are to have an amicable rencontre some evening soon at her lodgings,[4] and I have settled it in my own mind that l'Ami is to walk home with me—He having deposited his amiable person in apartments close by this street,[5] for the express purpose of being at hand to flirt with me whenever a snug and safe opportunity offered. Do not be alarmed however—for, as yet, he has only made a tender to me of one quarter of his heart, begging the other three parts might, at present, remain in your possession. I agree to the proposal at this moment, being really torn to pieces with sweet-hearts, & sweet-heartesses, all so eager to devour me after a ten months separation, that I scarcely know how to suffice so many craving souls.—Do you know that I am actually writing all this heap of rubbish to comply with l'Ami's request? He entreated me, being in prodigious doubt as to your opinion of him, to dispatch a <little> few well-timed insinuations in his favour—to compose a little recommendatory epistle in his behalf: and I, who am a good soul, always ready to comply with the reasonable wishes of my friends, gave a huge yawn, and sat down to the toilsome task. How have I acquitted myself?—

Lord, Lord! I have just discovered that at the back of this luminous performance the beginning of another letter is scrawled![6] I assure you, when I took this in hand, I knew nothing of the matter—for I began in mortal haste and trepidation, having, as if by the by, received a formidable lecture on Sunday from l'Ami on the subject of delays in writing to our friends. He pretended to be grumbling at a certain lazy sister of his[7]—but I, who am timid, and easily alarmed, applied every word of the philippic (have I spelt the word right?) to myself; and determined not to run the risk of having such a jobation addressed to me in direct terms.—And now, my dear, very dear Charlotte—Heaven bless you—Not one of your most zealous friends can more cordially wish you happiness than your truly

affectionate S: H: Burney.

1. Sarah is congratulating her niece on her engagement to Henry Barrett, a "love match" which Charlotte's mother now accepted as "inevitable," though not without fear of its financial imprudence: "he adores you so, that I am convinced there is no extravagance he w[d] not have committed rather than resign you." However, noting that "you have had so many Lovers, & no one but this that you liked," Mrs. Broome advises her daughter on how to break the news to a former suitor. The bride was twenty, her fiancé fifty (CBFB to CF, 16 May [1807], 22 May [1807], Barrett, Eg. 3700A, ff. 82–85v).

2. This appears to be a fabrication, as Mrs. Siddons was not then appearing in her famous role of Isabella in David Garrick's adaptation of Thomas Southerne's play, *The Fatal Marriage* (1694) (*Times*, 2 Apr.–21 May 1807). The heroine, believing her husband to be dead, remarries, the source of great misery when her first husband returns; she ultimately goes mad and kills herself.

3. This verse does not occur in the play, and its source, if there is one, has not been found.

4. Charlotte Broome was in London (lodging at 64 Stafford Place, Buckingham Gate) to arrange the marriage settlements and purchase clothes for her daughter (CBFB to CF, 16 May [1807], 22 May [1807], Barrett, Eg. 3700A, ff. 82–85v).

5. Henry Barrett was staying at 16 Dorset Street, Baker Street (see L. 34 below) which was near Upper Seymour Street, SHB's abode. That friction was developing over the contract is clear from Charlotte Broome's complaints that Barrett's "violent love & impetuous Disposition & Conduct" have prevented her from making proper enquiry into his affairs. In her opinion, "he ought to consider himself highly favourd in the match being suffer'd to go on" without satisfactory evidence of his property; however, she concludes that his apparent evasiveness is probably due to lack of information. Nevertheless, all would conclude well on 23 May 1807, and Mr. Barrett and Mrs. Broome would leave London a few days later (ibid.).

6. On the last page, the beginning of a letter in another hand has been scored through:

"Dearest
After receiving such benefit under your guidance and direction"

7. Henry Barrett's sister or half-sister, Julia (c. 1783–1809), who had married 13 August 1804 John Kingston (c. 1780–1839), the son of John Kingston (1736–1820), M.P. for Lymington, Hants. (Thorne; family tree in Barrett, Eg. 3707A, ff. 269–70v; *GM*, 74, Pt. 2 (1804): 783; NS 12 (1839), 545; *JL*, 11: 393, n. 8).

34. To Charlotte Francis

[Upper Seymour Street, 19] May [1807][1]
A.L.S., Berg
Address: Miss Francis / Mrs Cooke's / Exmouth / Devonshire

Tuesday May
the I don't know
what.—

My dearest Charlotte would not have been troubled again quite so immediately with a sheet of coarse paper, and the scratchings of a blunt-nibbed quill, were I not induced to it by sorrow and compassion for a suffering friend of hers, whom her unaccountable silence has almost rendered seriously indisposed—and quite driven to wretchedness and the extremest anxiety. My dear girl—this is no joke, I assure you. Poor Barrett went out of town on Saturday for a couple of days, already somewhat disturbed at your want of punctuality: but upon the whole, in tolerable contentment. On Monday early he returned, & called upon me with as anxious a face and heart as cruelty herself could have wished him to own. To day, I have seen him again—and really my heart ached for him. He has written to you every day since his arrival in town, & heard from you only twice.[2] I told him I had heard from you, and it afforded him some consolation to know, from that circumstance, that illness, at least, had no share in causing your taciturnity. But the poor sensitive soul, with feelings too susceptible for this heartless, and selfish age, torments himself with millions of terrors, doubts, & fearful phantasies[3]—His anxious mind preys upon his health—& seldom have I seen a countenance more ravaged by disquiet. Pray, pray my good girl, hasten to repair the mischief you have done—Account to him for your apparent neglect—If you torment this man a day longer, I shall really hate you.[4]

Your dear Mother and I have only been able to meet once,[5] so infernal has been the dirt & wet of these streets, the pretended golden pavement of which, three inches deep of mud has, for this last week, concealed. I will send you Sophy's address as soon as I know it: but though I have written to her this very day, I have been forced to send my letter to her mother to direct.[6] I mentioned in it your good intentions:[7] but I charge you write to no human creature (not even me) till you have bestowed a little consolation on the dear Ami.

Fanny Phillips has I believe atchieved a long letter to you,[8] so I say nothing more of her than that she looks blooming and pretty as ever.

Can you laugh after the well-merited trimming I have given you? If you can, I send you the following fragment, sublime in its kind, and in which certainly more is meant than meets the ear—

Somebody told Edward Burney that Madam Tussock[9] of Greenwich had had a threatening of the gout—

"Good God!" exclaimed he—"if she swells with the gout! . . . ." And there he stopped. Now is there not "much virtue in that if?"—Do you not admire the force & beauty, in this instance, of that most significant figure in rhetoric—the reticence; as the French term it?—Oh, it is inimitable!

So you want to know who the friend is, whom I told you dropped down from Heaven with the last batch of falling stars?[10]—She is a Miss James[11]—she lives within thirty doors of me—she is the joy, comfort & pride of my life. l'Ami has seen her but once—yet thinks he spied in her "that which passeth shew!"[12]—She is much too good to bestow her friendship upon such a little ugly, vulgar nincomepoop as I am: but somehow or other, she has done me the honour to take a fancy to my not un-honest heart; and we are sworn cronies I hope for life—A lovely brown Italian, who taught us both his delicious language,[13] first inspired in each a desire to know the other—She, blessed soul! made the premier pas—I met her advances with condescending benevolence—and found her all that is warm-hearted, genuinely sentimental, accomplished, polished, well-read, well-bred, & elegant!—You would adore her, if it was permitted you just now to adore any thing but Enrico. Some time or other ye shall meet—She often goes to Bath, & even remembers having there encountered, without knowing who he was, your Ami—I wonder any body should think it worth while to remember ever having seen such an ugly face!—

O yes, niece de mon coeur, I will come and gobble up your Devonshire cream,[14] & visit you in your little paradis terrestre with all the pleasure in the world—At least I will feast my imagination with the hope. As a party concerned, Nature & fortune seem to have placed happiness beyond my reach—but having happy particles in my composition, I intend they should catch fire, & burn bright & clear at the sight of every blessing engaged by those I love—and you and Barrett I certainly do love with all my heart. So I will go and visit you—and we will walk, talk, read & laugh together as merrily, as philosophically, or as sentimentally as you please.—

Addio—I leave you now to your rural delights—your little owlets, your chopped snails, & all the etceteras of Clement's enjoyments[15]—Write However, I charge you to N° 16, Dorset Street, Baker Street, London[16]—And thereupon, I give you my benediction.—Your devoted Enrichetta

Yes, I have seen, and am even in possession of some of his writings, which delight me—Love to Moll, & Clem.—

1. This letter was clearly written in May of 1807, preceding Charlotte's marriage, but subsequent to her engagement. It also follows SHB's previous letter of congratulations mailed on Wednesday, 6 May. Only two Tuesdays intervene before Barrett's departure on the twenty-sixth; judging from the fact that SHB has already received a (missing) reply, Tuesday, 19 May, seems the more likely.

2. Charlotte seems to have drawn back somewhat during this month, and is reportedly anxious lest her letters to her mother and cousin Fanny should be shared with her fiancé. Moreover, her former "unconditional promise" appears to have been retracted before 22 May 1807. However, the outcome is never seriously in doubt, and Mrs. Broome proceeds to order wedding clothes cut to the latest London fashion (CBFB to CF, 16 May [1807], 22 May [1807], Barrett, Eg. 3700A, ff. 82–85v).

3. The suitor's ardor impressed even the lawyer who declared that he "never saw one so much in love as Barrett!" (ibid.)

4. Charlotte may not have appreciated this interference on the part of her aunt who, it seems, had already prematurely introduced Barrett among the relatives (ibid.).

5. They had both dined at Chelsea on Sunday, 3 May 1807 (see above L. 33).

6. Sophia Burney had apparently left her governess post at Lord Brownlow's (L. 26), and taken up a new position with Mrs. Tyrwhitt Jones (see below L. 35).

7. Charlotte may have announced an intention to write to her cousin Sophia, perhaps in answer to a letter of congratulations. Her failure to respond to a similar letter from another cousin left the former well-wisher "highly indignant & sorely disappointed" (Sophia Elizabeth Burney to CFBt, 29 Nov. [1807], Berg).

8. The letter is missing; Fanny Phillips, who was then planning her own wedding, corresponded with her cousin Charlotte during this trying period, and advised her aunt Broome about bridal arrangements and outfits (CBFB to CF, 16 May [1807], 22 May [1807], Barrett, Eg. 3700A, ff. 82–85v).

9. Unidentified.

10. A similar phrase was used in SHB's letter of [6 May 1807] above.

11. Miss James (fl. 1807–52), who later lived with her two sisters in Bath (see below L. 172) has not been further traced.

12. William Shakespeare, *Hamlet*, I, ii, 85.

13. Gaetano Polidori, SHB's Italian master (L. 30, n. 27).

14. In a missing letter, Charlotte had apparently invited her aunt to visit her in her future home, which she may have expected would be in Exmouth, Devonshire, near her mother. The newlyweds did in fact return to Exmouth in the fall after a summer's traveling (MF to HLTP, 6 Oct. [1807], John Rylands).

15. Clement Francis, then aged fourteen, apparently had an affinity for animals and was endeavoring to tame a young owl he had caught in the woods. His sister, Marianne, describes his "whooting" to it "in a most romantic manner." Perhaps the chopped snails were food for his pet (MF to HLTP, 19 June 1807, John Rylands).

16. From the context, this would be Henry Barrett's address. Returning to London later with his bride, he would stay in Baker Street again (see below L. 36).

35. To Charlotte (Francis) Barrett

Upper Seymour Street, 26 June 1807
A.L.S., Berg
Address: Mrs Barrett / Charmouth / Dorsetshire
Postmarks: C JU / 27 / 807

Seymour Street
June 26th 1807

Why truly I must be in high favour indeed! Who would have expected a little couple just noosed,[1] and wandering about like the first pair in Paradise under bowers of delicious shade—who would have expected such blissful beings to remember the existence, and bestow a portion of their happy leisure, on poor Nell?[2]—Good creatures! I love you much for your kind recollection. It was my intention, at least pendant le mois de miel, not to intrude upon you a word either of congratulation or gossip—The first I thought you were too happy to require, and too just to imagine I omitted from indifference—and the latter I concluded you had a sufficient supply of within yourselves. But L'ami Barrett I find is a regular and faithful correspondent not only in theory but in practice—He exclaimed when in town against lingering letter-writers[3]—and I rejoice to perceive the good effect of his good principles upon that subject.—My dear friend Enrico—Do you know that your little bride used to be six or seven months hunting about for half an hour's leisure to write me half a page?[4] I swore by mine honour more than once that I w^d^ have nothing more to do with her as a correspondent—And then came an entertaining, chatty, funny letter that made my sides ache—And like Touchstone's, poor Knight, setting my honour aside, or, for the repose of my conscience, hoping I had none—immediately I was foresworn.[5]—

Your letter reached me at a moment when I happened to be extremely hungry—and the perpetual mention of the tantalizing word cake, made my mouth water, and caused me such twinges, that in or[de]r to allay the <Craven> gnawings of the gastric juice I was fain to hollow out for a huge slice of bread & butter.—But what is bread and butter compared to plumb cake—and that cake Bride cake too![6] In this respect you are better off than the charmed and charming first pair to whom I did you the honour of comparing you. I dare say Adam and Eve had no plumb cake—I question even whether they had any cake at all—and their diet considered, I sincerely hope they had not tender bowels.—

The Burney blood is thinned considerably within this last week. Maria Bourdois,[7] Richard & Blue, are off for Rimpton.[8] Fanny gone back to her bones at Lady Russell's[9]—Sophy snug with hers at Mrs Tyrwhitt Jones'[10]—and nothing remaining but John Street, and James Street people.[11] I saw Fanny Phillips last night, looking as ugly as usual, and walking home through Hyde Park followed by my father's hop-o'-my-thumb foot-boy; from some place she had been dining at in London. I breakfast at Chelsea on Sunday morning, and am to walk with her to see her Cottage[12]—She has roses in its garden! There's rural felicity for you!

Miss James has lent me, and I have been reading Alphonsine[13]—that is, the two first volumes—and it has completely bewitched me—I was such an old Ass as to sit up last night till three o'clock, reading—and then snuffed out my candle, and went to bed by day-light., The perfect originality of the plan upon which the story is founded, enchants me—and difficult as such an idea was to developpe, M^{de} de Genlis I think has done justice to her own design—a felicity many authors fail in attaining.—

Oh—(But now another day has passed, and I have finished the three volumes of Alphonsine—and the last disgraces the two first—Such a pack of higgledy piggledy stuff, without interest, finish, or any attempt at probability, I never read[14]—Whip the woman!—

You should quit your Devonshire shades were it only to share in the universal rage there is for going to Vauxhall[15]—I never knew any thing like it—The whole London World seems to be seized with a fit of the fool. I do not like Vauxhall—When induced to shew my fair face in any public place, I chuse to sit still and be amused without any trouble—If I must saunter about, and go staring round me for something that shall tickle my fancy, adieu to all real pleasure—I get tired, and yawn my heart out, & my feet burn, <as if on heated floors> and my eyes blink, & I am never easy till snug at home again.

What a pack, a heap, a mountain of insignificant trash have I scribbled. But what else can a poor D——l of a Governess write? Those I daily converse with, unknown to you, are tolerably uninteresting to me—I have no time to read any thing in London but a wide-printed fool of a Novel—and am born a mere Ass, but very affectionately yours, both,

S: H: Burney

1. Charlotte Francis and Henry Barrett were married 19 June 1807 at Exmouth, and set off after a wedding breakfast for Charmouth, then Lymington (where she was "enjoying herself every evening among Foreigners, who are her delight"), and finally the Isle of Wight. By the end of July they were back in London, and returned in September to Exmouth (MF to HLTP, 19 June 1807, 21 July [1807], 4 Sept. [1807], 6 Oct. [1807], John Rylands; 30 July [1807], Berg).

2. "Poor Nell," an expression which arose from a deathbed wish of Charles II in reference to his mistress Nell Gwynn ("Let not poor Nelly starve"), related by Gilbert Burnet, *Bishop Burnet's History of his own Time*, ed. M. J. Routh (Oxford: Clarendon Press, 1823), 2: 460.

3. For this "philippic" that SHB thought was meant for her, see above L. 33.

4. Sarah Harriet was often to voice these complaints about Charlotte's tardiness as a correspondent. See below passim.

5. Touchstone's knight is described in Shakespeare's *As You Like It*, I, ii, 72–74: "But if you swear by that that is not, you are not forsworn. No more was this knight, swearing by his honour, for he never had any."

6. Charlotte Broome had promised to have a "good Wedding Cake" prepared for her daughter at Exmouth (CBFB to CF, 22 May [1807], Barrett, Eg. 3700A, ff. 84–85v).

7. Maria Bourdois, Esther's eldest daughter, newly arrived from France where she had been living with her wealthy husband since April 1802. When he died intestate 6 August 1806, she stayed on to establish her claims to his estate, and then traveled home through Germany and Holland, arriving in London 22 May 1807; she was currently visiting among her relatives (*JL*, 1: lxix; 5: 205, n. 6, 322; 6: 472, 530, n. 2, 541–45, 560–62, 568, n. 1, 797–98; "Worcester Mem.," 56–57).

8. Richard Allen Burney, Esther's eldest son, B.A. Oxford (1799), M.A. (1807), Rector of Rimpton, Somerset (1802) and Master of St. Mary Magdalen Hospital, Winchester (1804). His maiden aunt, Elizabeth Warren Burney, "Blue" (1755–1832), was keeping his house (*JL*, 1: lxviii–lxix; *Alumni Oxon.*; "Worcester Mem.," 44, 55; *JL*, 5: 104 and n. 8, 107).

9. Esther's second daughter, Frances, was governess for Lady Russell, Anne Barbara née Whitworth (d. 1814), who had married on 23 July 1782 Henry Russell (1751–1836), Chief Justice at Bengal (1807–13), created Bt. (1812). They had five daughters (*DNB*; Burke, *LG*; *JL*, 1: lxix; 11: 371, n. 4).

10. Esther's third daughter, Sophia, had a new situation (since c. Jan.) with the family of Thomas (Tyrwhitt) Jones (1765–1811) of Stanley Hall, Salop, an independent and somewhat eccentric parliamentarian first elected in 1790; he was soon to be created a Bt. (3 Oct. 1808). He had married 25 April 1791 Harriet Rebecca Williams (d. 15 July 1824), by whom he had three sons and two daughters (EBB to CB Jr., 1 Mar. 1806 [1807], Osborn; *Alumni Cantab.*; Thorne; Burke, *LG* under Wilson-Tyrwhitt; Foster; *GM*, 81, Pt. 2 (1811): 590; "Appendix," *AR*, 66 (1824): 228).

11. Esther Burney, her husband, and daughter Amelia lived in John Street, while James Burney and his family were in James Street.

12. Fanny Phillips was living with her grandfather at Chelsea but was soon to marry (13 July 1807) Charles Chamier Raper (1777–1842), a clerk in the War Office. She was evidently showing off her future home (*GM*, 77, Pt. 2 (1807): 681; NS 18 (1842): 217; parish register, St. Luke, Chelsea; *JL*, 1: lxxi; 7: 423; 9: 22, n. 1).

13. Stéphanie-Félicité Brûlart (née Du Crest de Saint-Aubin) (1746–1830), marquise de Sillery, comtesse de Genlis, published *Alphonsine, ou la tendresse maternelle* in three volumes at Paris in 1806.

14. The first two volumes of *Alphonsine* are taken up with tales of enchantment, seduction, and adventure, as well as the central Gothic motif of an evil count who incarcerates his wife for twelve years. Her long narrative of the years of suffering, the daughter who was born to her, and the religious faith that sustained them both, closes the second volume. In the third, improbable complications and episodes are introduced to delay the final denouement—the reunion of Diana with her faithful lover and the marriage of her daughter.

15. Vauxhall Gardens (once known as the New Spring Garden), opened c. 1661, were altered and improved by Jonathan Tyers in 1732, and remained popular as a London pleasure resort for almost two centuries, closing in 1859. The spacious gardens, splendidly illuminated and decorated with statues, colonnades, and arches; the Grand Walk of lofty elms; the supper-boxes and pavilions adorned with paintings; and the Rotunda for musical concerts, are described at length in Warwick Wroth, *The London Pleasure Gardens of the Eighteenth Century* (1896; rpt., London: Macmillan, 1979), 286–326.

In 1806, "the most celebrated public gardens in Europe" charged an admission price of two shillings, or "three shillings on gala nights; when every thing that can captivate the fancy, is called into action to amuse and delight" (B. Lambert, *The History and Survey of London and its Environs* (London: T. Hughes, 1806), 4: 160–63).

One such "GRAND GALA" opened the season on 15 June, a concert followed by fireworks; on the evening of the twenty-sixth a "Rural Fete" was given, under the patronage of the Prince of Wales, which proved so successful that it was repeated a few days later: "An assemblage of not fewer than 5000 persons was the result . . . most of the first Nobility then in town graced the Gardens with their presence" (*Times*, 13, 15 June, 25 June–3 July 1807). These special events no doubt sparked an interest of which SHB was aware.

36. To Charlotte (Francis) Barrett and Henry Barrett

[Chelsea College], 25 August [1807]
A.L.S., Berg
Address: Mrs Barrett / Dorset Street / Baker Street / Portman Square / 37
Postmarks: [M]ewsR[Chel]sea / Un[paid] / Pe[nny Post]
7 o'Clock / 26 AU / 1807 NT

Charlotte, my love, and Henry, my Soul—

I have been entrusted by my dear father[1] with the very welcome commission of requesting you both to favour us with your company to dinner on Saturday next. I hope it is a day that will suit you, and promise myself the pleasure of seeing you early, though I think it but honest (in case you should have any morning engagement which an earlier hour might interfere with) to acquaint you, that our dinner hour will be half past four, or five. What a pother about hours, and earlies—

Have you recovered your Sunday fatigue?[2] I could not get up on Monday Morning till near eleven o'clock—Every toe I had ached to its very marrow. How fared it with yours? And with Caro Enrico's sore throat? Bring me good news of it, I entreat—A drunken man frightened me horribly in Sloane Street, after I got out of my gentle hackeney—So I seized fast hold of the foot-boy's arm, and griping it black & blue, darted off into the middle of the road, and ran against a chain suspended between two posts, which nearly tripped us both up—And then, before I reached home, it began raining kittens & puppies, at least, if not cats and dogs—and I arrived at our apartments in an admirable state to undergo a mopping—So hot, and so damp with rain—pah!

Have you seen Mr Latrobe[3] yet? Adieu, dear little Choux—I love you with all my heart—Amatemi, comandatemi, e vivete felice.

S: H: Burney

Tuesday Evening.
Aug^st^ 25th

1. This is the first letter that survives after Sarah Harriet's return to her father. She was reinstated through the mediation of Esther Burney, to whom she had written c. February 1807 expressing her regret for "her late rash & undutiful desertion of my Dear Father" and her desire "of making him all the reparation in her power by her future cares & attentions on this score."

Esther forwarded this appeal to her brother Charles, asking him how to promote Sarah Harriet's idea without offending Dr. Burney. Pointing out "how well she stands in the Opinion [*of the*] very respectable family with whom she is," she argued that it would be "more creditable to the family" for SHB to live at home than to work as a governess. Moreover, it would solve the problem of finding someone to succeed Fanny Phillips in looking after Dr. Burney: "will it not be forlorn & uncomfortable, & be a matter of Constant Anxiety to ourselves. for this Dear & Excellent Father to be left totally to the Care &&c of Servants" (EBB to CB Jr., 1 Mar. 1806 [1807], Osborn).

Apparently Charles concurred, and a "long audience" was arranged between Dr. Burney and his three children (Charles, Esther, and Sarah) (CB to CB Jr., [12 May 1807], Osborn). Soon after Fanny Phillips's wedding, Dr. Burney left for the country (16 July to c. 12 Aug. 1807), and Sarah moved into the apartment at Chelsea Hospital (CB to CBFB, 17 July 1807, Berg; CB to Edmond Malone, 23 July 1807, Bodleian, MS. Malone 38, ff. 137–38; CB to David Humphries, 15 Aug. 1807, Beinecke; MF to HLTP, 21 July [1807], John Rylands).

2. The Barretts, returning from their wedding journey, were staying in London and had apparently shared a Sunday's outing with Sarah Harriet.

3. Probably Christian Ignatius Latrobe, an old friend of the family, whose younger brother Benjamin, a favorite of Charlotte Broome's, had emigrated to America (see above L. 1, n. 21).

37. With Charles Burney to Charles Burney Jr.

Chelsea College, [December 1807][1]
A.L. CB with A.L.S. SHB, Burney-Cumming
Endorsed: 1807
[*The first 1½ pages consist of an A.L. CB to CB Jr., expressing concern for his son's weak eyes, and discussing a petition to the East India Company; the last part of his letter, containing a list of the directors of the company, is in SHB's hand.*]

My dear Brother

I received by means of your Charles, when he was here last, a pocket-book for the ensuing year—and thank you for it very sincerely—

Yours, my dear Brother, with great affection
S: H: B:

Wednesday Morn^g
Chel. Coll.

1. In the year of the endorsement (1807), the month of December is the most likely, from the subjects discussed by Charles Burney—cadetships for two grandchildren and trouble with his son's eyes. Both of these occupied Dr. Burney in late 1807 and early 1808 (CB to FC, 24–26 Dec. 1807, Jan. 1808, Osborn; CB to CPB, 9 Jan. 1808, Osborn).

38. To Charles Burney Jr.

Chelsea College, 1 February [1808]
A.L.S., Osborn
Address: Revd Dr Burney / Greenwich / Kent
Postmarks: [M]ewsRChels[ea] / Unpaid / Penny Post
12 o'Clock / [?] / [?]
4 o'Clock / FE 2 / 1808 E[V]

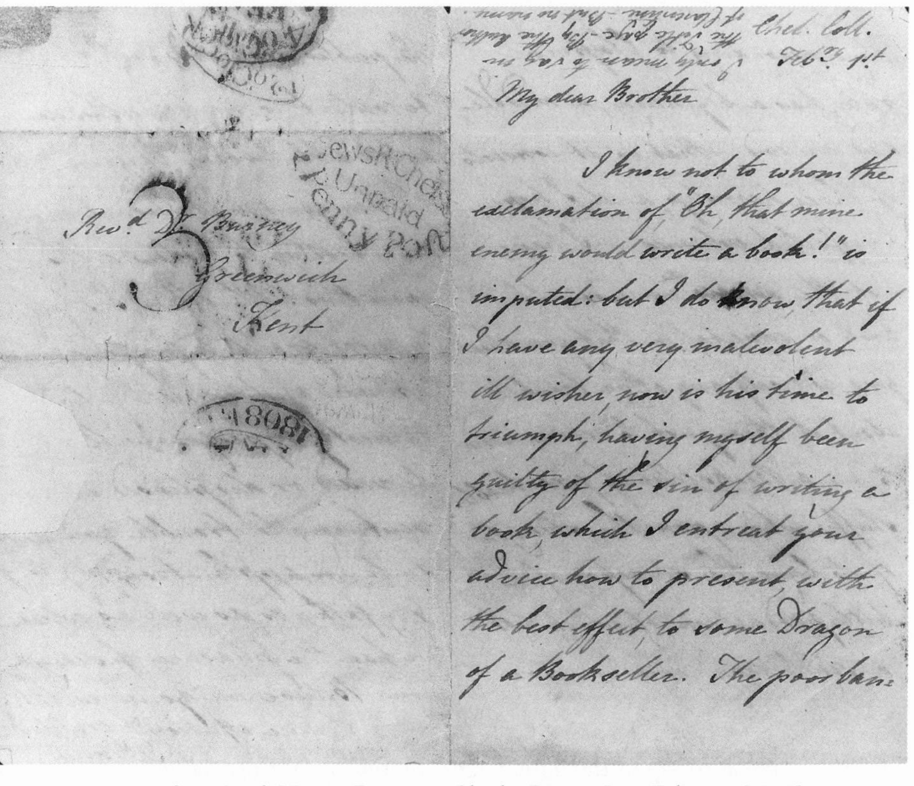

Rev.d Dr Burney
Greenwich
Kent

Chel. Coll.
Feb.y 1st

My dear Brother

I know not to whom the exclamation of "Oh, that mine enemy would write a book!" is imputed: but I do know, that if I have any very malevolent ill wisher, now is his time to triumph, having myself been guilty of the sin of writing a book, which I entreat your advice how to present, with the best effect, to some Dragon of a Bookseller. The poor bam=

I only mean to say in the title page — By the Author of Clarentine — But no name

Letter from Sarah Harriet Burney to Charles Burney Jr., 1 February [1808].
(Courtesy, James Marshall and Marie Louise Osborn Collection.)

Chel. Coll.
Feb^{ry} 1st

My dear Brother

I know not to whom the exclamation of, "Oh, that mine enemy would write a book!" is imputed:[1] but I do know, that if I have any very malevolent ill wisher, now is his time to triumph, having myself been guilty of the sin of writing a book, which I entreat your advice how to present, with the best effect, to some Dragon of a Bookseller.[2] The poor bantling, according to Classical rule, has a beginning, a middle, and an end—that is, it consists of three harmless, and, I hope, unaffected volumes.[3]—I have not the unreasonable wish or expectation that you should give yourself any other trouble about it, than just to recommend to me a Bookseller of practicable stuff; who, upon the strength of its being the successor of a little production of which not a single copy remains upon the publishers hands,[4] will be content to make with me a tolerably liberal bargain.—

When you are at leisure my dear brother to bestow a thought upon this little affair, I shall be most grateful for your opinion and counsel—And earnestly hope you will n[ot] be vexed or displeased at my venturing to trouble you with such an application.

My father is as well as when we had the pleasure of seeing you.[5] Believe me, yours with

Sincere affection & gratitude.
S: H: Burney

I only mean to say in the Title page—By the Author of Clarentine[6]—But no name.

1. The sentiment was originally Job's: "Oh that one would hear me! behold, my desire is, that the Almighty would answer me, and that mine adversary had written a book" (Job 31:35).

2. Charles Burney Jr. acted as intermediary between members of the Burney family and the booksellers, with whom he was supposed to have influence. "My son at Greenwich is used to printing, & has great weight with some of the principal publishers" (CB to JCH, 15 Aug. 1807, Osborn).

3. *Geraldine Fauconberg*, Sarah's second novel, was to be published in three volumes (see below L. 41).

4. SHB's first work, *Clarentine*, published by G. G. & J. Robinson in 1796. A second edition would later be printed by Henry Colburn with imprint date 1816, although the date of issue (according to the Colburn records) was actually 28 November 1815. It was first advertised on 27 December 1815 and still available in 1820 (*Times*, 27 Dec. 1815, 12, 15, 16 Feb. 1820). Between 1796 and 1816, the price for the three volumes would rise from 10s. 6d. to 21s. *Clarentine* would also be published in Ireland (Dublin: P. Wogan, 1797), America (Philadelphia: M. Cary & Son, 1818), and France, translated by Mme Élisabeth de Bon (Paris: Vve H. Perronneau, 1819). For its favorable critical reception, see above L. 13, n. 2.

5. Dr. Burney was not very well, and referred to himself later that month as "Old, infirm & almost bed-ridden," describing how he lay in bed "with blankets & flannels 'nine times round me'" to offset the severity of the winter. He had become virtually an invalid since a slight paralytic seizure in 1806 (CB to Edmond Malone, 24 Feb. 1808, Bodleian, MS. Malone 38, ff. 141–42; Lonsdale, 460–61).

6. This is exactly what appears on the title page.

39. [To Charles Burney Jr.]

Chelsea College, 12 February [1808][1]
A.L.S., Osborn

My dear Brother

I cannot deny myself the pleasure, even at the risk of being, perhaps, thought troublesome, of thanking you most cordially for the very kind and frank manner in which you have promised me your assistance. My expectations, when I ventured to apply to you for advice, by no means whatever went so far—and I cannot express to you the gratitude & satisfaction your note has afforded me.

I am desirous, if possible, of introducing my bantling to the world this season—The times are gloomy enough now—And Heaven knows what they may be! Works of this frivolous nature stand a worse chance of being read or sold every year—for even women are becoming politicians, and will speedily turn up their noses at every thing but a State Paper.—Whenever the obliging Bookseller is ready for me, I am ready for him—with this proviso—that he lets me correct the proofs—and gives me a few copies.

My father desires his best love to yourself and, C°, and is extremely sorry to hear it has been owing to the weakness of your eyes, he has not seen you.

Accept from me again the assurance of my sincere & hearty gratitude—Excuse my giving you the trouble of wearing your eyes out over this scrawl, & believe me, dear brother

Yours very affectionately
S: H: Burney.

Chel. Coll. Feb^ry^ 12th

1. The letter may be conjecturally dated to 1808 and addressed to Charles Burney Jr. by several features: the paper, watermarked 1805; the promised assistance in publishing a work, again referred to as a "bantling"; and the reference to a "weakness" of the eyes, a condition from which Charles suffered in 1808 (see, for example, CB to CPB, 9 Jan. 1808, Osborn; CB to CB Jr., 19 June [1808], Burney-Cumming; CB to CB Jr., 2 July [1808], Berg).

40. With Charles Burney to Dorothea, Lady Banks

[Chelsea College, spring 1808][1]
A.L.S. CB with A.L. SHB, [spring 1808], Hyde
Address: Lady Banks / Soho Square
[*The first 1⅓ pages consist of an A.L.S. CB to Lady Banks, dated only* "Monday Night," *thanking her for a visit and promising to look out some music for her.*]

Miss Burney presents her best respects to Lady Banks,[2] and begs leave to inform her, she has compared the index of her Ladyship's first volume of the History of Music, with that of her father's, and made a little list of additional articles that might be inserted,[3] which she will take an early opportunity of doing herself the honour of conveying or sending to Soho Square, with the delightful Engravings from Flaxman,[4] which, meanwhile, are most scrupulously defended from all mischief and injury.

1. The letter has been tentatively dated by Charles Burney's offer, in the warm spring weather, "to hunt after Tit-Bits, and airs of expression" suitable to a lady singer. Other letters on this subject, using similar phraseology, were written in the spring of 1808. On 25 February 1808, he had discussed the same song mentioned in his part of this letter, and offered to send his daughter with the music (CB to Lady Banks, 25 Feb. 1808, 11 Apr. 1808, 8 May 1808, Osborn).

2. Dorothea (1758–1828), the daughter of William Weston-Hugessen of Provender, Kent, had married 23 March 1779 Joseph Banks (1743–1820), the eminent botanist, created Bt. (1781), whose scientific pursuits took him around the world with Cook (1768–71). His house in Soho Square contained a valuable library and collections of natural history (*DNB;* see also Harold B. Carter, *Sir Joseph Banks* (London: British Museum (Natural History), 1988)).

3. Charles Burney published his *A General History of Music* in four volumes (1776–89). Conjecturally, SHB was supplementing this work with her father's musical articles for *The Cyclopaedia*, ed. Abraham Rees, 39 vols. (1802–19), an undertaking that had occupied Dr. Burney since 1801. Having compiled information from various sources, he may well have annotated his earlier publications with the new material. His biographer points out that his active involvement with the project diminished greatly after May 1808 (Lonsdale, 407–31), although apparently it did not cease completely; see below L. 57.

4. John Flaxman (1755–1826), sculptor, designer, and illustrator; his drawings for Homer, Aeschylus, and Dante were popular with contemporaries (*DNB;* David Irwin, *John Flaxman, 1755–1826* (London: Studio Vista, 1979)).

41. With Charles Burney to Charles Burney Jr.

[Chelsea College, 19 June 1808]
A.L. CB with A.L. SHB, Burney-Cumming
Address: Rev[d] D[r] Burney / Greenwich / Kent.
Postmarks: MewsRChels[ea] / Unpaid / Penny Po[st]
4 o'Clo[ck] / JU 19 / 1808 EV
[?] / [?] / 180[?]

[*The first 1½ pages consist of an A.L. CB to CB Jr., dated 19 June, reminding him of some business and closing:* "Sarah wishes to add 'a few pleasing words' to her worthy friends ever eager to perform their promises—"]

The worthy friends my father alludes to, are the dear Mess[rs] Robinsons,[1] of whom, however, I by no means think myself entitled to complain, though I should not be sorry if they were to recollect that the 16th of June is past—And if I might take the liberty of requesting them to begin Advertising[2]—The whole is now printed within 50 pages—

Adieu my dearest Brother
Yours most affectionately.

1. Sarah Harriet was probably thinking of the booksellers, George, George and John Robinson, who had published her first novel in 1796. The firm had gone bankrupt in 1804, however; John Robinson then joined George Wilkie in Paternoster Row, and it was this firm that was publishing her second work (Maxted, 191–92, 247; Nichols, *Anecdotes,* 3: 445–49).

2. Although SHB was "up to her chin in Booksellers" in March (MF to CFBt, 5 Mar. [4 Mar. 1808], Barrett, Eg. 3704A, ff. 12–18v), her three-volume novel would not come out until six months later (advertised to appear "In a few days" on 8 Sept. 1808 in the *Times*). Apparently considering her publishers too "supine," she was to market her third elsewhere (see below L. 66).

The reviewers of *Geraldine Fauconberg* bestowed mild praise: the *British Critic* 32 (1808): 520, called it a "superior performance" which "does not surprise, astonish, or electrify the reader, but it soothes into complacency." The *Critical Review,* 3rd ser. 16 (1809): 104–5, found it "elegant and well written. . . . a correct and faithful picture of genteel life." Both indicated that the authorship was an open secret.

A second edition (3 vols. at 21s.) would later be published by Henry Colburn; although the date of issue was 28 August 1812 (Colburn records), advertising would not begin until the autumn (*London Chronicle,* 24–26 Oct. 1812; *Times,* 13, 14 Nov. 1812). Still available in 1816 (*Times,* 16, 17 Apr. 1816), the novel would apparently be sold out by 1820, judging from its absence from advertisements listing all her other works (*Times*, 12, 15, 16 Feb. 1820).

There would be an American printing (Philadelphia: M. Carey and son, 1817) and a translation of the second edition into French as *Miss Fauconberg* (Genève: G. Paschaud, 1825).

42. To Charlotte (Burney) (Francis) Broome

[Chelsea College, 3 July 1808][1]
A.L.S., Barrett, Eg. 3700A, ff. 144–45v
Address: Mrs Broome / Mr Jay's, Dorset Street / Baker Street / 54
Postmarks: [M]ewsRChel[sea] / Unpaid / Penny [Post]
Endorsed: Sister Sarah / 1808

Sunday Night

Dearest Sister

My father read your note with the utmost pleasure, and bids me say there is no proposal he should have been more readily disposed to accept than the kind one made by Marianne[2] had he not, since I saw you, received information, that a visit will speedily be requested of him by the D. of Portland to Bulstrode,[3] and therefore a companion at Chelsea for the present becomes superfluous— But he charges to thank both you and Marianne very cordially for your offer, the kindness of which he seemed to feel, and to be much gratified by—

Heaven bless you, my dearest Sister—I envy myself the pleasure I shall enjoy in embracing Charlotte on Tuesday,[4] and wish Tuesday was already come—

Yours ever affectionately
S: H: Burney.

1. Endorsed "1808" by Mrs. Broome, the letter was probably written on Sunday, 3 July from the coincidence of an imminent invitation to Bulstrode with a visit of Sarah to the Barretts. See nn. 3, 4.

2. The note from Charlotte Broome is missing but probably contained an offer for her daughter, Marianne, to take care of Dr. Burney while Sarah Harriet, "his wonted Nurse, runs to the Country to recruit." However, presumably after this letter was received, Marianne would remark that "my meditated visit to Grandpap is given up" (MF to HLTP, 4 July [1808], 9 July [1808], John Rylands).

3. William Henry Cavendish Bentinck (1738–1809), 3rd Duke of Portland (1762), was then in his second term as prime minister. His friendship was highly gratifying to

Dr. Burney, who had enjoyed annual visits since 1802 to his country seat, Bulstrode, Bucks. (*DNB;* Gibbs; Lonsdale, 469–70).

On Saturday, 2 July 1808, Dr. Burney had learned that the powerful and wealthy aristocrat wished to invite him again; accordingly, he would visit the Duke on Monday, 4 July, accept the flattering invitation, and leave for a six-week stay c. Thursday, 14 July (CB to JCH, 2–[3] July 1808, [6 July 1808], Osborn; CB to CB Jr., 4–[5] July [1808], Comyn; CB to Lord Lonsdale, [6 July 1808], BL, C. 45, f. 4; CB to CB Jr., 16 Aug. 1808, Osborn; CB to Lady Banks, [11] Nov. [1808], Osborn).

4. On Tuesday, 5 July 1808, Sarah would leave for a fortnight's visit to the Barretts, who were renting Langley Cottage for four months. Located about three miles from Windsor, it was described as "very pretty" by Marianne Francis, who commended its features: "with a Lawn, & a Garden, & orchards, and fruit, without: and plenty of room, and a dear little hospitable way of making every body happy and comfortable, within" (CB to CB Jr., 4–[5] July [1808], Comyn; MF to HLTP, 10 June 1808, 4 July [1808], 23 July 1808, John Rylands).

---

43. [To Johann Christian Hüttner][1]

Chelsea College, 3 November 1808
A.L.S., Osborn
Endorsed: Miss Burney / November 3d 1808 / Chelsea, College

Sir

My father would have done himself the pleasure of answering your truly gratifying letter, but the state of his health, at this season of the year, always delicate,[2] must plead his apology. It gave us both very sincere satisfaction to find, that the indefatigable and extraordinary exertions you must have made in order to attain so speedily a knowledge of the Spanish language,[3] had proved so advantagoeus—and we have only to wish you health, and continued success in the pursuits in which you are engaged. I inclose Mr Canning's letter,[4] as it may be pleasant to you hereafter to look at it—I hope it is but the first of many you may continue to receive.

I have the honour to be
Sir
Your very obedient Servant
S. H. Burney.

Chelsea College
Novr 3d 1808

1. The letter was endorsed by Johann Christian Hüttner (c. 1765–1847) (*DNB*), the former tutor of Sir George Thomas Staunton (1781–1859), 2nd Bt. (1801), whom he accompanied on Lord Macartney's embassy to China (1792–94). Hüttner had helped gather materials on Chinese music for Dr. Burney, to whom he wrote early in 1807, explaining that he had been stranded in England without a livelihood. Dr. Burney showed his letter to Lord William Lowther (L. 44, n. 3), who recommended him for a position in the Foreign Office, and occasionally supplied him with money. Dr. Burney wrote to the ministry in support of his protégé whom he meanwhile encouraged to publish a translation. In May 1808, Hüttner was given a temporary post in the Pay Office, while awaiting something more suited to his talents. For an overview of CB's involvement with Hüttner, see CB to Edmond Malone, 10 June 1808, Bodleian MS. Malone 38, ff. 143–45; JCH to FBA, 18 Jan. 1833, Osborn; Lonsdale, 462–63, 465–66.

2. Since contracting a severe influenza in the winter of 1804, Dr. Burney dreaded the cold; his chronic cough had been revived by wet weather the previous month, and he now feared the onset of winter and the "suicidal" month of November (CB to FBA, 9 Oct. 1806, Berg; CB to Lord Cardigan, 29 Oct. 1808, CB to Lady Banks, [11] Nov. [1808], Osborn).

3. On 23 July 1808, George Canning (1770–1827) (*DNB*), the foreign minister, had fulfilled his long-standing promise by offering to employ Hüttner if he knew Spanish and Portuguese. Conjecturally, Hüttner asked for time to acquire fluency in these languages, possibly the improper "Proposals" that angered Dr. Burney. In October, he was able to translate into his native tongue the appeal of Don Pedro Cevallos to the Nations of Europe on Napoleon's invasion of Spain; widely circulated, this document was credited with arousing German sympathies for the Spanish cause (George Canning to CB, 23 July 1808, Osborn; CB to JCH, 26 July 1808, [Aug. 1808], Osborn; CB to Lady Mary Lowther, [Dec. 1808/Jan. 1809], Burney-Cumming; JCH to FBA, 18 Jan. 1833, Osborn; *GM*, NS 28 (1847): 99–100).

4. Presumably, Canning had written to CB in praise of this accomplishment for which Hüttner was remembered (*DNB*).

44. To Johann Christian Hüttner

Chelsea College, [16 January 1809]
A.L.S., Osborn
Address: John Huttner Esqr / Norfolk Street / Middlesex Hospital
Postmarks: 7 o'Clock / 16 JA / 1809 NT
Endorsed: Miss Burney / January 1809

Sir

I beg you will not attribute to negligence or indifference my silence, these two last days, to your truly welcome and interesting communication.[1] The evening it arrived, & the whole of the following day, I spent from home, & yesterday (Sunday) there was no post.

I would fain have persuaded my dear father to address a few lines of congratulation to you with his own hand: but though most cordially delighted by the intelligence you have sent us, he is grown more averse than ever from writing, & indeed, lies in bed so much, that he cannot guide a pen without the greatest difficulty.[2] But he <u>charged</u> me to assure you that, with all the truth and friendship of the heartiest well-wisher he participates in your satisfaction.

He wishes you to write to Lord Lonsdale yourself.[3] The last time he addressed any of the family, he related all he then knew of your promising prospects:[4] but now thinks it would give Lord L: more satisfaction to hear further particulars from yourself.

I can very safely assure you, from my own observation, that whatever little chagrine my father might once have harboured against you, is wholly done away[5]—& he speaks & thinks of you & your affairs with real friendship & pleasure.

I have the honour to be
Sir, Your obedient Servant
& sincere good wisher
S. Harriet Burney.

Chelsea Coll.
Monday Morn[g]

1. Hüttner's missing letter must have contained some good news—possibly the confirmation of his temporary appointment as translator to the Foreign Office, a position he was to fill with credit to the end of his life (JCH to FBA, 18 Jan. 1833, Osborn; *DNB; GM*, NS 28 (1847): 99–100).

2. Frequently in poor health and spirits, with failing eyesight and hands "crippled by gout, rheumatism or blight," the aging Charles Burney depended increasingly on Sarah Harriet's help as his "amanuensis" in reading, copying and taking letters from dictation (see e.g., CB to Lady Banks, 25 Feb. 1808, Osborn; CB to Samuel Wesley, 17 Oct. 1808, Osborn; CB to FBA, 12 Nov. 1808, Berg). More than one of his letters to Mr. Hüttner is at least partially in the hand of his daughter (CB to JCH, 4 Mar. 1808, 20 May 1808, 30 May 1808, Osborn).

3. William Lowther (1757–1844), created Earl of Lonsdale (1807), who had exerted his influence on the German's behalf. Hüttner apparently did write a letter expressing gratitude for his patronage, to which Lord Lonsdale replied graciously (Burke; Lord Lonsdale to JCH, 18 Jan. 1809, Osborn).

4. Dr. Burney had written to the Earl's daughter, describing Hüttner's responsibilities (CB to Lady Mary Lowther, [Dec. 1808/Jan. 1809], Burney-Cumming).

5. Through the spring and summer of 1808, some of Charles Burney's letters manifest a rising irritation at the endless negotiations and solicitations in which he was involved by Hüttner's affairs. Finally, when requested to respond to Canning's offer of employment, he exploded; in the draft of a letter labeled "Finale (It is hoped) to Huttner," he declined acting as intermediary any longer, a role that he himself had initiated and apparently for some time enjoyed. Hüttner attributed the reconciliation that later took place between the two men to "the intercession of good Miss Burney" (CB to JCH, 20 May 1808, 22 May 1808, [26 May 1808], [28–29 May 1808], 26 June 1808, 2–[3] July 1808, [Aug. 1808] and JCH to FBA, 18 Jan. 1833, Osborn).

---

45. To Charlotte (Francis) Barrett

[Chelsea College, 13 February 1809]
A.L.S., Berg
Address: M[rs] Barrett / Under the Hill / Richmond / Surry.
Postmarks: [MewsRChelsea] / [Unpaid] / [P]enny [Post]
[?] o'Clock / [1]4 FE / 1809 Nn

Monday Evening

My dearest Charlotte

I have this moment received your melancholy letter, and most truly lament its sad contents. I am sure you must both have been deeply wounded by such a blow, but poor Barrett's affliction I can very well picture to myself must be extreme. She was so sweet and interesting a creature that I can only be thankful I did not know more of her—What I did know is sufficient to leave upon my mind the sincerest regret for her premature end.[1]—Pray accept my unfeigned condolences, & seize the earliest opportunity that may occur of letting me know how poor dear Barrett & you both do. A single line will satisfy me.

Thank you for the account you give me of dear Baby[2]—I hope to see her ere she is much older, & to enrich her with my benediction. My father is tolerably well. Adieu, my dearest Charlotte

Yours very truly & affectionately
S: Harriet Burney.

1. Henry Barrett's sister or half-sister, Julia Kingston (L. 33, n. 7), had died on 9 February 1809 at age twenty-six. Their relationship as siblings is given in a family tree in the Barrett collection and confirmed by Charlotte Barrett's letters, which consistently refer to John Kingston as her husband's brother-in-law, and to the child of this marriage as his nephew (see e.g., CFBt to AY, 16 Apr. [1817], Barrett, Eg. 3703A, ff. 13–15v; CFBt & JBt to HBt, 30 June–6 July [1832], Berg). Despite the large discrepancy in their ages, therefore, there seems little basis for the supposition that Julia Kingston was "not Henry Barrett's sister Julia (who had married a Harvey) but her illegitimate daughter Julia by Sir Peter Nugent" (*JL*, 11: 393, n. 8). The references in Sir Peter Nugent's will to "the daughter or supposed daughter of the before mentioned Julia Harvey commonly called Barrett" may be explained by her mother's maiden name, which was Julia Harvey (legal documents, Berg; Barrett family tree, Barrett, Eg. 3707, ff. 269–70v).

2. Charlotte's first child, Julia Charlotte Barrett, born 21 October 1808, was four months old (MF to HLTP, 24 Oct. 1808, John Rylands; *JL*, 1: lxxii).

---

46. [To Johann Christian Hüttner]

Chelsea College, 28 February 1809
A.L.S., Osborn
Endorsed: Miss Burney / February 28. / 1809

Sir

Your letter, with its very punctual enclosure,[1] and the answer you received from Lord Londsdale,[2] I communicated to my father, on his return this day from one of his accustomed airings. Had I known, at the time, that the packet was brought by Mrs Huttner,[3] I should have had great pleasure in seeing her, and I am truly sorry she was not, at least, requested to walk in, and rest herself.—Your statement of the importunities you underwent with regard to the Marlow School,[4] fully justifies you to my father for the very natural wish you once expressed to obtain that situation. All, I hope, has turned out permanently for the best—and your present position must, in consideration of the liberty it allows you to cultivate an intercourse with your former friends, and to mix, at your pleasure, in society, be infinitely preferable, I should trust, to a confinement to the duties of a school.

Lord Londsdale's letter appears to me like himself—all politeness and benevolence. Every thing I hear or see relating to this Nobleman, confirms the exalted opinion my father long since taught me to entertain of his character;[5] and others, to whom I have occasionally mentioned his name, corroborate by innumerable testimonies of his worth and liberality, the high, but well-merited title to admiration which my father is always so happy in every opportunity of proclaiming.

I am especially commissioned to assure you of that dear father's most cordial good wishes, & to present to you, Dear Sir, his best and sincerest regards, and have the honour to be

With great esteem
Your obedient humble Servant
S: Harriet Burney

February 28th 1809.
Chelsea College

1. Possibly a quarterly payment on a loan; see below L. 49, n. 4.
2. Probably Lord Lonsdale's reply of 18 January 1809 (L. 44, n. 3).
3. Unidentified.
4. Conjecturally, Hüttner had sought employment at Great Marlow, Bucks., a market town situated thirty miles northwest of London, whose Free School was founded in 1624.
5. Charles Burney had a very "exalted opinion" of this aristocrat of whose friendship he was proud. Expatiating at length on the benevolence and delicacy of "this dear & adorable" nobleman, whom he considered the "source of all goodness," he finally concluded: "Compared with the rest of Mankind, Ld L. is a divinity" (CB to JCH, 14 Mar. [1807], Comyn; 29 Feb. 1808, [26 May 1808], [28–29 May 1808], Osborn).

47. To Charlotte (Francis) Barrett and Henry Barrett

[Chelsea College, 28 March 1809]
A.L.S., Berg
Address: Mrs Barrett / Under the Hill / Richmond / Surry.
Postmarks: 7 o'Clock / 29 MR / 1809 N[T]

My dear Charlotte & Barrett,

Instead of me, who in my own proper person, little as it is, am sometimes noisy and troublesome (especially when in the vicinity of that very mirror of tranquillity, honest Clement) be pleased to pay three pence for this quiet letter, which comes to tell you, with considerable regret, that my scheme of attending dear Fanny[1] on her visit to you, must be deferred. I hope this intelligence, if it does not <make> cause a crack in your heart, will absolutely shatter Clement's all to pieces! I never broke a male heart yet; and shall be proud, let the day come when it will, to hear I have at length effected so laudable an operation. It will be something to boast of, should I live, to your Julia's children; and depend upon it, the unique occurrence (for I never expect to break two hearts) will at no future time, slip my memory. I believe, after all, it was rather a lucky circumstance for mankind, that I was not born, nurtured, & exhibited to the world in the similitude of a Beauty—I should have delighted much in uniting to the power of charming all eyes, that of plaguing all hearts. As it is, I am compelled to simper & wheedle folks into decent endurance of me and my many repulsive qualities—and good nature, whenever I successfully labour for it, is less a virtue, than an act of policy.

Rather than not talk of Self, here am I holding forth about my own ugliness: but as my own, I believe I am half tempted to love it, particularly when I can somehow or other make it a subject of attention.

But the upshot of this three pennyworth which I am spinning out so notably, is this—

Fanny Burney[2] has either proposed and been rejected, or been invited & compelled to decline coming I know not how often in the course of the winter. I expected her last Sunday, and a nice tough leg of mutton was overroasted on purpose for her—but she could not come; and so the leg of mutton is to summon its brother for next Sunday. Fanny, wholly unsuspicious of my having any other scheme in my head, has written to offer us her company, and after so many delays, and cross hindrances, both my father and I are unwilling to put her off.—Will not this plead my excuse, dear Charlotte, for putting myself off? Especially, as I promise to make a bold push for the carriage before Easter is quite over—and try to come to you. If I do not, it will be no fault of mine, I assure you.

I never said a word to my father about the little embarrassments attending your return home the other evening—And I tried to persuade myself that if a rainy night did not fill all the Stages too full, you were clever enough to recur to such an expedient, and likely enough to succeed.—The rain perplexed me the most of any thing. But "All's Well that Ends Well"[3]—

This is the longest letter my poor right hand has written since its attack[4]—It is now quite tired, & with thanks to Marianne for her pleasant letter wishes you all Good Night—

Adieu dearest Charlotte
Yours affectionately
S. Harriet Burney

Tuesday Night.

1. Probably Sarah's niece, Fanny Raper, who lived nearby.
2. Esther's daughter, Frances or "Fanny" Burney.
3. Sarah Harriet's words often recall the plays of Shakespeare, whom she quotes more than any other author.
4. This is the first mention of a weakness of the right arm, which worsened in the cold weather; see below L. 57.

---

48. [To Unknown]

Chelsea College, 19 April [1809][1]
A.L.S., Osborn

April 19th
Chelsea College.

Madam

Your flattering letter has this moment come to hand, and, impressed with the liveliest gratitude for praise, which though so much beyond my due, I should yet have a heart of stone not to feel touched by in the most sensible manner, I instantly seize a pen not only to thank you for having written in terms so gratifying to my feelings, but for having done me the justice to find out so exactly what it was in my little work I most wished all good and well disposed minds to notice & approve. I aimed at nothing wonderful—I meant to delineate nothing extravagantly heroic, or inveterately wicked; I had no hopes of exciting admiration of <u>my</u> talents & genius—I simply wished to sketch such a character as the worthy might love, the young might advantageously imitate, and the rational might allow was not overstrained.[2]

The hints you have condescended to give me of your own enviable lot in life, unknown as we personally are to each other, warm and gladden my heart. I love to hear of happiness; and, to a certain extent, believe in its reality even here below: wherever it meets with a disposition willing to communicate as well as to enjoy it,—there I am convinced it prefers to dwell. May it long abide, & be cherished amongst you and yours, is the hearty wish, of Madam,

Your obliged and most truly grateful
S. Harriet Burney.

I might have troubled you with a longer letter, but that I am at this time most anxiously employed in attendance upon a very aged Father, who, for nearly a fortnight has been confined to a sick bed.

1. SHB is replying to what was obviously an admiring letter from one of her readers. The reference to her "attendance upon a very aged Father . . . confined to a sick bed" helps to fix the date. Dr. Burney suffered in the spring of 1809 from a serious illness (described in more detail below L. 49), and Sarah was fully occupied in nursing him. The work apparently referred to, *Geraldine Fauconberg*, was published anonymously in the autumn of 1808 but attributed to Miss Burney in the reviews (L. 41, n. 2).

2. Sarah Harriet's words echo the sentiment expressed in the dedication: "Geraldine has no brilliant qualities—she struggles through no tremendous difficulties—combats against no inordinate passions—but presents, in a probable situation, the calm virtues of domestic life . . . the only ones which are of daily utility and advantage" (p. vi). The reviewer concurs, recommending her as a pattern worthy of imitation to "any lady, who wishes her daughter to excel in that quiet elegance and correct *maniere* for which the heroine of this novel is famed" (*Critical Review*, 3rd ser. 16 (1809): 104–5).

---

49. To Johann Christian Hüttner

[Chelsea College], 28 May 1809
A.L.S., Osborn
Address: John Huttner Esqr / Norfolk Street / Midx Hospital
Postmarks: [M]ewsRChelsea / Unpaid / Penny Pos[t]
12 oClock / 1 JU / [*?*]
Endorsed: Miss Burney / May 28. 1809

Sir

I have little more to trouble you with than I wrote last night; yet am I unwilling that so concise & abrupt a note should be all the notice your obliging, and much-too-grateful letter should obtain. I had no leisure either to state what had been the nature of my father's recent disorder, than which nothing certainly could be more alarming and dangerous. He has miraculously recovered from a thrush, and a spasmodic hiccup, which, almost without cessation lasted four days and nights![1]—At eighty five[2] what a trial of strength!—But a finer constitution no man ever possessed—and better medical attendance no man could have obtained. The powerful doses of Musk and opium that were administered, seemed alone sufficient to kill him—but he has weathered the storm I trust; and has no other complaint at this moment but weakness (which I acknowledge is extreme) and a temporary disgust at the thoughts of animal food, occasioned by the strong operation upon his stomach of the palling drugs that were given him.

I am grieved to find your abilities in your present situation have drawn upon you the fate of all willing steeds, who by ungrateful men are ever overworked in proportion to their spirit & alacrity.[3] But I trust that when firmly established in your post, and your worth fully understood, some gentle remonstrance may be hazarded, calculated to ameliorate the unnecessary hardship's put upon you.

My father desires his kindest remembrances & good wishes—And if you wish it, I will hint to him the propriety of forwarding to you, now, a receipt in full for the £40.[4]

I have the honour to be
Sir
Your most obedient Servant
S: Harriet Burney

May 28th
1809.

1. Dr. Burney gives the details of this severe illness in his own letters: so sore was his throat that he was unable to eat and feared death by starvation; he also suffered for several weeks the loss of all sense of taste (CB to [Lady Manvers], 18 July 1809, Osborn).

2. Born 7 April (Old Style) 1726, her father was actually eighty-three.

3. Hüttner it seems had written to his former patron complaining of overwork, perhaps justifying CB's impatience at the peculiar temper of the man who was continually depressed by his ill fortune, but curiously passive in the face of it (CB to JCH, [Aug. 1808], Osborn; Lonsdale, 463).

4. On 26 May 1808, Hüttner had asked Dr. Burney if he could suggest any money-lender who would advance him £40. In his reply, Dr. Burney declined to give any advice on the subject and stressed that he was himself "very hard run by the increase of income tax . . . & have bills hanging over my head to pay." However, Sarah Harriet responded with more generosity to the appeal, offering to lend the money herself, interest-free, from her meager resources. (She was now receiving dividends of £38.0.6 per year in her account at Coutts, in addition to what she could make from her fiction.) Her father then agreed to meet her kind intentions, and they each lent £20 without interest, to be repaid within a year. Apparently, the debt was now discharged in full (JCH to CB, 26 May 1808, Osborn; CB to JCH, [26 May 1808], [28–29 May 1808], 30 May 1808, 1 June 1808, Osborn).

50. To Johann Christian Hüttner

[Chelsea College], 14 November 1809
A.L.S., Osborn
Address: Mr Huttner / Norfolk Street / Middlesex Hospital
Postmarks: 7 oClock / 14 NO / 1809 NT
Endorsed: Miss Burney / Novr 15. 1809

Dear Sir

My father was much gratified by the communication of the interesting paper you inclosed to him, and commissions me to transmit to you his best remembrance for such a proof of your remembrance of him. He has borne the approach of winter pretty well till now—but these fogs have renewed his cough, in addition to which bodily ailment, he has been under great mental affliction for the loss of his noble & faithful friend, the Duke of Portland.[1]—

My father was in some alarm lest these changes in the administration[2] should affect you in your office: but if my memory is correct, I think you once informed us that you held a permanent station under sanction of the King's own signature. I hope I am correct in this particular.

In the course of the Autumn my father had an interview with Mr Canning; and he thinks it will not displease you to hear that, when he mentioned your name, Mr C: cried out—"O, he is a very good fellow!"—The translation you sent, is, as you foretold, in to-day's paper[3]—but my father has greater pleasure in reading <it> your copy, which is so much better printed, and looks more official, though, in fact, the same thing.

I have the honour to be
Sir
Your very obedient humble Servt
S: Harriet Burney.

Tuesday 14th Novr
1809.

1. The Duke of Portland died 30 October 1809, just a month after CB's last visit to Bulstrode. Burney was indeed deeply grieved but described his loss as more than merely personal: "This is an irreparable loss to my heart,—& to my circumstances the losses are incalculable—a beautiful Park & Gardens for riding out and walking; one of the best rooms in the Mansion on the Ground floor—due South—a Table & dinner of my own chusing at 5 o'Clock, and a pair of horses for my own warm Vehicle, a careful driver for rides in the Park on fine days, when the Sun shines, with all free from rent, Taxes, or expences of any kind—so that all I c[d] possibly want in this abode was entirely my own" (CB to FC, [Nov. 1809], Osborn). Deprived of this hospitable refuge, the invalid "now retired completely to Chelsea College" (Lonsdale, 470).

2. The Duke of Portland had resigned in October, and Spencer Perceval (1762–1812) (*DNB*) formed the new administration (1809–12).

3. Hüttner had apparently translated the lengthy "Statement of the Tyrol Deputies" which filled several columns of the *Times*, 14 Nov. 1809. Unfortunately, his work drew negative comments in this newspaper: "We fear the translation, which has been made in the Foreign Office, does not do justice to the simplicity or spirit of the original narrative."

---

51. To Charlotte (Francis) Barrett

[Chelsea College, 29 December 1809]
A.L.S., Berg
Address: M[rs] Barrett / Under the Hill / Richmond / Surry.
Postmarks: TwoPy[Post] / Unpaid / Chelsea [R]
7 o'Clock / 29 DE / 1809 NT

Your well-packed, and well-stored basket, my best & kindest Charlotte, has just been safely delivered at our door, and has afforded me gratification of various kinds; first, in guessing, before it was opened, who it came from; for your usual running hand differs from the set one in which you write a direction; 2[dly] in conjecturing who could so patiently have packed & tied it up; 3[dly] as the things presented themselves to hand, one by one, wondering what each such packet contained—and lastly, spying the letter & loaf, food for the body and food for the mind, I gave a skip, and hardly knew which to devour first. If I had but happened, luckily, to be a little more lazy than usual, I might have eat of my loaf for breakfast—I had but just swallowed as much as I had room for of vile, chalky, white London bread! Was it not untoward, & a bad encouragement for early rising?—

I have been ashamed of myself, my dearest Char, and full of self-reproach ever since I sent off my last letter, on account of omitting to chat with you about our friend Feijoo.[1] I knew all the time I was writing it, I had some particular subject to discuss with you, and even after I had contrived to fill the whole sheet avec des fagots,[2] I still felt that there was something I intended and wished to say, which, however, for the life of me I could not dig out from the mass of rubbish heaped up in my stupid brains, till after the letter was sealed and delivered to Fanny to be sent to you in a parcel.[3] You must not attribute the omission to carelessness or indifference; honour bright, the very reverse was the occasion of it! This may sound problematical—but I have often experienced that out of two or three things I may wish to remember, the principal concern is the one I soonest forget. But now to business.—I hold strictly in the same mind, and have sounded Fanny with regard to our application to Dulau,[4] who has promised me the influence of her smiles and her beauty in support of my eloquence and argumentative powers. I will make the experiment as speedily as possible; but to-day (Friday) it is too late to give Fanny notice of my intention; & besides, old Coachy has solicited a holiday. Tomorrow (Saturday) Fanny, as she told me last night at Mrs Keates, (where we had a music party, made up of English Misses, all singing as if they held a sixpence between their teeth, & were afraid of dropping it) will be engaged herself the whole day; walking in the morning with Raper (it is his only weekly holiday, you know) and then something to be done about dining out, or people dining with her. Sunday no Bookseller opens his shop, of course; & Monday & Tuesday I spend in John Street, to go with them to Mrs Towers Allen,[5] and to sigh, whilst sleeping with fat Amelia, for a larger bed! But Wednesday or Thursday, I think I can manage it. I could do it sooner, but that I know what an useful aider and abettor Fanny's pretty face, & few joli mots will be in the business. Meanwhile, I shall read your translation in snug security: And the moment I have any thing to communicate, depend upon hearing from me.

Bobs, no![6] Do not speak to the James's[7] about Sister Burney! People who do not pay may danser, but they deserve not to chanter at our cost.[8] Besides, they live a great way off, and I have no particular fancy for putting myself or any of mine under obligation to them. I have ventured one application here in the College which I think may lead to "Someat as is good." Mr Yates, our second Chaplain,[9] is a worthy and active man, and knows every body, & I last night met him, & appointed him to call upon me this morning. He has been here, & I talked the matter over with him cooly & quietly, & he seemed to enter into it cordially, & promises to make diligent enquiries. I hail & accept your hint about Polidori;[10] who, I believe, once jumped into my head of his own accord,

& then jumped out again with as little ceremony as reason. I shall write to him without delay, and every other engine I can set to work, or you can set to work, or Fanny can set to work, ought to be actively employed.

Poor dear Tibbs's![11] I am truly concerned for them, though as matters stood when I left Richmond, not surprised at their failure! Lord Cardigan[12] has been to see my father since I came home; he spoke highly of Miss Tibbs: but I was gone to town, or I would have . . . . . done nothing, but aided in confirming a good opinion, which, though of no essential use *now*, it may be worth while to keep up.

Thank Barrett for his friendly Sweep-chimney intentions in my behalf. A *blacker* proof of friendship was never offered: but I take the *fair* side of the question, and, as it is not a set of features, or complexion alone that I admire, shall love and revere him in soot & ashes for the warmth of his intentions.

Dr Charles is going to Crewe Hall[13] as well as his son, & called here, I believe, I already told you to take leave, a night or two ago. His Abridgement of Pearson's Exposition of the Creed,[14] is printed, though not yet published. He gave to my father & me each a Copy. His Motto, I think a most happy one, taken from some work of the great Bentley's—"The most excellent Bishop Pearson—the very dust of whose writings is gold."[15]—I have read above half the volume; it is all a fudge to call it a book for the use of *young persons*—Unless they are such Young Persons as Moll, who reads Lock on the Human Understanding in two days, & says it is easy, & fancies she understands it[16]—And the same farce she played with regard to Butler's Analogy,[17] the toughest book (allowed by learned men) in the English language, which she spoke of with the familiar partiality I would speak of Tom Hickerthrift,[18] & bamboozleded me into trying to read—And, Good Lord! when I had pored over a dozen pages, & shook my ears, and asked myself—"Well, Sal, how dost like it? Dost understand one word?" "O, yes; all the *words*, but not one of their meanings when put together." "Why, then, Sal; put the book away; and say nothing about it; but say thy prayers in peace, & leave the reasons *why* thou art impelled to say them, and all the *fatras* of analyzation, to those who have more logical brains, or more leisure to read what they do not comprehend." But, however, a great part of Dr Charles's Abridgement, I flatter myself I *do* understand; and what is too deep for me, Moll may explain. He has retained a heap of hard words, which send me to Johnson's Dictionary[19] continually—Some of them, are expressive, & worth reviving; others, we have happier substitutes for, and it was ungraceful to admit them, and <a> shewed a false & pedantic taste. But all this is very pert, & my letter is very long—So adieu Dearest Char—Kiss dear Baby for me, & believe me ever affectionately Yours

S. H. Burney.

My father's best love, & a thousand thanks for your kind & <u>sweet</u> little remembrance of him.

1. Charlotte seems to have translated some work of Benito Jerónimo Feijóo y Montenegro (1676–1764), the well-known Spanish essayist, which SHB was trying to get published.

2. An echo from her reading of the letters of Mme de Sévigné; see below L. 60, n. 22.

3. Fanny Raper evidently had some way "of sending messages and parcels to Char more expeditiously than by the post" (L. 53).

4. A. B. Dulau and Co. were printers and booksellers at 37 Soho Square (1800–43) who specialized in French books (Maxted).

5. A friend of Sarah's mother, Mary (née Turner) Allen (c. 1745–1815), was the daughter of Charles Turner (d. 1792), twice Mayor of King's Lynn. In 1773, she had married the Rev. John Towers Allen (c. 1744–87), Rector of Barwick, Norfolk (1783–87) (*JL*, 4: 163, n. 5; *EJL*, 1: 9, n. 27, 244, n. 41; *Alumni Cantab.*; *GM*, 85, Pt. 1 (1815): 569).

6. Probably from the expression, "od's bobs," the possessive of a minced form of God, which (to avoid profanity) was very frequent in the early eighteenth century (*OED*).

7. Miss James, an acquaintance of Charlotte Barrett's, ran a boarding school for young ladies at Richmond; it is unlikely that this would be the same Miss James who had befriended Sarah Harriet (see above L. 34) (CFBt & HnBt to JBt, [1829], Barrett, Eg. 3702A, ff. 186–87v).

8. Possibly a reference to Jean de La Fontaine's fable of "La Cigale et La Fourmy" (1668). The grasshopper, who has spent his summer singing, has not laid by any food for the winter. She begs some from the industrious ant who refuses: "Vous chantiez? j'en suis fort aise. / Et bien, dansez maintenant" (Jean de La Fontaine, *Fables choisies mises en vers*, ed. Ferdinand Gohin (Paris: Société les Belles Lettres, 1934), 1: 37).

9. The Rev. Richard Yates (1769–1834), divine and antiquary, was Second Chaplain of Chelsea Hospital (1798–1834). On his appointment, he had been accommodating to Dr. Burney, whom he allowed to occupy the apartment destined for his own use (*DNB*; *Alumni Cantab.*; *GM*, NS 2 (1834): 437–39; Dean, 249, 275, 310; *JL*, 7: 384, n. 3).

10. Gaetano Polidori had been Sarah's Italian master; conjecturally, SHB may have been seeking ways to supplement her income by giving lessons. She would soon express anxiety about her financial position (L. 57 below) and was to be employed in this manner at a later period of her life (L. 89).

11. Miss or Misses Tibbs, friend(s) of Charlotte and Marianne at Richmond (referred to as "the good Tibbs" in a letter from MF to CFBt, 2 July 1813, Barrett, Eg. 3704A, ff. 97–102) may be related to William and Thomas Tibbs Senior, both listed as "music-master" in the *Universal British Directory* (1798) for Richmond, Surrey. They both appear (at different addresses) in the Richmond Rate Book for 1790, but only William is listed for 1800. In 1810, a "Mrs. Tibbs" occupies his Ormond Row address, lives at Duke's Court (1820) and on Little Green (1830). Misses Tibbs, "Richmond Green, Music," are listed in John Evans, *Richmond and its Vicinity* (Richmond: James Darrill, [1825]).

Thomas Tibbs wrote the music for the song, *Richmond Hill* [c. 1760], while William Tibbs composed *Eight Songs in Score. Arranged for the Voice and Piano Forte*, printed at

Richmond in [1797]. A William Tibbs of Richmond, Surrey, subscribed to the New Musical Fund in 1794 and was still a member in 1805. Doane's *Musical Directory* (London, 1794) shows William Tibbs as an organist of Richmond Church (information kindly supplied by Philip H. Highfill Jr.).

See further on Miss Tibbs L. 64.

12. James Brudenell (1725–1811), created Baron Brudenell (1780), 5th Earl Cardigan (1790) (Lodge).

13. Crewe Hall, Cheshire, the seat of Lord Crewe, whose wife, Frances Anne (née Greville), was a lifelong friend of Charles Burney (L. 27, n. 3). The Jacobean mansion, which impressed CB as a "noble house" (*Memoirs*, 3: 245), is described more fully below, L. 105, n. 8.

14. The Rev. Charles Burney, *The Exposition of the Creed, by J. Pearson . . . abridged for the use of young persons* (London: T. Cadell & W. Davies, 1810). The work of John Pearson (1613–86), Bishop of Chester, *An Exposition of the Creed* (1659), was a standard theological work.

15. Richard Bentley (1662–1742) (*DNB*), the classical scholar; Burney's motto is taken from *A Dissertation upon the Epistles of Phalaris* (London, 1699), 424–25. CB Jr. collected many works of and about him which were acquired by the British Museum at his death.

16. Marianne Francis, whose learning was regarded with some awe in the family, quoted approvingly from *An Essay concerning Humane Understanding* (1690), the philosophical treatise of John Locke (1632–1704), whose work she admired (MF to HLTP, 13 Aug. 1808, Rylands).

17. The theological work of Joseph Butler (1692–1752), Bishop of Durham, *The Analogy of Religion, Natural and Revealed, to the constitution and course of Nature* (1736).

18. Tom Hickathrift, a legendary strongman of the time of the conquest, reputed to have killed a giant (Ivor H. Evans, ed., *Brewer's Dictionary of Phrase and Fable*, rev. ed. (London: Cassell, 1981)).

19. Samuel Johnson (1709–84); his famous *A Dictionary of the English Language*, first published in two volumes in 1755, had already run through nine editions. Charles Burney owned two copies of the 1786 edition (*Misc. Lib.*, 28).

---

52. To Charlotte (Francis) Barrett

[Chelsea College, 6 January 1810]
A.L.S., Berg
Address: M[rs] Barrett / Under the Hill / Richmond / Surry
Postmarks: T[o Be] Delivered / by [?] o'Clock / on [S]und Morn
7 o'Clock / 6 JA / 1810 NT

My dearest Charlotte

I began a letter to you yesterday, but was interrupted before I could get it ready for the post. I wished to tell you that on Thursday, I believe it was, Fanny and I drove with your MS to Dulau's, and opened our commission to him with all the ability of which we were capable. Nothing could be more civil than he was: but he positively declined having any concern in the publication of *an English* translation: he advised us however to repeat the application at Hatchard's in Piccadilly;[1] authorized us to say we were sent and recommended by him; and promised, if Hatchard accepted & published it, to take twelve copies himself, & to disperse, and befriend its sale to the utmost of his power. I know something of Hatchard myself,[2] & the more readily therefore determined to try him. He gave but an indifferent account of the present popularity of Spanish literature, either original or translated—and all, I grieve to add, which we could, after a pretty long conference, obtain from him, was this recommendation—To apply to some other Bookseller who might be willing to <publish it on your own, & divide> print upon condition of dividing with you the profits of its sale: but he mentioned no one in particular, and we were too proud to solicit his unoffered patronage. But Dulau had told us, that if we were unsuccessful with Hatchard, he wished us to send the MS. to him, & he would consider of some method of becoming serviceable to us. I am sure he would have taken it, upon reasonable terms had your translation been made *in French*: we have therefore ventured, my dearest Char, to propose to him to get *our friend* to translate it afresh into that language; and are waiting for his answer. But I could not bear to keep you in total suspense; though I am so mortified at our failure, thus far, that it was almost painful to me to sit down and write to you. Believe us, my Charlotte, we were not slack in our endeavours—But beastly *fashion* determines or influences every thing; and since the Spanish Patriots have all turned out fools, knaves, or cowards,[3] Spanish is gone considerably out of fashion, & therefore the sale of books in that language is become precarious. I read your MS. with great and sincere admiration of its excellent style, which runs on as flowingly, & with as much spirit as an original work. Ah, would you had trusted to your abilities, & composed an original production, warm from the brain! Another thing I must tell you—Hatchard advised a change in the title; thinking that as it now stands, it might lead to bold misconstructions.

I will write again, & put you out of doubt as soon as we hear from Dulau—Meanwhile, with deep regret, but true affection, believe me truly yours

S. H. B.

1. At 190 Piccadilly, the bookselling firm of John Hatchard (1769–1849), Bookseller to the Queen (1800–19) (Maxted; *DNB;* Nichols, *Illustrations*, 8: 520–21).
2. SHB probably knew of him through Thomas Payne the bookseller (father-in-law to James Burney), whom Hatchard had once assisted (Maxted).
3. For the strained relations between Britain and her Spanish allies in 1809, see John M. Sherwig, *Guineas and Gunpowder* (Cambridge, Mass.: Harvard University Press, 1969), 216–38.

---

53. To Frances (Phillips) Raper

[Chelsea College, 1807–10][1]
A.L.S., Berg
Address: Mrs Charles Raper / Cromwell Cottage / Old Brampton

My dearest Fanny. To my utter surprise, my dear father, of his own accord, has this moment renewed the subject of the Richmond Concert, & even offered me the carriage if I chose to go. I am not asked, it is true, but somehow, I think they will try and poke me somewhere, & I cannot bear to throw a good chance away. Cannot you accompany me, & I will call for you tomorrow at what hour you like?—I take it for granted you will send me no positive answer before you have spoken to Mr Raper—but let me know in the evening, or early tomorrow morning. I shall not set off before twelve o'clock, & mean to write by to day's post, to let dear Char know what a plague of an intruder she may expect—Do you think my letter will get to her before my person bundles itself out at her door? And how will l'Ami Barrett relish my taking such a liberty? I had no serious thoughts of going, though it is certain I expressed a wish that I could go—And my dear Padre mistaking perhaps what I said, imagined I was asking permission, which now it is so indulgently granted, I cannot bear to throw to the dogs. But you cannot conceive how surprised I am to find myself grown so frisky—I have told my father you are invited, & he offered me George[2] to bring you this proposal of going with me—

Scratch me a line as soon as you can—

Ever yours most heartily, & liking you almost better than any body,

S: H: Burney.

Thursday Morning.

Is there not a way you often employ of sending messages and parcels to Char more expeditiously than by the post? If there is, I wish, dear Soul, you would scribble a line to her for me, to tell her of my impudence.

Pray pray Mr Raper let dear Fanny go,—It would double all my pleasure—

1. The letter can be dated only approximately; it must postdate Fanny's marriage of 16 July 1807, and predate 23 June 1810, when Sarah Harriet first speaks of the carriage being given up (L. 55). Mrs. Raper did live at Cromwell Cottage, Old Brompton during those years.

2. George, Charles Burney's servant, entered his service shortly before he made his will in January 1807 where he is referred to as "MY BOY, GEORGE, but lately come to me" (Scholes, 2: 263).

54. To Caroline Anne Bowles

[Chelsea College, 1807–10][1]
A.L.S., Fales
Address: Miss Bowles / 2. Bayner Place / Chelsea—

My dear Miss Bowles[2]

Please to hold yourself in readiness, on Saturday evening, to step into an elegant empty vehicle, wch will convey you, first, to the warehouse where it is to be filled with live stock, (including my little self); and thence, to enjoy the fun of our worthy friend Mathews.[3]—A little after six is the hour thought fittest for setting off from Chelsea.

With love to your host & hostess, & Co—Believe me yours truly.

S. H. Burney

1. The letter has been conjecturally dated by the coincidence of Sarah's residence at Chelsea, Charles Mathews's career, and Charles Burney's keeping of a carriage.

2. Caroline Anne Bowles (1786–1854), the daughter of Capt. Charles Bowles of the East India Company, who had married 23 July 1782 Anne Burrard (d. 1816) of Buckland Cottage, Hampshire. Miss Bowles harbored some literary aspirations, which later brought her into contact with Robert Southey, whom she eventually married (see further L. 162) (*DNB;* Burke under Burrard; parish register, Boldre, Hants.; IGI).

3. Probably Charles Mathews (1776–1835), the comedian, who made his London debut 16 May 1803. Later, he was to achieve fame for his one-man performances, "At Homes," in which he appeared before London audiences for the first time in 1817. His

career is described more fully in [Anne] Mathews, *Memoirs of Charles Mathews, Comedian* (London: Richard Bentley, 1838–39) and in Richard L. Klepac, *Mr. Mathews at Home* (London: Society for Theatre Research, 1979).

55. To Charlotte (Francis) Barrett

[23 June 1810, Chelsea College]
A.L.S., Berg
Address: Mrs Barrett / Under the Hill / Richmond / Surry.
Postmarks: To Be Delivered / by 10 o'Clock / on Sund Morn
7 o'Clock / 23 JU / 1810 NT

My dearest Charlotte

Were I so circumstanced as to be able, "free and unquestioned," to rove from place to place, or whithersoever I chose, you may depend upon it your letter would have sped me to Richmond in less than a day after receiving it. But I have to ask leave, an odious thing to me—And moreover, Fanny and I have not met so long, that I know nothing of her plans, or engagements, or what day, supposing, I at last get courage to speak about it to my father, will best suit <best> her to share in the frolic. I will not come upon you however by surprise, if I can any way avoid it—You shall at least have a day's notice to prepare for my important approach. And so much for your kind invitation, and my cowardly delay. Oh—if you did but know how I hate, face to face, asking for any thing! If my father was away, I could write—but to speak . . . .

Well, but, I have been reading, and am enchanted with The Lady of the Lake! It has all the spirit of either of its predecessors, (have you read it?) and ten times the interest. When I had finished it, I remained with such a relish for <William> Walter Scott upon my mind, that I immediately borrowed and sat down to a second perusal of Marmion.[1] I like the brave villain much for being so wholly divested of sneakingness—I admire his squabble with old Angus—his tranquil determination to gain possession of the Lady Clare, and her lands, coute qui coute;—And as for Constance de Beverley, and her infernal Trial, I think enough can never be said of her reprobate magnanimity, of the picturesque description of her person, of the surrounding gloomy objects—of scarcely any of the striking circumstances introduced throughout the whole harrowing scene.[2] But here am I telling you of an old book just the humdrum sort of stuff I often tell

THE WHILE, THE SPORTIVE FORMS WOULD TREAD
WITH LIGHT STEP ROUND HIS INFANT HEAD
AND FILL WITH DREAMS DIVINE THE FUTURE LAY.

Illustration to the poem "Spencer" in Richard Westall's *A Day in Spring*, designed by the author and engraved by James and Charles Heath, 1808.

myself with pen and ink in my little private reviews—And I wont say another word upon the subject. But have you seen a little volume of Westall's Poems, containing a Day in Spring, and other detatched pieces, with four lovely engravings from his own designs? One of them representing a youthful Spenser, dreaming about Knights, and Squires, & Dames of high degree, and Fairies, & other entertaining whimsies. And all these visionary personages are dancing around him in the prettiest groupes you can imagine[3]—

You will think me a deuce of a pedant to keep jabbering so much about books, when perhaps you would like to hear about people. But I see no people, and keep company continually with books—We have no carriage now, & I seldom get beyond our old College, except on Sunday evenings, when, if I can get any body to walk with me, I stump to different Chapels. In this manner I have been to the Magdalen,[4] and the Lock,[5] & I should like as long as the fine weather lasts, to go to such sort of places of honest resort every Sunday. The singing at the Magdalen is Heavenly—And a Clergyman preached there of the name of Stevens, one whom Dr Andrews is a great friend to,[6] I am told. He is very impressive, grave, full of reverence—has the clearest articulation I ever heard, and sufficient energy. At the Lock, I heard an old Mr Fry[7] preach a farewel sermon, with some touches of familiarity that astounded me! I believe, it was all extemporary—I know, at least, it was odd, though certainly in many respects good.

I have been with a nice little party of College friends, to see King John, and for a week after, I could do nothing but read Shakespear. Mrs Siddons was Magnificent[8]—When she tells the Duke of Austria he is a—Coward,[9] she makes a mouth as follows I could have done it better when I first came home—but it is a little like.

The story of Julia and the daisies is beautiful[10]—I read it to M F, (my father) and he liked it much. Tootty[11] is grown very sociable and dear—She likes no one better than Missah Barree.

Adieu, dearest Charlotte—My kind love to your dear Mother—and a kiss to Julia—& Believe me ever faithfully

S. H. Burney

1. Walter Scott's poem, *The Lady of the Lake,* which had come out the previous month (*Times,* 30 May 1810), "shattered all records for the sale of poetry." Its popularity eclipsed even the considerable success of two predecessors, *The Lay of the Last Minstrel* (1805) and *Marmion* (1808) (Johnson, 1: 225, 279, 335). The first of these SHB had already submitted to a "second perusal" (L. 30).

2. The trial scene in *Marmion* takes place in Canto 2, 17–33.

3. The artist, Richard Westall (1765–1836), designed the illustrations for his own book of poetry, *A Day in Spring* (1808), with plates engraved by James and Charles Heath (*DNB*). In the first stanza of "Spencer," he imagines the Elizabethan poet as a child, sleeping in a "deep sequester'd glade" (l. 1). "The while the sportive forms would tread / With light step round his infant head, / And fill with dreams divine the future lay" (ll. 4–6). These lines appear beneath the illustration described.

4. Magdalen Hospital, a charitable institution for the reclamation of prostitutes, was founded in 1758 and moved to a site in St. George's Fields in 1772. It became fashionable to attend the chapel services which, enhanced by the singing of an all-female choir, were successful in raising contributions (Henry B. Wheatley, *London Past and Present* (London: John Murray, 1891), 2: 454; *Survey of London*, 25: 66; John Timbs, *Curiosities of London*, 2nd ed. (London: Virtue, 1867), 539–40; Lambert, 3: 172–77; Walpole, 9: 273–74).

5. The Lock Hospital, created "for the cure of females suffering from disorders contracted by a vicious course of life," was established in Grosvenor Place in 1747. The chapel, added in 1764, was useful as a source of income and renowned for its preachers (Wheatley, 2: 412–13; Timbs, *Curiosities*, 438; Walter Besant, *London North of the Thames* (London: Adam & Charles Black, 1911), 183).

6. Dr. Gerrard Andrewes (1750–1825), D.D. (1807), the Dean of Canterbury (1809), was appointed to the Magdalen Hospital in 1791, and famed for his "full strong voice" when preaching (*DNB; Alumni Cantab.*). He had known the d'Arblays when he was Rector of Mickleham (1800–13) (*JL*, 5: 16, n. 2, 201).

His protégé might be Robert Stevens (c. 1778–1870) who, like Andrewes, had attended Westminster and Trinity College, Cambridge, D.D. (1821). A Lecturer at St. Margaret's, Westminster (1808–20), he would later become Dean of Rochester (1820–70) (*Westminsters; Alumni Cantab.*).

7. Unidentified.

8. A new production of Shakespeare's *King John* was presented at the New Theatre Royal, Covent Garden, on Saturday, 12 May 1810, and repeated on the seventeenth, twenty-fourth, and twenty-eighth of that month and on the eleventh and twenty-first of June. The play was strongly cast, with Mrs. Siddons as Constance, John Philip Kemble as King John, and another brother, Charles Kemble (1775–1854), playing Philip the Bastard. The reviewer in the *Times* also admired Mrs. Siddons's performance, which "was above our praise" (*Times*, 14 May 1810).

9. William Shakespeare, *King John*, III, i, 41.

10. Julia Charlotte Barrett, Charlotte's eldest child, was twenty months old. In a missing letter, Charlotte had probably told Sarah Harriet the same story that she related to her absent husband. The hay in some nearby fields had been mown and "when Julia went into the hay fields & saw that all her buttercups & daises were cut down she cried" (CFBt to HBt, 19 June [1810], Berg).

11. Probably Catherine Minette (1808–82), the two-year-old daughter of Frances (Phillips) Raper, who had married about the same time as her cousin Charlotte in 1807, and had a baby just seven months before her (*JL*, 1: lxxi; 6: 590, n. 10). The identification is confirmed by Mme d'Arblay's use of the nickname (20 April–16 May 1815) when she hopes that "sweet little Tooty is re-establishing" and has "been [frighten]ed at the alarming illness of her poor Mamma" (*JL*, 8: 124). Fanny Raper did suffer from

a "frightful illness" in the spring of 1815, and at the same time, her daughter was "not out of the wood" (see below L. 80).

While Hemlow attributes the nickname to Charlotte's daughter, Julia (n. 5), SHB's letter suggests otherwise. "Tootty" here is a child who refers to Charlotte's husband as "Missah Barree" (not "Papa"). Moreover, sandwiched between two references to Julia, "Tootty" is someone about whose welfare Charlotte is informed by Sarah (who lived near Fanny and Minette).

56. To Henry Barrett with Charlotte (Burney) (Francis) Broome to Charlotte (Francis) Barrett

[10 Chenies Street, 1 August 1810]
A.L.S. SHB to HBt with A.L.S. CBFB to CFBt, Berg
Address: Henry Barrett Esqr / Under the Hill / Richmond / Surry
Postmarks: TwoPyPost / Unpaid / Tottenham Ct
7 o'Clock / 1 AU / 1810 NT

If Moll's noise, for I am in Chenies Street,[1] and she is practising in the room, will allow me the use of my senses, I will now tell you my dear Barrett why I did not answer you sooner. Your kind letter was directed to Chelsea, and I have been a week or more in London between John and Chenies Streets, to give our Maids a fair opportunity of hunting bugs in my father's bed whilst he marches off into mine and keeps it aired for me whilst I am serving for meat to those which haunt the bedsteads in John Street—And a noble meal they have made of me! Cospetto di Bacco! They have not left a free place about my little person.—However, they are dislodged now I believe permanently for this summer, at least, and all owing to my useful grumbles: Amelia slept on, and never minded them: but I made such an outcry, that the Slaughter of the Innocents was finally determined on—and I had the pleasure of seeing a bottle of poison, a Charwoman, and an Upholsterer's prentice walk into the house to unite in storming their fort—attacking them in their strong holds,—and pursuing them into their darkest and most secret recesses.—Here, the house is as yet clear of such gentle lodgers—and long may it remain so.

I am in hourly expectation of a recall to Chelsea, as my father has some fishes for me to fry,[2] and I have now been absent from home above ten days. I will, however, and mean to come and see you while the Summer endures, but not till I have been at home first, at least a few days. I thank you gratefully for your kind and truly friendly invite—and what is better even than such thanks, sincere though they be—I kept it to myself whilst with those whom it did not concern.—Since an Irish journey[3] gives you such a pretty knack of writing cordial letters—a knack by the way which you were not greatly deficient in before—you shall go again whenever the fancy takes you. Bother of this great tear in my dear Sister Broome's cheap paper! [*A two-inch tear extends in from the bottom edge of the first leaf.*]

I met with two lines in the Rehearsal the other day which upon all wearisome occasions I solace myself with muttering in my sleeve, and they do me a great deal of good, and enable me to support a stick of a visitor better than I ever could do before I was provided with so comfortable a bit of spite to vent my disgust by—

> "Sir (or Ma'am) if you please, I
> should be glad to know
> How long you here will stay, how
> soon you'll go!"[4]—

Do not apply them to me when I go to you—Give my tenderest love to dear Char, and thanks for her kind addenda—I long to see lovely little Julia, and am ever most truly l'amie de l'ami

S. H. Burney.

Wednesday Morning

[*The last 5 lines consist of an A.L.S. CBFB to CFBt concerning the start of the school term.*]

1. Sarah was visiting her half-sister, Charlotte Broome, who had moved to No. 10 Chenies Street, Bedford Square, between 14 November and 11 December 1809 (MF to CFBt, 11 Dec. 1809, Berg; MF to HLTP, 14 Nov. 1809, 13 Dec. 1809, John Rylands).

2. Sarah was useful as a copyist to her elderly father, to whom writing had become a "laborious operation" (CB to FBA, [May 1810], Osborn); his dependence on her help is indicated by the fact that he refers to her as "my daughter, & amanuensis" (CB to Samuel Wesley, 17 Oct. 1808, Osborn). See further L. 57 below.

3. Henry Barrett had visited Dublin in June 1810 but curtailed his stay when one of his companions fell ill; he left for England on the twenty-second (CFBt to HBt, 19 June [1810], Berg; HBt to CFBt, 21 June 1810, Berg).

4. The words are those of King Usher (a Usurper) in *The Rehearsal* (1671) by George Villiers, Duke of Buckingham (1628–87) (IV, i, 239–40). The speech is offered by Bayes as that of "a well bred person . . . So modest, so gent!" Sarah has changed the "we" of the first line to an "I" and added in the "(or Ma'am)."

57. To Charlotte (Francis) Barrett

[Chelsea College], 15 August 1810
A.L.S., Berg
Address: Mrs Barrett / Under The Hill / Richmond / Surry.
Postmarks: TwoP[yPost] / Un[paid] / [Chelsea]
[*?*] [o'clock] / [15 AU] / 1810 NT

<July> Augst 15th 1810.

My dearest Charlotte

The sweet Catalani!—I should break my heart to hear her, when fancying herself in danger, singing like a dying Swan—taking so melodious a leave of the world, and piously appropriating her last musical exertions to the relief of the poor![1]—I assure you, all these ideas would make me contemplate and listen to her with sobs instead of animation—and I dare say I should behave like an old romantic fool, & expose myself to the sneers of half the room. But, however, this I would venture, since you and Barrett are so good as to ask me: only, being just returned from a fortnight's visit in town,[2] my father's daily allowance of scribbling has accumulated during my absence, and I am now surrounded up to my chin with foul copies of letters and notes I must transcribe for him—And I have from page 27 to p. 86 of the Cyclopedia Letter P:[3] to copy which he gives me daily hints I should do wisely to set about before the cold weather threatens again to deprive me of the use of my right hand.—This, I might bring or rather take with me to Richmond and work at under your roof—But I will put pride in my pocket, and tell you a secret which I only request may neither travel to John Street, nor Chenies Street, where it would obtain for me the reputation of being "one of the wicked."[4]—I have bought books more than I ought to have purchased, and spent money, which always burns holes in my pockets, faster than I ought to have spent it—And one day lately I took it in my head to reckon up all the one pounds, & two pounds, and three pounds I owed at different shops, & the amount, (which I shall not confess to Barrett, at least) frightened me horridly—And I instantly determined, and please the Lord, will rigidly adhere to the determination, not to buy sixpennyworth of any thing, or indulge myself in any maggots, till I had cleared myself of all twitching remembrances of foolish debts.[5] So, as a Cramp would cost me the D—— and all,—and the Concert half a guinea—and I must buy white gloves, &c, and, except longing to see you, and B: and Julia—I am so perfectly happy where I am, it seems to me no more than honest and just to maintain my good purposes inviolably, and stay where I am.

Now you have, without lies, or reserve, the whole truth, and nothing but the truth. I am a little ashamed of myself, but not quite so much as I should be if I did not hope and plainly foresee that half a year's persevering self denial will fully clear me. And the discomforts I witness in more than one family resulting from debts, make me nervous about my own—which yet however, I bless Heaven, are not of consequence enough to become objects of discussion in my own family, and I trust will never be mentioned to any one by you and l'Amico.

Adieu, my dearest Charlotte. May you be charmed to your heart's desire by the exquisite Catalani—I rejoice that you mean to go.—Remember me most kindly to Barrett—Give Julia a kiss for me, and believe me faithfully, &

admiringly and affectionately yours

S: H: Burney.

As I chose that my recent course of extravagance should die a melodious death, (like poor Catalani's talents) the last indulgence I gave it was the purchase of "The Lady of the Lake".[6] How sweet, and to my fancy, bewitching a poem it is!—Ever yours.

1. Angelica Catalani (1780–1849), an Italian soprano who had made her London debut in 1806, and enjoyed great success; she was engaged at the King's Theatre from 1810 to 1814 when she left for the continent, returning briefly in 1824 (*New Grove*).

Charlotte, who lived in Richmond, had probably invited Sarah Harriet to a "GRAND CONCERT" in the Assembly Room, Castle Tavern, on Saturday, 19 August at 8 P.M. Mme Catalani, who announced that this would be "positively the only Concert she will give this season," was dedicating the profits "to the relief of the most deserving families of this Parish during the severity of the ensuing winter, and towards the erecting a new Charity School, for the education of their necessitous offspring." Tickets were sold to subscribers at £1.1s. (for two or more) or 15s. each (*Times*, 11, 13 Aug. 1810).

2. To her half-sister Broome's (see above L. 56).

3. Sarah was evidently transcribing her father's contributions to Rees's *Cyclopaedia* (see above L. 40, n. 3), a task he had previously exacted of both his housekeeper and his granddaughter. SHB's help in reading the badly faded ink and making a fair copy was essential, as the articles had been written several years before. While Burney had completed his own work in 1805, he apparently retained the manuscript to make additions and corrections, supplying the publishers with each letter as requested (Lonsdale, Ch. 10, esp. 418–30; CB to FC, [Mar. 1808]; CB to FBA, 5 May 1810, Osborn). Although Lonsdale speculates (429–30) that CB had handed over all his material by 1808, this letter suggests otherwise.

The four volumes containing the letter "P" would be published between June 1813 and May 1814 (B. D. Jackson, "The Dates of Rees's Cyclopaedia," *Journal of Botany* 34 (1896): 307–11).

4. William Shakespeare, *1 Henry IV*, I, ii, 94.

5. SHB's modest income had remained stable since her return to her father: stock holdings of £1056.8.4 in 4 percents gave an annual yield of £38.0.6. In 1809 and 1810, her account at Coutts shows expenditures of £80.14s. and £60.18.6 respectively, made possible by a £50 deposit from James Burney and the surplus from previous years. The fact that her expenses were exceeding her income might have induced her to retrench.

6. Sarah must have bought Walter Scott's poem very soon after its publication in May, as she mentions reading it in her letter of [23 June 1810] (L. 55 above).

58. To Charlotte (Francis) Barrett

[Chelsea College, 29 January 1811][1]
A.L.S., Berg
Address: Mrs Barrett / Under the Hill / Richmond / Surry
Postmarks: 4 o'Clock / JA 30 / [18]11 [*?*]
12 oClock / 30 JA / 1811 [*?*]

Tuesday Night

My dearest Charlotte

I write to say that I am grown so invetarately dissipated, that my present shameless motto is—"In for a penny, in for a pound!"[2]—My friends ought to be either very angry with, or very much obliged to Mrs Hammond[3] for first setting my vis inertia in motion. But lately returned from her scene of revelry, I am more up to a repetition of such disorderly courses than I was at first to give into <it> them. The impetus (a'n't I very sublime in my terms?) is given:—stop it who can! So I mean to say, dearest Char, that since you are so very good as to desire it, & l'Ami Barrett is so very kind as to consent to my impudent plan of coming hither to fetch me, I will muster up all my eloquent powers and with "pleaded reasons"[4] poured into my father's ear, will supplicate him for leave to march myself off on Saturday morning at whatever hour dear good-natured Barrett can manage to come for me. If the weather is rainy, or otherwise unfavourable, grim, snowy, foggy, or blowing a huricane, I shall be rational enough neither to expect nor wish for him.

I must be allowed to bring some scribbling work for fagging at when you are in bed.

Your dear Madre dined here to-day, well, and sweet-tempered, and amiable, and good as ever—and Daddy was glad to see her, and cordial & hearty—and they fudged up old stories to sham grinning at—or perhaps they might grin in simple singleness of heart!—I am very apt to smirk at such grey <jokes> jockies rather hypocritically—Like Sir Joshua Reynolds' he, he, he, recorded in her Memoir of her husband by clever Mrs Opie.[5]

Oh—but I'll tell you a joke about Cauvini the new tenore at the Opera which is not old—They said that in the part of the Sultan in the new Opera[6] he sat cross-legged so ungracefully, and with such unhappy awkwardness of outline, that he looked like a taylor pondering upon his bad debts!

Price's business all settled, & the receipt delivered.[7]

If my father is not inexorable you will hear from me no more till you see me, and then, with a blessing upon my endeavours I mean that you shall hear enough!

Best love to Barrett from, (dearest kind goosy to be bothered with me!) Yours most lovingly & truly

S: H: Burney.

Thank Barrett for proposing to dance with me—the weather-cock with the Church steeple would hardly be <less> more out of proportion: but I decline no good offers for fear of le qu'en dira-on?—Too old a bird for that!

1. Postmarked 30 January 1811 (a Wednesday) and dated "Tuesday Night," the letter was probably written on the twenty-ninth.

2. A proverbial expression; Edward Ravenscroft used it in his play of 1695, *The Canterbury Guests* (V, i, 14–15); Walter Scott would quote it in his novel of 1815, *Guy Mannering* (Ch. 46), as if commonly known.

3. Ann Frances de la Fontaine (c. 1738–1818), who had married, on 12 April 1783, Thomas Hammond (c. 1754–1801), Clerk to the Secretary of the Royal Hospital, Chelsea (1775–1801) (*JL*, 1: 143, n. 17; *GM*, 71, Pt. 2 (1801): 863).

4. John Milton, *Paradise Lost* (1667), Bk. 7, l. 1147.

5. Amelia (née Alderson) Opie (1769–1853), in her memoir of her late husband, John Opie (1761–1807) (*DNB*), prefixed to his *Lectures on Painting* (London: Longman, Hurst, Rees and Orme, 1809). She describes an evasive technique of the painter, Sir Joshua Reynolds (1723–92): when asked to give an opinion, he "had a method of laughing a he! he! he! *so equivocally toned*, that the parties interested in understanding it favourably might do so without any great strength of self-flattery" (39–40).

6. A new opera, *Le Tre Sultane*, with music composed by Vincenzo Pucitta, opened at the King's Theatre on Tuesday, 22 January 1811. It featured Mme Catalani singing for the first time that season and Signor Cauvini making "his first appearance in this country." The reviewer in the *Times* thought the tenor showed promise: "his voice is sweet, but possessing little compass" (*Times*, 15, 23 Jan. 1811). The opera was repeated several times that season.

7. Sarah Harriet had apparently transacted some business for Charlotte Barrett at the well-known banking firm of Harrisons, Price, Kay, and Chapman, located at No. 1 Mansion House Street (Price, 133).

59. To Charlotte (Francis) Barrett

[Chelsea College, 26 June 1811]
A.L.S., Berg
Address: M[rs] Barrett / Under the Hill / Richmond / Surry.
Postmarks: 4 o'Clock / JU 26 / 1811 EV
[12 o'Clock] / 26 JU / 1811 Nn

No, darling Charlotte, I remember not a word in Milton about that dear little fallen Seraph that wandered about the universe, and could no where find rest for the sole of his white foot! But I should like to be made to remember it, for I love and am interested for the noble trespasser unsight, unseen. You do not, per chance, mean Abandona in Klopstock's Messiah?[1] Poor lovely melancholy Abandona always made me cry, even in a <cold *1 word*> stiff bombastical french translation[2]—And you who can read German, what comfortable pails full of tears you might shed![3] Well, and so I always do over Klopstock's Morte d'Adams, though I never read it but in Italian[4]—And I do believe it is, in both cases, as you say, because the noblest of their species, as Adam, created perfect by the Divinity, & living at first in bliss and innocence, and gifted with the highest powers mental and corporeal, lamentably fell—And the Seraph, that happiest & best of Celestial Spirits—he too degenerated;—But Klopstock represents him as sorry, confused, repentant for his fault—and sitting in loneliness and dejection—afraid to pray, yet abhorring to continue an associate of the inveterately wicked Spirits that seduced him—And I believe, at last, his penitence is accepted, and he is readmitted to favour in the Heavenly abodes. The Greeks had very pretty mythological inventions—but they had nothing half so touching as this.—See how the theme you supplied me, sets me chirping, to borrow your funny phrase, the instant your epistle (to speak à l'heroine) arrived. But I feel exactly as you do about fine, spirited, disinterested, thoughtless boys of the creation, who plunge themselves into such miserable difficulties before they have learnt the value of independence, & of character. Money difficulties though they seem so mean, and so little calculated to afflict the heart, do sting and pinch it, worse almost than half the other calamities incident to mankind—And some hearts—like that fine beautiful Brotherton Browne's, they really break. Do you know about poor Brotherton? Did you ever see him? He was the handsomest, & the most engaging creature I ever beheld or knew—He has been obliged to banish himself to India—to quit the King's service, & enter into the Military service of that purse-proud East India Company—He lives without health at some Fort up the Country, without society, without hope—for, let him come home when he will, unless possessed of thousands to pacify his creditors, he would be arrested, & thrown into the King's Bench for life! And he is only 6 or 7 and twenty! I knew him first when no more than fourteen or fifteen[5]—You will say, I always speak partially of boys—but the truth is, that except William Lock about the same age,[6] I never beheld so promising, so perfectly handsome, so sensible & sweet-tempered a creature.—And think of being buried for an indefinate term, perhaps for life, <to> in an asiatic Fort two or three hundred miles from the civilization even of Calcutta! And he has a Mother[7] here, adoring him, & breaking her heart by inches about him. But if this story was recapitulated to an extravagant headlong prodigal, it would do not the smallest good—for nothing but personal experience does succeed, & not always that, till age also brings steadiness and persevering principle. I am one who think that a great many people grow better by age, and who laugh at the pretended innocence of children as heartily as Capt. Burney, who asserts that almost every child, if it had strength proportioned to its malice, would have committed half a dozen murders before it was three years old!—I am glad to my heart however you partook of the noble Ganders festivities[8]—for tho' an idée noire came across you in the midst of the frolic, some notions couleur de rose, I hope hovered near you at least part of the time—And I like to think, that in such scenes, all are not lost to thought and morality—Perhaps, under a gay exterior, there were many other grave and reflecting hearts. Yours, dearest Charlotte, is the only sort of sentimentality I like. I cannot define it, but one of the appellations I would give it, would be that of genuine, and really virtuous & good sentimentality. Nervous hippishness is quite another thing—And Novel Romance makes me puke!—I have said nothing yet of poor dear Fanny, though my head and heart too, are full of her. She was here the other morning, & looked low, and had fits of silence and looks of absence that struck me very much. But, if it is as you say—If she has nobly taken courage and told the worst, why not now raise her eyes, and chearfully enjoy herself? Secresy is one, at least, of the severest stings <of> belonging to such a situation as hers—If that is at an end, exhort her, my dearest Char, to be merry and thankful. What signifies a little solitude? She has got a garden, and a healthy little girl, and many resources in her love of music, of reading, & of work. And if, when honest old Raper comes home, she can receive him with unapprehensive looks and feelings, a fig for the world, and a button for all the tempting shops in London or Paris to boot![9]—I ought to have been going on with my 523th page of Adela[10] instead of writing this long rigmarole to you—but having pen and ink, and Adela's kind of Copy paper before me,[11] and loving you in very truth, very much, I no sooner got to the end of your letter, than I began answering it.—I wish Fanny would speak out to me now, for I think she would afterwards feel more at ease with me—but on my own account, I am perfectly satisfied with the account you have goodnaturedly sent me.[12] Never fear my blabbing. About her affairs, I have always been cautious. But what a goose she is, if she wishes to be confidential and open-hearted with me, to hold back so queerly—Does she not know, I should honour and applaud her present resolution? And is it for me to tap so tender a subject? But Lady Crewe gives breakfasts, & invites poor Fanny to meet even the Princess of Wales[13]—How does she accept such invitations without incurring expence? But never mind—If Raper knows the heaviest part of the <debt> concern, he will watch a little now, I hope, to preserve her from incurring new difficulties. Love to Barrett—and believe me dear Char, affectionately yours—S. H. Burney.

It was I that first brought home the story of Mr Canning & the Portuguese Ambassador[14]—And only think of your having the impudence to make me swallow it again in writing, and in English too, which spoils it—La disette de vivres, sounds much better than scarcity of provisions.—Have you (I forget whether you ever told me) read the Curse of Kahama? I have seen two Reviews of it,[15] & now so well understand what it all seems to be about, I should like mightily to read the whole. Do not forget to tell me where to find the wandering Cherub the first time you write—And write very soon, pray do—I care not in what haste, nor how briefly, so that you do but write, & I will not always bother you with so prosy an answer.—Give a kiss to dear Ju for me, & another to little Hal[16]—

My long established favorite La Trobe called here the other morning. My father, to both our mortifications, would not see him: but he got over his vexation in a little while, & sat with me nearly an hour, & was entertaining, original, good & wise as ever. I was glad I had his book in the house to shew him I [was rea]ding it;[17] & he was pleased.—

I believe I go on Thursday to my Aunt Young. This is Tuesday. <the> Adieu

1. There is no such restless seraph in Milton's *Paradise Lost* or *Paradise Regain'd*, but in *Der Messias* (1748, 1773) by Friedrich Gottlieb Klopstock (1724–1803), the unquiet spirit of Abbadona regrets his role in the rebellion against Jehovah and subsequent fall from heaven.

2. An English translation of Klopstock's poem appeared in 1763, but Sarah seems to have preferred one of several French translations available since 1769.

3. Ten years later, Charlotte would read *Der Messias* in the original. Believing that it had never been rendered into "any meaner language than the German," she proposed to translate it into English herself (CFBt to MF, 20 Sept. [1821], Barrett, Eg. 3706D, ff. 12–13v).

4. Klopstock's *Der Tod Adams* (1757) was also translated into English in 1763; Sarah may have read the Italian translation of Gasparo Gozzi (1796).

5. Brotherton Browne, baptized 27 December 1781, the son of Thomas Gunter and Frances Browne (see n. 7). He joined the East India Company 10 December 1806 at the age of twenty-four and was assigned to the Madras Cavalry. He would resign 21 January 1812 after no further promotions (extract from parish register, St. John Zachary, London; list of *Cadets 1803 to 1806*, India Office Library; Dodwell and Miles, comps., *Alphabetical List of the Officers of the Madras Army* (London: Longman, Orme, Brown, 1838)).

He was actually turning thirty in 1811, but if SHB had met him twelve years before, it may have been in 1798 when she first mentions as an acquaintance his aunt, Emma (née Browne) Keate (L. 19, n. 5).

6. William Locke (1767–1847), eldest son of the arts patron William Locke (1732–1810) of Norbury Park, near Mickleham, Surrey (*DNB*). The Burneys had been acquainted with the Locke family since 1784, when young William was 17 (*HFB*, 183).

7. Frances (fl. 1777–1811), a daughter of bank director Lyde Browne, and sister to SHB's friend, Emma (née Browne) Keate (L. 19, n. 5). In September 1779, Frances Browne had eloped with Lt. Thomas Gunter Browne (1756–1834), later Capt. in the 60th Ft. (1781), who retired on half-pay in 1783. "Fanny Brown is run away—scampered off with a Cornet of Horse," commented Mrs. Thrale. "I hear he is a Gentleman & eminent for personal Beauty, deeply in Debt, a fashionable gay Fellow; probably worthless enough in every Sense of the Word" (*Thraliana*, 1: 222, 507; *EJL*, 3: 356).

Frances Browne's husband appears to have deserted her; by 1800, he was living in France with Anne Greene (c. 1762–1810), who also had a spouse living. FB's impressions of Miss Browne as a "good humoured, gay, Laughing" young woman are given in *EJL*, 3: 305 and passim. She is a more likely identification for the Mrs. Browne who called on Fanny at Chelsea in 1797 "to renew an acquaintance dropt for 16 years!" (*JL*, 3: 276 and n. 2; 7: 358, n. 9; *Westminsters; Alumni Cantab.* under Lyde Browne).

8. The gander-month was the one following a wife's confinement, when "it was held excusable for the husband to err" (in allusion to the gander's aimless wandering while the goose was sitting) (*OED;* Eric Partridge, *A Dictionary of Slang and Unconventional English*, 7th ed. (New York: Macmillan, 1970)). Traditionally, a gander-party would be male, but Charlotte Barrett seems to have attended some festivities in the month after giving birth to her second child (see below n. 16).

9. Fanny (Phillips) Raper appears to have fallen into debt, a situation that had troubled the family earlier, shortly before her marriage. Dr. Burney was reported to have

"settled £1000 on Fanny at his death, & p[d] all her Chelsea Bills . . .—if Phillips does not pay the London Bills. I suppose my poor Father will, rather than break off the Match, for Raper can't" (CBFB to CF, 16 May [1807], Barrett Eg. 3700A, ff. 82–83v). A month later, however, Fanny's affairs were still embarrassed; she then owed £270 which she hoped to discharge by using Dr. Burney's trousseau gift of £100, her father's pledge for £80 and a donation from her uncle Charles of £90.

How her debts were settled in the end is not clear, but it is possible that her own father, Lt.-Col. Phillips, took more responsibility than he has been credited with (*JL*, 5: 325, n. 3). Two years later, Dr. Burney complained of Fanny's defending her "worthless Father" in a "firm and peremptory" manner, and lauded his own generous intentions when "almost raising myself to settle F. Raper's affairs prior to her Marriage" (CB to CB Jr., 20 Oct. 1809, Osborn). His remark suggests that his assistance was not required.

In any case, Charles Raper was informed of his fiancée's financial difficulties at the time; he offered to help her himself, in order to expedite the wedding, and later sent a message of gratitude to Charles Burney Jr. for his aid (FP to CB Jr., 22 June [1807], [26 June 1807], 29 June [1807], Osborn).

10. Sarah Harriet was writing her third novel, the heroine of which was called Adela.

11. The paper is laid, watermarked H W / 1809, possibly manufactured by Henry Williams at Long Wick Mill or Saunderton Mill, Bucks. (Alfred H. Shorter, *Paper Mills and Paper Makers in England, 1495–1800* (Hilversum, Holland: Paper Publications Society, 1957), 130, 268).

12. Fanny appears to have confided in her cousin Charlotte, who had generously offered her help in previous financial difficulties (CBFB to CF, 16 May [1807], Barrett, Eg. 3700A, ff. 82–83v).

13. Caroline Amelia Elizabeth of Brunswick-Wolfenbüttel (1768–1821), consort to the Prince of Wales, then regent, was living apart from her estranged husband.

14. D. Domingos António de Sousa Coutinho (1760–1833), 1st Marquis de Funchal, was the ambassador of Portugal to England when George Canning was Secretary of State for Foreign Affairs (1807–9). The source of the anecdote was probably Johann Christian Hüttner, the protégé of Dr. Burney, who was employed at this time in the Foreign Office.

15. Robert Southey's poem, *The Curse of Kehama*, was published in 1810; of the numerous reviews, SHB might have read the *Monthly Review*, 2nd ser. 65 (1811): 55–69, 113–28, and the *Quarterly Review* 5 (1811): 40–61. Copies of these periodicals were in her father's library (*Misc. Lib.*, 16, 37).

16. "Hal," Henrietta Hester Barrett, Charlotte Barrett's second child, was born 9 April and baptized on 3 May 1811 (CFBt to FBA, 9 May [1828], Berg; IGI; *JL*, 1: lxxiii). After she recovered, Charlotte wrote to her aunt: "I suppose you will think my Henrietta a poor dab, but I mean to forgive that because you are so commendably alive to the merits of her sister. Ju behaves very well & takes people into the nursery to see the baby & then stands behind a chair watching with the most goodhumoured grin all the notice & kisses the baby gets & never minds when nobody speaks to herself" (CFBt to SHB, 17 May [1811], Berg).

17. Christian Ignatius Latrobe was an old friend of Charles Burney's. Of several published works, Sarah may have been reading his *A Concise account of the present state of the Missions established by the . . . United Brethren, among the Heathen* (1811).

Charlotte Barrett by Edward Burney, as published in R. Brimley Johnson, *Fanny Burney and the Burneys* (London, 1926).

60. To Charlotte (Francis) Barrett

[Chelsea College, 1 August 1811]
A.L.S., Berg
Address: Mrs Barrett / Under the Hill / Richmond / Surry
Postmarks: TwoPy[Post] / Unpaid / [Penny Post]
10 o'Clock / 1 AU / 1811 FN∩

I shall post no date to this letter, dearest Char, because I am ashamed you should know that I sit down to write it the very precise instant I have finished reading yours. It looks so like having no other correspondent to my back—and the fact is, I have none on earth I love half so well. I will tell you what, bien aimée; I have a great mind, if it will not plague you to pay for and read the trash, to make a bargain, that without your being obliged to answer more than one out of three, I shall be at liberty to relieve myself by sending you a letter as often as the fancy comes across me. How I must and do love you to dream even of such a proposal is untellable—for I in general detest letter-writing, and delight in letter receiving—from you s'entend.—

I have not read "Self-Controul,"[1] and am determined not to read it, till my own eternal rubbish is concluded. I was a week in the house, at John Street with the two first volumes, but never looked at them. Miss Jardine[2] lent them there. She spent a sociable evening with us, and made me laugh by observing that the book began with a sort of a ravishment that almost enclined her to shut it up after the first forty pages, and never to open it again.[3] Sister Burney likes it; not the ravishment, but the tout ensemble; but thinks the last volume flags.—The accounts flying about of "Thinks I to myself," are amusing to the last degree. May be, if I could get hold of it, I should read that, because it must be so unlike any thing I could clash with, & is so little in the way of a see saw Novel.[4]

Capt. Burney, I am wisely and kindly informed, openly, before all, the young t——ds of the family, calls poor Geraldine,[5] "London Milk & Water"; & the witticism was dispatched to Bath-Easton,[6] & to Richard's[7] &c &c—and Amelia Burney never sees a milk-pot and a kettle together without bursting into one of her constitutional laughs. I hate the fellow for speaking so plainly before these minxes.

I have a great deal more to chat to you about, but before I proceed to my mores, let me pause to tell you how very sincerely I feel for the anxiety you have been in about your little girl. I wish I had been with you, to nurse her, & chear you. Thank you for not sending off your letter till you could tell me she was better. It would break my heart that any thing distressing should happen to the children of a dear little Mother who knows so well how to manage them, & deserves that they should thrive, and be the comforts of her life.

The Keates, my neighbours who have been away four or five months, are come back. The Mother, poor heart, is a discontented dead weight upon her own hands, and every body's else: but I can give you no idea how much Emma, her eldest girl, suits and interests me—and the wonder is great, because our ages are so different, and I love so few modern acquaintances. We walk, whenever we can, tête a tête in our old College Garden, which has the merit of being safe even late in the evening, and snug and clean and airy. I would give much to see the nice girl well married. Her brother[8] is with Lord Wellington's army;[9] he writes to her such long military details as would surprise you, & she enjoys these letters, & I enjoy the <u>bonne</u> <u>amitiè</u> there is between them. She knows every inch of ground of the present seat of war by heart, & is so animated & well-informed on the subject, it is better to talk with her than to read a Gazette. Young Keate is enthousiastically proud of his noble Commander—& in one of his letters calls him—"the Fabius & Camillus of the age."[10] He went out not so partially disposed by any means—but Lord Wellington's great character has made him a zealous convert to his merit.

Sister Burney took the frank step yesterday to write to my father and invite Amelia to come here a few days on account of some painting and whitewashing their bugs are undergoing in the two John Street bed-rooms. The surprise of the thing abated its unpleasantness, and he consented with a tolerable good grace; but through the medium of <u>my</u> pen, which may perhaps not so well please my sister as his own.—This dear daddy is injuring himself, I am more and more persuaded by such close seclusion as he has doomed himself to—he wastes, and enfeebles, I think almost visibly: but he will bear not the slightest representation from any body on the subject—and to fret him would be worse than to see how thin he grows.[11]

I am sitting in such a snug corner of my exquisite bed room as you might almost envy even at Richmond. I see nothing but the tops of the trees and the western sky, though close to the window—and I have tea and bread and butter beside me, & drink a little, & write a little, & then drink again.

I have read some very delightful old books lately (for I now have just attained the wisdom to wish to make use of this ample library,[12] and reject all borrowed or hired books)—Amongst others, two collections of letters, Sevigné's to her daughter,[13] and Bussy Rabutin's to her and various others.[14] The celebrity of these letters makes one ashamed to praise them; it is like saying Shakespear was a clever fellow: but notwithstanding, I will say, that their wit, their facility, their original humour, their arch simplicity, their every possible epistolary merit, surpass even their reputation. Having read a good many French Memoirs of that time, I enjoy the court details, and the scandal and gossip as much as Mde de Grignan could—and the witty stories occasionally inserted, are impayable. Some mad Countess "maintenoit l'autre jour" she, (Sevigné) tells her daughter, "à Madame de Cornuel, que Monsieur un tel n'etoit point fou; elle lui repondit, bonne Comtesse, vous êtes comme les gens qui mangent de l'ail."[15]—Well, and Rabutin de Bussy in his little way, is also delightful. He held during the early part of Louis XIVth's reign a distinguished place at court and in the army, & was in high favour: but he wrote a pa pa book, les Amours des Gaules,[16] in which he unmercifully lampooned half the fine men and women in the Kingdom; he was thrust for a year into the Bastile, and then exiled to his estate in Burgogne. He had children he loved, and mental resources, and courage & philosophy, & so he jogged on many years in his retirement pretty happily. But on every public occasion, such as the breaking out of a war, the gain of a battle &c, he wrote direct to the King—and he sends Mde de Sevigné, who was his Cousin, copies of these letters, the most difficult to write, yet the most admi[*r*]ably written of any it is possible to imagine. The King never failed to read and re-read them; and my belief is, they retarded his recall, so well were they relished, & so desirous was he to receive more. It was a bright period for french intellects—Oh, how superior to the bright period of the Encyclopedists. At the time I am reading of, lived & wrote, Moliere, Corneille, Racine, la Rochfaucault, Boilleau[17] celebrated Divines a million, and who were really good Christians; & Sevigné, and all her witty cluster of friends—and no jargon, & no frippery, & false philosophy among them—but sterling stuff, too good almost to be French. Now I have given you a dose of the French, I have half a mind to give you about as long a one of the Greeks. I have been steadily & delightedly reading Mitford's History.[18] First of all, he is an Historian after my own heart, & I really believe a perfectly upright & honest man. He suffers not himself to be dazzled by the splendid qualities of the people he writes about—but, by turns, causes either an enthousiastic admiration of their magnanimity, or a just horror of their atrocity. <I believe I ought to put in *3 words*—I will look, when I have done my critique, in Entick.>[19] Individually they were the most glorious creatures, God ever permitted to shine upon earth—Collectively, they were infernal: and I take it, as good and honourable Mitford says, it was owing to their faulty religous & political institutions. But certainly the merit of this history is great, in proving, that bad as the world is now, even under Christian regulations., it is not nationally any where so bad as it was in Pagan Greece—except during the height and fury of the French Revolution—and still, and ever perhaps in Turkey. But left to his own Light of Nature, to his own groping stupid notions of futurity, Good Lord! what a diabolical beast is man![20] Blood, and the sufferings of others, and oppression, and a total senselessness of justice seem to be <their> his delight.—At all events, though I am sorry not to be as pretty as a Greek girl, I am mighty glad to be a Christened English dowdy. But with humiliation I now recollect that some of us christened dowdies, when we have the absolute command of an establishment of slaves in the West Indies, can be almost as infernal as the Spartans to their Helots.[21] Absolute power I fear will always be murder to the morality of vain, and selfish human creatures.

I am just come in from a delightful strole with my pretty young companion. Youth and prettiness, associated with sense and good manners, & symptoms of a heart, are mighty fascinating things. I long to be a Sultan, and to collect a troop of such favorites around me, who should think it no degradation, & whom I would honour & render happier than the inhabitants of any <former> previous Seraglio.—

Voila bien des fagotages, as M^de^ de Sevigné says[22]—but they have amused me to write, and at worst will not take you very long to read. Have you seen the little book, "Cottage dialogues," by Mrs Leadbeater? Edgeworths notes[23] are lively and nationationally [*nationally*] characteristic as ever: but I own, I tired a little of the receipts to make cheap dishes. Without half so much ceremony & fuss and trouble, I had rather dine upon that cheap dish, an egg boiled in the shell—or a good mess of gruel and onions.—My love to Barrett—When he likes to have me a day or two at Richmond, whisper to him to put on his seven league boots, & come here to walk with me to you & dear babes. How are the excellent Cambridges?[24]

Ever yours my dearest Char:
S. H. B.

1. *Self-control* (1811) was the successful first work of the Scottish novelist, [Mary Brunton (1778–1818) (*DNB*)], of which the third edition was soon to be advertised (*Times*, 10 Sept. 1811). Charlotte had praised it in her letter of 17 May: "I read Self Countroul & like it extremely all except some vulgarity meant to be jocular which tired me to death. but I think the principal character charming & well supported & the book really gives good lessons" (CFBt to SHB, 17 May [1811], Berg).

2. Joanne Jardine (c. 1769–1830), daughter of Lt.-Col. Alexander Jardine (d. 1799) of the Royal Invalid Artillery, whom Sarah knew from Chelsea Hospital (*DNB; JL*, 1: 70, n. 16; 11: 372, n. 7; *GM*, 100, Pt. 1 (1830): 284).

3. In the first forty pages of *Self-control* occur the attempted seduction of the heroine by Colonel Hargrave, followed by his proposal and rejection. These incidents lay the groundwork for his passionate pursuit throughout the remaining two volumes.

4. [Edward Nares (1762–1841)], *Think's-I-to-Myself. A serio-ludicro, tragico-comico tale, written by Think's-I-to-Myself Who?* (1811), was enormously successful, running through eight editions by 1812. A refreshing satire, "laughing with good humour at the follies and absurdities of the day," it was very different from the kind of novel that Sarah Harriet was writing (*DNB; GM*, 81, Pt. 2 (1811): 355–57; *British Critic* 38 (1811): 170–76).

5. Geraldine, the heroine of Sarah's second novel, *Geraldine Fauconberg* (1808).

6. The widowed Maria (Burney) Bourdois and her sister Sophia were living at Batheaston (*JL*, 6: 618, n. 1; 7: 25, n. 4; "Worcester Mem.," 57).

7. Richard Allen Burney, Rector of Rimpton, Somerset.

8. William Augustus Keate (d. 23 Nov. 1850) was with the Scots Fusilier Guards, of which he was Ens. (29 Aug. 1800), Capt. (24 May 1804), Lt.-Col. (9 Aug. 1813) and Col. (15 Sept. 1825). He served on the Peninsula from December 1808 to January 1813, including the passage of the Douro, the battle of Busaco, the sieges of Ciudad Rodrigo, the battle of Salamanca, and the siege of Burgos. For his service, he received the war medal with three clasps (*Army List* (1800–25); *Hart's Army List* (1841); *GM*, NS 35 (1851): 326).

9. Lt.-Gen. Arthur Wellesley (1769–1852), created 1st Viscount (1809) and later 1st Duke of Wellington (1814), was commanding the British troops against the French on the Iberian peninsula.

10. Two celebrated Roman generals: Marcus Furius Camillus, who saved Rome from the Gauls in the fourth century B.C.; and Quintus Fabius Maximus, who defended Rome against Hannibal in the Second Punic War (218–201 B.C.).

11. The last years of Dr. Burney's life were marked by his withdrawal from society into a sometimes gloomy seclusion; his state of mind could be rather morbid when subject to "the foul fiend Hypochondria." On her return from France in 1812, Mme d'Arblay found him much changed: "he now admits scarcely a Creature but of his Family, & will only see for a short time even his Children. He likes quietly reading, & lies almost constantly upon the sofa, & will NEVER eat but alone!" She tried to persuade him to allow the family to cheer his solitude, without success. Years later, she would recall the "gloomy retirement & seclusion into which that dear Father fell, & which embittered & harrassed & depressed many *years* of . . . [his] existence" (Lonsdale, 469–75; CB to Edmond Malone, 18 Dec. [1806], Bodleian MS. Malone 38, ff. 159–60; *JL*, 7: 11, 79–80; 11: 304).

12. Dr. Burney was very proud of his fine library, consisting of musical and nonmusical works, which netted a total of £2,353.19s. when sold after his death. In 1791 he began to make a catalogue of his collection, which he claimed contained upwards of twenty thousand volumes, a boast that was so much at variance with the list made for the sale, that Mme d'Arblay suspected foul play (Scholes, 2: 273–74; CB to Richard Cox, [28 Nov. 1791], Osborn; *JL*, 7: 326, n. 10, 505–6).

When trying to determine which books were available to Sarah in "this ample library," one must remember that Dr. Burney left a bookcase of French books to SHB and Mrs. Raper, whose titles would not appear in the auction catalogue of miscellaneous books (Scholes, 2: 268).

13. Marie (née de Rabutin-Chantal), marquise de Sévigné (1626–96). Her letters to

her daughter, Françoise-Marguerite (1646–1705), who married in 1669 the comte de Grignan and moved with him to Provence, were first published in 1725.

Which edition was in Charles Burney's library is unclear: the catalogue lists 7 volumes, published in 1738 and 1763 (*Misc. Lib.*, 50); however, the edition published in Paris in 1738 was in 6 volumes, and 8 volumes came out in 1763. Possibly CB's set was an amalgamation of the two, which had been depleted through loss or lending.

14. The letters of Roger de Rabutin, comte de Bussy (1618–93), cousin to Mme de Sévigné, were first published in 1697. Charles Burney owned 6 volumes, printed in 1700 (*Misc. Lib.*, 44).

15. Anne-Marie Cornuel (née Bigot) (1605–94) was renowned for her "bons mots." This one is recounted in a letter of 6 May [1676] in Mme de Sévigné, *Correspondance*, vol. 2, ed. Roger Duchêne (Paris: Gallimard, 1974), 286.

16. Comte de Bussy's *Histoire amoureuse des Gaules* was published in 1665.

17. The three French playwrights, "Molière," Jean-Baptiste Poquelin (1622–73), Pierre Corneille (1606–84), and Jean Racine (1639–99), and the writers François, duc de La Rochefoucauld (1613–80), and Nicolas Boileau-Despréaux (1636–1711).

Of these authors, Dr. Burney owned a two-volume edition of the *Oeuvres de Racine* (1736), a translation of La Rochefoucauld's *Moral Reflexions and Maxims* of 1706, and Boileau-Despréaux, *Oeuvres*, published in 1746 (*Misc. Lib.*, 8, 44, 45).

18. William Mitford (1744–1827), *The History of Greece*, 5 vols., 1784–[1818].

19. There are several reference works by the schoolmaster, John Entick (c. 1703–73), which Sarah might have wished to consult, including *The Present State of the British Empire* (1774) and the *History and Survey of London, Westminster, Southwark, and Places adjacent* (1766), a copy of which was in her father's library (*Misc. Lib.*, 17).

20. Perhaps a conscious inversion of Hamlet's famous words, "What a piece of work is a man! / how noble in reason!" (*Hamlet*, II, ii, 304–5).

21. The militaristic state of Sparta employed subjugated populations as slaves.

22. A characteristic phrase of Mme de Sévigné, who uses it, for instance (on 9 Sept. [1675]), to refer to "tout le fagotage de bagatelles" which fill her letters (Sévigné, 2: 95).

23. Novelist Maria Edgeworth (1767–1849) contributed notes and a preface to *Cottage Dialogues among the Irish Peasantry* (1811), by Mary Leadbeater (1758–1826).

24. The Rev. George Owen Cambridge (1756–1841), Prebendary of Ely (1795) and Archdeacon of Middlesex (1806), and his wife Cornelia (née Kuyck van Mierop) (c. 1768–1858), whom he had married 13 Jan. 1795 (*Alumni Oxon.*; *GM*, 65, Pt. 1 (1795): 81; NS 16 (1841): 214; "Appendix," *AR*, 100 (1858): 384; *JL*, 1: 2, n. 6; 4: 269, n. 5).

Once an admirer of SHB's half-sister, Fanny, he lived within walking distance of the Barretts over Richmond Bridge at "Meadowbank," a house that he had built in the grounds of his father's estate at Twickenham Meadows; see Borough of Twickenham Local History Society, *Twickenham, 1660–1900* (Twickenham: Twickenham Local History Society, 1981), 5–6; *JL*, 6: 712, n. 32; 8: 288, n. 7; *HFB*, 187–93).

61. To Charlotte (Francis) Barrett

[Chelsea College, 14–15 August 1811][1]
A.L.S., Berg
Address: Mrs Barrett / Under the Hill / Richmond / Surry
Postmarks: 7 o'Clock / 15 AU / 1811 NT

Wednesday 13th August.

I reckoned, my dearest Charlotte, without my Host, when so flippantly proposing myself to pay you a visit: and my disappointment now is proportioned to the sanguine hopes your kind letter excited. Imagine that during this last week, m[y] father has been quite in a fidget to know how to dispose [of me] whilst his bed was taken down, and he came into my room. Several schemes were started. I was to go to your Mother's: but a letter came to say she was herself setting out for Suffolk.[2] John Street was mentioned; but having already been there some days this summer, I was unwilling to invite myself <there> again,[3] and shewed a reluctance so to do, which being understood, my father proposed paying my board. This I knew would mortally offend my sister; so it was at last determined, I should ask our neighbour Mrs Keate to let me sleep a few nights at her house. To this she agreed; and to-day comes your letter, which I was fool enough to let my father perceive I was delighted with, and which I really thought he would be delighted with too:—But no; a little of the perverseness of 86[4] made him consider it as an untimely deranger of all "our <plays"> plans"—(I have no plans, Heaven knows with which it does not tally to perfection)—And in short, he grumbled so much at my preferring it to the scheme that had been settled "so comfortably" with Mrs Keate (whom, by the way, he hates), and wondered so much at my fickleness and caprice, that I told him I would give up the plan, & came out of his room quite sick. And so are the Maids—for they long to get me out of the house that they may take down and wash my bed too, after its having been stationary three years. But the dessous des cartes I verily believe is, that a nasty evening newspaper which that beast Lady Crewe took it into her head to persuade him to take, he makes me [read] aloud every evening, & he does not like me to leave home [for f]ear I should escape the sickening dose. I have talked to Becky,[5] <housekeeper,> and she who wants to get shoot of me as much as I want to be got shooted of, will try whether, for domestic reasons, she cannot bring him to a better way of thinking.—Till I know the result of her interference, I will keep this open.

Thursday Morning.

The result is unsatisfactory in the extreme. There is no arguing the point, but think how grievous to me it is to hear the two plans, that of sleeping at Keate's or coming to you, weighed in the mere scale of expediency. "The Keates' are the nearest, and you can be at home all day, and they have chearfully consented to admit you—and why should you wish a change?" To any one who can ask such a question, I deem it useless to make any answer. My dear father would not have dreamt of asking it some years ago; but matters of sentiment fade prodigeously in <their> his estimation now, and every thing is referred to convenience or interest.—He told me last night in a pet, that if I had set my heart upon the Richmond jaunt, he would not oppose it:—"I never set my heart upon any thing, Sir."—"That's a bold word!"—But in truth, it is almost a sincere one; though in cases where you are concerned, less so than any others. I should so have loved to have been with you and your dear babies, and to have enjoyed some lovely walks with Barrett and you, and to have inhabited the chearful garrett facing the river! And pray tell Barrett how very very kind I think it of him to have proposed to fetch me. I am sure he must like me, or he never could have meditated so good nature[d] an effort. Helas! How sorry I am that all these pleasure[s must] be exchanged for the ceaseless contradictions of "credible reports["] in one paper on purpose to make a refuting paragraph for the next. Mais il faut se soumêttre—And now I have shot my bolt, and told you all, I hope I shall submit with steady goodhumour. The moment I feel tempted to meditate too intensely on the subject, I snatch up a book—"Come dear mute companion of my life" I cry, "come and drive away care and regret for the breathing companions of whom I am deprived!"—

I have been frightened from taking up Hannah More's last book which Fanny lent me, by the dread that it would more than ever convince me what a worthless wretch I am without giving me the courage and virtue to become better. But last night, wanting to compose my wayward spirit, I ventured to open it, and read the first Chapter on Internal Christianity—And was agreeably surprised to find myself much pleased with it.[6]—I have finished all dear old Sevignés letters, and since then read Anquetils' "Louis XIV, Sa Cour, et le Regent."[7]—A most admirably entertaining work, in four moderate little volumes. He tells a story of le Regent truly characteristic—He was obliged to pass a few days in the country which he hated, & the people round him perceiving his ennui, proposed une partie de chasse—"Non, je n'aime pas la chasse"—A game at billiards—"Non, je n'aime pas le billiard"—Une lecture amusante—"Non, je n'aime pas la lecture." Then what should they do?—Why nothing—for to own the truth, he had no pleasure in innocent amusements. [His] words were—

"Je n'aime point les plaisirs innocents!"[8]—[The] laughable though desperate profligacy of this answer, makes me shout. James and his wife and Sally are at Ride in the Isle of Wight. She bore the fatigue of the journey very well. When I saw her last, there seemed none of the glare of internal fever in her eyes, and I thought she had upon the whole a promising look of approaching convalescence.[9]—Adieu dearest of Charlottes. With your two babes, and your hubby to attend to, and a thousand cares old maids know nothing about, I shall never be troublesome about exacting as long letters from you as my own—but I like to chat to you, & will whenever I have a mind. Adieu again—Love to l'ami Barrett, & am ever yours S. H. Burney

The politics seem changed again, and perhaps one out of the three days mentioned by dear Barrett I may be allowed to come—but I will write again—Hearing that my bed wants taking down has affected this change—How glad I shall be to be at a certainty.

1. SHB's date of "Wednesday 13th August" must be an error. Postmarked 15 August 1811 (a Thursday), the letter, if begun on the Wednesday, and continued on the Thursday, should be dated 14–15 August 1811.

2. Charlotte Broome was going to Bradfield Hall to visit Arthur Young with whom she had renewed acquaintance the previous year. Her daughter, Marianne, who joined her there early in September, reported they were both "enjoying the fresh air," and their visit was prolonged until mid-October. Thus began the warm friendship between Marianne Francis and the evangelical Young, which brightened the last years of his life (MF to HLTP, 22 Aug. 1811, 8 Sept. 1811, 24 Sept. 1811, 18 Oct. 1811, John Rylands; CBFB & MF to CFBt & Ralph Broome Jr., 12 Sept. 1811, 4 Oct. 1811, Berg; Gazley, 588–89 and passim).

3. SHB had visited Esther for a few days c. July (see above L. 60).

4. Born on 7 April (Old Style) 1726 (Lonsdale, 2), Charles Burney was actually eighty-five.

5. Rebecca More (fl. 1794–1819), Charles Burney's cook and later housekeeper. Sister to his former housekeeper, Mary More (L. 18), she was remembered in his will as "my Cook, who has served me with probity and diligence eleven [altered to '13'] years" (Scholes, 2: 263; *JL*, 5: 216, n. 1; 11: 142, n. 13).

6. Hannah More (1745–1833), *Practical Piety*, 2 vols. (London: T. Cadell and W. Davies, 1811). The first chapter "Christianity on Internal Principle" (1: 1–26) presents Christianity as "*The Religion of the heart*" (11). Perhaps Sarah took courage from More's view that the Christian need not despair over his imperfections; the sincere believer experiences a change of heart by which he is "transformed into the image of God" (3).

7. The work of the French historian, Louis-Pierre Anquetil (1723–1806), *Louis XIV, sa cour et le Régent*, was published in 4 volumes in 1789; Charles Burney owned a copy (*Misc. Lib.*, 2).

8. The passage would also be cited in SHB's novel, *Traits of Nature* (London: Henry Colburn, 1812), 4: 242, but the source has not been found.

9. James's wife, Sarah (Payne) Burney, was suffering from a very serious illness in the summer of 1811 but recovered after her stay on the Isle of Wight. James had taken his family there at least once before, in 1803. Their vacation was amusingly described in a joint letter with Charles Lamb, who accompanied him (Manwaring, 242, 218–21; *The Letters of Charles and Mary Anne Lamb*, ed. Edwin W. Marrs Jr., 3 vols. (Ithaca: Cornell University Press, 1975–78), 2: 121–22; 3: 77).

62. To Charlotte (Francis) Barrett

[Chelsea College, 4 October 1811][1]
A.L.S., Berg
Address: Mrs Barrett / Richmond / Surry
Postmarks: 4 o'Clock / OC 5 / 1811 EV
[12] o'Clock / 5 OC / 1811 N∩

My dearest Charlotte

I have just finished off a noble long rigmarole to Anna Wilbraham, to whom I was doubly in debt, and now, to make clear scores with my conscience, <sit> make use of the same pen to chirp (I like that word past expression) a little with you, in return for your last kind dispatch. I saw Fanny the day before yesterday—She perseveres in her agreeable literary frolic, but not at a very rapid rate—However, after admiring her noble constancy, I gave her the two or three chapters I had atchieved, and promised to furnish others if she could give me any good reasons for thinking it profitable.[2] Meanwhile, the second and third volumes are both in her custody; so if your Hugès man (as Dolf calls him)[3] should want them, apply in that quarter. I am sorry for the ink pye I have made underneath. [*There are two big ink-blots on the page.*] My writing-stand has just been replenished, being that it was mouldy, like poor Pacherotti's liver,[4] when I came home—and I now exercise my pen in Adela's service pretty regularly every evening. Morn[ings] I am forced, for the good of my internal and external body, to devote to walking & working.—I am also reading with great veneration, but some degree of despondency, Practical Piety. The Chapter on "Comparatively small Faults and Virtues" merits to be written in letters of gold, and comes home to the feelings with an aptness and force not to be resisted or described. All she says on Prayer, though but a new modification of her former sentiments delivered on this subject, is touching and beautiful:—in short, the first volume, which I have just finished, edifies and charms me.[5]—I have opened no other book, save the Monthly Review and Appendix[6] since I came home: my duds, as you honourably denominate them, being in woeful want of repairing and reinstating previous to the arrival of dreaded winter.—Richard Burney is to be married the tenth of this month.[7] Blue is now, or will shortly be paying a little visit to Maria Bourdois. She gives as a reason, her dislike to being present at any weddings.[8] Fanny[9] is at the sea with a neighbour of Richard's. James has been here once or twice since he came back to town[10]—I think he is looking remarkably well, with his little bit of honest sun burn.—As civil speeches from whatever quarter they proceed, always find their way at last to the ears of him or her of whom they were spoken—I was lately told, though not by Fanny, that when Marianne and Clement, after their walk to Richmond, stopt at Stanley Place,[11] Fanny said, "Aunt Sally is now with Charlotte, is'n't she? How does she do?"—"Oh, very well," cried Marianne, "and very pleasant and chatty, in her little way!"[12]—Ha, ha, ha!—

A book that I am sure would amuse Barrett, and perhaps you also, very much, is Jouhaud's Paris dans le dixneuvième Siecle. The account of it made me extremely desirous to see it.[13] There are in it descriptions of the present Parisien world—the state of Religion, of society, of amusements, of schools, fashions &c, &c—And all appears fairly done, and in a manly unaffected manner. pâté le 3eme [*A little hand points to an ink blot.*] I should like also excessively to see Catteau's Voyage en Allemagne et Suede.[14] The little I read about it, has made me so fond of the Swedes! Not the Swedish nobles, but the tiers état; the farmers, landholders, and peasantry: they resemble the Swiss at their best; but appear still more carefully educated at their provincial schools, and are quite dear things.

Pâté le second! [*A little hand points to another ink blot.*]—The deuce is in my over-stocked inkstand—I cannot apply to it the line in Grongar Hill—"Without o'erflowing, full".[15]—

I have largely profitted by your slight and too cautious hints for my old Ad:—Julius no longer gashes the dog's ear, but throws the scissars passionately at Amy when he sees her approaching to take them away,—and they fall by accident upon Frisk, who is wounded by their sharp points.[16] This is not so Zelucoish,[17] and yet answers my purpose of describing a spoilt, vehement brat.

7 o'clock, Friday. Here comes your letter. Let's see what is chantes.—I have read it.—Some part was answered before hand—other parts I will answer now. About Madam Young shewing off her shapes by the Cook's pattern, I remember she once about 12 years ago, confronted her legs to me by the housemaid's pattern, and was in a rage at the difference—Hers, she said so thin, the Suffolk Wenche's so well en embonpoint. But never mind her: let us talk of Eugenie

and Matilde.[18] It saddened, but did not make me cry. I foresaw it would end like a Turk, nay, I am not sure I did not peep, for I cannot bear to be gradually worked up into an agony by those dismal stories. It has not left upon my mind a strong impression of liking, and as long as I live shall I never desire to look into it again. But that is because of its melancholy cast, not because it is either dull or ill written. On the contrary, to those who have not the same objection with myself to hippish and mournful stories, it would be a treasure. I highly disapprove, however, the frequent insinuations thrown out, leading to a suspicion that Ladislaus means to commit suicide after losing his mistress—You are at last left in doubt whether he dispatches himself or not,[19] and the Author throws no condemnation on his impatience under suffering.—The name of the young man who wrote the Novel I spoke to Barrett and you about (Frederick de Montford) is Goldburne.[20] He is a spenthrift, and perhaps a bit of a rip—I never saw him, but Emma says he is inexpressibly entertaining, & knows every body, and keeps her and her mother in convulsions of laughter when he goes to see them. I mean to ask her to lend me his book. He gave her a copy of it. She does not much like it, but for the sake of her knowing the Author I will read it. A Dr Something, an Army Physician, just returned from Portugal, dined with the Keates lately. Amongst innumerable traits he recounted to them concerning Lord Wellington, he mentioned that at their messes, when the Officers are drinking their Commander's health, they always add to it that of his Nurse Dolly. Now, Nurse Dolly is an Irish Woman who brought him up, and when he went on this expedition would accompany him, & takes care of his tent, washes his linen, and when he comes back to <the Cam> his quarters at night harrassed to death, has always something comfortable ready for him, & they say has more than once been the means of preserving his life. She is adored in the Camp. Is not this like the Irish Nurse in Ennui?[21] Emma told me when I said so, that it had struck her directly. Well, and further, they say that whilst the Commissary General is eating off plate, Ld W. eats off Queen's ware[22]—and that two mules are able to carry all his luggage. Do you like to hear about him? If you do, I will send you more some day—He is my idol and hero, but I am not sure whether you care for him—I hope however you do, for he is a fine creature.

I wanted to have sent you a translation of the Epigram Flahault has introduced in her book. It is Johnson's, and inserted in Piozzi's anecdotes[23]—but my father has lent, & lost (often synonymous terms) his copy of that work, & I cannot immediately think of any body to apply to. There are no bookish people here—on the contrary, they seem to me to look with an evil eye on every reader of every production save a Newspaper. I am scandalized at Sal's[24] fal-lal taste in the literary way—only, but don't tell her, when I was a girl, I read as much such trash as most folks, mixed with a little French dramatic composition, & poetry whenever I could get hold of it. She ought by this time to like Pope's Homer[25]—try to persuade her of it, and make her take to the best periodical papers, and get Shakespear by heart & like Moliere, & something in short besides Sir Henry, and Seraphina,[26] & a parcel of stuff only good to put money in the writer's pocket. Adieu dearest own Char: kind love to l'Ami Barrett. Y[rs] ever S. H. Burney.

If my paper w[d] but have stretched, I had more to say. Pray give my respects to M[rs] Gundry[27] & M[rs] Baker,[28] my two prime Richmond favorites. Can't write to dear Clem.—

1. As the letter is postmarked 5 October 1811 (a Saturday), the Friday on which SHB writes was probably 4 October.

2. Sarah Harriet, at work on her third novel, was apparently inviting criticism from family and friends, which perhaps reflects a diffidence about her own literary judgment and abilities. She had submitted the manuscript for correction to Fanny Raper who may have considered herself a competent literary critic; Mrs. Raper would publish anonymously *Observations on Works of Fiction in General, and particularly those for Childhood and Adolescence* (1813), as well as a work of fiction (L. 75, n. 6).

3. Charlotte's half-brother, Ralph ("Dolf") Broome, aged ten, may have been referring to her husband, Henry Barrett, who was formed on a "fine large scale" (MF to CFBt, [1809], Barrett, Eg. 3704A, ff. 3–5v).

4. Gasparo Pacchiarotti (1740–1821), the Italian soprano castrato, who had met the Burney family in November 1778 during his first season in London. He left England in 1784, and returned for his last visit in 1791. Dr. Burney makes no mention of his liver problems, but reports, "He is not gifted with a very robust constitution" (*New Grove; EJL*, 3: 182–84; Charles Burney, *A General History of Music from the Earliest Ages to the Present Period*, vol. 4 (London: Payne and Son, 1789), 512).

5. Sarah first mentions reading Hannah More's *Practical Piety* in her letter of 14 August 1811 (L. 61). The chapter "On the comparatively small Faults and Virtues" is the last in the first volume (Ch. 11); "Prayer" is Ch. 5.

6. Charles Burney owned copies of the *Monthly Review* (1749–1814) (*Misc. Lib.*, 37).

7. SHB's nephew, Richard Allen Burney, Rector of Rimpton, Somerset (L. 35, n. 8), would marry on 10 October 1811 Elizabeth Layton Williams (1786–1862) (*JL*, 7: 29, n. 9; *GM*, 81, Pt. 2 (1811): 482).

8. "Blue" was Sarah's cousin, Elizabeth Warren Burney, a spinster (which may account for her aversion to weddings). She had been keeping Richard's house since his move to the Rimpton rectory in 1802. At the time of his marriage, she "took this opportunity of visiting her friends" at Bath Easton and Worcester. However, she would return to her nephew and remain under his protection to the end of her life ("Worcester Mem.," 55, 59–60, 83, 92, 95–96).

9. Sarah's niece, Fanny Burney.

10. James had been on the Isle of Wight with his daughter and convalescent wife (see above L. 61).

11. Stanley House and Stanley Grove, named after the former owner of the property, Sir Robert Stanley, stood at the northwest extremity of Chelsea parish. SHB's niece, Fanny Raper, lived nearby (*Survey of London*, 4: 43–44; W. W. Hutchings, *London Town Past & Present* (London: Cassell, 1900), 3: 804).

12. A certain amount of ambivalence is sometimes evident in the relations between Sarah Harriet and her niece Marianne Francis, whom she called the "Moll of all Molls" (L. 99). An example of a lefthanded compliment on Marianne's side is her remark to Charlotte Barrett that "Sally was more amusing & pleasant the day we were at Chelsea than I ever remember her" (MF to CFBt, 27 June [1808], Barrett Eg. 3704A, ff. 27–28v).

13. Pierre Jouhaud, *Paris dans le dix-neuvième siècle, ou Réflexions d'un observateur sur les nouvelles institutions, les embellissemens, l'esprit public, la société* (1809). Sarah may have read her father's copy of the *Monthly Review*, 2nd ser. 65 (1811): 484–93, which discussed the work in some detail, giving the titles of every chapter and summarizing or quoting from many.

14. Jean-Pierre-Guillaume Catteau-Calleville (1759–1819), French historian and geographer, published his *Voyage en Allemagne et en Suède* in 3 volumes in 1810. In the same issue of the *Monthly Review* (n. 13 above), 527–37, is a review of this work in which a long passage about the Swedish peasants is quoted (533–34).

15. The lines are not in fact taken from John Dyer's "Grongar Hill" (1726) but from Sir John Denham, *Cooper's Hill* (1642). Closing the four-line apostrophe to the Thames added into the 1655 edition (ll. 189–92), they were the most famous lines the poet ever wrote.

16. The scene, revised as described, occurs at the beginning of Sarah's novel *Traits of Nature* (London: Henry Colburn, 1812), 1: 46–52. It gives the reader his first view of Adela's brother, Julius Cleveland, and shows how the boy's character has been spoiled by his father's fond partiality.

17. The protagonist of [John Moore's] novel, *Zeluco* (1789) is a Sicilian nobleman brought up without restraint who follows evil courses.

18. [Adélaïde-Marie-Émilie (née Filleul), comtesse de Flahaut, later marquise de Souza-Botelho (1761–1836)] published *Eugénie et Mathilde* in 1811. The novel follows the fortunes of an émigré family as their troubles close around them. It ends with the death of Eugénie, a young nun whose order was disbanded, and who endured an enervating conflict between love and obedience to her vows.

19. Ladislaus, the admirer of Eugénie, frequently vows he will not survive her death; her last moments are filled with anguish about his fate, left indeterminate at the novel's end.

20. Edward Goulburn (1787–1868) published his novel *Frederick de Montford* anonymously in 1811 (advertised in the *Times*, 9, 10, 20 Sept. 1811). Having satirized some of his fellow officers in a poem, *The Blueviad* (1805), he withdrew from the army and entered the profession of law, in which his rise was owing largely to his brother's influence. After sitting briefly in parliament (1835–37), he was appointed a commissioner of the court of bankruptcy (1842) (*DNB*).

21. Ellinor, the old Irish nurse in Maria Edgeworth's "Ennui," vol. 1 of *Tales of Fash-*

ionable Life (1809), was supposedly patterned after the author's own (Marilyn Butler, *Maria Edgeworth* (Oxford: Clarendon Press, 1972), 249).

22. The story reflects Lord Wellington's well-known austerity, as "Queen's Ware" was a popular and relatively inexpensive creamware created by Josiah Wedgwood (Arthur Bryant, *The Great Duke or the Invincible General* (London: Collins, 1971), 85; Wolf Mankowitz, *Wedgwood*, 2nd ed. (London: Spring Books, 1966), 45–46).

23. Hester Lynch Piozzi, *Anecdotes of the late Samuel Johnson, LL.D., during the last twenty years of his life* (1786).

24. James Burney's fourteen-year-old daughter, Sarah, was attending Mrs. Budd's school at Richmond near Charlotte Barrett, and occasionally visited her aunt (CFBt to HBt, 19 June [1810], Berg).

25. The poet Alexander Pope (1688–1744) had collaborated in translating *The Odyssey of Homer* in 1725–26, but SHB was probably referring to his translation of *The Iliad of Homer* (1715–20), which had become standard.

26. Possibly the *History of Sir Henry Clarendon* (1785) and Caroline Burney's *Seraphina; or, a Winter in Town* (1809).

27. Probably Emma Clay (c. 1767–1824), daughter of a director of the Bank of England, Richard Clay; she had married on 23 December 1794 as his second wife Nathaniel Gundry (c. 1747–1830). Son of the M.P. and judge, Sir Nathaniel Gundry (1701–54), her husband had sold the lease of his paternal estate at Uddens, Dorsetshire, and was apparently living at Richmond (*DNB;* Namier & Brooke; *GM*, 45 (1775): 254; 61, Pt. 1 (1791): 282; 64, Pt. 2 (1794): 1149; 94, Pt. 1 (1824): 476; 100, Pt. 2 (1830): 93; W. G. C. Gundry, comp., Index of the Name Gundry, TS, 1929, Society of Genealogists, 219).

28. Sarah Baker (c. 1744–1835), known to the Burneys since 1784, was living at Richmond in a house owned by Charlotte's friend, the Archdeacon George Cambridge (*JL*, 1: 81, n. 6).

---

63. To Charlotte (Francis) Barrett

[Chelsea College, [c. 16] October [1811][1]
A.L.S., Berg
Address: Mrs Barrett / Richmond / Surry

Friday—lovely Octr Weather.

Behold Charlotte, my love, I send you a little fusty old book about English money, which, my father, having heard me say you were once a collector or collectrice of coins, is persuaded you will like to study; and you must assure him he was not mistaken when you return it; and you must neither return it too quick, nor be too tardy in its restoration; (It is <u>your</u> business to hit the right medium)—and you must thank him as if he had sent you a dowry for Julia, and a title and estate for yourself. So much for my friend Nummi.[2] Cheek by jowl, I send with him the Archdeacon's borrowed book about the Moravians,[3] and the cash I was forced to borrow of you and Barrett, when, tho' poor as a rat, you made me as happy as a Queen at blessed old Richmond. I touched the ready from Coutt's[4] only two days ago, and am paying it all away as fast as ever I can. Let me know exactly what I left owing at Allen's,[5] and if it is not a great, great, deal, perhaps he may come in for snacks.

I dare say you want to hear about Adela. I am sure it is a shame if you don't. "Well, my dear,—I remember it was about autumn,—the hottest weather that was ever known—I am sure I shall never forget it—heigh ho!—And as I was saying, I had left the Barretts about a week—heigh ho!—when I went to work with a fury surpassing all belief—I'm sure the maids must have thought me crazy."—The truth is, I have fagged very hard this fortnight or three weeks past—and what do you think is the consequence? Why I see daylight through the intricacies of my story with a clearness that now makes my path quite plain, and almost easy; I have exactly settled how it is all to terminate, and how every one is to have son pacquet,—that is to <may> say, is to have his or her little bit of poetical justice dealt <him> out. <to>—all but that spiteful toad Jemima. How shall I punish her?[6] Do think of something ludicrously mortifying for her, and let me send forth into the world at once the pickings of your brain, and the scrapings of my own. I have had two good long evening readings of the stuff with Emma Keate, whose hints, though too sparing, are sensible and truly useful.—She tells me, by the way, that in a second edition of "Thinks I to myself" the Author has inserted an additional scene.[7] That nasty little ricketty boy of Mrs Fidget's who frightened the bird, is to recite, during a morning visit, some fables and a speech or two from Shakespear. His mother vaunts his memory and intelligence, but owns he has one unfortunate disqualification for oratory which she is very solicitous to conquer—He cannot readily pronounce the letter R. For that reason, she selects passages that shall oblige him frequently to repeat it, and habit, she thinks, may enable him at last to do it with ease. He is to begin by King Lear's address to the Storm[8]—His Mamma and his sister sitting by to prompt him—

Child.—Blow, winds, and cack your cheeks" . . .

Mamma and Miss (in the same breath)—Crack, my dear, not Cack—

I never heard such a word!—Say it again—say Crrrack.'—

Child.—Blow, winds, and cwack your cheeks . . .

Mamma.—Thats wrong again!—not cwack—but crack.—Come try once more.

Child.—Blow, winds, and cvack your cheeks . . .
Mamma.—Well, that's better—but not quite the thing.—Now go on—
Child.—And Cvack your cheeks! Wage, blow, you catawacts, and huwicanoes . . .
Mamma.—Oh, shocking! You're incorrigible child—

And so it goes on most ridiculously, not only through this speech, but through part of Gay's first fable "Remote from cities" &c, and two or three other things, all murdered as inhumanly.[9] Emma tells it with great humour.

Who should spend the day with me on Monday, but Fanny Burney? She is thin, but looks clear, and is in good spirits, and was remarkably pleasant, and in Charity with all human kind. I must prevail on my father to let me invite her for a week—poor dear goose—she longs to come.—Her singing is clearer and sweeter than I ever heard it. You know she has been at the sea side, and bathing and sea air, I am persuaded clear the voice. She sings some lovely sentimental and pathetic ballads with exquisite unaffected feeling, and brought tears in my old eyes[10]—for which, by the way, I have no reason to thank her or any body, for tears horribly weaken and muddle the sight—and I want all the sight with which I can see, to scribble Adela, and to make some duds.

Martin is in love with noble Julia, and with great animation, and, I am sure, great sincerity, told me—"She is the most beautiful child I ever saw in all my life!"[11]—What a worthy creature that queer Martin is![12]—

My dear, I could not think of a word to write to poor Clem:[13]—A mere rational humdrum letter would not have been worth the postage—And like James, I am unable to furnish jokes on demand—and I had no Mrs Burney to apply to for some of hers. The truth is, I hardly ever write with perfect comfort and good/will to any body but such established and indulgent old correspondents as you.—I should like much to hear from you, & about your dear Mother—but not if you are busy, or not "i'the vein."[14]—No ceremony between you and me for pity's sake. It is far more the bane of good writing than the odious puzzle of third person, which young Charles lately assured me was the most deadly destroyer of eloquence.[15]—

Richard Burney is married—He wrote his Mother word—"I was to be espoused on the tenth—and on the tenth, accordingly, my espousals took place!"[16] Quaint enough and funny. Love to Barrett, and to the fine Ju, & the soft and gentle Etta[17]—Yours dearest of Charlottes

S. H. Burney.

1. The year of the letter is deduced from Richard Burney's marriage (of 10 Oct. 1811) having recently taken place; the day is conjectured from the bank deposit received "only two days ago" (n. 4).

2. Probably *Nummi Britannici Historia: or, an Historical account of English money*, a numismatical work [by Stephen Martin Leake (1702–73)]. Charles Burney owned both the first and second editions (1726, 1745) (*Misc. Lib.*, 29).

3. Sarah is probably returning a book through Charlotte to the Archdeacon Cambridge, possibly that of C. I. Latrobe (mentioned in her letter of 26 June 1811) about the Moravian missions.

4. The banking firm of Mr. Thomas Coutts, No. 59 in the Strand, with which S. H. Burney had opened an account on 10 July 1801. The ledgers at Coutts show that SHB's semiannual dividend of £19.0.3 was paid to her account on 14 October 1811. Almost immediately (Oct. 16), £20 was paid out to a Mr. Faulkner, the last entry of the year.

5. The *Universal British Directory* (1798) lists Jane Allen as a Haberdasher, and Edward Allen with a China Shop in Richmond. An Edward Alleyne is also "described as a Haberdasher and Milliner" who "once lived in Upper Hill Street" in "Retrospective Review," *Hiscoke's Richmond Notes* (Mar. 1963): 4–7.

6. At the end of *Traits of Nature*, the envious Jemima was "doomed to waste her youth, and pine over the decay of her beauty in a chamber of alternate languor and pain" (5: 248). However, through the purgatory of suffering, she achieves a more composed frame of mind.

7. The opening scene of [Edward Nares], *Thinks-I-to-Myself* was actually expanded in the third edition (not the second) in the manner described (16–26). This addition was also singled out for praise in the *Monthly Review*, 2nd ser. 66 (1811): 207–8.

8. William Shakespeare, *King Lear*, III, ii, 1–9, 14–24. In Nares's scene, the recitation ends at line 14.

9. In his comical spouting, the little boy stumbles at the fourth line of Alexander Pope's "The Universal Prayer" (which he renders "Jovajovalord!"), is discouraged from attempting Thomas Gray's "The Bard" which "put us too much in mind of *wumble* your belly-full," and finally bungles the opening of John Gay's *Fables* (1727).

10. Although Sarah refers to herself as "old," she was barely three and a half years older than her niece, Fanny Burney, who had been "at the sea with a neighbour of Richard's" (L. 62). Mme d'Arblay also noted her "extremely pleasing" singing voice (*JL*, 3: 251). Esther's daughter, Frances, would be invited to spend a week at Chelsea during the early winter (see below L. 64).

11. Julia Barrett, Charlotte's three-year-old daughter, was remarked for her beauty as a child and as a young woman (*JL*, 6: 590, n. 10).

12. Martin Burney, James's only son, seems to have been an eccentric but well-meaning young man; for a discussion of his wayward nature, his difficulties in finding and keeping employment, and his close friendship with the Lambs, see Manwaring, 291–306. For the irregularity of his later domestic life, see Phyllis G. Mann, "The Marriage of Martin Charles Burney," *Charles Lamb Society Bulletin*, no. 139 (Nov. 1957): 175–76; Winifred F. Courtney, "New Light on the Lambs and the Burneys," *Charles Lamb Bulletin*, NS no. 57 (Jan. 1987): 19–27.

13. Clement Francis, Charlotte's nineteen-year-old brother, was admitted to Caius College, Cambridge on 24 October 1811 (*Alumni Cantab.*). Sarah may have used the epithet "poor" in commiseration for his bad health, which he had been nursing at Brighton for six weeks (MF to HLTP, 8 Sept. 1811, John Rylands), or in pity for his difficulties in fixing a career. For his brief sojourns in the Navy and the City, see MF to HLTP, 1807–11, John Rylands Library, passim.

14. A Shakespearian phrase, it occurs in *Troilus and Cressida* (V, iii, 32) and *Richard III* (IV, ii, 121).

15. Charles Burney Jr.'s only son, Charles Parr Burney, an Oxonian (B.A. 1808; M.A. 1811), was acting as headmaster at his father's school at Greenwich. Perhaps this position had something to do with his decided views on grammar (*JL*, 1: lxxii; 7: 27, n. 11, 88, n. 1).

16. For the wedding of Esther Burney's only surviving son on 10 October 1811, see L. 62, n. 7.

17. I.e., Charlotte's husband, Henry Barrett, and her two children "Ju" (Julia) and "Etta" (Henrietta).

---

64. To Charlotte (Francis) Barrett

[Chelsea College], 20 January 1812
A.L.S., Berg
Address: M[rs] Barrett / Under the Hill / Richmond / Surry.
Postmarks: 12 o'Clock / 21 JA / 1812 N∩
4 [o']Clock / [*?* 2]1 / [*?*] EV

How very droll, dearest Charlotte, that your little thoughts, & my little thoughts should unconsciously take such identical leaps! Anch'io have been reading La Rochefaucould—and he has furnished me with an excellent Motto for my third Volume[1]—And what is more to the purpose, with some entertainment of the highest & most rational kind for my breakfast hours. I can only afford time now to read at my meals. Ah pauvre humanité—I am afraid he is very little too severe against it! Had man remained as the Deity originally created him, of course such a book, nay such thoughts could never have been conceived—But as man now is, its severest assertions I fear are just, till after long discipline, & much self-imposed restraint upon religious motives. He seldom writes as if he was hardened enough to exult in human depravity, but often as if he sadly, yet irresistibly felt its existence to be true—And such a book, it strikes me, properly considered, is calculated to produce infinite benefit. You will not mistake me for a gloomy fanatic, if I remind you, how closely it tallies with what is said of man in innumerable places in Scripture—Of the desparate wickedness of his heart—of his vanity—of his selfishness &c, &c. La Rochefoucould is none the worse for allowing what we all inwardly feel in some measure to be true—And to speak honestly, I revere, and I admire him—for I do not see why vain mortals should be forever trumpt up with undeserved praises of their unexisting goodness!—And so much for one of my long proses—But now do try, as James said about the picture, to like La Rochefaucould with me.—Dirty Deffand I have only read in the Reviews[2]—but I mean, I believe, one of these odd-come-shortlys to read her unreviewed.

Now I have another tedious prose for you, which though it is about myself, that is, about my book, I would not do any body but you the honour of relating just now, for fear of writing one word more than is prescribed in my bond.[3]—I have had it all to transcribe, and am now only a little way advanced in the fourth volume. Many alterations, additions, and I trust, improvements, have suggested themselves during the laborious occupation. Fanny Raper kindly offered to read and revise my fair copy—but poor heart, she lives such miles apart from me, that I am forced to let her take it home with her, and she makes pencil marks which I sometimes do not understand—and when we meet, she has almost forgotten herself why she made them—she forgets the conjunction of one set of chapters with the other—I hear none of her remarks as they strike her, pour ou contre, while she is reading; and she has no recollection of a word she thought, when at last we get together. This is thoroughly comfortless and mortifying, for she has taste & tact, & might do me very essential service. Well, now, as a grammatical critic, Martin comes and reads—but, hang the boy, he tries to gabble on for the sake of the story,[4] and I really believe, hardly knows whether it is written in English or High Dutch. I can get no really useful Critic, stuck down by my own fire side—So it must go as it is. Fanny Burney over-looked the first fifty pages during the week she was here, & was an excellent verbal and punctuation assistant—But (entre nous) I dare not ask for her to come again, as G.P. non molto la gradisca.[5] My title will be simply "Traits of Temper",[6] without the name of Adela. One of my little wise friends here, Mrs Haggitt,[7] advises me to leave that out, and I prefer it, I think, myself.—Every vol. has a different Motto, & though I say it that should not, they are all good ones, & from Sterling Authors—Shakespear, Martinus Scriblerus, (Pope s'entend) & La Rochefaucould.[8]—I made one, which I now have not the courage to prefix

"Take, Reader, an impartial author's vote,—

"This book's the best she yet has ever wrote.—"And bad" they would say, perhaps, "is the best!"[9]—

My poor right hand was ailing and painful for two or three days, and so now I write much slower, being forced to muffle it in warm gloves, and to not over-fatigue, but humour it.—You see by the mean shapelessness of this scrawl,[10] how it goes with me—However, I am thankful that, with ease, I can use it again in moderation.—

I long to come to you, though not for Tibbs,[11] though she is a good excuse to plead to Daddy—But you, dear soul, and yours, are my magnets, and not all the fiddles in Christendom. I will not stir, however, whilst this vile job hangs over my head. Should I complete it in time to plead Tibbs as a reason here, I will send you a line—But, honestly, I don't want to go to her—I only want to refresh myself with a sight of your dear faces.

I have behaved shamefully about poor Moll and her Irish jaunt,[12] which, ápropos de loving to meddle with what don't concern me, I half scared your Mother for having permitted—And took upon me to think, or rather to talk against, because of some disinclination to her companion which I heard in the summer was entertained by the Cams.[13] But I am sorry I vexed her with any such needless bother—And absolutely amazed at myself now, for having been so paltryly officious.[14] My father too joined me in grumbling at it, though in his heart, he cares not a snuff of a candle about the matter, & has now forgotten it. I wonder whether I should have been so mighty busy if I had not been an old Spinster.—Oh, by the way, Beckey says she was born the same year as myself, and is not forty till next time her birthday comes round[15]—So pray tell Barrett that I wronged my bloom by a whole twelvemonth.

Can you read this vile scratch—written with a tired, gloved-up hand?

I have, for Sunday reading, great delight in <reading> old South,[16] & I'll send you an epigram about him, & two of his axioms.—One is, "Nothing is great which it is great to despise"[17]—And the Other—"Sin never dies of old age".[18] He admirably illustrates both.—The epigram, founded on some degree of truth, is this—

Old South, the witty Churchman reckoned,
Was preaching once to Charles the Second:
But much too gravely for a court
That of all preaching made a sport.
The good and zealous man of God,
Seeing his audience yawn and nod,
And finding nothing would avail,
Cries to the Earl of Lauderdale[19]—
"My Lord, why 'tis a monstrous thing,—
"You snore so loud—you'll wake the King!"[20]

Adieu, dearest Charlotte. Love to Barrett, & Kisses to Ju & Etta from yours most honestly. S. B.

January 20th 1812.

P. S. Write whenever you can—I doat on hearing from you.

1. Charles Burney did own a translation of this author (L. 60, n. 17), but SHB quotes from the original French in the motto of her third volume: "S'il y a un amour pur et exempt du mélange de nos autres passions, c'est celui qui est caché au fond du coeur, et que nous ignorons nous-mêmes," the 69th of François de La Rochefoucauld's *Réflexions ou sentences et maximes morales*, 2nd ed. (1666).

2. Marie (née de Vichy-Chamrond), marquise du Deffand (1697–1780); she probably aroused Sarah's moral disapproval for her dissipated life and adulterous relations (see Benedetta Craveri, *Madame du Deffand e il suo mondo* (Milano: Adelphi, 1982)). The first edition of her *Correspondance* was published in Paris in 1809, but Sarah had probably read a review of the *Letters of the Marquise du Deffand to the Hon. Horace Walpole*, [ed. Mary Berry], 4 vols. (London: Longman, Hurst, Rees, and Orme, 1810). A copy of the *Monthly Review*, 2nd ser. 65 (1811): 28–36, was in Charles Burney's library (*Misc. Lib.*, 37).

3. The expression may refer to Shakespeare's play, *The Merchant of Venice*, in which Shylock tries to collect his bond of a pound of flesh, but is foiled by an exact legal interpretation of the words (IV, i).

4. Martin Burney's voracious reading habits were noted by Charles Lamb, who amusingly describes him making his way through *Clarissa* "by daily fragments" at a bookseller's stall (Charles Lamb, "Detached Thoughts on Books and Reading," *The Last Essays of Elia* (1833); Manwaring, 303).

5. "G.P.," an abbreviation for Dr. Burney (Grandpapa), who was apparently not fond of his granddaughter, Frances Burney.

6. The novel would be published under a slightly different title, apparently at the publisher's suggestion (see below L. 66).

7. Sarah Chambers (c. 1763–1827) had married 6 April 1785 the Rev. William Haggitt (1756–1834), Chaplain to Chelsea Hospital (1798) and Rector of Byfleet, Surrey (1798–1834) (*Alumni Cantab.;* Dean, 309; *GM*, NS 1 (1834): 663; gravestone, Royal Hospital Chelsea).

8. Sarah actually took mottoes for each of her five volumes from "Martinus Scriblerus" (the pseudonym adopted by the Scriblerus Club), Voltaire, François de La Rochefoucauld, Jean de La Bruyère, and William Shakespeare.

9. SHB's remark is curiously prophetic. While unquestionably her most successful novel commercially (running to a second edition in four months; see L. 66, n. 9), *Traits of Nature* was somewhat coolly received by the critics, who perceived too close a resemblance to Mme d'Arblay's early novels. The *Critical Review*, 4th ser. 42 (1812): 519–27, warned readers that "this is not a novel in which they are to expect any great *novelty*. Though every character in the work is well drawn, and ably supported, yet these characters appear (at least to us) *old acquaintances* only in *different situations.*" The *Monthly Review*, 2nd ser. 71 (1813): 102–3, also remarked on the "family-likeness in this lady's productions" and took her to task besides for incidents that were "rather *dramatic* than natural," a "negligent" style and a "fondness for hard words." The *British Critic* 41 (1813): 643, was the most favorable, though hardly flattering, noting briefly the popularity of the novel.

10. The "shapelessness of her scrawl" is more imaginary than real; the handwriting of SHB's letter is perfectly legible and clear, although the lines are perhaps slightly uneven.

11. For Miss Tibbs, a friend of Charlotte Barrett at Richmond, who seems to have been connected to a local family of musicians, see L. 51, n. 11. Charlotte had probably invited Sarah Harriet (as she had her sister, Marianne) to "MISS TIBBS' CONCERT (under the patronage of His Royal Highness the Duke of CLARENCE)" to be held 24 February 1812 at the Assembly Room, Castle Tavern, Richmond (later postponed to 26 February). Tickets for this benefit concert, priced at half a guinea, could be obtained from Miss Tibbs of Ormond Row (*Times*, 20 Jan., 6 Feb., 2 Mar. 1812; MF to CFBt, 31 Jan. [1812], Barrett, Eg. 3704A, ff. 83–84v).

12. Marianne Francis accompanied to Ireland a friend of Mrs. Piozzi's, Anna Maria (1780–1843), the eldest daughter of John Blaquiere (1732–1812), 1st Baron de Blaquiere (1800). She had married 18 August 1802 John Hamilton FitzMaurice (1778–1820), styled Viscount Kirkwall, only son of the Countess of Orkney. Lady Kirkwall had been sent for by her dying father, and left 3 December 1811 to join him near Dublin (Burke; Gibbs; *DNB; GM*, 82, Pt. 2 (1812): 298; MF to HLTP, 3 Dec. 1811, John Rylands).

13. The Cam[bridge]s (L. 60, n. 24) may have heard some gossip about Lady Kirkwall's marriage which ended in a separation in 1809, with the husband taking the children. Marianne ardently supported her friend who "has been so wickedly used—suffers so cruelly about her Babies." She believed that "Lord Kirkwall is all that is cruel & cross" while his wife's "uprightness stood her in good stead" (MF to HLTP, 27 May 1811, 8 Sept. 1811, John Rylands).

In 1817 Lady Kirkwall would institute proceedings for a divorce, charging her husband with adultery, a suit which was undetermined at the time of his death (*Times*, 26 Apr., 5 July 1817). The fact that blame might still accrue to the wife is indicated by Mme d'Arblay's reaction to the situation: "I have been really shocked to see the charge that elegant woman, Lady Kirkwell, has permitted herself to make against her husband. I doubt not its truth: but surely there are boundaries even of Veracity which a delicate woman should not touch. How does Marian defend her?" (*JL*, 10: 541–42).

14. Sarah's interference seems to have had some effect on Mrs. Broome, who at the end of five weeks wrote to her daughter, asking her to come home. Marianne relayed her mother's request for her immediate departure to her hostess, who was rather taken aback: "I was not quite prepared for it to happen so suddenly . . . I really am so taken by surprise I know not how hardly to write another word" (MF & Viscountess Kirkwall to HLTP, 15 Jan. 1812, John Rylands).

15. "Beckey" is probably Rebecca More, Dr. Burney's servant (L. 61, n. 5). She was born in 1772 if she were the same age as Sarah Harriet, who was born on 29 August and christened on 25 September of that year (parish register, St. Nicholas, King's Lynn).

16. Robert South, D.D. (1634–1716), the divine, famous for the wit and humour of his sermons, of which Charles Burney owned 11 volumes (1727) (*DNB; Misc. Lib.*, 51).

17. This may be a paraphrase of one or more paradoxes expressed in a sermon on the text of Titus 2:15: "Reputation is Power, and consequently to despise is to weaken. For where there is Contempt, there can be no Awe; and where there is no Awe, there will be no Subjection. . . . It is a Proposition of eternal Verity, that none can govern while he is despised. We may as well imagine that there may be a King without Majesty, a Supreme without Sovereignty" (Robert South, *Twelve Sermons Preached upon Several Occasions*, 5th ed., vol. 1 (London: Jonah Bowyer, 1722), 200–201).

18. This epigram is based on a passage in South's second sermon on Romans 1:32,

where he warns of the fallacy of believing that virtue will become easier with age: "For this is a Maxim of Eternal Truth; *That nothing grows weak with Age, but that which will at length die with Age;* which Sin never does" (South, 2: 228).

19. John Maitland (1616–82), 2nd Earl (1645) and 1st Duke of Lauderdale (1672), a Scottish lord, intimate of King Charles II, and member of the "cabal" of 1667 (*DNB;* Burke).

20. "A Court Audience," *The Festoon: A Collection of Epigrams, Ancient and Modern,* [ed. Richard Graves] (London: Robinson and Roberts, 1766), 192. The original differs slightly:

Old South, a witty churchman reckon'd,
Was preaching once to Charles the Second,
But much too serious for a court,
Who at all preaching made a sport:
He soon perceiv'd his audience nod,
Deaf to the zealous man of God.
The doctor stopp'd; began to call,
"Pray 'wake the earl of Lauderdale:
"My lord! why, 'tis a monstrous thing!
"You snore so loud—you'll 'wake the king."

---

65. To Charlotte (Francis) Barrett

[Chelsea College], 19 February [1812][1]
A.L.S., Berg
Address: M[rs] Barrett / Under the Hill / Richmond / Surry
Postmarks: 7 o'Clock / [?] / 18[?] NT

Wednesday 19th Feb[y]

Dearest Char—Last night, or rather, this morning at one o'clock, I finished my (I began to think it) interminable job.[2] But not a word more about it, till I have said all my say about the kind cart loads of good things, brought and sent and begged and nobly bestowed upon my poor dear daddy. It has gone bitterly against me to let so many days elapse without shewing signs of Christian gratitude, or Christian compassion for poor aching Barrett. But so muddled and tired and desparately determined was I to get through with my long plague that I defied though I could not silence all the twitings of my conscience—And half wished that you had been on a trip with Astolpho to the Moon,[3] rather than employed, just at such a time, in catering for one who referred all his thanks to me to deliver.[4] I had commissioned Fanny Raper, and I think dear my Sister,[5] to entreat that you would make no application for any of her good messes to Mrs Cambridge—But lo, you have—And I am sure it would vex him to know it—So I have lain the damson cheese without pots, and the damson cheese with pots, all at your door, and not said a word to him about any body else. He would fret & fume at the idea of the fine letter of thanks it ought to cost him—and perhaps never write it.[6]—Now, dear Char, this would not have happened, I know, if I had written to you sooner; but, I really have much to plead in my defence—and you must either tell the truth to M^rs C: (about my father's dislike to writing, and my sneaking silence relating to her thereupon), or you must invent speeches of gratitude for him, and those that he now charges me to send to you (to keep, as children say) pass on to her.—Do you understand all this mean mess, darling? And do you forgive me for not having stopped your hand in time? But who could have dreamt, that after all that your Mother brought, and the dear little pottikin which you had sent on my first application, you could ever have thought of still foraging for more?—About his likings and preferings—My Daddy likes the consistency of M^rs C's stuff best, but the taste and spirit of yours is wanting—And what my sister brought, I fear is hardly firm or spirited enough to please him equally with either of the others.

Sweetheart mine, your last letter was the quintessence of all good fun, and pleased me Mightily. The mild <sauceyness> perfections of Ju and Etta, the one fighting for sugar, the other requiring flagellation for "an aggregate of misdemeanours," have never been out of the laughing quarter of my imagination since I read about them. Now, that I can crasher letter for letter with you, haud not your haund,[7] good friend. It would be the summit of all spite, only to be a diligent correspondent when I am least able to answer; and to stop the instant I can give you tit for tat.—

Yes indeed; I most truly, warmly, and applaudingly rejoice at dear Fanny's new schemes of retrenchment,[8] which albeit (as you hint) carried too far, and adopted perhaps too abruptly by fusty Raper, it will be to her honour beyond any other circumstance, chearfully to enter into. She is one, who, to know and value as she fully merits, one should see intimately and habitually—The casket is fair, but the inside is still fairer—And when the casket has cut too great a dash, and dazzled ones eyes, and made one 'critical', it is comfortable to <manages> them to have it gently opened, and to see all the intrinsic, but mild gems within, quietly revealed.[9]—If I could always live with dear Fan, I should always be in perfect humour with every thing she did, and often should truly honour and respect her. Nobodys retired hours are so good—Nobodys harum-scarum passing visits so unsatisfactory, and oversetting of all one's high-wrought good will. As a passing vision, indeed, she confuses me with mixed and heaped up blues, and greens, and yellows, and produces upon me the effect of looking too long at an Argant lamp,[10] or a glaring and sunny white wall. I like her in shade—Not unhappy, but still <and silent> shade.—I hope, out of Norfolk, from my good Sister Allen,[11] to get her a Maiden of a thousand—And I meanwhile 'say nothing to nobody' but to you, about it;—I Don't quite love Raper's rough dockings, but repress all grumbling before dear Fanny, & heartily wish her as rich as she would be liberal—as prudent as she is poor.

Tonight's the night, I speak it with great terror, that I mean to make my application to Dr Charles to sell my good little Adela[12]—whose morality after all is of the kind Barrett won't dislike[13]—I like her much myself! Ha, ha! I have no idea, dearest, when I shall be able to come to you.—Certainly not at present—but I keep the blessed project in view, and will come as soon as I can disentangle myself from certain bothers too numerous to mention. I shall have proofs to correct—and there are beastly debates to read in the evening paper—and my stockings want darning—and all my caps and chemises are spotted with ink—and I have five dozen old pens to mend of daddy's and <mine> my own—and rigmaroles without end to look after, but send me the earliest violets you can gather, and Ju & Etta in a basket to kiss. And tell poor dear Barrett how heartily sorry for his sufferings is your affectionate. S. H. Burney

1. The letter is conjecturally dated 1812, when 19 February did indeed fall on a Wednesday. The year is confirmed by other factors: the references to Dr. Burney's reluctance to write, Frances Raper's debts and, most revealing, the marketing of Sarah's novel about Adela.

2. The completion of SHB's third novel, *Traits of Nature.*

3. In Ludovico Ariosto's *Orlando furioso* (1532), Astolpho visits the moon, where he discovers Orlando's lost wits (Cantos 34–35). Sarah could have read the epic in her father's library in the original Italian (published in 1713 and 1746), in John Hoole's popular translation of 1783, or in an edition which printed both Italian and English [trans. William Huggins et al.] (1757) (*Misc. Lib.*, 3, 5).

4. Her father, Charles Burney; for his dependence on Sarah as an amanuensis, see L. 56, n. 2; L. 57. Writing was a chore for the eighty-five-year-old man whose hand was "crippled by gout, rheumatism or blight" (CB to FBA, [post 11 July 1810], Osborn). Just a few days earlier, he had complained of the "nervous debility of my hand, & the decay of sight & memory" which made the task difficult (CB to Lady Bruce, 6 Feb. [1812], Osborn).

5. Probably Charlotte Barrett's mother, Charlotte (Burney) Broome, who had also sent some damson cheese to Dr. Burney (see below).

6. Sarah's reasoning is difficult to follow here, for she claims to have omitted mention of the Cambridges to spare her father, who would fret over the necessity of writing a letter of thanks. But if he really "referred all his thanks to me to deliver," it was her own labor she was saving and not his.

7. A Scotticism, perhaps derived from Sarah's reading of Walter Scott.

8. Fanny Raper was practicing economy, after finding herself in financial difficulties (see above L. 59, n. 9).

9. SHB's analogy is reminiscent of the casket scenes in *The Merchant of Venice*, a play that was quoted in her letter of 20 January 1812 (L. 64).

Susan (Burney) Phillips had described her daughter's character in similar terms when she was a child: "Her faults . . . rise all to view, & shew themselves <u>more</u> to strangers—but I think the deeper one sees into her, the more <u>elle</u> <u>est</u> <u>approfondue</u>, the better she will always be found" (SBP to FB, 21 Dec. 1787–22 Jan. 1788, Osborn).

10. Invented about 1782 and named after the inventor, an Argand lamp had a cylindrical wick, which allowed air to circulate both inside and outside the flame, thus creating a brighter light (*OED*).

11. Susanna née Sharpin, the wife of SHB's half-brother, Stephen Allen.

12. Charles Burney Jr. often acted as intermediary between his sisters and the booksellers. He had offered to help Sarah with *Geraldine Fauconberg* (see above LL. 38, 39) and had been active in marketing Mme d'Arblay's *Camilla* and *The Wanderer* (*JL*, 3: 135, n. 1 and passim; 7: 148, n. 4 and passim).

13. The reviewers would concur with the author that the morality of her work was unexceptionable. The *Critical Review*, 4th ser. 42 (1812): 519–27, found "many excellent lessons" and "sensible reflections" therein, while the *Monthly Review*, 2nd ser. 71 (1813): 102–3, pointed out that "the fable is blended with excellent moral lessons; and, while the mind is amused, it is also improved."

---

66. To Charlotte (Francis) Barrett

[Chelsea College, 1 April 1812]
A.L.S., Berg
Address: M[rs] Barrett / Under the Hill / Richmond / Surry.
Postmarks: 7 o'Clock / 1 AP / 1812 NT

Wednesday.

I thank you, my dearest Charlotte, for the dispatch with which you have answered me.—I wrote to D[r] Charles immediately on receiving your letter, and in confirmation of what I had advanced from memory, quoted you as speaking to the same purpose from <u>written</u> <u>documents</u>, as well as verbal information. If I hear nothing further from him, I shall now let the matter rest; for, without absolute necessity, I could not endure to communicate Charles' letter to poor Fan:—He uses such horribly strong expressions, that they shock me even whilst I dispise them; and allowing much for tasteless exaggeration, I always substract from them two thirds of their real meaning. But applied to myself, I know not that I could thus coolly dissect them—Nor might Fanny. I asked him the very question that occurred to you—"What more can she do to retreive than she is now vigourously doing?"[1]—If I hear any thing more on this unfortunate subject, you shall know.

I am glad you approve my application to Colburn.[2] We agree like a pair of turtles. He <agrees> subscribes to my demand of £50 a volume, and pays down £100 immediately; the other £100 he is to give me his note of hand for, payable in six months.[3] But neither he nor any of them will take it without the Author's name in the title-page. I held out stoutly against it for two or three letters backwards and forwards: but, at last, half persuaded, read Colburn's arguments to my father, whom they satisfied;[4] and then I gave my consent. Colburn has begged me to alter the title "Traits of Temper," because Mrs Opie is coming out with a Novel called "Temper."[5]—I gave him his choice of "The Case is Altered," or of "Early Prejudice."—He does not seem satisfied with either, but wants me to call it "Traits of Nature"[6]—I think that title arrogates too much on the part of the Author, and will be thought conceited. I wish I could have your opinion—But Colburn is coming here tomorrow to talk about proofs, and to settle some other matters, and so then, I suppose, I must give him my final answer. He talks of advertising that I am the Miss Burney who have nothing to do with Miss Caroline Burney[7]—And perhaps will put vulgar puffing stuff in the Newspapers which will half kill me with shame. Certainly the Robinsons were too supine[8]—but I dread this man's being too quackish, and making me sick with overpushing. How strange it is, that a just medium is always so much more difficult to find, than vulgar extremes of activity, or disheartening extremes of indolence.[9]

What French party were you at, dear love, when you found my letter on your return? Were you with that sweet soul we sat next at the ball, who says of Barrett, Monr aime un peu à étoufer? Tell me about her if you were, and restore to my recollection her name, which I shame to say, is gone from me.—Oh, & I want to hear how you like Gertrude, or modes of discipline, by Miss Hawkins,[10] daughter of Sir John Hawkins who sent a man to prison for calling him Codger. If you disbelieve the anecdote, apply to Charlotte Barret from whom I have heard it as often as Sir J. Hawkin's name has been mentioned in her presence.[11] The book Gertrude has been well spoken of I am told by Mr Parsons,[12] a gentleman much looked up to by some people here for his reading and taste.—I am reading Bartelemi's Anacharsis,[13] which forms a sort of Appendix or rather Commentary to the Grecian History I was so much taken up with last summer.[14] Without such a previous brushing up of the memory, about all those Grecian chaps, I should not have enjoyed Anacharsis at all. He and Mitford seldom agree in their principles, and not always in their details. Barthelemi is a professed democrat, à tort et à travers, and Mitford hates the wrangles and turbulence, and stupid factions of democracy—And loves Pericles better than all the demagogues, soi-disant patriots, of antiquity.[15]—Don't you?—

Adieu dearest—Love to Barrett, & am y[rs] devotedly

S. H. Burney.

1. Charlotte Barrett's letter to Sarah, Sarah's to Charles Burney Jr., and his reply are all missing, but conjecturally, he had been asked for advice about Fanny Raper's debts. He may have been unsympathetic to a predicament into which she had fallen before and from which he himself had helped to extricate her (L. 59, n. 9). Fanny herself had tempted fate when writing to thank him for his generosity, declaring: "I shall now I trust do very well & if I incur another Debt may I lose the too well tried & proved affection of my dearest, kindest Uncle" (FP to CB Jr., [26 June 1807], Osborn).

2. Henry Colburn (d. 1855) of Conduit Street, who would soon become "the principal publisher of novels and light literature of his time. . . . He had a keen perception of what the public required; and of the market value of the article offered. He was liberal and punctual in his dealings with authors, and most skilful in the art of advertising" ("Appendix," *AR*, 97 (1855): 300; see also *DNB*). SHB was negotiating with him the sale of her third novel.

3. Although the financial arrangements imply a four-volume work, the novel would be published in five. On April 27, 1812, £50 was paid into Miss Burney's account at Coutts; some time after 14 October of that year, she was able to increase her stock by £150.

4. Charles Burney was protective of his daughters and their literary reputations. Early in Frances Burney's career, he helped stifle her play, *The Witlings*, whose satire he feared might earn her enemies; even after her marriage, she incurred his "most afflicting displeasure" by risking her reputation on the stage (*HFB*, 132–38; *EJL*, 3: passim; *JL*, 4: 394–95). This would be the first novel that Sarah Harriet would publish under her name (and *not* her next, as in *JL*, 9: 36–37, n. 14), which she agreed to only after receiving her father's consent.

5. Amelia Opie would publish a novel called *Temper, or Domestic Scenes: A Tale* (1812), reviewed in June in the *Monthly Review*, 2nd ser. 68 (1812): 217.

6. Colburn must have prevailed, as the novel was published as *Traits of Nature*.

7. Miss Caroline Burney (no relation to Sarah Harriet) was the author of *Seraphina; or, a Winter in town* (1809), a novel Sarah held in low esteem (see L. 62). The publisher's disclaimer dissociating the two authors does appear in some copies of SHB's work.

8. SHB's first novel, *Clarentine* (1796), had been published by G. G. and J. Robin-

son, and her second, *Geraldine Fauconberg* (1808), by G. Wilkie and J. Robinson. She may have considered the latter firm "supine" when she herself had to write to request them to advertise (L. 41).

9. SHB's third work of fiction, *Traits of Nature*, 5 vols., at 30s., was published on 25 April 1812 (Colburn records), advertised the previous day in the *London Chronicle*. Four months later, a second edition (4 vols., 28s.) was printed, according to Colburn's records on 28 August 1812, although advertising would not begin until later in the season (*London Chronicle*, 24–26 Oct. 1812; *Times*, 13, 14 Nov. 1812). The novel would still be available in 1820 (*Times*, 12, 15, 16 Feb. 1820).

Traits of Nature was also published in an American edition (1812), and translated into French as *Le Jeune Cleveland, ou Traits de nature* (1819).

10. Laetitia Matilda Hawkins (c. 1759–1835), *The Countess and Gertrude; or, Modes of Discipline* (1811) (*GM*, NS 5 (1836): 100). Charlotte Barrett knew the author and developed a theory about this work's having an autobiographical basis (see further L. 73).

11. Sir John Hawkins (1719–89), magistrate and author, who had published a rival history to Dr. Burney's in the same year (1776). This anecdote is not related in either of his biographies, but such stubbornness and contentiousness would not be uncharacteristic. See Percy A. Scholes, *The Life and Activities of Sir John Hawkins* (London: Oxford University Press, 1953); Bertram H. Davis, *A Proof of Eminence* (Bloomington: Indiana University Press, 1973).

The incident (or something like it) may have occurred while he was a Middlesex justice from 1761 to 1781. Charlotte Barrett might have heard the anecdote at Twickenham, where Hawkins lived from 1760 to 1771 and where his litigiousness aroused enmity. His relations with his neighbors, seen through the eyes of his daughter, are presented in D. H. Simpson, *The Twickenham of Laetitia Hawkins, 1760–1835* (Twickenham: Twickenham Local History Society, 1978).

12. Unidentified.

13. Jean-Jacques Barthélemy (1716–95), *Voyage du jeune Anacharsis en Grèce* (1788); Charles Burney owned the 2nd ed. of 1789 (*Misc. Lib.*, 2). It is not clear whether Sarah realized that the Scythian traveler in Barthélemy's work, although named for an historical figure, was purely fictitious.

14. In her letter of 1 August 1811 (L. 60), SHB had discussed at some length William Mitford's *The History of Greece*.

15. Pericles, the Athenian statesman (c. 495–429 B.C.). Barthélemy presents him as a tyrant who pretended to populist principles to attain power, and contributed to the corruption of the Athenian state. Mitford, on the other hand, believes that "Athens, in that age, reached a perfection of taste that no country hath since surpassed" (Abbé [Jean-Jacques] Barthélemy, *Travels of Anacharsis the Younger in Greece* [trans. William Beaumont] (London: G. G. and J. Robinson, 1796), 1: 178–80, 218–20; William Mitford, *The History of Greece*, 3rd ed., vol. 3 (London: T. Cadell, 1795), 288).

67. To Charles Burney Jr.

[Chelsea College], 21 July 1812
A.L.S., Osborn
Address: Revd Dr Burney / Greenwich / Kent
Postmarks: [Tw]oPy[Post] / [Unp]aid / [Ch]elsea
12 o'Clock / 22 JY / 1812 N∩
4 o'Clock / JY 22 / 1812 EV

My dearest Brother

That French-headed, fluttering bustler, M^{de} Solvyn,[1] sent here last week her brother,[2] with a commission to deliver to me in private a letter from our beloved sister d'Arblay, and an intimation, given verbally, and in presence of my father, <that she was> of her being actually upon her journey to England![3] The letter I but too well guessed was such as it would require all my own strong spirits to read without being broken-hearted,[4] & having already a suspicion of its tragical nature, I immediately put it out of sight, and gave not to my father the slightest reason to believe I had received it. But the intelligence of my sister's impending arrival, occupied his mind the whole day, and believing at that time, that M^{de} Solvyn had full authority for what she had asserted,[5] we worked ourselves up to expect dear Fanny's appearance even in the course of the next twenty four hours. My father, ignorant of her late dreadful sufferings, was in the highest spirits at the prospect of seeing her; and all Friday & Saturday neither he nor I could think or talk of any thing else. On Sunday, I called upon M^{de} Solvyn, at Henderson's Hotel[6]—and how did the uncertainty with which she then spoke, let me down in my wedding shoes! Her reason for believing that M^{de} d'Arblay was en route to Chelsea, was simply this: A vessel from Dunkirk was said in the Newspapers to have arrived at an English port,[7] and she thought that my sister might have come over in it. She seemed very much shocked when she found that my father knew the report which she had procured to be conveyed to Chelsea, and said that she had promised you not to mention the subject of M^{de} d'Arblay's journey prematurely to him. Her brother, then, certainly misunderstood his cue; for he spoke of it in the library without any appearance of mystery—And my father's disappointment is now proportioned to his preceeding delight. Whip the woman! Why not write a line to me, rather than dispatch an half-instructed verbal messenger?—

But what, my dear Brother, is your opinion of our dear sister's plans? I write unknown to my father, who is subsiding into gradual incredulity of the whole report.—Mosely[8] has strenuously urged me to go for bathing to the sea-side, & previous to receiving this news, I had engaged to set out the 1st week in August[9] with a friend who has secured me a lodging, & whose company on the road would be particularly desirable. Yet, were I going merely for amusement, I would at once give up the excursion rather than run the slightest hazard of losing my sister's society even for a single day.[10] But every sensation of my <rhumatic> relaxed little frame, tells me that bathing and change of air are almost indispensably requisite to enable me to get through the ensuing winter with tolerable comfort. I have been a cripple till within this last fortnight, ever since February, and even now am wearing what Mosely calls a warm plaister, and am often as rhumatic as an old hedger and ditcher.—I am in a cleft stick, and long to hear how you would advise me to manage. I should not mind forfeiting my lodging, but I should mind losing the opportunity of travelling with a friendly companion; being but a cowardly dab, and of late years, little used to "moving accidents, by flood, or field".[11]

A line addressed to S. H. Burney, Chaplain's Apartments Chelsea College, will be thankfully received by, my dear brother, yours ever most affectionately

S. H. Burney.

July 21st 1812.

Six o'clock

I open my letter to say, that a note from you is just arrived of which, saving and excepting the allusions to "stools and pots," I understand not one syllable. Perchance it is designed for one of the S. Burneys in James Street?[12]—At all events, the cap fits not me. Adieu.

1. Mary Ann (née Greenwood) Solvyns (1781–1844) had married in 1807 a French man, François-Balthazar Solvyns (1760–1824). She had met Dr. Burney in the spring of 1810, bringing him news of his election to the Institut de France, and had conveyed letters back to France to his daughter, Mme d'Arblay (*JL*, 6: 587, and n. 2; CB to FBA, 5 May 1810, [May 1810], [post 11 July 1810], Osborn; CB to CB Jr., 7 May [1810], [9 May 1810], 1 June 1810, Berg; CB to Mme Solvyns, 4 undated letters, Osborn).

She was to serve the d'Arblays in this way for some time, especially between August 1812 and May 1813 when husband and wife were separated. Though initially impressed by her charm and grateful for her services, Mme d'Arblay was to conclude: "She is a good humoured, pleasing, friendly, lively woman, but without *tact*, or discretion" (*JL*, 7: 130, 228, n. 8 and passim).

2. Probably Charles Gregory Greenwood (c. 1787–1856), Mme Solvyns's elder brother who resided in Sloane Street, Chelsea (*JL*, 7: 129, n. 11; *GM*, NS 45 (1856): 551).

3. With travel between England and France restricted by the war, Mme d'Arblay had not seen her family for ten years. She had now succeeded in obtaining a passport for

herself and her son, and was planning to sail on an American ship that would make a surreptitious stop in England. They left Paris on 4 July 1812 for Dunkirk, arriving on the evening of the sixth, but found the voyage of the *Mary Ann* delayed. At the time of Sarah's letter, they were waiting in Dunkirk for the ship to set sail, which it eventually would do on 13 August 1812 (*JL*, 6: 627, n. 1, 629, n. 1, 676, n. 7; *HFB*, 324–25).

4. Sarah may be referring to the mastectomy that Fanny had undergone on 30 September 1811, described to Esther in a letter written c. 22 March 1812 but not sent before June. For this detailed and chilling account, see *JL*, 6: L. 595.

5. Mme Solvyns did have some authority for announcing Fanny's return. She appears to have left Paris herself about the same time, but sailed from Ostend. Mme d'Arblay reports receiving a letter at Dunkirk (c. 13 July) shortly before Mme Solvyns's departure in which "she kindly promised to be my herald" (*JL*, 6: 648).

6. The "King's Arms tavern & hotel, Bridge-st. Westminster" is listed under the name Henderson in Holden's Annual London and County Directory.

7. Mme Solvyns may have seen the report in the *Times* on 16 July 1812: "An American vessel has arrived at Dover from Dunkirk, where she had been detained two years, until liberated by the decision of the Prize Court. She has brought several passengers, who report, that the coast of France was entirely stripped of troops to augment the Grand Army in the North. Provisions at Dunkirk were very dear."

8. Dr. Benjamin Moseley (1742–1819), M.D. (1784), Physician to the Royal Hospital, Chelsea (1788–1819). He would act as pallbearer at Dr. Burney's funeral (DNB; Dean, 311; JL, 7: 290, n. 5).

9. SHB's account at Coutts shows that she would withdraw £35 on 6 August 1812, presumably to bear the expenses of this journey.

10. But see below L. 69 where Sarah prolongs her stay at the seaside for another fortnight despite news of her half-sister's arrival.

11. William Shakespeare, *Othello*, I, iii, 134.

12. James Burney's wife and daughter were both named Sarah.

---

68. To Charlotte (Francis) Barrett

Lymington, 14–17 August [1812][1]
A.L.S., Berg
Address: Mrs Barrett / Richmond / Surry

Lymington,[2] at
Mrs Pardy's Nelson's Place
Augst 14th

My dearest Charlotte

Your letter to Mde Gomer[3] procured me a visit from her the very day after I arrived, but unfortunately I was out walking; I saw her, however, in the evening at a ball given in honour of the Regent's Birthday,[4] and where I also saw all the beauty and fashion of the place. Mr Burrard[5] introduced me to Major Gomer, who brought his charming wife to me, and we chatted together the whole evening. Afterwards, M. la Chapelle[6] came in, and his sister introduced me to him. They thanked me over and over again for the letters which you and Barrett had given me to bring, and spoke of you both with real friendship and cordiality. I have returned M^de Gomer's visit, but she also was out, being gone to a wedding. We have therefore met only once; but M. la Chapelle has called, and sat here nearly an hour. He has been very ill, but is recovering, and his eyes are certainly the handsomest I ever saw. Mr John Kingston[7] and his brother Henry,[8] & their two wives, and Lady Rooke,[9] & two Miss Rookes[10] were at the ball. John Kingston either did not, or would not know me, though our eyes met once or twice. His wife is not half so amiable-looking as Mrs Henry Kingston, and nobody here seems very partial to her.

Aug^st 17th—My lodging I am told is within a few doors of the one which you and Barrett occupied, but nearer to the water side, and with a better view. Mr C. Raper gave me a letter to a friend of his who lives just opposite, and whose wife and five boys, I like extremely. They admit me at all times, and are perfectly free from form or ceremony, and very cultivated nice people.—I drank tea at M. de Chapelle's Cottage on Saturday with a complete French party. C'etoit la fête de la vielle M^de de Chapelle,[11] & her daughter carried her a bouquet, and we all made her a little civil speech. M. de Chapelle has an excellent small Broadwood,[12] & he sung French, English & Italian songs delightfully, and was relieved de tems en tems by M^de d'Orfeuil, who was a Mlle de Choiseiul, and is married here to a young officer,[13] said to be a great fool, but very good-natured. Le Major Gomer is particularly liked in this place, and was with us at the Cottage; but before the old lady, he scarcely ever speaks; and to say the truth, she gives but little time for any body to put in a word even edgeways. Mlle Clementine[14] is a fine sensible looking girl, with beautiful eyes: but she is short and thick-built, and has nothing of a French degagée look. Her drawings are very clever, and I have begged one as a present for you, and am to take charge of it when I leave this place.

As for reading, or the improvement of my mind, I have really no time for either, though I rise earlier than I have done for years. But bathing before breakfast, and then a walk, & then coming home to brush and dry my wet shock head; and then going to Market (which amuses me exceedingly) and then meeting people to lounge about the town with; & then making or receiving idle visits, and dressing to dine out, fills up e[very minute. I] am in terrible want of a sofa for a little spra[wl after m]y stroll—but I make the bed pay for it. I have been [to s]pend a morning at Walhampton the house and grounds of Sir Harry Nield,[15] and have dined at Milford, about four or five miles from hence, where there is an excellent beech, on which we wandered during the whole evening, and where we had an admirable view of the Needle rocks,[16] and a wide extent of sea.—The bathing, which I have now tried three times, seems to agree with me perfectly well, and gives me spirits and activity.

M. de Bourblanc,[17] whom probably Barrett knows, has been here for a couple of days, (I believe at M. de Chapelle's) but I missed seeing him, which I regret, for he is not only an old acquaintance, but an old favorite of mine.—

M[de] Gomer enquired a great deal after your little girls, & la maisonette at Richmond, and told me of your assisting to milk the cow for a syllabub—And many other frolics which I must defer recording till another opportunity being now called away to a visitor—

Adieu my dearest Charlotte

Yours ever most affectionately

S: H: Burney.

1. The letter has been dated by Sarah Harriet's visit to Lymington, Hampshire (see L. 69).

2. At Lymington, SHB was associating with a group of French émigrés, who had been landing on the southwest coast of England since 1792. The English government organized some of these refugees into several corps stationed at Lymington because of its strategic position on the Channel coast. The emigrant corps took part in an unsuccessful landing in Brittany in 1795 when large numbers were killed. The survivors were incorporated into other foreign regiments (mostly German) who were later billeted in the town, in addition to "large bodies of militia [who] were constantly moving about during the summer months" (Edward King, *Old Times Re-visited in the Borough and Parish of Lymington*, 2nd ed. (1900; rpt., Winchester: Barry Shurlock, 1976), 138–49).

The Barretts had stayed at Lymington on their honeymoon, when Charlotte reportedly "was enjoying herself every evening among Foreigners, who are her delight: whole shoals of German & Swiss Officers being in the place" (MF to HLTP, 21 July [1807], John Rylands).

3. Probably Agathe Breton des Chapelles (fl. 1797–1823), who had married on 27 March 1797 Antoine-François-Gabriel, comte de Gomer (b. 5 Aug. 1770). Originally in the French military, he had fled his own country and served in the British army, Capt. (1796), Maj. (1808), Lt.-Col. (1814). He would resign his commission in 1817 and join the artillery corps in France (*Nobiliaire universel*, 13: 474–76). However, it seems that Mme de Gomer would remain in Lymington (Agathe de Gomer to CFBt, 7 May 1821, 12 Dec. 1822, 19 Jan. 1823, Berg).

4. The Prince Regent and future King George IV (1762–1830) turned forty on 12 August 1812. It had become a custom for him to celebrate his birthday at Brighton.

5. Probably Philip Burrard (c. 1763–1842), Mayor of Lymington (1809), only brother to Sir Harry Burrard (1755–1813) (*DNB*), who was created a Bt. (1807) for military service; Mr. Burrard was uncle to Sarah's friend Caroline Anne Bowles (L. 54, n. 2) (Burke; *GM*, NS 17 (1842): 337; King, 185).

6. The brother of Agathe de Gomer (n. 3), M. Breton des Chapelles; their father was Lt.-Gen. and Commander at Santo Domingo (*Nobiliaire universel*, 13: 475–76).

7. John Kingston was Barrett's brother-in-law, having married his sister Julia, who died in 1809 (L. 33, n. 7; L. 45, n. 1). On 7 April 1812, John Kingston married as his second wife Harriet Ann (1788–1860), the eldest daughter of Sir Giles Rooke (see n. 9) (*GM*, 3rd ser. 8 (1860): 419; parish register, Lymington, Hants.; IGI).

8. John Kingston's brother, Lucy Henry Kingston (d. 9 July 1851), had married at Lymington on 25 February 1812 the second daughter of Sir Giles Rooke, Frances Sophia (b. 19 April 1789) (*GM*, 82, Pt. 1 (1812): 188; NS 36 (1851): 330; parish register, Lymington, Hants.).

9. Harriet Sophia Burrard (c. 1765–1839), daughter of Col. William Burrard (1712–80) and sister to Sir Harry (Burrard) Neale, 2nd Bt. (n. 15) (Burke; *GM*, NS 11 (1839): 668). Renowned for her beauty, she had married 15 August 1785 Giles Rooke (1743–1808), who was appointed judge of the Court of Common Pleas and knighted (1793) (*DNB;* IGI; Charles Percy Jones, *History of Lymington* (Lymington: Charles King, 1930), 199).

10. Lady Rooke's two younger daughters: Mary Anne (1793–1867) who would marry on 28 March 1818 Maj.-Gen. Sir Charles Ashworth (d. 1832) and secondly, on 5 October 1836, Capt. Charles Kerr Macdonald, 42nd Regt; and Caroline (1795–1865), who would not marry until 1843 Capt. John Barclay, R.N. (Col. H. W. Rooke, comp., "Pedigree of the Descendants of Giles Rooke," *Genealogist*, NS 37 (January 1921); *GM*, 88, Pt. 1 (1818): 368; NS 6 (1836): 538; NS 19 (1843): 644).

11. Marie-Claude-Eleanor-Alexandrine Guiton Breton des Chapelles (fl. 1797–1817), a widow, who had given consent to the marriage of her daughter (a minor) with M. de Gomer (chapel register, Royal Hospital Chelsea). Later she would stay with her daughter in a cottage on Arthur Young's estate (CFBt to AY, [16 Jan. 1817], Barrett, Eg. 3703A, ff. 4–5v).

12. A piano manufactured by the English firm of John Broadwood (1732–1812) (*New Grove*).

13. Louise-Marie-Françoise-Charlotte de Choiseul-Beaupré, daughter of Charles-Antoine-Étienne (b. 1739), marquis de Choiseul-Beaupré, Lt.-Gen. des armées du Roi. Mlle Choiseul had married in London on 13 December 1810 Arthur-Marie-Edouard d'Orfeuille, comte d'Orfeuille-Foucaud, who had emigrated to England in 1791, and was serving in the 60th Regiment. Their daughter, Mary Pauline, was baptized in 1811 at Boldre, Hants. (*Nobiliaire universel*, 9: 108–9; parish register, Boldre, Hants., cited in King, 140; information kindly supplied by Prof. David Smith, University of Toronto).

14. Adélaïde-Clémentine de Gomer, only child of the de Gomers (n. 3 above) was born in London 2 October 1798 and would be confirmed on 23 September 1817 at Sopley, near Lymington (*Nobiliaire universel*, 13: 476; Catholic register, Sopley, Hants.; information supplied by the Hampshire Record Office).

15. Sir Harry Burrard (afterwards Neale) (1765–1840), who succeeded his uncle as 2nd Bt. (1791), was cousin to Sir Harry Burrard (see n. 5 above). He assumed the name

and arms of Neale on his marriage (15 April 1795) to Grace Elizabeth Neale (c. 1774–1856). He represented Lymington in many parliaments and also had a distinguished naval career, becoming Admiral (1830). The family estate of Walhampton had the honor of visits from George III (whom Neale served as Groom of the Bedchamber) in 1801 and 1804 (*DNB;* Burke; Thorne; *GM,* 65, Pt. 1 (1795): 346; NS 45 (1856): 210).

16. The famous Needles are outlying fragments of a chalk-barrier of which the Purbeck Downs and the ridge on the Isle of Wight are other survivals (A. Temple Patterson, *Hampshire and the Isle of Wight* (London: B. T. Batsford, 1976), 156).

17. Possibly Charles-Marie-Henri de Bourblanc (b. 29 Nov. 1766), dit le marquis d'Apreville, who came from a distinguished family staunchly loyal to the royalist cause. He had joined the French navy in 1782, became Lt. (1789) and emigrated in 1791 (*Nobiliaire universel,* 8: 342).

---

69. To Charlotte (Francis) Barrett

[Lymington], 7 September 1812
A.L.S., Berg
Address: M[rs] Barrett / Richmond / Surry.

Sept[r] 7th 1812.

My dearest Charlotte

I am an ungrateful wretch to have left your delightful long letter so shamelessly unanswered. The intelligence which it contained relative to my dearest sister d'Arblay, though not wholly new to me, was still most welcome and precious. Fanny had given me previous particulars, but different to yours, and that made yours almost completely new. You may wonder that thus doubly assured of my dearest sister's arrival,[1] I do not immediately speed back to Chelsea: but I likewise hear that her stay in England will not be very short;[2] that she is now scarcely ever at the College; is unable to obtain a bed there,[3] and that at present, there is scarcely one in our apartments for myself. These reasons, added to the strong persuasions of every body here to bestow upon myself another fortnight's bathing, whilst the weather is so fine; and the difficulty I always find to get leave of absence, determine me whilst I am on the spot to avail myself of its advantages to the utmost; especially, as a cold obliged me to forfeit one entire week's bathing, and I have not yet gained strength enough in my hand wholly to cut away the warm plaister with which I brought it down, covered up.—My kind sister, I well know will give due weight to such motives, & not attribute my prolonged stay for ten days or a fortnight to want of affection.

Your amiable friends Mde de Gomer and Monr de Chapelle have jointly with myself met with a subject of vexation which has engaged considerably more of our thoughts that in itself it was on any account worth. The story is too long to tell in detail: but its abridgment is this. An elderly woman married to a very young man passed last week through Lymington in their way to the Isle of White. Monr de Chapelle had known the young man in London previous to his marriage, and was accosted by him here, and introduced to his wife, whom he called Lady Flemming.[4] The young husband was once a professed musician, and plays as well as sings, admirably. Well, somehow or other, he got himself and his Lady Flemming invited to M. de Chapelle's cottage to spend an evening, and Mde de Gomer engaged me and several others to be of the party. All this seemed to me perfectly natural, and after hearing the young man perform with great admiration, and looking at his nasty old wife with great contempt for marrying such a boy, I came home in the carriage of this ill-assorted pair, thanked them for their civility, went to bed, and thought no more about them.—The next day, the story got wind with enlaidisements and additions. I received a very impertinent letter about keeping bad company &c, &c, from a little odious old Frenchman, the husband of my father's Mrs Le Noir.[5] The only thing for which I take blame to myself in the whole business is, that I was persuaded by Mde de Gomer to answer his stupid stuff. Then he re-wrote folio pages of self-justification, to which I returned laconic answers of two lines. Then he bothered for a quart' d'heure's entretient, and I <tiring> pleaded business and declined it. But the Gomers and I have been worn to death by hearing so much of this disagreeable story; and through Mrs Le Noir, I am in a great fright, lest the old Frenchman should spread it to My father, to whom it would take a year to explain it clearly.—Meanwhile, I wish the old meddling chap was at Sumatra.—But, I should tell you, that Lady Flemming as she now calls herself, was once discreditably known as Lady Worsley,[6] and that her former fame got blazoned here unknown to the Gomers, at the very time they were shewing her the most civility.—

Ten thousand thanks dearest Charlotte, for your hospitable invitation to meet my Sister at Richmond. I know enough of the matter to be well aware that at Richmond or at your dear Mother's only, could I thoroughly enjoy her company[7]—but at present, I can say nothing as to accepting or declining your truly kind plan. Best love to Barrett, and believe me ever my

dear Charlotte, yrs S. H. Burney.

1. Mme d'Arblay reached Chelsea on 20 August 1812 to be reunited with her aged father and other members of the family. Fanny Raper saw her the next day, Charlotte Barrett soon thereafter (*JL*, 7: 10–12).

2. Mme d'Arblay had originally planned to stay three months, but the visit was prolonged, for one reason or another, until November 1814, when M. d'Arblay came over from France and accompanied her back (*JL*, 6: 662; 7: 491).

3. As Dr. Burney's apartment could only accommodate one visitor (in Sarah's empty room), Mme d'Arblay and her son Alex stayed in "2 very pretty rooms" elsewhere in Chelsea Hospital. However, she soon began visiting among friends and relatives and found that "every moment is filled up with interviews, family parties, & Letters!" (*JL*, 7: 11, 14).

4. Seymour Dorothy Fleming was the daughter of Sir John Fleming, Bt. (c. 1701–63) of Brompton Park, Middx. She had married on 20 September 1775 Sir Richard Worsley (1751–1805), 7th Bt. (1768). Her husband died intestate with no male issue on 8 August 1805; thereupon, a jointure of £70,000 reverted to his wife, although his estates went elsewhere. A month later (12 Sept.) she married J. Louis Couchet, having reverted in the meantime to her maiden name, probably to escape her notoriety (see n. 6) (Cokayne; Burke, *Extinct; GM,* 75, Pt. 2 (1805): 781–82, 874–75).

5. Elizabeth Ann Smart (1754–1841) (*DNB*), the daughter of Christopher Smart, the poet, an early London associate of Charles Burney's. She had married in 1795 a French émigré, Jean Baptiste Le Noir de la Brosse (c. 1753–1833). In 1804, she had sent a copy of her second novel, *Village Anecdotes* (1804), to Dr. Burney, who promoted her work among his friends (Arthur Sherbo, *Christopher Smart* (East Lansing: Michigan State University Press, 1967), 59, 100 and passim; Lonsdale, 25–28, 33–34, 66–70; CB to Thomas Twining, 10 May 1804, Osborn; CB to FC, 4 July 1807, 27 July 1807, Berg).

However, some misunderstanding would later cloud their friendship, and Charles Burney was hoping in 1813 to "get rid of a correspondence that has long been very troublesome to me and try to forget all ab[t] it" (CB to CB Jr., 9 Mar. 1813, Osborn).

6. On 21 February 1782, Sir Richard Worsley brought an action for "criminal conversation" against Maurice George Bisset (c. 1757–1821). The defense contended that the baronet was not entitled to exemplary damages, as he had himself both acquiesced in and encouraged his wife's incontinence. To substantiate this claim, several "*sprightly* men of the *ton*" were examined who had "been *criminally* acquainted with her Ladyship" as well as a doctor who had apparently treated her for venereal disease. Another witness testified that Sir Richard himself had hoisted Capt. Bisset on his shoulders to peep at his wife in the bath. The evidence established beyond a reasonable doubt "that the Lady was *flighty* before her present connexion." The jury found a verdict for the plaintiff, but reduced the damages to one shilling (which did not include costs). The trial, which attracted much attention, was covered in detail in the *Whitehall Evening Post,* 21–23 Feb. 1782 and described by Horace Walpole (Walpole, 25: 227–28 and 245–46).

7. Sarah Harriet might be constrained in meeting her half-sister at Chelsea by the presence of her father, who could in his old age be difficult.

70. With Frances (Burney) d'Arblay to Charles Burney Jr.

[Chelsea College], 13 October [1812]
A.L.S. FBA with A.L.S. SHB, Berg
Published: JL, 7: *L. 648*
Postmarks: 4 o'[Clock] / O[C] / 1812 [?]
[?] / [?] / 1812 NT
[*The first page consists of an A.L.S. FBA to CB Jr., dated 13 October, apparently responding to an invitation to Deptford.*]

My dearest Brother, I must make use of this little corner, to entreat that, if you ever invite me to Deptford,[1] it may on no account be whilst that disagreeable person, Sister d'Arblay is with you![2]

Ever most affectionately yours
S. H. Burney.

Kindest love
to Mrs Burney.

1. Charles Burney Jr. was Vicar of St. Paul's, Deptford (1811), and lived in the rectory (*JL*, 7: 27, n. 10).

2. After 2 September 1812, Mme d'Arblay left Chelsea Hospital and visited among her relatives. She did spend much of the fall at Deptford with Charles (*JL*, 7: 20, n. 5, 21, n. 14).

71. To Richard Allen Burney

Chelsea College, 7 October 1813
A.L.S., Osborn
Address: [?] Burney / [?]n / [?]born / [?]tshire
Postmarks: Two[Penny] / U[npaid] / Chel[sea]
A OC / 7 / 813
Endorsed: Sarah Harriet Burney

Chelsea Coll. Octr 7th
1813

My dear Richard

With regard to the whole mess discussed in your letter,[1] I am as innocent as the babe unborn, & as ignorant too. I have been absent from home seven weeks on the Kentish Coast, with my brother Charles and the dear Barretts, and only returned four days ago.[2] My father, since I came back, has never said one word on the subject of any books that have been sent to Rympton[3]—nor did I know, till I read your letter, that he had at last been the honest man to keep his long-standing promise, or rather offer, to you about them. I am heartily glad the books are in your possession; heartily glad that you like them; & heartily desirous that you should retain them. He never made me any tender of the volumes you speak of, nor did I even dream that he ever meant me to have them. Be assured that I have no hanker after them, <but> and that you are well entitled to cherish and protect them to your life's end, with a clear conscience.

So much for Biography.

If you gave Mrs Burney[4] as satisfactory and striking a likeness of me, as you have sent me of her, she must have an astonishingly accurate an idea of my parts and person! After so masterly a description, I dare say I should know her at the first glance, wherever I might meet her. Meanwhile, present to her my best love and compliments, and tell her, that I shall much rejoice to know her if the fates and destinies ever permit me that pleasure.

To Mrs Hawkins[5] and dear Cecy,[6] say every thing for me that is most kind and affectionate. I dreamt that Miss Cholmondeley[7] thought them so unhappy to have lost her, that she meditated to pay them a consoling visit! My best and cordial love to dear Blue[8]—

Farewel my dear bookish correspondent. I will set every thing relating to the Dictionary right with my father—do you set it right upon your shelves—

Ever with sincere regard & good wishes,
Dear Richard yours,
S. H. Burney.

1. The letter from Esther's son, Richard Allen Burney, is missing, but one gathers that Charles Burney had sent him some books that Richard feared may have been intended for Sarah Harriet.

2. Sarah Harriet spent seven weeks at the seaside in August and September 1813, joining the Barretts and her half-brother Charles at Sandgate, which she left on 20 September (*JL*, 7: 153, 156, n. 2, 183, n. 2).

3. Rimpton, Somerset, where Richard Burney was Rector.

4. Elizabeth Layton (née Williams), Richard's wife of two years (L. 62, n. 7), whom

apparently Sarah Harriet had not yet met. The marriage seems to have had a shaky start, judging from a curious comment made by Mme d'Arblay in 1817: "Mrs. R[ichard] B[urney] is greatly improved in manner & conversation, by all I can gather, since her marriage; &, what is happiest of all, in the estimation of her husband, who now pays her all that attention that seems the result of attachment. I believe them to be among the very few who go on better than they began" (*JL*, 9: 417).

5. Eldest daughter of Sarah's uncle Richard, Ann or "Nancy" Burney (1749–1819), had married on 27 January 1781 John Hawkins (d. 19 June 1804) of Nash Court, Kent. Formerly a Catholic priest, he was professed at Douai Abbey in 1761, but apostasized early in the 1780s and joined the Church of England. Author of some devotional and apologetic works, he became Rector of Hinton Ampner, Hants. (1789), and of Halstead, Essex (1791) (*JL*, 1: lxxiv–lxxv; IGI; "Worcester Mem.," 16, 26–27, 34, 56, 67; *GM*, 74, Pt. 2 (1804): 692; information kindly sent by Mr. Geoffrey Scott, Douai Abbey, Upper Woolhampton, Reading, Berks.).

6. Cecilia Charlotte Esther, the fourth of Esther Burney's five daughters, was virtually adopted by her childless aunt Hawkins, with whom she had lived since 1794 (*JL*, 3: 60; 9: 5, n. 3; "Worcester Mem.," 67).

7. Probably Harriet Cholmondeley (1798–1814), the daughter of George James Cholmondeley (1752–1830), commissioner of excise (1782–1801), by his first wife, Marcia (née Pitt) (d. 1808), whom he had married 7 August 1790. This would be the "cousin to Lord Cholmondeley, a widower with one daughter," who in 1808 "was looking out for some respectable Lady that he could trust his daughter with, as sea bathing was . . . particularly recommended for her." She joined Mrs. Hawkins and Cecilia at Brighton for the winter, and accompanied them to Malvern the following summer, a pattern which was repeated more than once. Their responsibility for her seems to have ended late in 1813, but she had not long to live and would die 12 June 1814, a month after her father's second marriage (Burke; "Worcester Mem.," 58–59, 61; *GM*, 60, Pt. 2 (1790): 764; 84, Pt. 1 (1814): 621, 700; 100, Pt. 2 (1830): 567; parish register, St. Marylebone).

8. "Blue," Elizabeth Warren Burney, sister to Mrs. Hawkins, lived with her nephew Richard both before and after his marriage (L. 35, n. 8; L. 62, n. 8).

72. To Charlotte (Francis) Barrett

[Chelsea College], 10 November 1813
A.L.S., Berg
Address: M[rs] Barrett / Lower Road / Richmond / Surry
Postmarks: 7 o'Clock / 11 NO / 1813 NT
Two[PyPost] / Unpaid / Chelsea E C

Nov[r] 10th 1813

Dearest Charlotte

I too am reading Mme de Staal,[1] and am such a Goth, that I catch myself yawning over it! Probably I am not formed to love "les plaisirs dissertant." The book is like a long Review, and all about the same set of objects; and I tire for want of connection, and something either to interest my feelings, or amuse my imagination. Yet, I have extracted some delightful, and some most wise little passages; and I read, though with fatigue, still with admiration, such a copious series of well-expressed reflections. Being no great hand at reflection myself, however, I look for something more narré, more tangible, &—bref—as I said before, crack my jaws for very weariness.—I told my sister d'Arblay to-night, how glad I was that our best English writers, meaning Adison, Swift, Johnson[2] &c, had not written like M^de de Staal; for if they had, as sure as a gun, I should never have loved reading—I should never have opened a book. I have finished vol 1. & shall probably read II & III, out of vanity, & just to say I have read them; all the while making the mortifying discovery about myself which Sir Hugh so ruefully makes about Indiana, when he exclaims—"My dear Brother,—do you know that Dr Orkborn says, poor Indiana has got no brains!"[3]—I have no brains to relish five hundred pages of critical & philosophical, & now and then rhapsodical disquisition.[4]—Basta così.

I cannot for my life send you F. Raper's direction, for, not having seen her this fortnight, and only hearing her say it was in Cook's Grounds,[5] I was this day forced to forward a letter to her from Sister d'Arblay through the medium of old Mrs Raper,[6] to whom I sent it to convey or give to her as soon as possible. Her little Tale of Laura[7] (I believe she will call it) will be excellent: but when I had read it, & returned it to her, it made me write to her—"Ah, dear Fanny, you who know so well what is right, & I who feel it so well when reading your representation—how great is our responsibility!—"

My Sister has a lodging in little Sloane Street,[8] & in coming backwards & forwards, has hitherto escaped cold. But the nights are terribly damp, & I tremble for her. She reads Newspapers from morning till night: but Newspapers of three or four weeks back,[9] & will not let you say a word to her of present events. "O, don't tell me—I shall come to it—I am reading up to it!" And by the time she has read up to it, some newer intelligence will probably have arrived, which will make what we are now rejoicing at appear stale, & put it all out of our heads. Thus she loses to herself and others all the pleasure of participation; for who can take great delight in hearing her conjectures and exclamations relative to matters which are now decided? Who can be much interested to hear her talking so big of a partial skirmish, who knows that a momentous general engagement has so recently taken place?—These are oddities that are—that are—rather—odd!—

I will write instantly, my dearest, about the Whalebone. I own I had forgotten it; like the woman de Staal tells of, that lamented how prone her nature was to forget les absents.[10] Henrietta Larkin's[11] pretty bonnet was out of my sight, & so the materials of which such bonnets are made, went out of my thoughts. But I trust you shall hear good tidings of the whalebone speedily. I am alive to tell of it: but one day last week I went to dine at the Hulse's[12] beyond Shooter's Hill & Blackheath[13] with a gentleman & lady who took me in a Cramp, & we did not get home till half past one! Only think of being on such a thievish road at such hours.—Love to Barrett, Sister, Marianne, Doppy, & your three[14]

Ever dear Char y[rs] S. H. B.

1. Sarah, as it appears later (see L. 73), was reading the work of Anne-Louise-Germaine (née Necker), baronne de Staël-Holstein (1766–1817), *De l'Allemagne*, finally published in 3 volumes in London in October 1813, after Napoleon had banned its publication in 1810.

2. Joseph Addison (1672–1719), Jonathan Swift (1667–1745), and Samuel Johnson (1709–84).

3. In Mme d'Arblay's novel, *Camilla* (1796), Sir Hugh Tyrold makes the remark when giving up his attempt to have the beautiful but shallow girl educated; Dr. Orkburne was her tutor (Vol. 1, Bk. 1, Ch. 6).

4. Charlotte Barrett may have sympathized with this point of view; another work of Mme de Staël's she found "sagacious & brilliant & beautiful, though in general I have no great taste for deep books. Adam Smith's wealth of nations, spoiled my digestion for them" (CFBt to AY, [24 Feb. 1819], Barrett, Eg. 3703A, ff. 92–93v).

5. Fanny Raper, who had started her married life in Cromwell Cottage in 1807, had moved in with her mother-in-law (see next note) c. August 1812. Apparently, she and her husband had now moved again, probably to Cook's Grounds, King's Road, Chelsea, where they would be living the following August (L. 35; CB to CB Jr., 17 June [1808], Berg; CFBt to MF, 26 [Aug. 1812], Barrett, Eg. 3702A, ff. 162–63v; *JL*, 7: 423).

6. "Old Mrs. Raper" was Fanny Raper's mother-in-law, Katherine (née Shepherd) (1735–1823), who had married Henry Raper (1717–89) on 3 September 1763. In 1807, the elderly widow was residing in Chelsea near St. Luke's Church (CB to CBFB, 17 July 1807, Berg; *Alumni Oxon.*; *GM*, 33 (1763): 465; 93, Pt. 2 (1823): 477; Raper family tree, Barrett, Eg. 3707, ff. 269–70v).

7. Fanny Raper's work was probably *Laura Valcheret: a tale for adolescence*, which would soon be published anonymously by Henry Colburn (see below L. 75). The tale is discussed in the Introduction.

8. Mme d'Arblay, who had been sharing accommodation with her sister Charlotte Broome at 23 Chenies Street, had now moved to 63 Lower Sloane Street in Chelsea (*JL*, 7: 21, n. 13, 201).

9. After ten years in Napoleonic France, Mme d'Arblay was out of touch with events that had occurred in England during her absence. Soon after her arrival, her father began to supply her with back issues of periodicals and newspapers. In December 1813, however, she was still three weeks behind; the practice of reading out-of-date news seems

to have become a habit, to which her son refers in 1816 (*JL*, 7: 43–44, n. 10, 132, n. 19, 197, 206).

10. In her chapter on "Les Femmes," Mme de Staël uses this remark as an example of an affected sentimentality among German women: "Une femme allemande disait avec une expression mélancolique: 'Je ne sais à quoi cela tient, mais les absents me passent de l'âme.' Une Française aurait exprimé cette idée plus gaiement, mais le fond eût été le même" (Germaine de Staël, *De l'Allemagne*, ed. Simone Balayé (Paris: Garnier-Flammarion, 1968), 1: 67).

11. Unidentified, but possibly related to John Pascal Larkins (1781–1856) (L. 76, n. 4), whose son Henry (c. 1796–1820) attended Charles Burney Jr.'s school (*Times*, 6 Apr. 1820; *Alumni Oxon.*; *GM*, 91, Pt. 1 (1821): 186, 189).

12. Samuel Hulse (1747–1837), P.C., G.C.H. (1819), Kt. (1821), and his wife, Charlotte (d. 1842). Son of the 2nd Bt., Sir Edward Hulse (1715–1800) of Breamore, Hants., he was Colonel of the 62nd Foot, Gen. (1803), and later Field-Marshal (1830). Lt.-Gov. of Chelsea Hospital since 25 February 1807, he would become Governor on 19 February 1820 (*DNB;* Burke; Shaw, 1: 449; 2: 323; Dean, 303, 305). For a description of his house, see below L. 77.

13. Blackheath, crossed by Shooter's Hill Road, was known for its highwaymen and footpads (Ben Weinreb and Christopher Hibbert, eds., *The London Encyclopaedia* (London: Macmillan, 1983), 69–70, 784).

14. Sarah sends her love to Henry Barrett, Charlotte Broome, Marianne Francis, Ralph Broome, and Charlotte Barrett's three children—the third, Richard Arthur Francis, having been born 13 December 1812 (baptismal certificate, Barrett, Eg. 3708, f. 16).

---

73. To [Elizabeth] Carrick[1]

Chelsea College, 6 December 1813
A.L.S., National Library Wales
Address: Mrs Carrick / Dr Carrick's / Clifton / Bristol / Somersetshire
Postmarks: 7 o'Clock / 6 DE / [1]813 N[T]
A D / 6 / 81[3]

Chelsea Coll. Decr 6th 1813.

Dear Madam

I will weary you with no apologies for my long silence, but give you a little history of myself since I last wrote, and thank you most heartily for the truly amusing letter which you were kind enough to address to me (I blush to record it!) in the month of August! And this is December!—What a fool, and an enemy to myself I am! The vile spirit of procrastination, how lamentably it too often possesses me! I would not forfeit your correspondence for the world, and yet I seem by the tardiness with which I take up my pen, as if I attached to it scarcely any value. I forget who it is that says with frightful strength and truth "Hell is paved with good resolutions!"[2] My mind, I know, is most ineffectually stored with them; and I sometimes wish, since it is so difficult to perform all I intend, that such useless projects of reformation would never enter my head. They only fret me, and destroy the <enjoyment> comfort with which I might otherwise <derive from> indulge my laziness.

But this is even worse than an apology, and this is not giving you the history I promised.—My Summer was spent in rambling along the beautiful coast of Kent.[3] I was scarcely acquainted till then with that charming county. I made the longest stay at Sandgate, a tranquil and as yet unhackneyed bathing-place, which has but one draw-back: the shore is composed of shingles, and I can only enjoy a walk by the sea side on smooth sands. The country at the back of the little town is delicious, verdant, hilly, well-wooded, and smiling with peace and plenty. Mr Wilberforce and his family were the principal residents in the place.[4] He visited the relation I was with,[5] and (for a Saint!) appeared to me really a deserving, animated, and pleasing man. I don't love, generally speaking, Separatists,[6] and men, who instead of communing with their own hearts, in their chambers, and on their beds, make a sort of parade of their religion, and are never easy till they have established a public reputation for sanctity. Except amongst clergyman, I think a man's religion should be between himself and his God. However, Mr Wilberforce, as the open enemy of the Slave Trade,[7] is entitled, whatever other objections may be made to him, to the highest veneration—the most sincere applause.—Miss Hawkins, (and as a friend of mine always adds, "the daughter of Sir John Hawkins, Justice of the Peace, who sent a man to prison for calling him a Codger",)[8] was likewise at Sandgate. She is, as you know, the Authoress and the Heroine of Gertrude and the Countess.[9] A more fluent, and long-winded speaker I scarcely ever encountered; and with the features and strong-boned figure of a man, she is now and then romantic—always enthusiastic, and by way of variety, sometimes pathetic. She tires me, I own: but I believe her to be perfectly upright, and well-principled, & benevolent.—

I heartily exult and rejoice in the speedy prospect of a new work from the pen of Miss Edgworth, under the title you wrote me word of: "Patronage". I saw it Advertized yesterday.[10] My Sister d'Arblay's first Vol. is in the press.[11] We do not know ourselves, yet, what its title is. She says that half the bloom of novelty is taken off an expected work, by mentioning its name, extent, or any thing relating to it before it is published.[12]

Yes; I have read the book you speak of, "Pride & Prejudice",[13] and I could quite rave about it! How well you define one of its characterestics when you say of it, that it breaths a spirit of "careless originality."—It is charming.—Nothing was ever better conducted than the fable; nothing can be more piquant than its dialogues; more distinct than its characters. Do, I entreat, tell me by whom it is written; and tell me, if your health will allow you, soon. I die to know. Some say it is by Mrs Dorset, who wrote that clever little bijou, "the Peacock at Home".[14] Is it so? Pray, pray tell me. I have the three vols now in the house, and know not how to part with them. I have only just finished, and could begin them all over again with pleasure.—

I am not sufficiently fond of dissertations, of eternal analysis, of eloquent bubbles, to be a warm partizan of M^de^ de Staal. Between friends—but don't mention it—I yawned over her Allemagne[15]—and yet, here and there, was electrified by a flash of sublimity. Do you agree with me in thinking, that with all her brilliant varnish, she is corrupt at heart? Had Satan himself written "Pauline", one of the Stories published with "Zulma",[16] he could have produced nothing more offensive to decency—more detestably disgusting. But adieu dear Madam, I can only add that I am y^rs^ ever

S. H. Burney.

Pray write soon, & give me all the gossip you can about books, & clever people.

My dear Father is tolerably well. M^rs^ d'Arblay is in Chelsea near us, & dines here twice or thrice a week.[17] She is too busy correcting the press to come oftener.[18]

1. Elizabeth Carrick (d. 10 June 1817) was the wife of Andrew Carrick (1767–1837), M.D. of Clifton, who graduated in medicine from Edinburgh in 1787 and began his practice in Bristol in 1789. Elected a Physician to the Infirmary in 1810, he would become the Senior Physician in 1816 until his retirement in 1834 when he "was unanimously chosen Honorary Physician" (*GM*, NS 8 (1837): 100; 87, Pt. 1 (1817): 573; *List of Graduates in Medicine in the University of Edinburgh from 1765 to 1866* (Edinburgh: Neill, 1867)).

2. The expression is proverbial, but its currency was perhaps owing to Johnson's pronouncement, on 16 April 1775, that "Hell is paved with good intentions," as quoted in James Boswell's *Life of Samuel Johnson, LL.D.* (1791).

3. For SHB's seven-week vacation, some of which was spent at Sandgate with her half-brother Charles and the Barretts, see L. 71.

4. William Wilberforce (1759–1833), philanthropist and politician (*DNB*), had married on 30 May 1797 Barbara Spooner, by whom he had four sons and two daughters. For Wilberforce's association with Sandgate, where he spent four summers (1812–14 and 1825), see Linda Rene-Martin, "Wilberforce's Sandgate Summers," *Country Life*, 29 May 1975, 1402–3.

5. The Wilberforces were close friends of Sarah's Evangelical niece, Marianne Fran-

cis, who had met them in 1811 through Arthur Young, and wished to accompany them on their summer excursion (MF to HLTP, 16 Dec. 1812, John Rylands; Gazley, 602, 622, and passim). The relation Mr. Wilberforce was visiting at Sandgate, however, was probably Dr. Charles Burney Jr., scholar and divine, who introduced him to Mme d'Arblay (*JL*, 7: 181).

6. In 1785, Wilberforce became Evangelical in outlook, but did not in fact separate from the established church; for an account of his conversion and its effect on his personal and political life, see Robin Furneaux, *William Wilberforce* (London: Hamish Hamilton, 1974), Chs. 3 and 4.

7. During his long parliamentary career (1780–1825), Wilberforce fought for the abolition of slavery. A major victory came on 25 March 1807 when a bill prohibiting the slave trade in the British West Indies became law. Active in organizing the Anti-Slavery Society, he died shortly before the Bill for the Abolition of Slavery was passed. For a detailed record of his parliamentary career, see Thorne; two recent biographies are by Furneaux and John Pollock, *Wilberforce* (London: Constable, 1977).

8. Sarah Harriet had recounted this anecdote of Charlotte Barrett's in her letter of 1 April 1812 (L. 66).

9. The idea that Laetitia Hawkins's novel, *The Countess and Gertrude*, was autobiographical probably also originated with Mrs. Barrett. Marianne Francis reports that "Charlotte, who knows Miss Hawkins, declares, that the Countess must have been meant for her Mother, & Gertrude for herself" (MF to HLTP, 17 Feb. 1812, John Rylands).

10. Maria Edgeworth's novel, *Patronage* (1814), which the *Times* began advertising on 6 December 1813 as "in the press, and will be published about Christmas."

11. Mme d'Arblay's novel had been at the press since 4 November 1813 (*JL*, 7: 208–9); she believed that the first and second volumes were printed by Christmas, but this may not have been the case (*JL*, 7: 222 and n. 7, 238 and n. 6). The novel would appear on 28 March 1814 (*JL*, 7: 256 and n. 2).

12. Early in her career, Frances Burney had been advised by her mentor, Samuel Crisp, to keep her work "an impenetrable Secret" until finished. Samuel Johnson had also admonished her "not to *whisper* even the *Name* of it to my *Bedfellow*,—to raise no expectations of it, which were *always* prejudicial" (*EJL*, 3: 180, 250).

She was now being disturbed by the expectations raised for *The Wanderer*, which were so high that the publishers began to circulate surreptitious copies of the first volume before the whole was printed (*JL*, 7: 209, 237–38). Later she would blame its failure at least partly on an erroneous impression of its subject matter, "the false expectation universally spread that the Book would be a picture of France," as well as on envy over its commercial success (*JL*, 7: 478–79; 8: 317–18).

13. The second novel published by Jane Austen, *Pride and Prejudice*, appeared anonymously in January of 1813. Immediately successful, the first edition sold out within six months, and a second edition appeared in the autumn (John Halperin, *The Life of Jane Austen* (Baltimore: Johns Hopkins University Press, 1984), 209–11; for the publishing history, see David Gilson, *A Bibliography of Jane Austen* (Oxford: Clarendon Press, 1982), 23–37).

14. The rumor was a current one (Gilson, 25–26). Sarah seems to have enjoyed speculating about the authors of anonymous works, which she did when *The Peacock "at home"* came out in 1807. According to Charles Burney, "my dafter Sarah thinks that it must have been written by Charlotte Smith's Sister, who is a great Naturalist & full of learn-

ing, Spirit, & genius" (CB to FC, Jan. 1808, Osborn). In this case she proved to be right; the writer of the children's poem was Catherine Ann Dorset (c. 1750–c. 1817) (*DNB*), the sister of Charlotte Smith.

15. Sarah discusses Mme de Staël's work, which she was "yawning over," in her letter of 10 November 1813 (L. 72).

16. "Pauline" appears in Mme de Staël's, *Zulma, et trois nouvelles* (London: Colburn, 1813), 131–267. The heroine, a woman with a past, fails to tell her austere husband of her faults. After he kills her seducer in a duel, she dies repentant, vindicated by the narrator.

17. Mme d'Arblay was living in lodgings in Lower Sloane Street near the Chelsea Hospital (see above L. 72).

18. She was correcting the proofs of her novel *The Wanderer* (n. 11).

---

74. To Charles Burney Jr.

[Chelsea College], 8 December 1813
A.L.S., Comyn
Address: Revd Dr Burney / Deptford Rectory / Kent
Postmarks: 7 o'Clock / 9 DE / 1813 NT
[?] Py Post / [?] / [?]

December 8th 1813

We are in a very poor way here, my dear brother, and at our wits end to know what we <should> can do to rouse my poor father's spirits. He has had for some time, a very severe cold, and other teasing complaints have followed it which render him so low, that it is shocking to see him. I want you to come and cheer him up a little. You have more novelty to talk to him about than I have, and would not so easily be silenced. He says he hates to be spoken to—but that is a fib: he only hates it when the speaker has nothing amusing to talk about. That is a good deal my case at present; yet, I do my best, with the help of Newspapers and tittle tattle to make myself agreeable.—Come and try your own hand, and meanwhile, I will say nothing about expecting you, for fear business should prevent your leaving home.

My kindest love to Mrs Burney.
Adieu, my dear brother,
yours ever affectionately
S. H. Burney.

Mother Dab is still at Windsor.[1] All the worse for us!—

1. Mme d'Arblay, who had served as Second Keeper of the Robes to Queen Charlotte (1786–91), was occasionally invited to Windsor. She was there on 6 December 1813, but back again in Sloane Street by the eleventh (*JL*, 7: 199, 201).

75. To Henry Colburn

[Chelsea College], 24 January 1814
A.L.S., Bodleian, MS. Montagu d. 6, ff. 319–20v
Address: Mr Colburn

January 24th 1814

Dear Sir

I hope, that considering the thickness of the Volumes, and the impossibility of reading any work of Miss Edgeworth's with the carelessness and haste a common Novel may be skimmed over with, I shall not be thought to have detained "Patronage"[1] a very unreasonable time. I thank you most cordially for the loan. Nobody more thoroughly venerates the admirable Author than I do—And in this last work, she really has excelled herself! Every young man ought particularly to study it—but it contains many hints useful and good for all ages, conditions, and characters. She is the pride of English female writers—and I do positively believe, the most useful author, whether male or female, now existing.[2]

I am also extremely grateful to you for the pretty bound copy you have been so good as to send me of Mrs Hervey's book.[3] I hear it very generally well spoken of, and hope that, in every way, it will prove an advantageous publication to you.

Your plans for the New Magazine,[4] I keep at hand to distribute as I imagine will be most useful. They are exceedingly well drawn up, & hold forth the most desirable promises of impartiality combined with amusement and instruction. My porte-feuille alas! can supply you with nothing. I can never scribble but with the aim of gradually developing the intricacies of some long-winded story. Neither Tale nor Essay could I ever atchieve in my life—But I have often felt an earnest impulse, after reading a new work, to sit down and analyze or Review it. For my own use, this, indeed, has been a practice I have observed for many years.[5] If, in that branch of the business I could ever be of any use to you, I shall be happy to do my best. Do you ever mean to deal in Reviews of foreign books, french or Italian, <in> before they appear as translations? I might, in such a case, assist you—And, I fear, that is all I can venture to undertake.

Mrs C. Raper's little book reads most agreeably in its printed form.[6] I hope it will take.

I shall, in a very few days, return the last box of books which was sent me[7]—Between ourselves, it was a miserable selection—There were not more than three or four in the whole set of those that had been put down in my own list—And nothing newer than the "Heroine".[8] I shall, this time, <send> inclose a longer list, & do trust they will be sent—genuine.

I am, Dear Sir, your much obliged humble Servant

S. H. Burney.

1. Sarah expressed her interest in Maria Edgeworth's latest novel in her letter of 6 December 1813.

2. Maria Edgeworth "was undoubtedly the most commercially successful and prestigious novelist of her heyday, 1800–14." For *Patronage* she earned £2100, which compared favorably to Scott's £700 for *Waverley* (1814) and Jane Austen's £300 for *Emma* (1816). "For contemporary women, the most significant fact about M[aria] E[dgeworth] may well have been her successful competition with men," a view apparently borne out by SHB's remark that she was "the most useful author, whether male or female, now existing" (Marilyn Butler, "Edgeworth, Maria," *A Dictionary of British and American Women Writers, 1660–1800*, ed. Janet Todd (Totowa, N.J.: Rowman & Allenheld, 1985)).

3. Elizabeth (née March) Hervey (c. 1748–c. 1820) (Todd, *Dictionary*). Her last known work, *Amabel; or Memoirs of a Woman of Fashion*, was published by Henry Colburn in 1814, with a second edition in 1818.

4. Henry Colburn would soon publish the *New Monthly Magazine and Universal Register*, a rival to the *Monthly Magazine* of Sir Richard Phillips. The new periodical, the first issue of which would appear on 1 February 1814, "had a long career of success, and numbered among its editors and contributors many of the most illustrious *literati*" ("Appendix," *AR*, 97 (1855): 300; see also *DNB;* Michael Sadleir, *Nineteenth-Century Fiction* (London: Constable, 1951), 2: 112–13).

5. Sarah Harriet speaks of her practice of writing "little private reviews" in her letter of [23 June 1810] (L. 55).

6. Probably *Laura Valcheret* (L. 72, n. 7), which had just been published by Colburn and was advertised for the first time in the *Times* on 11 January 1814.

7. Henry Colburn assisted in and eventually succeeded to the proprietorship of Morgan's Circulating Library in Conduit Street, but was advertising his "English and Foreign Subscription Library" as early as 1807 (*DNB;* Sadleir, 2: 112). He may have lent books from this store "*Gratis*" to Sarah Harriet as one of his published authors, a courtesy which he apparently extended to her father (*JL*, 7: 104). If she paid for the privilege, she might belong to one of several classes of subscribers: those subscribing £10.10s. were entitled to "the immediate perusal of every new work desired," while those paying the lowest rate of £3.3s. were "not entitled to the perusal of new works" (according to an advertisement in the *Times* of 6 April 1820).

8. *The Heroine; or Adventures of a Fair Romance Reader*, a mock romance by Eaton Stannard Barrett (1786–1820) (*DNB*), was published by Henry Colburn late in 1813 and reviewed in the *British Critic* in November.

76. To Charles Burney Jr.

[Chelsea College], 26 January 1814
A.L.S., Osborn

My dearest Carluce

You remember, I hope, the good-natured assurance you lately gave me, that you should never be vexed at my applying to you for any thing I wished to have done—since you would but refuse if it was not a feasible matter, and there would be an end of it.—

Now, in as few words as I can, I will tell you what the above is recalled to your memory for.

I find my new protegé from India, John Burney,[1] a very worthy, active, considerate lad, & grow anxious to be of lasting and substantial service to him. He has, at present, no prospect but of serving on board an East Indiaman as a Midshipman, with £2,,5, per month, out of which he must pay his quota to the mess, cloath himself, and when in port, pay his laundress &c. Upon this slender salary he must continue a Midshipman five years, at the end of which, he may come to be a fourth Mate, and get on a little better. But now comes the rub—Whilst sailing backwards & forwards from India to England, during the above five years, he will generally be in an English port six months after every voyage, without a farthing to live upon till the ship is again taken up for a fresh trip. He receives no pay but just while in actual employment. Who is to maintain him in England at the end of each Voyage?—It makes me sweat (saving your presence) to think of it!—Now, it has been suggested to me that you might perhaps be able to procure for him an East India Cadetship. I cannot make my father act, as he did when such resources were obtained for this boy's two brothers[2]—And James has already had such trouble with the other Cub who was here last year,[3] that I am ashamed to ask him. But if you know any East India Director, or any leading clue to guide towards a Director, it might be done for only (what we all hate bad enough, but must sometimes do) for only asking. If I thought Mr Larkins[4] could do any thing for me, or put me in the way, & it would save you trouble, I would e'en venture with a bold face to apply to him. But turn it over in your mind, dearest Brother. A Cadetship is an assured & permanent support for the lad—a Midshipman's situation only maintains him whilst at sea, and he cannot be at sea above half his time.[5] My father is much as when I wrote last. Is it true that your sweet little Bright-blossom[6] has the measles? I fear this is a bad time for such a complaint—

but may she have it favourably, and soon be smiling and playing around you again!—

My kindest love to Mrs Burney—And hate to your Gout:—

"The Sofa suits

"The gouty limb, 'tis true; but gouty limb

"Though on a Sofa, may I never feel!"[7]—

Yours ever affectionately, my dear Brother

S. H. Burney.

January 26th 1814

1. John Burney (1799–1837), one of the numerous offspring of Sarah's late brother, Richard Thomas, in India. John had worked his passage to England arriving pre May 1813, and was attending a school run by Daniel Simpson in Mendlesham, Suffolk. Apparently, Charles Burney had offered to pay for his education, and this intention was reluctantly fulfilled by his residuary legatee, Mme d'Arblay. She refused, however, an order for clothes made for John before he had seen any of his English relatives (*JL*, 7: 481–82 and n. 5).

2. Richard's two eldest sons, Richard and Henry, had been sent to be educated in England c. 1804 (L. 28, n. 10). In 1807, Richard Thomas asked his father to help to procure them cadetships in the East India Company, which "with infinite trouble and difficulty," he was able to do (CB to FBA, 12 Nov. 1808, Berg). Both boys joined the company in England in 1807 and returned to India on 14 August 1808, where they would lead successful careers in the Bengal Army (Hodson; see further LL. 162, 174).

Although he did act on the request of his son, Charles Burney did not do so without protest. He complained bitterly of the "constant plague, vexation, disappointment, letter writing & dictating" involved in the business, which he felt was "the most cruel task that c^d^ have been imposed upon me" (CB to CPB, 9 Jan. 1808, Osborn). It is hardly surprising that Sarah would shrink from requesting help from her eighty-seven-year-old father.

3. James Christian Burney (1797–post 1828), another of Richard's sons, had been in England early in 1813 when James tried to assist him. He in turn had asked Dr. Burney to write a soliciting letter which "so extremely | disturbed & harrassed" the old man "that it has almost made him ill!—&, at last, my Brother only could procure it, by writing word for word what he wished, & which, at length, he consented to copy" (*JL*, 7: 74, and n. 6). Apparently, these efforts were unavailing and James Christian returned to India where he joined the East India Company in 1819, became Ens. in the Bengal Army in 1820, Lt. in 1823, and retired in 1826 (Hodson).

4. Probably related to John Pascal Larkins (1781–1856) of the Bengal Civil Service (1796–1827), who was currently a member of the Board of Trade and Superintendent of Silk Investments; when he retired from the East India Company in 1827, he was a senior member of one board and president of another (Dodwell and Miles, comps., *Alphabetical List of the Honourable East India Company's Bengal Civil Servants, from the year 1780, to the year 1838* (London: Longman, Orme, Brown, 1839); *GM*, NS 46 (1856): 526–27).

5. It would seem that Sarah's efforts were unsuccessful, and John Burney would sail back to India c. May 1814, his mess being paid from his grandfather's estate (*JL*, 7: 481–82). He would obtain a cadetship in 1819, however, when he joined the E.I.C. in India; like his brothers before him, he became an officer in the Bengal Army (Ens. 1820; Lt. 1823), and retired in 1828 (Hodson).

6. "Brightblossom" was CB Jr.'s fond name for his granddaughter, Frances Anne (1812–60), eldest child of his only son Charles Parr and his wife, Frances Bentley (née Young) (c. 1792–1878), whom he had married 24 December 1810 (*JL*, 1: lxxii; 7: 166, n. 14; *GM*, 80 (1810): 586).

7. William Cowper, *The Task* (1785), Bk. 1, ll. 106–8.

---

77. To Charlotte (Francis) Barrett

Dartford, Kent, 10 September [1814]
A.L.S., Berg
Address: Mrs Barrett / Richmond / Surry
Postmarks: DARTFORD / 15
10 o'Clock / SP 12 / 1814 FN∩
[?] / [?] SE 12 / 1814

Septr 10th
at General Hulses
Westheath,
near Darford, Kent.

My dearest Charlotte

Oh, the bustles and fusses that I was in, on <my> reaching Chelsea on Wednesday!—There was the Court so full of Soldiers waiting for their discharge from the Board, that I could scarcely make my way up to Erswell's[1] door.—General Hulse I heard was in the Board-room, and in order to know at what hour he would return to Westheath, I sent a note to him which he had only time to answer at the back "At half past three—Yours truly, S. Hulse."—So I bustled and looked sharp, & aired and changed, and turned over all my drawers for half mourning garments,[2] and eat luncheon, & was as busy as a bee; and at half past three, in a pouring rain, I got into the General's carriage, and away I hied. Mrs Hulse received me most kindly; her very dogs were civil; her dinner excellent—And our evening was chatty and social. We never go out till two o'clock, and then wander about the grounds, and through the neighbouring Village—and gather flowers, and look at prospects, and enjoy ourselves mightily. We have a most extensive view from almost every window in the house—The Thames runs in full sight, and we can trace its windings almost down to the Nore. Yesterday I was very grand, and dined at Belvedere,[3] the seat of Lord Eardly[4] with <three> four noblemen, an honourable, a Lady, and an honourable Miss.—The noblemen were, Lord Eardley, Lord Say and Sele,[5] Lord Headford,[6] and Lord Hindon;[7]—the Honble was Mr Eardley,[8] the Lady was Lady Say and Sele; & her daughter, Miss Twistleton,[9] was the Honble Miss. All these fine folks were very civil and pleasant. Mrs Hulse is the best chaperon I ever went out with, and takes as much pains to secure attention for you abroad as at home. The pictures at Lord Eardley's I did not see very well because they (not the pictures) dined so late, that the carriage was not ordered to take us thither till half past six—but I am to go again, and see them by daylight. Miss Twistleton is one of the best bred young women of fashion I have ever met with; she paid great attention both to Miss Brander[10] and me—played and sung to us delightfully; has [cop]ied out two or three airs which I liked, and sent them to me this morning—and what is best of all, I am told that she is uncommonly good and charitable. She superintends a school in her Grandfather's neighbourhood, and walks to it every day to hear the children read, and to look at their work. She makes a hundred ingenious things which she gives to poor people to sell; and she is very very pretty, and perfectly unaffected, and not yet twenty. Mrs Hulse says she never sees her without planning a match for her with the Duke of Devonshire;[11]—she really would make a good and most amiable little Duchess.—

I have heard an anecdote or two of Lady Cecilia Johnson[12]—One is, that about two years ago, after being at a crouded drawing-room in the morning, and at the play in the evening, somebody said—"Was not your Ladyship dreadfully fatigued?"—"Fatigued! No, not at all;—I was not one of the performers."—She calls Hampton Court, where she and many other high but poor dames, has or had apartments—"The Quality Workhouse."—Oh, and I heard to-night, that Welje, the Prince of Wales' Confectioner, being sick, sent for a lawyer to make his will; the lawyer asked him for a brief sketch of his testamentary dispositions—"Why the whole matter" said Wellje "is that I mean to leave all I have to my posteriors."[13]—My kindest love to Barrett & my two dear Sisters—Pray write soon—Adieu dearest Charlotte, ever y^{rs} S. H. B

Love to Julia, to Etta, and "How do? Shake hands"—

1. Sarah's landlady, Elizabeth Erswell (fl. 1795–1821), the wife of Joseph Erswell (c. 1774–1842), who had been appointed Master Butler of the Royal Hospital Chelsea in 1811 (L. 79; chapel register, Royal Hospital Chelsea).

2. This is the first surviving letter of Sarah's since the death of her father on 12 April 1814 (Scholes, 2: 253–60). During the following month, Sarah moved to another apartment in Chelsea Hospital where she was established by 27 May (*JL*, 7: 348, n. 15, 512).

From her father, Sarah inherited "One thousand Pounds and one hundred Pounds more for a wedding Garment if ever she marries." She was also left a glazed bookcase, an edition of Shakespeare and "any other of the duplicates lent to Lady Crewe which she does not wish to retain." With Frances Raper, she was to share some French books "except the works of Voltaire many of which are unfit for the perusal of Females." A miniature portrait of her mother, a one-third share in the proceeds of a "curious Merlin Table," and a small Broadwood piano, completed her bequests. (For a copy of the will, see Scholes, 2: 262–75.) Apparently these intentions were fulfilled when £1,089 was deposited to her account at Coutts on 10 June 1814; invested almost immediately in 4 percents, it brought her total investments to £2,410.14.4, yielding approximately £85 per annum.

At least one member of the family would comment on the paucity of provision for his youngest daughter, the only one left unmarried, who had cared for her father in his old age (MAR to FBA, 21 June [1814], Barrett, Eg. 3697, f. 305). Charles Burney's will was a curious one in any case. The property was by no means equitably divided among his children: James, Charlotte, and Charles each received £200; Susan's daughter, "heiress to my affection and designs in her mother's favor," inherited £1,200 in all, while Esther and Fanny were given £1,000 each and shared the residue of the estate, which included a valuable library. Of the second generation, Charlotte Broome's children (and some of Richard's) were not mentioned even for tokens of remembrance.

Mme d'Arblay defended her father and the kindness of his intentions: "who had ever a right to make a Will by his Choice, if HE who himself inherited NOTHING; whose whole possessions were the result of his labours & his talents, might not do it?" (*JL*, 7: 352). Nevertheless, she and Esther made efforts to distribute the property more evenly (see e.g., *JL*, 7: LL. 774, 777, 781, 784). As she herself acknowledged: "The distinction, however, shewn me by my dearest Father . . . seems to have cast a kind of general though undefinable cloud over the Family Harmony" (*JL*, 7: 352). James refused to act as executor (*JL*, 7: 325), and Charlotte Broome "takes her cutting off quite to heart for the unkindness still more than the loss" (CFBt to MF, 7 May [1814], Berg).

Fanny's belief that her father had acquired nothing except through his own industry would later be challenged by Mrs. Burney's son. Stephen Allen alleged that Charles Burney had benefited considerably from his second marriage, and estimated the value of Mrs. Burney's property at £4,000. While the exact amount of her contribution cannot be determined, she probably had sufficient funds to purchase the family home and set up a carriage (*JL*, 12: 781, n. 7, 789; CB, *Memoirs*, 181–82).

While there was no legal constraint on Dr. Burney's inclinations, there may have been a moral obligation to provide for the sole surviving child of that second union, before distributing the property among his other children. It also appears that he failed to honor fully the testamentary intentions of Sarah's maternal grandmother (see above L. 9, n. 2). Although she makes no complaint in her surviving letters, Sarah clearly suffered under considerable financial constraint after losing her home with her father.

3. Belvidere House, near the village of Erith, Kent, originally erected by George Hayley, was later much improved by Sampson Gideon (c. 1699–1762), a wealthy Jewish stockbroker, who left it to his son (see n. 4; Cokayne; Gibbs). "It stands on an eminence about a mile and a half from the Thames, and commands a very extensive prospect of the surrounding country, which is beautifully diversified by the appearance of the river through different openings." It was noted for a valuable art collection of old masters (Lambert, 4: 349; Edward Hasted, *The History and Topographical Survey of the County of Kent*, 2nd ed., vol. 2 (1797; rpt., Canterbury: E. P. Publishing, 1972), 248–49).

4. Sampson (formerly Gideon) Eardley (1745–1824), only son of Sampson Gideon (n. 3), was created a baronet through his father's influence (1759), and succeeded to his immense estates in 1762; he was M.P. (1770–1802). By royal licence in 1789, he took the name of Eardley and was shortly afterwards created Baron Eardley in the peerage of Ireland. He married 6 December 1766 Maria Marow (then a minor), eldest daughter of Sir John Eardley Wilmot (1709–92), Chief Justice of the Common Pleas (*DNB*). As his sons predeceased him, his honors became extinct (Cokayne; Gibbs; Namier & Brooke; Thorne).

5. Gregory William Twistleton (1769–1844) (afterwards Eardley-Twistleton-Fiennes), 14th Baron Saye and Sele (1788), married 8 September 1794 Maria Marow (1767–1834), the eldest daughter of Lord Eardley. By Royal licence, February 1825, he assumed the name of Fiennes and in March of that year took the name of Eardley, in consequence of his wife's descent (Burke; Gibbs).

6. Thomas Taylour (1757–1829), 2nd Earl of Bective (1795), created 1st Marquess of Headfort (1800) in the peerage of Ireland (Burke; Gibbs; Lodge).

7. John Poulett (1783–1864), styled Viscount Hinton, until he would succeed his father as 5th Earl Poulett in 1819 (Burke; Lodge).

8. Probably Lord Eardley's eldest son, Sampson Eardley, born 29 December 1770, who would die unmarried at Belvidere in 1824 (Cokayne).

9. Maria Elizabeth Twistleton (1795–1826), only daughter of Lord and Lady Saye and Sele (n. 5) (Burke; Lodge).

10. Possibly Georgiana-Bulkeley Brander, who would marry on 14 September 1826 the Rev. Richard Davies, Vicar of Erith Kent (1808–49). She was the eldest daughter of John Spicker Brander (d. pre 1839) of Somerford Grange, Hants., who inherited the fortune of his uncle, Gustavus Brander (1720–87) (*DNB*), a bank director and wealthy collector (*Alumni Cantab.; GM*, 59, Pt. 2 (1789): 1147; 96, Pt. 2 (1826): 365; NS 12 (1839): 324).

11. William George Spencer Cavendish (1790–1858), 6th Duke of Devonshire (1811) (*DNB*), would die unmarried, while the Hon. Miss Twistleton would wed on 31 August 1825 George Ernest (b. 22 Oct. 1795), Count Von Gersdorff of Prussia, only to die the following year (Burke; Cokayne). Perhaps the idea of a match occurred because the two families were closely associated; William Cavendish (1720–64), 4th Duke of Devonshire, had been left the executorship and reversion of her grandfather's estate.

12. Lady Henrietta Cecilia West (1727–1817), daughter of John West (1693–1766), 7th Baron, created 1st Earl De La Warr (1761). She married 5 May 1763 Col. (later Gen.) James Johnston (c. 1724–97). She was known for her wit as well as her caustic tongue (Burke; *Westminsters;* Walpole, 9: 28, n. 19; 11: 18, n. 27; 12: 145; *GM*, 67, Pt. 2 (1797): 1077).

13. The German-born Louis Weltje (c. 1745–1800) was appointed to the Prince of Wales's household c. 1783 as Clerk of the Kitchen and Cellars. The anecdote, typifying his butchery of the English tongue, was a current one (Henry D. Roberts, *A History of the Royal Pavilion Brighton* (London: Country Life, 1939), 18–23); Joanna Richardson, *George IV: A Portrait* (London: Sidgwick & Jackson, 1966), 19).

---

78. [To William Ayrton][1]

Chelsea College, 3 December 1814
A.L.S., Ayrton, BL Add. MS. 52339, ff. 25–26v

Chelsea Coll.
Decr 3d
1814

Dear Sir

When poor Frank Hammond[2] was in prosperity, nobody enjoyed a little grin at his expence more heartily than myself: but now, I think, the time to indulge this grinning disposition about him is passed. Forgive me, therefore, if, at the earnest entreaty of one of his few remaining friends, I take the liberty of stating to you his present plan, and request you, if possible, to <offer to him some assistance in order to> benefit him by some recommendation. He wishes to be employed as an instrument-tuner: but what will be far more difficult to accomplish, he also is most anxious to be engaged as a vocal performer at one or other of the approaching Oratorios. The elder Ashley,[3] to whom Mr Graham[4] would have applied for him, is gone to Paris—And I have been so totally out of the way of public places, and public men, that it is madness to ask me to write or speak upon such a subject to any one but such an old friend as you, who, perhaps, will just hint at some practicable method of getting this poor boy heard, and if he has talents, of enabling them to earn a scanty maintainance. I can say nothing of the Mother—but poor Frank, I heartily pity.—

I shall not plague you with apologies—I dare say you think it quite enough to have been plagued by this application. If you hate writing more than you hate a muddy walk, I shall rejoice in receiving a verbal answer, and in shewing you how snugly I am housed in the old College at Mr Erswell's, Master Butler

Pray present my kind regards to Mrs Ayrton,[5] and believe me, Dear Sir, Yours very truly

S. H. Burney

1. Preserved in the Ayrton Collection of the British Library, the letter is probably addressed to William Ayrton, the influential music critic, who was neighbor to Sarah's half-brother James (L. 25, nn. 5 and 6).

2. Possibly the only son of the late Thomas Hammond, the former Clerk to the Secretary of Chelsea Hospital, and his wife, Ann Frances (L. 58, n. 3).

3. Probably Charles Ashley (1770–1818), the eldest of four sons of the musician, John Ashley (c. 1734–1805), all of whom followed their father's profession. Charles achieved some fame as a violinist, but retired as a man of means shortly after his marriage in 1804 (*DNB; New Grove; GM*, 88, Pt. 2 (1818): 378).

4. Richard Robert Graham (c. 1734–1816), who succeeded his father Daniel (d. 1778) as Apothecary at the Royal Hospital, Chelsea, though without training of any kind (Dean, 221, 312; Walpole, 31: 28, n. 6).

5. Marianne Arnold (d. 25 Jan. 1836), daughter of the composer Samuel Arnold (1740–1802) (*New Grove; DNB*), had married William Ayrton on 17 May 1803 (*GM*, 73, Pt. 1 (1803): 478; NS 5 (1836): 331).

---

79. To Charlotte (Francis) Barrett

[Chelsea College], 28 January 1815
A.L.S., Berg
Address: M[rs] Barrett / Lower Road / Richmond / Surry
Postmarks: [*?*] / 26 JA / 1815 NT

January 28th 1815

My dearest Charlotte

I have scarcely been at home a day for these last six weeks, and when absent from my own fire side, my own writing desk, and my own inkstand, I seem to myself absent from my own powers of thinking, and never can endure the idea of taking up a pen. My trips from home however, have not been of that merry sort to drive away all reflection by gaiety and disipation. I have been nursing and trying to chear my poor Anna Wilbraham,[1] who, subsequent to a jaundice, has been attacked by gall stones, and has suffered dreadfully. This is the tenth week that she has been confined to her room; often to her bed, and though the violence of the disorder appears abated, it still hangs about her, and may, for weeks or even months to come, harass and distress her. She is very thin, but still looks pretty; and her patience, courage & chearfulness are admirable. D[r] Baillie,[2] and your friend Chilver[3] attend her, and shew much compassion for her sufferings, and great admiration of her fortitude. I always slept in her room whilst in Seymour Street, and wholly devoted myself to her solace and amusement (at least, when she was sufficiently free from pain to be amused). One evening only did I leave her, tempted by the prospect of meeting Miss Holford[4] and Miss Baillie[5] at Mr Sotherby's.[6] The latter fulfilled her engagement; Miss Holford pleaded indisposition and staid away; but a younger married sister of hers, Mrs Walker,[7] came, and really struck poor dear Mrs Wilbraham all of a heap! She was a Chester girl, and such infamous stories were known of her previous to her marriage, that, to see her now received in good company—to behold her gay, unconcerned, and perfectly at her ease, disgusted and astonished the Wilbraham party beyond all description. Mrs Sotherby who has two grown up daughters[8] has been admitted into the secret of this young woman's past history, and the acquaintance will gradually drop.—But of this frail fair one, enough. I must tell you how sincerely I was pleased by the gentle, quiet, unpretending deportment of Miss Baillie. It was a crouded party, & I did not get near enough to hear her converse: but I watched her manners and her looks, and liked all that I observed. She appears to be about fifty, or rather more; is short, neither fat nor lean—never can have been pretty, but has a sensible though not brilliant, or even very animated, countenance. There was also a Sir John Malcolm of the par[ty] who has been in Persia and, [I beli]eve, Arabia—and was very communicative and entertaining upon the subject of his travels.[9] Mrs William Spencer, wife to "The Year of Sorrow" poet,[10] was also there, with a very pretty daughter,[11] had it not been for the formal and odd effect that was given to her face by a nose descending in a straight line from her forehead like a grecian profile, and then, all at once curving into a roman bend.—I never saw any thing so heterogeneous, so <u>anomalous</u> (Hannah More would say)[12] in my life.—

My good landlady, Mrs Erswell, is in the straw. She brought into the world on Tuesday night a very pretty little girl, to whom I am to be God Mamma[13]—And if my Nephews and Nieces do not behave to my mind, let them look to it, for I shall certainly cut them out of my Will, and adopt this little Harriet for my Heiress!—When you have leisure to write, let me know <u>particularly</u> how poor dear Clem does.[14] And how are you yourself, my sweet Charlotte? You are spoilt by so many babies,[15] Heaven knows, for a correspondent such as you used to be, and I no longer expect to find you such—But a bill of health you may now & then send me. I have not been able to get to poor Fanny for ages. Thanks for Gardiner's pretty card,[16] & the seal impressions. Adieu—

Kind love to Barrett, your Mother &c, &c, & am ever

Your certainly most loving Aunt
S. H. Burney

I have written to Alex for news of his father & Mother, but get no answer.[17]

Colburn has just sent me the L^{d} of the Isles,[18] some of which I read in Seymour Street,[19] & liked.—

1. Anna Wilbraham, Sarah Harriet's former pupil (L. 29, n. 5).

2. Matthew Baillie (1761–1823), M.D., F.R.S. (1789), physician extraordinary to George III, who had an extensive practice. Author of a pioneering work on morbid anatomy, he was "the first to define exactly the condition of the liver now known as cirrhosis" (*DNB*). He was consulted by various Burneys, including Charles Burney Jr., Charlotte Broome for her son Ralph, and James's daughter Sarah (*JL*, 9: 130, 376, n. 22; 11: 357).

3. Probably Samuel Chilver, a surgeon (d. 16 Feb. 1824) of 14 New Burlington Street, who had been a pupil of Sir Walter Farquhar and had a successful practice; he later treated Mme d'Arblay (*List of the Fellows and Members of the Royal College of Surgeons of England* (London: R. Carpenter, 1822); GM, 94, Pt. 1 (1824): 284; *JL*, 11: 157, n. 6 and passim).

4. Margaret Holford (1778–1852), authoress, the daughter of Allen Holford (c. 1755–88) of Davenham, and Margaret (née Wrench) (c. 1761–1834), his wife, also a writer. Miss Holford had published in 1809, *Wallace; or the Fight of Falkirk*, and in 1811 a collection of *Poems*. She would marry (as his second wife) on 16 October 1826 the Rev. Septimus Hodson (1768–1833), Rector of Thrapston, Northants., and chaplain-in-ordinary to the Prince of Wales (*DNB;* Ormerod, 1: 300; 3: 239).

5. Joanna Baillie (1762–1851), poet and dramatist (sister to Dr. Baillie above), lived with her sister at Hampstead. She had first published in 1790, and had by now produced her most important work, which was known as *Plays on the Passions* (1798–1812); her achievement as a dramatist was considered unusual for a woman (*DNB;* Todd, *Dictionary*).

6. Probably William Sotheby (1757–1833), F.R.S., F.S.A. (1794), a versatile author and member of the Dilettante Society, who entertained in his home the leading literary figures of the day, including Joanna Baillie (*DNB*).

7. Margaret Holford's younger sister, Anna Maria, had married 18 December 1805 Joshua Walker (1786–1862) of Portland Place and Hendon Place, Middx., M.P. (1818–29) (Ormerod, 3: 239; Burke, *DLG;* Thorne).

8. Mary Isted (1759–1834), youngest daughter of Ambrose Isted (c. 1717–81) of Ecton, Northants. She had married William Sotheby on 17 July 1780; her two daughters, Maria Elizabeth (d. 30 March 1852) and Harriet Louisa (d. 1865) would remain unmarried (Burke, *LG* under Sotheby; *GM*, 69, Pt. 1 (1799): 353; NS 37 (1852): 534).

9. Sir John Malcolm (1769–1833), Kt. (1812), Indian administrator and diplomatist, soldier and historian, had been to Persia more than once in the course of his varied career, the subject of a life by John William Kaye, *The Life and Correspondence of Major-General Sir John Malcolm*, 2 vols. (London: Smith Elder, 1856). After returning to England in 1812, he made various literary contacts and would soon publish (in July 1815) his *History of Persia* (*DNB;* Shaw, 2: 312).

10. Susan (née Jenison) (fl. 1791–1815), daughter of Count Francis Jenison Walworth

(1764–1824) (*DNB*) and widow of Count Spreti, who allegedly committed suicide to enable her to marry (on 13 Dec. 1791) her second husband. This was William Robert Spencer (1769–1834), a popular poet and wit in London society, who had published *The Year of Sorrow* in 1804 (*DNB*).

11. The Spencers had two daughters: the elder, Louisa Georgina (c. 1792–1854), married Edward Canning; the younger, Harriet, was to wed on 9 October 1819 at Ratisbon her cousin Count Charles Westerholt (*DNB; GM*, 89, Pt. 2 (1819): 458; NS 42 (1854): 638).

12. Hannah More frequently perceives anomalies, as in her discussion of "A Devotional Spirit": "To bring a proud temper to an humble prayer, a luxurious habit to a self-denying prayer, or a worldly disposition to a spiritually minded prayer, is a positive anomaly" (Hannah More, *Practical Piety* (London: T. Cadell and W. Davies, 1811), 1: 131).

13. Harriett, the daughter of Joseph and Elizabeth Erswell (L. 77, n. 1), was baptized in the chapel of Chelsea Hospital on 9 April 1815 (chapel register, Royal Hospital Chelsea).

14. Clement Francis, Charlotte Francis's brother, was a student at Cambridge; his health was deteriorating, perhaps through overwork (*JL*, 8: 15, n. 12).

15. Charlotte Barrett had given birth to her fourth child in six years, Henry John Richard, on 11 October 1814 (baptismal certificate, Barrett, Eg. 3708, f. 17).

16. Possibly a design by William Nelson Gardiner (1766–1814), artist and engraver (*DNB*).

17. M. and Mme d'Arblay had left London 10 November 1814 to return to France, leaving behind their son Alex at Cambridge (*JL*, 7: 485, n. 1). The family lost touch with her until mid-February, when she sent a letter to Esther, explaining that ill health, low spirits, and constant occupation had prevented her from writing (*JL*, 8: L. 838). Alex's failure to reply to his aunt's letter was not uncharacteristic; his mother frequently complained of his negligence in correspondence (e.g., *JL*, 8: 59).

18. Walter Scott's poem, *The Lord of the Isles*, composed rapidly in a few weeks, had been published on 8 January 1815 (Johnson, 1: 460–67).

19. 56 Upper Seymour Street was the London address of the Wilbraham family (L. 31, n. 2).

80. To Charlotte (Francis) Barrett

[Chelsea College], 5 April 1815
A.L.S., Berg
Address: M[rs] Barrett / Lower Road / Richmond / Surry
Postmarks: [*?*] Post / [Un]paid / [Chel]sea C O
7 o'Clock / 5 AP / [1815] NT

April 5th 1815

If ever you do me the undeserved honour to think of me at all, my dearest Charlotte, what a wretch you must by this time have learnt to believe me! Two dear kind letters of yours have remained unanswered I am ashamed to remember how long. I have nothing to say for myself but this—and a poor shabby say it is! Colburn and I are in negociation together, and I have been toiling for him like a dragon, and I meant to have been in readiness with a Tale, an' please you, in one fat volume, for the press in May.[1] And so, I have toiled for I know not how long till three and four in the morning, and I was beginning to see daylight not only through my windows, but through my job,—And I should have been ready at the time proposed,—And I should have written to you a folio of comfortable nonsense,—and I should have enjoyed myself in idleness through the Summer, when, lo! Anna Wilbraham, poor heart, is ordered to Cheltenham, and comes over to me last Sunday to implore me to go with her, Madam not being able to accompany her. Had any thing but health been concerned in the business, I should flatly have said No! For above a month past I have refused every allurement to go out except for exercise in the morning, & no less than three times, I sent the Wilbrahams away bootless when they came to fetch me, and wanted me to sleep and bother at their house. This has been since Anna has been better. When she was ill, I went to her without a word. For the same reason, I must now go with her to Chelt: and I like the plan mainly in itself, but I do not like, when I am so industriously in the working vein, to knock all my labour on the head,—set my brains a wool-gathering, and then to have the trouble of taking up, one by one, all the threads of my ravelled thoughts.—I might as well have written to you, my darling, as have fagged thus unmercifully to meet in an instant with such a stumbling block. And that fool Colburn had begun on the backs of Reviews advertising.[2] He must draw in his horns, and I must draw in my crow-quill; for though they tell me that I may work at

Chelt: I know it is a lie. Early morning hours are indispensable there,—and constant exercise; and we shall have William Wilbraham, her Sailor brother[3] with us, and the greatest Mag, bating myself, in the King's dominions,—& I shall no more be able to sit down and compose any thing but dull bulletins to her Mother, than I shall fly.

And so much for my own individual history.

Believe me, I am not the shirking stinkard about visiting Fanny that you seem to suspect. I have been to her since her frightful illness[4] three or four times, and I went to her even before, oftener than to James Street, or to any other relation. Fanny Burney is quite at war with me, for I have never yet been to see her and her lodging at all.—But to return to poor M[rs] Raper. I saw her on Sunday, and she was in pain and looking wan and very indifferent. I mean certainly to make her another long visit before I set off for Cheltenham. She complains that I never go alone; but why should she? I take only pleasant people with me, people that she knows—and she used to litter my rooms with Reynolds'[5] and any kind of strange trash she could pick up. I should now feel embarrassed at being tête a tête with Fanny; I only love to converse with her upon general subjects, and if we were alone, I should be in a constant fright lest she should touch upon her own affairs;[6] which, however, for ought I know, are going on well: but she has told me, and others have repeated so many tarradiddles of hers, that I am sure my looks would convince her that I was not believing a word she said.

M[r] Keate begins to think much better of poor little Catherine:[7] but he says she is not out of the wood.

Have you seen Guy Mannering?[8] I perfectly doat upon it. There is such skill in the management of the fable, & it is so eminently original in its characters and descriptions, that I think it bears the stamp of real genius. "Discipline" people tell me to read, but I have no stomach to it, I believe because of the name, fool that I am!—But one thing is, that I did not like the other book by that author, Self Controul, and so I have no appetite to try the second.[9] Gossip Wraxall is going to publish Historical Memoirs of his own Times.[10] I shall like to read that, for to give him his due, he always knew how to write entertainingly.—I have seen Alex twice. He looks well, but he hears nothing from his poor Father or Mother. O, my dear Charlotte what must be their situation! Where do you suppose him to be? With the King, or in Paris?[11]—I am very anxious as we must all be about them.—But my paper bids me say adieu. Give my kindest love to Barrett, to your Mother, Marianne, the children and yourself, & believe me ever

affectionately y[rs] S. H. B.

1. Despite her initial resistance to the idea (L. 75), Sarah Harriet was working on the first of a series of tales, a genre made popular by Maria Edgeworth in her *Tales of Fashionable Life* (1809–12) and Mrs. Opie with *Tales of Real Life* (1813); hers would be called *Tales of Fancy* (see below L. 81, n. 1).

2. In the 1 April issue of the *New Monthly Magazine* 3 (1815): 245, it was announced that "Miss BURNEY, Author of Traits of Nature, Geraldine Fauconberg, &c. has in the press Tales of Fancy."

3. William Wilbraham (1781–1824), third son of George Wilbraham, and Anna's elder brother. He received his first commission in the Royal Navy on 24 February 1801, becoming Comdr. (12 Aug. 1807) and promoted to Capt. (13 Jan. 1809) (Burke, *LG;* Marshall, *Suppl.* Pt. 1, 432; The Commissioned Sea-Officers of the Royal Navy 1660–1815, TS, Society of Genealogists).

4. Frances (Phillips) Raper apparently suffered from a severe illness in the spring of 1815 (L. 55, n. 11).

5. Possibly one of the three daughters of Frances Riddell Reynolds (c. 1771–1846), a wealthy brewer of Great Yarmouth, Norfolk, whose eldest son, John Preston Reynolds (1794–1861), was apparently well known to Fanny Raper. The father's occupation may account for Sarah's distaste (*GM*, NS 27 (1847): 219, 431–32; 3rd ser. 11 (1861): 93; IGI; *Alumni Cantab.; JL*, 9: 51 and n. 2).

6. For Fanny Raper's financial difficulties since her marriage, see above LL. 59, 65, 66.

7. Mrs. Raper's daughter, Catherine, seven years old. Her medical adviser might be Thomas Keate, Surgeon to Chelsea Hospital (L. 19, n. 5), or possibly his nephew and apprentice, Robert Keate (1777–1857), who became "Hospital Mate" at Chelsea in 1794, and succeeded his uncle as Surgeon of St. George's Hospital (1813) (*DNB*).

8. The second novel "By the Author of Waverley" [Walter Scott], *Guy Mannering*, appeared 28 February 1815 and was sold out the day after publication (Johnson, 1:468).

9. The second novel by the Scottish novelist, Mary Brunton, *Discipline*, was published anonymously in December 1814. Her first novel, *Self-control*, was referred to by SHB soon after its appearance in 1811 (L. 60).

10. Sir Nathaniel William Wraxall (1751–1831), created Bt. (1813). He would soon publish the *Historical Memoirs of my own Time* (1815). The first edition sold out in a month, but the sale was arrested by an action for libel, for which the author was sentenced to a fine and imprisonment (*DNB*). The work was attacked fiercely in the *British Critic*, NS 4 (1815): 17–31; the *Quarterly Review* 13 (1815): 193–215; and the *Edinburgh Review* 25 (1815): 168–220.

11. The d'Arblays were residing in Paris when Napoleon escaped from Elba and landed in France 1 March 1815. An officer in the Garde du Corps of Louis XVIII, M. d'Arblay withdrew from Paris with the troops still loyal to the King, marched to the Belgian frontier, and joined the King at Ghent. Mme d'Arblay fled from Paris the same night (19 March) to await news of her husband at Brussels. At this time, husband and wife were together at Brussels where M. d'Arblay had a ten-day congé for his health (*JL*, 8: 103). For their experiences throughout the Hundred Days, see *JL*, 8.

Mme d'Arblay wrote to members of her family in early April, assuring them of her safety, and asking for news of her son. She commented on 16 May on the replies she had received: "Every body has written now—. . . All but Sarah" (*JL*, 8: 124–25).

81. To Sarah (Rose) Burney

[Chelsea College], 4 October 1815
A.L.S., Osborn
Address: M[rs] Burney / Rectory House / Deptford / Kent.
Postmarks: TwoPyPost / Unpaid / Chelsea C O
4 o'Clock / OC 4 / 1815 EV
12 o'Clock / 4 OC / 1815 Nn

My dear and very good M[rs] Burney—

It is possible that you may receive the duplicate of this bright epistle in the course of the day, for I wrote an answer to yours and my brother's kind proposal last night, which in its way to the post (by the hands of a child) I am told has been lost. So I must tell my story over again; which story is, that I am just at present so much employed in correcting proofs &c (and for an old work too, partly)[1] that I was forced to tear myself away, after two days stay, from poor dear Esther at Turnham Green. She is still in bed, where she has now lain upwards of a month—and the improvement in her hand has been so gradual as scarcely to be perceptible. The chief pain now lies in her arm and shoulder, but her hand is as helpless and as much swelled as ever.[2]—But by bringing up her name, I meant to imply, that if I was able to say no to her who so much wanted me, it would be scandalous that I should not say no to you whose proposed frolic I should so much like. Yet thank you heartily both for remembering me—Nothing little nobodies like better than to be remembered. Adieu dear M[rs] Burney. I sincerely wish you and my brother every gratification from your intended jaunt, and am most affectionately yours and his

S. H. Burney

Oct[r] 4th 1815.

1. The first volume of S. H. Burney's *Tales of Fancy*, called *The Shipwreck*, would soon be published by Henry Colburn at 7s. 6d.; although it bears the imprint date 1816, the actual date of issue was 28 November 1815 (Colburn records). It was entered into the registers of the Worshipful Company of Stationers on 4 December and advertised as "This day is published" on 27 December 1815 (*Times*) along with "new editions" of her first three novels. The tale would be translated into French as *Le Naufrage* in 1816 (of which there was a second edition the same year) and into German as *Der Schiffbruch* in 1821.

In her Dedication to Lady Crewe, the author pleads that "the *possibility*, at least, of the leading circumstance of my story" (a shipwreck on a deserted and hitherto undiscovered island) be accepted, and cites in her favor the "well qualified" opinion of "a naval officer" (presumably James Burney). The *Augustan Review* 2 (1816): 247–50, approves a genre with "the marvellous in narrative blending with the natural in sentiment," while the *Monthly Review*, 2nd ser. 79 (1816): 214–15, finds the title of *Tales of Fancy* an apt description. The *British Lady's Magazine* 3 (1816): 25–28, considers it "a pretty little story, very well told . . . well calculated to *amuse*, though not to *strike*."

2. Esther and her husband, Charles Rousseau Burney, both suffering from poor health, were benefiting from the "country air" at Turnham Green, Middlesex, where they had moved in July 1814. From an unspecified complaint (though suspected to be some form of gout) Esther had lost the use of her right hand (*JL*, 7: 416, n. 13; 9: 5 and n. 2, 8, 21).

82. To Charlotte (Francis) Barrett

[Chelsea College], 23 [November 1815][1]
A.L.S., Berg
Address: Mrs Barrett / Lower Road / Richmond / Surry.
Postmarks: TwoP[yPost] / Unpaid / Chelsea [*?*]
4 o'Clock / NO [*?*] / 1815 EV
12 o'Clock / [*?*] NO / 1815 [*?*]

Thursday. Octr 23^d^

My own dear Charlotte

Ten millions of thanks for telling me so many particulars of that interesting family of the Soupers.[2] How glad I am that you saw and liked the dear admirable wife,—And, my excellent Charlotte, how glad I am that you drew so good a moral from the view of her troubles. They are indeed such as to make ordinary matters dwindle into nothing. She has only two supports under her harassing cares; but they are hosts:—She is very religious; and she loves poor Souper as if he had not a fault in the world. Heaven knows, he has plenty! But the chap (at least when I knew him) was engaging with all his misdemeanours. I am sorry to have so completely lost sight of them; for altho' I do not keep up a barren correspondence with her, I never loved any body, nor respected any body more truly than that warm-hearted, liberal creature.

Do you know that the Wilbrahams are your neighbours? They have taken for three months a house on the Green, next door I think to Dundas's;[3] and they want me after my first foolery is published (after 1st Dec^r^)[4] to spend some time with them. And think how glad I should be to kill two birds with one stone; To be with them, who have house-room, and to see you continually, who have only heart-room. And yet, this visit at present will be terribly inconvenient to me. I must scribble, or I cannot live; and being engaged with a bookseller I like, and who likes me, it is my interest to keep him in good humour. It was originally meant, that two volumes of Tales <were to> should appear at once;— I could only get one ready this year, having been lazy all the fine summer weather; and that one, he engaged to print immediately, upon condition I would prepare the second for publication soon after Christmas.[5] That second, I am consequently now at work upon, and it will destroy me to be taken off in the very midst of it, to go gallanting, and making merry, as if I were an independent gentlewoman. I expect, at least, I fear, little by little, to lose all my friends;— for I am too poor to go near them, and they think it is indifference; whereas, it is prudence in the shape pen and ink, my only means of keeping out of Marglandism.[6]

There—You have now my whole dish of bother. At least nearly so.—Colburn is to give me £100 a vol: and twenty five a vol: on a second edition:—and if the two first vols: take, he is to give me £300 for the two next; for I have promised him four, under the running title of "Tales of Fancy",[7] but each Tale to have a separate title.—The second will be called "The Secret."

I shall state some of the dirty particulars I have plagued you with, to the Wilbrahams, and if I lose their good will because I do not give up my bread and cheese to go and see them whenever they ask me, why even their good will is not genuine, and I must stick to the solid, and give up the shewy. But I have not in my heart any real fear of them. They will be considerate, and accept my company, such as it is, another time.—I hope in the summer to have earned a right to a holyday; at least, to be so far set forward in my undertaking, that a temporary intermission <of my> will do me no material harm.—

Richard Burney and, I fancy, his wife, are in town.[8] They called very kindly the other morning, and I was unlucky gone out to 'fetch a walk'. To-day, James, (Captain) has invited me to meet them at his house to dinner: but—the coming home! Diantre! what a night frolic!—Or the sleeping out for one night— Diabolique! So, I was fain to decline. But, let me decline frolics and invitations ever so much, I live here amongst such a set of idle and heavy-bottomed old and young women, that, of a morning, my time is never my own. Our Street door opens with a latch; and people who know me intimately, think themselves priveleged to walk up stairs without ringing, and catch me, sometimes at breakfast, sometimes dressing by the fire, sometimes airing a chemise—and often wishing them at Jericho.[9] I am forced therefore to avoid as much as possible all ungenteel jobs; and as I reckon scribbling by trade very ungenteel, I never set too with comfort, till candles come, & visitors cease.

To night, I am going with Mrs Hulse, who brings me back and takes me, scot and lot free, to see Hannah More's Tragedy of Percy,[10] and Miss O'Neil as heroine.[11] I would not stir over the threshold to go to the play if it cost me money, or mobbing, or trouble,—but in this easy, quiet way, and into a private box, I doat upon the business.

God bless you my dearest Char. You did my heart good by telling me that all your young fry were "well and good." My love to Julia, and tell her that I could have heard nothing that would have pleased me more. Mes amours à l'Ami Barrett. I hope he liked dear Mrs Souper. Adieu. I had a nice snug visit from your Madre lately. Have you heard lately of Sister Burney? I have not since she went to Brighton.[12] Yours at last affectionately

S. H. Burney.

May I trouble you my dear Charlotte, as the W——'s are new comers to let one of your maids find out whether I have directed the inclosed right.

1. SHB dated her letter Thursday 23 October, but it is postmarked November 1815. She probably mistook the month rather than the day; the 23 November was indeed a Thursday in 1815, whereas the 23 October was a Monday. This supposition is confirmed by the reference to Esther Burney; on 23 October 1815 she was still in London, but at Brighton in November (*JL*, 9: 5, 21). Further corroboration is the date of the performance of Hannah More's play (see n. 10).

2. Unidentified.

3. Probably Sir David Dundas (1749–1826), Sergeant-Surgeon to the King (1791), created Bt. (1815), who lived at Richmond Green (*JL*, 3: 251; Walpole, 11: 373).

4. *The Shipwreck*, vol. 1 of *Tales of Fancy* (L. 81, n. 1).

5. In Colburn's *New Monthly Magazine* 5 (1816): 66, after comparing *The Shipwreck* to *The Tempest* and *Paul et Virginie*, the reviewer concludes: "we shall look for the continuance of Miss Burney's Tales with eager impatience, anticipating from this specimen equal delight and edification."

6. Miss Margland, the soured governess in Mme d'Arblay's novel, *Camilla* (1796). The family significance of this expression is discussed above (L. 7, n. 12).

7. SHB would realize some but not all of these anticipated profits. On 13 December 1815, £100 was paid into her account at Coutts, £25 of which was sent to her immediately, and the remaining £75 used to purchase more stock. However, her second and last tale in 2 volumes would not be published until 1819, with a second edition of both tales appearing shortly thereafter (see further L. 90, n. 2; L. 92, n. 5).

8. SHB's nephew, Richard Allen Burney, Rector of Rimpton, and his wife Elizabeth. In 1815, he was offered the curacy of Brightwell, Berkshire, and the use of the rectory, to which he had moved in April ("Worcester Mem.," 61–62; *JL*, 8: 281, n. 20; 9: 206, n. 12).

9. The colloquial expression for a place far away arose from 2 Samuel 10:5, when David bade his servants to "Tarry at Jericho until your beards be grown."

10. Hannah More's successful tragedy, *Percy*, first performed in 1777, was playing at the Theatre Royal, Covent Garden on 23 November 1815 (*Times*, 23 Nov. 1815).

11. The role of Elwina was played by Eliza O'Neill (1791–1872), the daughter of an Irish actor, who had created a sensation when she made her London debut on 6 October 1814. During her five years as "reigning favourite," she revitalized the tragic roles played by Mrs. Siddons, with whom she was often compared. On 18 December 1819, she would marry William Wrixon (later Becher) (1780–1850), an Irish M.P. and "a Gentleman of very considerable property," created Bt. (1831); she never returned to the stage (*DNB; GM*, 89, Pt. 2 (1819): 635; Thorne).

12. For the lameness in her right arm (L. 81), Esther Burney was trying the sea air at Brighton, accompanied by her daughter, Maria Bourdois. She left for the coast after 23 October 1815, and remained for at least a month; by 26 February 1816, she was back at Turnham Green, somewhat recovered (*JL*, 9: 5, 49, 74).

83. [To Henry Colburn][1]

[Chelsea College, Early 1816][2]
A.L.S., Pierpont Morgan

Wednesday Evening.

Dear Sir

You will be concerned to hear, that since I last did myself the pleasure of addressing you, I have been much indisposed, and still continue in a very ailing state. All application to my pen is at present out of the question; and as health must with every one be the first consideration, I am obliged to add, that the second volume of Tales which I had promised myself <to> should be prepared for you about this time, must necessarily <be deferred> wait till I am in a fitter state for the employment.

Many thanks for the loan of "Emma",[3] which, even <in much> amidst languor and depression, forced from me a smile, & afforded me much amusement. Books, indeed, are now so desirable a resource to me, at those intervals when I am able to read, that it will be a real kindness if you will occasionally have the goodness to supply me, either with French or English novelties.—

Believe me, dear Sir,
Yours very truly
S. H. Burney

1. Sarah Harriet's publisher, Henry Colburn, would be the most likely recipient, judging from the reference to a volume of tales which should have been "prepared for you" and the loan of a new publication (LL. 75, 82 and n. 7).

2. The letter can be dated to early 1816 from the mention of an indisposition (see below L. 84), which prevented SHB from meeting a deadline for a second volume of Tales. In her letter of 23 November 1815, she discusses the agreement by which she was preparing "the second [Tale] for publication soon after Christmas," while in this letter her tale should have been ready "about this time." The loan of *Emma* as a newly published work confirms this conjecture (n. 3).

3. Jane Austen's fourth (anonymously published) novel, *Emma* (1816), came out in early January 1816 (Gilson, 68). Colburn may have sent it to SHB as the work of a kindred spirit, and she was much struck with it (L. 84).

---

84. To Charlotte (Francis) Barrett

[Chelsea College], 1 March 1816
A.L.S., Berg
Address: Mrs Barrett / Under the Hill / Richmond / Surry
Postmarks: To Be [Delivered] / by [?] / on Sund[?]
[? P]ost / [Unp]aid / [Chels]ea C O

March 1st 1816

I do begin, my dearest, humbly to flatter myself that God purposes to spare me, in his mercy, the very severe trial to which I, at one period, terrified myself with an idea that I was condemned.[1] What I have now to pray for is, that the remembrance of his mercy may be as effectual towards my amendment as the chastisement with which I beheld myself threatened. I ought to be, and indeed <u>am</u> very profoundly grateful; and gratitude upon a nature at all inclined to good, will sometimes effect as much as fear. Heaven grant that I may prove capable of retaining the sentiments which at the present moment, most sincerely animate me.[2] Mr Keate acknowledges that his first opinion was very unfavourable: but now speaks of me as of one making even more progress towards recovery than he could have expected.

Now I am ill, I feel aware that "Missess" (as the girls call Mrs W:)[3] asks to hear or to see every word I write to them; & that throws a constraint over my mind which makes it unpleasant to me to address them. So, I was glad to fob them off with a mere weekly bulletin, without contradicting their proposal of forwarding the dry morcel to you. Writing to you is no effort to me;—but to the lady who burnt Parisina,[4] the property of a daughter nearly thirty years old, I must own it is always a trying and dull task. She is squeamishness so over-strained, that she makes me sick: but, bien bonne in the main, though.—

Fanny Raper and my little fellow-patient Katherine, have just been here, looking fresh, and rosy, and just as people ought to look <upon> newly come out of the Spring air. Fanny desired me to tell you, that she would execute your commission to Marianne, and thanks you for your letter.

Within these two days, I have procured a regular assistant, to dress me, and put my coals on, and spare me every species of exertion, Mr K——[5] forbidding my lifting my left hand to my head, or putting it behind me. She is a nice quiet honest person, whom I have often employed before to do needlework by the day; and she has been used to wait upon a sick mistress, and can manage leeches better than any one. An illness like mine that drags out to such a length, can scarcely continue to receive the requisite degree of attention without some one appropriate assistant. Mrs Erswell and her maid have been as solicitous, and handy, and willing, as any people so circumstanced could be: but when it came to my not being allowed to wait upon myself, even to cut a slice of bread, it would have been too inconsiderate to have gone on without a helper—as there are five children in the house, one of them cutting teeth, and very unwel, and the poor Mother in a family way again.

I am so glad you like what you have read of "Emma," and the dear old man's "gentle selfishness."[6]—Was there ever a happier expression?—I have read no story book with such glee, since the days of "Waverley" and "Mannering," and, by the same Author as "Emma," my prime favorite of all modern Novels "Pride & Prejudice."[7]—Fanny Raper likes to languish over stories stuffed, as she says herself, as full of love as a rich plum pudding is full of plums. I never insert love but to oblige my readers: if I could give them humour and wit, however, I should make bold to skip the love, and think them well off into the bargain. But writing for the press, is like writing to the conflagratress of Parisina; it cramps my genius, & makes me weigh my words, and write as you call it mawning.[8] Do not betray that I thus amuse myself in scribbling rubbish to you—not even to my own family, for, bless the dull dogs & dog-esses—the Amelias and Dr Charles'[9] &c; I cut them all off as short as I mean soon to cut off my own hair, to save myself the trouble of long combings, and reaching up my arms to fasten it in fine knots.

I have read both Scott's visits,[10] and Mrs Hulse has just lent me the Life of John Sobieski, K. of Poland.[11] I have only just begun it, but it promises facility of style, & I think I shall like it. I tried Pallas's Travels in Russia[12] lately: but there was too much about progressive improvements in agriculture, & manufactures amongst the grown-up Muscovite babies, & I got tired, as I easily do of all that relates to half civilized nations. Give me a whole Savage, or no Savage at all.—

Adieu, Dearest Charlotte. My kindest love to Barrett & my Sister—Keep up my interest with Miss Hotham,[13] and believe me ever most affectionately yours

S. H. Burney

1. In the winter and spring of 1816, Sarah Harriet suffered from a serious illness that alarmed her family (*JL*, 9: 117) but is difficult at this distance to diagnose. Mme d'Arblay speaks of "a large bulbous neck's swelling" which "not cancerous . . . proves merely glandular" (*JL*, 10: 584). FBA may have suspected cancer, however, as she compares Sarah's complaint to her own (diagnosed as cancer of the breast), and sends her a letter of advice on the authority of "so near a fellow sufferer" (*JL*, 6: 607; 9: 124 and n. 19, L. 1049).

Charlotte Barrett, on the other hand, understood that her aunt's illness was "rather a scrophulous case" which (according to the article on "Medicine" in the *Encyclopaedia Britannica* [1771]) was "attended with hard, scirrhous, and often indolent tumours . . . most commonly seated in the neck." In June she reported that "the tumour she says has almost disappeared" (CFBt to FBA, [15 June 1816], Berg).

2. These pious sentiments, expressed in this or a later letter, were repeated approvingly by Charlotte Barrett: "You will be pleased that my aunt Sarah Burney is quite recovered, & has written me a very comfortable letter, full of gratitude for the mercy which has been shewn her, and of desires that the serious impressions produced by her illness may not wear off but that she may be enabled to live to the glory of God in future" (CFBt to AY, [16 Jan. 1817], Barrett, Eg. 3703A, ff. 4–5v).

3. Mrs. W[ilbraham], SHB's former employer.

4. A poem by George Gordon (1788–1824), 6th Baron Byron (1791), *Parisina* was published with *The Siege of Corinth* in February 1816. It dramatizes a domestic tragedy in which the Marquis of Este discovers the adulterous and incestuous love of his wife Parisina for his illegitimate son, whom he executes.

5. Mr. K[eate], SHB's medical adviser (L. 80, n. 7).

6. The phrase occurs in the opening chapter of Austen's *Emma*, describing the valetudinarian Mr. Woodhouse as "a nervous man, easily depressed . . . hating change of every kind."

7. [Walter Scott's] first and second novels, *Waverley* (1814) and *Guy Mannering* (1815). The latter was mentioned in L. 80; for [Jane Austen], *Pride and Prejudice* (1813), see L. 73.

8. "Mawning" is not in the *OED*, but Charlotte Barrett may have coined it from "mawmish" meaning mawkish or maudlin.

9. Amelia Maria, Esther's youngest child, and Sarah's half-brother, Charles, who received a D.D. (Lambeth) in 1812 (*JL*, 1: lxix, lxxi). Relations with her somewhat lordly half-brother appear to have been cordial rather than warm.

10. John Scott (1783–1821) (*DNB*), later editor of the *London Magazine*, published in 1815 *A Visit to Paris in 1814* and in 1816 *Paris revisited in 1815 by way of Brussels.*

11. Alicia Tindal Palmer (fl. 1810) (*DNB*), an English novelist, published her *Authentic Memoirs of the Life of John Sobieski* in 1815.

12. Pierre-Simon Pallas (1741–1811), German naturalist and ethnographer, who had lived in Russia 1768–1809. Of his several publications, Sarah may have read *Travels through the Southern Provinces of the Russian Empire in 1793 and 1794*, [trans. F. W. Blagdon], 2nd ed. (London: John Stockdale, 1812).

13. Henrietta Gertrude Hotham (1753–1816), the only child of Sir Charles Hotham (1729–94), 8th Bt. (1771), by his wife Lady Dorothy née Hobart (d. 1798). In 1793, she inherited Marble Hill, a villa in Twickenham which had belonged to her great-aunt, Lady Suffolk, and a smaller house nearby where she preferred to live. Before 1811, she had moved to Richmond where "she has taken a house . . . and fitted it up most delightfully, wth books, pictures, prints and every thing that can make it amusing." Charlotte Barrett and Sarah Harriet had visited her there in March 1813 (CB to CB Jr., 9 Mar. 1813, Osborn; Walpole, 11: 236, n. 11; 12: 36; 42: 483–84; *Twickenham, 1600–1900*, 11).

85. To Charlotte (Francis) Barrett with P.S. Frances (Phillips) Raper

Malvern Wells, 4 September 1816
A.L.S. SHB with P.S. FPR, Berg
Address: Mrs Barrett / Bradfield Cottage / Bury / Suffolk
Postmarks: A SE / 12 / 816

Malvern Wells,[1] Septr 4th
1816

How many sweet, and cordial, and amusing letters, my ever dear Charlotte, am I in your arrears for!—In arrears even of thanks; at least, thanks expressed. During a long period, I forbore writing in some degree, from prudential motives, connected with my complaint; these last three weeks, I have been silent because I would not fag your eyes, or take up your time whilst the former were perhaps weak, and the latter required to be spent in nursing either yourself, or your dear new baby.[2] I congratulate you most sincerely, dearest, on having prosperously, I trust, got through your late Hockley adventure; and I congratulate Barrett on having again got a convalescent wife, and enlarged his honours of paternity. Is not this last sentence a little in his own worst style?—My love to him, and ask him.

You have probably heard from F. R.[3] how much I am pleased with this lovely place, the benefit of which I feel more and more sensible of every week;—I mean principally in regard to general health. The local complaint still at times requires leeches, but has been very quiet for upwards of a fortnight.—You would make many delightful drawings were you here. The views are beautiful, and as varied as they are beautiful. I can find but one fault with the place; the dearness of lodgings. I pay for a sitting room, bed chamber, and garret for the maid, two guineas a week, and 9d a day for the use of the kitchen fire, 6d a day if I have a parlour fire; and the weather has really been such, as scarcely to allow my being without one, during some part of every day that I have been here. I have no mind however to go back to Chelsea yet; so, what does me. I, but sally forth upon a Donkey to the Western side of the hills, facing lovely Herefordshire, and ferret out a sort of a farm-cottage containing a neat little sitting room with a delicious view, and two tidyish little garrets, and a doll's kitchen, and hire the whole for a fortnight at one guinea per week. And I purpose removing to it next Wednesday. I shall be within easy reach of the Wells, and the frequented part of the hills, either on foot, or upon a Donkey, but I shall be removed from the houses which fashion makes expensive; and by a saving of a guinea a week, I mean to eke out a short purse into a long one,[4] and so to obtain the power of remaining in this country, <is> or going to the sea side in Wales and abiding there till about the end of October. My Maid,[5] a civil, conformable, and truly comfortable creature, is agreeable to every thing I propose, and seems to regard the solitude of our future abode no more than her mistress. I never mind being alone, so long as I know that there are inhabitants in the house who may preserve me from having my throat cut; and one end of the new residence I have chosen, is occupied by—a Taylor—an old Woman—and a Prentice boy. Yet, I shall sincerely regret quitting the society of two charming fellow-lodgers now under the roof with me; a Mrs Stuart,[6] and her cousin, Miss Sullivan.[7] Mrs Stuart is only eight and twenty, and has been deprived of the use of her limbs for nearly seven years by a sort of dead palsy. She is carried up and Down stairs by a man servant, and has a little travelling folding-up sort of sofa, with portable cushions and pillows, on which she is obliged to lie whenever she is not in bed. But a creature so angelically patient, submissive and amiable, I never met with. Her face is beautiful, and continually reminds me of an exquisite Madona of Carlo Dolci's.[8] She contrives, by resting on a little horizontal frame attached occasionally to her sofa, to write, work, and employ herself as industriously as if she were in health. She is Sister in law, somebody told me, to Sir Charles Stewart,[9] who, I believe, was, or is, Minister of some foreign court. Her father, is the Honble something Sullivan M. P.[10]—

But none of the pride of family appears about her which many without half her pretensions display.[11] She is deeply, fervently, and heartfully—if I may be allowed such an expression—a Christian; and never has the influence of real Christianity struck me in a more endearing, gracious, and exemplary point of view. Every evening, we all, servants, landlord and landlady, assemble to prayers in her parlour. Miss Sullivan reads them, after having first read a portion of Scriptures. These little religious assemblages are extremely interesting to my feelings; and it will grieve me when worldly prudence compels me to give them up. Miss Sullivan has nearly as many attractive points about her, as her invalid companion. One circumstance in which she and I most perfectly agree, is her partiality for the worthy and dear Moravians. She spent four months last year at one of their Settlements in Derbyshire with a Mrs Bates,[12] who, though not <one> a Moravian herself, resides amongst them, and dedicates a large portion of a handsome fortune to their service in different ways. Miss Sullivan has read me many parts of letters which she receives from various of the Sister or Brotherhood. They are admirable, both in point of primitiveness and simplicity, as well as genuine piety. She knows, and very much likes M^r^ La Trobe; and that unites us also. Pity that one must leave such beings!—

I have had Amelia with me from Worcester for a week, and then Cecilia another week, and then, for a third week, my Sister Burney, who was so taken with the place, and the Donkeys, that she has procured a lodging not far from me for a fortnight more of it. She took possession to-day with Amelia, and left Richard and Blue at Mr Sandford's in their place.[13] Poor Blue has been suffering with that vile tedious complaint the Shingles; & having been ill managed by a country Apothecary, is come to Worcester to be under the care of Mr Sandford. Entre nous soit dit, I like Mrs Sandford[14] almost the very best of the Cousin race of Burneys; and I admire her too, for she really has much information, originality, & goodness; besides a tournure vraiment comme il faut. Pray say for me many grateful & kind things to Mr Young, with thanks for his dear Baxter,[15] which I brought here with me, & read with pleasure very frequently. My friends in the opposite parlour have lent me another abridged work of Baxter's, edited by Benjamin Fawcett, & entitled "Converse with God in Solitude."[16] The chapter on friends taken from us by Death is worthy to be written in letters of gold; the rest, I have not yet read: but hope to like.—

There is here a Mrs Hutton of Birmingham with whom I have struck up an acquaintance because she wrote a clever amusing little book called "The Miser Married"[17]—And I like her plain, unaffected manners and conversation very much. Exclusive of her, I visit no one, but I bow and curtsy and simper in passing to some who, I suppose simpered first, but whose names I hardly know.

Did I tell you that, health and circumstances permitting, I have promised to pay Maria Bourdois[18] a visit before I return to Chelsea? This is the third year she has been so kind as to ask me, and I think I shall like the visit very much; all but the plague of being obliged to leave off my wrapping gowns, and my thorough dowdy dress. I do love to be a clean dowdy!

Love to l'Ami Barrett, & best remembrances to Mary Young,[19] & kisses to the children. Yours dearest Charlotte with most grateful & affectionate feelings. S. H. B.

[*The letter concludes with a P.S. signed F. Raper which ends:* "If ever you let my Aunt Broome pay more than 3d for her letters, I think it a shame."]

1. For her complaint, Sarah was advised "to try the waters of Malvern, by Medical ordinance" and was to leave "not later than the beginning of July" (*JL*, 9: 166; CFBt to FBA, [15 June 1816], Berg). The Malvern waters were considered particularly efficacious for diseases of the skin. See Brian S. Smith, *A History of Malvern* (Gloucester: Alan Sutton & the Malvern Bookshop, 1978), 174–75).

2. Charlotte Barrett gave birth to her fifth and last child, Arthur Charles Barrett (1816–80), on 10 August 1816. Her "little 'original sin'" would be christened on 22 January 1817, a ceremony that SHB was well enough to attend (*JL*, 1: lxxiii; baptismal certificate, Barrett, Eg. 3708, f. 18; CFBt to AY, 27 Dec. 1816, Barrett, Eg. 3703A, ff. 1–3v; *JL*, 9: 318).

3. Frances Raper was with her aunt at Malvern and added a postscript to the end of the letter.

4. SHB's illness was a drain on her resources: the ledgers at Coutts bank show her selling £100 of her bonds in the summer of 1816 and a further £62.10s. early in 1817. She was also sent £10 by Mme d'Arblay on 26 June 1816 (*JL*, 9: 117, n. 7).

5. SHB had taken with her to Malvern a "very pleasing female attendant whom Fanny has procured and recommended to her" who proved to be "a most trusty & valuable nurse in a maid" (CFBt to FBA, [15 June 1816], Berg; *JL*, 9: 166).

6. Albinia (née Sullivan) Stuart (d. 3 June 1827), who had married 26 September 1807 John James Stuart (1782–1811), Capt. R.N. and grandson of John Stuart, 3rd Earl of Bute. A widow, she would marry again in September 1825 as his second wife the Rev. Marmaduke Thompson (c. 1776–1851), Chaplain to the East India Co. (1806–19). By a curious coincidence, he would be appointed Rector of Brightwell, Berks. (1831–51) over Richard Allen Burney, who had been acting as curate since 1815, despoiling him at the same time of his home in the rectory (Burke under Bute, Sullivan; *Alumni Cantab.*; *GM*, 77, Pt. 2 (1807): 976; 81, Pt. 1 (1811): 399; 97, Pt. 1 (1827): 646–47; NS 35 (1851): 677; "Worcester Mem.," 91–92; *JL*, 8: 281, n. 20).

7. Miss Sullivan might be Mrs. Stuart's cousin Charlotte (d. 28 March 1873), the daughter of Sir Richard Joseph Sullivan (1752–1806) (*DNB*), created Bt. (1804). She would marry on 28 Dec. 1824 William Hale of King's Walden, Herts.

Alternatively, Miss Sullivan could be one of two daughters of another uncle, Sir Benjamin Sullivan (1747–1810), judge of the supreme court of Madras, Kt. (1801): Margaret Mary (b. 21 April 1792) who would marry Capt. Robert Ashworth, or Harriet (b.

25 April 1795) who would marry on 6 May 1824 Lt.-Col. Francis de Vismes (1793–1869) (Burke under Sullivan, De Visme; Foster; IGI).

8. Carlo Dolci (1616–86), the Florentine artist, painted a number of Madonnas in a highly finished style.

9. Capt. Stuart's elder brother, Sir Charles Stuart (1779–1845), G.C.B. (1812), who had been in the diplomatic service at Madrid (1808) and Portugal (1810), was minister at the Hague (1815–16) and ambassador to Paris (1815–30). He would later be created Baron Stuart de Rothesay (1828) and serve as ambassador to St. Petersburg (1841–45) (Burke under Bute; *DNB*).

10. Mrs. Stuart's father was the Rt. Hon. John Sullivan (1749–1839) of Richings Park, Bucks., who, after a career in the East India Company (1765–85), served as M.P. Old Sarum (1790–96), Aldborough (1802–6) and Ashburton (1811–18) and Under-sec. of State for War and Colonies (1801–4) (Burke; Thorne).

11. The obituary of Albinia (Stuart) Thompson dwells in some detail on her family connections on her mother's side: "She was dau. of the Right Hon. John Sullivan, of Richings, by Lady Henrietta-Anne-Barbara-Hobart, second dau. of George, third Earl of Buckinghamshire, and twin-sister to Lady Maria-Mary, Countess of Guilford, the mother of the Marchioness of Bute, to whom, and to the present Earl of Buckinghamshire, Mrs. Thompson was accordingly first cousin. She received the name of Albinia, after her maternal aunt, Lady Albinia, wife of Richard Cumberland, esq" (*GM*, 97, Pt. 1 (1827): 646–47).

12. Possibly Mary Bates (fl. 1787–1840) who had married pre 1787 Joseph Bates (c. 1761–1817) of Buxton Hall, Buxton, Derbyshire. As a widow she is the only Bates who appears in the list of subscribers to the 1829 *History, Gazetteer and Directory of the County of Derby* (The Register at Buxton, TS, transcr. F. A. Forster and D. W. Woodheard, Society of Genealogists).

13. The "Worcester Mem." describes this gathering of the clan at Worcester (eight miles from Malvern) while Sarah Harriet was there. Esther Burney and her daughter Amelia were visiting Mr. and Mrs. Sandford (see next note) in Bridge Street. Mrs. Hawkins and Cecilia lived nearby. To this party were added on 29 August 1816 Esther's son, Richard, and his aunt "Blue," who was seeking a change of air. The family group enjoyed "frequent pleasant intercourses." After Richard left on 6 September and Esther on 23 September, Sarah spent five days with the Sandfords in Bridge Street and left on 13 November 1816 with her cousin "Blue" and niece Cecilia for Brightwell. She enjoyed a short stay there and then continued on to London ("Worcester Mem.," 61–63; *JL*, 9: 173 and n. 12, 252).

14. Rebecca (Burney) Sandford (1758–1835), third daughter of Charles Burney's older brother Richard. She had married 24 March 1788 a Worcester surgeon, William Sandford (1759–1823) (*JL*, 1: lxxv; "Worcester Mem.," 24–25, 81). Other comments on cousin Rebecca are equally favorable: lively and gay as a young woman, "her Temper is very sweet, her Heart affectionate, & her Head mighty well laden with natural stores of good understanding & sense" (*EJL*, 2: 232–33).

15. Arthur Young published a volume of excerpts of the seventeenth-century divine and prolific writer, Richard Baxter (1615–91) (*DNB*), called *Baxteriana* (1815) (Gazley, 633, 647, 706).

16. Benjamin Fawcett (1715–80), a dissenting minister (*DNB*), published several

abridgments of the writings of Baxter. The third of three treatises in Baxter's *The Divine Life* (1664), "Of Coversing [*sic*] with God in solitude" was abridged by Fawcett as *Converse with God in solitude* (1761).

17. Catherine Hutton (1756–1846) (*DNB*), only daughter of William Hutton (1723–1815), a miscellaneous writer, published *The Miser Married* in 1813.

18. Esther's daughters, the widowed Maria (Burney) Bourdois, and her younger sister, Sophia, lived at 5 Ainslie's Belvedere, Bath (*JL*, 9: 5, n. 4, 9, n. 13).

19. Mary Young, Arthur Young's eldest daughter (L. 1, n. 1). To economise, the Barretts were spending a second summer in a cottage on Arthur Young's estate at Bradfield. Charlotte's son Arthur was born there and named after her host; the family stayed until 5 December 1816 (Gazley, 642–45, 663–64, 681).

86. To Charlotte (Francis) Barrett

[Chelsea College], 16 December 1817
A.L., Berg
Address: Mrs Barrett / Lower Road / Richmond / Surry.
Postmarks: Tw[o]PyPost / [Un]paid / Chelsea C O
7 oClock / 17 DE / 1817 NT

December 16th 1817.

Well, how do you do, my dearest Charlotte? I suppose you are at Richmond again by this time,[1] and I hope that you begin to feel a little settled, and are all well and comfortable. Yes, poor Bone stumps off the very day that her third quarter is up: the 5th January.[2] You perceive therefore that I shall be punctually delivered at my nine months end, and of a large, sturdy, &, vulgarly called, fine child as ever was seen. With her will go my good wishes for her future welfare, for I know no other harm of her than her being radically low-minded, sulky, sly, and maid-servanty in her ways and notions. She suits me and I her about as well as a dull but selfish Dutchman would suit a petulant but sprightly Frenchman. For the experience I have gained through her means, I shall be always thankful: she has taught me the folly and hazard of accepting (for any remuneration) an inmate whose temper, understanding and habits <were> are unknown; & she has taught me, moreover, how many millions of times better it is to have no companion at all, than to possess one from whom the heart recoils. Well, that little bit of experience I will put by in cotton, and take the greatest care of: but ten to one whether I shall ever be called upon to bring it into use. I always find that my judgment is more appealed to in cases wholly new to my consideration, than in such as have already occurred. Thus it is, that in the variety of events in this life, we are always condemned to be feeling our way in new and indistinct tracts; & that it so rarely happens, that the experience of yesterday can be of any benefit to us to day.—The wisdom of the above reflection, strikes me now I have written it, to be a little of the je pretend-moi cast: but never mind; it is assuredly not the less true for being stale; and it is really a relief to me to think, when told that I did an unadvised thing in receiving a stranger under my roof—"Well, however true that may be, wiser folks than me will commit blunders quite as clumsy; for scarcely any individuals profit by experience which is not of their own hard earning; and when they have earned it on one point by the sweat of their brow, they are speedily obliged to toil for it again on another, where the preceeding labour can be turned to no account."—

We are now all assembled for the winter in the College, Hulses,[3] Spicers,[4] Haggitts,[5] Keates[6] &c. And we have a new & comme il faut family, named Neave,[7] established amongst us. The husband I can say nothing about; I have been in a room with him but once, & then he was at cards: but the wife is the most complete Noodle I have seen for many a day. Her plan, as she told me, on coming here, was "to please and be pleased;" so, she is all intimacy, and cordiality at the very first interview. She professes to be enchanted by the College and all its appurtenances. She is so impatient to do the civil thing, that she gives her first party tomorrow night before half the inhabitants have had opportunity to invite her; and she literally called upon me, and others, I suppose, before I had paid her my first visit. She calls herself and a toady Miss Payne[8] who lives with her, "The Forresters," because they have lately left a house on the borders of Epsom Forrest. She says, her husband is so clever, that it is impossible to puzzle him; he knows every thing;—he knows seven languages;—"I ought not to say it, perhaps, of my own husband, but my dear Miss Burney, he is . . . Oh, pray, do you draw?—I suppose you are a good Italian scholar?—If I was not ashamed, I should like to take a few lessons"—&c, &c, &c. Poor Goosecappy, however, will be patiently borne with, as long as affability and good nature are her cue: but woe be to her, if she gives herself airs, or should happen to be capricious.—An excellent device has been adopted for the improvement of our winter parties. A Sedan chair has been set up,[9] for which one guinea is subscribed the first year, & a shilling out and home is to be paid for every jaunt it takes in the College. Something more is to be paid, if the men are to go beyond the walls.—Till now, we have had to send to Sloane Street for a chair, & merely to be carried into the adjoining court, cost three or four shillings.

The C. Rapers and I dine to day with Lady Crewe; the last little party of hers that we shall be at previous to her leaving town for Liverpool. She was very chearful and pleasant when I dined there last, about three weeks ago, and spoke much more distinctly than in the summer.[10]

To make up for the silliness of our new comer, I discover in another resident of longer standing, but of reserved manners wch prevented my knowing her value till lately, a very amiable as well as truly estimable creature. I am speaking of Mrs Spicer. Never was a person of whom it might more truly be said, that she is always at her post, and that post is always the right one. Moreover, she can be very funny and entertaining, and she is so unquackishly well-informed, that it is an improvement and advantage to apply to her on all puzzling matters, particularly such as relate to Natural History, to painting, and to a hundred other things of far more consequence. She gives away at Christmas good things to the poor, and she has brought me three tickets (for beef and vegetables to be served out at her own house on that day) to give to "my own particular beggars;" and besides that, a letter for a lying-in woman entitling her to medical attendance, a Nurse (at home) gruel, medecines, and sometimes a <set> suit of baby linen. And I happen to know a poor young woman I want to serve, so this letter (unsolicited) is a treasure.—Is not Mrs Spicer a Dear?

Read, read, read M.Leod's Narrative of the Voyage of the Alceste to China,[11] & her wreck in coming home. Ellis's Account of the Embassy is comparatively dull,[12] but I had it lent me, & was glad to swap. I have just got the first volume of Godwin's Mandeville,[13] but have not yet opened it.—Saw poor Mrs James Burney last week. She is slowly recovering,[14] but has had a terribly trying & weakening attack. My kindest love to Barrett, my Sister, Marianne, the childer, as Mrs Erswell says & yourself.—

I am trying to understand something about Minerealogy, and Mrs Spicer helps me, & has given me specimens, & Anna Wilbraham has lent me a little cabinet of minerals: but I <miss> feel my ignorance in chimestry very sensibly.—

I have eight shillings odd pence of yours, for Gingham wch could never be procured exactly like the chosen pattern. It shall be forwarded to you first opportunity.

1. The Barretts had been in a cottage at Bradfield from early July to early December 1817, while SHB herself had been at Brighton with Charlotte Broome for at least a month c. August (Gazley, 681; *JL*, 10: 542, 584, 645, 774).

2. It appears that Sarah Harriet, from motives of economy, had shared her apartment at Chelsea for nine months, an arrangement that was not a success.

3. Gen. Samuel Hulse, Lt.-Gov. of Chelsea Hospital, and his wife Charlotte (L. 72, n. 12).

4. Possibly Lt.-Col. William Henry Spicer (fl. 1796–1829) of the 2nd Regiment of Life Guards, who had married 20 January 1810 Maria Charlotte (1780–1855), only daughter of Sir George William Prescott (d. 1801), 1st Bt. (1794) (*Army List;* IGI; *GM*, 80, Pt. 1 (1810): 86; 95, Pt. 2 (1825): 66; 99, Pt. 1 (1829): 418; NS 44 (1855): 555; Burke).

The Spicers also knew Charlotte Barrett, who refers to Col. Spicer as an old friend of her husband's (CFBt to AY, 6 Apr. 1818, Barrett, Eg. 3703A, ff. 40–41v).

5. The Rev. William Haggitt, Chaplain of Chelsea Hospital, and his wife Sarah (L. 64, n. 7).

6. Thomas Keate, Surgeon at the Hospital, and his wife Emma (L. 19, n. 5).

7. Richard Neave (1773–1858), youngest son of Sir Richard Neave (1731–1814), 1st Bt. (1795), Governor of the Bank of England. He had married on 2 July 1807 Sarah née Irvine (c. 1782–1826), and had four children. He was also connected to the Spicers (n. 4), his sister having married Mrs. Spicer's uncle. A barrister, Richard Neave had been appointed on 28 July 1816 deputy-paymaster to the forces, and secretary and registrar of the Royal Hospital, Chelsea. Both he and his wife would remain at the hospital for the rest of their lives (Burke; *GM*, 77, Pt. 2 (1807): 681; 96, Pt. 2 (1826): 284; 99, Pt. 1 (1829): 418; 3rd ser. 4 (1858): 230).

8. Unidentified.

9. A sedan chair was provided at Chelsea Hospital to transport the sick to a new Infirmary, which was completed in 1816 (Dean, 259).

10. A longtime family friend (L. 27, n. 3), Lady Crewe had suffered a paralytic stroke c. January 1817 from which she had not fully recovered in the summer (*JL*, 9: 306, 346, 362 and n. 9, 446).

11. John McLeod (c. 1777–1820), M.D. (1818), was a naval surgeon who served on the ship which carried Lord Amherst as ambassador to China (1816) and was wrecked on the way home. He published in 1817 his *Narrative of a Voyage in His Majesty's late ship Alceste to the Yellow Sea*, which ran to three editions (*DNB*).

12. Henry Ellis (1777–1855), K.C.B. (1848), was one of the commissioners on Lord Amherst's embassy to China. His *Journal of the proceedings of the late embassy to China* (1817) was the "authorised narrative" (*DNB*); it cannot have been considered dull by all its readers, as a second edition was published the following year.

13. *Mandeville* (1817), the recently published novel by William Godwin (1756–1836) (*DNB*).

14. James's wife, Sarah, convalescing from a severe illness, was now in a "promising way of amendment" (JB to FBA, 21 Dec. 1817, Berg).

87. [To Frances (Burney) d'Arblay][1]

[Chelsea College], 6 May 1818
A.L.S., Berg
Annotated by FBA: "a most kindly appropriate Letter from my dear Sarah on my Heart's dechermont" *and dated:* "6. May, 1818"

How shall I, my most dear Sister, find courage to address you at such a moment?[2]—And yet how can I be silent?—Oh, that you could but know how deeply, how sincerely my heart aches for you!—It is an event, the very most distant idea of which was so dreadful to me, than I never dared allow my thoughts to rest upon it;—I shuddered when it came across me; for could I be ignorant what you and my poor dear Alexander would feel!—Adored, venerated, admired as He was by us all, we can but too easily represent to ourselves what must now be your sufferings!—My poor, poor Sister! I can only grieve from the bottom of my heart for you—and offer up prayers to God to support you through a trial the heaviest and the greatest that could have befallen you!—The heaviest and the greatest that could have befallen any human being—for who ever meritted to be beloved and regretted like Him! Every sweet, every noble, every generous and high-minded quality was His.—I never thought in so exalted a manner of any other living soul—and I loved, I honoured Him, I may almost say, as he deserved to be loved and honoured!—Certain it is, that all the warmth of attachment and respect of which my heart is capable, were more devotedly and uniformly His, than they ever were, or can be any one's else.—I hope I do not pain you, my already too deeply afflicted sister, by this address.—Ill expressed as it is, my sympathy comes from my heart—And as I ever thought you the happiest and most enviable of women whilst so united, so now I mourn for you as the most smitten and pitiable.

May God Almighty uphold you, and strengthen, and succour you and my dearest Alexander, is the heartfelt prayer, my loved Sister, of your deeply commiserating

S. H. Burney

May 6th 1818.

I hope some of my dear family at Bath[3] will soon give me intelligence of you.—

1. A letter of condolence, obviously addressed to Sarah Harriet's half-sister, Frances (Burney) d'Arblay, on the death of her husband. It has been dated and annotated in FBA's hand.

2. Alexandre-Jean-Baptiste Piochard d'Arblay died on 3 May 1818 after suffering a painful disease of the bowels. Mme d'Arblay's grief is described in *HFB*, 408–13; see also the "Narrative of the Last Illness and Death of General d'Arblay" (*JL*, 10: L. 1170).

3. Besides Maria Bourdois and her sister Sophia, who lived at 5 Ainslie's Belvedere (L. 85, n. 18), Esther and Charles Rousseau Burney had moved to Bath in the spring of 1817. They were living at 5 Lark Hall Place with their youngest daughter, Amelia (*JL*, 9: 357, 362, 405, n. 7, 462; 10: 773).

---

88. [To Richard Clark]

Brighton, 26 November 1818

L., Published: Richard Clark, ed., *An Account of the National Anthem Entitled God Save the King!* (London: W. Wright, 1822), 53–54.[1]

Brighton, Nov. 26th, 1818.

Sir,

I am much concerned that I have it not in my power to communicate to you any information worth receiving, on the subject of our national air.[2] I have no recollection of ever having heard my father mention the name of its composer: on the contrary, I seem to have a confused remembrance of having heard him declare, that he did not himself know whom to ascribe it to. I am so perfectly assured, however, that he believed it to have been originally sung in honour of King James, that though, in general, unwilling to trust to my memory, I would not, on this point, scruple to speak in the most positive manner.

I am, Sir, your very obedient servant,

S. H. Burney.

1. The letter is cited by Richard Clark (1780–1856) (*DNB*) in his discussion of the origin of "God Save the King." Clark believes that it was composed by John Bull (c. 1563–1628) (*DNB; New Grove*) for James I, to commemorate his escape from the Gunpowder Plot, and performed for the first time on 16 July 1607, in the hall of the Merchant Tailors' Company (Clark, xiii–xvi).

As an historian of music and the apprentice of Dr. Arne (who arranged the anthem in 1745 when it became popular), Charles Burney was asked his opinion of the authorship. His view, reported in Clark (39–40) as well as the *Morning Post* (2 Nov. 1814) and *GM*, 84, Pt. 2 (1814): 99–100 (and also expressed in his letters), was that the unknown composer had lived in the reign of James II and that the earliest copy began "God save great James our King." Clark appeals to Dr. Burney's authority for the words but claims they apply to James I rather than James II (54).

Percy A. Scholes in a more recent discussion of the controversy supports Clark's view, although he suspects him of altering the Bull manuscript in his possession to make it more closely resemble the tune (Percy A. Scholes, *"God Save the King!" Its History and Its Romance* (London: Oxford University Press, 1942), 21–24; and *God Save the Queen! The History and Romance of the World's First National Anthem* (London: Oxford University Press, 1954), 92–103).

2. According to Richard Clark (53), "I wrote to Miss Burney, requesting she would do me the favour to give me such information on the subject as she could, who very politely sent me the following account."

---

89. To Charlotte (Burney) (Francis) Broome

Chelsea College, 30 March 1819
A.L.S., Berg
Address: Mrs Broome / 6 German Place / Brighton / Sussex
Postmarks: Chelsea C O
7 [o]Clock / [31 MR] / [AT] 18[*?*]
7 oClock / 31 [*?*] / [*?*]
C MR / 31 / 819
Endorsed: Sister Sarah / March 1819

Chelsea College
March 30th 1819

No, no, my kindest of Sisters—Nor no such a think! And for this plain, politic, provident, and unsentimental reason: i,e: that were I to consent to let you transform a loan <debt> into a gift, I never should have the face, in any future embarrassment, to apply to you again;—and I like to keep a sound string to my bow. Besides,—had I ever meant to do so shabby a thing, I would have dealt openly with you, and not sneaked the money out of your pocket under pretence of borrowing: but fairly at once have said—"If you can possibly spare it, my dear Sister, do pray give me seven or eight pounds."—To be sure I would! But when I use the words borrow, debt, and loan, I mean, sooner or later, to abide by said words.—You know, dearest, that I am not subject to fits of false delicacy, and a little friendly present never yet threw my pride into a fever, if it came from one I love. But I cannot be mean, my kind heart, even to gratify your generous spirit; and so, you will really and truly oblige me by accepting the money now in our Charlotte's hands, & <permitting> allowing me to remit the rest as I may find convenient. Had all things turned out as I expected, I should, long since, have been able to discharge this debt: but Miss Gell,[1] very soon after our return to Chelsea,[2] became too ill to go on regularly with our lessons; and finding that she often missed four days out of the seven, and yet brought me no message from her Mother proposing to give up these irregular studies, I thought that they were silent from motives of delicacy, and therefore determined to make the proposal myself. It turned out that I was right, though they would not acknowledge it; for, on my suggesting the discontinuance of the plan, it was abandoned: but the whole quarter's salary was sent to me all the same. However, I could not, you know, for very shame, accept it, considering how very little I had been enabled to do towards earning it; so, after a tough battle, I made Mrs G: take back all but one third of the money—and that, dearest, being a circumstance which I had neglected to calculate upon, it left me, of course, rather poorer than I had intended to be, and rather deranged my Christmas accounts.[3] But all these matters are now getting right again, and I have no cause to lament the temporary pinch I have suffered, since it has taught me, I hope, the wisdom never again to reckon upon my chickens before they are hatched. An income depending in any degree upon contingencies—upon the health either of others or of oneself—an income, in short, not secured from <the> every species of uncertainty, ought, least of any, to be forestalled—And that, I trust, I shall hereafter never forget.—I bother you with all this, my sweet Sister, to account for my long delay, and to set your heart at rest with regard to my present ways and means. I have no debt now, but the remaining four pounds to you,—And I have good prospects for the remainder of this year by the sale of my scribble[4]—And after my next Birthday, in August, I mean to sink my little property, for which I shall then be old enough to receive eight per cent[5]—And that, with prudent management, will make me easy, without scholars, or compulsory Authorship, the rest of my days. And you will be glad I know—and my children will never reproach me!

Yes—I heard that dear Julia was with you, and rejoiced for both.[6] Her sweet Mother and I chatted side by side a whole evening lately at a ball given my Mrs Gell in celebration of lovely Emma's seventeenth birth-day. And Barrett was there in high good humour, and they both came with pretty Emma Woodbridge.[7] Charlotte I hope liked her evening—She looked very interesting and lady-like, and every body took a fancy to her, and admired her eyes, and countenance, and polished white throat:[8] but she hides her hair with caps, fitter for you or me, & wears her gowns too high—but that she says is to avoid colds in her chest, so I must not scold.—I see no outlet to the scrawling maze I have got into: but every thing by perseverance may be brought to an end. <at last.> Does not Imlac tell us, that “He that shall walk with vigour three hours a day, will pass in seven years a space equal to the circumference of the globe?”[9]—

Adieu my own dear—And thank you a thousand times for your generous offer and your kind letter. My affectionate love to Julia.—Oh—And your blue cloth has made me such a nice pelisse! every body thinks it new. Ever Yours S. H. Burney.

1. Emma Harmar Gell (1802–23) of Chelsea, only child of John Henry Gell (c. 1770–1856), coroner of Westminster, and his wife (m. 23 March 1801), Charlotte (née Harmar). Apparently of delicate health, young Emma would die four years later at the age of twenty-one, after marrying Lt. George Hawkins (d. 23 Aug. 1846) of the 86th Foot (parish register, St. Luke, Chelsea; *GM*, 93, Pt. 1 (1823): 189; NS 26 (1846): 444; 3rd ser. 1 (1856): 662; *Westminsters;* Burke under Hawkins).

2. Sarah Harriet had been with her half-sister, Charlotte Broome, at Brighton in October 1818 (*JL*, 11: 4, 27) when apparently she had borrowed some money. However, the joint letter signed “S. Burney” which has been attributed to her, and used to date her visit there as early as August (in *JL*, 11: 27, n. 5) is not in her hand. Moreover, the familial relationships of the writer (to whom Charlotte Broome is “my dear Aunt” and Marianne Francis a “Cousin”) clearly establish her identity as James’s daughter, Sarah (CBFB & Sarah Burney to MF & HnBt, 24 Aug. [1818], Berg).

3. SHB’s account at Coutts shows a withdrawal of £20 on 28 December 1818, and it would appear that 1819 was a hard year financially. Judging from the dividends deposited in her account, her stock holdings were effectively reduced by £232 between 8 April and 13 October 1819.

4. This is the first mention of the second of SHB’s *Tales of Fancy* which would soon be published (see below L. 90). The financial arrangements with her publisher were discussed in her letter of 23 [Nov. 1815] (L. 82).

5. On 29 August 1819, Sarah Harriet would be turning forty-seven. Whatever may have been her intentions (whether serious or not), her stock holdings do not change over the next three years; from £2,041.6.8 invested in 4 percents, she receives half-yearly dividends of £40.16.6, the only income that enters her account at Coutts.

6. Julia, Charlotte Barrett’s ten-year-old daughter, had gone to Brighton to visit her grandmother c. 19 February 1819 and returned home on 1 May. Mrs. Broome, recovering from fatigue and grief after the death of her consumptive son Ralph, found the sea air reviving. She would remain at Brighton until August (*JL*, 11: 79, n. 1, 81, 119, n. 1; CFBt to AY, 22 Apr. [1819], 10 May [1819], Barrett, Eg. 3703A, ff. 98–103v; MF to AY, 25 Apr. 1819, 14 Aug. 1819, Barrett, Eg. 3703B, ff. 135–36v, 152–53v).

7. Probably Emma Woodbridge (d. 1877), the youngest daughter of the late James Woodbridge of Richmond (c. 1739–1805). She would marry 22 November 1819 George Barttelot Smyth (later Barttelot) (1788–1872) of Stopham House, Sussex (*GM*, 75, Pt. 2 (1805): 685; 89, Pt. 2 (1819): 563; Burke under Barttelot).

8. Alexander d'Arblay had made the same remark a few months earlier; seeing his cousin Charlotte at a ball, he declared that "nobody was half as elegant as Charlotte" (*JL*, 11: 81).

9. Imlac makes the remark in Ch. 13 of Samuel Johnson's work, *The Prince of Abissinia. A Tale* (1759), later called *The History of Rasselas, Prince of Abyssinia.*

90. To Henry Colburn

[Chelsea College, 6 January] 1820
A.L.S., Osborn
Address: Mr Colburn

Twelfth Night
1820.—

Dear Sir

I venture to inclose a fresh list of books, & return, with many thanks, the parcel of those lately lent to me.—I was much gratified by learning that you had been kind enough to supply Miss F. Burney[1] with two copies of Country Neighbours.[2] I hope your purchase does not hang in hand.—When opportunity serves, do not forget that I am to be the purchaser of second hand copies of Waverley, Mannering &c—& the Tales of my Landlord.[3]—& if possible, let me also have Southey's poetical works.[4]—

A happy New Year to you
& believe me Dear Sir
yours truly S. H. Burney.

1. Sarah Harriet's niece, Frances Burney.

2. *Country Neighbours; or The Secret*, completed S. H. Burney's *Tales of Fancy* as volumes 2 and 3 (for vol. 1, see L. 81, n. 1). Colburn advertised extensively, starting in December 1819: "MISS BURNEY'S NEW NOVEL—In the Press, and speedily will be published" (*Times*, 17 Dec. 1819). The actual date of issue was 30 December 1819 (Colburn records), advertised as "This day is published" early in the new year (e.g., *Times*, 8 Jan. 1820). Almost immediately, a "new" edition in 3 volumes, 24s., appeared; entered in Colburn's records on 13 January 1820, it was advertised on 15 January 1820 in the *Morning Chronicle.* The last 2 volumes only were entered as a second edition into the registers of the Worshipful Company of Stationers on 27 January 1820. *Country Neighbours* was published in New York (1820), and in Paris as *Les Voisins de campagne, ou le Secret* (1820).

The reviews were favorable: the *Monthly Review*, 2nd ser. 91 (1820): 320–21, was pleased that Miss Burney had reverted from tales of "fancy" to a more natural genre, "the relation of natural incidents, well put together." Indeed, "she has the power of throwing a charm over the incidents of familiar life,—of displaying with true effect the naïveté of youth,—of reporting conversations with characteristic humour." Her work also figured well in two concerns of Colburn: the *New Monthly Magazine* 13 (1820): 597, which found "in every page the traces of a mind elegantly cultivated, and correctly regulated"; and the *Literary Gazette*, no. 156 (15 Jan. 1820): 38–40, which believed Miss Burney's forte to be "accurate observation on life and manners, and lively delineation of character." "Country Neighbours" inspired a sonnet by Charles Lamb, published in the *Morning Chronicle*, 13 July 1820 (see Appendix 2).

3. [Walter Scott's] first and second novels, *Waverley* (1814) and *Guy Mannering* (1815), and *Tales of my Landlord*, of which three series had appeared (1816–19).

4. Robert Southey (1774–1843), poet laureate (1813).

---

91. To Charlotte (Burney) (Francis) Broome

[Chelsea College], 7 June 1820
A.L.S., Berg
Address: M[rs] Broome / Henry Barrett's Esq[r] / Lower Road / Richmond Surry.
Postmarks: Chels[ea] C O
12 o'Clock / 8 JU / 1820 N∩
4 o'Clock / JU 8 / 1820 EV
Endorsed: Sister Sarah / duplicate of Cheltenham / Springs—

June 7th 1820.

When I saw you last, my dear Sister, and mentioned the account which I had heard of a mineral Spring similar to that at Cheltenham, but situated in the neighbourhood of London, you expressed a wish to hear more upon the subject; and the result of my enquiries is, that there are <u>two</u> such Springs; one called the Wells at East Acton, on the Ealing Road, four miles from town, and an easy drive from Richmond; the other, is St. Chad's Well, Gray's Inn Lane.[1] Both of these, as I am informed, are as effectual as either Leamington or Cheltenham; and lodgings might be taken in the neighbourhood of either.

I am, from the persevering disposition to pain in my face, still a very poor wrapt-up creature. I hope amendment from change of air, & warmer weather; & propose a trip, as soon as we are blessed with a few dry days, to Cheltenham, trusting that the very journey itself will do me good.—Yours dear Sister, with kindest love to Charlotte & Co. most affectionately, S. H. Burney.

I cannot accurately recollect your direction—So address this to you at Mr Barrett's.—Ormond Row,[2] is it?

1. Two of the many wells in the London area: the Acton Wells, whose "purging waters" were said to be "second only to Cheltenham's in potency"; and St. Chad's Well on Gray's Inn Road, also recommended for its purgative qualities (William Addison, *English Spas* (London: B. T. Batsford, 1951), 50, 35–36; Lambert, 4: 226–27, 295; *Survey of London*, 24: 66–67, 112).

2. Charlotte Broome had returned from Brighton and settled by mid-August 1819 at 6 Ormond Place, Richmond, a five minutes' walk from her daughter Charlotte (MF to AY, 14 Aug. 1819, Barrett, Eg. 3703B, ff. 152–53v; *JL*, 11: 24–25, n. 1, 119). The house, in a pretty row of terrace-houses dating from the early eighteenth century, is still standing.

92. To Frances (Burney) d'Arblay

[Chelsea College, pre 3 August 1820][1]
A.L.S., Barrett, Eg. 3698, ff. 82–83v
Address: M[rs] d'Arblay
Annotated by FBA: Cheltenham / Sarah-Harriet. / Aug[st] 1820

My poor Alex[2] came in, Dearest Sister, miserably hot—But a quiet little wholesome morcel of refreshment, & resting himself with his feet up upon my chaise longue, took off his weariness, and cooled & comforted him: besides having the pleasure of seeing how rejoiced I was to behold him.—Oh, this delightful fine weather! It is the first time I have felt tolerably secure from pain since January:[3] I cannot tell you how I sit enjoying the heat & glow which every body else is ready to gasp at.—But before I say another word, let me thank you, and take shame to myself for not having done it sooner, for your most noble & generous offer of a loan in case I should be under difficulties on account of money for my Cheltenham journey.[4] Would it not, however, be inexcusable to labour under such difficulties this year?—Out of my friend Colburn's punctual payments, I have put by a moderate sum purposely for the expenses of this journey;[5] & therefore, (with renewed & most grateful thanks to you) I have it fully in my power to avoid drawing upon your liberality.—In about ten days time I shall probably set out, and a young friend, who like myself is but an invalid, goes with me from the next door—

Excuse all this dry stuff—while I am writing I want to be talking, & that makes me probably do <u>both</u> ill—

Adieu—I dare say nothing about the <u>when</u> I shall get to you—but I do mean it, & that soon—And so believe your ever affectionate

S. H. B.

Saturday Evening

And Alex talking to me—

1. SHB's letter is written ten days previous to her setting out on a journey to Cheltenham, financed by the proceeds of her fiction. Such a journey did take place in the summer months of 1820; although endorsed by Mme d'Arblay "Augt 1820," the letter must at least predate 3 August when Sarah was reported "yet at Cheltenham," and was probably written earlier. In any case, by 3 September 1820 she was back in London (*JL*, 11: 170, 175).

2. FBA's only child, Alexander, was elected Fellow of Christ's College, Cambridge (1818). Ordained as a deacon (1818) and a priest (1819), he would not obtain a curacy until 1824. When not at Cambridge, he stayed with his mother at 11 Bolton Street, Piccadilly (*JL*, 1: lxx; 11: 1, n. 1, 12, n. 4).

3. On 11 May 1820, Mme d'Arblay wrote: "I have seen nothing of Sarah-Harriet this age. She has been mu[ch] a sufferer from pains of various sorts: but I hope this [*cut*] weather will re-instate her" (*JL*, 11: 158).

4. Fanny had sent her half-sister £10 (either as a loan or gift) on a previous occasion when illness was draining her resources (L. 85, n. 4). She may have been acting on the feeling of compunction she expressed when acknowledging her own favoured position in her father's will and trying to share some of the money more equitably: "I | only regret that we are not sufficiently rich to do the same by Sarah—but I have no right to forget That what my dearest Father bequeathed to ME, he meant should be also, as my peculiar portion, ENJOYED by my honoured Partner, and INHERITED by our Son" (*JL*, 9: 49). Her "honoured Partner" had by this time died.

5. By the terms outlined in her letter of 23 November 1815 (L. 82), Sarah Harriet would realize at least £100 for her second tale and £50 for the second edition (it is not clear whether the payment per volume would double for a single tale that took up two volumes). As no deposit appears in her account at Coutts, it seems likely that she did pay the expenses of her journey with her earnings.

93. To Charlotte (Francis) Barrett

[Chelsea College], 27 October [1820]
A.L.S., Berg
Address: Mrs Barrett / Henry Barrett's Esqr / Lower Road / Richmond.
Postmarks: C[hel]sea C O
7 o'Clock / [?] / 18[?]

Octr 27th

My dearest Char—for sundry reasons, too tedious to ennumerate, I did not honour the Greenwich party with my presence—so I am glad that you were not there. I will do what in me lies about the Alfred Club:[1] but I suspect that *our* Revd Wm Haggitt is not the *D^{r}* Haggitt[2] whom you mention: time and due enquiry however will shew; & if I can find any body to whom an application from me can be of any avail,[3] I shall be glad. I have been most remarkably well during my late sojourn at Brighton:[4] but, would you believe it? have never had the sense & resolution to stir from my own door since I came back. I miss the pleasant, friendly little *coterie* to which I belonged whilst there; and so little attraction has Chelsea and its present inhabitants, that I feel quite a distaste to the idea of sallying forth and making myself visible to the few Cats, male & female, now residing here. Haggitts & Keates are absent.—Tell me more of your Mrs Barnard's[5] "good girl!" *Is* she a *good girl*? That is, good tempered, & good mannered? I am half tempted to wish to try the situation myself. My eyes are not so well fitted for constant reading & writing as they have been; and a life of more sociability than I can enjoy by living by myself would I think suit both my spirits & my health better than the solitary paradise which I now inhabit. I care little about <the> salary. By saving house-rent, coals, &c, I should be able perhaps to put by £50 a year, or 40, & pay for dress & washing with the remainder of my little income.[6] In fact, my chief object would be chearful, well disposed, & well bred associates. A motive for going out more than I do, would be of advantage to me; particularly, if there was no danger of my being wanted to sail forth through mud through mire, on my ten toes, at night. Night air & I are at deadly variance, & have been any time these fifteen years.—See what can be done about this business, dearest. Think for me, & advise me—and learn all you can of the temper & character of the parties in question. As I am a little upon the fidget since this idea has struck me, I shall be heartily obliged to you to be as expeditious as you can in gaining farther intelligence for me.—Mum, meanwhile, to all whom the matter may not concern.—

Little Rob[7] will perhaps tell you that she saw me at Brighton, and asked me to dinner, wch I declined for merrier fishes which I had to fry. Our first meeting would have been more in character had she and I reversed occupations: she found me, arm in arm with another lady, admiring caps & bonnets at a shop window. The thing is, that what with Mrs Barclay, & others who invited me, I went out more than usual, & was forced to make merry among the cap venders whether I would or no. What a nasty little displaying wonder is Jessy Barclay![8] I admire, & hate (almost), & pity, & sometimes love her. The Mother is unpardonable—the child, a coquette the most determined, with, I believe, a naturally good disposition which they are spoiling as fast as flattery, finery, shewing-off, & vanity-feeding can effect.—I am glad you like your new house, & have got into it before winter.[9]—I am glad also that in your letter you say not one word of the pending trial.[10] It is refreshing to read or to think of any and every thing sooner than that.

Do you remember a Mrs Jennings to whom you were introduced two or three years ago, & who raves of you & your children, & who knew Barrett before he married, & loves & admires him? She lives at Kensington with her married son, a Lawyer,[11] & she was in the Boarding House with me, West Cliff, Brighton. She is a dear old Lady—We were just five good-humoured womenkind, all widows but me, & grew quite friendly & cordial before we parted, & had our own visitors, & p^d^ our own visits, & were independent without being unsociable. Adieu, love to y^r^ Mother & Barrett & childer.

Y^rs^

S. B.

1. The Alfred Club at No. 23 Albemarle Street was established in 1808. Originally patronized by travelers and men of letters (of which Lord Byron was one), it also attracted members of the higher clergy and the legal profession (John Timbs, *Club Life of London* (London: Richard Bentley, 1866), 1: 237–39).

2. The Rev. William Haggitt, Chaplain to Chelsea Hospital (L. 64, n. 7), was not to be confused with the Rev. Francis Haggitt (1759–1825), D.D. (1808), Rector of Nuneham Courtenay, Oxon. (1786), Chaplain to the King (1787), Prebendary of Durham (1794). Charlotte may have expected Dr. Haggitt, as a church dignitary, to belong to the Alfred Club (*Alumni Cantab.; GM*, 95, Pt. 2 (1825): 283).

3. It seems that Charlotte Barrett was asking her friends to canvass influential churchmen in favor of her brother Clement, who may have been seeking preferment in the church, or some emolument within his college at Cambridge (see further, L. 94). After taking his B.A. (1817) at Caius College (M.A. 1820), Clement would become a Fellow

(1820–29), Dean (1821–22), and Bursar (1827–28). He was also ordained as deacon (1820) and priest (1821) (*Alumni Cantab.*).

4. Shortly after returning from her summer sojourn at Cheltenham, SHB had left for Brighton, where she was by 24 October 1820 (*JL*, 11: 176).

5. Possibly the Hon. Louisa Barnard (1769–1835), daughter of John Peyto Verney (1738–1816), 14th Baron Willoughby de Broke (1752). She had married on 31 October 1793 the Rev. Robert Barnard (1760–1834), Rector of Lighthorne, Warws. (1787) and Prebendary of Winchester (1793). She sometimes stayed at her father's house in Richmond and may be the same Mrs. Barnard whose theatrical evenings CFBt would recall attending (Burke; Lodge; Venn; *GM*, 78, Pt. 2 (1798): 902; 82, Pt. 1 (1812): 588; CFBt to HBt, 25 Apr. [1833], Barrett, Eg. 3702A, ff. 88–89v).

6. Sarah Harriet was earning £81.13s. per annum from her stock holdings, but may have had other income from writing or giving lessons.

7. "Rob" or "Robby," a friend of Charlotte Barrett's at Richmond, is probably Marianne (1770–1839), the daughter of Sir William Wake (1742–85), 8th Bt. (1765) of Courteenhall, co. Northampton, who had married on 15 October 1801 Col. Roger Eliot Roberts of the Bengal Establishment. This "innocent old friend" was to die suddenly (as CFBt would inform SHB) in March 1839 (Burke; *Debrett's Baronetage of England*, 5th ed. (London, 1824), 1: 87; *GM*, 71, Pt. 2 (1801): 959; CFBt to MF, 26 [Aug. 1812], 21 Oct. [1824–28], CFBt to JBt, 12 Apr. [1829], Barrett, Eg. 3702A, ff. 162–63v, 176–77v, 188–89v; CFBt to SHB, 4 May [April 1839], Barrett, Eg. 3702A, ff. 157–60v).

8. Mrs. Barclay may be the same acquaintance whom Charlotte later mentions as planning a trip to Italy; she and her daughter Jessy have not been further identified (CFBt to Matilda Aufrère, 11 Feb. [1833], Berg).

9. For some time past, Henry Barrett, with a reduced income and five children to support, had been renting out the house at Richmond, while living more cheaply in a cottage at Bradfield or (13 July–12 Oct. 1818) on the continent. The family would soon leave (in mid-May) for Ghent, "making their Rent pay for their travels" (*JL*, 9: 140, n. 9, 261, n. 2; 11: 4, n. 13, 356 and n. 2).

10. A Bill of Pains and Penalties "to deprive her Majesty Caroline Amelia Elizabeth of the title, prerogatives, rights, privileges, and pretensions of Queen Consort of this realm, and to dissolve the marriage between his Majesty and the said Queen" was introduced in the House of Lords on 5 July 1820. On the third reading (10 Nov. 1820), 108 voted in favour and 99 against, which led to the virtual abandonment of the bill and was hailed as a victory for the Queen. Her trial is the subject of a recent book by Roger Fulford, *The Trial of Queen Caroline* (London: B. T. Batsford, 1967).

11. Possibly Ann Jennings (d. 11 Aug. 1838), the widow of D. Jennings of Shaftesbury House, Kensington (*GM*, NS 10 (1838): 338). Her lawyer son may be one of several Jennings listed in the *New Law List* (1812–24). Marianne Francis also spoke of a Dr. and Mrs. Jennings who were staying at Brighton (Catherine Minette Raper to HnBt, 22 Feb. [n.d.], Barrett, Eg. 3707, ff. 172–73v).

94. To Charlotte (Francis) Barrett

[Chelsea College, 1 November 1820]
A.L.S., Berg
Address: Mrs Barrett / Lower Road / Richmond / Surry
Postmarks: 7 o'Clock / 1 NO / NT 1820
C NO / 1 / 820

No, my dearest, I do not by any means think that you have been precipitate in naming me.[1] There is no shame in what I propose, therefore no need of mystery—especially between me and the other party concerned. As for blaring about my own affairs to every chance comer, I have respect enough for myself to know, that I deserve better than to be made the subject of a heartless article of gossip either at the beginning, the middle, or the end of an idle half hour's visit. Those who really care about me, or those whose business it is to know something of me, are as welcome to the information as the flowers in May.

As to the wholesale Druggistship. I am ashamed, my dear Char, ever to have given you cause to think that I should be so insolent as to make such a matter a subject of objection. I have sundry recollections of past flippancies on the topic of tradesmen, shops, &c, &c—and in my heart, cannot but allow, that you are justified in having entertained such a distrust of me. But it is never too late to learn, nor to amend. I have been thrown by circumstances, recently, more into the society of traders, city people, and manufacturers than I ever was before—and my vulgar astonishment at their good manners, information, and liberality of mind, was, even to myself, perfectly ridiculous!—At a Boarding-House at Brighton, I met two young ladies so remarkable for their intelligence, so accomplished, and well bred, that I quite admired and delighted in them. Where should they come from but—London Wall?—A Mrs Jerdein was likewise there, the widow and Mother of Wholesale Tobacconists, and residing close to their own warehouses in Fore Street.[2] She was amiable, gentle, Lady-like, & kind-hearted in the highest degree; and all these folks became so sociable with me, that I received from them the most pressing invitations to visit them, and keep up the acquaintance; a circumstance I should like very much, but for the distance at which they reside.

Excuse my costing you another threepence for this rigmarole; but I thought you would not be sorry to hear, that all that you have done appears to me right & proper. Who likes to meddle with a pig in a poke?—Neither S. H. Burney, nor Johnny Hodgekinson,[3] you may be sure.—When I know what my own plans can be, I will endeavour to give myself the treat of spending a day with you. Perhaps, when Mrs Gell[4] returns from the sea side, she may have an inclination to a drive as far as Richmond, in which case, I will make interest with her for a cast. The Wilbrahams, now at Tunbridge, mean to spend Christmas at Brighton, & have written to ask me to join their party. I know nothing about the matter yet—but am glad of such a string to my bow, for my late frolics have made me agog for more—& this place is the ne plus ultra of stupidity, just now. The Keates however come back in about a week, & they are my sheet anchors—and then, soon, the Haggitts will return, merry & happy, I hope, for the eldest girl is about to be married.[5]—Adieu dearest. I have got the promise of one member of the Alfred (Mr Neave)[6] to be favorable to Clem:—Neither our Yates nor Haggitt belong to it.[7]

Yours & Cos ever
Affectionate
S. H. B.

Wednesday Morning

1. In her missing letter, Charlotte apparently responded to her aunt's appeal (L. 93) to "think for me, & advise me" about finding a situation. It would seem that Charlotte had approached a potential employer (John Hodgkinson; see n. 3) but feared she had been precipitate in naming her aunt.

2. Probably Margaret Jerdein (d. 1825), the widow of Michael Jerdein, a tobacconist, who took over his business at 70 Fore Street in 1819, would share it with her son in 1824, and disappear from the firm name after 1825. At the end of that year on 12 December, "Mrs. Jerdien, of Fore-street" died at Brighton. Her sons John Inglis and Michael would continue to operate from the same address until 1834 when they disappear from the London directories (London directories, 1798–1837; *GM*, 95, Pt. 2 (1825): 574).

3. A firm of wholesale druggists appears in the London directories under the name Brandram Hodgkinson & Co. between 1815 and 1833 at 213 Upper Thames Street. Presumably, a member of the family was seeking a governess, but Charlotte feared that Sarah's apparent prejudice against tradesmen might preclude her interest in the position.

4. For Mrs. Gell of Chelsea, see L. 89, n. 1.

5. The Haggitts' eldest daughter, Sarah (b. 27 July 1797), would marry on 3 April 1821 Capt. Henderson Bain (c. 1776–1862), who had entered the Royal Navy in 1793 and served in the war with France as Lt. (1800) and Capt. (1813). He would later be promoted Rear-Admiral (1846) (chapel register, Royal Hospital Chelsea; *GM*, 91, Pt. 1 (1821): 372; 3rd ser. 12 (1862), 242; Marshall, *Suppl.* Pt. 3, 123–24; William R. O'Byrne, *A Naval Biographical Dictionary* (London: John Murray, 1849)).

6. Richard Neave, secretary and registrar of the Chelsea Hospital (L. 86, n. 7). A barrister, he belonged to the Alfred Club and had apparently been canvassed to use his

vote or influence in favor of Clement Francis. The subject was first raised in SHB's letter of 27 October 1820 (L. 93, nn. 1, 2, 3).

7. The Rev. Richard Yates, Second Chaplain (L. 51, n. 9), and the Rev. William Haggitt might be expected as churchmen to belong to the club, but apparently they did not.

---

95. To Frances (Burney) d'Arblay

[Chelsea College], 7 December 1820
A.L.S. with typescript, Barrett, Eg. 3698, ff. 84–87v
Address: M[rs] d'Arblay / 11. Bolton Street / Piccadilly
Postmarks: Chelsea C O
[*?* oClo]ck / 8 DE / 1820 NT
Annotated by FBA: on / leaving / Chelsea College—/ M[rs] Delany's / Letters. / Wilbrahams

Dec[r] 7th 1820.

My dearest Sister

I take a sheet of letter, not of note paper, because it is not a little that I mean to say to you. I am, to begin, sick of Chelsea College. In itself it has sundry stupefying properties: but <what> the climax of all its abominations is, its distance from my family & many of my best friends, & the difficulty (without giving a day's previous notice) of procuring any sort of conveyance to town.—M[rs] Wilbraham advises me, almost seriously, to establish myself in London lodgings during the three winter months, that I may be got at! How well that would suit my pocket, whatever it might do my inclination, is a matter deserving some consideration. I am sorry, however, upon the whole, that I took root in this focus of inconvenience and dullness. I seem just to have discovered that it is neither town nor country; that the air is moist & relaxing; the society miserably confined, and when the Haggitts and Keates are away, which is the case full six months in the year, is reduced to—no society at all, of a cordial, & intimate kind. Have I not taken my time to discern all these obvious objections? Who can say I have been hasty in conceiving a spite against the place?—The truth is, that during the summer, I got into such pleasant domestic society both at Cheltenham and Brighton by having adopted the plan of boarding as well as lodging where I took up my quarters, that I now feel the solitude of my situation more keenly than I almost ever did before. However, for the present, I must be resigned; and if I could but settle my mind sufficiently to become industrious as I was last winter, I should live in a little ideal world of my own,[1] and care nothing about the humdrum of surrounding realities.—My poor Brother James has sent me a pamphlet of his, about La Perouse, which tho' well written, I am afraid will be thought to come a day after the fair, & will do little more than excite a smile. Have you seen it?—Am I mistaken in my opinion of it?—I shall really be glad to find that I am; for now, I grieve at what appears to me a serious and unconscious fudge![2]—

The Hulses[3] have been reading Mrs Delany's Letters,[4] & never were so interested, they say, nor even affected in some parts of it, by any book in their lives.—You will feel a degree of pleasure, for the sake of the family, though I believe you scarcely know Miss Haggitt personally, in hearing that she is shortly to be married, & much to the satisfaction of her dear Mother and father. The gentleman is a Post Captain, and an intimate friend of Colonel & Mrs Spicer.[5] Kate, the youngest sister,[6] is nearly recovered, and in good looks, and still better spirits. Miss Keate says, (you must have College gossip in a letter from the College) that all the single women in the establishment ought to present a vote of thanks to Miss Haggitt for enticing Hymen to come within the walls!—We think this a very witty idea.—See what we are brought to.—

The Wilbrahams put me in a rage. They have been at Tunbridge two or three months, amongst Tankervilles & Bennetts, and are come back so corrupted by evil communication (all but the Mother, a stanch Tory, born and bred,) that they are perfect Radicals, and for fear of a quarrel, we have agreed never to touch again upon politics.[7]—However, Anna, the youngest, may, perhaps, mend her notions, by going with Lady Cholmondeley[8] into Norfolk: but a fig for such cameleon principles!—Do you know that when I get with very violent party people, either one way or the other, the spirit of contradiction is so strong within me, that I give way less than I should with moderate folks, and set myself sturdily to resist their puffs, and rather to break than bend.—I hope you sometimes, if not always, see the New Times,[9] and have read Cato's Letters,[10] & some other excellent ones from a female monitress—said to be admirable Mrs Fry, the Quaker Howard.[11]—Adieu my dearest Sister. Best love to Alex.

Ever yours
S. H. B.

1. I.e., while writing the second of her *Tales of Fancy*, which was published early in 1820; see above L. 90, n. 2.

2. James Burney's *A Memoir on the Voyage of d'Entrecasteaux, in search of La Pérouse* was privately printed in November 1820. In it, he urged the British government to discover the fate of this explorer, as a gesture of goodwill to France.

Jean François de Galaup, comte de La Pérouse (1741–88), never returned from his 1785 voyage of exploration and was last heard of in 1788 at Botany Bay. In 1791 another French navigator, Joseph Antoine Bruni d'Entrecasteaux (1739–93), set out to discover his fate, without success. The mystery would be solved by an expedition sent in January 1827 by the East India Co. under the command of Peter Dillon (1788–1847), who discovered the remains of the boats wrecked on Vanikoro Island; his findings were soon confirmed for the French by Jules Sebastien Cesar Dumont d'Urville (1790–1842). Besides the published contemporary accounts of the voyages, see J. W. Davidson, *Peter Dillon of Vanikoro: Chevalier of the South Seas* (Melbourne: Oxford University Press, 1975).

3. Gen. Sir Samuel Hulse, Gov. of Chelsea Hospital, and his wife (L. 72, n. 12).

4. Mary (née Granville) (Pendarves) Delany (1700–88) (*DNB*); her *Letters from Mrs. Delany . . . to Mrs. Frances Hamilton, from the year 1779, to the year 1788* were published in 1820. Mme d'Arblay would be interested in this work as she had known Mrs. Delany in her old age, a friendship which had resulted in Fanny's appointment in the Queen's household (see *HFB*, 167–68, 194–95; *DL*, 2 and 3 passim).

5. For Col. and Mrs. Spicer who lived at Chelsea Hospital, see L. 86, n. 4.

6. Catharine, daughter of the Rev. William and Sarah Haggitt, was born 4 December 1795 and baptized 14 January 1796 at the Royal Hospital, Chelsea, by her own father, who was Chaplain (chapel register).

7. Charles Bennet, 4th Earl of Tankerville, had married Mrs. Wilbraham's cousin (L. 27, n. 7). His two sons, Charles Augustus (1776–1859), styled Lord Ossulston, and Henry Grey (1777–1836), were both M.P.'s and strong adherents of the Whigs; for the record of their parliamentary careers, see Thorne.

8. Georgiana Charlotte (née Bertie), wife of the 1st Marquess of Cholmondeley (L. 32, n. 16), whose principal seat was near the Wilbrahams at Nantwich, Cheshire. Lady Cholmondeley's eldest son, George Horatio (1792–1870), M.P. for Castle Rising (1817–21), was Tory, but her husband was known as a Whig (Thorne).

9. A rival daily to the *Times* with staunch Tory tendencies, the *New Times* was started in 1817 under the editorship of Dr. (later Sir) John Stoddart (1773–1856) (*DNB;* Stephen Koss, *The Nineteenth Century*, vol. 1 of *The Rise and Fall of the Political Press in Britain* (London: Hamish Hamilton, 1981), 42).

10. Among others, *Cato's Letter to the People of England*, a political pamphlet, was reprinted from the *New Times* in 1821.

11. Elizabeth (née Gurney) Fry (1780–1845); her exertions on behalf of prison reform recalled those of John Howard (c. 1726–90) (*DNB* under Howard and Fry; *GM*, NS 24 (1845): 644–46).

96. To Charlotte (Francis) Barrett

[Chelsea College], 27 February 1821
A.L.S., Berg
Address: Mrs Barrett / Lower Road / Richmond / Surry.
Postmarks: 12 o'Clock / 28 FE / 1821 N∩
4 o'Clock / FE 28 / 1821 EV
[Chelsea CO]

Feby 27th 1821.

My dearest—That part of your letter which related to the business of your excellent Charlotte,[1] I have done the best in my little power to do: <which> I have read it in the presence of three brides-elect whom it was reasonable to suppose might be joyful to snap at such a treasure; and to sundry married ladies, who, I am sorry to say all seem determined to rest satisfied with their present, I doubt not, very inferior attendants. The Wilbrahams are at Brighton: but when I saw them last, spoke with satisfaction of the young woman now waiting upon them. Thus far then, I have been successless in my wishes to serve your worthy Nurse: but I will not lose thought of the matter, and shall be most truly glad if any opportunity occurs to speak of her to more purpose.—

I long to know the light in which you and Barrett consider Sarah Burney's approaching marriage.[2] To me, I own, it is a pill that wanted far brighter gilding than it is likely to have, to make it go down without some degree of nausea.—I cannot comprehend her motives for accepting him, deeming, as I do, that she is no more in love with him than I am, and that she sees most clearly a great probability of losing cast by the union, and of having, for an entirely indefinite period, the *désagrement* of being dependent upon old Payne's liberality,[3] and the prospect of being any thing but affluent.—She is ill calculated, I fear, to give grace to straightened circumstances. She has lately spent a week with me, and I could have mourned over her disorderly habits, her wasteful neglect of her cloaths, and her slatternly morning appearance. She is (to me) a very engaging creature: but to make her *domestically* Lady-like, she required to be placed in a situation <where> in which she might have possessed, as a matter of course, every advantage of steady, experienced, personal attendants.[4] To lament, thus seriously, over mere untidiness, may seem ridiculous: but I dread what such a defect, combined with a certain degree of vanity, and a limitted income, may lead to.—Debts are not unfrequently incurred through such causes; and, exclusive of that frightful evil, a thousand lesser disadvantages, marring to happiness and respectability, are apt to arise from them.—These are odd reflections to make on the prospect of a girl's marriage: but I love her too well not to feel anxious for the consequences that may result from <her> such a marriage, with the faults in grain that stamp her character.—I am perplexed also as to the class of society to which she will henceforth find herself restricted. Admired & liked as she is, will her pill be swallowed in consideration of the sweetener she can administer with it?—How will your Richmond folks stand <disposed> affected on this subject?[5] How, even, will the higher description of her own present associates deport and comport themselves on the occasion? The proud militaries here, I grieve to think, will all hold aloof: or what is worse, I am such a coward from my conscious insignificance, that I shall dare make no effort to induce them to come forward. This is being a pretty kind of Aunt!—I am ashamed of myself—but yet, when you think of my known poverty—of the obligations which I am perpetually receiving in the way of invitations, without the ability to return one of them, some little excuse may be found for me.

Of course you have read Kenilworth Castle, and I trust, liked it. I greatly prefer it to the Monastery, & am almost as much pleased with it as with the Abbot:[6] but not quite; the catastrophe is painful, & Elizabeth figures not so appropriately in a Romance, as her beautiful Rival; <might> neither is the false varnish given to Leicester's character capable of making one forget his historical turpitude. The introduction of Raleigh is a delightful relief; and I wanted Sir Philip Sidney to boot; and more about several others only incidentally mentioned. It would perhaps have been too hazardous to have brought in dear Shakespear: I cannot, however, but wish that he had adventured it. May be, I am a fool, and Scott's[7] enemy for desiring it: but with his versatility of power; his happy embodyings of fictitious character, he might surely have given form and pressure (if any man could) to the realities of Shakespear mind, and manners, & person.—At all events, Raleigh being so well delineated, I hope he will soon take some other historical personage in hand.—I have just begun Belzoni,[8] & like his simple style very much. Miss Porter (Anna Maria) has published a new Novel, The Village of Mariendorpt,[9] full of the most touching passages, but, as a whole, it drags. Her knowledge of military details appears to me marvellous; the period at which she makes her people act and talk, is during the Protestant War in Germany; she carries you to the dreadful siege of Magdebourg, & takes you into the camp and tent of Forstenson, Konigsmark, and I cannot tell you how many others, & seems to know more of warriors and warfare than, as a woman myself, I can at all account for.—My own trash stands stock still a little beyond p. 80.[10] Un de ces beaux jours perhaps it may see light again. Glad you like your new house. My love to Barrett—to your Madre, & the dear children. Ever affectionately yours, S. H. Burney

1. Charlotte Barrett was trying to place one of her servants, "my poor Charlotte . . . [*who is*] very trusty & useful. I must lose her, & therefore should be glad to consign her to a good mistress" (CFBt to Sarah Burney, [1821], Berg). She would succeed in recommending her to a recent bride (L. 99 below).

2. James Burney's daughter, Sarah, would marry 14 April 1821 her cousin, John Thomas Payne (c. 1796–1880), the natural son of a bookseller. The ceremony was said to form the basis of Charles Lamb's essay, "The Wedding," *The Last Essays of Elia* (1833); see *JL*, 11: 222, n. 2; Manwaring, 264–78; *HFB*, 425.

There was certainly no want of cordiality in the letter of congratulation sent on the wedding day by d'Arblays, Barretts, and other members of the family (*JL*, 11: L. 1247), but eyebrows were raised at her marriage to a tradesman. Esther Burney, hearing of the match through Mme d'Arblay, "lament[*ed*] that the party is not likely to raise her consequence in the Eye of the World" (EBB to FBA, Barrett, Eg. 3690, ff. 138–39v). Mrs. Barrett told of one lady who dropped their acquaintance on learning "whom Sarah had married" as she "does not admire the connection. . . . even I am ashamed to speak of it." Sarah "is a clever & delightful creature, & might have made a better match if she had wishd."

On the other hand, Charlotte admired John Payne's generosity to his bride in paying off all her debts (as well as those of her relatives), in agreeing to live with his in-laws to help their finances, and in denying himself in order to indulge his wife; "he seems to me to have behaved in all matters most nobly, generously & affectionately—I quite forgive him for being a bookseller—& wish Sally may like him. he doats upon her & sends the tenderest letters, full of money." In short, "Johnny cannot help it [*being in trade*], & is such an excellent fellow that one must love & honour him, as well as make the best of it all to poor Sally, now she has married him" (CFBt to CBFB, 9 Sept. [1822], 14 Sept. [1822], 4 Oct. [1822], CFBt to FPR, 22 Sept. [1822], Barrett, Eg. 3706D, ff. 39v–49v).

3. John Payne took over in 1825 the bookselling business of Thomas Payne the younger (1752–1831) (*DNB*), who acknowledged him in his will as his natural son, and left him the residue of an estate whose value was sworn to be under thirty thousand pounds (*JL*, 11: 47, n. 5, 222, n. 2; Phyllis G. Mann, "A New Gloss for 'The Wedding,'" *Charles Lamb Society Bulletin*, no. 170 (Mar. 1963): 402–3).

4. Sarah Burney's unsteadiness of character and her need for "some one to help her through the thorny paths of life as a Guide," was also noted by her aunt d'Arblay, when alarmed by her own son's attraction to her (*JL*, 8: 234).

5. Charlotte would report that her cousin Sarah "says that Aunt d'Arblay praised Mr J P.s manners as 'being gentlemanly & elegant.['] Poor dear Sall! I hope she will be happy, & she is such a clever & good tempered girl, & has such good sense withal, that I think she will not miss of it" (CFBt to SHB, 5 Oct [1821], Barrett, Eg. 3706D, ff. 20–22v).

6. The three latest historical novels of [Sir Walter Scott]: *The Monastery*, published at the beginning of March 1820, *The Abbot*, which came out 2 September 1820, and *Ke-*

nilworth, which appeared in January 1821. The latter was set in the time of Queen Elizabeth I and concerned the Earl of Leicester's marriage to the beautiful Amy Robsart (Johnson, 1: 700, 714, 723).

7. Sir Walter Scott (created Bt. 30 March 1820) was still maintaining his anonymity, but his authorship of the novels was widely assumed.

8. Giovanni Baptista Belzoni (1778–1823) (*DNB*), the results of whose excavations in Egypt were published in his *Narrative of the Operations and Recent Discoveries within the pyramids, temples, tombs, and excavations, in Egypt and Nubia* (1820).

9. The prolific novelist, Anna Maria Porter (1780–1832) (*DNB*), whose work, *The Village of Mariendorpt*, appeared in 1821.

10. SHB may have begun a third tale, which was never finished. In any case, she would publish no more fiction until 1839.

97. To Frances (Burney) d'Arblay

[26 Cadogan Place, 28] April [1821]
A.L.S. with typescript, Barrett, Eg. 3698, ff. 88–91v
Address: M[rs] d'Arblay / 11 Bolton Street / Piccadilly
Postmarks: 7 o'Clock / 28 AP / 1821 NT
N O Sloane St
Annotated by FBA: on / Miss & Mrs. / Gregor, / 1821

Saturday Morning
April—

My dearest Sister

I was very much in hopes that I should still find you at Richmond,[1] whither I was conveyed for a few hours about a week since by a friend who was going there on business:—but you had left the place the very day before. I had much to say to you, which I have now hardly time to say intelligibly. The upshot of the whole, however, is, that I have left the College, not to be in lodgings, but to have the charge of a young Lady (residing with an Aunt named Gregor,)[2] who comes of age in June, but, meanwhile, from ill health, is entirely deprived of all the <gay wor> amusements of the gay world, and was advised to engage some Lady to reside with her as a friend and associate who could occasionally supply the place of her Aunt,[3] and who had good spirits to talk, and read, and walk and draw with her—In short, to be what I find myself perfectly happy to be—her messmate and female Pylades.[4] She is extremely sweet tempered and well bred—And all that I have hitherto seen of her Aunt delights me. She has (the Aunt) travelled, nay even resided in Italy—is fond of books, painting, music—has a very chosen circle of acquaintance; and I am made, on all occasions, quite one of the family, and most kindly as well as politely treated. We are at present in Upper Cadogan Place, N° 26—But if Miss Gregor can be dismissed by her physicians, are soon (that is, after her affairs are settled on her coming of age)[5] to remove into the country. I have been here ten or twelve days, and hitherto, see nothing but what I have reason to be gratified by.—I shall be able to devote a day to you I hope ere long, and will then gladly fill up t[his] hasty sketch—My most affectionate love to dear Alex—And believe me, dearest Sister Yours ever in all truth & love

S. H. Burney

1. Mme d'Arblay had been visiting her sister Charlotte Broome at Richmond c. 8–18 April and went back again on the twenty-sixth for three days (*JL*, 11: 223 and n. 1, 225, n. 5).

2. Jane (née Urquhart) (c. 1770–1854), the eldest daughter of William Urquhart (fl. 1756–91) of Craigston, Aberdeenshire, and Margaret (née Irvine), his wife. Jane married on 9 October 1795, as his second wife, Francis Gregor (1760–1815) of Trewarthenick, Cornwall, M.P. for the county (1790–1806) (*GM*, 65, Pt. 2 (1795): 877; 76, Pt. 2 (1806): 879; 85, Pt. 2 (1815): 185; NS 41 (1854): 670; *Alumni Cantab.;* Thorne; Burke, *DLG* under Urquhart, Gregor).

3. A childless widow, Mrs. Gregor was living with the only child of her husband's younger brother, the Rev. William Gregor (1761–1817) (*DNB*), a mineralogist, and his wife (m. 1790), Charlotte Anne (née Gwatkin) (d. 11 Sept. 1819).

An orphan, Charlotte Anne Gregor (1800–25) inherited considerable wealth. Delicate in health (and apparently epileptic) she would die unmarried in 1825. In her will, dated 12 March 1822 and witnessed by Sarah Harriet Burney, she disposed of more than £24,000 before leaving the family mansion and residue of the estate to a distant relative (*GM*, 95, Pt. 2 (1825): 559; Burke, *DLG;* will of Charlotte Anne Gregor, dated 12 March 1822, proved 2 April 1825, PRO/PROB/11/1697/198).

4. I.e., faithful friend, from the proverbially close friendship of Pylades and Orestes of Greek myth.

5. Charlotte Anne Gregor would turn twenty-one on 10 June 1821 (information supplied by the Cornwall County Record Office).

98. To Henry Colburn

Stanley Grove, 29 June 1821
A.L.S., Osborn
Address: Private / Henry Colburn Esqr / Conduit Street

Stanley Grove
Kings Road, Chelsea
June 29th 1821.

Dear Sir

I am leading just now a very secluded life with a sick friend near Parson's Green, and it would be great charity to supply me occasionally with a few new books.[1] Lady Morgan's Italy[2] is one I am particularly desirous to see, and the third Vol. of Rome in the Nineteenth Century[3]—I have read the two first wch I had from your house, & return them with thanks. I have never read Maria Graham's Three Months in the Mountains near Rome[4]—Nor "An Autumn near the Rhine"[5]—Nor Mrs Stodart's Letters from Normandy[6]—Nor Southey's Vision of Judgment,[7] Nor "Valerius, a Roman Story."[8]—Any of these would be most acceptable—but it is vain to apply to your Shopmen, for they do not know me, and will not be wrought upon to supply me with what I ask for—

Excuse haste, & believe me Dear Sir, very truly yours

S. H. Burney

1. SHB's "sick friend" was undoubtedly her charge, Charlotte Anne Gregor. It would seem that her sojourn with Mrs. Gregor, who had resided in Italy, was influencing her reading, and she requests from Colburn several works on travel. With one exception, none of the requested works was published by him, and they probably came from his circulating library (L. 75, n. 7).

2. The successful Irish novelist, Sydney Owenson (L. 32, n. 12), had married in 1812 Sir Thomas Charles Morgan (1783–1843). On the strength of the popularity of her observations on *France* (1817), she was offered £2,000 by Henry Colburn for a similar work on *Italy*, which had just come out (20 June 1821) (*DNB*).

3. [Charlotte Ann Waldie (later Eaton) (1788–1859) (*DNB*)], *Rome in the nineteenth century*, 3 vols. (1820).

4. Maria (née Dundas) Graham (later Lady Callcott) (1785–1842) published popular accounts of her travels, one of which was *Three Months passed in the Mountains east of Rome, during the year 1819* (1820) (*DNB*).

5. *An autumn near the Rhine, or sketches of courts, society, scenery, &c. in some of the German states bordering on the Rhine* was published anonymously in 1818.

6. Anna Eliza (née Kempe) Stothard (later Bray) (1790–1883) (*DNB*), *Letters written during a tour through Normandy, Brittany, and other parts of France in 1818* (1820).
7. Robert Southey's laureate poem, *The Vision of Judgment* (1821), later satirized by Byron.
8. [John Gibson Lockhart (1794–1854)], *Valerius; a Roman story* (1821).

---

99. To Charlotte (Francis) Barrett

Stanley Grove, 7 September 1821
A.L.S., Berg
Address: A / Madame Barrett

Stanley Grove, King's Road, Sepr 7th 1821.—

I write, dearest Charlotte, for the interested sake of obtaining a letter from you, which I well know your conscience will force you to endite, however little worthy the bribe may be which I am now offering to you.[1] The extreme seclusion in which all who inhabit this house pass their lives, affords no subject matter for l'éloquence, either du billet, or de la lettre. I shall not, however, weary you with a description of the uniformity of our existence; but give you an assurance which I am certain will afford you pleasure—and that is, that except the illness of poor Miss G—— I find no one thing in this family which I would wish to alter. M^rs^ G—— is all that I could desire, & far more than I could ever have expected. Frank, liberal-minded, considerate, unpretending, and provided with a thousand resources against the ennui of solitude and monotony. Her sister, Miss Urquhart,[2] is often from home: but whenever here, is a pleasing addition, tho' not altogether quite so winning a character as her sanguine and animated hostess.—The house we are in belongs to the Under Secretary of State, William Hamilton Esqr, who was in Greece with Lord Elgin, and has placed, as a frize to a magnificent library of his own building, casts of the fine reliefs brought from the Parthenon at Athens,[3]—and three of the Metopes the originals of which are in the Museum. There are likewise casts, as large as the marbles, of the famous Statues of Theseus and of the River God Illisus[4]—And many genuine antique Vases perfectly entire—And busts and statues by Canova,[5] with whom Mr Hamilton is very intimate. Altogether, the place is calculated to excite a taste for the antique which I never dreamt of experiencing in so strong a manner. We have the free use of all the books and prints in the library, and have been studying Wilkins' Vitruvius, and Vignola, and Stuart's Athenian Antiquities;[6] & I wd have you to know, that I am become a very pretty Architect, and take great delight now when driving about town, in looking at all our Church Porticoes, or at any odd bit of architecture I can cast my eye upon. I have had lessons (never too late to learn, if the will is there) from Miss Nicholson,[7] and can at length draw and shade a tree pretty decently in pencil. Drawing is a quiet amusement wch does better in a sick house than any thing, save needle work, and that is not an occupation my fingers love to <pursue> dwell upon.—But a lead pencil, a piece of card paper, Indian rubber, and a penknife, go into as small a compass as a thimble, a pr of scissars, and a parcel of cotton-balls; and are just as portable. Besides, I can draw by candle-light far better than I can thread those old torments, needles; and we have the resource of Chess also, and now and then a little music: but at this last, we are none of us great hands: Miss Urquhart was originally the best; but she has neglected it, and her voice, a very sweet one, is, however, fallen into "the sear, the yellow leaf"[8] and not so gratifying to hear as it *has* been.—We are all *has beens* here, except Miss G——, who, poor soul, is now only a *would be*.—I had a great treat last Monday, wch was a drive to Richmond, and a dinner at your dear Madre's. Clement, though complaining of recent illness, looks better than I almost ever saw him;[9] his cheeks are filled out, and do not, as formerly, shew through the skin every sinew and <string> fibre that held them together. He was cordial, and glad I believe to see his "lovely boob", and I was very truly rejoiced to see him. Your Mother was her own placid sweet self, and made me right welcome; and the Moll of all Molls allowed Clem to say Grace (much to my greater edification) and gave up the pleasure of a dinner at Lady Cardigan's[10] for the honour of dining with me!—After this, what may I not expect in the way of preferment and distinction?—I heard through a side channel, that Mrs Painter is quite pleased with her new Maid, your Charlotte.[11] She praised her to a Lady Hunter,[12] a friend of Mrs Gregor, at whose house I made a five minutes visit before I left Richmond.—Fanny Raper and I are very near each other,[13] and she has been three or four times to see me;—I cannot so well go to her. She looks quite the thing with respect to health: but has her summer hue on, and is tanned tawny—and will never become clear white again, I fear. Do not let your girls expose themselves to such unnecessary dyings. The skin does not thoroughly recover its natural colour; and a tanned *throat*, particularly, looks vulgar.—Pray admire my improvement in the science of education, and thank me for my edifying hint.—Were you not glad of my poor Brother's advancement in title, and improvement in income?[14]—It will be nearly two hundred per ann: addition to his "means of giving", as he says, "bread and cheese to his old cronies".—I called upon him on hearing the news, and seeing him look sleeker and happier than he had done for a long time past, complimented him on his appearance of health.—"I do not know, dear James, when I have seen you with a smugger face:—you are really looking quite well."—"And what's the harm of that?" said he—And then took a characteristic spin round upon his heel, and called out to his wife—"Mother Burney—can't you give me an apple?"—Sarah came back from her Tour[15] two evenings since; I have not yet seen her, but the servant at my brother's told me she was well when I called there yesterday. They were all out.—Sister d'Arblay is after some mysterious business, and though in town and avowedly well, will see no one all this week.[16] My secret idea is, that she and the dentist are having a little private intrigue. She, however, has promised to admit my M^rs^ G—— to the honour of her acquaintance; and actually has condescended to become acquainted with the Wilbrahams. These last, often enquire about you and Barrett.[17] They have lately had a terrible alarm, from a sudden seizure of their Mother's—something threatening Apoplexy!—She has gone through much severe discipline, and, I trust, is recovering. Their house in Seymour Street is painting, and they were going into Essex: but to be near medical assistance, they have taken a place at Highgate for a short time. And now, dearest Char—my paper and my subjects draw to a close together—So Heaven bless you—And give my love to Barrett, and to both or either of the girls who like to accept of the same, & believe me most truly & affectionately yours S. H. B.

1. In her reply to this letter, Charlotte politely responded: "Your kind & beautiful letter only arrived today. . . . But you see I lose no time in answering it because I like to shew you the efficacy of such a bribe whenever you chuse to employ it for the purpose of setting me scribbling" (CFBt to SHB, 5 Oct. [1821], Barrett, Eg. 3706D, ff. 20–22v).

2. Mrs. Gregor's younger sister, Eleanor Urquhart (c. 1770–1848), who would remain with her sister to the end of her life (Burke, *DLG; GM*, NS 29 (1848): 560; NS 41 (1854): 670).

3. William Richard Hamilton (1777–1859), private secretary to Thomas Bruce (1766–1841), 7th Earl of Elgin (1771), Ambassador at Constantinople (1799). Hamilton superintended the removal of marbles from the Acropolis of Athens, and their transportation back to England; the "Elgin marbles" were bought in 1816 by the government and housed in the British Museum (*DNB;* Burke; Christopher Hitchens, *The Elgin Marbles* (London: Chatto & Windus, 1987); William St. Clair, *Lord Elgin and the Marbles* (London: Oxford University Press, 1967)).

William Hamilton had bought c. 1815 Stanley House, Chelsea, formerly the residence of Sir Robert Stanley, on the north side of King's Road. To this mansion, he added a large hall on the east side, inserting some casts of the Elgin marbles into the frieze (*Survey of London*, 4: 43–44).

4. The "metopes" of the Parthenon were sculptured blocks inserted into the "metopae," the spaces left between the ends of the roof-beams. Of the original ninety-two, Lord Elgin brought back fourteen, all taken from the south side of the building, depicting the contest between Centaurs and Lapiths.

In the pediments at either end of the Parthenon were statues carved in the round, whose identities are largely conjectural: a figure lying on an animal skin on the eastern pediment, formerly identified as Theseus, the legendary hero of Attica, is now seen as either Dionysos or Herakles. A male figure reclining in the left angle of the western pediment, recognized as a river-god, is conventionally named Ilissos, a river of Athens (B. F. Cook, *The Elgin Marbles* (London: British Museum Publications, 1984), 11, 18–24, 40–52).

5. Antonio Canova (1757–1822), the famous Italian neoclassical sculptor, had been approached by Lord Elgin in 1803 to restore the statues, but refused, believing it would be sacrilege to touch them. In Paris in 1815, while seeking to reclaim for the Pope the art treasures taken by Napoleon, he had recourse to Hamilton, who is largely credited with ensuring their return. Canova subsequently visited London in November 1815 and admired the Elgin marbles, which are thought to have influenced his later style (St. Clair, 152, 226–27; Joseph Farington, *The Farington Diary*, vol. 8, ed. James Greig (New York: George H. Doran Co., 1928), 46–47).

6. Perhaps affected by her surroundings, Sarah was studying influential works on the Greek Revival in England: that of "Athenian" James Stuart (1713–88) and Nicholas Revett (1720–1804), *The Antiquities of Athens* (1762–1830), of which 4 volumes had been published by 1816; and a translation of *The Civil Architecture of Vitruvius* (1812) by William Wilkins (1778–1839). She was also reading the important treatise on architecture by Giacomo Barozzi "Vignola" (1507–73), *La regola delli cinque ordini dell'architettura* (1562), which had been translated into English several times.

7. Possibly Marianne Nicholson (1792–1854), daughter of Francis Nicholson (1753–1844), a prominent watercolor artist. Like her father and brother, she probably gave drawing lessons; in 1830, she would marry Thomas Crofton Croker (1798–1854), an Irish antiquary (*DNB* under Nicholson, Croker; H. L. Mallalieu, *The Dictionary of British Watercolour Artists up to 1920*, 2nd ed. (Woodbridge, Suffolk: Antique Collectors' Club, 1986)).

8. William Shakespeare, *Macbeth*, V, iii, 25.

9. In her reply of 5 October [1821], Charlotte confided: "entrenous, I fancy Clemkin likes nursing when he can get it, for he always takes a poorly fit when he goes home, and sets Mama cooking & coddling & cooing over him—And yet, sometimes in the midst of his most ailing & languishing moments, if a spirt comes, he forgets his complaints and jumps over the Moon & back again" (CFBt to SHB, 5 Oct. [1821], Barrett, Eg. 3706D, ff. 20–22v).

10. Penelope Anne (c. 1770–1826), daughter of George John Cooke, who married 8 March 1794 Robert Brudenell (1769–1837), 6th Earl of Cardigan (1811). She associated with Marianne in benevolent activities, forming one of a "Committee of Cooks" in a "Soup society for the poor" (Gibbs; Lodge; CFBt to FBA, 19 Dec. [1820], Barrett, Eg. 3702A, ff. 41–42v).

11. Mary Penn (1785–1863), second daughter of Richard Penn (1736–1811), M.P., Deputy-Governor of Pennsylvania (1771–73), and great granddaughter of William Penn,

the founder of Pennsylvania. She married on 14 June 1821 as his second wife Samuel Paynter (1774–1844) of Camborne House, Richmond (Burke, *LG* under Paynter; *DNB*; Thorne; *GM*, 3rd ser. 14 (1863): 669; *JL*, 11: 392, n. 2).

Charlotte Barrett, who was friendly with the Penn family at Richmond, had mentioned the forthcoming marriage when she was trying to place her servant Charlotte (CFBt to Sarah Burney, [1821], Berg; see above L. 96, n. 1); she had apparently succeeded in doing so.

12. Penelope Maria (née Free) (d. 1840) had married 16 July 1797 Sir Claudius Stephen Hunter (1775–1851), Lord Mayor of London (1811), created Bt. (1812) (Burke; *DNB*).

13. Frances (Phillips) Raper, Sarah's niece, also lived in Chelsea near King's Road (L. 72, n. 5).

14. On 19 July 1821, Capt. James Burney was appointed Rear-Admiral on the Retired list, the news reaching him 14 August. The promotion entitled him to the pension (half pay) of the higher rank (Manwaring, 281, 284; *HFB*, 425–27; *JL*, 11: 241, n. 3, 242, n. 1).

15. After their wedding on 14 April 1821 (L. 96, n. 2), Sarah and John Payne had left for the Continent; the bride "returned improved in looks, & in all sort of amiability." Mrs. Barrett reported that she "seems to have been much liked & admired abroad" (*JL*, 11: 222, n. 2, 243, n. 2, 280–81; CFBt to SHB, 5 Oct. [1821], Barrett, Eg. 3706D, ff. 20–22v).

16. The mystery is solved in Mme d'Arblay's letters. On 23 August 1821, she was summoned by the Princess Sophia to visit her at Kensington Palace, where the Princess was sitting for her portrait. Invited to attend every sitting, she was called to Kensington Palace on 6, 7, 8, 13, and 14 September. To keep her mornings free in readiness for a call, Mme d'Arblay regretfully declined the proposed visit: "And what is provokuss also is a Note from Sarah-Harriet to offer to come to me to-morrow; & receive her I cannot—nor all the Week—*at least*." On 17 September 1821 she was still unable to see her, and a month later would report, "I have been forced, very reluctantly, to keep aloof dear aunt Sarah—for these, now, nameless reasons" (*JL*, 11: 275 and n. 1, 279–81, 285).

17. Sarah's former employers, the Wilbrahams, had already met other members of her family. They seem to have been friends of Esther Burney; in 1819 SHB introduced them to her half-sister Broome, and they would probably have known the Barretts when they lived at Richmond in 1815 (L. 82; *JL*, 11: 40–41, 379).

100. To Charlotte (Francis) Barrett

Stanley Grove, 10 March 1822
A.L.S., Berg
Address: Mrs Barrett / Under the Hill / Richmond / Surry
Postmarks: T P / W O Chelsea
[? o'Clo]ck / [?] MR / [?] NT

My dearest, I write to you, under the rose,[1] to enquire how the land lies at Richmond—in short, to know, whether Clement or my Sister d'Arblay are at your Mother's[2]—and whether my projected visit there, about this time, would be in any degree inconvenient. I expect you to answer me with perfect openness, and not, on any account, to let me come at an unsuitable moment. I can very well bear a delay—but I should like to know about what period I might be beginning to prepare for the little excursion.—Mrs Gregor is now returned from a fortnight's visit paid in Sussex, and is so much improved by the change of air, that I shall be quite glad to try the same experiment. I was well pleased, however, to remain stationary during her absence, as Miss Urquhart was left behind, and my company might, en defaut de toute autre, be of some value to her. Hitherto, Miss Gregor has only appeared down stairs in the evening; her early dinner hour not suiting with the usual time for the family meals: but she is, though her nerves remain in a very tremulous state, quite recovered; and a few weeks hence, will probably set out on some expedition to confirm her amendment. They do not tell me so, dear people, but I have reason to think, that the long illness I have had,[3] and the precautions respecting <diet &c,> quiet, regimen, &c, which I am still obliged to observe, frighten Mrs Gregor and her sister, and lead them to apprehend that my strength is not equal to the calls that would be made upon it, were I to remain with their young inmate. They are too delicate to express themselves in any way that could hurt my feelings, or lower my spirits;—from certain words, however, that have dropped, when talking over future plans, I have had clear intimations of their state of mind upon the subject: and therefore, to save both them and myself the pain <and> of being more explicit, I have arranged in my own noddle, a scheme for the summer which will take me handsomely out of their way—and the winter, if I live, must <be> provide<d> for <afterwards> itself.—My notion is, after a moderate stay at Richmond (by way of trying my wings) to take a trip into Norfolk, from whence I have received a most warm and pressing invitation, the joint production of my brother Allen & his daughters.[4] From thence, when I think it time they should be quit of me, I may, perhaps, repair to Brightwell,[5] where I was under an engagement to go last summer: but broke through it, owing to <my> the arrangement into which I had entered here. What more I may undertake—or whether all or any of these <plans> schemes will come to pass, time and health must decide: but, it is pleasanter to act, or, at least, to endeavour to act upon some fixed plan, than to twirl about in the air like a gossamer-web, never knowing when or where to alight.—Adieu, my dearest—forgive the complete egotism of this letter—It has been a relief to me to write it—for, to tell you the truth, the impending break-up of the projects to which I had looked forward by remaining here—the hopes of travelling—of enjoining agreeable domestic society—of cultivating more and more intimately the regard of my excellent Mrs Gregor,—the smash of all these anticipated pleasures, saddens, disappoints, and mortifies me[6]—How true it is that

The purpose of to-day,
Woven with "joy" into our plan,
Tomorrow rends away![7]—

My love to Barrett—And believe me, dearest, though just now a little querulous, your most affectionate, &, upon the whole, contented

S. H. Burney.

March 10th 1822
Stanley Grove.

1. I.e., privately, in strict confidence, from the Latin sub rosa (*OED*).

2. Mme d'Arblay had been visiting her sister, Charlotte Broome, at Richmond early in the New Year, but returned home at the beginning of March (*JL*, 11: 337).

3. It had been a hard winter for Sarah Harriet, who suffered from a liver complaint, compounded perhaps by her grief at the sudden death of her half-brother James on 17 November 1821 (*JL*, 11: 294, n. 1). Soon after his death, she was reportedly "quite overwhelmed with grief, & still very ill. . . . 'tis the *most* severe stroke to Her, she avows, that misfortune has ever inflicted." Mending "slowly" in January, in a "weak & precarious state" through the winter, she was said to be "wonderfully recovered" by March, and somewhat less susceptible to a loss "the most heart-piercing she has ever endured" (*JL*, 11: 316, 321, 340).

4. For Sarah's half-brother, the Rev. Stephen Allen, and his daughters, see above L. 28, n. 8.

5. At Brightwell SHB would no doubt visit her nephew, Richard Burney, who was curate there and lived in the rectory (L. 82, n. 8).

6. Financial considerations might have been another factor; SHB's bank account at Coutts

shows that in 1821–22, the time she spent with the Gregors, she was living quite easily within her income of £80.13s., without either adding to or diminishing her stockholdings.

7. William Cowper, "Human Frailty," *Poems* (1782), ll. 2–4. The original version reads "pains" instead of "joy" and "his" for "our."

101. To Charlotte (Burney) (Francis) Broome

Stanley Grove, 14 March [1822]
A.L.S., Berg
Address: Mrs Broome / Under the Hill / Richmond / Surry.
Postmarks: [T P] / Piccadilly
7 o'[Clock] / 14 MR / 1822 N[?]

Thursday 14th March
Stanley Grove.

Tell our sweet Charlotte, my dear Sister, that I have received, and thank her most heartily for her kind letter;—and you, above all, I thank for being so affectionately willing to receive me.[1] I trust that now, I shall occasion you but few of the plagues attached to invalidism. I rise to breakfast like other people; walk out an hour or more at a time, and do most of the things which the rest of the world does, except in the article of eating. Even there, however, I require very little consideration; a little light pudding, or a bit of innocent boiled fish, or a dab of mashed potatoes, is all I want, or am allowed. If you hear nothing further from me, expect me, my dear Sister, on Tuesday next: Mrs Gregor is so good as to say, that she will bring me out to Richmond herself, and take that opportunity of paying you and Mrs Barrett a visit. I believe I told Charlotte, that I meditate a journey into Norfolk in the Summer; and have various other schemes in my head, if, after being a little while at Richmond, I find myself strong enough for such enterprizes.—But my stomach is such a rag-of-my-Dame's, that it will keep me weak and washy, perhaps, for the remainder of my life. Would not any body think that I was now paying for former habits of intemperance?—I wonder why my liver should be "mouldy," as poor Pach^otti^[2] said of his "lights"!—I am sure I never soaked it either in Ale, Wine, or Spirits!—

Adieu my kind and sisterly sister—My warmest love to the Charlotte of Charlottes—and believe me most gratefully yours

S. H. Burney.

1. Charlotte Barrett's reply to SHB's letter of 10 March 1822 above (L. 100) is missing, but apparently it contained an assurance that Sarah would be welcome to stay with her half-sister, Mrs. Broome.

2. SHB had remarked before "it was mouldy, like poor Pacherotti's liver" (L. 62), perhaps quoting an expression of this old family friend. Gasparo Pacchiarotti, the castrato singer, had recently reentered the orbit of the Burney family when Sarah (Burney) Payne met him in Rome on her wedding trip, occasioning a renewal of correspondence with Mme d'Arblay (*JL*, 11: 243, n. 2, 292–93).

102. To Charlotte (Burney) (Francis) Broome

Stanley Grove, 17 March 1822
A.L.S., Barrett, Eg. 3700A, ff. 146–47v
Address: M[rs] Broome / Under the Hill / [R]ichmond / Surry
Postmarks: T P / W O Chelsea
7 o'Clock / 18 MR / 1822 NT
Endorsed: Sister Sarah / 1822

I might have saved you much plague, my dear Sister, in making arrangements to enable you to receive me, had I foreseen the plan that now offers itself to my acceptance, and which, regard to my health induces me to prefer even to a Richmond visit. M[rs] Gregor, for a complaint a little similar to mine—one, at least, connected with liver—is ordered to Cheltenham; and D[r] Paris[1] says, that <it> is the place of all others to do me good. My kind M[rs] Gregor urges me, therefore, to accompany her, and we shall probably set out the latter end of this week, or beginning of the next.—Accept, meanwhile my heartiest thanks for the hospitality you were so willing to extend to me, and believe me perfectly sincere in assuring you, that had all circumstances conspired to make it convenient, there is no place, person, or neighbourhood I should have delighted in so much as Richmond, yourself, and Charlotte.—I hope on my return to make myself amends for losing the pleasure of seeing you now—and in the interim, let me ask you whether you could assist in putting M[rs] Gregor into the way of applying to any East India Director for a Nephew of hers who wants a Cadetship.[2] Have you not some City friends, or old cronies of M[r] Broome's,[3] who are acquainted with India folks?—Could the Garrats[4] do any thing? Do you know M[r] Twining?[5] Has he any interest?—I cannot describe to you how happy it would make me, were it possible to succeed in this business through the interferance of any of my family!—Mrs Gregor deserves so much from me, that I never had a thing more warmly at heart. Could Clement lend a helping hand, by writing to any body connected with India affairs?—Do turn the matter over in your mind, my dearest Sister, and aid & abet my anxious wishes, if it be within the power of possibility.—

My most affectionate love to Charlotte, Barrett, & Co—and believe me ever most gratefully yours

S. H. Burney.

March 17th 1822
Stanley Grove

1. Dr. John Ayrton Paris (1785–1856), M.D. (1813), who had practiced in Cornwall 1813–17 and written *A Memoir of the Life and Scientific Labours of the Late Rev. W. Gregor* (1818), Miss Gregor's father. He returned to London in 1817, and rose to prominence in his profession, serving as president of the College of Physicians from 1844 until his death (*DNB; Alumni Cantab.*). Just five days previously, with Sarah Harriet Burney, he had witnessed Charlotte Anne Gregor's will (L. 97, n. 3).

2. A nephew of Mrs. Gregor seeking a cadetship in the East India Company may be a son of her only brother John Urquhart (d. 1821), who had married on 26 March 1799 Isabella Moir. John's second son, George, would in fact die unmarried in India; he may be the same George Urquhart who joined the E.I.C. as a cadet in 1822, became 2nd Lt. in the Bengal Army (1822), Lt. (1825) and resigned in 1836. However, Mrs. Gregor also had a half-brother and half-sisters from her father's second marriage, to whose sons she might also refer as nephews (Burke, *DLG; GM*, 69, Pt. 1 (1799): 524; Hodson).

3. Charlotte Broome's second husband, Ralph Broome, had lived in India and would presumably have had contacts in the East India Company (*JL*, 4: 33, n. 11).

4. There were several Garretts at this time in both the civil service and military establishment of the East India Company. Captain (later Vice-Admiral) Henry Garrett (1774–1846), Governor of Haslar Hospital (1820–38), was in charge of the victualling depot at Deptford until 1820 and had three sons in the company's service (O'Byrne; Hodson).

5. Probably an old family friend, Richard Twining (1749–1824), head of the tea business in the Strand and a director of the East India Company (1793–1816); he passed the last decade of his life at Dial House, Twickenham. SHB might also be referring to one of his sons, Richard (1772–1857), who had joined the family firm in 1794, or Thomas (1776–1861), who had been with the East India Company since 1792 (*DNB; JL*, 11: 342, n. 17; *Twickenham, 1660–1900*, 25).

103. To Anna Wilbraham

5 Ainslies Belvedere, Bath, 2 June [1822][1]
A.L.S., Berg
Address: Miss Anna Wilbraham / 56 Upper Seymour Street / Portman Square

5 Ainslies Belvedere, Bath.
June 2d

My dearest of Dears

Our Mrs Gregor leaves this place, I grieve to say, two days hence, and I cannot let her go empty-handed to you. Are you benefitted, satisfactorily, by your Cheltenham journey? Did you find Mrs Wilbraham going on to your heart's content? Had you a comfortable journey? Are you "looking pretty, and dressing for the Cansert," as poor dear Cecilia used, when a child, to say of her Sister Maria?[2]—I am looking dowdy, and dressing three evenings out of seven for the Play. I delight in this quiet, clean, easily-accessible Bath Theatre,[3] and have 'ticed all around me, Mrs Gregor, Maria & Sophy to accompany me, and to be as dissipated as myself whenever any thing tempting <was> is announced. We have a Queen Elizabeth here, as <represented> described in Kenilworth, who deserves that every body who loves good acting should take a journey to Bath purposely to see her.—She was Miss Somerville, now Mrs Bunn;[4] and really shews admirable originality of talent in the part she is <now personifying> representing.—This is a marvellous pretty place, though fatiguing to walk in from its being so hilly.—Maria's house is at once <u>in</u> & <u>out</u> of the town.—I mean that it has an unobstructed view of hills & dales from its back windows, and from those in front looks to a Street.—I arrived in time to see my Sister Burney with comfort both here and at her own pretty snug litle residence, about a mile out of Bath.[5] She is now at Richmond, and thence goes to spend a fortnight or three weeks in London. She enquired anxiously after your whole family. I am in admiration at her activity and chearfulness, and clearness of intellect at the age to which she has attained, and considering all the wear and tear her mind and body has gone through.[6] She is now seventy three, and more alert, & stronger than any of her daughters. Our Mrs Gregor drank tea at her house with me one evening, and was delighted with her.—I have been so much better since I came here, that I have not yet made up my mind to send for Dr Gibbs,[7] and begin to flatter myself that I may do without him. When I get to

Worcester, I shall state my case to Mr Sandford[8] at whose house I shall be staying, & in whom I have just and great confidence; and meanwhile, I go on taking from time to time Dr Newell's[9] nastiness, and scrupulously abstaining from meat, wine, pastry, & malt liquor; and I do hope, I shall toddle on as well as most of the young Spinsters of my age who flourish in this ungrateful generation.—Lord bless me! What heaps of cotemporaries I <do> meet with here at every turn!—It is their old bones, I verily believe, that makes the soil all around so white and pulverized.—In our way hither, Mrs Gregor and I saw Badminton, the seat of the Duke of Beaufort.[10] I wish you had been with us. The drive through the Park was beautiful; it is level ground, indeed, but magnificently wooded, and full of deer; and the house, & a small Church attached to it, interested us by the pictures & monuments they contain, & were shewn by an old-fashioned Housekeeper, who talked of every thing as if part-owner in it—talking of our family—and we built that—and that belongs to us, &c, in the most thing-of-course-way you can imagine.—Pray, how was your pocket volume approved? And my friend Napoleon & his family?[11]—Oh—Mrs Trannick's[12] darling, Spot, has been very ill, as she learned by a letter from her lover—& she was in tears for two or three days: but is now charming well again, for Spot was taken to the Doctor you had recommended to Mrs Gregor (she wrote to desire it) and the dear Doctor has done the dear Spot much good, & hopes are entertained that he will eventually effect a cure. Trannick sends love to your "Pretty cretur". I have eat "chick'n" two or three times at her boarding-house with ones Gregor, and met some of her nice Scottish friends, Gordons & Campbells',[13] and laughed at her Bath Waiters as much as I did at our first Cheltenham ones. I hate the thoughts of her going away, though I am no longer in the same house with her—Bath will lose with her, one of its prime attractions in my estimation.—I have read the first volume of The Fortunes of Nigel, which I like much better than the Pirate.[14] I never could feel perfectly reconciled to having a Freebooter for a Hero, and a romantic, half crazy girl falling in love with him from mistaking him for an honest bold man.—And now "mine own," farewell—tell me that you enjoy yourself—tell me about Mrs Wilbraham—and remember me in the most grateful and affectionate manner to your dear Sisters—and direct to me Miss S. H. Burney, being, that I am now to represent the youngest of the party—Ever yours —

1. The letter is dated from the context, Sarah Harriet's visit to Cheltenham and Bath with Mrs. Gregor in 1822 (*JL*, 11: 358). She is staying with her niece, Maria Bourdois, at 5 Ainslie's Belvedere, and remains behind when Mrs. Gregor leaves. SHB's position with the Gregors apparently terminates at this time, perhaps because of her ill health; however, the separation seems amicable enough, and Miss Urquhart would later commend her in flattering terms (CFBt to FPR, 22 Sept. [1822], Barrett, Eg. 3706D, ff. 45–48v).

2. A family expression originating with Cecilia Burney, Esther's seventh child, watching her eldest sister Maria preparing to go out (*JL*, 9: 329, n. 25; CB to SBP, 8 May 1795, Osborn). "Poor dear Cecilia" had died of consumption the previous year on 3 April 1821 at the age of thirty-three (*JL*, 11: 220, n. 1).

3. The Theatre-Royal in Beaufort Square opened in 1805.

4. Margaret Agnes Somerville (1799–1883), who had married in 1819 theatrical manager Alfred Bunn (c. 1796–1860), was famous for her role of Queen Elizabeth in Scott's *Kenilworth*. A modified production of Thomas J. Dibdin's adaptation of the novel played to great acclaim at the Theatre-Royal in Bath during the winter season of 1821–22 (*DNB*; Henry Adelbert White, *Sir Walter Scott's Novels on the Stage* (New Haven: Yale University Press, 1927), 124–27).

5. At Lark Hall Place near Bath (see above L. 87, n. 3).

6. Esther had endured in recent years the death of her husband, Charles Rousseau Burney, on 23 September 1819 after a long painful illness, and of her daughter Cecilia in 1821. Other fatalities which must have left their mark were the deaths of her two brothers, Charles (on 28 Dec. 1817), and James (17 Nov. 1821), and of her sister-in-law and cousin Ann Hawkins on 16 January 1819 (*JL*, 10: 766, n. 2; 11: 38, n. 1, 128, n. 1, 220, n. 1, 294, n. 1; "Worcester Mem.," 68–73).

7. Sir George Smith Gibbes (1771–1851), M.D. (1799), a prominent physician at Bath, had published two treatises on the Bath waters (1800, 1803). Physician-extraordinary to the Queen (1818), he was knighted (1820) (Munk's Roll, 3: 13–14; *Alumni Oxon.; DNB; JL*, 9: 275, n. 4).

8. The Worcester surgeon, William Sandford, husband of SHB's cousin, Rebecca (L. 85, n. 14), had moved on 4 April 1820 from Bridge Street, Worcester, to "a small house pleasantly situated on Rainbow Hill about 3 qrs. of a mile from the centre of the town." On 18 February 1822, he had "sold his house in Bridge Street, Coachhouse, Stable, etc. . . . for little less than the original purchase, after having lived in it for 25 years." Sarah Harriet would visit the Sandfords at their new home, "Rainbow Villa," from 3 to 19 July 1822, her stay coinciding with that of her cousin "Blue" and great-nephew Henry ("Worcester Mem.," 71, 78).

9. Probably Thomas Newell, M.D. (c. 1765–1836), a medical practitioner at Cheltenham for more than forty years and a magistrate for the county (*GM*, NS 6 (1836): 333; *Gloucestershire Notes and Queries* 3 (1887): 614).

10. Henry Charles Somerset (1766–1835), 6th Duke of Beaufort (1803) (Burke; Lodge; Gibbs). His family seat of Badminton House, Chippenham, co. Gloucester, was a Palladian-style mansion built in 1682 (T. A. Ryder, *Portrait of Gloucestershire* (London: Robert Hale, 1966), 197). The magnificent grounds and splendid church of 1793, connected to the house by an underground passage, are described in H. P. R. Finberg, *The Gloucestershire Landscape*, rev. ed. (London: Hodder & Stoughton, 1975), 93–96). The

fine collection of pictures is also noted in *A Series of Picturesque Views of Seats of the Noblemen and Gentlemen of Great Britain and Ireland*, ed. Rev. F. O. Morris (London: William Mackenzie, n.d.), 2: 75.

11. Judging from the context, Napoleon might be a pet dog.

12. Mrs. Trannick (or Tranick) may have been a housekeeper or companion to Mrs. Gregor (see L. 181 below) but has not been further identified.

13. Unidentified.

14. Two novels by [Sir Walter Scott], *The Pirate* and *The Fortunes of Nigel*, both published in 1822.

104. To Charlotte (Francis) Barrett

[29 Park Street], 13 June [1823][1]
A.L.S., Berg
Address: Mrs Barrett / Under the Hill / Richmond / Surry.
Postmarks: T P / Park St[reet]
[?] NOON / 14 [?] / [18]23

I am quite disappointed, dearest, at your talking of <u>one</u> <u>night</u>, and a nasty officious Steam-boat![2]—I had reckoned upon you for a week, or more; & nothing upon my honour, can be more perfectly convenient than your being here. So pray think about it again, & if you possibly <u>can</u>, do delight me by a longer visit, & Barrett also, & my dear Hetty. I have beds plenty, & you will like our house, & my merry little Annabel;[3] & I will make you all as comfortable as possible.—We have <plenty> lots of room in the carriage to bring Barrett as well as yourself & Hett—for it is a wide Barouch, chosen for travelling.—If the weather is fine—that is, if it does not rain cats & dogs—we hope to be with you about two o'clock on Tuesday—If not, still earlier on Wednesday; or else (as Annie goes to a dancing Academy that day) we will set out after our own early two o'clock dinner, & be with you before four. But, I trust, Tuesday may be the day.—I want you to join me in a visit to Greenwich, where I wish to shew Annie the Park—& then call upon Charles[4]—And you ought to stay with me for the Exhibition,[5] & fifty things besides.—

I grieve at my dear Clement's suffering complaint[6]—And for the anxiety of my poor Sister—Will not this warm weather assist his recovery? I earnestly hope it. Adieu Dear<u>est</u>, if you stay longer with me—<u>Dear</u> only, if you Steamboat it.—for I meant to treat myself and Annie with a drive back with you, after keeping you as long as I could. Dear Lord Crewe[7] gave us horses on purpose for my relief and accommodation whilst in town—and what better accommodation can I squeeze out of them than to bring you & Co. here. Love to Barrett, who is a good boy for consenting to come—

Ever yours
S. H. Burney

June 13th Annie's 9th Birthday.[8]

1. This is the first letter written after Sarah Harriet's appointment to a new position c. September 1822. On 14 September Charlotte Barrett rejoiced at the "great news" that "Lord Crewe had been desirous of Miss Burney's taking charge of his grandchildren who are wards in Chancery, & the Master, Mr Courtney has nominated her to the care of them. She is to have a house in Park Street kept up for her, they are placed under her control quite independently of Lord Crewe & they are to have a Swiss governess who is to be under her direction & who will undertake all the drudgery of education, walk out with them, &c." In other words, "no more trouble than if she were the mother of these young Ladies, with every earthly Comfort." Under these ideal conditions, "having a french bonne under her direction & being placed with these young people on so independent a footing I think she will preserve her liking for them & with it her good humour & all the charms of manner & conversation which make her so pleasing when pleased." In short, "I think the present prospects of poor dear Aunt Sarah better than any she has ever had."

In September 1822, SHB was "on a visit at Crewe Hall, making acquaintance with her young charges," and spoke of her "great contentment in her new abode." During the winter, she was reported "in high Spirits & Feather at Crewe Hall"; in March 1823, she returned to London to preside over 29 Park Street, Grosvenor Square, the house provided by Lord Crewe for his granddaughters (CFBt to CBFB, 14 Sept. [1822], CFBt to FPR, CFBt to MF, 22 Sept. [1822], Barrett, Eg. 3706D, ff. 42–48v; *JL*, 11: 383, 387, 416).

Charlotte Barrett's enthusiastic prediction (in her letter of 14 September) of the financial benefits to her aunt, £300 a year and "a provision for life" (cited as fact in *JL*, 11: 366–67, n. 4, 372, n. 7), proved to be only partially correct; by her own account (L. 118), SHB's salary was fixed at £300 at first, but in the end there would be no annuity. Moreover, her bank account shows no regular payment of such an amount. Starting in 1823, deposits are received from the Master in Chancery (usually in semiannual amounts of approximately £266), but these are offset by expenses apparently related to her responsibilities. During seven years with the Crewe family (and before receiving her final pay), she would invest only £500 in total, which compares with the £250 she accumulated in half that time with the Wilbrahams. See further, L. 105, n. 27; L. 118, n. 5.

2. The first steamer to ply for hire on the Thames was in 1814 the *Richmond*, which ran between Richmond and London (Peter H. Chaplin, *The Thames from Source to Tideway* (Weybridge, Surrey: Whittet Books, 1982), 102). *Pigot and Co.'s London & Provincial Directory* (1823–24) under "Middlesex" notes that a Steam Packet leaves London

for Richmond "from the White Cross, Water-lane, every evening, from May to October" (63), and in 1826–27 describes the same leaving "from Richmond Bridge every evening at eight" in the summer (485). By 1838, there were four daily runs.

3. Annabella Hungerford Crewe (1814–74), youngest daughter of John Crewe (1772–1835), later 2nd Baron Crewe (1829), by his wife (m. 5 May 1807) Henrietta Maria Anne (née Hungerford) (c. 1772–1820). Annabella's mother had died and her father spent much of his time on the continent (Burke; Lodge; Gibbs; *JL*, 4: 64, n. 4).

4. The Rev. Charles Parr Burney, only son of Charles Burney Jr., had succeeded his father at the Greenwich school (1813–34) (*JL*, 1: lxxii).

5. Probably the 55th Exhibition of the Royal Academy, which had opened on 5 May 1823.

6. Charlotte Broome was at Brighton nursing her son Clement, who suffered from rheumatism (among other complaints), making him nervous and irritable. Her daughter expressed concern that Mrs. Broome was "sadly harrassed" in caring for her son (MF to CFBt, 15 Aug. 1823, 29 Sept. 1823, Barrett, Eg. 3704A, ff. 112–25v; *JL*, 11: 435).

7. The elderly Lord Crewe (then 80) was grandfather to SHB's charges; his wife, Frances Anne, was a longtime friend of the Burneys (L. 27, n. 3). "One of the most brilliant constellations in the hemisphere of fashion," she had died in 1818 (*GM*, 88, Pt. 2 (1818): 646).

8. Annabella Crewe was born on 13 June 1814 (Lodge).

---

105. To Charlotte (Francis) Barrett

Crewe Hall, 2 December 1823
A.L.S., Berg
Address: Mrs Barrett / Colege / Ely
Franked: Crewe / Nantwich third Decr. 1823
Postmarks: AMPTWICH / [?]
FREE / 5 DE 5 / 1823

Why your impurance and your insurance! Think of your reproaching me for not writing! Did'n't I, in <writing> a letter to Miss Penn[1] about some poor woman Ld Crewe was good to, beg to know whether she could tell me how to direct to you?[2] And did I ever hear a single word from her afterwards?—Hold your peace then, Hussey—for, this time, I am as blameless as a lamb.—

How glad I am poor dear Clem has regained ease and better spirits. He has had a fearful long bout of suffering, and my poor Sister a terrible period of anxiety & fatigue. Thank God, their burthens are lightened, for both must have been heavy to bear.[3]—

I have always understood that the society you have got amongst, ranked the highest almost of any for information, good breeding, and general agreeability.[4] Mrs Sandford, poor soul, when at Worcester, mixed a great deal with the Prebendaries and their set, and those I saw at her house, or called upon with her,[5] were elegant and accomplished people, far above the usual style of country town inhabitants. Such folks are worthy of you, and I am happy to know you so well circumstanced at least on the score of associates. Poor Richard at Brightwell, has, generally speaking, a mortal rum set around him—with the exception of a family named Durrel[6] connected with the Bishop of Durham, and the venerable old Bishop himself,[7] who is fond of music & of Richard.—Here, as I live with the girls all the morning, I put myself in mind of being at a large Hotel,[8] where I endeavour to remain snug & detached from the other inmates till called to the Table-d'Hôte, where, as in a Magic-Lanthorn, new people pass in review before me who stay for a night or two, and then are off. I begin to grow hardened to the horror of seeing so many strange faces, for, on going into the gallery before dinner, I always expect to behold three or four new phizes, which the second or third day (at farthest), give place to three or four others.—As I do not think it would be prudent or profitable to learn either to love or hate any of these birds of passage, I persuade myself these transient periods of intercourse are just the thing. We have now here S^r^ Ch^s^ & Lady Rowley and an unmarried daughter.[9] I remember seeing her with her Sister, Lady Hammond,[10] at some Richmond Concerts—She then lived at Petersham. She is a wonderful woman. Had her children all lived, she would now have had twenty! Yet she is a pretty woman still, with the finest jet-black, shining hair, good teeth, & fashionable tournure.[11] We have become extremely well acquainted, probably to part tomorrow, and meet no more. Thus with her married daughter Mrs Longford Brook,[12] three weeks ago—and thus of all the rest, except some superfines, who never debase themselves by bestowing more than an <u>unlooking</u> <u>look</u> upon me. Do you know what I mean? One of those sort of looks you cast upon a fire-skreen or a hearth-broom, and are not sure you have ever cast at all.—There is here now a dandy of the first water, a Mr Sneyd,[13] who looks like a pretty china figure for a chimney-piece, with pale roses in his cheeks, a highly-scented pocket handkerchief, a brilliant ring on his little finger, and a rose-coloured velvet underwaistcoat, who talks more affectedly than Hotspur's finical Courtier[14]—and yet (deuce take him) is clever & entertaining to a degree where & when he lists, and keeps his chosen neighbour at dinner in continual laughter: but the vulgar herd is never admitted to hear a word he says, and eyes he has none save for the purpose of seeing who he shall <u>not</u> see.[15]—We are expecting old Lady Cork[16] in the course of this month. She wrote to propose herself, and has been accepted, upon condition she came on a certain appointed day, and departed in like manner, Lord Crewe pretending an engagement at the end of that time. Think of agreeing to such terms!—

What our plans must be in the Spring, I am yet wholly ignorant. The probability is, we shall be in lodgings near Lord Crewe, and at his expence, as we are now for every thing. The Park Street house, I trust, is only given up for two years, there being a prospect that by that time things will have mended.[17] Your scheme,[18] my dearest would suit Annie and me to a nicety; she grew very fond of your Henrietta, and talks of her frequently; and the mere sound of the word Richmond, makes her face brighten, and her eyes sparkle. She was very ill, poor child, soon after you saw her; but now, with good bathing at Park Gate, and plenty of exercise, and great caution respecting diet, she is looking better than I have almost ever seen her. She is a well-disposed, engaging little thing, & has wound herself round my heart very closely. We are now tête a tète in the School-room, her Sister[19] being in Wales with Mrs Cunliffe,[20] who, on the point of removing from their present house, had only furniture enough left in it to receive one girl, & thought she could manage better with the elder by herself, than with the little one, having no accomodations for a Maid, &c—I care not how much the Aunt and Niece are together, since the time is so fast approaching when Harriet will become the charge of Mrs Cunliffe far more than mine. She is nearly sixteen, & dying to be amongst the quite grown-ups; and when that is the case, <our> the arm soon aches with holding in the reins. I shall be glad to resign the authority which now it is my reluctant duty to <exert> maintain; and at first, poor creature, she will be in extasies to feel herself at liberty: but, if we live, I should not be at all surprised were she, a year after, to come back of her own accord to the old stall. The privileges for wch she is craving, soon pall upon the fancy; and a girl of twenty will often submit to restraints by choice, which at sixteen she is continually seeking to elude. My little Annie, meanwhile, creeps into my pocket, and cares not how much she is under my eye—partly from being more shy of strangers—and partly from feeling no jealousy yet of her own consequence. And besides, there may be more natural docility in her character.

The Wilbrahams write to me as often as they can, and ever affectionately. They are in a Cottage at Petersham, and talk of Brighton about Christmas, & in the Spring, a little trip to Cheltenham for poor Anna. What will then be their plan, I know not.—My kind Mrs Gregor is on a visit in Sussex, at some Park (I forget the name) where, a few years ago, the <best> most perfect remains in England of mosaic pavements, &c, were discovered supposed to have belonged to some Roman Villa. I have seen drawings of them which <are so

wonderfully entire> shew they are in wonderful preservation.—I beleive the place is called Bignor.[21]—Pray did you ever hear of some remarkably fine Orange trees at a gentleman's place in S: Wales, which are said to have been sent from Spain & destined for Philip 2^{d} whilst the Husband of our Mary—but being wrecked on the Welsh coast, were seized upon by the L^{d} of the Manor as his right, and are still in most flourishing condition.[22] A visitor was here lately, who spoke of, and had actually seen them, and said they were magnificent.—Lady Rowley was talking last night of Mrs Siddons with whom she is well acquainted. That Lady understands no French, and hearing a regret expressed for some poor ci-devant at Paris, who had been turned out of his Bureau, she mistook it for an escritoir, and said very compassionately—"Poor man! And how gat he there?"—Mr Sneyd, my little China figure, I overheard speaking to his next neighbour of Mary Bury (the well-known talkative eldest Miss Bury)[23] of whom he quaintly said: <she talks so much> "One hears her voice so incessantly, that I could almost imagine she has a sounding-board in her mouth that echoes her own words."—Was it not a comical thought?—Adieu, dearest Charlotte, I can think of no more odds and ends to send you, except a humble little pun of mine own[24]—(I do not often trespass in that way).—The Newspapers have been stuffed with details of the Murder of Wear, <the> of barbarous wooden etchings of the suspected culprits, of the pond, the Cottage, and the "fatal spot,"[25]—and so much, in short, has been printed & talked about it, that I advise to read for "Wear's murder", wearing murder!—I am half ashamed of my flat, Cousin-Inny-joke,[26] now I have given it you—but let it pass.

Two or three of my friends have been afraid, that as money was become scarce with these girls, my salary would be difficult to procure: but no such thing. Mr Cunliffe considerately mentioned his apprehensions to my dear generous old Lord Crewe, and the very next day he sent me up by his daughter a draft for £300 out of his own pocket.[27]—

My hearty love to Barrett, and the younkers—Annie sends many affectionate remembrances to Etta, and to "that nice little Arthur"[28]—And I am, and shall be ever thine

S. H. B.

Crewe Hall

Decr 2^{d} 1823.

Is not poor old Mrs Raper[29] dead? Somebody told me so, either in a letter, or by seeing it in the papers.—I hope Fanny may in some way be the better for what she may have left, or at least may tend to save by her decease.—Kindest love to your dear Mother, & best re[spects] to your excellent friends the Archdeacon & Mrs Cambridge.[30]—

I just now met a housemaid carrying coals upstairs, & asked how many fires there were to keep up? "Three and twenty, Ma'am".—And yet, the house is not now so full as I have known it, and the Hall stove is not included.[31]

Oh, pray send us the versified English Chronology.[32]

1. Hannah Penn (d. 1856), eldest daughter of Richard Penn and sister to Mrs. Paynter (L. 99, n. 11), the friend of CFBt. Miss Penn lived at Richmond, where she would die unmarried on 16 July 1856 (Burke, *LG; GM*, 3rd ser. 1 (1856): 263).

2. In 1823–24, probably through the mediation of their friend, the Rev. G. O. Cambridge (L. 60, n. 24), the Barretts were occupying a vacant prebendary house at Ely, while renting out their own house at Richmond (*JL*, 11: 415, 447; CFBt to FBA, [1 Apr. 1823], Berg; CFBt to CBFB, 16 Sept. [1823], Barrett, Eg. 3706D, ff. 57–58). Sarah's remark suggests that her correspondence with Mrs. Barrett had lapsed for at least three months, as the Barretts were certainly at Ely before 31 August 1823 (CFBt to MF, 31 Aug. [1823], Barrett, Eg. 3706D, ff. 53v–54v).

3. Clement had been ill in the summer and was nursed assiduously by his mother at Brighton, "who is so kind & anxious that she gives herself double the trouble that she ought." His health was slightly improved in October and "much better" in November, allowing him to return to his duties at Caius College, Cambridge (MF to CFBt, 29 Sept. 1823, 31 Oct. 1823, Barrett, Eg. 3704A, ff. 118–33v; MF to CFBt & HBt, 19 Nov. 1823, Barrett, Eg. 3704A, ff. 136–42; *JL*, 11: 458, 470).

4. Mrs. Barrett had some trouble adjusting to Ely society, finding the prebendaries sociable, "fat & goodnatured," but somewhat provincial. "Read your Bible and mind your cards . . . has become a sort of Ely aphorism comprehending the whole duty of man applicable to all soaring geniuses who stretch beyond the Card table," she comments, although trying to keep up a good front: "on the whole I think we like Ely better than we did at first" (CFBt to Caroline Holland, 7 Sept. [1823], CFBt to CBFB, 16 Sept. [1823], Barrett, Eg. 3706D, ff. 55–58v).

5. Probably during SHB's visit to her cousin, Rebecca (Burney) Sandford, of 3 to 19 July 1822 (see L. 103, n. 8).

6. Probably the Rev. David Durell (c. 1763–1852), B.A. Oxford (1785), M.A. (1789), Prebendary of Durham (1801–52), who was remembered with other "much-valued and esteemed friends" in the will of the Bishop of Durham (see next note) (*Alumni Oxon.; Westminsters; GM*, 96, Pt. 1 (1826): 518–20, 606–8).

7. Shute Barrington (1734–1826), youngest son of John Shute (1678–1734), 1st Viscount Barrington (1720), was created successively Bishop of Llandaff (1769), Salisbury (1782) and Durham (1791) (Burke; *DNB*). Formerly a friend of Charles Burney and Charles Burney Jr., he was "healthy, benevolent, & chearful, as well as honourable and venerable" (*JL*, 11: 359, n. 13, 370).

8. The family seat, Crewe Hall, Cheshire (see below), built between 1615 and 1636, was admired as a splendid mansion of early Tudor style: "it is chiefly of brick . . . . The hall, the staircase, and several of the rooms, remain in their original state; the roof of the dining-room has pendant ornaments, the wainscot is enriched with terms, and other sculptured ornaments . . . the ceilings and wainscots of several of the rooms, as well as the principal stair-case, retain their original decorations. The gallery, which is one hundred feet in length, is fitted up as a library, and contains many family portraits" (Daniel

and Samuel Lysons, *Magna Britannia*, vol. 2, pt. 2 (London: T. Cadell and W. Davies, 1810), 458–59, 502).

9. Elizabeth King (d. 11 Jan. 1838), daughter of Admiral Sir Richard King (1730–1806), 1st Bt. (1792). On 7 Dec. 1797, she had married Charles Rowley (1770–1845), Rear-Admiral (1814), K.C.B. (1815), later 1st Bt. (1836), and Admiral (1841). Of six surviving children, the unmarried daughter would be Louisa Burton (d. 6 March 1885), who would soon marry (17 Aug. 1824) Thomas Robert Hay (1785–1866), 11th Earl of Kinnoull (1804) (Burke; *DNB;* Gibbs; *GM,* 67, Pt. 2 (1797): 1069; 94, Pt. 2 (1824): 368; NS 9 (1838): 217).

10. Lady Rowley's elder sister, Louisa (d. 31 Aug. 1853), had married on 26 June 1803 Col. Francis Thomas Hammond (fl. 1803–37), Lt.-Gen. (1814), Kt. (1819), and later Lt.-Gov. of Edinburgh Castle (1831), and Gen. (1837) (Burke; *GM,* 73, Pt. 1 (1803): 595; 84, Pt. 1 (1814): 696; 101, Pt. 2 (1831): 170; NS 7 (1837): 199; NS 40 (1853): 429; Shaw, 1: 450, 454; 2: 321).

11. The beauty of Lady Rowley and her two elder sisters was celebrated in an anonymous poem "To a Friend, who desired me to write in Praise of a Lady whom he had seen, but knew not that there are Three Sisters. 1791" (*GM,* 80, Pt. 2 (1810): 359–60).

12. Lady Rowley's eldest daughter, Elizabeth Sophia (d. 1835), had married on 1 July 1818 Peter Langford Brooke (1793–1840) of Mere Hall, co. Chester (Burke; Burke, *DLG; GM,* 88, Pt. 2 (1818): 81; NS 13 (1840): 217).

13. Possibly Ralph Sneyd (1793–1870), eldest son of Lt.-Col. Walter Sneyd (1752–1829), of Keele Hall, Staffordshire. He attended Eton, and matriculated at Christ Church, Oxford in 1818, but left without taking a degree. He would die unmarried after an apparently uneventful life (Burke, *LG; Alumni Oxon.;* Ormerod, 3: 493).

14. A "certain lord, neat, and trimly dress'd, / Fresh as a bridegroom" and "perfumed like a milliner," is described contemptuously by Hotspur in Shakespeare's *1 Henry IV,* I, iii, 32–35.

15. Possibly echoing a phrase in Luke 8:10, "that seeing they might not see."

16. Mary Monckton (1748–1840), the daughter of John Monckton (1695–1751), 1st Viscount Galway (1727); she had married 17 June 1786 as his second wife Edmund Boyle (1742–98), 7th Earl of Cork and Orrery (1764). Known for her wit in her youth, when she formed part of the "blue-stocking" circle, she was noted for her eccentricities in her old age (Burke; Gibbs; *DNB*).

17. Sarah Harriet was abruptly called (c. Aug. 1823) from the residence in Park Street to return with her pupils to Crewe Hall. "A sudden failure of the West India remittances forced this measure, greatly to poor Sarah's discomforture, though the disappointment was borne with commendable fortitude" (*JL,* 11: 448). The year that the separate establishment was given up, only one of the usual half-yearly payments from the Master of Chancery was made to her account at Coutts. Winter in the country she found "rather *morne,*" according to FBA: "The dullness of her life seems to require all her judgement for endurance" (*JL,* 11: 466).

18. The reference to a "scheme" of Charlotte Barrett's is lost with her letter, but possibly she had some intention of taking on pupils in an informal way, as she would do later (L. 113, n. 4).

19. The elder of Sarah Harriet's two charges, Anna's sister, Henrietta Mary Hungerford Offley Crewe (1808–79) (Burke; Lodge).

20. Elizabeth Emma Crewe (c. 1781–1850), the only daughter of John, 1st Lord

Crewe, had married 21 April 1809 Foster Cunliffe (later Offley) (1782–1832), M.P. for Chester (1831–32), the eldest son of Sir Foster Cunliffe, 3rd Bt. (L. 30, n. 4) (Burke; Foster; *GM*, 102, Pt. 1 (1832): 477; death certificate, 15 Feb. 1850, GRO).

21. The ruins of the Roman villa at Bignor, Sussex, one of the largest in England, with its fine mosaic pavements, are described in *The Victoria History of the County of Sussex*, ed. L. F. Salzman, vol. 3 (London: University of London Institute of Historical Research, 1935), 20–23. The remains were discovered c. 1811 in Bignor Park, then owned by John Hawkins (d. 1841), and were excavated "for many years, and with unusual success" (Dudley George Cary Elwes, *A History of the Castles, Mansions, and Manors of Western Sussex* (London: Longmans, 1876), 32–33; Burke, *DLG*).

22. Possibly the Margam Orangery in South Glamorgan at the former seat of the Mansel family, who acquired the estates of the medieval abbey of Margam. The origin of the famous collection of citrus trees is unknown, but the orangery which housed it was the longest building of its kind in England, constructed mainly in 1787–90. For a description, see the Royal Commission on Ancient and Historical Monuments in Wales, *Domestic Architecture from the Reformation to the Industrial Revolution*, Pt. 1: *The Greater Houses*, vol. 4 of *An Inventory of the Ancient Monuments in Glamorgan* (Cardiff: HMSO, 1981), 323–31).

23. Possibly the authoress, Mary Berry (1763–1852), who, with her younger sister, Agnes (1764–1852), was a friend of Horace Walpole (*DNB;* Walpole, 11 and 12, passim).

24. Charlotte Barrett's mother, Charlotte Broome, was known as the family punster (*DL*, 2: 252; CB to CBF, 15 Aug. 1795, Barrett, Eg. 3700A, ff. 11–12; *JL*, 12: 612, n. 1).

25. The murder on 24 October 1823 of William Weare at Aldenham, Hertfordshire, had aroused strong public interest. The evidence examined by the magistrates after the arrests of the twenty-eighth and twenty-ninth and the results of the Coroner's Inquest were minutely detailed in the *Times* (31 Oct. 1823). Throughout November 1823, the newspapers carried daily accounts of the latest developments, retailed gossip about the prisoners' earlier lives and present demeanor, and reported on the notoriety of the scene of the crime. Hundreds of sightseers paid a shilling each to view the cottage where the suspects had stayed and the pond where the corpse was hidden; moreover, "the part of the hedge in the lane through which Weare's body was dragged after the murder no longer remains, having been cut away piecemeal by the persons who have visited the spot" (*Times*, 13 Nov. 1823).

The stream of publicity abated after a warning from the judge on 5 December 1823 against calumnious publication; however, excitement rose again at the time of the trial on 6 and 7 January 1824, when the murderer, John Thurtell (1794–1824), made an eloquent speech in his own defense. He was nevertheless convicted and hanged on 9 January before enormous crowds, earning himself a place in the *DNB*. The Gill's Hill tragedy has been enacted on the stage and narrated in ballads; the trial is documented in *The Trial of Thurtell and Hunt*, ed. Eric R. Watson (Edinburgh: William Hodge, 1920).

26. "Inny" was the family nickname for Sarah's cousin, Edward Burney, the artist; see above L. 27, nn. 12, 14.

27. This may be the bill for £300 drawn on Gosling & Co., which was credited to SHB's account at Coutts on 6 February 1824, and used the same day to buy £333.16s. of Consols. A comparable amount (£400) was deposited on 31 December 1822, which could conceivably cover her salary for the last four months of 1822 and the year 1823

(L. 104, n. 1). For the next three years, there is no evidence in SHB's account of her salary being paid; regular payments are made from the Court of Chancery, but these are apparently used to pay living expenses of the two wards—although in 1828, part of this money (£252.18s.) is used to buy Consols. Then, shortly before Sarah leaves the Crewes, a final £600 is credited to her account (see below L. 118, n. 5).

28. Sarah sends her love to Charlotte's husband and five children; her pupil Anna asks to be remembered to "Etty," Henrietta, aged twelve and Arthur, almost eleven.

29. Fanny Raper's mother-in-law, Katherine Raper (L. 72, n. 6), died on 12 November 1823, aged eighty-eight (*GM*, 93, Pt. 2 (1823): 477). In St. Luke Church, Chelsea is a memorial tablet to her and her husband, Henry.

30. The Rev. George Owen Cambridge and his wife, Cornelia, who had helped to arrange the Barretts' stay in Ely (n. 2) and were also in Ely in early December (*JL*, 11: 465).

31. Horace Walpole remarked on this feature of the "brave mansion," which he visited in 1763: in the hall was a "very fine chimney of different coloured marble to the top of the room, a monumental style of architecture and would ruin any estate in fuel that was not within six miles of the coal-pits" (Walpole, 10: 96).

32. Possibly *The Heads of Chronology, in English Verse* (Oxford/London: Parker/Whittaker, 1822) which may have been produced for children or schools. The editor thanks Prof. J. R. de J. Jackson for suggesting this work, which is listed in his *Annals of English Verse, 1770–1835* (New York: Garland, 1985), 481.

---

106. To Dr. [John Ayrton] Paris[1]

18 Grosvenor Street, 30 March [1824][2]
A.L.S., Pforzheimer
Address: Dr Paris / Dover Street / Piccadilly

Dear Sir

Mrs Gregor has informed me of her kindness in making so ill a report of my beautiful looks to you—and of your goodness in saying you would call any day and hour I appointed, & endeavour to repair my damaged charms. Now the fact is, I <u>have</u> had a severe feverish cold, & a great internal discomfort from, I believe, indigestion; so, I have starved & physicked myself into a fright of the first water: but I feel better—and sleep better—and, to say truth, never am so near well as when looking fit for a sick bed. I always plump up a little just before I have an attack, on purpose to give fever a better feast—and while any thing remains upon my bones to pick, Fever never leaves the pleasing banquet.

We go in about a week or ten days to a lodging at 24 Green Street—but meanwhile, I shall be most happy to see you even here, tho, I own, I shall enjoy a visit from you much more in my own habitation than in this, where I am perpetually liable to interruptions, & have but one room for dinners, & teas, & Masters, & visitors, and tradesfolks, &c, &c—

I shall seize the earliest opportunity of paying my personal devoirs to Mrs Paris[3]—and in the interval, beseech you to believe me

Ever most gratefully & truly yours
S. H. Burney

March 30th
18 Grosvenor Street

1. For Dr. John Ayrton Paris of Dover Street, see L. 102, n. 1.

2. The letter is conjecturally dated from the reference to SHB's severe illness, her reduced state, and a consultation with Dr. Paris, which occurred in the spring and summer of 1824. So ill was Sarah Harriet in June that she was forced to give up her responsibilities and try sea-bathing at Brighton, while her two charges went with another guardian to Ramsgate, Kent. Her condition did not improve at Brighton; returning to London c. 10 July, she remained under the care of Dr. Paris. In October, she was still too ill to venture out, but recovered sufficiently in November to return to her duties at Crewe Hall. The story unfolds in Mme d'Arblay's letters (*JL*, 11: 519, 536, 538, 542, 557, 561, 565); however, the editor is mistaken in suggesting that she was also at Ramsgate in June (*JL*, 11: 519, n. 9, 536, n. 5), a visit that would take place the following year (L. 107 below), or that on her return to London, she stayed in Park Street (*JL*, 11: 542, n. 3, 557, n. 9), a residence that had been given up by the Crewe family (see above L. 105).

3. Mary Catherine (d. 24 June 1855), the daughter of Francis Noble of Fordham Abbey, Cambs., had married John Ayrton Paris 11 December 1809 (*DNB; Alumni Cantab.; GM*, NS 44 (1855): 221).

---

107. To Charlotte (Francis) Barrett

7 Nelson's Crescent, Ramsgate, 19 June [1825][1]
A.L.S., Berg

June 19th
7 Nelson's Crescent
Ramsgate.

My dear Charlotte was kind enough to say she should like to hear from me whilst I was here;—so, here goes. I am truly thankful to Providence for being able to tell you, that I have in no way suffered from the excursion.—Far from being sleepless and restless as I was last year, I get excellent nights; wake of my own accord between seven and eight—set about my business without langour or fatigue—eat with good appetite, & avoid nothing that other people do, save and except rough winds, & walks too much prolonged.

Now, though it goes to my heart to fail, year after year, in seeing you as much, even in part, as I could wish, I must honestly confess that I am mighty glad not to have been driven to Richmond by illness!—Any other obliging motive that would offer itself I should most joyously snatch hold of—such as Julia's marriage to a Duke or Marquis—but illness is a bridge I can never wish to go over, even to arrive at the most agreeable journeys end.—I cannot tell you, my dearest, how I was struck, and Harriet Crewe also, as well as the very Music-Mistress then teaching Annie, with your Julia's[2] beauty the day you brought her to Green Street.[3] I saw my Sister d'Arblay that or the next evening,[4] & she was as much impressed. Upon my word, such a fine creature as that, ought to marry the Duke of Devonshire[5]—and I dare say she would, if he could but see her.—

We know nobody at this place—but we are a snug contented little party—Miss Mary Hesketh[6] forms one of it, and is a very desirable associate. She and Annie bathe every morning. Harriet is, for the third season, affected by the most extraordinary complaint brought on by the sea-air. Three or four times a day, she is seized with ungovernable fits of sneezing—water pours from her eyes and nose—and a tingling comes on all over her head something like the feel every body has experienced from what is called pins & needles in the feet.—When these attacks subside, no cold remains behind them, and she appears as well as usual.—Lord Crewe goes into a warm sea bath for eight minutes every day, & it agrees delightfully with him.—

Annie begs me to send her best love to Etty;—she was very sorry to see her for so short a time, & in the midst of a lesson. My kind love to Barrett—Heaven bless you and yours, dearest Charlotte, is the hearty prayer of your most affectionate

S. H. Burney.

1. The letter is dated conjecturally to 1825, by the reference to Sarah's visit to Ramsgate with her two pupils, which took place that summer (L. 108). Her health had somewhat improved at Crewe Hall over the winter and she was with her pupils in London in May 1825. They left for a month at Ramsgate in June, returning on 8 July; she was reported "wonderfully *better*" in August (*JL*, 12: 577, 589, 596, 611, 618).

2. Julia Charlotte, Charlotte Barrett's eldest daughter, sixteen years old.

3. SHB was living with her pupils at 6 Green Street, Grosvenor Square (*JL*, 12: 589); the year before they had stayed at No. 24 (L. 106).

4. Mme d'Arblay reported that Sarah had "drunk tea with me 3 times" during her stay in London in May and June (*JL*, 12: 596).

5. In 1814, Sarah Harriet had reported that Mrs. Hulse wished to match the Hon. Miss Twistleton with the enormously wealthy 6th Duke of Devonshire (L. 77), who remained, nevertheless, a lifelong bachelor.

6. Possibly Anna Maria Martha Hesketh (1808–86), only surviving daughter of Robert Hesketh (1764–1824) by his wife (m. 11 Sept. 1790) Maria née Rawlinson (d. 3 July 1824) (Burke, *LG*). Miss Hesketh was six years older than Annabella Crewe.

---

108. To Charlotte (Francis) Barrett

18 Grosvenor Street, 11 July 1825
A.L.S., Berg
Address: Mrs Barrett

18 Grosvenor Street
July 11th 1825

My dear Charlotte

I have fumbled over your puzzle, and found out, before I looked at your method, a way of my own to do it, which way I send you, marked with a printed S.—Moreover, I send you, another sort of puzzle given me by M[r] Willoughby Crewe,[1] and explained at the back, & dotted where it is to be cut, in front. And moreover & besides, I send 6 others, somewhat differing in shape from yours, but on the same principle—one is marked with an X, another with a G—another with a D—another with an A—another with a C—and another with a B—all the produce of M[r] W. Crewe's perseverance. We have had a great deal of amusement whilst poking out these things, which tho' neither of my girls care for, I do, and may often meet with others, who, like good-humoured Willoughby Crewe, take an interest in them for an evening or so.—I drank tea with Sister d'Arblay on Saturday, & being on my good behaviour now, that is, writing and calling as often as I can, I get very graciously received.[2]—We leave town early on Wednesday morning, and only arrived here from Ramsgate to a late dinner on Friday last. The lots of packing and unpacking, and dividing cloaths for the journey, & cloaths to go by water, & all that bother, so often renewed, plagues me mortally.—The Wilbrahams embarked at the Tower Stairs for Boulogne on Saturday morning. I like pretty chearful Ramsgate—The effects of the sea-air never remitted upon Miss Crewe the whole month we were there—but now she is quite well.—I have read with much pleasure The Betrothed, and am au beau millieu of the Talisman[3]—And a second-rate thing fell into my hands by Mary Charlton, which in many parts has extraordinary merit—but the heroine is too great a fury, & sometimes the dialogue, where meaning to be witty, is obscure & studied.—It calls itself Grandeur & Meanness.[4]—

Best love to Barrett, & the dear girls—thank you for the masterly portraits. You have great merit in being so clear-sighted in what relates to such objects—I am tired, but miraculously well, considering. Thousand loves to my dearest Sister—Ever thine

S. H. B.

1. The Rev. Willoughby Crewe (1792–1850), youngest son of Maj.-Gen. Richard Crewe (1749–1814), younger brother to Lord Crewe. Of St. Alban's Hall, Oxford, B.C.L. (1819), he was presently Rector of Warmingham (1816), and of Barthomley, Cheshire (1819), but would resign these livings in 1830 when he became Rector of Mucklestone, Salop, and later of Astbury, Cheshire (1836) (Burke; *Alumni Oxon.;* Ormerod, 3: 314; *GM*, NS 33 (1850): 678; Rev. Edward Hinchliffe, *Barthomley: In Letters from a Former Rector to his Eldest Son* (London: Longman, Brown, Green, and Longmans, 1856), 1: 42).

2. Mme d'Arblay complained of Sarah's inattentiveness: "She has her share of this rising generation, for she likes to write or to let it alone; to visit, or to drop the Ceremony, as well from impulse & the humour of the day, as her dutiful nephews & nieces." The theme recurs with some frequency: "*Sarah Harriet* is at Crewe Hall: but has written to none of us in these parts since she left town"; "Sarah Harriet is *mute*, again" or, more wryly: "Sarah Harriet is at Crew Hall, & I hope prosperous, though not communicative" (*JL*, 11: 358–59, 444, 493, 504).

3. "The Betrothed" and "The Talisman," which constituted [Sir Walter Scott's] *Tales of the Crusaders*, came out in June 1825 (Johnson, 2: 901).

4. Mary Charlton (fl. 1794–1830) (Todd, *Dictionary*) who published *Grandeur and Meanness; or, Domestic persecution* in 1824.

109. To Charlotte (Francis) Barrett

Crewe Hall, 10 November [1825][1]
A.L.S., Berg

Novr 10th Crewe Hall.

My dearest Charlotte, notwithstanding your unconscionable impudence in asking with such plausible gravity what I had been doing, and where I had been?—Why pray Miss, if you come to that, what have you been doing?—So long ago as last July, did I not write you an incomparable letter from Grosvenor Street, giving a most entertaining account of a recent excursion I had made to <Buxton> Ramsgate, and containing, moreover, sundry mathematical puzzles, each unique in its kind? And did you ever respond a single line to my amusing performance?—I am ashamed of you, my dear!—The artifice of trying to shift off upon my shoulders your own burthen of misdemeanors is too shallow and palpable to escape detection even a single half second! Come now—be honest, and own yourself a scrubby sly-boots.

I was very unwell from a severe feverish cold when your letter arrived, and in bed—and though delighted to have it, its poetical first page was read by me with most prosaïc dullness, and not found out to be poetical till this very morning, when I again looked over the letter to see what might most require an answer.[2]—If rhyme can be read as prose, and found to contain reason, let me tell you, its merit is most extraordinarily inhanced—and such is the case with regard to yours, for I found nothing queer in it whilst mistaking it for prose, but on the contrary, got thereby at two or three valuable bits of news, told as I thought in a plain and good current style.—You are very clever, you creature, to run off such a rigmarole with such ease.—

Annie and I went in August & beginning Septr for a fortnight to Buxton[3] with Lord Crewe. Harriet spent the interval with a friend in Wales. I enjoyed the trip extremely, but medled neither with Baths nor Pumps. But the hilly walks & fine air—and the pleasant people I either made or renewed acquaintance with—and the entire novelty of a table-d'Hôte, all amused & did me good. My poor dear old Lord took a spite against the slippery material of the Baths (polished marble) and almost from the second day of his arrival, did nothing but grumble and scold, and vow that Buxton was the most abominable place under the sun. I did not mind him, however, as he let me laugh at him without being affronted—and Annie and I went on enjoying it all very much to our heart's content.—There was a Revd Mr Barlow[4] (I think his name was) and his wife at our Hotel, who made up to me—because I knew Arch^{n} & Mrs Cambridge. However, I am by no means sure I have told you the name right, for they were not folks of much mark or likelihood,[5] & made a very superficial impression upon my memory. *He* was pompous, & vain—and *she*, a little chiffon of a woman, born an heiress, and bred (for her size) an uncommonly good feeder.[6]—Mrs Coutts and her Duke & Duke's Sister[7] came to the Hotel adjoining ours three days before we left—and with other Gape-Seed folks, I <went> walked about to have a look at them—and a buxom, good-humoured dame she is—and a handsome little dull looking man is he—and a fine *comme il faut* girl is the Sister.—Moreover, Ld Crewe took us to Chatsworth; the drive thither from Buxton is magnificent—Chatsworth itself is all higgledypiggledy just now—they are building new wings as large as the main habitation, and at present there is no fine library, or Statue Gallery, or collection of pictures—and the park is flat, & the grounds about the house formal—and the Gobelin Tapestry is almost the only very curious thing to be seen,[8] <there>, except a Statue, I believe by Canova, of Madame Mere, Nap's Mamma.[9] She looks like a Colossul Juno, very regular, and with much of the air antique.

I have not much more to say, my Charlotte, except that, much to my surprise and pleasure, I lately had a long and very chearful letter from poor dear Sister Burney—quite recovered,[10] & using her goose-quill as firmly, freely, & funnily as ever. I am glad you have somewhat favourable tidings of your kind Mother & poor Clem[11]—But the Invalid Diary Man says Lucca is far better for delicate people than either Nice, Naples, or Montpellier.[12]

Of course you have read Segur,[13] & Pepys,[14] and with the latter are perhaps "mightily" weary now & then, but on the whole amused—There is an interesting History of the Tower of London lately published,[15] which read when you can, for its historical anecdotes—and also (if you like Tours) read John Russel's Tour in Germany in 1820, 21, 22.[16]—

Adieu my best & dearest Charlotte. Always love to Barrett, who has always been friendly and kind to me—and heartily wishing you & yours all good & prosperity,

believe me faithfully yours
S. H. Burney.

Lady Ann[17] & Mr Wilbraham were at Buxton, & told me their Sisters meant to winter at Rome.—

When you write to your dear Madre, pray thank her for the few lines she sent me on the eve of her departure—and add my cordial love & good wishes to Clem.

What paltry stuff the Memoirs of poor vain Genlis are![18]

1. The letter gives many clues as to its date. The reference to a previous letter written in July after a recent stay at Ramsgate, and containing puzzles, seems to describe SHB's letter of 11 July 1825. This supposition is confirmed by other events that all point to 1825: Mrs. Coutts's northern tour, Esther Burney's recovery, Clement Francis's journey with his mother to warmer climes, and the recent publication of the *Memoirs* of Pepys and de Genlis.

2. This rhyming letter of Charlotte Barrett's does not survive, but another poetical missive does, which closes with greetings "From the girls in the parlour to boys in the Garrett / Your very affectionate niece Charlotte Barrett" (CFBt to SHB, 18 Apr. [1826], Barrett, Eg. 3702A, ff. 149–50v).

3. Buxton, Derbyshire, a spa with a thermal spring discovered by the Romans. Frequently compared to Bath, it also boasted a Royal Crescent (completed in 1786) but its "social life developed slowly. . . . Its pride is in its buildings and its open spaces" (Addison, 85–91).

4. Probably William Barlow (1789–1848), second son of Admiral Sir Robert Barlow (1757–1843) (*DNB;* Burke). Of Trinity College, Cambridge, B.A. (1811), M.A. (1820), he was ordained in 1820 and became Vicar of St. Mary Bredin, Canterbury (1824–48) and Rector of Weston-super-Mare, Somerset (1829–40). Later he would become Canon of Chester (1834–48), Rector of Coddington (1834–40), and finally Rector of Northenden, Cheshire (1840–48) (*Alumni Cantab.; GM,* NS 31 (1849): 214).

5. William Shakespeare, *1 Henry IV* (III, ii, 45): "A fellow of no mark nor likelihood."

6. William Barlow's first wife, whom he had married 25 November 1824 was Louisa (d. 7 April 1838), daughter of Robert Jones Adeane (d. 10 Jan. 1823) of Babraham, Cambs. (Burke, *LG; GM,* 93, Pt. 1 (1823): 383; 94, Pt. 2 (1824): 640; NS 9 (1838): 558).

7. Harriet Mellon (c. 1777–1837), an actress, had married on 18 January 1815 as his second wife, the banker Thomas Coutts (1735–1822) (*DNB*), who bequeathed to her the bulk of his vast fortune (*GM,* NS 8 (1837): 419–21; Ernest Hartley Coleridge, *The Life of Thomas Coutts Banker* (London: John Lane, 1920), 2: Ch. 28 and passim).

She was probably traveling north to Scotland with William Aubrey de Vere Beauclerk (1801–49), 9th Duke of St. Albans (1825), and his sister, Lady Charlotte Beauclerk (d. 12 Aug. 1842), where they would visit Sir Walter Scott at Abbotsford (25–28 Oct. 1825). By her own account, Mrs. Coutts had already refused the Duke twice; they would eventually marry on 16 June 1827 (Burke; Gibbs; Lockhart, 8: 54–61, 95–96).

8. Chatsworth Hall, Derbyshire, begun in 1552 and rebuilt 1686–1707, was the seat of the 6th Duke of Devonshire, who spent much of his time and fortune improving the estate, and wrote a *Handbook to Chatsworth and Hardwick* (1845). The house boasted several fine tapestries, one of which was apparently created in the famous French factory (Lysons, *Magna Britannia,* 5: 149–55; Duchess of Devonshire, *The House: A Portrait of Chatsworth* (London: Macmillan, 1982)).

9. The Italian sculptor Antonio Canova (L. 99, n. 5), of whose art the Duke of Devonshire was "the most fervent of all English collectors" (F. J. B. Watson, "Canova and the English," *Architectural Review* 122 (1957): 403–6). The seated statue of Laetitia Bonaparte, Napoleon's mother, was housed in the sculpture gallery at Chatsworth: "Madame Mère! first acquired treasure, next to Endymion the most valued!" (Duke of Devonshire, *Handbook,* as quoted in Duchess of Devonshire, *The House,* 187).

10. Esther Burney had suffered in the summer of 1825 from some complaint of the bowels (*JL*, 12: 614–16), but recovered in the autumn, when she found herself "better in health . . . in good Spirits, as good as ever" (EBB to CFBt, 23 Oct. 1825, Berg).

11. Charlotte Broome and her son, Clement Francis, had left England in October 1825 seeking a milder climate to restore Clement's health. She would write in late November from Hyères in the south of France, where they were enjoying the balmy air, which was apparently beneficial: "Clem^{t} is stronger since he came, & has better nights, & more appetite" (*JL*, 12: 628, n. 2, 629, n. 5; CBFB to FBA, 28 Nov.–9 Dec. [1825], Barrett, Eg. 3693, ff. 95–96v).

12. Henry Mathews, *The Diary of an Invalid being the Journal of a Tour in pursuit of health in Portugal Italy Switzerland and France in the years 1817 1818 and 1819* (London: John Murray, 1820). Mathews commended the "warm, mild, and muggy" air of Pisa as "the very best . . . during the winter for complaints of the chest." The climate of Nice was "the very worst," and the sharp winds of Naples and Montpellier were irritating to weak lungs (12, 20 Feb., 11–18 Oct. 1818).

13. The French general and historian, Philippe-Paul, comte de Ségur (1780–1873), wrote an *Histoire de Napoléon et de la grande armée, pendant l'année 1812* (1824).

14. The diary of Samuel Pepys (1633–1703), written 1660–69, was first published as *Memoirs of Samuel Pepys*, ed. Richard Lord Braybrooke, 2 vols. (London: H. Colburn, 1825). Pepys is often "mightily pleased," particularly by performances of plays or the sight of beautiful women; see e.g., 19 Oct. 1667 (2: 142).

15. John Bayley, *The History and Antiquities of the Tower of London*, 2 pts. (1821, 1825).

16. [John Russell], *A Tour in Germany, and some of the Southern provinces of the Austrian Empire, in . . . 1820, 1821, 1822* (1824).

17. Lady Anne Fortescue (1787–1864), third daughter of Hugh (1753–1841), 1st Earl Fortescue (1789), had married on 3 September 1814 George Wilbraham the younger (L. 112, n. 12), so was sister-in-law to Emma, Elizabeth, and Anna Wilbraham (Burke, *LG* under Wilbraham; Burke, Gibbs, Lodge under Fortescue; Ormerod, 2: 138; *GM*, 3rd ser. 16 (1864): 539).

18. Stéphanie-Félicité Brûlart (née du Crest de Saint-Aubin), comtesse de Genlis, published her *Mémoires* in Paris in 1825; they were published in London by Henry Colburn the same year.

---

110. To Charlotte (Francis) Barrett

Crewe Hall, 26 November 1826

A.L.S., Berg

Address: <Madame Barrett> / <22 Place d'Alton> / <Boulogne>

readdressed to: Miss Barrett, / At Miss M. Francis's / Richmond Green, / Richmond, Surry / p^{t} p^{d} / to be forwarded

Postmarks: Pic[cadi]ll[y] / 3pyPPaid
18 Paid 26 / 29 NO / 8 MORN 8
[?] NOON / NO 29 / 26 o[?]

Novr 26th 1826
Crewe Hall.

Dearest Charlotte

"Send you the letter that I owe you," quoth'a?[1]—I verily suspect, that is a most invidious sort of insinuation. I have been persuading myself these hundred years that you were my debtor, and when at last I had the satisfaction of seeing the nice long letter just received, I hailed it merely as my due.—However, if I really have been the debtor all this time, the more generous you—and the more <shameless> graceless I.—To make further speeches about the matter, would only be making bad worse.—Yes, dear Charlotte—I was indeed most cordially gratified by the appearance, manners, and excellent countenance of your fine Eton lad.[2] He is quite what I like a boy to be—natural, intelligent, and modest without being sheepish. Harriet Crewe was extremely struck by him. I wish poor dear Hungerford Crewe[3] was altogether just such an other—but though I love him much (as I am rather apt to prefer the he gender in boyhood) yet, I cannot but allow, that he is often childish, and always awkward—and I fear will hereafter be extremely subject to being led by the nose!—The trimmings you talk of, have been most correctly announced to you,[4] and I trust, are by this time ready to be put into Julia's hands.[5] When I left town nearly a month ago, they were at a Dress-Maker's, to whom I had committed the charge of mounting them upon muslin skirts, so that your dear girls might have no other trouble than that of making up the waists to their own shape. When finished, the creature (an affected cat) had orders to send them in a neat flat bandbox to 11 Bolton Street,[6] and I apprized my Sister of the circumstance, requesting her to give them house-room, till there occurred a safe opportunity of getting them conveyed to their destined owners. Harriet Crewe is quite flattered by the manner in which you accept her little offering, and entreats me to forward her best compliments to you as well as your daughters. And now, to close the chapter of Dress-makers, and Bandboxes, I must repeat to you an absurdity just communicated to me from the breakfast table where Lord Crewe always opens his franks. There was one to-day, addressed under cover to his Lordship, "Mr Watson, Silver Department, Crewe Hall, Cheshire"[7]—and after incredible puzzling, who and what do you think this meant?—Why, it was for a person we all call for distinction, Long Thomas, who is Under Butler, and cleans the plate!—There's for you—Can any thing be grander?—It made me, like Touchstone, "laugh till my lungs did crow like chanticleer".[8]—

Miserable cattle your company at Boulogne![9]—We have something here not a great deal better. A clergyman whose Living is about four miles off,[10] but who chiefly lives at this house, where he now and then gallops through the Sunday Service in the domestic Chapel, spending the rest of the week in playing billiards, hunting, lounging on a Sofa with a Novel, playing Whist, letting himself be made love to by an artful girl who wants to be married, and disdains not to take all the trouble of <being> becoming so upon herself,—eating good dinners, making sneering jokes, and taking snuff!—How do you like him?—Yet, this cypher is called a good creature—and said always to mean well. He certainly picks no pockets, nor cuts any throats!—

Pray when you write to dear old Clem remind him that there is such a little body as me about the world, and give him my love, and tell him I often think of him, and have felt most sincere concern for his long sufferings.[11] Sister Broome fond of Paris!—I wonder what will happen next!—Had it been Sister Burney, I should not at all have wondered.—Had it been Sister Sarah, I should have wondered had <the> she not liked it—but Sister Broome, somehow, not speaking fluently the language, and so truly English in all her habits—it is marvellous![12]—You say not a word of your health—let me then flatter myself it is much amended[13]—as for me, I ought to be on my knees twenty times a day, to thank God for the wonderful restoration He has vouchsafed me. I have not been better for years.—My little girl is getting quite a companionable age, and take her for all in all, is a very satisfactory child, and promises well for hereafter. Harriet and I are very friendly—and my good old Lord is hand and glove with me. So—any little occasional rubs, and they really seldom occur, may be patiently borne.—

My love to Barrett—I yet hope that we may meet to renew some of our former friendly wrangles—though, if we do, tell him he will not find me one jot less stanch to my own opinion than in days of yore. I get tougher than ever here, as I meet with more and more wrong-notioned folks—at least, such as I think so.—At Easter, if we are all alive, I hope Dick will come and see me in London. Best love to Henrietta.—Adieu dearest—I am sorry such stuff as this should cost you any thing, mais qui faire?

S. H. B.

1. On 19 November [1826], Charlotte Barrett had written to her aunt: "I have long been wishing to write, though not 'in answer to your last kind letter,' which I fear still remains in your head. However, that is a very improving place for it, and the longer it stays there the more agreable & valuable I may expect it to be—Yet, my dearest, there is reason in roasting of oysters, and and [*sic*] as I have been very patient, you will not think me importunate if I beg you to send me my letter that you owe me, at your earliest leisure" (Barrett, Eg. 3702A, ff. 152–53v).

Mrs. Barrett was writing from Boulogne where she, her husband, and two of their children were spending the winter; they had been there since August, having rented out their house at Richmond for ten months (MF to CFBt & HnBt, 23 Aug. 1826, Berg; CFBt to CBFB, 3 Nov. [1826], Barrett Eg. 3702A, ff. 135–36v).

2. Charlotte Barrett's thirteen-year-old son, Richard Arthur Francis, was attending Eton College (baptismal certificate, Barrett, Eg. 3708, f. 16; H. E. C. Stapylton, *The Eton School Lists from 1791 to 1877* (Eton: R. Ingalton Drake, 1885), 119b). In her letter, Charlotte had thanked her aunt for her kindness in visiting her boy at Eton: "He wrote me word of his pleasant visit to you." She had also heard through her daughter Julia that Aunt Sarah was very impressed with Dick's "gentlemanly behaviour" and improvement (CFBt to SHB, 19 Nov. [1826], Barrett, Eg. 3702A, ff. 152–53v; CBFB & JBt to CFBt, 29–31 Oct. 1826, Barrett, Eg. 3700A, ff. 98–99v).

3. Hungerford Crewe (1812–94), later 3rd Baron Crewe (1835), the only son of John Crewe (L. 104, n. 3), and younger brother to Harriet Crewe (L. 105, n. 19). SHB had accompanied Miss Crewe to Eton to visit her brother, who compared unfavorably to Dick Barrett (CBFB & JBt to CFBt, 29–31 Oct. 1826, Barrett, Eg. 3700A, ff. 98–99v).

4. Charlotte Barrett had heard through Dick "that Miss Crewe has been so very good as to employ herself in some beautiful work for my two girls. If this is really true, & Dick made no mistake,—do pray my dearest Aunt Sarah say everything for us all that can best express our sense of so kind & pretty a thought, originating doubtless in regard for you,—and trebly welcome to us for that very reason" (CFBt to SHB, 19 Nov. [1826], Barrett, Eg. 3702A, ff. 152–53v).

5. Julia Barrett was in England with her grandmother, Charlotte Broome, but would join her parents at Christmas (ibid.; CBFB, MF, & JBt to CFBt, [18 Dec. 1826], Berg).

6. 11 Bolton Street, Piccadilly, where Mme d'Arblay had lived since 8 October 1818 (*JL*, 11: 1, n. 1).

7. Unidentified.

8. It was actually Jaques who laughed, meeting Touchstone, the "motley fool" in the forest: "My lungs began to crow like chanticleer" (William Shakespeare, *As You Like It*, II, vii, 30).

9. Charlotte had complained of her society: "We have very few acquaintances at Boulogne, as I avoid any whom I have not known else where . . . even the best, of the real Boulogne residents, appear to me in such a questionable shape, that I think the less one mixes with them the better." After illustrating her remarks with a gambling baronet and a card-playing clergyman, she concludes, "I never knew a set of people received in society whose conduct was so open to censure as that of most who appear at Boulogne" (CFBt to SHB, 19 Nov. [1826], Barrett, Eg. 3702A, ff. 152–53v).

10. Probably the Rev. Willoughby Crewe, uncle to Sarah's pupils, Rector of Warmingham, about five miles northwest of Crewe Hall, and of Barthomley, about three miles

southeast (L. 108, n. 1), of which Lord Crewe was patron. The trifling clergyman with a living nearby is named in her letter of 17 February 1828 below (L. 112).

11. Charlotte had informed Sarah Harriet about her apparently consumptive brother who was wintering for a second year in the south of France: "Clem is at Hiéres near Toulon, for the winter; & finds great benefit from that mild climate & the Baths of Barege which he took in the summer. He has friends who are very kind & attentive to him—but we all regret the immense distance which separates him from us, & makes our reunion impossible at present" (CFBt to SHB, 19 Nov. [1826], Barrett, Eg. 3702A, ff. 152–53v). Mrs. Broome would soon hear from her son who "does not mention his Santè so we must conclude no news is good news" (CBFB, MF & JBt to CFBt, [18 Dec. 1826], Berg). He would not return to England until June 1827 (MF to CFBt, 22 June 1827, Barrett, Eg. 3704A, ff. 163–64v).

12. In her letter to her aunt, Charlotte Barrett had remarked that her mother "is grown quite fond of France; knows Paris as well as London, and falls, with cordial good will, into every harmless french custom." Mrs. Broome had spent some months in Paris in 1826, and wrote in good spirits about her amusements in the capital (CBFB to FBA & CFBt & MF, 4 Mar. 1826, Barrett, Eg. 3693, ff. 97–98v; CBFB to CFBt, 20 Apr. [1826], Barrett, Eg. 3700A, ff. 96–97v; *JL*, 12: 641, 644, 650, n. 2). Mme d'Arblay also marvelled at Charlotte's ability to cope, considering "her ignorance of the Language of the Country where she was confined, & her utter inexperience in all foreign travelling & customs, &c" (*JL*, 12: 670).

13. Charlotte Barrett was apparently unwell in the autumn of 1826. Mme d'Arblay had reported (possibly with some exaggeration) that she was "in a state of health so precarious, & so frequently alarming" that there was "*no hope* of her restoration, except under the Maternal Eye" (*JL*, 12: 671). Charlotte's brother, Clement, had kindly invited her to winter with him, but she was not in "a state of health to make such a change of climate essential." She found Boulogne mild enough: "therefore I think the best way is to take care, keep warm, avoid mistrale, and remain here" (CFBt to CBFB, 3 Nov. [1826], Barrett, Eg. 3702A, ff. 135–36v).

---

111. To Charlotte (Francis) Barrett

Crewe Hall, 12 February 1827
A.L.S., Berg

Crewe Hall. Feby 12th 1827.

My dearest Charlotte—Julia's well bred, and unaffected little note, was received with great pleasure, and drew forth an immediate answer, which has been baking in my possession above a week, but will at length go in the same frank with this. I had not the heart to write sooner, for listening to my own dear grunts, with a huge blister on my stomach, and a due degree of soreness attending thereon. I am better now—but have, for the present, at least, given up dining with the family, as I find myself tempted, little as I eat, now and then to take more or better things than I ought; & so then, I get well punished. Now, by dining with Annie at two o'clock, I keep out of the way of these hazardous "creature comforts", and have a better chance of escaping severer after-discipline.—

We begin to hear a good deal on the subject of impending hostility between the two illustrious noodles St. Dennis and St. George.[1] Individually, men do get wiser perhaps—but when will nations become so, and abstain from going to logger-heads on every paltry pretext?—My belief is—the world, old as we think it, is yet in its babyhood. As for such peace, and gentleness, and wisdom as the Scriptures foretell, to our shame be it spoken, we see nothing of them yet—collectively. We only, now and then, hear of an individual so gifted, who mourns over the faults & follies of his fellow men. Like me!

Tor Hill,[2] I have read—and was amused to find myself en pays de connoisance. Many years ago, I walked with my poor Brother James & Martin,[3] from a little village in Somersetshire called Uphill, to Glastonbury, and thence three miles farther, to visit Glastonbury Tor, on the Summit of a high hill. The local descriptions are very accurate, at least as far as I remember—and there are some interesting sketches of character—of personages who attach—but the concluding part of the story is wretchedly huddled together—the attempts at facetiousness beneath contempt—and throughout, there is a hardness of manner which gives to the book what the earliest Masters gave to their paintings, dryness, meagerness & want of gradual light & shade.—He cope with the Author of Waverley!—He be hanged! Brambletye Hall or House,[4] I have not read, though every body else here has—but few were pleased with it, and I can well believe it to have all the demerits you speak of. The most spirit-stirring Author, next to the Great Unknown,[5] that I have met with, is the American who has written the Spy, and the Last of the Mohicans, & various others.[6] He copies nobody, & he has an energy, a power of developing what he has previously enveloped, and of keeping the interest upon the stretch, that is admirable.—

I have bought a book lately full of general information, & written in a good spirit—that is, containing a happy mixture of religious feeling with Science. Its title is "Good's Book of Nature." Have you heard of it? It is by a Dr Good, an M.D.F.R.S. who delivered Lectures at the London Institution.[7]—

You know I have seldom availed myself of the materials furnished by the individuals around me for filling my letters.—I think such doings hardly fair: but without naming names, I may allow myself to describe a scene now passing daily before my eyes, which astonishes my weak mind. A young Lady is here who is known to be engaged, and is actually to be married in May. She writes three or four times a week to her absent love—talks of him—wears his gifts—in short is open and unreserved about him as heart could wish. There is however another young Youth in the house, very idle, very fond of gossip and child's play, & my engaged friend is after him all day and all evening; learns French of him—whispers, giggles, plays tricks to him and with him—sits in his pocket—follows him to whatever part of the room he goes—carries on, in short, such a systematic flirtation with him, that if the Mind's eye of her absent Henry could see what she is at, I suspect he might be half tempted to wash his hands of her. Altogether, the proceeding is past my comprehension; for she is supposed to be desparately in love, and marries her man in direct opposition to the wishes of an Uncle she lives with, two brothers, and a brother-in-law![8]—

I must very soon concoct a letter to my Sister d'Arblay—She never concocts any to me, and yet the unconscionable woman exacts <of> under the penalty of being lectured to death, the tribute which of all others she knows I least like to pay—writing letters to which I know I never shall receive an answer.[9]—But, I suppose it must be done. My best love to Barrett—and kind greetings from Annie to Henrietta—Yours dearest Charlotte ever most affectionately S. H. Burney—

1. I.e., France and England. In December 1826, five thousand British troops were sent to Portugal to defend the constitutional regime against the various insurgents backed by Spain, and to counterbalance the presence of the French army in the peninsula. For the intricacies of Canning's foreign policy, see Wendy Hinde, *George Canning* (London: Collins, 1973), 375–83, 411–25.

2. The historical novel, *The Tor Hill* (1826), work of the parodist [Horatio (or Horace) Smith (1779–1849)] (*DNB*).

3. Probably between 1799 and 1801 when Sarah Harriet lived with her half-brother James and nephew Martin near Bristol (see above L. 23, n. 4).

4. Another anonymously published novel by Horatio Smith, *Brambletye House, or Cavaliers and Roundheads* (1826), an imitation of Scott.

5. The "Great Unknown" was the anonymous author of the *Waverley Novels*, until Sir Walter Scott publicly acknowledged his authorship at a dinner on 23 February 1827 (Johnson, 2: 1008–9).

6. James Fenimore Cooper (1789–1851), then at the height of his fame, had published anonymously *The Spy* (1821) and *The Last of the Mohicans* (1826) (*DAB*).

7. John Mason Good (1764–1827), physician and miscellaneous writer, F.R.S. (1805), M.D. (1820), had given three courses of lectures at the Surrey Institution, which were later published as *The Book of Nature* (1826) (*DNB*).

8. The "very idle" youth and the lazy clergyman who was "letting himself be made love to by an artful girl who wants to be married" (in L. 110 above) may be one and the same, probably the Rev. Willoughby Crewe (see further L. 112). The young lady is pos-

sibly Mary Hesketh (L. 107, n. 6), nineteen years old, and a frequent houseguest of the Crewes (L. 113). Some of the details seem to fit: both her parents had died in 1824, so she might well live with an uncle; she had only two surviving brothers, Peter Hesketh (later Fleetwood) (d. 12 April 1866), of Ronsall Hall, Lancs., and the Rev. Charles Hesketh (1804–76). However, the brother-in-law remains unidentified, and she was not to marry until 17 September 1828, Thomas John Knowlys of Heysham Tower, Lancs. (Burke, *LG*).

9. Mme d'Arblay claimed from her family an unequal exchange of correspondence: "Three Letters were agreed upon as the industrious premium for one *tardy return.*" While ever anxious to receive "these Letters I so prize," Fanny herself could not be expected to reply regularly. In her widowhood, she claimed that writing was difficult because "*recollective,*" a rationale she had used years before, when the death of her favourite sister, Susan, "had made the very action of writing laborious—painful—almost anguish to me" (*JL*, 11: 15, 251; 12: 662; 4: 408). In actual fact, she had insisted on the generous indulgence of this foible long before the death of Susan (see e.g., FB to Rosette Burney, 22 Mar. [1786–91], Osborn; *JL*, 2: 12; 3: 7, 90, 316–17).

---

112. To Charlotte (Francis) Barrett and Charlotte (Burney) (Francis) Broome

Crewe Hall, 17 February 1828
A.L.S., Berg
Address: Mrs Barrett / 6 Burlington Street / Brighton
franked: Crewe /—Nantwich twenty fourth Feb^ry^ 1828
Postmarks: FREE / 26FE26 / 1828

Crewe Hall
Feby 17th 1828.

Ye are, both Mother and Daughter, most charming persons, and your joint letter[1] did me a power of good. Lest I should frighten you by answering it too quickly, I shall hold this back some days after it is written; for I know what it is to be put into debt again the moment one has fancied oneself quite clear: but it is a pleasure to me to write while the cold of my iron pen is warmed by the influence of your kindness.—

Thanks, dearest, for your little family bulletin.—Barrett's new verb, "Babooning" makes me laugh whether alone or in company, by night and by day whenever it occurs to me!—Do you know, that softened into "Monkey-ing," it would apply sadly well to my poor Annabel? She is growing miserably affected in attitudes, language, and expression of countenance. All here perceive, and twite her with it, except her Aunt,[2] who being affected herself, either does not or will not see it. She is growing up however a very nice girl, and will be very popular, I make no doubt—but her head is warmer than her heart. She will never love much, but she will flirt à corps perdu! But I trust she will be well principled—I know she will have a liberal and charitable spirit towards the poor—she will, mostly, speak the truth—and, when pleased, will be very agreeable and good-humoured. Don't laugh at this qualified praise;—know you not many who never can be agreeable whether pleased or not?—The other Sister, with an exterior of ice, has feelings the most fervent.[3] She is, by those she loves, and who understand something of her disposition, the most easy and comfortable person to live with in the world. She is made up of charity, and adored throughout the neighbourhood. Her tastes are simple, and thoroughly countryfied. No two creatures were ever more unlike than she and her Aunt, and they never can be long at ease together. To tell you the truth, I am not often at ease with [(a)][4]Mad^{me} Pernelle[5] myself. She has much real with still more imaginary penetration, and is <was> "finding out meanings never meant,"[6] all day long, and suspecting that one never drinks one's tea without a stratagem.[7] Besides, in the true Pernelle spirit, she is so fond of setting every body to rights—invents so many new devices, and affects to think every difficulty so easy to overcome!—But enough of this prosing. I know not how the deuce my pen fell into such a vein—and I am afraid, after all, I have not done the right thing, quite, in making these, my present inmates, so much my theme. To you however, dearest, I have less scruple in letting it go, than I should have to any one else—and you will do me the justice to own, I have seldom if ever, got into such gossip before.

I am enchanted to hear of dear Clement's recovery. Tell him that Willoughby Crewe, an old school-fellow of his (one of those who was mainly concerned in throwing brick-bats at poor Dr Charles during The grand school-rebellion)[8] has often talked to me about him, and enquired after him very cordially. He is now a clergyman, amply preferred—idle as Creole blood can make him (his Mother was a West Indian dawdling beauty)[9] doing no manner of useful thing, but luckily, abstaining from vice. His living is not more than seven miles from hence, and he may in fact be said to live here. He is a widower, with two charming little boys,[10] now at school with a Lady (they are very young) in Wales. His wife died after I came here, and certainly her loss has contributed to make him more reckless, and nonchalant than before. She was a lovely creature, and I believe he was as much attached to her as his nature will permit him to be to any body.—

My poor Anna Wilbraham has been these two or three years in Italy, and was on the point of marriage with a young Roman Count Roberti,[11] an accomplished, good-looking, and moderately-well-off cavalier. Uncle Roger[12] had stormed in vain—Brother George[13] had recommended prudence, but with great kindness—other friends had wished the R. Catholic Lover at Jericho—when lo! after the day was almost fixed, the Pope interferes, and imposes such conditions upon the protestant wife, before he will give his consent, that Anna's conscience recoils from agreeing to them—and the match is broken off. I cannot much regret that circumstance; but I grieve at the sorrow it must cost her—and I honour her motives of action beyond expression. Instead of coming to England in the Spring, as they intended, to spend a year amongst her friends, she has prevailed upon her sisters to pass another year abroad: but not to be in the vicinity of Count Roberti, for they are going into Germany, to Vienna, and even as far as Berlin.—Eliza will enjoy it as a musician—and Anna as a Mineraologist.

I have behaved ill-naturedly to Marianne,—but she really put so strong a temptation in my way, that I had not the virtue to resist it. She wrote last Spring a long rigmarole to Lord Crewe (aged 85) in a hand difficult to read, recommending somebody to his charity, & introducing herself to him as "Dr Burney's Grand-daughter"—and he made a bother of the business—and fancied she was the widow in distress, and asked every body in the house who this G.daughter of Dr Burney was, &c, &c? At last, the enquiry was addressed to me. I told him the whole was a mistake (not of his, however, for I dare not) and I offered to answer the letter for him. He had half torn it up, intending to burn it. But it was hunted for and found—and some time or other perhaps, I may find opportunity to shew you both that, and my very pert answer. But really, in the true spirit of self-justification to which we are all so prone, I must say, that considering Marianne's utter want of personal acquaintance with Lord Crewe—considering his age—and considering the much greater propriety with which she might have applied to him through me, actually under the roof with him, she did a most obtrusive and inconvenente thing, and one that made me heartily ashamed. To this minute Ld. C: either really believes or affects to believe that he had a begging letter from a G.daughter of Dr Burney whom I am a little shy of acknowledging, and dislike to talk about.—Of course, she has never taken any notice of my impudent persiflage, and thereby has only realized my anticipations.—<When> I wish that roomy head of hers would give admission to a little bit of judgment.—

I am lame of my left hand, and have worn it in a sling for nearly ten weeks, from the obstinate effects of a long-neglected sprain.—Mr R. Keate,[14] to whom I have written, has directed me how to manage it. The inflamation is deep-seated, and I expect little good from any of his prescriptions except leeches, poultices, rest, time, and warm-weather. The cold kills it.—I have had the perseverance to read Sir W. Scotts Boney[15]—and hackneyed as is the subject, I was lured on from page to page, with unwearied interest and entertainment. I am longing for Bishop Heber's Journal. Did you read, in one of the Quarterly's, <a Review>, an Article relating to him, remarkably well written, and worthy in all respects of its subject.—It must be now nearly a year ago that it appeared. I wish you could get it—and there is also a more recent article, published in the very last Review—quite excellent.[16]

Now a word to your dear Mother.

Lady—Deem not so wrongfully of the truest of thy friends, as to opine, even for a moment, that she could forget thy many kindnesses, or thy long-tried affection. She sits and grieves, 'tis true, full oft, at the distance that separates hearts so well united—or rather, the frail forms that enclose those hearts: but judging by her own, she knows that when thy pen is silent, thy thoughts are not therefore estranged; and she never frets at not hearing but because she wants to know that thou art well, and all thy belongings so to boot. In sooth, we are a fragile set—Yet, the amendment of thy Clementius, and the recovery of thy Charlottina, are sweetening drops in thy cup, which must make thee very thankful.—Poor dear William Phillips'[17] is a history which, sorry as one may be for him, it is not in nature to forbear a smile at, and every creature who has written to me about it, has irresistibly mingled the ludicrous with the grave.—How glad I am, my dearest Sister, that we have at last a prospect of seeing each other in Spring!—You, who have been a Dame Parisienne must tell me lots of your adventures amongst the Parlez-vous. I shall have nothing to relate, but loads to hear, and for once I suspect, I may find it pleasanter to listen than to talk. Heaven bless you dearest Sister, prays your ever heartily affectionate S. H. Burney.

Dearest Charlotte, I must say good by here at the top, for I have left no room below: Love to Barrett, and my dear girls—and waggon loads of them to yourself.—

1. Charlotte Broome was with the Barretts at Brighton. The joint letter to SHB is missing, but Mrs. Barrett had written from 6 Burlington Street on 9 December 1827, a few weeks after their arrival, describing their efforts to "make our tiny house habitable," and pleased that "the air suits my dearest Mother so well" (CFBt to FBA, 9 Dec. [1827], Berg).

2. Annabella Crewe's aunt, Elizabeth Emma (née Crewe) Cunliffe (L. 105, n. 20). This is the first indication of the tension that would develop between Sarah Harriet and Mrs. Cunliffe over the Crewe children (see further LL. 113, 118). Childless her-

self, and later widowed, Mrs. Cunliffe was much occupied with her youngest niece: "The Annabel saves her life at least, its only cheerful endurance" was FBA's later comment (*JL*, 12: 892).

3. At the age of thirty-seven, Annabella Crewe would marry on 31 July 1851, Richard Monckton Milnes (1809–85), created 1st Baron Houghton (1863) (*GM*, NS 36 (1851), 424–25; *DNB;* Gibbs). Her elder sister Harriet would remain a spinster.

4. "(a) Vide, Tartuffe." is SHB's footnote.

5. The mother of Orgon in Molière's play, *Le Tartuffe* (1664); the ardent defender of Tartuffe, she is easily duped by his hypocritical zeal.

6. Possibly an allusion to William Cowper, *The Task* (1785), "charge / His mind with meanings that he never had" (Bk. 3, ll. 148–49). The same expression is quoted in two of SHB's novels.

7. Edward Young, *Love of Fame: The Universal Passion: in Seven Characteristical Satires* (1728), Satire 6, 188. It was quoted and applied to Pope in Johnson's life of the poet.

8. The rebellion of about fifty schoolboys, unhappy with the strict discipline at Charles Burney Jr.'s school, is described in an undated letter from one pupil to his mother (cited in *JL*, 10: 796, n. 6). After providing themselves with food, chessboards, cards, and weapons, the boys barricaded themselves in. "Then Burney came and told them to open the door but they said it was not shut to be opened. he then got a ladder & got at top of the door where he could see them all . . . till at last as the door was going to be cut open they unfastened it, when Burney rushed in. at first they hit him with their sticks but he knocked them about till at last they were quiet & Burney very generously gave them the choice of being expelled or forgiven above 40 were forgiven and 2 expelled."

9. Willoughby Crewe's father, Maj.-Gen. Richard Crewe (1749–1814), had married at Kingston, Jamaica, in 1780 Milborough, the daughter of Samuel Allpress (Burke; Ormerod, 3: 314; *GM*, 74, Pt. 1 (1814): 701).

10. Catherine (d. post 1823), the daughter of J. Harvey, had married the Rev. Willoughby Crewe in Aug. 1816, leaving at her death two sons. The eldest of these, Offley, was eight years old (Burke; *GM*, 86, Pt. 2 (1816): 176; *Alumni Oxon.*).

11. Unidentified.

12. Roger Wilbraham (1743–1829), younger brother to Anna's father, George (L. 27, n. 1). After a distinguished career at Cambridge (B.A. 4th Wrangler 1765, Fellow 1767, M.A. 1768), he was elected F.R.S. (1782), served in Parliament (1786–96), and became "well known as a patron of literature and science" (*GM*, 99, Pt. 1 (1829): 569; Burke, *LG;* Namier & Brooke; Thorne; *Alumni Cantab.;* Ormerod, 2: 138).

13. George Wilbraham (1779–1852) attended Rugby and matriculated at Trinity College, Cambridge (1796), but left without taking a degree. Fifteen years an M.P. (1826–41), he served as High Sheriff of Cheshire (1844). Twelve years Anna's senior, he had succeeded his father in 1813, and so was head of the family (Burke, *LG;* Stenton; *Alumni Cantab.; GM*, NS 37 (1852): 302–3).

14. Robert Keate, nephew and apprentice to Thomas Keate, Surgeon of Chelsea Hospital, who had died in 1821 (L. 80, n. 7; L. 19, n. 5).

15. [Sir Walter Scott's] massive *The Life of Napoleon Buonaparte* was published in 9 volumes in 1827 (Johnson, 2: 1017).

16. Reginald Heber (1783–1826), Bishop of Calcutta (1822–26) (*DNB*), whose *Narrative of a Journey through the Upper Provinces of India, from Calcutta to Bombay, 1824–25*

(1828) was treated in a long review in the *Quarterly Review* 37 (1828): 100–47; an article commemorating his life and work in the Church in India had appeared in the same periodical, 35 (1827), 445–81.

17. Sarah's nephew, John William James Phillips (1791–1832), Susan's youngest child, who joined the Navy in 1805 and rose to the rank of Lt. (1815). His active career in the Navy ended in 1818, after which he apparently sailed on merchant ships trading to the Far East, and was to die at Canton. The reference to his history is lost with the letter, but he was visiting his relatives in England in 1828, and left after August for New South Wales (*JL*, 11: 445, n. 8; MF to CFBt, 15 Aug. 1828, Barrett, Eg. 3704A, ff. 196–97v).

---

113. To Charlotte (Francis) Barrett

18 Grosvenor Street, 25 April 1828
A.L.S., Berg
Address: Mrs Barrett / 6 Burlington Street / Brighton
Postmarks: EAP / 26 / 1828

18 Grosvenor Street
April 25th 1828

Dearest Charlotte

I have been in town about a month,[1] with only part of the family however, Mr & Mrs Cunliffe, and Annabel. They came for their diversion, and brought me for advice, face to face, <with> from some good London Surgeon. I saw Mr Keate in the first instance, and the progress I made under him, not satisfying their expectations, I consented to see Mr Brodie.[2] He did not dispute that a sprain might have been the origin of the mischief: but its obstinacy, and other symptoms, he imputed to constitutional debility; advised me to take Camomile-tea and Salvolatile two or three times a day, and to use a steam-bath for my hand <for> half an hour every morning and night—and to keep it warm and quiet.—The swelling and feverish heat are now much reduced,—but the weakness and utter helplessness remain,—it will not bear even the lightest rubbing, and the stiffness is like that of wood. He has seen me twice, and bids me persevere, assuring me of eventual recovery. So, what is to be done, except to pray for patience?—He never knew any but women attacked in a similar way, and only one who never regained the use of her limb. They were all persons of delicate and nervous habits—and the melancholy exception he mentioned, was a Lady not only in bad health, but overwhelmed about the same time by domestic afflictions.—

Now Mr Keate was treating the thing as a sprain only, and recommending merely local applications, without reference to the general health.—Dr Holland[3] has also been prescribing for me, and trying to give a little tone to my flimsy inside, & with, perhaps, some little success: but after all, I have the best hopes from change of air, and fine weather—no tonic for me like what comes <up> out of Father Neptune's shop—and I look forward with some impatience to our usual removal to Ramsgate.

There, dearest,—I have given you a sickening dish of ailments, and of egotism—but I am sure you wanted to know all about me, and having now once turned my bag inside out, I will proceed to other subjects.

I admire and most warmly applaud (however I may grieve at its necessity) your present truly meritorious plan.[4] Oh my dearest Charlotte, how many there must be, who, if they could but know of such a situation, would spring mast high to seize upon it for their young people!—Be assured, my well-beloved, that being now acquainted with the plan, I shall let pass no opportunity of giving any furtherance to it I may be able. Such opportunities may however, I fear, be rare. All the creatures I see here as visitors and intimates of Mde Pernelle,[5] are, like herself, completely thoughtless, dashing women of ton. My own few acquaintances, I have discouraged from visiting me, more than ever this year, from having no private room to receive them in. We are packed here as closely as bees in a hive; at least, shall be after Wednesday, when Ld Crewe, and Harriet arrive from Cheshire, bringing with them a Niece, Mary Hesketh,[6] and a tribe of Servants—and Brook Greville[7] is also expected from Paris—and every floor will have two or three bed-rooms, and every bed-room two or three beds.—In the country I sometimes do see a rational family-sort of body or two: but here never. Day is turned into night—conversation <into> is only gossip or scandal—dress and dissipation is all there seems time to think of. To tell you the truth—the whole style of the thing makes me sick. Last night, Mde Pernelle, under pretence of giving a Child's ball for Annabel, had Two hundred and odd persons here—chalked floors, hot-house flowers, a regular supper &c, &c—And conceive her madness—In less than one fortnight, she has taken the poor little consequential, vain child, to the Opera, to two balls, besides her own, to the play, and to I know not how many morning visits, when she drives about, nominally for air and exercise. The little creature is so set up by all this, that she chimes in on all subjects, and makes herself a party in every conversation,—and would verily, I believe give her opinion in a debate on politics or mathematics!—It is melancholy to see all the prevailing foibles of a poor self-sufficient little scatter-brain thus cruelly fostered. Many months of regularity and retirement will not undo the mischief that is now working in this hot-bed of folly.

I saw with very great pleasure and interest, your Dick in James Street the other day, where I dined. There is in him an un-tricked-up look of honourable, and manly simplicity that I like indescribably. With us, he had no awkward shyness, but a mild, composed, sensible manner, the most genuine and the most satisfactory I have met with for a long time. I feel that I <shall> should grow amazingly fond of him were I to see more of him.—You are a fortunate Mother, at least, my dear Charlotte!—

I get to my Sister d'Arblay's now and then, indeed pretty often, of an evening, and I think my little talkie's do her good. Alex is in excellent looks—and dresses like a <rum> gentleman—and goes into good society, and is remarked for his clever countenance; and in favour with those he gets into conversation with.—All this, I heard, by a side wind, & from a quarter not to be distrusted.

I have had the gratification of being in the same room with Sir Walter Scott,[8] and of even being introduced to him, and hearing a little of his inartificial, unparading talk;—and I have also been in a room with Mr Cooper,[9] the Author of the Spy, & the Mohican &c. He <u>has</u> a look of genius—a meditative eye, that <seems upon> seems, as it looks upward, to be receiving inspiration from some invisible agent!—He is gentle and quiet in his manner and tone of voice, though the fine folks, who are making a lion of him for the season, pretend there is abruptness about him—he is certainly not rubbed down to their insipid smooth-shilling standard.—Adieu my most dear—love to Barrett, & your nice girls—And love the warmest to your Mumsy.—

ever affectionately
S. H. Burney.

Poor dear Fanny! I can scarcely yet persuade myself she is really gone![10]—

1. Sarah had been in London on 31 March 1828 when her half-sister d'Arblay reported, "Poor Sarah Harriet is in town, & far from prosperous! but amending. I expect her to night to tea" (*JL*, 12: 713).

2. Benjamin Collins Brodie (1783–1862), later Sergeant-Surgeon to the King (1832), created Bt. (1834), had published a treatise on diseases of the joints (1818) and would later lecture on "local nervous affections" (*DNB*).

3. Henry Holland (1788–1873), M.D. (1811), F.R.S. (1816), F.R.C.P. (1828), was an extremely fashionable practitioner who would become physician-in-ordinary to Queen Victoria (1852) and a Bt. (1853) (*DNB*).

4. Charlotte Barrett had a "new scheme" to help the family finances: "It is to take charge during the next two or three years, of a young lady. . . . She is Hettys age, and about as <u>accomplished</u> as Hetty, so, they may finish their education together. Julia and I shall do what we can—. . . Masters will do the rest" (CFBt to FBA, 9 Dec. [1827], Berg).

5. Sarah Harriet's nickname for Mrs. Cunliffe, first used in her letter of 17 February

1828 above. Her remarks here confirm the significance of her fanciful name, since the Cunliffes are the "only part of the family" now present, and at the same time, Sarah sees only the "visitors and intimates of M^{de} Pernelle, [*who*] are, like herself, completely thoughtless, dashing women of ton." Sarah's opponent in the struggle over Annabella's education is clearly the aunt and not (as in *JL*, 12: 740, n. 4) the "Swiss (or French) governess." See further, L. 118.

6. For a possible identification of Mary Hesketh, see L. 107, n. 6. The family connection to the Crewes has not been traced.

7. Lady Crewe's nephew, Brooke Greville (1798–1884), third surviving son of her brother Lt.-Col. Henry Francis Greville (1760–1816). Having taken his B.A. from Cambridge (1821), Brooke Greville was perhaps on the grand tour; he would later marry on 23 October 1856 Emilie Anne Bouchez (d. 3 Nov. 1875) (Burke, Lodge under Warwick; *Alumni Cantab.*).

8. Sir Walter Scott was in London for a seven weeks' visit from 9 April 1828 (Johnson, 2: 1049–54, 1080).

9. James Fenimore Cooper was in England for several months from February to June 1828, during which time he renewed his acquaintance with Sir Walter Scott (Robert E. Spiller, *Fenimore Cooper: Critic of His Times* (New York: Minton, Balch, 1931), 135–41).

10. Frances Burney, Esther's second daughter, who was "subject to violent attacks of pain in the stomach; attended with extreme sickness, & followed by Jaundice," had died at Bath on 28 March 1828, at the age of fifty-two ("Worcester Mem.," 84–85; *JL*, 12: 712 and n. 1).

---

114. To Charlotte (Francis) Barrett

7 Nelson's Crescent, Ramsgate, 17 [June] 1828
A.L.S., Berg

You have not surprised me, dearest Charlotte, though you have awakened in me much regret by your answer. I thought it was not likely that a scheme so very delightful to me, would take place without any lets and hindrances. I am only afraid, now, that my poor Mrs Burney should think herself tied to come to me through thick and thin, at the expence of all health and comfort. Of course, I could not bear that she should run any risk, and you must assist me, dear Charlotte, in trying to impress this fact upon her.—When I first proposed her coming to Ramsgate I had no suspicion she was going to Brighton—and I really hate having any hand in hastening her removal from it.—I need not say, how infinitely I should prefer being near you, to remaining here—But it won't do, my Charlotte—I have a house and maid upon my hands, and must abide by my bargain. If you know of any very agreeable houseless wanderer, pray send him or her to help to fill the wretched vacancies in my establishment. I wish Sarah Payne could be persuaded that there is no air would agree with her so well as that of Ramsgate. Pray urge her Mother to inforce that doctrine.

I like your Capt. Franklin mainly—and his manly & respectful commendation of my poor dear James, is charming.[1]—I am (though a little ashamed to own it) not fond, in general, of Voyages. Many women are, and I wish I were one—for the more innocent amusements we have the better. But when scientific purposes are to be answered by such voyages, I have great respect for them, and only wish I could get at their marrow, without being obliged to read about the gluttonous, dirty, lying, cruel, thieving, and brutal Savages!—To think that such creatures are really our fellow-beings, and that we might have been such as they are, but for the favour of God, is to me the most melancholy consideration in the world—I hardly dare hate them, and yet I shrink with horror from their ferociousness, and can hardly indure to think they are of my own species.—Do you know that poor little Monkeys have been seen to display qualities far better than some of these barbarous tribes of men? And I am sure that Elephants, Dogs, and even some horses, are ten times more amiable as well as more sagacious.

I did not see the cover of your letter—but the proper direction is, To The Lord Crewe, 7 Nelson's Crescent, Ramsgate.—He will be gone however on Friday or Saturday next.

Adieu dearest Charlotte—Best love to Barrett, and am ever yours

S. H. Burney.

Thanks to Henrietta for wishing me to be at Brighton. Send her with Mrs Burney (if she comes) for a little change to Ramsgate. I will take excellent care of her.

Tuesday 17th 1828.

1. Capt. John Franklin (1786–1847), Kt. (1829), the Arctic explorer, whose expeditions helped to chart the northern regions, and who was eventually credited with the discovery of the Northwest Passage (*DNB*). The account of his first exploratory voyage, *Narrative of a Journey to the Shores of the Polar Sea in the years 1819, 20, 21, and 22* (1823), became a classic, and a second account, *Narrative of a Second Expedition to the Shores of the Polar Sea, in the years 1825, 1826, and 1827*, was published in 1828. In it, he acknowledged his indebtedness to "the descriptions of Cook and Burney" (160) in navigating the Pacific coast. Charlotte may have reported a remark made by Franklin, with whom she was acquainted (CFBt to FBA, 9 Oct. [1828], Berg).

115. To Charlotte (Burney) (Francis) Broome

Crewe Hall, 22 February 1829
A.L.S., Berg
Address: Mrs Broome / <care of Henry Barrett Esq> / <6. Burlington Street> / <Marine Parade> / <Brighton> /
readdressed to: Caius College / Cambridge
and Mrs Broome / Caius College / Cambridge.
Postmarks: [*?*] FE / 25 / 1829
BRIGHTON / FE 27 / 1829
A / 28FE28 / 1829
Endorsed: Sister Sarah Harriet / Feb—1829 ans^{d}

Oh my dearest Sister! I can find no words to tell you how my heart aches for you! If I loved him so dearly, if I regret him so bitterly, how must you have loved—how must you inconsolably bewail him![1]—Let me grieve with you though at this distance;—would I were within reach of you, that we might shed our tears together.—My poor Sister! The pity I feel for you makes me almost pity myself, for it is really painful. And my dearest Charlotte, too—I can too well judge what she must be feeling, she who was so devotedly fond of him![2] May Heaven support you all—There must be your reliance, for at this moment, what is there on earth that can give you comfort!—I thank Marianne for her letter—pray give her my kind regards—

God bless, and strengthen, and enable you to acquiesce in His dispensations, prays, my most dear Sister, Your ever affectionate and sympathizing

S. H. Burney

Crewe Hall
Feb. 22^{d} 1829.

1. After a long battle with tuberculosis, Charlotte Broome's only remaining son, Clement Francis, finally succumbed to the disease, and died at Cambridge 17 February 1829 at the age of thirty-six (*JL*, 12: 729–33; *GM*, 99, Pt. 1 (1829): 649). Mrs. Broome, who had nursed him devotedly for years, had difficulty accepting his death: "Poor dearest Mama could scarcely believe he was in danger & cannot now shed tears—she is quite stunned & I pray that this dreadful loss may not have some terrible effect upon her" (CFBt to HBt, 17–18 Feb. 1829, Berg).

2. Clement's sister, Charlotte Barrett, "who is a nonpareile as a nurse . . . the only one he can bring himself to admit," was with him at the end (CBFB to FBA, [13 Feb.

1829], Barrett, Eg. 3693, f. 107). It seems the strain did tell on her; the morning after her brother's death, she wrote to her husband: "I am very ill, head & chest, & very hysterical I dont know what I shall do" (CFBt to HBt, 17–18 Feb. 1829, Berg).

116. To Charlotte (Francis) Barrett

Crewe Hall, 22 March [1829][1]
A.L.S., Berg

Crewe Hall
March 22d
1828

Dearest Charlotte, how kind of you to remember the probable anxiety I should feel to hear of you, and, as you say, to learn some of the details, however melancholy, you might be able to give me. To me they are very precious—and though sad, not gloomy. The piety of the dear sufferer, and the knowledge of his state of mind long previous to, and at his decease, consoles and sooths one.[2]—Except his ill health, there is nothing to reflect upon, connected with dear Clement, that is not pleasant—He was mirthful, affectionate, and the most exhilarating of companions. His mind had laid in a large store of information, and his conversation the last time or two I saw him, charmed me by its variety, and the great extent of observation it evinced. He called upon me one morning at Stanley Grove, and Mrs Gregor, who had been abroad not long before, got with him upon the subject of foreign towns, and <roads>, curiosities, and prospects, and customs—and they kept up the dialogue with mutual good will for above an hour—Mrs Gregor remaining quite bewitched by him, and always speaking of him afterwards with distinction and real regard.—

But, alas! my dear Charlotte, your kind Mother—how bereaved she must feel! I have heard from her, excellent soul, and am <in> lost, I will not say in admiration, but in something higher than admiration, at her touching and unparading resignation!—I could cry over the bare thought of what she must have felt, and long <u>will</u> feel.[3] Most earnestly do I hope it may be in my power ere long to become domesticated with her for some little time. I have every reason to anticipate that my residence in this family is drawing to a close. Many disagreeables have occurred within the last twelvemonths, and I think the measure will soon be full.[4] I trust I shall know in a day or two how it will all end.

Meanwhile, one circumstance is positively settled. I <shall> have declared that I will not be with Annabel during her stay in London. M[rs] James Burney is kind enough to offer me house-room for a few weeks, during which I shall turn over various little plans in my head, and if I do not come down again to Crewe Hall (which I think it most probable I shall not) I purpose, after allowing myself a brief holiday, to set up a small school, perhaps—or to try for day pupils at home—In short, whilst I have strength and spirits, to be doing something active & useful—for the dull, monotonous, and lonely home I had at Chelsea would never do for me again. But none of my schemes are ripe yet—All that I have hitherto resolved upon is, not to live in London; and, if possible, not to live alone.—

We have had dreadful colds even in this westerly part of England—At Brighton, the east winds must have been tremendous—I hope your removal to Hastings with poor dear Henrietta[5] has been of service. I have heard that some parts of that place are as sheltered and warm as any thing in Devonshire.—May be, dearest, I may have it in my power to refresh myself by taking a peep at you somewhere or other in the course of the Spring or Summer. In that hope, my own dear Charlotte, I bid you farewell with a thousand love and good wishes to Henrietta, in w[ch] Annabel cordially joins—

Yours ever affectionately S. H. Burney.

1. Sarah dated her letter 1828 apparently in error for 1829, since she refers to Clement Francis's last illness and death (which took place 17 February 1829) and to Charlotte Barrett's sojourn at Hastings (see n. 5).

2. Charlotte Barrett told of Clement's pious resignation to his fate: "in all his troubles he never murmured. & once, when I pitied him, he wrote on his paper tablet, 'Dont complain—pray, and trust.'. . . he appeared to die without much suffering. I thank God for that. and far more, for all the faithful trust he put in his Saviour & the firm humble faith I am sure he had" (CFBt to HBt, 17–18 Feb. 1829, Berg).

3. Mrs. Barrett wrote of her mother's health on 29 March 1829: "Poor dearest Mama is low & nervous, and sleeps ill, yet all these symptoms are not <u>so</u> violent as I feared they would be. She does all she can to regain tranquillity and strength." She also described her state of mind, "her resignation & submission—they are beautiful and admirable—but I must watch lest sad thoughts should prey too much on her dear mind even in consequence of the piety with which she restrains their outward expression" (CFBt to FBA, 29 Mar. [1829], Berg).

In the ensuing months, Mrs. Broome would be disturbed by "self upbraidings" that she had not done more for her son at the last. Her daughter considered these to be "causeless regrets. . . . how could she possibly have been more kind and tender and indulgent to him than she was?" (CFBt to FBA, 28–30 Jan. 1830, Berg).

4. Possibly an echo of Matthew 23:32, "Fill ye up then the measure of your fathers."

5. Charlotte Barrett had gone to Hastings in March with her daughter, Henrietta, who was beginning to show signs of a possible consumption: "her pulse is at 100—she has restless nights—no appetite, and is so pale and changée that I cannot think her safe." Her doctor advised her to go abroad to a warmer climate, but for the moment Charlotte believed: "My poor Henrietta is better. . . . She coughs much less, and is less faint and low than when I first brought her hither. . . . doubtless the change of air was a great advantage" (CFBt to FBA, 29 Mar. [1829], Berg).

117. To Charlotte (Francis) Barrett

[Crewe Hall, 24 March 1829]
A.L., Berg
Address: Mrs Barrett / 8 York Buildings / Hastings
Franked: Crewe /—Nantwich twenty second March 1829
Postmarks: Free / 24MR24 / 1829

Need I tell you how sensibly gratified and even affected I was by your report of dear Clement's kind mention of me, after we had been so very long separated? He knew how well I had loved, and how much I had enjoyed being with him—and amongst the thousand blessings that attend our loving any one, is that of exciting (generally speaking) love in return.

It is purposed here to set out for London the third of April—We hope to reach our journey's end on the fifth, which I am sorry to say will be on a Sunday. I intend going the same day to James Street.[1]

I wish any School or Pupil plan could occur to us, in which we might mutually embark, and benefit each other.[2]—

1. Mrs. Barrett's reply to this letter is missing, but on receiving it she wrote to her husband: "I have heard from Aunt Sarah. she does not like to remain with Lord Crewe's party while they are in London, therefore she is going to Mrs Burney's in James Street for 6 weeks, when they leave Crewe Hall;—she expects to arrive in Town with the family on the 5th April" (CFBt to HBt, [Apr. 1829], Berg).

2. The Barretts' financial position was worrying, precariously based as it was on property in the West Indies (CFBt to MF, 4 Jan. [pre 1829], Berg). Writing on 12 April, and expressing her concern to her husband for his "bad Jamaica news," Charlotte hopes that she can retrieve the family fortunes by taking on pupils: "I shall no doubt be able to meet with some little girls to educate & help to make out our income" (CFBt to JBt, 12 Apr. [1829], Barrett, Eg. 3702A, ff. 188–89v).

118. To Charlotte (Francis) Barrett

James Street, 6–7 April 1829
A.L.S., Berg

April 6th 1829
James Street

Your dear letter, my kind Charlotte, reached me the very morning I left Crewe Hall, about five minutes before I got into the carriage. I am much comforted to hear that Dr Batty, so skillful and experienced a physician, "does not allow that there is any danger": but I am not the less persuaded of the indispensable necessity of taking her abroad.[1] I shall, individually, be a severe loser by such a plan; since, though now a poor gentlewoman at large, I shall be as much separated from you as whilst tied by the leg amongst <by> my fine folks. But if your dear girl is to benefit by it, I will try to avoid repining. Sarah Payne[2] received me with all cordiality and affection. She is not looking very ill, but she has been a tremendous sufferer, and in a most annoying way.—I hope my being with her a little, may do her good.—You will be glad to hear that my separation from the Crewe family has been attended by no quarrel or crash. We have parted more than civilly, and are supposed to intend often to meet—and so, for a little while, we may: but there is too little real deep-seated esteem between us, to <mellow the> allow our causes of mutual complaint to mellow into permanent future friendship. Madame Pernelle is not like some, who whilst you live with them torment you by their odd tempers, but when you are divided <from them> leave so many kind recollections upon the mind that you forget whatever was amiss, and almost wonder how you could ever have been dissatisfied;—she is, on the contrary, a person whose manoeuvring, and subtlety, and love of cabal, must recur to the memory continually, and strike with even more force on reflection than at the moment when plausibly carrying on her wretched deceptive system.—But, in as few words as I can, I will tell you, that after <getting> going down to Crewe again at the end of last Spring, I was able to get Annabel once more into such right and steady ways, that I began to think I might contentedly remain with her, at least in the country; and that when she went back to London, something might be deducted from my salary to pay a day Governess for three months. I accordingly proposed this—and the offer was accepted, and the thing, I concluded, arranged. Meanwhile, the eldest Miss Crewe came of age;[3] and I was then (about three weeks since) told, that the small remaining independance the two girls derive from their almost ruined West India property was henceforward to be divided between them, and would only amount to about £250 <and> each.[4] It was therefore coolly proposed to me to retain my post at—£100 a year in lieu of the original £300![5]—After a nearly seven years assiduous performance of the duties I had undertaken, I thought this a little too uninviting—and civilly declined the obliging offer. So here I am—and probably, Madame, without chusing to say so, is well pleased that there I am no longer: but rejoices that she should have succeeded in making the thing appear my own act and deed.—

Thank you, my dearest, for interesting yourself so kindly about my future plans.[6] What you throw out concerning the Greenwich family[7] is not to be thought of a moment, and for this powerful, most powerful reason—they are relations!—Whoever I may place myself in dependence under, I trust it will never be a relation.

I purpose going to-day to see my Sister d'Arblay, & will keep this open till tomorrow, to tell you how I find her.

April 7th

I got to her between two and three,—she was just come down from her bedchamber. She does not look so ill as might have been expected: but she has certainly considerable indisposition still hanging upon her.[8] She has seen an eminent (nameless) physician, who assures her that her pulse is good, and that there is no danger in her case. It hurts her to talk, and she professed an intention to be only a hearer during my visit: but, for want of due inertia, she did talk perhaps more than she ought, and I resolutely abridged my stay.—

I feel mighty queer, and all at sixes and sevens on this sudden change of pursuits, of persons, of places, and of occupations. London, which under all circumstances, strikes me as a dingy, disagreeable abode, looks dirtier and more to be recoiled from now than it ever did before. I can hardly persuade myself to drink its water, or eat its bread, or inhale its nasty air. I long to be out of it; but for the present must thankfully avail myself of the hospitality of Sarah and her husband, & remain perforce till all my accounts and business with the Crewe family shall be concluded.

And now, my dearest Charlotte, recommending to you most earnestly to say every thing for me to your kind Mother that is most affectionate & sisterly, & offering up for you a thousand, thousand good wishes, believe me now and ever Yours truly

S. H. Burney.

1. Robert Batty (c. 1763–1849), M.D. (1797), a London obstetrician and amateur artist (*DNB*). He was "an old friend" of Mrs. Barrett's, who consulted him at Hastings about her daughter's health. "He says there is nothing (he believes,) decidedly wrong in the chest, at present" but advised her to seek a warm climate (CFBt to FBA, 29 Mar. [1829], Berg). A few days later, as Henrietta worsened (refusing food, tiring easily, and coughing continually), he would speak more strongly: "He told me today, that if she was his child he would take her abroad into the vine countries as soon as the weather gets warm & settled enough for travelling" (CFBt to HBt, [5 Apr. 1829], Berg).

2. Sarah (Burney) Payne, James's daughter; Sarah Harriet was staying "a few weeks" in the James Street house at the invitation of James's widow (L. 116). Presumably, John and Sarah Payne were still living in the family home, as they had arranged to do in 1822 (L. 96, n. 2).

3. Henrietta Crewe turned twenty-one on 30 March 1829 (Lodge).

4. Within a few weeks, the girls' financial position may have been further affected by the death of Lord Crewe (28 April 1829). As Sarah's nephew would remark, "the death of the good old Peer has broken up all that Establishment" (Lodge; CPB to Robert Finch, 13 Nov. 1829, Bodleian MS. Finch, d. 3, ff. 346–48v).

5. Sarah Harriet's account at Coutts does not clearly confirm a salary of £300 paid over seven years (a total of £2,100) (L. 104, n. 1; L. 105, n. 27). From the time of her appointment, the sums which are credited to her in large round amounts, or which are used to increase her stock holdings, would amount to no more than £952. A deposit of £600 made on 15 April 1829, used immediately to buy a £500 Exchange Bill, may represent a form of severance pay or a settling of accounts.

At the end of her seven-year sojourn with the Crewes, Sarah's financial position shows moderate but not marked improvement. Having sold £50 of her previously held stock, she owned £1,991.19s., to which she added £628.5.11 in Consols and the £500 Exchange Bill. From these investments, she could expect an annual yield of approximately £100, an increase of £20 from her former income.

6. Charlotte Barrett passed on this news to her family: "Aunt Sarah has left the Crewes & is now in James Street. She left them all in friendship, but she has left them. I had a letter from her yesterday. Miss Crewe is of age—& their W. India property is dwindled almost to nothing" (CFBt to JBt, 12 Apr. [1829], Barrett, Eg. 3702A, ff. 188–89v).

7. Charlotte seems to have suggested some arrangement with Charles Parr Burney, who succeeded his father at the lucrative Greenwich school (1813–33) and lived at Croom's Hill, Greenwich (*JL*, 7: 27, n. 11, 88, n. 1; 12: 890, n. 1).

8. Mme d'Arblay had suffered in February from "accumulated Colds & a Cough" which confined her to her bedroom; in March she developed "a feverish languor & lassitude" for which she was finally persuaded to seek medical advice (*JL*, 12: 729–30, 732–34).

119. To Charlotte (Burney) (Francis) Broome

26 James Street, [25] June 1829[1]
A.L.S., Berg
Address: Mrs Broome / 11 Burlington Street / Brighton
Postmarks: F JU / 25 / 1829
Endorsed: Sister Sarah Harriet / June 1829 / ansd

Thursday 26th June 1829
26 James Street

My dearest Sister

I will venture to say, that I am not undeserving of the kind, the very kind mark of regard you have shewn me. It has pleased and touched me—and I accept it with the most sincere gratitude. Send me, my dearest, our Clement's pencils, at least if their case is marked H, for then they will fit my silver case. If not, I shall be most thankful for the inkstand.[2] Indeed, any thing that has been his, will be welcome to me, and always valued—for his memory will be always dear to me, and your deeply-felt and enduring grief (knowing both you and him so thoroughly) can never excite my surprise, much as I may lament it. That you should not, dearest sister, immediately after the first stunning blow, and whilst obliged to exert yourself on matters of business, have felt quite so distinctly the desolation of heart you now suffer, I can well understand. There are some sorrows over which Time scarcely seems to have its accustomed effect: but even then, there is one solemn thought, <granted> suggested I doubt not, by a merciful Providence, that affords some balm to the poor mourner—"I shall go to him, though he cannot return to me,"[3] are words which no afflicted Mother can repeat to herself unmoved—and they are Scriptural words, and such as she cannot mistrust. How much do they comprise both of individual and general comfort!—Who can read them without considering them as an inspired promise of a future state—of one, too, in which dear friends will again recognize each other, and be re-united?—

There is a probability (life and health permitting) that I may go abroad early in September with my kind & faithful friends) the Misses Wilbraham. They are now in England after a four years residence on the Continent, and purpose returning thither as I said, early in the Autumn. Pray tell Henrietta that they enquired most kindly after her, and really spoke of her as if they quite loved her. They say she was so good to their little nieces;[4] and these nieces they doat upon. I wish we could all meet abroad—but that, I fear is unlikely, as the Wilbrahams will winter in Italy, and Charlotte will probably go no further than the South of France.[5]

I drank tea lately with our dear Sister d'Arblay, who was looking quite herself again, and had been that morning to see one of her Princesses.[6] Alex was to set off the next morning for Cambridge. He had a violent cold, which the harum-scarum fellow had attempted to bully away by taking, the night before, four Analeptic pills—and then going about the house the next day, into drafts & all sorts of mischief, as if he had only taken powder of post.[7] My poor Sister was sadly annoyed by these mad proceedings: but, I am happy to say, unnecessarily, for I have seen him since, and he seemed much as usual.

Sarah Payne does nothing flagrant—but she does not know how to be prudent though she means it, and is perpetually over-doing things, and bringing on returns of indisposition by want of judgment, and want of moderation. Half the world suffers from much the same cause; for nothing seems so difficult to hit as the blessed Golden-mean.

I do not wish that just at present, my dearest, any thing should be said respecting my projected Tour.[8] The Wilbrahams, for some reason best known to themselves requested me to speak about it as little as possible—so, I have only written about it to Bath & to Brighton![9]—

And now dearest Sister, adieu—and may God bless & uphold you—

M[rs] Burney has had a dreadful cough & cold in addition to her other ailments, but is a little better again.

Your most affectionate sister

S. H. Burney

I hardly dare touch upon the subject of my darling Charlotte—but she has few friends who have felt more deeply and sincerely for her than I have!—I grieve at the account you give of poor dear Minette's[10] sufferings, and continued indisposition. May she soon be restored to health, & her parents to comfort!—Adieu.

1. SHB's date of "Thursday 26th June" appears to be an error; Thursday was the twenty-fifth of June in 1829, the date of the postmark.

2. It seems that Charlotte Broome had proposed a keepsake of Sarah's nephew, Clement Francis, who had died in February 1829 (see L. 115). She probably did send the pencil case to Sarah, as the inkstand was later offered to Robert Southey, who composed the epitaph (*JL*, 12: 743, n. 5).

3. "But now he is dead, wherefore should I fast? can I bring him back again? I shall go to him, but he shall not return to me" (2 Samuel 12:23).

4. Probably the daughters of their brother, Capt. William Wilbraham (L. 80, n. 3),

who had married 16 January 1817 Julia Fanny (d. 23 June 1836), youngest daughter of Lewis Montolieu. William had died at age forty-three on 29 November 1824, leaving behind him a son and three daughters: Julia, Emily, and Louisa. William's widow had married a second time on 8 July 1826 a veteran of the Peninsular War, Maj.-Gen. Sir Henry Frederick Bouverie (1783–1853), K.C.B. (1815), later Lt.-Gen. (1838), and Governor of Malta (1836–43) (Burke, *LG;* Marshall, *Suppl.* Pt. 1, 432; *GM*, 96, Pt. 2 (1826): 77; NS 6 (1836): 222; NS 39 (1853): 92–93).

5. On the advice of her physician, Charlotte Barrett was taking her consumptive daughter Henrietta abroad to a warmer climate (L. 118, n. 1). She left Brighton with Julia and Hetty on 30 June 1829 for Boulogne, where they would remain a month "to take the hot sea Baths, & after that, proceed to Fontainebleau to live upon grapes, till she adjourns to a warm winter residence" (CFBt to FBA, 7 July [1829], Berg). They were at Nice by October 16, and a month later at Pisa, Italy, where they would spend the winter (CBFB to CFBt, 5 Dec. 1829, Barrett, Eg. 3700A, ff. 108–9v; CFBt to FBA, 28–30 Jan. 1830, Berg).

6. For Mme d'Arblay's continued association with the royal family after the resignation of her position as Second Keeper of the Robes, see *HFB*, 420; *JL*, passim.

7. "Analeptic pills" were a restorative, while "powder of post" was a neutral medicine (*OED*).

8. All of this paragraph, and part of the second above referring to SHB's plans for a continental Tour, have been scored through lightly, as if to suppress what should not be repeated.

9. Esther Burney and her three surviving daughters lived at Bath; SHB was addressing Charlotte Broome at Brighton, where the Barretts also lived.

10. Frances Raper's daughter, Catherine Minette, twenty-one years old.

120. To Robert Finch

[Rome],[1] 28 November [1829]
A.L.S., Bodleian, MS. Finch, d. 3, ff. 349–51v
Address: Rob[t] Finch, Esq[r] / Palazzo di Prussia
Endorsed: Rec[d] Nov[r] 28th 1829. Ans[d] 30[o] / Burney

Dear Sir[2]

I know not how to thank you sufficiently for so cordial a welcome. It will give me infinite pleasure, when your health permits it,[3] to express my gratitude in person: but I entreat M[rs] Finch[4] will make no effort on my account that might be prejudicial to her—particularly, as I hope to remain in Rome some time.—I have taken to-day a most interesting round with M[r] Robinson,[5] who was so good as to dedicate a whole morning to shewing me some of the most celebrated amongst the many celebrated remains of this venerable city—and, to-night I am enjoying the whole treat over again with maps and books.—

I shall be very happy to make acquaintance with Mr Mayer,[6] and hope to hear from him a more favourable account of yours & Mrs Finch's health[7]—

I am, dear Sir,
Your greatly obliged
and obedient Servant
S. H. Burney.

Novr 28th

Perhaps Mr Mayer may be allowed to encourage me to trouble you with a short visit?

1. This is the first surviving letter of Sarah Harriet's, following her journey from England to Italy by vetturino (described below L. 177). She probably left London soon after 22 July 1829, when she withdrew £250.15.6 from Coutts; she had arrived in Rome by 25 November (HCR, 25 Nov. 1829, Travel Journals).

2. Robert Finch (1783–1830), an antiquary of Balliol College, Oxford, B.A. (1805), M.A. (1809). He held some minor posts in the church and acted as a tutor until his father's death in 1810 freed him from the necessity of employment. He went abroad in 1814 and lived chiefly at Florence and Rome after 1820. Characterized by a strange "infirmity . . . of braggadocio lyeing," he had conferred a fictitious military title on himself and cut a somewhat ludicrous figure (*DNB;* Elizabeth Nitchie, *The Reverend Colonel Finch* (New York: Columbia University Press, 1940), 61–62 and passim; *GM,* 100, Pt. 2 (1830): 567–68; *The Letters of Mary Wollstonecraft Shelley*, ed. Betty T. Bennett, vol. 1 (Baltimore: Johns Hopkins University Press, 1980), 94–95).

Not only did he boast an intimacy with SHB's father (HCR, cited in Nitchie, 4), Robert Finch was also friend to her nephew, Charles Parr Burney, who had provided her with a letter of introduction: "An Aunt of mine . . . is at Lausanne on her way to the eternal City. She is no beauty,—but most agreeable; full of talent,—& by my orders, will find her way to you & your's:—when she has found it—she will make it good" (CPB to Robert Finch, 13 Nov. 1829, Bodleian, MS. Finch, d. 3, ff. 346–48v).

Throughout her stay in Rome, Sarah Harriet would benefit from Robert Finch's liberal hospitality (see below passim). His diary for 1829 shows that he wrote to her on 28 November 1829 and received her reply the same day. He wrote again on the thirtieth and she called on him the next day, 1 December (Finch, 28 Nov.–1 Dec. 1829, Diaries).

3. Mr. Finch was somewhat of an invalid all his life and looked much older than his years (Nitchie, 7).

4. Maria (d. 11 Mar. 1839), the eldest daughter of Frederick Thomson of Kensington, had married Robert Finch in November 1820 at Florence (Nitchie, 59; *GM,* NS 11 (1839): 444).

5. Henry Crabb Robinson (1775–1867), a lawyer, journalist and diarist who culti-

vated the friendship of literary men, including Wordsworth, Coleridge, Lamb and Southey (*DNB; GM*, 4th ser. 3 (1867): 533–35). Robinson's travel journal notes his meeting with Miss Burney in Rome on November 25 (see L. 121, n. 2) and their frequent encounters thereafter; during the four months they both spent in the city, he was often seeing her daily. On 28 November 1829, he took Sarah Harriet to see the church of S. Maria Maggiore: "And by the Coloseum thro' the Forum back losing my way & so seeing the Pantheon. It was her first visit to these objects. And I had great pleasure in observing her enjoyment of them" (HCR, 28 Nov. 1829, Travel Journals).

6. Henry (or "Enrico") Mayer (b. c. 1806), a German boy whom Mr. Finch had met in 1819 and in whom he took a paternal interest. In 1827 Finch rewrote his will, making provision for his protégé, whom he virtually adopted and who came to live with him as his secretary after 1828. He was later to have a distinguished career in Italy as a man of letters (Nitchie, 49–50; E. R. P. Vincent, "Robert Finch and Enrico Mayer," *Modern Language Review* 29 (1934): 150–55).

7. On 28 November 1829, Henry Crabb Robinson took a letter (presumably this one) from S. H. Burney to the Finches, "but the family were all ill." He would accompany her to the Finches on 1 December (n. 1), and would also enjoy the family's hospitality during his stay in Rome (HCR, 28 Nov., 1, 6 Dec. 1829 and passim, Travel Journals; Finch, Nov. 1829–Mar. 1830, Diaries, passim).

---

121. To [William] Ayrton[1]

Rome, 30 November 1829
A.L.S., Ayrton, BL Add. MS. 52339, f. 18–v
Endorsed: From Miss S. Burney, / daughter of Dr Burney, Mus.D.

For Mr Ayrton. Rome. Novr 30th 1829.

I have the happiness to tell you that I am, my dear Sir, under the same roof with your kind and excellent friend, Mr Robinson, who has honoured your letter of introduction in the most cordial manner possible. I hardly deserved that he should, for I was stupid enough when I saw him at Florence not to recollect that the name of one of your friends was Robinson; and having put my two or three letters for Rome carefully by till I should reach that place, I never detected my omission till the day I arrived here.[2]—He has done, and is doing every hour, all the friendly things in his power, and I deem myself truly fortunate to have made such an acquaintance.[3] Sir Rufane Donkin[4] called this morning, and appeared to me an agreeable, off-hand, animated man. He came a second time, after I was out, with some tall young Signore Inglese, as the man of the house told me, but left no message. I am curious to know who the Inglese

Bust of Henry Crabb Robinson, executed by Ewing in Rome c. 1831. (By permission Dr. Williams's Library, London.)

is.—I have had a most prosperous journey, & met with good & kind souls every where. Rome would be perfect had it but an Opera. Instead, there is a mortal deal of evening visiting. My best regards & good wishes to Mrs Ayrton.[5] Adieu Adieu—yours gratefully. S. H. B.

1. William Ayrton, the music critic, a friend of James Burney (L. 25, nn. 5, 6).

2. William Ayrton had apparently given SHB a letter of introduction to Henry Crabb Robinson, an intimate friend whom he had known since 1810. Robinson gives a similar account of his meeting with Miss Burney:

> When I passed through Florence I was told by a stranger that he had been travelling with Miss Burney, a younger sister of Madame d'Arblay: he gave a promis-

ing account of her, and I begged him to introduce me. On my telling her of being well acquainted with her brother, the admiral, my vanity was a little hurt by finding that she had never heard of me. . . . I said we should be sure to meet there [*at Rome*], and offered her my services when we should meet again, which she accepted at once. I had not forgotten her, when to-day on coming home, I found upon my table a letter from Ayrton to me, introducing Miss Burney. 'Who brought this?' said I to our landlord. 'The lady.'—'What lady?'—'The lady who is occupying the rooms below.'—'Is she at home?'—'Yes.' I went down, and was received by her with a hearty laugh. She told me that, bringing many letters from England, she had separated them into bundles, and not opened those addressed to Rome until now. Our irregular introduction to each other was now legalized, and we became well acquainted, as will appear hereafter. Our acquaintance ripened into friendship, which did not end but with her life. She was a very amiable person, of whom I think with great respect. (HCR, *Reminiscences,* 1: 299–300; 2: 452–53)

The travelers were both staying at 66 Piazza di Spagna, which Sarah Harriet found unsatisfactory for the fleas, dirt, and inflated rent; she would move after the first month (on 24 Dec. 1829) to 31 Via Condotta (LL. 122, 139; HCR, 24 Dec. 1829, Travel Journals).

3. Robinson explained that:

She at once confessed that she was obliged to be economical, and I made an arrangement for her which reduced her expenses considerably. I had before this time found that the German artists dined at a respectable, but cheap restaurant in the Corso, and I occasionally saw ladies there—Italian, not English. There were several rooms, one of them small, with a single table, which our party could nearly fill. This I frequently engaged, and I introduced Miss Burney to our party. She became our *pet,* and generally dined with us. When I was engaged elsewhere, there were several proud to take her. (HCR, *Reminiscences,* 2: 453–54)

Robinson's Travel Journals bear ample testimony to the attentions he showed Miss Burney—accompanying her to the sights, theaters, and cafés of Rome, joining her on walks, visiting her, and introducing her to several of his acquaintances.

4. Lt.-Gen. (later Gen.) Sir Rufane Shaw Donkin (1773–1841), K.C.B. (1818), G.C.H. (1825), who had retired from active service and followed literary pursuits (*DNB; GM,* NS 16 (1841): 318–19; Burke, *DLG*). His civility to Sarah Harriet may have owed something to her family's literary reputation; according to Crabb Robinson, he "made peculiar enquiries . . . abo[t] Miss B: whether or not she was an authoress" (HCR, 27 Nov., 11 Dec. 1829, Travel Journals).

5. Marianne (née Arnold) Ayrton (L. 78, n. 5).

122. To Anna Wilbraham

Rome, 11 December 1829
A.L.S., Berg
Address: Miss Anna Wilbraham / Poste Restante / Fiorenza

My dear Anna

Very bad weather—very atrocious smells—very inevitable mud—very gluttinous fleas—very inhuman pavement for walkers—very slovenly lodging-house people—very imposing shop-keepers—very good eating and drinking—very bad supply, or rather, no supply, of books—Such are a few of the modern characteristics of illustrious Rome. But, with all its faults, I love it still.[1] I have seen an immensity, for I have always three, often four, male escorts,[2] and I put my gentility in my pocket (where, by the way, it is not of such magnitude as to be much incumbrance) and away I go (I wish I could also put my nose in my pocket) and see, either ruins, or villas, or Churches, or Galleries, till I have not an eye to look out of, or a foot to stand upon! Should you desire to know where I have been, I am sure I could not tell you without having recourse to my journal. I have only a general impression of having unmurmuringly tramped through more nastiness, and seen more perfection than in my wildest moments of enthusiastic expectation, I had ventured to anticipate!—And still—I seem to have seen nothing, for even yet, I have not been to the Vatican—and but a small portion of the fine things at the Capitol—and not a third of the Churches—and none of the Thermae.[3] But the thing is, we all have a fancy for going to some of the places again and again—and so, while we are re-admiring what we have already beheld, we cannot, somehow, be looking at new things too![4]—I have heard yet but one little bit of goodish music—and that was in a side Chapel at admirable St. Peters. What a building is that! How satisfactory, how complete, how irreproachable in all its parts! I verily believe that if I heard any one pick a hole in its coat, tho' ever so small, I should wish for the strength of Samson to knock him down. It would really give me pain.

Who do you think I dined with a day or two ago? Mrs Morier.[5] She is here with him, and her boy, & his nurse, and her Maid, &c—And they have a house with a delightful view—and he is in great request—and altogether, they seem comfortable, & are pleasant to see. And I have a M^r^ & Mrs Finch to my back, living in the Palazzo di Prussia,[6] on Monte Cavallo—and a Mr Boddington & his daughter Mrs Webster[7]—and sundry others, all very civil—but my male escorts, Sir Wm Fletcher,[8] Mr Robinson, (in the same house with me) and Dr Harwood,[9] are worth a thousand dinner-giving, and smart cap-requiring folks.—My health, I am most thankful of heart for it, has been faultless. I can laugh at all minor difficulties!—

Adieu my dearest Anna—I enter into no details with you, who are so much more of a Roman than I am—I only must beg leave to say that poor dear Raffaello's Fornerina[10] gives me no pleasure to look at, except from her being finely painted—And that one of the things I have beheld with most admiration is the Maddelena, detta delle Radici, of Guido[11] in the Palazzo Sciarra, and a St. John the Baptist about to drink out of a shell, by Guercino, in the Palazzo Doria. Do you remember them? And Guercino's Prodigal Son, in the same collection?[12] How exquisite!

My best love to your Sisters. When shall we four meet again?[13] Thank Mrs Gregor for her kind letter when you see her—and believe me ever, dear Anna yours most affectionately

S. H. Burney

Decr 11th 1829
66 Piazza di Spagna.

1. Possibly an allusion to William Cowper's *The Task* (1785): "England, with all thy faults, I love thee still—/ My Country!" (Bk. 2, ll. 206–7).

2. For the usual party which dined together, friends of Henry Crabb Robinson, see below.

3. On 7 December 1829, Robinson describes visiting the museum on the Capitol with "Miss Burney &c": "The most noticeable part is the gallery of busts, arranged in classes. That of the philosophers afforded a trial of skill to Miss Burney and myself in guessing." Two days later, "our usual party" went to see the Barberini Palace (HCR, 7, 9 Dec. 1829, Travel Journals; *Reminiscences*, 2: 456). Several more sightseeing expeditions would be made before the wet weather set in.

4. On 24 February 1830, Crabb Robinson would take Miss Burney on "a walk among the Roman antiquities that she had yet to see," which included the Temple of Vesta, the Arch of Janus, and the Theater of Marcellus (HCR, 24 Feb. 1830, Travel Journals).

5. Lady Crewe's niece, Harriet (d. 11 May 1858), the eldest daughter of Capt. William Fulke Greville, R.N. (1751–1837), had married 15 June 1820 James Justinian Morier (c. 1780–1849), diplomat, traveler, and novelist. They had one son, Greville, aged five (Burke under Warwick; *DNB; Alumni Oxon.* under Morier; *GM,* 90, Pt. 1 (1820): 636; NS 7 (1837): 220; 3rd ser. 4 (1858): 686). Charlotte Barrett remarked that Mrs. Morier was Aunt Sarah's "chief crony" at Rome (CFBt to FBA, 28–30 Jan. 1830, Berg).

6. Since August 1829 the Finches had resided in the Palazzo del Re di Prussia through an arrangement with the Prussian envoy to the Vatican (Nitchie, 61–62). Robinson would attend the first "large party" held at Mr. Finch's new house on 12 February 1830 (HCR, 12 Feb. 1830, Travel Journals).

7. Samuel Boddington (1766–1843), a West India merchant and director of the South Sea Company, an M.P. in 1807. He had at first opposed the marriage of his only daughter, Grace (c. 1797–1866), on 23 October 1824 to Maj. Henry Vassal Webster (c. 1793–1847), Lt.-Col. (1831), Kt. (1843). A friend of Mr. Finch, Maj. Webster was named as a trustee in his will; H. C. Robinson mentions dining with Mr. Boddington and the Websters on 18 December 1829 (Thorne; Burke; *Army List* (1817–29); *GM*, NS 28 (1847): 93; 4th ser. 1 (1866): 760; Shaw, 2: 345; HCR, 4 May 1839, Diaries; 18 Dec. 1829, Travel Journals).

8. Possibly William Alexander Fletcher of Londonderry, created an Irish K.B. on 9 September 1811 (Shaw, 2: 310). This may be the "Irish Baronet[s]" described as one of SHB's acquaintances at Rome (CFBt to FBA, 28–30 Jan. 1830, Berg). SHB shared accommodation with him at both Rome addresses, and he figures frequently in Robinson's journal as part of "our usual party" until his departure on 26 January 1830 for Naples (L. 139; HCR, 25 Nov., 9, 12 Dec. 1829, 26 Jan. 1830 and passim, Travel Journals).

9. Identified in Robinson's diary as an M.D. of Sheffield, Dr. Harwood may be the English medical student, Henry Harwood, who took his degree in medicine from Edinburgh in 1828, and is probably the Dr. Harwood of the Sheffield Dispensary listed in the *Medical Almanac* in the 1840s. He appears as one of the "usual party" of friends in Rome until 26 January 1830 when he leaves with Sir William Fletcher for Naples. However, Robinson is soon offended by the "lateness & shortness" of a letter from him and later grumbles at a "not very welcome call" from Dr. Harwood in London (HCR, 4 Nov., 9 Dec. 1829, 26 Jan., 7 Mar. 1830 and passim, Travel Journals; 24 Feb. 1836, Diaries; *List of Graduates . . . Edinburgh*).

10. *Portrait of a Young Woman* (c. 1518–19), known as the "Fornarina," was traditionally attributed to Raphaël (1483–1520) and said to depict his mistress. The identity of both the subject and the artist have been disputed (Jean-Pierre Cuzin, *Raphaël* (Fribourg, Switzerland: Office du Livre, 1983), 233–36). Crabb Robinson went to see the famous painting on 9 December 1829 but found that "in spight of my predilection for everything of Raphael—this picture was offensive to me" (HCR, 9 Dec. 1829, Travel Journals).

11. *The Magdalen* (1631–32) of Guido Reni (1575–1642) was at that time (between 1812 and 1891–92) in the Sciarra collection, which Sarah would visit again with Crabb Robinson and "our party" on 29 December 1829. Robinson explained how the full-length portrait of Mary Magdalen was called the "Maddalena delle radici from the radishes lying near her" (Pepper, 267; HCR, 29 Dec. 1829, Travel Journals).

12. Among several paintings by Giovanni Francesco Barbieri, "Il Guercino" (1591–1666), in the Palazzo Doria are his *Return of the Prodigal Son* and *St. John the Baptist in the Desert* (1652) (see Eduard A. Safarik and Giorgio Torselli, *La Galleria Doria Pamphilj a Roma* (Roma: Fratelli Palombi, 1982), 124–25).

13. "When shall we three meet again," Shakespeare, *Macbeth*, I, i, 1.

123. To Maria & Robert Finch

[Rome, 18 December 1829][1]
A.L., Bodleian, MS. Finch, d. 3, ff. 64–65v
Address: Mrs Finch
Endorsed: Rec^d^. Decr 19° 1829. / Burney.

Miss Burney presents her best compliments to M^r^ & Mrs Finch, and will have great pleasure in accepting their obliging invitation for the 27th

Miss Burney has many apologies to make for deferring so long to call again upon M^r^ & Mrs Finch—but the skies "are more in fault than she."[2]—

Friday Morn^g^

1. Although endorsed 19 December 1829, the letter was written on "Friday Morn^g^," which actually fell on the eighteenth that year. Robert Finch's diary correctly notes the date on which this note was received (Finch, 18 Dec. 1829, Diaries).

2. Possibly a misquotation of the lines from Shakespeare's *Cymbeline*, V, vi, 63–64: "Mine eyes / Were not in fault, for she was beautiful."

124. To Maria & Robert Finch

[Rome], 9 [January 1830][1]
A.L., Bodleian, MS. Finch, d. 3, ff. 354–55v
Address: Mrs Finch / Palazzo Cambiaso / Monte Cavallo
Endorsed: Rec^d^ Jany 9° 1830. / Burney.

Saturday 9th

Miss Burney presents her best compliments to M^r^ & Mrs Finch, and is extremely sorry that she is pre-engaged for Jany 14th

1. Robert Finch wrote to Sarah Harriet Burney on 8 and 9 January 1830, perhaps inviting her in one of these notes for the fourteenth. Although endorsed 9 January, her letter is listed with five others on 10 January in his diary, which shows frequent contact with her throughout the month. SHB called on the Finches on 2 and 7 January, took tea with them on the twenty-second and dined (in company with Henry Crabb Robinson) on the twenty-fourth; in addition, Robert Finch heard from her on 5 January and wrote to her on the twenty-eighth (Finch, 1–28 Jan. 1830, Diaries).

---

125. To Henry Crabb Robinson

Florence, 19 March [1830]
A.L.S., Dr. Williams'
Published: Morley
Address: Al Coltissimo Signor / Il Signor E. C. Robinson / Signor Inglese / Ferma in Posta / Napoli
return address: Direct a la Signora / Sig[ra] S. E. Burney / Poste Restante / Firenze
Postmarks: FIRENZE
NAP 1830 / 25 MAR
Endorsed: 19 March 1830 / Miss Burney. / Miss B: was the / younger Sister of / Madame d'Arblay
The first leaf has torn and frayed, evidently since Morley's transcription of 1941, which is used to confirm conjectural readings.

Florence, Friday 19th
March.

My kind and dear M[r] Robinson

It will be pleasant to you if I begin my letter by telling you that my poor invalid niece is somewhat better. I have not yet heard directly from her Mother since I arrived at Florence: but I have seen a letter from Pisa in which the Barretts are mentioned, and the dear girl is stated to be amending.[1] This was received the day before yesterday. I am almost certain there will be a letter for me at the Post to-day, but I would not wait for its reception to begin a little chat with you.—The journey from Rome was uneventful,[2] but sociable and good humoured. We had the most favourable weather possible; plenty of room, a very civil Vetturino, and much better accommodations at the Inns than on the Siena Road I had been induced to expect. I could have travelled on very contentedly with the Doctor and Madam—they rather grew upon me—but their demoiselle was a cheat—she appeared for the first day, or half day, rational and pleasing—but afterwards betrayed herself to be vapid, and empty-headed, and a spoilt-child—and she annoyed me by the most insufferable tittering laughs, shrill and causeless, that I ever remember. I was glad to get quit of her, though her name is made classical by W. Scott—She is a descendant of his Catherine Seton, and herself a Catherine Seton.[3]

We all put up on arriving at Featherstone's Hotel d'Europe, where the Kirklands[4] still remain. But they leave Florence tomorrow, and go as far as Pisa or Leghorn with Miss Seton and her brother. They then part, the Setons to cross the Simplon, the Kirklands to go by Genoa to Paris. I am staying with my friends the Wilbrahams, till I hear from Mrs Barrett.[5] Florence is in great beauty, and I think looks more like what Florence ought to be than when I saw it before. Yet the season is extraordinarily backward: but the sky is blue, and the sun is bright, and there are indications of approaching foliage which I hope will in due time keep their sign of promise.—Now tell me about yourself and Co.—Had you a pleasant journey? Did you set out the day you had appointed? Were you comfortable at your resting places? Were you robbed, or murdered, or poisoned by Mal-aria on the Pontine Marshes? Is Naples gay and lovely, and noisy and dirty as represented?[6] Have you likeable lodgings?[7]—And what have you gone out for to see?[8]—I want to hear all how and about it.—By the way, I forgot to tell you that we spent half a day at Siena, and visited the Cathedral, and Baptistry, and the great fountain—and, if it had not been for Roman remembrances, still so fresh in <ones> our memory, such sights would have been very much more satisfactory.—

Your young companions[9] I trust, have comported themselves like good boys, and are still held worthy to be well thumped about, and well laughed at—and do not lose their talent of making toast well, nor their zeal for sight-seeing, nor any other of their recommendable qualities. Remember me to them in the most friendly, grateful, and Aunt-like manner. I always look upon sociable and good-humoured young men as Nephews,—and thereby am paying a compliment I think to my real Nephews.

Have you seen any thing of the loving Dr Harwood, or his Sir William?[10]—

Remember if you come to Florence that I may be heard of till the month of May at Casa Pepe, Via Pepe, the residence of the Misses Wilbraham, who from thence mean to establish themselves in some Villa a few miles out of Florence for the Summer—such residences being very bearable in this part of Italy even in hot weather.

Adieu my dear friend. May all health, and spirits, and enjoyment of what you are seeing attend you. Write soon, and believe me ever most truly yours

S. H. Burney.

1. Charlotte Barrett was with her two daughters at Pisa (L. 119, n. 5), where in January Henrietta was suffering from a "pain in her side and quickness of pulse. . . . She grows thinner & weaker—and is so susceptible of cold that she has never quitted the house without increasing her cough, all through the winter." Her mother hoped that warmer weather and a more aggressive treatment prescribed by her physician might restore her daughter (CFBt to FBA, 28–30 Jan. 1830, Berg).

In the spring, however, the invalid relapsed, with "such heat in the chest & oppression of the breath & pain" that she was obliged to be bled. She recovered sufficiently to take a brief airing on a pony, which renewed hopes of her improvement (CFBt to HBt, 23–30 Apr. [1830], Berg).

Robinson had noted in his diary on 2 March that Miss Burney was "out of spirits hav[g] sad tidings abo[t] her great niece Miss Barrett at Pisa" (HCR, 2 Mar. 1830, Travel Journals), which may explain SHB's present assurances.

2. Sarah Harriet left Rome on 10 March 1830 for Florence; H. C. Robinson noted in his diary on the eve of her departure that "Miss B: is a person I feel a regard for. And with whom I have no doubt I shall continue to be acquainted." The next day he saw her off on her journey and commented: "Miss B: I hope to see again" (HCR, 9, 10 Mar. 1830, Travel Journals).

3. In Sir Walter Scott's novel, *The Abbot* (1820), Catherine Seyton is the daughter of George (1531–86), 5th Lord Seton (1549), a faithful servant to Queen Mary. The main branch of the family had died out, and the identity of SHB's travel companion is unknown (*Scots Peerage*).

4. The Kirklands, who left Rome with Sarah Harriet (HCR, 10 Mar. 1830, Travel Journals) have not been further traced.

5. Charlotte Barrett wrote that her aunt Sarah "gives me hopes that she will pass the summer at whatever place <u>we</u> select, and her society will be a great comfort to us all. I am advised to carry Hetty during the Summer to the Baths of Lucca, only 30 miles from Pisa—they tell me that Lucca is a cool & healthy residence—we have taken our apartment here till May—but <u>after</u> the beginning of May Pisa is said to become insupportable from the heat" (CFBt to FBA, 28–30 Jan. 1830, Berg).

6. Henry Crabb Robinson set out from Rome on 13 March 1830: "Our days ride was, as the whole journey was, rendered delightful by the very best of weather." On the second day of the journey, he passed by the Pontine Marshes which "emit no vapour at this season—And they afford fine colours for the painter." On the third day, he was faced with the "glorious view of the city & bay" of Naples, but suspected that his first enthusiastic impression of the city would be the best (HCR, 13–15 Mar. 1830, Travel Journals).

7. Robinson did like his Neapolitan lodgings, which he took on 17 March: "I have a terrace walk which gives me a view of the whole bay. I see Vesuvius without lifting my head from my pillow And am awakened by the rays of the [*sun*] . . . and the rest of the day my terrace is in shade!!!" (HCR to Robert Finch, 23 Mar. 1830, Bodleian, MS. Finch, d. 14, ff. 171–72v).

8. Matthew 11:8.

During his three weeks in Naples, Robinson would make several sightseeing excursions in the city and its environs, e.g., to Pompeii, Amalfi, Herculaneum, Sorrento, and Capri (HCR, 15 Mar.–6 Apr. 1830, Travel Journals). For an account of some of his experiences, see HCR, *Reminiscences*, 2: 461–65.

9. Henry Crabb Robinson was in Naples with three young friends, Mr. Richmond, Mr. Westphal, and Mr. Smith, who were often joined by another acquaintance, Mr. von Sacken, making a party of five (HCR, 13 Mar.–6 Apr. 1830, Travel Journals).

10. Dr. Harwood and Sir William Fletcher had left Rome for Naples two months before (L. 122, nn. 8, 9). Robinson's party would meet Dr. Harwood again in Sicily; however, having previously offended the diarist, Harwood would be "repressed by the coolness of my reception" (HCR, 6 Apr. 1830, Travel Journals).

126. To Henry Crabb Robinson

Florence, 19 May 1830
A.L.S., Dr. Williams'
Published: Morley
Address: H. C. Robinson Esq[r] / Poste Restante / Roma
Postmarks: FIREN[ZE]
MAR 1830 / 27 MAO
29
29 M[A]
Endorsed: 19 May 1830 / Miss Burney

Florence, May 19th, 1830.

My dear Sir,

I begin with the due formality of which your "dear Madam," set me the example—otherwise, I should naturally have begun with "My dear friend."—However, I will not quarrel with such a letter as yours whatever may have been its beginning or its end;—for its middle—its body was charming, like a Torso repaired at the extremities by an inferior artist, but perfect as far as its original Sculptor had carried it. You are worthy to travel and to see lovely countries, for you do enjoy such sights with true spirit. I followed you step by step (on the Map s'entend) and I promise you that if ever I proceed so far as Naples, I shall make your letter the companion of my way[1]—I have been very stationary since my last, not even having yet been to Pisa. Poor M[rs] Barrett frankly told me that her lodging was too confined to admit me when I first arrived here[2]—and though she has often hoped during Henrietta's gleams of amendment, to get her either to the Baths of St. Giuliano, near Pisa, or to the Baths of Lucca, or to the Village of Saravezza,[3] at any of which places I was to have joined her, the poor girl has always disappointed her expectations by some fresh attack, and they are still at Pisa, and I am still at Florence.[4] I might indeed have taken a lodging near them—but the young invalid was forbidden to speak, at one time forbidden to see any one but her Mother or Sister, and every moment of that poor Mother's time was necessarily devoted to her girl. My friends here therefore advised and persuaded me to stay with them—and but for the very variable and often very alarming accounts from Pisa, I should have been extremely comfortable. Florence has improved upon me by seeing it in the Spring. It has justified its name and its dedication to Flora, and been a perfect Garden of all colours, all forms, and all delicious odours. The Gallery is within an easy distance, and I go to it two or three times a week. The Pitti Palace is also an inexhaustible resource;[5] and there are some smaller collections well worth examination—and many lovely Villa's and Gardens to which, in the Wilbrahams carriage, I am able to gain easy access. Besides these inducements to like Florence, I have had, and still have a renewal of an old mania; a drawing mania, and instead of a language master, have treated myself with a drawing Master, and fagged as hard as if fagging for bread. One amongst my many imperfections is that of never being able to engage in any pursuit with healthy and rational moderation. "The Cynthia of the minute"[6] swallows me up, crust and crumb, body and mind. I have repeatedly drawn from seven o'clock with only brief intervals of rest for meals, till six or seven in the evening. Do not suppose I mean this as a boast, for seriously speaking, I know it to be absurd: but, rather than not talk of Self, one tells even what would be more to ones credit to conceal.—Whilst Lord Burghursh[7] remained, there was the additional amusement of Theatricals at his Private Theatre. Talk of <u>my</u> exclusive devotion to a favorite pursuit!—It is a joke compared to his frenzy for Music!—The day never passed without Rehearsals, sometimes of eight hours duration, never less than three or four. There were generally two Representations a week, and of such a length, that I have actually been from eight in the evening till half past one detained as weary spectatrice of his Operas. I went to two, both of his own composing. One was the favorite and pretty Opera of The Siege of Belgrade, originally set by Storace, and <u>new</u> <u>set</u> by Lord Burghursh!![8] The Chorus Singers were all Italians, and at their wits end to know how to pronounce the words they had to sing;—so, many of them put words of their own to the notes, such as "Oibo," or "Ahimé"—and in the general hubbub, they did very well. The other Opera was Italian, and if it had not been so desparately long, would have gone off <very well> triumphantly. There were luckily plenty of ices, and when all was over, a good supper for those who liked it.—Another night, I went to see <u>Lady</u> Burghursh[9] act in an Italian Play. She pronounced her part admirably, but was not a very clear speaker, for none but first-rate actors are. She performed with good sense, and her deportment was Lady-like—but the character was too young for her, & she often made it harsh instead of playfully capricious. Of course, she was much applauded, & by no one more, nor sooner, than by her good-natured husband.—There seems a doubt whether his Lordship will return to his long-held situation here (he has been English Ambassador at Florence twelve years) and the Natives appear to regret him extremely.[10]—How shocked you must have been by the sudden death of Lady Northampton![11]—It was a most afflicting event to her husband & family.

Who should start up before me at the Gallery the other day, but Mr Botherington![12]—He gave me the latest news of you I could hope to receive, and the sight of him, for once, gave me pleasure, for he reminded me of my friends at Rome and of Rome itself.—I have very comfortable letters from England; one, especially, from Mad^me^ d'Arblay written in excellent spirits.[13]—In the course of June, I am likely, at last, to join Mrs Barrett. My friends the Wilbrahams will be going themselves about the middle of the month to attend the Illuminazione at Pisa, a festival that occurs only once in three years, and will this summer be more brilliant than usual.[14] They will take me to Pisa with them, after I shall have spent with them about a fortnight at a Villa two or three miles from hence which they have engaged for three months. By that time I trust Mrs Barrett may be able to remove her poor girl to Lucca. I should be sorry to spend much time at Pisa in hot weather.—Thank Mr Richmond[15] for the agreeable little addition he made to your letter, and give my kind regards to him either in writing, if you are parted, or by word of mouth. The Moriers will be detained another winter in Italy by the delicate state of health of their dear boy. They are now at Castel a Mare. Mrs Payne I hear nothing of except from my Sister d'Arblay who says she is gay & well.[16] We have had the most Splendid and interesting Ballet at the Pergola[17] I ever witnessed—It is founded on the Mournful story of Ines de Castro[18]—and the principal Actrice performed so admirably that she made me cry like a child!—The news of our poor King are a little better, and I cannot but hope he may yet rally, for we have nothing better to supply his place, & I have always had a sneaking kindness for him.[19] If you want light easy Italian reading, get Giraud's Commedie[20]—They are excessively amusing—Some are farcical & some are grave, but all full of action, & with a good deal of character well delineated & well supported—Books are so cheap here, that I bought Nota's Comedies,[21] which are in great repute & often acted, and are printed in eight duodecimo volumes for Six Pauls!

Adieu my dear friend. Still when you favour me with your remembrance direct Poste Restante Firenze. Yours most truly,

S. H. Burney

1. After receiving SHB's "very friendly letter" of 19 March 1830 above, Robinson replied on 28 March from Naples: "I gave her a short account of my journey hither—And subsequent towns with hints that may be useful to any of her friends" (HCR, 28 Mar. 1830, Travel Journals).

2. Charlotte Barrett describes their winter lodgings in Pisa: "from our windows we can see the Appennines 5 miles off. We are on the bank of the Arno, but too high up, on a secondo Piano, to be in danger from its damps" (CFBt to FBA, 28–30 Jan. [1830], Berg).

3. San Giuliano, a small spa near Pisa; the Bagni di Lucca, with thermal mineral springs; and Seravezza, a mountain village, were being considered for the invalid.

4. Mrs. Barrett's original plan to summer at Lucca had been changed by 23 April 1830 when she realized that her daughter would be too weak to travel so far. Instead, they intended to go to "the Baths of Pisa, a village five miles hence, where . . . the air is mild and fine" until Hetty was able to proceed further. "But we must pray that there may be occasion for all these removals. the poor darling is so ill at present that I never look at her sweet thin face without anxious and fearful forebodings" (CFBt to HBt, 23–30 Apr. [1830], Berg).

5. The Via Pepi where Sarah Harriet was staying was northeast of the Gallerie degli Uffizi (constructed 1560–74), one of the great art museums in Italy. Across the river was the Palazzo Pitti, a fifteenth-century palace whose magnificent collection was begun by the Medici family in the seventeenth century, and was opened regularly to the public in 1828 (Claudio Pescio, *Complete Guide for visiting the Uffizi* and *Complete Guide for visiting Pitti Palace* (Firenze: Il Turismo, 1979, 1981)).

6. Alexander Pope, *Of the Characters of Women* (Moral Essay 2) (1735), l. 20.

7. Maj.-Gen. John Fane (1784–1859), styled Lord Burghersh, who would afterwards succeed his father as 11th Earl of Westmorland (1841). A distinguished military officer and diplomat, he was currently serving as Envoy Extraordinary and Minister Plenipotentiary to Florence (1814–30) as well as to Parma, Lucca and Modena (1818–31), although he resided at Florence (Burke; Gibbs; Lodge; *DNB;* see *Correspondence of Lord Burghersh afterwards Eleventh Earl of Westmorland, 1808–1840*, ed. Rachel Weigall (London: John Murray, 1912)).

8. Passionately fond of music, of which he was himself an amateur performer, Lord Burghersh had founded the Royal Academy of Music (1823) and composed seven operas, including the favorite *Catarina, ossia L'Assedio di Belgrado*, which was first performed on 15 April 1830 at his residence in Florence. As *Catherine, or The Austrian Captive*, it was publicly rehearsed by the pupils of the Royal Academy of Music in October 1830. The music for James Cobb's *The Siege of Belgrade*, which opened at Drury Lane 1 January 1791, had been principally composed by Stephen Storace (1762–96) (*New Grove* under Storace, Burghersh; *DNB* under Fane; *London Stage*, Pt. 5, Vol. 2, 1313).

9. Priscilla Anne (1793–1879), third daughter of William Wellesley-Pole (formerly Wellesley) (1763–1845), 3rd Earl of Mornington (1842), and niece to the Duke of Wellington. She had married Lord Burghersh 26 June 1811 and was considered to hold her social position with grace and ease (Burke; Lodge; Gibbs).

10. In November 1830, Lord Burghersh was gazetted Envoy Extraordinary to Naples, but the appointment was revoked. The next post he held was that of Envoy Extraordinary and Minister Plenipotentiary at Berlin 1841–51 (*DNB;* Gibbs).

11. Margaret, the eldest daughter of Maj.-Gen. Douglas Maclean Clephane, had married 24 July 1815 Spencer Joshua Alwyne Compton (1790–1851), 2nd Marquess of Northampton (1828). They had lived in Italy since 1820 where their house became a center of attraction and influence. During his winter in Rome, Robinson had attended their parties, which "were of weekly occurrence," and liked both host and hostess: "Lord N: pleased me His manners are agreeable & he talks of virtue pleasantly enough My lady . . . is a fine woman and had great dignity." Lady Northampton died in Rome on 2 April 1830, shortly after giving birth to her sixth child (*DNB;* Burke; Lodge; Gibbs; HCR, *Reminiscences,* 2: 458; HCR, 27 Nov. 1829, Travel Journals).

12. Possibly a humorous name for Robert Finch (L. 120, n. 2), a somewhat eccentric acquaintance in Rome, who did indeed pass through Florence between 21 and 23 April 1830 and again at the end of May (Finch, 21–23 Apr., May 1830, Diaries). During one of these visits, he called on S. H. Burney; see further, L. 128.

13. This may be the "one Poor letter in answer to 1.2.3. charming ones" which Mme d'Arblay speaks of having written to her half-sister before 25 April 1830 (*JL,* 12: 745).

14. The "Luminaria" at Pisa, a festival held every three years on 17 June to commemorate St. Ranieri (d. 1160), the patron saint of Pisa. The original custom of placing candles in windows developed into the display of elaborate illuminations, and the celebration acquired patriotic significance (Giorgio del Guerra, *Pisa attraverso i secoli* ([Pisa]: Giardini, [1967]), 281–83; *Bibliotheca Sanctorum,* vol. 11 ([Roma]: Istituto Giovanni XXIII nella Pontificia Universita lateranense, 1968), 39–40).

15. James Cook Richmond (1808–66), a young American, had graduated from Harvard in 1828 and then studied in Göttingen and Halle. After his return home from Europe, he would be ordained in the Episcopal Church as deacon (1832) and priest (1833) (James Grant Wilson and John Fiske, eds., *Appletons' Cyclopaedia of American Biography,* vol. 5 (New York: D. Appleton, 1888), 246).

He met Robinson in Italy, and they became almost inseparable companions. They were currently returning from Naples and Sicily to Rome, which Richmond would leave three weeks later. Robinson, rather forlorn at losing "my sole permanent companion for these last 8 months," was pleased to meet him again at Siena and Florence (L. 134, n. 14), and they planned to travel to England together in the spring. However, years later when Richmond visited him in London, Robinson was less than hospitable (see below L. 175, n. 1) (HCR, 22 Nov. 1829, 24 May, 11, 25 June, 6 July, 22, 28, 31 Aug. 1830 and passim, Travel Journals; HCR, *Reminiscences,* 2: 465–67).

16. Crabb Robinson would be interested in news of Sarah's niece, Sarah (Burney) Payne, the daughter of James Burney, with whom he was well acquainted. Mrs. Payne had in fact furnished him with a letter of introduction to Robert Finch (HCR, *Reminiscences,* 2: 452–54).

17. The Teatro della Pergola; the original theater, built of wood in 1656 and renovated in the mid-eighteenth century, was well adapted for lyrical drama (Piero Bargellini, *La città di Firenze* ([Firenze]: Bonechi, 1979), 263–67).

18. The subject of Inés de Castro was a fertile one in the Spanish literary tradition, inspiring several plays and poems. The mistress of Prince Pedro of Portugal was murdered in 1355 by order of the King, his father, but avenged and honored after Pedro's accession to the throne in 1357.

19. King George IV of England, who was suffering from dropsy and other complaints,

was then in his last illness and would die on 26 June 1830, to be succeeded by his brother, King William IV (1765–1837).

20. Giovanni Giraud (1776–1834), Italian comic dramatist. An edition of his plays under the title *Commedie* was published in Rome in 1808; another collection, *Commedie scelte*, was printed in Paris in 1829.

21. Alberto Nota (1775–1847), contemporary and rival to Giraud. Several editions of his *Commedie* had been published by 1830.

---

127. To Henry Crabb Robinson

[Florence], 5 June [1830][1]
A.L.S., Dr. Williams'
Published: Morley
Address: Allo Signor / Signor H. C. Robinson / Poste Restante / Roma
Postmarks: FIRENZE
Endorsed: 5 June 1830 / Miss Burney

Saturday, June 5th
1826.

My dear Friend

Business must take the lead—I therefore begin by telling you that the Illuminare at Pisa is to be on the 16th—That the gayities at that place, whatever they may be, are to last three or four days.[2] That I was offered a bed at a private house, in the Lung'Arno for three or six nights, at the price of 3 zecchiné. Probably accommodations would be cheaper in other parts of the town, but they try to make a good harvest every where.—Mrs Barrett is chearing up with the hope that her poor girl is doing better, and if the present amendment continues, she writes that her "present plan is to set off next Monday, the 7th for the Baths of Lucca, making two days journey of the thirty miles thither, and putting a mattress in the carriage for Henrietta to rest upon."[3]—The Baths of San Juliano, it appears by this, will not be resorted to, the Physician thinking that the weather would soon become too hot for them. Should Henrietta actually <atchieve> accomplish the removal, I shall join her Mother at the Baths of Lucca without troubling my head about the Illuminare at all. Till I really hear however, that the poor girl has been able to undertake and positively to succeed in terminating the journey, I shall not quit Florence, or at least its neighbourhood;—I am now at about a mile and a half from the Porta Pinti, at Villa

Niccolini, in full sight of Fiesole, in a large and cool house, where I should be well content to remain some time.—My friends here, however, go themselves on the 15th to Pisa—but with a party, and there would be no convenient means of taking me and my luggage with them.[4] If, when they depart, Mrs Barrett has not established herself at Lucca, I shall repair to my old quarters at Florence, (the Hotel de l'Europe) and there await her movements, or return hither with the Miss Wilbrahams when they come back from the Illuminare.—I should tell you, as you are good enough to take so warm an interest in Henrietta, that Dr Peebles[5] who spends his Summers at Geneva, called upon Mrs Barrett in his way thither, and confirmed, by the opinions he gave, all that had been asserted by her Italian Physician, giving her confidence in her present adviser, and a glimmering of hope from the influence of climate, change of scene, & chearful associates. He and many others, think that her complaints are in part spasmodic, and on the nerves—The improvement at the present moment is this—that they are able, when pain and inflamation attack her, to substitute leeches for bleeding with a lancet. The latter method always weakens far the most.[6]

Our friend Richmond's request about letters shall be most punctually attended to.—How glad I should be if circumstances caused us to meet again! I would compound for losing, at sight of him in a new place, some of the Roman associations of ideas connected in my mind at present with his name and remembrance. Why should it not be as well to think of Mr Richmond <in basking or> amidst sun-shine, hot weather, and rural scenery, as <in> amidst frost, & snow and rain and mud, in cold palaces and in starving galleries. But still somehow, tho' I abused them at the time, I love the recollection (almost) of the very dirt of Rome, and of its spouts, and I had nearly said of its smells and fleas!—Your coming to the Baths of Lucca I will not hold to be impossible. All I have heard induces me to think you might find the situation very eligible. You wd have as cool air as you can reasonably expect in Italy. Very good & accessible society; newspapers and Reading Rooms,—and you would have the pleasure of giving pleasure to a friend—myself.

I congratulate you on the enjoyment you must have derived from your delightful Tour.[7] How enviable I thought you all the time I was reading your little account.—It made me exclaim with Shakespear's Beatrice—"Oh that I were a man!"[8]

There is no "Feast of Flowers" at Pisa, but there is one between Rome and Florence, at Monte Fiascone I believe: but the exact time I do not find easy to learn.[9]—By the way, do not regret too much the not having seen the Aqueduct at Maddelena,[10] wch tho' I dare say very fine, you will be sure to hear is finer than any thing else the moment you are found out not to have visited it!—I hardly ever speak of any beautiful object that I am not asked if I have seen another at such or such a place, and then assured that the one I have seen is not worth looking at in comparison.—Where do you lodge at Rome?[11] Have you ever seen again my good little Columba?[12] What have you done with Mr Smyth?[13] Is Mr Goetzenberg[14] (I do not know how to spell the name) at present in the Great City. If you see him, give him my best regards & good wishes. Adieu my dear friend—Yours here & every where most truly Y^rs^ S. H. B.

P.S. The Miss Wilbrahams would welcome you most readily—They know you thro' me.—

1. Dated by Sarah Harriet "Saturday 5 June 1826," the year is clearly a mistake. The endorsement and the context establish 1830, her first year in Italy as the correct year; 5 June does fall on Saturday in 1830, but on Monday in 1826.

2. Crabb Robinson had written to SHB on 1 June 1830, making "inquiries," and received her reply on the 9th. After wavering for several days, he would eventually decide not to attend the Illuminare "as I c^d^ not bear the fatigue of travell^g^ 3 nights with^t^ intermission"; his friends would set off without him on 11 June (HCR, 1, 9–11 June 1830, Travel Journals).

3. The letter to SHB from Charlotte Barrett is missing, but on 18 June 1830 Mrs. Barrett would write from the Baths of Lucca, whither she had "with much difficulty conveyed my poor Hetty . . . taking two days to travel 30 miles." She was then expecting her Aunt Sarah's imminent arrival: "she waits for companions & opportunities of travelling with some protection. her society will be a very great comfort and acquisition to us" (CFBt to FBA, 18–20 June [1830], Berg).

4. Charlotte Barrett felt this was unfriendly in Sarah's hostesses: "We think her Wilbrahams ought to have taken her with them to the Pisa Illuminations and then brought her hither, as they project making the same tour for their own amusement. . . . She however makes no complaints, and I have no right to blame them without knowing more of the circumstances." She would change her mind after meeting the Wilbrahams, who "spoke of Sarah Harriet with the most affectionate admiration, regretting that her dislike to crowds &c, prevented her accompanying them to the Pisa festival. I think I did them great injustice by my previous strictures" (CFBt to FBA, 18–20 June [1830], Berg).

5. Perhaps John Peebles, who graduated in medicine from the University of Edinburgh in 1817, or Dr. John Home Peebles, Fellow of the Royal College of Physicians of Edinburgh, who died in 1867 (*List of Graduates . . . Edinburgh; GM*, 3rd ser. 22 (1867): 690).

6. Henrietta's physician believed she suffered from "Chronic Inflammation very obstinate and deeply seated," which must be treated by "depletion &c, to subdue the paroxysms." During the "periodical exacerbations" of the disease, "there is nothing to be done but bleeding" (CFBt to HBt, 23–30 Apr. [1830], Berg). Hetty improved in May and June, and her mother was thankful that she "has now been six weeks without any violent attack of Inflammation" (CFBt to FBA, 18–20 June [1830], Berg).

7. In his letter of 1 June 1830, HCR gave Miss Burney an account of his journey from Naples to Sicily 5–7 April, his circuit of the island by mule (13 April–5 May), the voyage back to Naples (10–13 May) and his return to Rome (17–20 May) (HCR, 1 June 1830, Travel Journals). His adventurous tour of Sicily, which he recommended as "the finale, as it would be the crown and completion, of every Italian tour," is described in HCR, *Reminiscences,* 2: 465–67; 5 Apr.–20 May 1830, Travel Journals.

8. *Much Ado About Nothing,* IV, i, 304.

9. In the same letter (n. 7), Robinson told of his intended journey to the mountains to attend the "Feast of Flowers" in Genzana, where the streets were "paved with flowers . . . . in the form of temples, altars, crosses, and other sacred symbols" (HCR, *Reminiscences,* 2: 470–71; 1–18 June 1830, Travel Journals).

10. The aqueduct Carolino was constructed 1752–62 by the Italian architect Luigi Vanvitelli (1700–73) to carry water from Maddaloni 25 miles to Naples (Luigi Vanvitelli Jr., *Vita di Luigi Vanvitelli* (Napoletana: Società Editrice, 1975), 194–99).

11. On 20 May 1830, when he arrived back in Rome after an absence of two months, Robinson had gone back "to my old apartments in the Piazza di Spagna. . . . I preferred to bear 'the ills I had, than fly to others that I knew not of'" (HCR, *Reminiscences,* 2: 467–68).

12. Sarah Harriet's housemaid in Rome, distinguished by her ability to make excellent coffee (see below L. 139).

13. Sydney Smith (c. 1807–80), a young man whom Robinson befriended in Rome, and would later look up in London. He matriculated at Cambridge in 1828, but did not take his degree. After a period of travel, he returned to England c. 26 May 1830 and joined the firm of his father, George Smith, an architect. However, in 1840, he would take his B.A. at Cambridge and be ordained as a priest, eventually to become perpetual curate of Worth, Kent (1854–80) (*Alumni Cantab.; Pigot's Directory* (1827); HCR, 26 May 1830 and passim, Travel Journals; HCR, 14 Oct. 1831, 26 Oct. 1836, Diaries).

14. Jacob Götzenberger (1800–66), an historical painter, who had visited Robinson in London in 1827 and had been at Rome since 1828. He is probably one of the "clever artists" described as SHB's associates in Rome. On 2 January 1830, she had accompanied Robinson to Götzenberger's studio to look at his "great cartoon" (*Bryan's;* Thième-Becker; CFBt to FBA, 28–30 Jan. 1830, Berg; HCR, *Reminiscences,* 2: 379; HCR, 2 Jan. 1830, Travel Journals).

128. To Henry Crabb Robinson

Baths of Lucca, 19 July 1830
A.L.S., Dr. Williams'
Published: Morley
Address: Allo Signor / Signor H. C. Robinson / Poste Restante / Firenze
Postmarks: LUCCA
22 / 10 JL 10 / 1830
Endorsed: 19 July—1830 / Miss / Burney

My kind and uncapricious Friend

To be what I have called you is a great merit—I am not sure that (in some cases) it is a merit to which I myself have any title to lay claim!—Were I put to the Bar it would puzzle me <to> how to deny that I do occasionally exhibit very pretty specimens of this fashionable failing, particularly towards newly-formed acquaintances—people that have pleased me on meeting them for a time or two, and then been thought of and wished for no more.—Such folks however, I never dreamt of classing amongst my friends, as I now venture confidently to class you.—But something too much of this.—Let me tell you of Lucca Baths, & Henrietta Barrett, and a little English gossip in letters from thence.

We are in a little Paradice. Nothing can be more lovely than our surrounding scenery, which reminds me at once of the hanging woods and Avon River at Bristol Hotwells, and of the terraced walks, and gushing waters, <and> or cascatellini, and shady clumps of Malvern Hills.[1]—Evenings and early mornings are deliciously cool, and nobody stirs till near seven o'clock, and many are out by four, A.M. and return at eight to lie down again, & sleep if they can.—Our invalid by very slow degrees we hope improves: but inflamation will return from fortnight to fortnight, & then fresh bleeding (Cautiously performed however)—becomes indispensable. She is generally in good spirits, and looks better than you would expect, but very very pale.[2]—Her dear Mother lets no one be her nurse but herself, and it is wonderful to see what extraordinary fatigue mother-love carries her through.[3] She is well, sweet soul, and rather enjoys this hot weather, <and> at least, likes it much better than our English soi-disant summers. Barrett writes from Brighton, 6th July—"We are inundated with rain, and have continual storms."—If you delay your meditated visit hither till September, dear friend, two evils will happen, one to you, and one to us—

The rains here will have set in, and you will be able to enjoy none of the beauties of the place—and, furthermore, we shall have left it, probably for Florence, and shall thereby miss seeing you at either place. So, do try and make the little scapata towards the end of August. You may travel cool, by setting out in the evening, and jogging on all night. I came with a jewel of a Vetturino, named Bastiano,[4] recommended at M^de^ Hombert's Hotel,[5] & tho' I believe not the cheapest of his race, he was the most good-humoured, and had an easy, clean carriage, and good horses, and we performed the journey in a day, arriving here a little after ten, and leaving Florence at ½ 5. Bastiano took a liking to me, as in duty bound for the liking I took to him, and comes to see me whenever he brings new live-cargoes to this place.—My dear friend, my Italian speaking is here quite at a dead stand, for I see none but English people, except our Maid and occasionally a Shop-keeper. But I read only Italian books—and have just finished Niccolini's Foscarini[6] which is a fine masculine, energetic performance, & gave me much pleasure, and makes me admire and respect the Author.—If I were not here, I should like to be with you at Florence, getting acquainted with the looks at least of clever people,[7] and hearing the Tuscan language hourly spoken in its perfection. But after all, the Roman accent for my money! The Florentines despise it greatly however, and perhaps they may be right: yet to foreign ears it is far the most agreeable, and I always have found it easier to understand.

We are very little incommoded by gnats. I am sorry they so torment you.[8] It is to make up for all the unaccountable impunity with which you escaped through the plague of fleas at Rome. Never was such a thing known as an uncomplaining Englishman the first year of facing the myriads of Roman fleas!—

Pray, if you have no particular reason for not doing it, read Alfieri's Auto-Biography, were it only to admire his truly respectable industry at an advanced period of life, and his success in acquiring Greek from its very beginning after he was turned I believe of fifty.[9] His style is clear and easy, very unlike his Tragic diction.—

You are aware, I believe, that another year in Italy is prescribed for our sick girl, & I think it very probable she, and we all may winter at Rome.[10] I leave them to their own discussions about it—but I must own it would give me very great pleasure to revisit that place again, and your being there we All look forward to as a special inducement, for we hope you would come and chat at evenings by our fire side, & now and then accompany us to some favorite haunt.[11]

You will be glad to hear that Bertollini's[12] nose is a little out of joint. A young German from Manheim, (a picture dealer, I believe) who shewed the Paynes civility when abroad, is now in London, reigning paramount in Sarah's good graces. He is said to be handsome, and well-mannered, and goes a great deal to James Street, where moreover, we have been taking a new series of dancing lessons of a crack Master, and we perform surpassingly at all our second-rate balls!—Che roba!—

Do you remember (I do not) the following Epitaph in Poets Corner? It was sent us by one who lately went over the Abbey. "Spes, vermes, et Ego."[13]—How quaint & queer—Yet one may think it into good sense.—The Pavillion at Brighton is left by the late King to his reigning brother, and it is supposed the present Sovereign will reside there a good deal.[14]—

I delight in Mr Finch's kindness to young Heely.[15] As for his affront against me, dear Man,[16] I can only laugh. Who ever heard of returning Gentlemens visits, unless old & infirm, or habitual invalids like Dr Nott,[17] unable even to pay a visit at all, though glad to receive them. I shall be writing soon to Mrs Finch, & without seeming to know of her husband's miff, shall tell her how much I regretted not seeing him when he called, & how sorry I was that custom prevented my doing myself the pleasure of returning the visit he so kindly paid me.

I have met here again two of the English ladies I knew at Rome—Mrs Bertie, and Mrs Heath.[18] Mrs Berties history is a very singular one. She was married at eighteen by a young man of high family who took her I believe off a country stage. She has always conducted herself irreproachably, though very beautiful, and very generally admired. But the connexions of her husband have never forgiven the match & stirred themselves so effectually to separate them, that they got him appointed to a Ship shortly after the union; he sailed, leaving her in a family way—and neither he nor the Vessel have ever been heard of since!—Her child died—soon after its birth, & she poor thing, with broken health & Spirits, remains a widow, having no object to attach her to life but a brother who is in the Medical profession in England, and attended her to Italy when she first came half dying <here>, & supposed to be in a Consumption.[19] Since I met her at Rome she has been at Naples—then went back early in June to Rome, and caught the Mal-aria fever, and is now at these Baths—slowly recovering.—

I hope the story you promise me will be gayer than mine—but it cannot be truer, and that must give it merit, if Arthur Barrett,[20] my Niece's youngest boy is right. A lady offered him for his holiday reading, a Novel or a Volume of History, & he chose the History because "Novels don't prove what they tell, and Histories do."—sometimes, he might have added.—

Mrs Barrett & her dear girls desire their best compliments to you. Always remember me kindly to Mr Richmond, & believe me ever your obliged and affectionate friend & servant

S. H. Burney.

One of my namesake's letters came to me at Florence[21]—It was in German, & I declare I will not betray any of the secrets it contained! Her Christian name I found was Eliza.—But for that name, I might have suspected it to be a love-letter to myself from Mr Goetzenberg—

July 19th
Casa Lena, Ponte Seraglio
Bagni di Lucca

I fancy you could look up as a young Roman Gent: did when asked at a party how he did, and answer with a sentimental shrug—"Sudo!"—I asked at a shop whether they anticipated any greater heat than we had last Friday—"Perchè no?" said the man, proud of his Italian sun.—

19 July—1830

1. Charlotte Barrett had expected her aunt to "be charmed with this lovely scenery" at the Baths of Lucca, which was considered "one of the picturesque beauties & wonders of Italy. We are embosomed in Mountains & chesnut groves with the river Serchio forming a thousand cascades and vines hanging in airy festoons along its banks" (CFBt to FBA, 18–20 June [1830], Berg).

2. Hetty's mother also believed in her slow progress, and that she had "grown rather stronger" since arriving at Lucca; in early August, Charlotte was "thankful to say she has not now been bled either with Lancet or Leeches since the 16th of July, a longer respite than she has had yet." However, "she is so weak that I cannot get her into the air as much as I wish. . . . But whenever she does make any extra exertion she is always feverish" (ibid.; CFBt to HBt, 7–8 Aug. [1830], Berg).

3. At Lucca, Mrs. Barrett was "entirely confined at home with Henrietta," although not quite so much as during the winter at Pisa when "I never opened my eyes on any thing but her poor little self" (CFBt to FBA, 18–20 June [1830], Berg).

4. Unidentified.

5. The "Grand Hôtel de Madme Hombert" stood on the "rue Porta rossa, Palais Torrigiani, prés du Cabinet litteraire et de l'Etablissement des Bains à Florence," according to a bill from this establishment, endorsed 22 April 1830 by Robert Finch (Bodleian, MS. Finch, d. 3, f. 24).

6. Giovanni Battista Niccolini (1782–1861), Florentine poet; his *Antonio Foscarini* appeared in 1827.

7. Robinson had arrived in Florence for the summer on 15 July 1830, and took lodgings with "two elderly ladies, highly respectable, who let their best apartments." His daily routine was to read Italian authors at home all morning, "lounge over the papers at the Reading-room" in the afternoon, attend an evening gathering with "the most distinguished literati in Italy," and finish the day at home with a conversazione, which the poet Niccolini always attended. He wrote to SHB on 16–17 July, informing her of

his situation (HCR, *Reminiscences*, 2: 473–74; HCR, 2, 15–17, 27 July 1830, Travel Journals).

8. In his journal, Robinson noted the one drawback to his accommodation, a "great-curtain" around his bed to protect against insects; considering the heat of the Florentine summer, "I have some apprehension the remedy may be itself a disease" (HCR, 15 July 1830, Travel Journals).

9. Vittorio Alfieri (1749–1803), Italian poet and dramatist, spent the last eleven years of his life studying Greek. The *Vita . . . scritta da esso* was published posthumously (1804).

10. Hetty had been so weak all winter that her mother realized "even if she begins to recover, that we shall be obliged to keep her abroad another winter" (CFBt to FBA, 28–30 Jan. 1830, Berg). They planned to leave the Baths of Lucca in September when "the rainy season among these mountains sets in," spend a month in Florence, and proceed to Rome towards the end of October (CFBt to HBt, 7–8 Aug. [1830], Berg).

11. Crabb Robinson received this "friendly letter from Miss Burney" on 24 July, and noted in his journal: "I have the prospect of her company at Rome—It will be a great pleasure" (HCR, 24 July 1830, Travel Journals).

12. A London music-master. According to Charlotte Barrett, "Sarah has got a new singing master, Bertolini, a most excellent one, who has some very creditable pupils, but this is his first season & so he is only charging 3[s.] a lesson" (CFBt to [Unknown], 22 Feb. [n.d.], Barrett, Eg. 3707, ff. 165–66v).

13. The epitaph "Spes, vermis, et ego" belongs, not to the poets' corner of Westminster Abbey, but to the marble tomb of Thomas Owen of Condover (d. 1598), Justice of the Common Pleas, in the south aisle of the choir (Arthur Penrhyn Stanley, *Historical Memorials of Westminster Abbey* (London: John Murray, 1868), 204).

14. The Pavilion at Brighton, originally built in 1787 and altered by John Nash in 1815–21 in splendid Oriental style, was left by King George IV to his brother and successor. William IV visited it for the first time as King in August 1830, made some improvements, and entertained there frequently during his seven-year reign (Clifford Musgrave, *Royal Pavilion* (London: Leonard Hill, 1959); Philip Ziegler, *King William IV* (London: Collins, 1971), 157).

15. A Captain Hely, "poor & almost friendless," who regarded Mr. Finch as a "patron," has not been further identified. Robinson had told SHB something of Mr. Finch's "patronage of Hely" in his letter of 16–17 July (HCR, 16–17 July, 15 Nov. 1830, Travel Journals; Nitchie, 4, 17–18).

16. Robert Finch was of a somewhat irascible temper, and quick to take offense at suspected social slights (see Nitchie, 17–19, 33–35, 55). He had passed through Florence between 21 and 23 April 1830 and again at the end of May (L. 126, n. 12), when he was offended at SHB's "not answering his card" (HCR, 16–17 July 1830, Travel Journals). It is interesting to note that Sarah's kinsman, M. d'Arblay, was once guilty of a similar oversight, and received from Finch an "insolent letter in French, reproving him for his bad manners" (Nitchie, 41); this incident is not mentioned in the account of their relations in *JL*, 7: 391, n. 6, 438, n. 2.

17. George Frederick Nott (1767–1841), D.D. (1807), divine and author; as prebendary of Winchester, he was supervising repairs to the Cathedral in 1817, when he sustained severe head injuries from which he never fully recovered. Dr. Nott retired

thereafter to Italy where he collected books, artwork, and coins, giving religious services at Pisa, which Mary Shelley attended in 1821–22. He was in Rome when Sarah Harriet was there; Crabb Robinson, who visited him, called him "the victim of ill health & gout" (*DNB; The Journals of Mary Shelley, 1814–1844*, ed. Paula R. Feldman and Diana Scott-Kilvert (Oxford: Clarendon Press, 1987), 1: 386, 400 and nn.; HCR, 21 Dec. 1829, Travel Journals).

18. Agnes Wallace (1788–1874) had married at Fort St. George, Madras, on 9 May 1811 Maj. Charles Heath (1776–1819) of the 1st Battalion of the 7th Regiment of Native Infantry. Three children were born to her in India before her husband, who became Lt.-Col. (1817), died on 18 February 1819 in camp at Ajunta. An "intelligent & very hospitable" woman, she was in Italy with her family: "She is a great admirer of Miss Burney and prefers her as an authoress to Mad: Darblay!" noted H. C. Robinson (Dodwell and Miles, comps., *Alphabetical List of the Officers of the Indian Army* (London: Longman, Orme, Brown, 1838); *East India Register and Directory* (1810–19); *GM*, 89, Pt. 2 (1819): 281; Madras Ecclesiastical Returns, Madras Military Fund, Early Cadet Papers, India Office Library; HCR, 7–8 Aug. 1831, Travel Journals).

19. As "Miss Fisher," Catherine Jane Saunders (d. 1850) was well-known as an actress at the Plymouth and other provincial theaters. On 26 November 1808, she married the Hon. Willoughby Bertie (1787–1810), second son of the 4th Earl of Abingdon. Her husband was placed in command of H.M.S. *Satellite*, which sailed from Spithead 17 December 1810 and was lost in a gale. "In one of these sudden gusts . . . she is supposed to have upset, and every soul on board perished. The next morning her boats, some spars, &c. which were upon her deck, were picked up . . . but no other vestige of her has ever been seen." Capt. Bertie was assumed dead, while his widow "in daily expectation of her *accouchement*, was waiting his return at one of the sea-ports." A posthumous son, named for his father, was born 20 April 1811, but died 31 July 1812 (Burke; *GM*, 78, Pt. 2 (1808): 1125; 80, Pt. 2 (1810): 656; 81, Pt. 1 (1811): 489; 82, Pt. 2 (1812): 189).

The story ends happily, however, as Mrs. Bertie would eventually marry in 1837 as his second wife, the Rev. William Sheepshanks-Burgess (d. 1853) (*GM*, NS 8 (1837): 417, 648; NS 39 (1853): 672; *Alumni Cantab.*).

20. Charlotte's thirteen-year-old son, Arthur Barrett, was attending Charles Parr Burney's school at Greenwich. He was not always a model student, judging from the headmaster's complaints of Arthur's "idleness & impertinence," faults which his mother felt were "the necessary consequence of his [CPB's] having abolished flogging at Greenwich" (CFBt to HBt, 7–8 Aug. [1830], Berg).

21. Sarah was having trouble with the misdirection of her mail to a "Miss B. of Rome, who has opened various of her Epistles" (*JL*, 12: 745).

129. To Henry Crabb Robinson

Baths of Lucca, 12 August 1830
A.L.S., Dr. Williams'
Published: Morley
Address: Allo Signor / Signor H. C. Robinson / Poste Restante / Firenze
Postmarks: LUCCA
14 / [?] STO / [?] 30
Endorsed: 12 Augt. 1830 / Miss Burney / Enquiry ab^t^ French / News.—/ Ans^d^ same day

Dear Friend

We are inexpressably anxious to hear the opinion of some sensible man on the subject of the probable consequences of the ferment in France.[1] Here we see only twaddling women, as ignorant and perhaps even more prejudiced than ourselves. Mrs Barrett, after the 7th or 15 of September thinks of repairing for some time to Florence; and thence, if deemed advisable by abler judges than herself, to Rome for the winter.—Are you inclined to think such a project judicious for unprotected women?—England she is afraid of carrying her invalid back to this winter; and Florence would be too cold for her. There remains little choice between Pisa and Rome, and the only advantage of the former over the latter is, that it is nearer Leghorn, from whence, in case of rational alarm, means of embarkation for England might with <more> comparative facility be obtained. Have the charity, dear friend, to give us a little bit of a notion of the light in which this business appears to you. Will the European Powers be wicked enough to interfere in the internal affairs of France? Or, if they forbear, will the leven work in other oppressed States, & render the spirit of Insurrection the general order of the day?—Amongst the innumerable <u>on-dits</u> of the moment, it is said that Piedmont is already in great disburbance; that the infatuated Charles X^th^ means to take refuge at Rome; that the English are held in the bitterest abhorrence throughout France; and that very probably discontents may break out at Milan, &c, &c, &c.[2]—We hear and say little, for we are all as unknowing as the Babes in the Wood:[3] but we want to have a little sense put into us, and we entreat you to do us the good office of trying to perform that service for us. Perhaps it is yet early days to ask you in what aspect public affairs present themselves to your mind: but even your confusion of ideas on the subject will be clearer than our utter darkness; and so, write my dear friend, & above all, tell us whether you meditate any change in your own plans.—And tell us also where to hear of you when we get to Florence.[4]

Mrs Barrett and her daughters send their best compliments. It would give them very sincere pleasure to see you again; and you would have a kind pleasure also in seeing the progress (gradual though it may be) that our dear Henrietta is making.

Believe me ever, my dear Mr Robinson,
Your obliged and attached friend
S. H. Burney.

Have they not got a funny, stump-about, populace King in Billy IV?[5]
August 12th 1830.
Casa Lena, Ponte Seraglio
Bagni di Lucca

1. Charles X (1757–1836), King of France since 1824, issued on 25 July 1830 ordinances suspending liberty of the press, restricting the franchise, and dissolving the newly elected Chamber of Deputies. Violent protests in Paris on 27–29 July resulted in the abdication of the King.

News of the revolution reached Lucca on 7 August, including an unfounded report that the French King had been shot. Mrs. Barrett immediately wrote to her husband, asking for his "advice & opinion as to our best plan when we quit the Lucca Baths. tell me whether you think <u>Rome</u> liable to disturbances on acc^t^ of this french insurrection. <u>You</u> see & hear more in England than <u>I</u> can" (CFBt to HBt, 7–8 Aug. [1830], Berg).

2. Crabb Robinson, who learned of the ordinances at Florence on 4 August 1830, described the effect on his Italian friends, who were "all alike confounded. . . . Next day was lost to all ordinary occupations; nothing thought or talked of but what we expected to hear every hour. . . . The reports were ludicrously contradictory." Three days later, the news of the insurrection arrived, and the liberal society frequented by Robinson "was full of joy & hopes as to other countries from the great & salutary change in France" (HCR, *Reminiscences,* 2: 479–80; HCR, 18 Aug. 1830, Travel Journals).

3. The story of the Children in the Wood was the subject of an old ballad included in *Reliques of Ancient English Poetry,* [ed. Thomas Percy] (1765).

4. Robinson was staying at 4131 Via della Vigna Nuova, the home of Mme Carlotta Certellini and her sister, Mlle Gertrude, where SHB herself would later stay (HCR, 15 July 1830, 23–24 May 1831, Travel Journals; HCR, *Reminiscences,* 2: 473–74; see further below, L. 136, n. 7; L. 138).

5. King William IV, who "made a merit of his ordinariness" and whose reign was characterized by "informality, economy and patriotism," was a genuinely popular king (Ziegler, 151).

130. To Henry Crabb Robinson

Baths of Lucca, 30 August [1830]
A.L.S., Dr. Williams'
Published: Morley
Address: Allo Signor / Signor H.C. Robinson / Poste Restante / Firenze
Postmarks: LUCCA
[?] RE
Endorsed: 30 Augt 1830. / Miss Burney—

August 30th
Bagni di Lucca.

My dear friend

Mr Richmond gave me yesterday afternoon a very agreeable surprise by suddenly making his appearance here, & delivering to me your kind little note.[1]—After sitting with us some time, he expressed a wish to call upon Mrs Heath up at the Bagni Caldi, and glad of a walk, I accompanied him to shew him the way. He returned afterwards to tea here, and was very pleasant and made a highly favourable impression upon Mrs Barrett & her girls, who were, as well as myself, quite sorry he could not make a longer stay amongst us.—

And so, you naughty Varlet, you will not come and take a peep at us!—Well then, the mouse must come to you heavy-sterned mountain. I am intending to be at Florence about the 7th or 8th Septr a week sooner than my present associates, for the sake of seeing more of my friends the Wilbrahams, who will be leaving their Villa Nicolini about that time, to spend a few days in Florence previous to setting their faces homewards. I have not decided yet where I shall lodge if I make any stay at Florence, but purpose sleeping at least one night at Mad^{me} Hombert's Hotel,[2] where I was well treated and reasonably charged on my former residence.—To say the truth (entre nous, be it spoken) I have had rurality enough, and to spare—and shall be very glad to see you, and the Venus dè Medeci[3] and the Pitti Palace, and the Theatres, and a hundred other Urbane delights, in exchange for vineyards and vipers, Cottages and scorpions, and other such inviting Italian pastorals.[4]—

I am very thankful to you for your proposed scheme for getting me access to Gagliani's paper:[5] but I had already subscribed for it at a shop kept here by an Englishman who lets it out <for> at so much a month, and sends it to me very regularly for two hours each time. I warmly and admiringly approve of all the French have done hitherto—May the Spaniards acquit themselves only half as well![6]—

M[rs] Barrett and her girls will I trust be able to follow me to Florence before the middle of the month—Henrietta gains ground very slowly—Her present physician, with all due hatred of bleeding, was however compelled two days ago to take from her ten ounces.—

Adieu my dear friend. All here join with me in kindest regards,—

Yours ever truly

S. H. Burney.

My <party> companions have given up, I believe, all thoughts of Rome for this winter.—Nobody encourages M[rs] Barrett to go there for various reasons.—

1. James Cook Richmond arrived unexpectedly at Florence 22 August 1830, visited with his friend Robinson, and left on the twenty-eighth for the Baths of Lucca, bearing with him a letter from HCR to Miss Burney. He sent an "interesting acc[t]" of his call on the Barretts back to Robinson, who was also pleased to receive this "friendly little note from Miss Burney" (HCR, 22 Aug.–1 Sept. 1830, Travel Journals).

2. On 9 September 1830, Crabb Robinson would call on Sarah Harriet Burney at Mme Hombert's Hotel and find her "in good health & spirits. I spent an hour with her." Later, "after a lounge in the Evening," they attended the theater; the next morning, he introduced her to his landladies. On 12 September, Robinson in turn would meet the Wilbrahams, and comment, "three old maids," although he was impressed by the fact that "they are quite gentlewomen" (HCR, 9–12 Sept. 1830, Travel Journals).

3. The famous Medici Venus, attributed to Cleomenes (middle of the first century B.C.), a copy of an original by Praxiteles dating from the fourth century B.C. It was brought to the Uffizi in 1717 by Cosimo III de' Medici (Pescio, *Uffizi*, 67).

4. Robinson's journal over the next six weeks shows almost daily meetings with SHB, including outings to galleries, museums and the theater, chats at her lodgings, or most frequently "a walk & ice" (HCR, 9 Sept.–26 Oct. 1830, passim, Travel Journals).

5. *Galignani's Messenger*, a newspaper founded in 1814 by Giovanni Antonio Galignani (1757–1821) and continued by his sons John Anthony (1796–1873) and William (1798–1882) (*DNB*). Published in Paris, it was written in English and contained political, literary, and commercial news extracted from other newspapers, and circulated among Englishmen living abroad. See *A Famous Bookstore* (Paris: Galignani Library, 1970).

6. With little bloodshed, the July Revolution brought to the throne of France Louis-Philippe (1773–1850), duc d'Orléans (1793), known for his liberal views. In Spain, a succession crisis was developing as King Ferdinand VII's third wife was expecting a child, who would disappoint the dynastic ambitions of his brother, Don Carlos (1788–1855). At Ferdinand's death in 1833, his infant daughter Isabella would be proclaimed queen, provoking a civil war.

131. To Charlotte (Francis) Barrett

[Florence], 19 October 1830
A.L. with typescript, incomplete, Barrett, Eg. 3705, ff. 41–44
Address: Alla Signora / Signora Barrett / Casa Pettini / <Poste Restante> / Lung' Arno / Pisa

19th October, 1830.

The above has lain by me some days. Take it with all its imperfections on its head; and accept my thanks for your kindness in giving yourself the trouble to copy so long an extract. I am deeply sensible of Mr Methuen's interest for my spiritual welfare;[1] and grieved that I can make no other return for it than cavils and objections.—But something whispers me, that there may be much in his doctrine which had I sense rightly to understand, I yet might be induced to acquiesce in.—

I am ashamed dear Charlotte to have allowed my debt to you so long to have remained uncancelled. I am inclined to hope that a safe opportunity will occur this week of forwarding to you the money <this week>—and if so, I will not neglect it. I accompanied my friend Marchettini[2] one evening lately to the house of an Italian Lady who gave a Soirée. There were about thirty persons present in a large stone-floored room with no furniture save chairs, a looking Glass, one table, and a Patent lamp. Many very pretty girls were of the party. The gentlemen were chiefly professional—Painters, Lawyers, language Masters, men holding offices under Government, and a very handsome young Banker. The evening began with Christmas Games, such as I hardly remember the names of, but have seen played in England. Then came forfeits, and impromptu verses, and ridiculous commands still more ridiculously executed. When they were all well warmed and tired, the Director of the School for Declamation at the Accademia <di belle arte> delle Arti e Mestieri,[3] was applied to for permission to call upon two of his pupils, then present, to recite. He consented. The chairs were instantly whisked to one end of the room in rows one behind the other, and a space being thus left for the young ladies, they stood up, and modestly but courageously began a scene from [*The letter is fragmentary and incomplete; the following passage begins overleaf.*] I begin to be somewhat uneasily surprised at the failure of all intelligence from the Wilbrahams, who seriously promised me to write from Geneva.[4]—I saw last night two ladies from Naples whom I knew at Rome, and who give excellent accounts of the restored health of the Morier's fine little boy.—This was at a grand party at Lady Dorothea Campbell's,[5] who opens a very fine house every Monday Evening. I was introduced to her by our friend Mrs Slater,[6] & have received a general invitation for the season. Last night was her second meeting. The kind Shuldhams[7] took me, & sent me home. A hack does not do well for such set-outs. It was very full, but not hot, I promise you! The stuccued floors are the deuce, & there was no fire.—A Milanese was there who played upon an exacrable instrument—a Mandoline—I had never heard one before, and except in his hands never desire to hear one again. He did wonders with it. It is smaller than a guitar, and played with a quill. The energy, neatness, brilliancy, & even fine expression of the performer were perfectly marvellous—but what a pity to throw so much time almost away upon a catgutty, wirery, tinkling toad of a machine scarcely better in itself than a tail-comb and a bit of paper. Mr Robinson is still here, but goes to Rome on Saturday.[8] We were both much shocked to hear of the sudden and unexpected death of poor Mr Finch. I forget whether I told you of it in my last.—He seems to have died of a billious fever, & some say he was not well managed.[9]—Adieu my dearest Charlotte.

At any odd intervals of spare time, if ever you have such, pray let me hear from you. The Irelands[10] are still here, and always ask kindly after you when I see them. My best love to your two dear girls. I hope Julia is all the better for her bathings, & that poor Het is at least not worse than when you wrote.—Again adieu, & loves a million.—

1. The Rev. John Andrew Methuen (c. 1794–1869), Vicar of Corsham, Wilts., and spiritual adviser to Charlotte Barrett, who it seems had quoted a passage to him from a letter of SHB's. In his reply, he expressed concern for Sarah Harriet's spiritual welfare, particularly in "that divided trust partly on H partly on self, which seems to be your poor dear Aunt's stumbling-block. . . . looking to the work wrought in her, instead of the work done for her" (*Alumni Oxon.;* Burke; A. Methuen to CFBt, [Oct. 1830], Berg; John A. Methuen to CFBt, 4 Dec. 1830, Barrett, Eg. 3705, ff. 139–40; CFBt to HBt, 6 Feb. [1833], Berg). Apparently, Mrs. Barrett had passed on this opinion.

2. Marchettini, SHB's "kind-hearted and sensible" drawing-master, gave her lessons twice a week; with his wife, he would occasionally accompany Sarah Harriet to the opera or theater (LL. 133, 138 and passim).

3. The conservatorio tecnologico per le arti ed i mestieri was set up in Florence under the French imperial government (1807–14) (*L'Accademia di belle arti di Firenze* (Firenze: Accademia di belle arti di Firenze, 1984), 86).

4. The Wilbrahams had left Florence c. 20 September 1830, about ten days after Sarah Harriet's arrival (HCR, 19 Sept. 1830, Travel Journals).

5. Dorothea Louisa, the youngest daughter of Otway Cuffe (d. 1804), 1st Earl of Desart (1793); she had married 18 March 1817 Col. James Campbell (c. 1773–1835),

who had served with distinction in India and Spain. Her husband was promoted Maj.-Gen. (1819), made a K.C.B. (1822) and would die at Paris 6 May 1835 (Burke; Lodge; *DNB* under Campbell; *GM*, NS 4 (1835): 90).

6. Unidentified.

7. Edmund William Shuldham (1778–1852) of Dunmanway, co. Cork, joined the E.I.C. as a cadet in 1797 and rose through the ranks to Col. (1829), later Maj.-Gen. (1838) and finally Lt.-Gen.; for some years, he was Quarter-master general at Bombay. His wife, whom he married 3 December 1816, Harriet Eliza Bonar (d. 31 July 1847), youngest daughter of Thomas Rundell of Bath, gave birth to a son at Florence in 1828 (Sir Bernard Burke, *A Genealogical and Heraldic History of the Landed Gentry of Ireland*, 10th ed., ed. Ashworth P. Burke (London: Harrison & Sons, 1904); *Alumni Oxon.; Alphabetical List . . . Indian Army; GM*, 86, Pt. 2 (1816): 562; 98, Pt. 2 (1828): 171; NS 10 (1838): 317; NS 39 (1853): 200–201; Early Cadet Papers, Register of Cadets 1775–1779, India Office Library).

8. Henry Crabb Robinson would actually leave Florence on Tuesday, 26 October 1830, reaching Rome three days later (HCR, 26–29 Oct. 1830, Travel Journals).

9. Robert Finch died on 16 September 1830 of a severe chill that developed into rheumatic fever, and was buried on the twentieth in the Protestant Cemetery in Rome (Nitchie, 2, 63). Sarah Harriet undoubtedly learned of his demise when she "took a walk & ice" on 21 September with Mr. Robinson, who had just received the news. The idea that he was the "victim of mismanagement," based on the opinion that "bleeding & bark can never be at the same time the proper remedies," was expressed by a "party" to whom Robinson read the account of his death (HCR, 21–26 Sept. 1830, Travel Journals).

10. Probably Thomas James Ireland (1792–1863) of Owsden Hall, co. Suffolk. A graduate of Cambridge (M.A. 1817), he would later sit briefly in Parliament (1847–48) and act as county magistrate. He was recently married, on 17 February 1829 to Elizabeth, daughter of Sir William Earle Welby; his wife gave birth to their first child in Florence on 27 November 1829 (Burke, *DLG; Alumni Cantab.;* Stenton; *GM*, 99, Pt. 1 (1829): 268; 99, Pt. 2 (1829): 558; NS 19 (1843): 669; 3rd ser. 15 (1863): 248).

132. To Anna Wilbraham

[Florence], 13 November 1830
A.L., incomplete, Berg

I shall be just before I am generous; so remember, my dearest Anna, that the other half of the sheet is for Sister Eliza. Ye may pay the postage between ye,—I dare say ye will be able to afford it.—

Why, mercy, mercy, will ye not be very cold at Geneva all the winter?—To be sure it is better than running your heads into places full of turmoil and confusion: but I must say, that provided there had been a fire-place in Miss Emma's room, I wish ye were still in Casa Pepe!—And how many people there are here wishing the same thing. Poor Bati[1] for one, who, as yet, has got no permanent situation, but now and then gets employed for a few days by persons passing through Florence, and putting up at the Quatres Nations, or other Locandi where he is known. For about a week, he escorted a party of no fewer than six young German Students. They repaired to the Gallery daily at nine o'clock, and remained till three; they then visited the Churches, or private collections—dined, and went off again whilst there was light seeing all that could be seen—and ended the day at the Theatre. I saw them once at the Gallery; there was not a pair of whiskers amongst them darker than Terra Gialla—they were as national in appearance as they well could be; but looked like good intelligent and inquisitive lads.—La Serefina[2] has got something of a place, which by her account of it to Sig^r Marchettini, whom she met lately, is no great shakes: but he persuaded her to retain it whilst in doubt of getting any thing better; and I hope she will be wise enough to follow his advice. The Scrub of the world, Sussini[3] (was that his name)?—He with the pink sattin pelisse wife, honoured me with a visit; but I did myself the honour to decline receiving him—for though I pity his poverty, I despair of doing any good to one so foolish.—

We have heard at length from Mrs Gregor, who is housed safely in England, at the Rectory House, Ockley, Dorking, Surrey. She is near some intimate relations, or friends, perhaps both, the Arburthnots,[4] and seems pleased with her residence, and neighbourhood. She was ill on the road, and sent to Vichy by an English Physician, and got much better: but then poor Nelly[5] fell sick, and very seriously, and they were detained in France a long time.—The Chandlers[6] are gone back, or are on their road to Rome without passing through Florence. Except the Shuldhams, <unless by accident *1/4 line*> I seldom see any of the people you knew unless by accident. Lady Dorothea Campbell opens her house every Monday evening, and was civil enough to give me a general invitation. I have been once, and spent a pleasant evening—but it was bitter cold, for she had neither fire nor carpets, and half her visitors caught bad colds. Since then, she has I am told made a complete reform; and moreover, she has set the young persons dancing, which enlivens the meeting, without making a regular fussy ball of it.—There I saw all your old friends, Bowyers,[7] & Mason,[8] and Walkers,[9] & Douglass'[10]—Mrs Walker has called upon me, good-humouredly exempting me from the necessity of returning her visit. Mrs Mason asked me where I lived—and has made a forget of it, and there the matter rests. The Locks[11] and I smile and bow when we pass in the street, or see each other at

Church, and neither take, nor give <each other> any further trouble. Some of my Lucca Baths friends keep up their intercourse with me, and though not persons I have any long-standing regard for, yet I find them chatty and pleasant.—

I shall procure for your Sister-Em the information about Farenheit's Thermometer[12] from some Professore whom Marchettini knows, and who has the best instruments in Florence.—Your scamp of a flower-vender, seemed almost to recognize me one evening whilst I was eating ice at a Coffée House with Mr Robinson and offered me his beautiful basket to chuse from, but I only shook my head at him and laughed, and he looked somewhat perplexed as if he hardly knew whether to laugh too, or to be angry.—I draw at a great rate, and have regular lessons twice a week—My present sketch is from Guido's Cleopatra,[13] and very prit she is. Col. Shuldham has bought Marchettini's own drawing.—

In the Bobili Gardens[14] one evening I met Marchettini with his wife, and Child. The latter is a fine sturdy young thing, & the wife is very pretty, and modest-looking and gentle—but poor thing, her front teeth are spoiling.—I see la Sigra Mancini[15] pretty often—She has promised to come and read a play to me—for I have been told upon high authority (Niccolini the Tragedian) that she recites admirably. Mr Robinson knew Niccolini well, and I was once honoured with a visit from him, and might go whenever I like to a house where he spends all his evenings[16]—Mais a quoi bon? He speaks so fast and so thick that I do not understand one word in twenty that he utters[17]—and so I have never been.—But I would go if I had any companion to encourage me.—Adieu once more my dears All—

Oh—I have sent Miss Chandler word that you are to be written to Poste Restante Geneve if there is any thing to write about.

November 13th 1830.

1. Probably a servant of the Wilbrahams during their stay in Florence, he is often mentioned when SHB writes to them (see LL. 140, 142, 145 below).

2. Serafina or Seraphina may be the former housemaid of the Wilbrahams in Florence (also "the wife of Mr Landor's Coachman") who continues to visit Sarah Harriet Burney after their departure (L. 135; see also LL. 140, 142).

3. Unidentified.

4. Jane Gregor's grandfather, Capt. John Urquhart of Craigston, had purchased the estate of Cromarty and married his cousin Jean, daughter of William Urquhart of Meldrum, thus bringing the two related families together. His daughter Mary (Jane Gregor's aunt) married Robert Arbuthnot of Haddo, Aberdeen, whose son William (1766–1829) was created 1st Bt. (1822) and had a numerous family (Burke; Burke, *DLG*).

5. Probably Mrs. Gregor's younger sister, Eleanor (L. 99, n. 2).

6. Possibly Benigna née Dorrien, widow of the traveler and antiquary, Richard Chandler (1738–1810), and her children, William Berkeley (c. 1789–1867) and Georgina Benigna (d. 24 Feb. 1857); the latter was certainly in Italy in May 1832 when she would marry Dr. David McManus (d. 1848) (*DNB; GM*, NS 29 (1848): 559; 3rd ser. 2 (1857): 499; 4th ser. 3 (1867): 829; CFBt & JBt & HnBt to HBt, 16–17 May [1832], Barrett, Eg. 3702A, ff. 78–79v).

7. Probably Sir George Bowyer (1783–1860), 6th and 2nd Bt. (1800), and his wife (m. 19 Nov. 1808) Anne Hammond née Douglas (d. 1844). Outlawed as a debtor, he, as well as his wife, would die abroad. His mother, Henrietta, the Dowager Lady Bowyer (c. 1752–1845) would die at Florence in 1845 (Burke; Thorne; *GM*, NS 23 (1845): 223; NS 25 (1846): 446–47).

8. Mrs. Mason, whom Sarah Harriet later refers to as a "restless gad-about" (L. 140), has not been further identified.

9. Charles Montagu Walker (1779–1833), Capt., R.N. (1825), who married 5 October 1811 Anna Maria (d. 22 Feb. 1859), daughter of Walter Riddell of Glen Riddell, Dumfries (Burke; Burke, *DLG;* Marshall, Vol. 3, Pt. 1, 225–27; *GM*, 103, Pt. 2 (1833): 369–70).

10. Probably Admiral Sir Andrew Snape Douglas (d. pre 1845), K.B. (1789), father of Lady Bowyer (n. 7), who may be the Admiral Douglass with whom Crabb Robinson would dine at Rome in 1831 (Burke; *GM*, NS 23 (1845): 223; Shaw, 2: 300; HCR, 11 Feb. 1831, Travel Journals).

11. Lt.-Gen. John Locke (d. 1837) and his wife Matilda Jane née Courtenay (1778–1848) (Burke, Lodge under Devon; *GM*, NS 30 (1848): 334). The General was "an old friend of Sallys at Sir Joseph Banks" (CFBt to HBt, 7–8 Aug. 1831, Berg).

12. The thermometric scale introduced by physicist Daniel Gabriel Fahrenheit (1686–1736), who also invented the mercury thermometer c. 1714.

13. Of several paintings of *Cleopatra* by Guido Reni, SHB may have been copying the one which hung in the Palazzo Pitti in Florence, dated 1638–39 (Pepper, 283).

14. The magnificent Bóboli Gardens on the hillside behind the Palazzo Pitti were laid out in the sixteenth century, extended in the seventeenth, and opened to the public for the first time in 1766.

15. Unidentified.

16. The home of Mme Carlotta Certellini and her sister Gertrude on Via della Vigna Nuova, where Henry Crabb Robinson had lodged during his stay in Florence; her evening gatherings of friends included the poet Niccolini (L. 128, n. 7; L. 129, n. 4). Robinson introduced Sarah Harriet to these ladies 10 September 1830 and took her home to the conversazione on at least one occasion (e.g., HCR, 10, 28 Sept. 1830, Travel Journals).

17. Robinson would agree that Niccolini "is the worst speaker of Italian I ever heard . . . I am content to conceal my want of comprehension by trying to look wise—Sometimes I give a look of despair to the ladies—And one of them repeats to me" (HCR to Robert Finch, 24 July 1830, Bodleian, MS. Finch, d. 14, ff. 177–78v).

133. To Henry Crabb Robinson

Florence, 28 November 1830
A.L.S., Dr. Williams'
Published: Morley
Address: All' Signor / Signor H. C. Robinson / Poste Restante / Roma
Postmarks: FIRENZE
DECEMB
Endorsed: 28 Nov. 1830 / Miss Burney

November 28th 1830. Florence.

My dear friend

There was a passage in your letter that made me start and grin with satisfaction,—it was this—"unless I can meet with agreeable apartments, I shall cut and run—either Southwards to Naples, or Northwards to Florence."—But that maladetta Minerva Library has spoilt my sport, and there you are, I suppose for the winter.[1] Well—I wish you comfortable, and if you can find the way of becoming so, I will e'en reconcile myself to your absence: but I do miss you much, though we were not in the same house. I gradually withdraw myself from the few English fine gents I am bound to bow to when they pass, (always excepting the good and friendly Shuldhams) and have fallen into a little sociable set, where I can drink tea in my bonnet, and hear a little rational talk which being in French, I am able to chime in with. A Mde La Riviere, a Swiss, who is very musical, and gives lessons when she can get scholars—and a Mde and Mlle Le Brun,[2] the latter a clever painter, or paintress, or paintrice (which should it be?) are my new associates, not forgetting Monr La Riviere[3] who is a Negociant, and a civil and not ill-informed man. We laugh, and chat, and are at ease together, and give each other Swiss Goutés, and walk home like scrubs, and wear no fine cloaths. And at Lady Dorothea's I see heaps of folks with mines of wealth on their backs, and not a real cordial face amongst them.—Then there is my Marchettini, the drawing-Master, a kind hearted and sensible man with whom I now and then trudge to the Opera or Play, and who is soon to get me tickets for the Goldoni Theatre[4] where an expert set of dilletanti performers will be giving their representations. These sort of doings amuse me fifty times more than seeing fine caps and hats, and eating ices in a circle with men and women who all seem to be made of ice too.—

The Wilbrahams have got no further than Geneva, and there pitched their tent, an' please you, for the winter!—They took fright at the state of Paris during the cries for the condemnation of the Polignac Ministry;[5] and now they have got into a set they like, with Sismondi,[6] the Author, at its head, and their brother will not be coming to meet them at Paris as they expected; and so they are fixtures like Mont Blanc, though not perhaps quite so permanently.—There is, or was lately at Geneva, a young Russian Lady, very beautiful, acquainted with all languages, an Improvisatrice, turning all heads by her talents, winning all hearts by her manners—and, in short, the Corinne[7] of her day. They were to meet her at M^de^ Sismondi's,[8] and, I own, I did envy them the treat. Here there is nothing to distinguish one Jack or one Gill from another.

Are you fond of Monkeys?—Prince Demidoff who built a fine Villa near Florence, chose to furnish it with outlandish animals of various sorts,[9] such as Reindeer, Siberian Dogs, Cockatoos, Eagles, and tho' last not least, a whole legion of Monkeys. An English party of Ladies and children, went lately to see this precious Repository, and one of the poor children held forth to a Monkey in its wooden cage, a walnut—the brute seized her hand, and tore it so unmercifully that there is danger of her losing forever the use of one finger and her thumb!—So much for ferocious pets!—We have had another shocking adventure here. A young Englishman who had established a large Straw-hat manufactory, quarrelled with some of his work people and dismissed them. He received sundry anonymous letters threatening his life if he did not take back at least some of the set. These he disregarded; & being a stout-bodied and stout-hearted man, went about fearlessly and at all hours unarmed. He slept always at a little Villa about a mile from one of the gates, & in going towards it last Sunday Night, he was attacked by six ruffians, and literally hacked to pieces by their knives, for there was scarcely a part of his body unwounded. Two, if not three of the Assassins have been taken; and one of these has some of his front teeth knocked out by the vigorous blows which in self-defence the poor victim dealt about him. Col. Shuldham says he was one of the handsomest men almost ever seen, and was but eight and twenty.

If you see Dr Nott, pray present my compliments to him, and tell him I heard lately from my kind friend Mrs Gregor, who has got a pleasant house and garden near Dorking in Surry, and seems much pleased with her new home, and with its friendly neighbourhood.

I am told in a letter from England that M^r^ and Mrs Morier mean to spend the winter at Nice, but by your having seen him so lately at Rome,[10] I imagine they must have given up that intention.—They and you, are almost the only folks I should feel intimate with at Rome.—I really wonder at, and am sorry that our tastes differ so much that you do not like Pignotti[11] though I like him so very much. I have read as far as the beginning of the seventh vol: and every day my interest in the work encreases. His reflexions indeed are not very brilliant, deep, or new, but they are sagacious and just; and independently of the style, the subject is, to my thinking, highly curious, and chiefly from its extraordinary resemblance to the turbulent spirit of the little Grecian Republics, who, like the Florentines, the inhabitants of Pisa, Genoa, and Venice, were always at daggers drawn, and yet flourishing, wealthy, and devotedly fond of the fine arts. To be sure, the Greeks fought their own battles, whereas the Italians hired mercinaries & entrusted their command to Condottieri. Amongst these scamps of the world, were some remark[*ab*]ly clever, and not wholly undeserving men—I mean in a moral point of view. It is also interesting to trace the slow and yet uninterrupted progress of the Medeci family. You first hear of them the latter end of the eleventh century—they lie by for some twenty or thirty years; then starts up another of the race, & another, and another; and they are always popular, and some of the early ones, were truly patriotic.—One volume, and not the least interesting, <is dedicated to giving> gives an account of the revival of science and literature, and a summary of the life of some of the most distinguished amongst the early Poets, Mathematicians, Lawyers & Artists, &c.[12]—I must say, that the Florentines were less inexcusable in their conduct towards Dante than I had supposed.[13] But you know all that, & so, basta così.—

Write again, my dear friend, as often as the Spirit moves you, and tell me when and what you have heard of Mr Richmond.[14] Give my compliments to Mynheer Goetzenberg, & believe me ever truly yours

S. H. Burney

We have beautiful weather—a little cold, but fine for walking—How does mud flourish this year at Rome?

—The accounts from Pisa are much the same. Mrs Barrett & her girls was were [*sic*] delighted to hear of the arrival there of the father & sons of the "wearisome wife" who came with you to call upon me one morning. Hang me if I have not forgotten her name! The Barretts are fond of Entymology—but the Lady they presently found out to be a mere Goody.[15]—I fancy folks are more sociable & less fine at Pisa than here.

1. Henry Crabb Robinson began a letter to Sarah Harriet on 20 November 1830 (sent on the twenty-second), informing her of "my uncomfortable state here on acc[t] of bad lodgings." He also complained that Rome itself was sufficient "only for a learned man" and that he was suffering for "want of a congenial companion." When he continued his letter two days later, however, he was feeling "in a better humour" and told her of the Minerva library, in which he had found "a recourse ag[t] bad weather & bad temper at once."

He had made his first visit to this institution on 16 November and thought it would be "a charming place to read in." On the nineteenth, he records that he read there from half-past eight until eleven and on the twenty-second, rose at 7 A.M. and read at the library until eleven "as usual" (HCR, 16–22 Nov. 1830, Travel Journals).

2. Probably Marie-Louise-Élisabeth (née Vigée) (1755–1842), the well-known portraitist who in 1776 had married Jean-Baptiste-Pierre Le Brun (1748–1813), an artist, by whom she had one daughter before they divorced. Favored by Marie Antoinette, whom she painted numerous times, she was admitted to the Académie in 1783, but fled to Italy when the Revolution began. She later lived at Vienna, at St. Petersburg, in England and in Switzerland, but after 1815 stayed mostly in Paris where she held a salon (*Bryan's;* Bénézit).

3. M. and Mme La Rivière have not been identified.

4. The neoclassical Teatro Goldoni, designed by the architect Giuseppe Del Rosso, was located in the Via Santa Maria in Florence.

5. Jules-Auguste-Armand-Marie, Prince de Polignac (1780–1847), minister (1829) under Charles X; his reactionary policies were unpopular.

6. Jean-Charles-Léonard Simonde de Sismondi (1773–1842), Swiss economist and historian, friend of Mme de Staël. He was writing his monumental *Histoire des Français* in thirty-one volumes (1821–44). See Jean-R. de Salis, *Sismondi, 1773–1842* (Paris: Librairie Ancienne, 1932).

7. Corinne (or Corinna), the beautiful poetess of ancient Greece; also the female paragon and protagonist of a novel by Anne-Louise-Germaine, Baronne de Stäel-Holstein, *Corinne ou l'Italie* (1807).

8. Jessie Allen (1777–1853), seventh daughter of John Bartlett Allen (1733–1803) of Cresselly, Pembrokeshire, had married Sismondi on 15 April 1819. She settled with her husband at Geneva, where she entertained select groups in her home on Thursday evenings (Burke, *LG;* de Salis, 377–81, 387–90; *Emma Darwin: A Century of Family Letters, 1792–1896*, ed. Henrietta Litchfield (London: John Murray, 1915), 1: xxii–xxiii, 1–5, 151–54).

9. Nicolaï Nikitich Demidov (b. 1773), a wealthy Russian aristocrat, who died at Florence in 1828; at his sumptuous villa near the city, he had formed valuable collections of art and natural history.

10. Robinson had mentioned the Moriers (L. 122, n. 5) in his letter to SHB, sent on 22 November 1830 (n. 1 above).

11. Lorenzo Pignotti (1739–1812), Italian poet and historian, whose *Storia della Toscana sino al principato* was published in nine volumes in 1813–14.

12. The last volume.

13. Pignotti implies that Dante's exile from Florence was a mild fate compared to

the fierce reprisals suffered by others of the same faction, and that any hope of return was lost through his own indiscretion (Bk. 3, Ch. 8).

14. Robinson passed on SHB's polite enquiry when he wrote to Richmond on 18 December 1830 (HCR, 18 Dec. 1830, Travel Journals).

15. Probably Elizabeth Spence (c. 1781–1855), the wife of William Spence (1783–1860), the entomologist, who lived with his family on the Continent 1826–33, mostly in Italy and Switzerland (*DNB; GM*, NS 43 (1855): 550; 3rd ser. 8 (1860): 631–32). Sarah Harriet would refer to "that weariful woman, M[rs] Spence, whom you insisted upon my knowing" in a later letter (L. 163 below). Crabb Robinson had met them at Florence on 16 October 1830 and was "very favourably impressed"; he soon considered them to be "in the first line of my friends" (HCR, 16 Oct. 1830, Travel Journals; HCR, *Reminiscences*, 2: 486). Charlotte Barrett also speaks of them as valued acquaintances in several letters from April 1831 on, and admired the diligence of the Spence boys who rose at 5 A.M. to study (CFBt to HBt, 28–30 Apr. [1831], 13–20 Aug. [1832], Berg).

134. To Anna Wilbraham

[Florence], 29 November 1830
A.L.S., Berg
Address: A / Mademoiselle / Mademoiselle Anna Wilbraham / Poste Restante / Geneve
Postmarks: FIREN[ZE]
GENEVE / 8 xbre 1830
LT

"If you do write;"—I wonder at your assurance, M[rs] Nannie—Why, when was I ever a slack correspondent in regard to you?—I can always write to those it is no trouble to write to—folks who desire not that I should stand upon ceremony, and will let me run on as long and as unconnectedly as I please.—So you are to know that wanting sadly to <know> hear something about my poor dear Harriet Crewe, I wrote to Amelie Hinchliffe,[1] who I thought likely to have the means of giving me better information than any one else I could apply to.—She very good-humouredly answered me immediately. The material point in her letter is, that Harriet is safe, and in England—the rest, poor girl, was a rigmarole history as long as the nose of Prince Cheri[2] of the difficulties Edward Hinchliffe[3] encountered in his way from Leige to the confines of Belgium. I care about as much for Edward Hinchliffe as you do for Tom Thumb, and it provoked me that so much of a single sheet of paper should have been wasted upon him, when there were such a quantity of other things and other people (besides telling me more about Harriet herself) <which> she might have talked of.—However, one must take the will for the deed:—she meant to be kind, but it is her nature to be prosy, and what she will be if she lives to be old there is no guessing, since already she is so long-windedly tedious.—She knows I have a horror of her many words, so to save herself a bullying she begins by saying she remembers how I hate long prefaces, and therefore will immediately come to the point—And lo! that point is Ed Hinchliffe!

Of Lady Combermere she very succinctly says: "I suppose you have heard of the separation of Lord & Lady Combermere from incompatibility of temper."[4]—However, even that little sentence gave me comfort, as it entirely did away with all idea of infidelity and crime. I always hoped that it might be so, for Lady Combermere is one of the few people who with all her faults has in my eyes such redeeming qualities that the thought of her being seriously guilty went to my very heart.

But now what think you Amélie tells me next? Why, that "Edward Davenport was married yesterday (the day before Lord Mayor's no Shew)[5] to a Miss Hurt or Hunt, (I cannot very well decipher which), a very pretty girl of five and twenty."[6]—She says no more, and I suppose thinks it quite natural that a very plain infirm man, upwards of fifty should marry so flourishingly—and with none of the best of tempers into the bargain.—The weather in London is so like Spring, or was early in November, that Mr Hinchliffe caught himself enquiring of somebody how his sick daughter had borne the winter?—Poor Lady Anson has had another dreadfully severe domestic calamity,—the death of another son, and the best of them all, after three days illness. That pitiable woman seems to be marked out for affliction.[7]—Well might be applied to her the words of St. Paul "if in this life only she had hope. . . .[8]

Do you remember the Demidoff hideous Monkeys? An English party of Ladies, children, and Maids went to see the Villa, and likewise paid a visit to those nauseous animals. A good-natured little girl offered one of the beasts a walnut: it seized, not the nut, but her hand, & bit it so dreadfully that the Shuldhams told me she would probably lose the use of the thumb & one finger for life!

Ma'am, I went lately to a Swiss Gouté, and was made much of, and spent a very pleasant evening; and Ma'am, I give a Gouté in return tomorrow, and expect three ladies and a gentleman; and we are to chat, and eat, and drink, and chat again, and I dare say we shall all like the fun very well.—

Lady Dorothea Campbell goes on with her Monday evenings; it is now always a dance. I went a second time about a fortnight ago, and got well acquainted with the Mother of Miss Stewart[9] who used to draw in the Gallery when Miss Eliza went there to paint. She has called upon me, and I have returned the visit, and if we meet again we shall both express great concern at not having found each other at home.—Pour tout le reste, the party was much the same as the time before, with rather a better, at least a fuller attendance of men. I was angry to see so many young Englishmen manufacturing themselves to look like Italians. One aimed, and with some success, at resembling the Duke of Lucca,[10] and quantities had so very foreign an appearance that on my asking Lady Dorothea how she had been able to bring together so many young Italians willing to forsake their own countrywomen for ours, she laughed, and said there was not one Italian in the room!—She lets her five children, the youngest only three years old, sit up the whole evening, becurled, be-ribboned, be-necklaced and be-braceleted as smartly as the best of them.—

Marchettini comes to me still regularly every Tuesday and Friday at nine o'clock, and I like my lessons as well as ever, & him better and better, for he is a good creature I really believe. He represented to me that the poverty & long illness of his friend Maghelli[11] had involved him in difficulties that rendered a little immediate assistance so necessary for him, that tho' any thing but rich, he felt that he should hardly be able to deny him a small loan. I hope my dear Miss Eliza will forgive my officiousness, but on hearing this, I could not forbear offering him an advance upon what she will have to pay him when the picture is finished.—To me, it appears admirably done—and persons who were standing round looking at it, expressed the highest admiration.—My advance to him was three Napoleons. If I have done wrong I am very sorry—and you must intercede for me, my dear Annie. But I know that however generous a person may be, it is not pleasant to be acted for without authority given.

I am much interested by Pignotti's History, which though I bought, I am reading, and have got into the seventh volume. The squabbles and turbulence of the little Italian Republics, puts one in mind of the Greeks, where so much of the same spirit reigned. The gradual progress to celebrity of the Medeci family keeps up ones attention, and the little that is interspersed concerning the other Italian rulers, the Visconti, the Gonzagni, the Sforza family, & the great Condottieri of the day, is all very entertaining.—

The accounts from Pisa are much the same—in the last letter, rather better.—Mr Robinson is by no means so cock-a-hoop at Rome as he was last year. Most of his cronies have dispersed—Mr Finch, poor man, is dead[12]—Lord Northampton out of spirits[13]—Mr Richmond gone to Paris,[14] and Rome itself no longer such an astounding novelty. However, he has gained admittance to the Minerva Library—a Monastic establishment, where he spends his mornings in greater comfort than he had at first expected.—So, with kindest love to your Sisters, believe me ever my dear Annie's most affectionate S. H. Burney

The Devil take Capt. Sotherby![15]—I am provoked beyond measure.—What in the world did Mrs Isted mean?[16]—I saw Mrs Paterson[17] lately, looking ten years younger than when she left Florence; she says Geneva is the healthiest air in the world—However, if I leave Italy next year, I think I should prefer Lausanne unless ye were still in your present quarters, for I know not a soul at one of the places, and have lots of folks at the other.

This is written the 29th day of Novr 1830.—Marchettini sends respects.—

1. Possibly Emma Maria, the daughter of the Rev. Edward Hinchliffe (c. 1772–1819), Rector of Barthomley (1796) and of Acton, Cheshire (1798), and granddaughter of John Hinchliffe (1731–94), Bishop of Peterborough (1769) (*DNB*), who had married Lord Crewe's sister, Elizabeth (c. 1744–1826). Baptized on 26 November 1808 at Barthomley, Emma Maria was the same age as Harriet Crewe and may have been called "Amelie" in the family (*Westminsters; Alumni Cantab.;* parish register, Barthomley, Cheshire; *JL*, 5: 208, n. 5).

2. The story by the well-known fairy-tale writer, Marie-Catherine Le Jumel de Barneville, comtesse d'Aulnoy (c. 1650–1705), "La Princesse Belle-Étoile et le Prince Chéri"; a translation was included in *A Collection of Novels and Tales of the Fairies, Written by that Celebrated Wit of France, Countess D'Anois* (1728), but it was also published separately as *The Renowned History of Prince Chery and Princess Fair-Star* (1800). Mme d'Arblay had read it with her six-year-old son in 1801 (*JL*, 4: 473, n. 1; Andrew Block, *The English Novel, 1740–1850* (London: Dawsons, 1961), 196).

3. The Rev. Edward Hinchliffe (c. 1801–78), brother to Emma Maria (n. 1 above), had attended Oxford, B.A. (1823), M.A. (1826), and would be appointed Rector of Barthomley, Cheshire (1836–50) on the resignation of Willoughby Crewe (L. 108, n. 1) (*Westminsters; Alumni Oxon.*).

4. Second daughter of Capt. William Fulke Greville, and sister to Mrs. Morier (L. 122, n. 5), Caroline (c. 1793–1837) had married 18 June 1814 as his second wife Lt.-Gen. Sir Stapleton Cotton (1773–1865), 6th Bt. (1809), a hero of the Peninsular War. As a result of his distinguished military career, he was created Baron Combermere (1814), Viscount (1827), Field Marshal (1855). In 1825, he was appointed Commander in Chief in India, where he helped to restore English supremacy by the capture of Bhurtpore (*DNB;* Gibbs). His wife did not accompany him to India, and they separated on his return in April 1830, living apart until her death seven years later. "The cause of their disunion could not be ascertained. . . . Incompatibility of tastes and habits may latterly have estranged this couple, once so attached, and perhaps the independence which each had enjoyed during Lord Combermere's stay in India unfitted them for the mutual concessions required in married life" (*Memoirs and Correspondence of Field-Marshal Viscount Combermere*, ed. Mary, Viscountess Combermere [and W. W. Knollys] (London: Hurst and Blackett, 1866), 2: 226).

5. The Lord Mayor's Show, the annual procession in London on the occasion of the

Lord Mayor's taking his oath of office, was traditionally held on 9 November. In 1830, the festival was canceled for fear of "disorder and tumult" (*Times*, 8–9 Nov. 1830).

6. Edward Davies Davenport (1778–1847) of Capesthorpe, Cheshire, married on 8 November 1830 Caroline Anne (c. 1809–97), eldest daughter of Richard Hurt (b. 1785) of Wirksworth, Derbyshire. The bride was about twenty-one; after her husband's death, she would marry as his second wife 11 February 1852 Edward John Littleton (1791–1863), 1st Baron Hatherton (1835) (Burke, *LG;* Burke, *DLG;* Gibbs; Burke).

7. The Dowager Viscountess Anson, Anne Margaret (1779–1843), the second daughter of Thomas William Coke (1754–1842), 1st Earl of Leicester (1837). She had married 15 September 1794 Thomas Anson (1767–1818), created 1st Viscount Anson (1806), M.P. (1789–1806). Eight of her fourteen children had died, the latest being her fourth son Capt. William Anson (1801–30) on 19 October 1830 (Burke; Lodge; Gibbs; *GM*, 100, Pt. 2 (1830): 476–77).

8. "If in this life only we have hope in Christ, we are of all men most miserable" (1 Corinthians 15:19).

9. Possibly the same Stewarts with whom H. C. Robinson dined on 11 February 1831 in Rome, and who were about to leave Italy on 2 April. "They are very amiable persons. And she is a superior woman" the diarist commented (HCR, 11 Feb., 2 Apr. 1831, Travel Journals).

10. Charles-Louis (1799–1883), Duke of Lucca, later Charles II of Parma. Charlotte Barrett, who passed the summer at Lucca, considered him to be "very handsome but a great vaut-rien. . . . always surrounded by gay idle young englishmen" (CFBt to FBA, 18–20 June [1830], Berg).

11. Unidentified.

12. At Robert Finch's unexpected death on 16 September 1830 (L. 131, n. 9), Robinson felt a sense of personal loss: "M[r] Finch was a very kind & hospitable man. And his ample library would have been my great resource. . . . These are sad interruptions in one's course. In life we expect them—But on a tour of a few months we do not look for them" (HCR, 21 Sept. 1830, Travel Journals).

13. The 2nd Marquess of Northampton was "out of spirits" after the sudden death of his wife 2 April 1830 (L. 126, n. 11). During his second winter at Rome, Crabb Robinson felt the "loss of Lord Northampton's house, which was not opened to parties during the season" (HCR, *Reminiscences*, 2: 490).

14. Robinson's last parting with his travel companion took place on 28 August 1830 in Florence; that day, he felt "unsettled as Richmond was getting ready to go away" but comforted himself with the hope that "we shall meet in the spring I have no doubt" (HCR, 28 Aug. 1830, Travel Journals).

15. Charles Sotheby (d. 20 Jan. 1854), Capt., R.N. (1812), eldest surviving son of William Sotheby, a friend of the Wilbrahams (L. 79 and n. 6). He helped to suppress piracy in the Mediterranean (1824–27) and would attain flag-rank (1848). He had recently married for a second time, on 18 November 1830, his cousin, Mary Anne Sotheby (d. 1881) (O'Byrne; Burke, *LG; GM*, 100, Pt. 2 (1830): 560; NS 42 (1854): 191–92).

16. Possibly Charles Sotheby's maiden aunt, Rose Sarah Isted (c. 1761–1847), the elder sister of his mother Mary (L. 79, n. 8) and daughter to Ambrose Isted (c. 1717–81) of Ecton, Northants. (Burke, *LG; GM*, NS 18 (1847): 221). But Mrs. Isted could also

be the wife (m. 20 Oct. 1795) of Charles's uncle Samuel Isted (1751–1827), Barbara née Percy (c. 1762–1834) (Burke, *DLG; GM,* 65, Pt. 2 (1795): 878; NS 2 (1834): 220).

The context suggests that Mrs. Isted had heard of Capt. Sotheby's recent marriage and imagined the bride to be Sarah Harriet Burney.

17. Possibly Elisabeth Patterson (1785–1879), the daughter of a wealthy Baltimore businessman, William Patterson (d. 1835), and repudiated wife of Jérôme Bonaparte (1784–1860), Napoleon's youngest brother. Their marriage of 24 December 1803, never recognized by the Emperor, was declared null in Paris in 1806, and Jérôme wed Princess Catherine of Württemberg the following year. Refused entry into French domains, Elisabeth returned with her son to America, where she was pensioned by Napoleon on condition that she renounce the name of Bonaparte. Since his defeat in 1815, "Mrs. Patterson" had been residing chiefly in Europe, and was certainly at Florence in 1829; she also spent some time at Geneva, where she attended the evening-gatherings of the Sismondis (L. 133, n. 8) (*Emma Darwin,* 1: 241; Bernardine Melchior-Bonnet, *Jérôme Bonaparte ou l'envers de l'épopée* ([Paris]: Librairie Académique Perrin, 1979), 41–61, 324–30, 339–42; Philip W. Sergeant, *The Burlesque Napoleon* (London: T. Werner Laurie, 1905), 64–112, 360–64).

---

135. To Henry Crabb Robinson

[Florence], 6–11 February [1831]
A.L.S., Dr. Williams'
Published: Morley
Address: H. C. Robinson Esqr / Poste Restante / Roma
Postmarks: FIRENZE
14 FE [*?*]
Endorsed: Reced 15th Feb: 1831 / Miss Burney

My dear friend

In these "spirit-stirring times,"[1] I thought a letter from one who leads so monotonous a life as I do, <will> would come with singular disadvantage; so I have been waiting to hear from one or other of my few correspondents in England, hoping to glean out of their letter something to insert in my own. A few days since, I received a good-humoured & amusing-enough despatch from Sarah Payne. A Mr Manning (do you know him?—I do not) a Persian traveller, and a friend of my late dear brother,[2] has been spending a little time with them; and they have had a Soirée at which Southey[3] attended, and other worthies;

and the aspect of public affairs brought politics upon the tapis, more than literature or any other subject. Mr Southey thinks that in ten years, there will be no House of Lords. Little ignorant S. H. Burney, had thought long before she heard this, that such a circumstance is likely to occur much sooner. Were that the worst we have to fear, I should be too happy. In Cromwell's time, Government went on powerfully and steadily with no House of Lords. But in these days, though hypocrisy is hardly so prevalent, there is more misery to excite the people to mischief, and more daring, open licentiousness than in the very worst times of the Commonwealth. Tell me, am I wrong in thinking, that the mass of the lower order of Englishmen is corrupt—unpatriotic—un every thing but poor, and thievish?—The land cannot maintain the population, I am afraid; and if that is the case, how can the evils they suffer under be redressed by any Reform, or any attempt at retrenchment made by Government?—Altogether, my poor addled head is full of confused apprehensions;—I grieve for the desparation that seems to have led to the destruction of so much property by fires,—and I grieve for those who, with good intentions, like our present Minesters, have to combat against evils that are perhaps incurable.[4]—The papers are sent to me very regularly by the kind Shuldhams, and I read them with indescribable eagerness: but they take away my spirits for the rest of the day. The affairs of Ireland—the horrors that appear to be hanging over the heads of the poor dear Poles[5]—the Conflagrations in England, &c, &c—All these, are tremendous circumstances. Hunt, the new M.P., you find, means to become a genteel and pretty-behaved legislator, and says he will hold no more raggamuffin Meetings, but will carry the petitions of his Constituents and lay them before Parliament, Constitutionally.[6] And so the poor rogue will lose his popularity, and be called a turn-coat.—Is it not pity they, I mean the Lord Leuttenant and Co., snapped up O'Connel so soon, without giving him, or leaving him rope enough to do his own business for his own neck?[7]—How you must grin at my wise political talk!—But remember, I see no one to set me right in my crude opinions. The weather has been bad, and the Shuldhams, my only English friends here, have been, like myself, lothe to stir out for some weeks. All therefore that I have now favoured you with, is the produce of my own solitary meditations.

Your Signora, where you boarded (name forgotten),[8] sent one of her tidy damsels to me lately to enquire when I had heard from you?—I mentioned the date of your last letter, and said I should be writing to you soon; whereupon the damsel, holding a pretty little good-natured white lap-dog in her arms all the time, requested me in the name of her Mistress, to present a thousand compliments and kind remembrances to you.—I was glad to find you had conducted yourself so prettily as to deserve all these civilities!—

I like you much, my dear friend, for your kindness to your poor young Italian Master![9] It is a pity-moving case, and I wish I was his Scholar too. If you wish to add a mite to the greater good you have done him, find out some way of laying out upon him, (for me,) the trifling amount of a Sovereign. "I would do more, but that my hand lacks means."[10]—

I began this on Sunday the 6th Feb: and here is Friday the 11th. "Nothing can come of nothing."[11] I really cannot think of a word to add.—Oh, yes!—I saw yesterday the wife of Mr Landor's Coachman; she was housemaid at the Wilbrahams, and often comes to see me.[12] Mr Landor, by her account, is just like too many of your discontented liberty-boys,—he likes no tyranny but his own.[13] If she (the Maid) is to be believed, he has had 16 Coachmen in one year! I dare say she lyes by at least ten: but the <truth> fact probably is undeniable that he is a harsh and intolerant Master, and is much disliked in the servile class.[14] His wife,[15] they say, is mild and good, but has little influence, and not an atom of authority.

We have begun Spring weather since last Sunday, and nothing can surpass the splendid blue of our clear sky, nor the vivifying and delightful feel of the air. The Carnaval Tom-fooleries go on pretty spiritedly. There was yesterday a sort of Corso you do not see at Rome—very gay and brilliant. Under the Uffizio, which was cleared of its Exeter-Change shops, the G. Duke, Duchess,[16] &c, &c, walked a reasonable time, surrounded by well dressed company, including an immense proportion of Masks. At night, he went with his family to the Pergola, which was crouded to excess. All this I heard of, but did not see,—except as the Masks passed my windows.—

I have thoughts of making a little trip to Pisa, when the Spring is more advanced. When do you return from Rome? I am heartily ready to go back to England, if I knew how to manage it in safe and good company. I dread the heat of another Italian Summer. If Switzerland were quiet, it might suit me—but I can decide upon nothing yet. Italy is to me like the plums in a Grocer's shop to a new 'prentice boy;—it is very irresistable at first, but palls after a while.—If I get back according to my wishes, I shall always be glad to have made the excursion—but I would not by choice reside here on any account.

I am reading Michaud's Histoire des Croisades,[17] well written, and en[*ter*]taining; and I have just finished Monti's fine Tragedy of Caius Gracchus. I like it much better than his Aristodemus—and suspect I shall also prefer it to his Galeotto Manfredi,[18] tho' the opening scene of this last is admirable. The story however is an odious one, and all the worse for being true.—I forgive you for going a cooing to another old Maid:[19] as long as you keep to the genus, you cannot be taxed with inconstancy.

We hear of disturbances at Bologna, and throughout Romania[20]—As little as may be transpires, and nothing detailed has yet reached us. Your new Pope is in all our shop windows—He is not lovely it must be confessed.[21]—Adieu. Pity me for being reduced to write such a dull dog of a letter, which, if you never answer, you would really be perfectly excusable.—

Once more, Adieu—Ever truly yours

S. H. Burney.

1. Perhaps a reference to Walter Scott's *The Lord of the Isles* (Edinburgh: James Ballantyne, 1815), Canto 6, 1–2: "O who, that shared them, ever shall forget, / The emotions of the spirit-rousing time."

2. Thomas Manning (1772–1840), who was not in fact a Persian traveler, but the first Englishman to enter Lhasa, Tibet (1811); he accompanied Lord Amherst's embassy to China (1816) and was noted as a scholar of the Chinese language and civilization (*DNB; GM*, NS 14 (1840): 97–100; Marchand Bishop, "Lamb's Mr. M: The First Englishman in Lhasa," *Cornhill Magazine*, no. 1046 (Winter 1965–66): 96–112). He was a close friend of Charles Lamb, through whom he had met Robinson and probably James Burney. HCR, on his return to England, would dine with Manning at the Paynes, and finding him "taciturn," suspect that he was credited with more ability than he had (HCR, *Reminiscences*, 1: 349; 2: 81, 269; HCR, 19 Mar. 1832, Diaries).

3. Robert Southey (1774–1843).

4. In the latter half of 1830 and early 1831, England was experiencing popular agitation for reform, industrial unrest, and a wave of arson, rioting, and machine-breaking in rural areas.

5. The Polish uprising of 29 November 1830 and the ensuing war with Russia (Jan.–Sept. 1831) evoked sympathy and financial aid from other countries in Europe, but would end in defeat.

6. Henry Hunt (1773–1835), the radical reformer, who was chief speaker at the "Peterloo Massacre" of 1819 and was sentenced to two years' imprisonment. Elected in December 1830 to represent Preston, North Lancs., in Parliament, he advocated universal suffrage, annual parliaments and the secret ballot. He lost his seat in the next election (1833) and thereafter retired from politics (*DNB;* J. C. Belchem, "Henry Hunt and the Evolution of the Mass Platform," *English Historical Review* 93 (1978): 739–73).

7. Daniel O'Connell (1775–1847), called the "Liberator" for his role in securing Catholic emancipation (1829). An Irish M.P. (1829–47), he led the agitation for the Repeal of the Union. On 19 January 1831, he had been arrested in Dublin for breaches of the Act for the Suppression of Illegal Associations, charges to which he agreed to plead guilty if judgment were postponed. He returned to London to support the Reform Bill, which passed a second reading with a majority of one; before O'Connell could be sentenced, however, Parliament was dissolved, and with it expired the Act under which he had been indicted, enabling him to escape punishment (Denis Gwynn, *Daniel O'Connell*, rev. ed. (Oxford: B. H. Blackwell, 1947), 201–4).

8. Mme Carlotta Certellini (L. 128, n. 7; L. 129, n. 4).

9. Robinson had written to SHB, 6–8 January 1831, telling her of his lessons in Ital-

ian from a master called Gatti and lamenting his "slow progress." There is no mention in his journal of any charitable act (HCR, 6–8 Jan. 1831 and passim, Travel Journals).

10. Shakespeare, *As You Like It*, I, ii, 236.

11. Shakespeare, *King Lear*, I, i, 90.

12. Possibly Seraphina, news of whom is regularly passed on by SHB to Anna Wilbraham (LL. 132, 140, 142).

13. Walter Savage Landor (1775–1864), to whom Robinson was introduced on 16 August 1830 as the friend of Wordsworth and Southey: "Met to-day the one man living in Florence whom I was anxious to know." Landor, who had been living in Florence since 1821, immediately invited him to visit his villa: "To Landor's society I owed much of my highest enjoyment during my stay at Florence." The following summer, Robinson would introduce Sarah Harriet Burney to Landor, who would call her "one of the most agreeable and intelligent women I have met abroad" (HCR, *Reminiscences*, 2: 481–84, 502, 521; HCR, 16 Aug., 20 Aug., 9 Sept., 9 Oct. 1830, 11, 25 July 1831 and passim, Travel Journals; see also *Henry Crabb Robinson on Books and Their Writers*, ed. Edith J. Morley (London: J. M. Dent & Sons, 1938), 1: 378–93; Malcolm Elwin, *Landor* (London: Macdonald, 1958), 244–45; R. H. Super, *Walter Savage Landor* (New York: New York University Press, 1954), 216–18).

14. Landor was reported to have thrown a servant out of the window in a fit of temper, expressing solicitude only for the trampled flowerbed (Elwin, 276–77). Robinson maintained that while the Italians were afraid of him, he was "respected universally. . . . He was conscious of his own infirmity of temper, and told me he saw few persons because he could not bear contradiction" (HCR, *Reminiscences*, 2: 483).

15. Landor had married on 24 May 1811 Julia Thuillier (c. 1794–1879), the daughter of a Swiss banker, Jean-Pierre Thuillier (1760–1836). The marriage ultimately failed, and Landor left his wife and children in April 1835, never to be reconciled. For differing accounts of the separation, see R. H. Super, 252–59; Elwin, 273–80.

16. Leopold II (1797–1870), the last reigning Grand Duke of Tuscany (1824–59), and his wife, Maria Anna of Saxony (d. 1832).

17. Joseph-François Michaud (1767–1839), *Histoire des Croisades* (1812–22).

18. The three tragedies of the Italian poet Vincenzo Monti (1754–1828): *Aristodemo* (1786), *Galeotto Manfredi* (1788) and *Caio Gracco* (1800).

19. In his letter of 6–8 January 1831, Robinson had mentioned his acquaintance with Frances Mackenzie (d. 1840), a younger daughter of Frances Humberston Mackenzie (1754–1815), cr. Lord Seaforth, Baron Mackenzie (1797). He was introduced to her as a friend of Wordsworth on 2 December 1830, and soon considered her his closest associate in Rome, enjoying hospitality at her house all winter (HCR, 2, 4, 10, 26 Dec. 1830, 4 Jan. 1831, Travel Journals; HCR, *Reminiscences*, 2: 489–90; *The Letters of William and Dorothy Wordsworth*, ed. Allan G. Hill, 2d ed., vol. 6 (Oxford: Clarendon Press, 1982), 395, n. 4; *Scots Peerage*).

20. On 4 February 1831, a revolt against Papal rule in the Romagna spread rapidly through the Papal States, and a provisional government was set up at Bologna.

21. Robinson was in Rome when Pope Pius VIII died (30 Nov. 1830) and his successor proclaimed, Pope Gregory XVI (1765–1846), on 2 February 1831. He would agree that the new Pope was "a plain & vulgar man in his appearance" but found that "the election gave general satisfaction" (HCR, 1 Dec. 1830–6 Feb. 1831, Travel Journals; HCR, *Reminiscences*, 2: 487–88, 493–96).

136. To Henry Crabb Robinson

[Florence], [27] March 1831[1]
A.L.S., Dr. Williams'
Published: Morley
Address: All' Signor / Sig[r] H. C. Robinson / Poste Restante / Roma
Postmarks: FIRENZE
31 MAR [?]
Endorsed: 28 March 1831 / Miss Burney

My dear Friend

Mais arrivez-donc!—I have been hoping to hear of your arrival, or to see you enter my Salotto, poste haste, every day, nay almost every hour, for this month past.[2] They told me it might be as well not to write in the present state of affairs[3]—but I begin to think it would have done no harm to have minded them not a whit! Such extravagant lies are current, that it would make you stare to hear of them. At first, we cannot be sure they are lies; so they perplex and alarm us; and afterwards, they make us hold ourselves cheap for having paid any attention to them. I think of going to Pisa, for a little while, the beginning of April.[4] My journey thither would have taken place sooner, but all the Locande at Pisa were crouded, and no bed could have been procured for me. Charlotte Barrett had none to offer me—so here I remained, where I have had the comfort of seeing M[r] & M[rs] Morier; they are still at the Quatres Nations on the Lung'Arno; and I go to them pretty often.—My dear friend, I know nothing about your ancient lodging; I have been ashamed to go near them after so complete a cut[5]—But this is a time of the year when they are very likely to be vacant, for many foreigners leave Florence, if not for their own country, at least for some Villa, as the Wilbrahams did last year, and the city gets gradually thinned.—The Wilbrahams I should tell you write word that they purpose departing from Geneva the Monday after Easter.—I lead so uniform a life that I have not a thing to tell you. Parties I utterly renounced early in the winter, and as soon as I drew my little stick out of the water, the circle closed round the spot it had occupied, and I remained, "The world forgetting, by the world forgot."[6]—If I live another season here, however, I will not condemn myself to such complete solitude. My plan is, to board with a Swiss family, keeping the comfort of a separate sitting-room, but joining them occasionally, and taking my meals in company with them.[7] But the style of society (I will not say here only, but, in these times, every where) puts me quite hors de combat. The dress, and the lateness of the hours, and the inevitable expense of carriage hire, &c suit neither my taste nor my pocket; and bad for me as it is, to depend solely upon myself for amusement, I had rather a thousand times lead over again such a monotonous winter as the last, than enter into the troublesome soi-disant gayeties of the many here.

You, I hope, have had a more animated time of it. I shall be truly rejoiced to see you—and if you can let them have a peep at you at Pisa they will be very glad—

Meanwhile—Believe me ever most sincerely Yours
S. H. Burney.

I have not heard from home, except through Charlotte Barrett's letters from her Mother and husband, since I wrote last.—We have a very cold Spring compared with the last.

Palm Sunday
March 28th 1831.

1. SHB appears to have made an error in the date of her letter, as "Palm Sunday" was 27 (and not 28) March in 1831.

2. Henry Crabb Robinson was planning to pass through Florence on his homeward journey; he had written to SHB on 12 March 1831, telling her that the "uncertainty of my plans depend on the conduct of the French." He was still in Rome six weeks later when he wrote to inform her of his "intended departure at the end of a month." In the end, he would leave the Holy City on 6 May 1831, remarking that "I have lived 11 happy months within its walls." Taking a circuitous route, he would reach Florence on the twenty-third (HCR, 12 Mar., 21 Apr., 6–23 May 1831, Travel Journals; HCR, *Reminiscences*, 2: 501–2).

3. The Revolution in the Papal States was being subdued by Austrian troops who overran Parma and Modena (25 Feb. to 6 March) and entered Bologna (21 March). On 27 March 1831, the provisional government capitulated and the three-week-old revolt was over.

4. Sarah Harriet would spend a fortnight at the end of April at Pisa, staying at a hotel near the Barretts and spending her days with them. Charlotte wrote to her husband on 29 April 1831: "Rain again today so Hett must stay at home and content herself with listening to Sallys new manuscript which is very pretty & amusing" (CFBt to HBt, 28–30 Apr. [1831], Berg).

5. In his letter of 12 March 1831, Crabb Robinson had inquired about his Florentine landladies, Mme Certellini and her sister, whom he had introduced to Sarah Harriet. She had attended with him at least one of their conversaziones and was apparently given a general invitation, but was loath to go alone (L. 132 and n. 16). In her own letter of 6–11 February [1831], she told Robinson that the ladies had sent to inquire after him.

6. Alexander Pope, "Eloisa to Abelard," l. 208.

7. SHB was lodging with a "swiss Lady" in Florence that winter (CFBt to HBt, 28–30 Apr. [1831], Berg), which may account for the "little sociable set" of Swiss acquaintance mentioned in her letters of 28 and 29 November 1830. She would adopt a different plan, however, apparently moving at the beginning of May 1831. When Robinson arrived in Florence later that month, he was "surprised" to find Sarah Harriet at his old lodgings. "She was tired of the solitude of her former lodging. And has taken apartm^{ts} here. She is delighted with the goodness of her hostesses. And says she will remain here as long as she stays in Italy" (HCR, 23 May 1831, Travel Journals). For a full description of life on the Via della Vigna Nuova, see below L. 138.

137. To Charlotte (Francis) Barrett

[Florence], 2 June 1831
A.L.S. with typescript, Barrett, Eg. 3705, ff. 45–48v
Address: Alla Signora / Signora Barrett / Ponte di Seraglio / Bagni di Lucca
Postmarks: FIRENZE

4131 <Casa> Via della Vigna Nuova
2° piano. June 2^{d} 1831.

Many thanks, my dearest Charlotte, for the enquiries you have made concerning Diodati's Bible,[1]—And as I think it, (that you speak of) must be the same, bating the slight difference in the Title-page, with that I have seen here, I am exceedingly glad you have purchased it, and shall be upon the look-out for an opportunity of getting it brought to me.—I am sorely disappointed at not having the pleasure of receiving Julia; though you try to <relieve lighten> soften the unwelcome information by the conditional assurance that "if an opportunity should ever offer" to send her to Florence, you will allow her to profit from it. I have the evil habit of placing but small reliance upon these iffs! But after all, mistake me not—I have no intention to scold, for I am sure that if circumstances had permitted it, you would willingly have sent her. What was it that finally induced you to renounce (as you appear to have done) your Sea Voyage?[2]—I am sorry the clean house you were in last year at Lucca Baths is engaged:[3] but try for something a little like the chearful residence of your Italian Physician, whose name, as usual, I have of course forgotten.[4] Mr Robinson will probably take a peep at you, as he talks of a flying visit to Pisa, Lucca, & the Baths.[5] I have been reading, with great amusement, a series of seven or eight long letters from young Richmond to Mr Robinson, the two last of which are written from Greece, one dated Navarino, the other Napoli di Romania. Two or three are from Paris, and contain amongst other curious particulars, an account of his meeting the bright-eyed Quaker, as he calls her, M[rs] Opie, at Gen[l] La Fayette's,[6] and presenting to her a few lines of introduction sent to him by M[r] Robinson. She received him charmingly; invited him, when he visited England, to go and see her at Norwich, &c.[7] La Fayette was of course very courteous to an American. His Soirees are, or were, enormously crouded.—I was much concerned to hear last night that the papers contain an account of the robbery of two young Travellers, (an American and a Swede) not far from Argos. The names are not mentioned—but it is probable M[r] Richmond may have been one of the parties, and his companion (a Dane, not a Swede) may have been the other. I hope they suffered nothing beyond the loss of their effects, (bad enough, that!)—But such an untoward circumstance may entirely disable him from prosecuting his intended plan of visiting most of the celebrated parts of Greece. Athens, luckily, he had early secured a peep at—but I think he meant to go thither again. You will like to hear that the poor fellow during his journey in the Diligence from Paris to Marseilles, met with a gay, pretty young Frenchwoman, from whose conversation he had reason to believe she was an unbeliever. He spoke French but imperfectly; however, he undertook the difficult task of talking to her, in defiance of her laughter and mockery, and that of some others. By degrees, she became attentive, and more serious—and it ended by her saying to him when they parted—"Monsieur, je n'oublierais jamais les bons conseils que vous m'avez donné"—And she shook hands with him most cordially. May he not have been the appointed instrument to begin the conversion of this poor soul?—

Now I will give you a bit of politics, extracted from a letter received this morning by Mr Robinson.—Speaking of the recent Cornish Election, the writer says: "We gained a glorious victory over the Borough-Mongers, on their own dunghills. We had 1300 votes unpolled when they resigned; whereas they had brought up their last man. The anti-reformers had abundance of money, and spent it freely, and they had all other appliances which usually command success;—on our side there was great zeal in a good cause, and the result proved its force and value; we have reason to be delighted not only with the victory, but with the way in which it was won. There was much to try the temper and the patience of our party, and much to tempt the virtue of the poorer voters: but in no instance did they break either the peace, or their promises; and though brought into close and continual contact with their opponents, and that too under feelings very strongly excited, there was neither an insult nor a quarrel, and all the candidates, and their friends, were able to mix indiscriminately in the crowd without being exposed to the slightest molestation. The Borough-mongers had engaged the only Inn and every Pot-house in the place (Lest-withiel). There is an old ruined palace of the Ancient Dukes of Cornwal which our party were fortunately able to <engage> hire;—in this they fitted up a kitchen, cellar, &c, killed 20 oxen, and 100 sheep, and renewed scenes of good cheer and festivity such as the old walls had not witnessed for three centuries; 1200 persons were entertained there daily during the Election",[8] &c.—But I want to ask whether there is not <corruption> bribery in all this feasting?—Adieu dearest Charlotte. You may perceive by my borrowing so largely from others, that I have little to say for myself. I continue to like my Signoras very much. Nicolini would be charming were he but less sleepy every evening. He is about to publish a new Tragedy, "Procida", to whose family the Island so called belonged, and who was the principal instigator of the conspiracy against the French which led to the Sicilian Vespers.[9] Sigra Carlotta Certellini,[10] who has heard it read, says he has written nothing equal to it—not even his Foscarini.[11]—Mr Robinson sends his best regards—Give my cordial love to your girls, & believe me ever most affectionately Yours

S. H. Burney

1. Giovanni Diodati (1576–1649), a Biblical scholar of Geneva who translated the Bible into Italian (1607); it was reprinted throughout the nineteenth century.

2. In the spring of 1831, Charlotte Barrett was planning to take Hetty on a sea voyage to strengthen her, and Sarah Harriet "kindly offered to take charge of Julia while we are at sea." The journey to Leghorn was accomplished in May, but instead of benefiting Hetty, the sea air "brought back all her pain & irritation of the lungs." After a fortnight's stay, the sea voyage was given up, and the Barretts traveled instead, before 8 June 1831, to the Baths of Lucca where they now planned to spend the summer. Julia, therefore, did not go to Florence (CFBt to HBt, 14 Apr. [1831], 28–30 Apr. [1831], 6 May [1831], CFBt to HBt & ABt, 8–13 June [1831], Berg).

3. The previous summer, the Barretts had stayed at Casa Lena, Ponte di Seraglio, Bagni di Lucca, where they at least had interesting neighbours: "Countess Guiccioli is here with her brother & lives opposite to us. She was, you know, Lord Byrons favourite. She is fair with thick light hair, & very like our cook Caroline—pretty, but rather a rustic beauty." In the summer of 1831, they found "a pretty lodging with a garden very near our old house of last year" (CFBt to FBA, 18–20 June [1830], CFBt to HBt, 7–8 Aug. [1830], 8 June [1831], Berg).

4. During a year and a half spent in Italy, Charlotte Barrett had consulted five physicians about her daughter Hetty's health; the name of their doctor at the Baths of Lucca was Franceschi (CFBt to HBt, 7–8 Aug. [1830], Berg).

5. Crabb Robinson would soon leave Italy on his homeward journey; on 25 July 1831, he recorded his "serious regret" in parting from Niccolini, "as well as Miss B[urney] and the Mesdames Certellini." He left Florence that evening, and arrived at Lucca Baths

the next day, where he called on Mrs. Barrett and had "a very pleasant chat." He left on 31 July for Pisa where he saw SHB's friend, Mrs. Heath, and the next day (8 Aug.) wrote to Sarah Harriet, giving her "an acc[t] of my adventures—a message from M[rs] Heath." He pursued his journey home, arriving in London on 7 October 1831 (HCR, 25 July–7 Oct. 1831, Travel Journals; see also HCR, *Reminiscences*, 2: 509–13).

6. Marie-Joseph-Paul-Yves-Roch-Gilbert du Motier, marquis de La Fayette (1757–1834), famous French general and politician.

7. The writer, Amelia Opie (1769–1853), occasionally visited Paris but owned a house in Norwich. In 1825, she had been received into the Society of Friends; an attractive and vivacious woman, she apparently contrived to look fashionable even in the plain Quaker garb (*DNB*). Robinson thought that "her becoming a quaker gave her a sort of éclat; yet she was not conscious I dare say, of any unworthy motive" (HCR, *Reminiscences*, 2: 277).

8. The election of two M.P.s for the county of Cornwall was a tough contest and the expenditure of the two Tory candidates enormous. After the poll had been open for five days, these two—Richard Rawlinson Vyvyan (1800–79), 8th Bt. (1820) and Ernest Augustus Edgcumbe (1797–1861), styled Viscount Valletort (1818–39), later 3rd Earl of Mount Edgcumbe (1839)—retired. They had been soundly beaten by the two Whigs, Edward William Wynne Pendarves (c. 1775–1853) and Charles Lemon (1784–1868), 2nd Bt. (1825), who continued to represent the county for years. Vyvyan found refuge in a pocket borough and continued his fight against the Reform Bill, while Lord Valletort briefly represented Lostwithiel, a borough soon to be disenfranchised when the bill was passed (1832) (Henry Stooks Smith, *The Parliaments of England From 1715 to 1847*, 2nd ed., ed. F. W. S. Craig (Chichester: Political Reference Publications, 1973), 36, 490; *DNB;* Burke, Cokayne under Vyvyan; Gibbs, Thorne under Edgcumbe; Burke, *LG*, *Alumni Oxon.* under Pendarves; Stenton under Lemon).

9. Giovanni Battista Niccolini's drama, *Giovanni da Procida* (1830), is based on the life of the supposed leader of the Sicilian uprising of 1282, which began with the slaughter of French soldiers at Easter vespers in Palermo, known as the "Sicilian Vespers."

10. SHB's landlady, a personal friend of Niccolini's.

11. In her letter of 19 July 1830, Sarah Harriet had spoken of her pleasure in reading Niccolini's *Antonio Foscarini* (1827), which she admired as a "fine masculine, energetic performance."

138. To Frances (Burney) d'Arblay

Florence, 8 August 1831
A.L.S., Berg
Address: A / Madame / Madame d'Arblay / 1. Half-Moon Street / Piccadilly / London / Inghilterra
Postmarks: Verona / 11∧[?]
FIRENZE
LL
FPO [A]U22 / 1831

Florence, August. 8th
1831

My dearest Sister

I have been silent so long, that it were vain to attempt any excuse; so, suffer me at once, to make believe I have never misbehaved, and to spare both you and myself the ennui of an unconvincing apology. I own that I have nothing satisfactory to plead in my own defence, and therefore have no resource but to throw myself upon your mercy.—However, I have this to say at least in mitigation of my offence;—though you seldom heard of me, I was continually hearing of you through the medium of our Charlotte Barrett, who in all her letters inserted little extracts from those written by her dear Mother, or Mr Barrett; & thus, without the necessity of exertion, I was kept au courant of what I most valued, family intelligence.—

The first fervour with which I looked about me on entering Italy, and above all, Rome, having gradually abated, I felt convinced that my letters would lose much of their interest, and yet would cost a mint of money.—Here we pay little for foreign letters,[1] so you may write as often as you please, my dear Sister, without the fear of ruining me; and I know how much you enjoy the employment!—Almost as much as I do myself.

My winter was spent here in Florence with tranquillity, and a certain degree of bodily comfort, but with much want of sociability. I scarcely knew any Italians, and the English deal in large, and dressy, and late, and tiresome parties: but not in friendly, unceremonious intercourse. I accepted two or three invitations in the early part of the season, which turned out to be Balls, and cost me much more than they were worth in <hiring> carriage hire, and smart cloaths. After these essays, I declined all subsequent engagements, and never went out in the evening, except now and then, in a quiet unceremonious way, to the Opera with my worthy Drawing Master and his pretty modest wife. We chose fine, calm nights, and walked to and from the Theatre, paid our 3 pauls (1/6) at the door, got excellent places, with backs to our seats, saw and heard with undisturbed convenience, and got home well pleased a little before midnight.—Once too, I went with the same persons to an Italian Soirée, and never was better amused. Amongst the company present was the Professor who teaches Declamation at the Academy of the Fine Arts,—and two of his best and favorite pupils, one of them his Niece. He was good enough to prevail upon them at different intervals in the course of the evening, to recite various scenes from Alfieri, from Goldoni,[2] and other Authors as well Tragic as Comic. They acquitted themselves admirably: but what I was even more struck by than their grace, and correctness, and expression, was their good humoured unaffectedness, their modest composure. They were young ladies, and not intended for public performers, yet they equally were exempted from bashfulness or boldness. In short, I never saw girls with more pleasing, and natural good manners. Indeed I can find but one fault with the few Italian ladies I have been introduced to,—they have the harshest and loudest voices in the world. On entering a room, it is difficult not to believe, if there are four or five ladies present, that they are quarrelling; they really bawl and scream—yet, if you look at them, you find that they are smiling, and in perfect amity, although every vein in their throat and forehead is swelled with the effort of forcing themselves to outdo their companions in vehemence.—To me, this is a most repulsive fault; I do not so much mind the loudness as the bad quality of that loudness;—it is not full-toned & rich—but piercing & grating;—in short, it is vilainous, and whenever I speak to an Italian woman, if she attempts to answer me before I have done, I am so unequal to cope with her, that I immediately stop short, and give the matter up, well knowing the uselessness of trying to be heard to the end of my little speech. This makes no difference to them, for as they never listen to any thing but the beginning of what you meant to say, they go on arguing upon that, & fancy that you are silenced by their irresistible logic. I have now lived long enough to endure with patience not to be listened to, upon the principle that in all probability those I am with are better entertained by talking themselves than by being talked to; and if that is the case, why should I <fatigue myself in order to be heard by people who like so much better to> not let them "do all the talking themselves," as a young American[3] said when asked how he could bear to dine so often with a companion notoriously dull?—"Oh, I don't mind his dullness—I do all the talking myself!"—

During these last three months I have been upon a new plan, boarding and lodging in an Italian family, consisting of two ladies, d'un certain age, one a widow, the other single; and two excellent and kind-hearted female servants who have lived with them for years. I have a lofty and handsome drawing-room, & a bed-chamber adjoining; and am welcomed with cordiality whenever I join their party in their own quarter of the house. They seldom go out except for a walk, or to one of the Theatres, but they invariably have one, two, or three friends dropping in without form of an evening. The most constant of these, is the Signor Niccolini, the most successful Tragic Poet now in Italy. He is full of erudition; understands modern as well as ancient languages, is a devoted admirer of our Shakespear—and moreover, an upright, honourable, & modest man;—but—"Would he were leaner!"[4]—Poor soul, he is short & thick, rises early, studies hard, takes much exercise; and by the time he arrives here at half past eight, or nine, he is so sleepy, that he can scarcely keep his eyes open two minutes together. Moreover, when he does converse, I lose much of what he says by his rapid mode of utterance, and the thickness of his voice. But the most comical perplexity he throws me into, is when he chuses to read English to me; he understands & construes every thing perfectly, but his pronounciation is so any thing but English, that I really can scarcely tell what language he is reading in.—As he has taught himself entirely without any help but from books, this is not to be marvelled at—but it does not make my case less pitiable when I am called upon to listen to him. My Widow Lady is pretty well read in the literature of her own country, & a little in that of France, and her memory is stored with much poetry which I should like to ask her to recite were it not for the tiresome sing-song monotony with which to my ear she spoils the finest passages. Her Sister, is a notable needlewoman, who makes all the gowns and caps that are worn in the family; goes to bed & sleeps an hour regularly every day after dinner; towards evening takes her lap-dog upon her knee, & reads a chapter or two in her Italian Bible, and spends the remainder of her time till we all retire for the night, in nursing said dog, & lounging upon a sofa, without a cap (at fifty years old) and now that the weather is hot without other garments than a gown & shift! even her stockings only come up to the calf of her leg, like a half boot. In winter, she tells me, that both she & her sister, knit all the evening[.] The heat during the last three weeks (it is now the eighth of August) has been most trying. Eighty four or eighty three of Farenheits thermometre has been the usual standard. At night we are obliged to sleep under a mosquito net which corrects one evil by the infliction of another—we are less stung but more stifled. And after all the beasts contrive to sting me even by broad day-light, and particularly attack my hands, obliging me almost constantly to wear gloves.—

Charlotte Barrett, poor thing, writes in far better spirits, & seems to have every reason to flatter herself that her long-suffering girl will eventually recover.[5]—She has informed me that there is some prospect of seeing Sarah Payne & her husband in this country.[6] I hardly think that in these unsettled times such a thing is very likely, but if it should occur, it will be a great treat to us to see them and hear all their English news.—I often, oh how often wish myself at home again,[7] for every reason but one—viz: the cheapness with which I can live here compared with what the same method of existence would cost in England.—I spend not now, lodging, board, and every personal expence included, twenty pounds a quarter![8]—Certainly this is no trifling recommendation but it by no means makes me amends for other privations—such as that of seeing those I know and love, & living <with> where the climate is more temperate, and the Country more inviting.—An Italian City has many charms—but an Italian Country house is to me detestable, abounding in venemous reptiles, and devoid of every domestic comfort we are are accustomed to enjoy.

I have two or three English good natured neighbours, and one family in particular living in a large Palazzo just opposite who are very kind to me. Their names are Layard[9]—They lend me Newspapers and books, and encourage me to visit them sans façon in bonnet & shawl and spend an evening with them as often as I like.—I hope to enjoy this very evening a little sociable country drive with Mrs Layard, and then to return with her for an evening chat to her own cool & beautiful house. She has introduced me to many clever people, chiefly Artists, English as well as foreign, & their conversation is full of interest.—

If you should say to yourself Here is Sarah wishing to return to England, & yet remaining abroad—Why does she do so?—Because—I am anxious to join some respectable party, & have not the courage to travel as I did before under the sole protection of a Voiturier.

And now my dearest Sister I must bring this rambling letter to a conclusion. Do not omit I beseech you to give my best love to my two dear Sisters, Burney and Broome. Remember me most kindly to Cousin Edward—How often have I wished for him!—Do not forget me when you see Martin—Say every thing affectionate for me to dear Alex. And to Maria & Sophy entreat my Sister Burney to give my love—Adieu, & adieu my most dear Sister—Yours ever most affectionately, S. H. Burney.

Whoever may be kind enough to wish to write to me, may direct alla Signora Signora Burney S. E. Burney, Poste Restante Firenze—Italia.

To my unutterable surprise, my poor dear Harriet Crewe has—turned Roman Catholic![10] She has been in England during the Belgian disturbances,[11] & has made her formal profession of the new faith she has adopted.—I believe her to be now gone back to [Liege].—

1. Charlotte Barrett wrote from Lucca that "every letter we receive costs me 3/6 sometimes more," an expense considerable enough to make her wish to exercise restraint, but Mrs. Barrett probably received more English letters than SHB (CFBt & HnBt to HBt, 7 Aug. [1831], Berg).

2. Vittorio Alfieri (1749–1803), the Italian tragedian, and the comic playwright, Carlo Goldoni (1707–93).

3. Possibly J. C. Richmond, Crabb Robinson's young American friend (L. 126, n. 15).

4. An inversion of Julius Caesar's observation, "Would he were fatter!" in Shakespeare's play, I, ii, 199.

5. Charlotte Barrett believed her daughter's disease to be "chronic inflammation," which it was necessary to subdue with "a great deal of bleeding and severe weakening diet." Despite her daughter's increasing debility, she still wrote confidently of her eventual recovery. In May she took comfort in the fact that her arms "have gained half an inch in circumference since December." In June she reported that "she took a very short walk—her poor knees are very weak . . . she sat down at the end of 150 steps." In August she found that Hetty "is so weak that it gives her great pain to sit for a quarter of an hour in a chair or to lie on a sofa." Nevertheless, she still thought it possible that another winter might complete her cure "if Hetty should continue mending" (CFBt to HBt, 6 May [1831], CFBt to HBt & ABt, 8 June [1831], CFBt & HnBt to HBt, 7 Aug. [1831], Berg).

6. During Sarah Harriet's visit to her niece in the spring, Charlotte had written her husband asking "Have you heard yet . . . whether John & Sarah are coming abroad?" The Paynes seem to have left England by early August when Mrs. Barrett wrote thanking Henry Barrett for "all the nice things you send us by Sarah" and added "I hope Sarah Payne will write to us when she arrives at the Lake of Como" (CFBt to HBt, 28–30 Apr. [1831], CFBt & HnBt to HBt, 7 Aug. [1831], Berg).

7. Mme d'Arblay passed on this message to Anna Wilbraham, who had now reached England and inquired with "affectionate anxiety" about Sarah Harriet. Fanny told her that in a "Letter from the dear Wanderer . . . the wish of return 'creeps out,'—nay, more than creeps, it almost gallops" (*JL*, 12: 753–54).

8. SHB initially withdrew £250 before setting out on her journey (22 July 1829); another £150 was sent to her by Coutts the following year (9 Nov. 1830); on 7 July 1832 a final £100 was taken from her account, bringing the total debited for the three-and-a-half-year period she spent abroad to £500 (Coutts ledgers).

9. Henry Peter John Layard (1789–1834), who had gone to Ceylon with his younger brother in 1803–4 and joined the Civil Service, becoming Second Assistant to the Agent of Revenue, Jaffna. He held various appointments, such as Sitting Magistrate, Batticaloa, Collector and Provincial Judge, Matara, before retiring 1 January 1814. The following year, he married at St. Lawrence, Isle of Thanet, Marianne (1789–1879), the only daughter of Nathaniel Austen, a banker. In 1831 they were renting a floor of the Rucellai Palace in Florence where they entertained hospitably (Gordon Waterfield, *Layard of Nineveh* (London: John Murray, 1963), 11–14, 430; J. Perry Lewis, *List of Inscriptions on Tombstones and Monuments in Ceylon* (Columbo: H. C. Cottle, 1913), 25; *GM*, 85, Pt. 1 (1815): 177).

10. Apparently, the conversion took place when Harriet Crewe was in Belgium: "in

Flanders she heard the Bishop of Liege preach, sought private conversation & discussion with him, and finally became persuaded that she ought to acknowledge the authority of the Old Church in all things" (CFBt to HBt, 28–30 Apr. [1831], Berg).

11. Disturbances which broke out at Brussels on 25 August 1830 and spread to the provinces led to the overthrow of the dynasty and the establishment of an independent Belgian state.

139. To Charlotte (Francis) Barrett

[Florence], 1 September 1831
A.L.S., Berg
Address: Alla Signora / Signora Barrett / Casa Morganti / Bagni di Lucca
Postmarks: FIRENZE

Septr 1st 1831

My dearest Charlotte

Before I allow myself any of my usual gossip, I will give a categorical answer to all your demands.

No; I have yet heard nothing of our Paynes,[1] as you call them;—and in one sense, that of aches, I do not care how long it may be before I do hear of them. Should I learn any tidings of them, I will let you know: but you are likely to receive the first news from them, as they are quite unacquainted with my address; and I am no subscriber at the Gabinetto Letterario[2] by reason of the ample supply of books I get from the Layard's, and occasionally from Niccolini; so they will not find my name in their list.—Should your projected journey to Rome take place[3] (and I heartily wish you may be able to enjoy that indulgence) you will hear of my poor good Columba at her Sister's Brigitta Belini,[4] Stiratrice, N° 35 Via di Bocca di Leone, Roma. I forget her family name, but ask for Columba, and that will do. She often works by the week or month at the Upholsterers, and when the distance is great to come home at night, sleeps at her employer's. Remember me to her with great cordiality. She will help you all she can: but I fear will never suit you as a permanent servant. I am not sure she even understands any thing of cooking. She has only been used to act as housemaid. She makes excellent Coffée, though.—Now for houses. I had a sitting-room, and two bed-rooms (because Sr Wm Fletcher was with me) for twenty scudi a month at N° 31 via Condotta, a wholesome Street, between the Piazza di Spagna and the Corso. During the Carnaval it was as gay and as thronged with carriages as the Corso itself. But the apartment w^{d} not suit you, unless the Padrona would turn out, and let you have the kitchen and the adjoining little bed-room; and even then, without a large skreen it would never do for you, as the drawing-room is a passage room: but they provided me such a skreen, and it did very well, and shut out both cold, and prying eyes. Mrs Morier had a warm, pleasant house, at N° 22. via Gregoriana, but what they paid I do not know. Whatever you do, go not to the Arch-rogue Brunetti, 66 Piazza di Spagna.[5] His house has but one recommendation—its situation. It is full of fleas (for that matter, so is all Rome) & of dirt; and he is full of lies and imposition. I was with him the first month, and paid at least double what I afterwards was asked.—I wish I could tell you more, my dearest.[6] Poor Mrs Chandler!—Her house, if vacant, might perhaps suit you, and is very clean, and I believe not dear.—It is N° 98 Via dé 4 Fontane.—

As for my presumptuous objection to your calling the Sister of Lord Courtney Lady Matilda, I find I was all in the wrong, in point of fact, though right in point of propriety. Her brother has lately obtained an exaltation in the peerage, and is become an Earl, either by the revival of an old claim, or the grant of a new one. But her father never was an Earl, and it is a thing unheard of that Sisters should derive titles from brothers. Here she is much laughed at for her assumption of this collateral honour.[7]—I am glad you like her girls; they seemed to me nice creatures, full of talent, and industry; and perseverance; and, as you say, they are very unaffected.—I think the Mother a bore,—and the father dull.—Mrs Layard is gone into the country to recruit her strength, and I hear she is better. Her youngest boy is with her; the eldest stays here with his father.[8] I quite like, almost love them both,—her especially. She seems thoroughly good, and is cultivated and agreeable.—

Oh, mercy, mercy! what should I have done with your ten Scorpions? The very name of queste benedette bestie makes me shiver!—One of my ladies, la Geltrude,[9] told me, that being in the country some years ago, and sleeping, as usual, in an uncarpetted room, she heard after she was in bed some live creature stepping about upon the floor, as if its little feet had had nut-shells fastened to them. She rung the bell that somebody might come and see what this was; and behold! two large Scorpions were discovered, taking their nocturnal walk. Frightened out of her wits, she instantly got up, and went to a room in the floor above, and never has consented to sleep in any ground-floor room since. What struck me in this little relation, was the circumstance of these creatures having feet that may be heard patting along when on the bare stones.—

I like—I admire the Italian translation of the Gospels & Psalms,[10] which are what I have hitherto read. If the Prophetical books are not so well rendered, I will abide by my dear English version. Mr Layard has lent me Sir Humphrey Davy's "Consolations in Travel, or the Last Days of a Philosopher." It is a posthumous publication, & the Editor says that "Had his life been prolonged, it is probable that some additions and some changes would have been made".[11] —There are many fanciful and unwarranted ideas on the subject of the creation of this world, & the state of existence in the next: but, on the whole, it is a most interesting work, and shews a mind anxious to discern the right, and well prepared to love and glorify its Creator.—Another book of a very different character has amused me mightily; it is entitled "Tablettes Romaines," and is full of wit and vivacity, and gives a very just and true picture of modern Rome, at least, as far as I am competent to judge. I wish you could get it. The pretended name of the Author is Santo Domingo, but, somehow, I suspect that to be a fudge. It was printed at Bruselles, for neither in Italy nor at Paris would such free opinions have been allowed to see the light[12]—at least, during the Carlists[13] day.—

I congratulate you most zealously in the improvement of your dear invalid.[14] Give my best love to her, and to my dear Julia—Margaret I intend to new model,[15] retaining such parts as seem to me a little worth it, and altering what relates to the family & origin of the heroine. You shall see that I materially improve it.—Adieu my very dear Carlotta—Always give my affectionate love to your dear Mother. Ever yours S. H. B.

1. John and Sarah Payne, who were traveling on the continent, did arrive in Italy soon afterwards and spent some time with Sarah at Florence (CFBt to CBFB, 21 Oct. [1831], Berg).

2. The Gabinetto Letterario, which kept Italian and foreign newspapers, periodicals and books, was opened in 1819 by Jean-Pierre Vieusseux (1779–1863). It became the center of liberal intellectuals in Florence, who gathered at the conversazione held three times a week on the premises, and contributed articles to Vieusseux's journal *Antologia* until its suppression in 1833. Crabb Robinson resorted daily to the Gabinetto during his stay in Florence, and frequently attended the evening gatherings (HCR, 15, 27 July, 18 Aug. 1831, Travel Journals; HCR, *Reminiscences*, 2: 474 and n.; HCR to Robert Finch, 24 July 1830, Bodleian, MS. Finch, d. 14, ff. 177–78v).

3. For the second year in a row (above L. 128, n. 10), Charlotte Barrett was considering spending the winter at Rome: "Julia & Hetty both wish extremely to go," and their desire was supported by a physician's opinion that the change would be good for Hetty, and "the air of Rome really preferable." They intended to return to Pisa about mid-September, and at the end of the month embark from Leghorn "in the Steam Vessel which goes to Civita Vecchia" and from thence to Rome (CFBt & HnBt to HBt, 7 Aug. [1831], CFBt to CBFB, 9–12 Sept. 1831, Berg).

The journey was accomplished, but the change did not prove salutary; writing from

Rome 21 October, Mrs. Barrett was "near wishing we had never left Pisa." All three had caught a severe influenza, and she found Rome both colder and more expensive than expected, "though, if Hetty finds this air better, that will make amends for most things. Hitherto she has scarcely been aware what the air is" (CFBt to CBFB, 21 Oct. [1831], Berg).

4. SHB's former maid, Columba, and her sister Brigitta Belini have not been identified.

5. For the lodgings where Sarah Harriet had stayed on first arriving in Rome, see above L. 121, n. 2. Henry Crabb Robinson, who also lodged there, shared her low opinion of the landlord, a "cowardly knave," whom he had detected in two attempts to cheat him (HCR, 13 Mar. 1830, Travel Journals).

6. Mrs. Barrett would write home of the confusion of their arrival in Rome when all three fell sick and "in the midst of all this we had to look for houses. . . . We have now I think fixed ourselves in a tolerable apartment—dirty and out of condition, but rather cheaper on that account—and I shall clean it up myself, by degrees" (CFBt to CBFB, 21 Oct. [1831], Berg). This was 99 Via del Corso, Rome, where they would remain all winter.

7. Lady Matilda Jane Locke (L. 132, n. 11) was sister to William Courtenay (1768–1835), 3rd Viscount Courtenay (1788), who established his right before parliament to the Earldom of Devon, he being heir to the grantee in a remote collateral line. By an extraordinary decision of the House of Lords on 15 March 1831, he was declared 9th Earl of Devon, the title having been dormant since 1556; his surviving sisters (of thirteen) thereupon assumed the rank and title of Earl's daughters, "their father having been unquestionably entitled to that dignity" (Burke, Lodge, under Devon; Cokayne under Courtenay).

The moving spirit behind the "astonishing decision" was apparently William Courtenay (1777–1859), a clerk in parliament, third cousin to the 9th Earl, who would inherit the title on the latter's death. When this occurred (26 May 1835), the sisters and brothers of the 10th Earl also laid claim to the "same titles and precedence as if their late father had survived" (Gibbs, under Courtenay, Devon; *GM*, NS 4 (1835): 89, 645).

8. The Layards had four sons: Henry Austen (1817–94), Frederick (c. 1819–91), Arthur John (c. 1820–55) and Edgar. The two eldest were sent to school in England in 1829, so only Arthur and Edgar were presently with their parents on the continent (Waterfield, 12, 14–15, 477; *GM*, NS 44 (1855): 441).

9. Mlle Gertrude, sister to Mme Certellini, who rented out lodgings to Sarah Harriet (LL. 129, n. 4; 136, n. 7; 138).

10. Probably the translation by Giovanni Diodati, purchased for SHB by Charlotte Barrett pre 2 June 1831 (L. 137 and n. 1).

11. Sir Humphry Davy (1778–1829) (*DNB*), *Consolations in Travel, or the Last Days of a Philosopher*, [ed. John Davy] (London: John Murray, 1830), consists of a series of philosophical dialogues. The sentence SHB quotes occurs on the very first page; the story of the author's illness is given in his own Preface, dated Rome, 21 February 1829, within a few months of his death.

12. [Count J. H. de Santo-Domingo], *Tablettes romaines; contenant des faits, des anecdotes et des observations sur les moeurs, les usages, les cérémonies, le gouvernement de Rome.* Editions were published at both Paris and Brussels in 1824.

Charlotte was not grateful for the recommendation, which led her into an embarrassing situation, as she informed her mother: "Aunt Sally . . . recommended a book to me in one of her late letters, as being extremely entertaining &c—it was called Tablettes Romaines I recommended it to L^{y} C. Morrison who bought it on my word, and it proves to be very indelicate, rather profane, not very clever, but such a work that L^{y} C. when she lent it to Julia for us, charged her not to read a certain chapter because it was too bad for any young person—I am quite ashamed of my recommendation, & vexed at Sally for bringing me into such a scrape I shall not take her word about books again" (CFBt to CBFB, 19 Jan. [1832], Berg).

Charlotte may have objected to the tone of the work, which is irreligious throughout; probably the offending chapter is the one entitled "Des Romaines" (161–71), which discusses the voluptuousness of Italian women, illustrated by the story of a beautiful Italian woman who seduces a young French man, but is offended by his impertinence at asking her name: "livrer sa personne et refuser de dire son nom est un trait caractéristique." A second anecdote shows that illicit affairs were accepted and treated lightly in Italian society.

13. The partisans of Charles X who ruled France (1824–30) in an authoritarian manner.

14. For Mrs. Barrett's unwavering belief in her daughter's improvement in health, see L. 138, n. 5.

15. Possibly the "new manuscript," which SHB was reading to the Barretts in the spring (L. 136, n. 4), and probably the same work that she would put "the finishing stroke to" in December 1832. Titled *The Renunciation*, the heroine's name would be changed to Emily (L. 145 below) and eventually to Agnes.

---

140. To Anna (Wilbraham) Grosvenor

Florence, 15 January 1832
A.L.S., Berg
Address: Mrs Grosvenor / <General Grosvenors> / <Grosvenor Square> / <London> / Inghilterra
readdressed to: Ambrose, Isteds Esqr. / Ecton / Northampton
and Ecton / Northampton
Postmarks: FIRENZE
2 A NOON 2 / JA 30 / 1832
FPO / JA 30 / 1832

January 15th 1832
Florence

Buon giorno, la mia carissima Sposina.—Are your bridal festivities[1] sufficiently gone through to give you time and give you heart to sit quietly down to the perusal of a humdrum letter from an old humdrum friend?—I had much rather say my say to you viva voce, I can tell you, having had quite enough of the charms of brilliant Italy. I am much enclined to agree with a recent English Traveller, who thus expresses himself—"Saving a little more settled weather, we have the best part of Italy in books; and this we can enjoy in England. Give me Tuscany in Somersetshire or in Surrey. Bocaccio shall build a bower for us out of his books; and we will have daisies and fresh meadows besides. An Italian may prefer his own country—and he is right. But to me, Italy has a certain hard taste in the mouth. Its mountains are too bare, its outlines too sharp, its lanes too stony, its voices too loud, its long summers too dusty. I <long> sigh to bathe myself in the grassy balm of my own country."[2]—How like you my Traveller's notions?—They tally so exactly with my own, that I am jealous of the pen that endited them, thereby robbing me of the pleasure of being the first to express them. As soon, please God, as I can attach myself to any good folks on the journey home, I shall be too happy to take my leave of this refulgent land.—The few natives in it that I have become acquainted with, are worthy and kind-hearted: but I hold no real community of sentiment with them. How should I? Their customs, their manners, their Religion, their subjects of conversation are all so diametrically opposite to any thing I have ever been used to, that we are reduced perforce to confine ourselves to general common-places. They can take no interest in what interests me, et ma foi, no more can I in what interests them. Amongst the men, I now and then meet with a clever fellow who is more than my match: but commonly speaking, they are free-thinkers, and let out opinions that pain me to hear.—In short—though human nature may be alike every where in the main there certainly are dissimilarities in the pursuits, the tastes, & the, prejudices of different nations, that render them as uncongenial one with the other, as if of another species.—But I did not mean to treat you with a dissertation when I begun this letter. I intended rather to communicate to you the various felicitations with which I have been charged. I met lately Mrs Walker and her Gertrude[3] (who, if she did not, from weakness, become round shouldered, would be prettier than ever) and was entreated by her to wish you joy most sincerely. At the same party was present Lady Bowyer and her daughter,[4] who send you a thousand kind and polite messages; Lady Matilda Lock and two of her accomplished girls, were profusse in their congratulations; so were Colonel & Mrs Shuldham; and last, not least, that figure of fun, Mrs Mason, who goes, without chick or child, to every ball that is given, is always the first to arrive, and the last to depart. She vows that the moment she heard your marriage announced, she did not wait for the name of the bridegroom, but immediately called out—"Oh, she is married to General Grosvenor!"—Is she a witch as well as a restless gad-about? She could give no reason for her strange anticipation; but only says that she had a presentiment General Grosvenor was the man!—I suppose, and hope your sister Eliza received my immediate answer to the communication you and she (jointly) gave me so much pleasure by forwarding.—Since that was written, little has occurred under my observation likely to afford you much amusement.—Marchettini, poor man, has another bambino, born during la notte del Natale, and had it been precisely at midnight, he would have been entitled to a little premium from Government!—His new baby is to have, or probably has already, the ugly name of Giovacchino, from his maternal grandfather. Bati is still, I hope, in place; Seraphina at present, not; but she has been pretty fortunate.—Krepps[5] comes to see me occasionally, & is now quite the the pink of fine men about town. He dines at the Table d'Hôte at Mad^me^ Hombert's with ladies and gentlemen lodging in the house. He has an apartment near the Piazza Sta Trinità, where he has been visited by the Cavaliere Pepe, e la Signora Marchesa;[6] he was lately at a dance and supper with a family living over my rooms—and, in short, he is enjoying his dolce far niente with I trust equal dignity and idleness. —I told you, I remember, that he had escaped all loss from the failure of Donat Orsi.—I am in love with a Mr Sloane (a lineal descendant from Sir Hans)[7] who is also a little bit, as de raison, smitten with me, and comes and coses with me for an hour or so very agreeably.—Col. de Courcy[8] and I are very good friends too, but I should not know his wife from Mrs Punch. Mr Apthorpe[9] has become acquainted with me (also without the incumbrance of his womenkind) and whatever he may be as a preacher, is sensible, well informed, and well-bred as a companion. I am in general very glad to skip the wives and daughters of my friends, because they occasion a thousand times more suggeszione than the husbands. However, a gentleman of the name of Irving,[10] first introduced to me by Mr Robinson, after paying me sundry morning visits, and always making himself very acceptable, came in one day rather out of breath, and hastily said—"I have brought my Mother to see you!"—Bless the man, I did not even know he had a Mother; however, I stroked down my bib and tucker, and rose to receive the nicest, gentle, most amiable-looking person I had seen for many a day. She was accompanied by a lady-like daughter, not so engaging quite as the Mother, but of whom it might have been said non ci è male; and a little niece of twelve or fourteen, with eyes like the deep blue of a midnight sky—I never saw more glorious eyes!—I tumbled headlong in love with them all, and kept up the intercourse with real delight as long as they staid in Florence—but, whip them! they are off to Rome now. I have hopes of seeing them again, if I live, in the summer. They talk of coming back then to Sienna, and I think I should like a little trip thither very much. Sienna is cool, has no mosquitoes, contains many pleasant English families, and suits me better than the right down country, which in Italy is my horror, on account of Scorpions, vipers, and other detestable reptiles.—The Buccanans[11] are wintering here,—but till the weather is a little better we can meet but seldom, as I give no evening parties, and refuse as much as possible to go to any.—I have an intimate friend just opposite, in the Palazzo Rucclai,[12] that I can run over to whenever I like without the plague of dressing and buying fly-caps,—and I either chat and work with the wife, or play at chess and get well beaten by the husband.—My last letters from Rome gave me excellent accounts of Henrietta;[13] the Coleseum, and St. Peters, &c, &c, agree with her complaint;—in short, she is amused.

Adieu my Carina—When thou hast time write, but write less sprawlily, like a good ragazza, & tell me a great deal of self & Sisters, & all that you think I shall like.

Ever thine S. H. B.

1. On 15 October 1831, Anna Wilbraham became the second wife of Gen. Thomas Grosvenor (1764–1851), Field-Marshal (1846). Of a younger branch of an ancient and wealthy Cheshire family, he replaced his father as M.P. for Chester in the family interest (1795–1826), and then represented Stockbridge (1826–30); he was cousin to Robert Grosvenor (1767–1845), 1st Marquess of Westminster (1831) (Ormerod, 2: 138; *GM*, 101, Pt. 2 (1831): 464; *DNB;* Thorne; Burke).

2. Slightly altered and abridged from a passage in Leigh Hunt, *Lord Byron and some of his contemporaries; with recollections of the author's life, and of his visit to Italy* (London: Henry Colburn, 1828), 500.

3. Anna Maria, the wife of Capt. Walker (L. 132, n. 9); their eldest daughter, Henrietta Gertrude, would marry on 1 April 1835 at Florence, John Andrew McDouall (d. 1889) of Logan, Wigtownshire, and again on 28 June 1849 Count Antonio Baldelli of Florence (Burke; Burke, *DLG; GM*, NS 23 (1849): 200).

4. Lady Bowyer (L. 132, n. 7) had two daughters, Caroline (d. 21 June 1881) and Mary (d. 28 Oct. 1898) (Burke).

5. Krepps or Kreft, as the name is spelled below (L. 146), appears to have served the Wilbrahams in some capacity during their stay in Florence and to have since retired. He is a faithful visitor to Sarah Harriet for the rest of her stay in Italy (see below passim).

6. The Wilbrahams had stayed at the Casa Pepe, Via Pepe, in Florence (L. 125). The owner of the house may have been Gabriele Pepe (1779–1849), a political and military man; exiled from Naples and living in Florence since 1823, he offered lessons in Italian to notable foreign residents.

7. Possibly William Sloane-Stanley (1781–1860) of Paultons, Hampshire, M.P. (1807–12; 1830–31), eldest surviving son of Hans Sloane (1739–1827). His father had been great-nephew to the eminent physician, Sir Hans Sloane, Bt. (1660–1753), and inherited the family estates from his cousin in 1780. Both father and son assumed the additional name of Stanley in December 1821 (Burke, *LG; Alumni Cantab.;* Thorne).

8. Gerald de Courcy (d. Oct. 1848), Lt.-Col. (1814), a younger son of John de Courcy (d. 24 May 1822), 26th Baron Kingsale (1776), had married 29 January 1807 Elizabeth Carlyon (d. 1855), daughter of John Bishop. One of his daughters would marry at Florence in 1840 (Burke; Lodge; *GM*, NS 13 (1840): 536; *Army List* (1801–24)).

9. The Rev. Frederick Apthorpe (c. 1778–1853) of Jesus College, Cambridge, B.A. (1799), M.A. (1802), who had married on 2 April 1803 Susan Hubbard (c. 1784–1865), niece to Sir George Pretyman Tomline, Bishop of Lincoln (L. 157, n. 2). In 1802, the Rev. Mr. Apthorpe was collated to a prebendal stall in that cathedral and also to the vicarage of Bicker, Lincs. In 1807 he was appointed to the rectory of Gumley, Leics., and in 1809 to the vicarage of Farndon, Notts. (*Alumni Cantab.* under Apthorpe, Hubbard; Burke, *LG* under Pretyman; *GM*, 72, Pt. 2 (1802): 1218; 73, Pt. 1 (1803): 380; 77, Pt. 2 (1807): 662; 79, Pt. 1 (1809): 576; NS 41 (1854): 551; 3rd ser. 19 (1865): 258).

10. Crabb Robinson met a Mr. Irving on 29 June 1831 at a dinner party in Florence, and traveled with this "gentlemanly young man" from Florence to Leghorn. Soon after this letter was written, he remarks that Miss Burney is "pleased with the Irvings—the mother and sisters of my companion at Leghorn" (HCR, 29 June, 25 July 1831, Travel Journals; HCR, 24 Feb. 1832, Diaries).

11. Henry Crabb Robinson accompanied Sarah Harriet to Mrs. Buchanan's one evening in Rome; the family is otherwise unidentified (HCR, 24 Feb. 1830, Travel Journals).

12. The Layard family (L. 138, n. 9), who lived in the Palazzo Rucellai, built c. 1446–51 for the wealthy merchant, Giovanni Rucellai (1403–81).

13. It is difficult to reconcile this account of Hetty's health with that of Mrs. Barrett's: "Hetty creeps on towards the Spring counting each day of winter that passes over, and coughing while she counts" (CFBt to CBFB, 19 Jan.–4 Feb. [1832], Berg).

---

141. To Frances (Burney) d'Arblay

Florence, 30 March 1832
A.L.S., Berg
Address: Madame d'Arblay / 1 Half-Moon Street / Piccadilly / London / Inghilterra
Postmarks: FIRENZE
FPO / AP12 / 1832

4131 Via della Vigna Nuova, Firenze
March 30th 1832

Oh my poor Sister! How little dare I think of my own sorrow, when I reflect upon that which you must feel!—The habits of confidence and attachment of so many years—the recollections of past times, when in your girlhood you were companions, and when life, tricked in its gayest colours was opening before you[1]—the subsequent unfeigned admiration with which each looked up to the talents of the other—the similarity of affection that united you both so strongly to the other dear Sister you so much earlier lost[2]—All, all these are links which when thus torn assunder, must make you feel to the very quick the keenness of the wound you now Suffer!—I grieve for you, and with you, my beloved Sister!—And, oh how painfully do I feel for the additional calamity which has since fallen upon our dearly-loved Sister Broome!—Sorrow has indeed been busy with her! One after the other, what a succession of trials she has gone through! 'Tis wretched to think that she is now deprived of the consolation of being with her chief-surviving blessing, dearest Charlotte. I am almost tempted to say, that if ever poor frail mortal could be detached from life by the loss gradually of all that could render it valuable, she is that being![3]—But I know she will be unmurmuring and humbly submissive. Sarah Payne writes me word[4] that at least, as yet, she has borne up wonderfully. The blow will be heavy to our dear Charlotte. I heard from her a day or two ago; her letter was dated March 20th and she speaks in it of poor Marianne without the most distant shadow of a suspicion that even illness, much less Death, had been at work to rob her of one she loved so much.[5]—I often wonder how we dare place such dependance upon the lives of others or our own—how we dare form schemes for so uncertain a future—in short, how we can dare to think so little of our state to come, and so habitually occupy ourselves with the fleeting concerns of this world. Yet, that such should be our nature, I know upon consideration, is wisely provided by Providence to preserve us from disgust, to give us activity, and to avert from us the useless gloom that a perpetual reference to Death would unavoidably, to the greatest number, occasion. There are and have been those Angelic Spirits that could meditate upon their own mortality with more than resignation—with even chearfulness, and a sincere wish to be emancipated; and yet could at the same time take an interest in the beings and affairs of this life. I revere such blessed individuals—but, alas! I own myself to be far far from the same enviable state of mind. Death to me is a subject of awful thought, which nothing sooths but the remembrance of the Atonement & Mediation—the Compassion and Love of Jesus Christ. When I anchor there, I become calm, and even venture to hope.—Would that such remembrances, with their blessed effects, were more continually, more habitually present to my soul!—

It has long been my earnest wish to revisit dear England, never so dear as since I have resided at so great a distance from it. Projects I form none, for I become daily more sensible how little we are able to foresee what we may be able to do;—but hopes I indulge that some opportunity may offer of returning home under respectable and friendly convoy in the course of the ensuing Summer. I am quietly and kindly domesticated with two very worthy Sisters, and their excellent servants, one of whom has lived with them two and twenty, the other, eight years. If any thing is the matter with me, they are all attention and care; and such is my security with respect to money-matters, cloaths, &c, that I lock up nothing, and have no more distrust than if Becky and Maria were still living with me.[6] Opposite reside a M^{r} and Mrs Layard.—The father of the former was Dean of Bristol,[7] and knew you well, I believe at Windsor. His son remembers his talking of you much, and with great respect and admiration. An Italian Lady, now at Rome, an Improvisatrice of some celebrity, is preparing a translation of Cecilia. How extraordinary that what the Germans and other Continental people executed so long ago, should not yet have been effected by the Italians![8]—But our literature is in general little known amongst them.

Most of my useless time I employ in drawing or painting. Books are less difficult to get at since I became acquainted with the kind Layards. To-day all Florence is in gloom, it being the appointed day for the burial procession of the good and amiable Grand Duchess.[9] She was much and deservedly loved, and the poor, above all, will severely feel her loss. Poor thing, she died of a lingering decline aged hardly six and thirty. Already I hear people conjecturing who is to be her successor, she having left only daughters.[10]—

I hear frequently and affectionately from Harriet Crewe, now again residing with her father near Liege, after spending a year amongst her various friends in England during the unsettled state of <affairs> the Belgium affairs. She invites me very pressingly to pay her a visit on my return homewards, not in her own name only, but also in that of her father![11] I am obliged to her for the favorable manner in which she must have represented me.—From dear Annabel I hear less often, but always with great pleasure to myself, and with apparently undiminished regard on hers.—

Adieu my dearest Sister—Give my kind love to Alex, with many cordial remembrances to Cousin Edward, and to any other friends who are good enough to think of me—Ever most affectionately

Yours S. H. Burney.

1. The eldest daughter of Dr. Burney's first marriage, Esther (Burney) Burney, had died of influenza on 17 February 1832 aged eighty-two (*JL*, 12: 756, n. 2). "She possessed all the attractions both mental & personal to make her company desirable to a large and admiring acquaintance, & her affectionate disposition to her family, was returned by reciprocal attachment on their side," ("Worcester Mem.," 93). For the record of Fanny and Esther Burney's entrance into young womanhood together, see *EJL*, vol. 1.

2. Susan (Burney) Phillips had died on 6 January 1800 (L. 20, n. 3).

3. Charlotte Broome had already endured the loss of two husbands and two of her four children; now her youngest daughter, Marianne Francis, had also died c. 15 March 1832 at age forty-two (*JL*, 12: 756, n. 2). Her only surviving child, Charlotte Barrett, was in Italy nursing her own sick daughter. Mrs. Barrett had expressed her concern at leaving her mother even before this latest blow: "I hoped that my children and all whom I left in England would try to supply my place to her, and cherish and comfort her now that circumstances have removed me to so great a distance" (CFBt to HBt & ABt, 8 June [1831], Berg).

4. The Paynes had returned to London shortly before 29 January 1832, when they informed Henry Crabb Robinson that Sarah Harriet was "in excellent health and spirits . . . still very comfortable at Mad. Certellini. Niccolini seems a great favourite with her" (HCR, 29 Jan. 1832, Diaries).

5. Mrs. Barrett's letter of 20 March 1832 to SHB does not survive, nor does one from her daughter Julia written before 6 April to announce Marianne's demise, and prevent a repetition of the family oversight which followed Esther's death: "nobody had written to Aunt Sarah at Florence on that melancholy subject & she had the shock of reading her sisters death first in the public papers—I suppose they all forgot her in the moment of sorrow."

Although her sister's death was a severe blow, Charlotte Barrett found "unspeakable consolation in the full certainty that my dearest Marianne was a redeemed Child & servant of God" (CFBt to HBt, 6–7 Apr. [1832], Barrett, Eg. 3702A, ff. 70–71v).

6. Rebecca and Mary More, Charles Burney's servants at Chelsea Hospital (L. 18, n. 1; L. 61, n. 5). Henry Crabb Robinson had felt the same security when he lodged with Mme Certellini and her sister: "I had a confidence in their integrity in which I was not disappointed." He also commended the two servants "who seem to be like their mistresses respectable" (HCR, *Reminiscences*, 2: 474; HCR, 15 July 1830, Travel Journals).

7. Charles Peter Layard (1748–1803), D.D. (1787), Dean of Bristol (1800), had been Chaplain-in-Ordinary to the King (1790–1800). Twice married, he had ten children; Henry Peter John Layard, Sarah's acquaintance in Florence (L. 138, n. 9), was his second son. Mme d'Arblay commented that "the Layards are esteemed in general" (*JL*, 5: 414; *DNB* under Daniel Peter Layard; *Alumni Cantab.*; *GM*, 73, Pt. 1 (1803): 481).

8. Sarah's source was probably Julia Barrett, who had met the previous month "a great curiosity" at Rome, Mme Dionigi Orfei, improvisatrice and authoress, who intended to translate Mme d'Arblay's second novel into Italian (CFBt to CBFB, 19 Jan.–4 Feb. [1832], Berg). *Cecilia, or Memoirs of an Heiress* (1782) was translated into French and German almost immediately (1783, 1784–85) and even into Swedish (1795–97), but never, it seems, into Italian (Joseph A. Grau, *Fanny Burney: An Annotated Bibliography* (New York: Garland, 1981), 7–10).

9. Maria Anna of Saxony had married in 1817 the Grand Duke Leopold II. Delicate

in health, she died on 24 March 1832 in Pisa; the funeral procession bringing her remains to Florence arrived on the afternoon of the twenty-ninth, and passed along the Via della Vigna Nuova where SHB lived (Giorgio Cucentrentoli, *Gli ultimi Granduchi di Toscana* (Bologna: La perseveranza, 1975), 57–68).

10. The Grand Duchess had three daughters, all of whom died young. However, the year after her death, Leopold II married Maria Antonia of the Two Sicilies (1814–98), who would give birth on 10 June 1835 to a son and heir, Ferdinand, and have ten children in all (ibid.).

11. Sarah Harriet, who was hired in 1822 by John, 1st Baron Crewe, to care for his granddaughters, Henrietta and Annabella, apparently did not know the girls' father, John, 2nd Baron Crewe (1829), who had spent much of his life on the continent (L. 104, nn. 1, 3, 7; L. 105, n. 19).

---

142. To Anna (Wilbraham) Grosvenor

Florence, 9 May 1832
A.L., Berg
Address: M[rs] Grosvenor / <Grosvenor Square> / <London> / Inghilterra
readdressed to: Hare Park / Newmarket
Postmarks: FIRENZE
12 NOON 12 / MY 24 / 1832
O / MY 24 / 18[?]
O / MY [?] / 1832
FPO / MY 24 / 1832

Florence, May 9th 1832
4131 Via della Vigna Nuova.

Oh my dearest Nannie, how you (I mean your letter) do stink!!—I am forced to keep you at a most respectful distance, holding you at arm's length, and dabbing my nose with Eau de Cologne (the only thing by way of perfume in my possession). All letters and Newspapers that cross the Alps, are subjected to the agreeable process that gives them the mixt scent of Sulphur, garlic, and asoefoetedoe[1] (how do you spell that same?) However—I am of Vespasian's mind, though I certainly do not like him think their gold can convert a stink into a perfume[2]—but a letter from a friend must be sweet, though to the nose a little unsavory.—Yes—tell dear Sister Emma that I did receive from her a nice long letter for w[ch] I heartily thank her: but tell her moreover, that my mode of life is so monotonous, that she must have the charity to forgive my not undertaking a separate answer to you and to her. It is all I can do to find matter for one correspondent;—to write to two, living nearly under the same roof, is more than flesh & blood (mine at least) is equal to. I delight in receiving as many letters as you may be kind enough to send me, and so I should were there a dozen of you: but I do trust you will permit me to address all I have to say in return to one only, though meaning it gratefully to all.—Am I understood, and forgiven?—I have seen Squire Krepps (I never shall make any thing but a hodgepodge of that name "which nobody can speak, and nobody can spell").[3] Nina, he says is no longer at his disposition: but she is doing well, and is fat and in good case; he saw her as he passed through Geneva. Were any negociation attempted with her present possessor, he would not know how to be extravagant enough in his demands—and besides, Krepps says she is too old for the service to which you would put her; she would neither take care of the foal of another, nor produce any of her own. I forget what age he said she was, but it sounded to me rather venerable.[4]—To Miss Eliza I was to say, that the money she speaks of had arrived safe.—And then there is something about stuffed dicky birds, which he is to expound more fully before this letter sets off. And so much for Krepps, who is a good creature, and in high feather and song, only a little prosy.—Will you believe, that I not only have been so circumstanced as to be under the necessity of letting myself be introduced to M^r^ & Mrs Apthorpe, but that—I actually like him!—Her I care nothing about; she lets her daughters dress indecently,[5] and seems a good-natured, frivolous, motherly body. But he is positively pleasant in society, and extremely well informed, which, considering his funny provincialisms I should by no means have expected.—Poor Bati was here a day or two ago. He has just left his place at Lady Warrender's,[6] who had, or rather has, he says, il core duro come marmo, and led him a very unhappy life during the eight or ten months he staid with her. I hope he will ere long meet with some better situation. Krepps I dare say will help him if he can. Seraphina has been housemaid at Ld Wm Russel's,[7] and hopes to return to him again when he comes back from a tour he is making in Germany. She got capital wages, and he expressed himself well satisfied with her.—Marchettini alas! has another bimbo, born on Christmas Day; I wish it had come to your shop instead!—I have left off being his scholar, and am painting miniatures with a certain cheap, and humble, but not unclever Martini;[8] and we have been copying a fine portrait by Giorgione,[9] he on one ivory and I on another. Mr Layard lent me the original, which is incomparable. We are now at work on our respective copies of a picture of "Giovanni delle bande neri," by Allori,[10] lent me by Sig^r^ Niccolini. Not so fine a painting as the other, but interesting from its representing so celebrated a character, and from the likeness also to Buonaparte which is so remarkable in all Giovanni's portraits.[11]—Well, and moreover as I hate parties and goings out, I divert myself by reading lots. The Layards lend me books, and I subscribe to Vieusseu's Reading Room, and now and then get a tidy thing or two. The Italian little evening circles at my Signora <lombardini> Padrona's, tire me to death, and I have quite given up going to join them. Nothing but talky, talky, from eight o'clock to eleven, by the light of one wick of a high Tuscan lamp, is quite too much for me.—A game at Commerce with Mrs Layard's boys is worth a thousand such evenings. We play for roba dolce from the Confectioner's; and it is delightful to see the triumph of the boys when they win the great prize, a candied lime, perhaps, or some such good thing, which they would hardly care a rush about but for the pride of having won it.—I dare say I have told you that these friendly Layards live just opposite in Palazzo Ruclai; and she hates parties as much as I do, and is always at home unless now and then tempted to the Theatre. We have had a very good set at the Pergola this spring. Anna Bullen[12] has been performed with great success, and was well got up. The prima donna is a German, Madame Ungher,[13] and sings in good taste and always in tune, & great charm: but her voice is not very capital. She is fair with dark hair & eyes, tall & well made, & has much unaffected dignity. The man I like best (for David[14] is my bête d'aversion) is a certain Luigi Duprez,[15] a Frenchman, and please you, but Italianized by a long residence in the country, & to my taste a very charming, and often truly pathetic singer.—The accounts from the Barretts at Rome announce that poor Henrietta's amendment, tho' very gradual, is going on:[16] but I have heard nothing very recently except from Julia—the poor Mother was in too much sorrow at the loss of her Sister, Marianne Francis, to be able to write. Where they will spend their summer I know not: perhaps at Castelamare, or Sorrento. As for me, I intend to write to the King (W^{m} IVth) to beg him to send one of his best sailing Frigates for me to Livorno, commanded by a good-humoured, Captain, and manned by an able and intelligent crew, with orders to convey me safe to the nearest English port. I have offered my friend Mrs Layard a free passage with me for herself and children, and she thinks it a very pretty scheme! Don't you?—At the first word I say about it, I dare say the King will comply Meanwhile, being of opinion with Pope, that:

> Fixed to no place is happiness sincere;
> 'Tis no where to be found, or every where:[17]—

I make myself as contented as I can, till Providence puts it in my power to undertake the journey homewards in something like a satisfactory and promising manner. A thousand thanks for your hospitable offers. I long to see you all, and my own dear land, though I fight hard against depression at being detained from it so long. France is not a country one would wish to travel through at present; and Lord help me! what should I do vagabonding through Germany with a Vetturino and a parcel of strangers?—Adieu my dearest Nannie—"Oh Nannie wilt thou gang with Me?"[18] Aye troth, would I, if I could.

1. An epidemic of cholera that broke out in India in 1826 soon spread to Russia and to eastern and central Europe. By 1831, the disease was raging in most European capitals, despite attempts to control it by cordons and quarantine (Norman Longmate, *King Cholera* (London: Hamish Hamilton, 1966), 1–19). Charlotte Barrett at Rome complained that her letters from England arrived "cut & slashed for fumigation, lest you should slyly send us the cholera. . . . as yet, it has not been seen in Rome, nor farther south than Milan" (CFBt to CBFB, 21 Oct. [1831], Berg).

2. Titus Flavius Vespasianus (A.D. 9–79), Emperor of Rome (A.D. 69–79); he is credited with the introduction of public urinals in Rome, but more likely instituted a tax on the collection of urine, used to make ammonia. Another tradition associates him with the remark "money does not smell."

3. Robert Southey, "The March to Moscow," *Courier*, 23 June 1814; rpt., *The Poetical Works of Robert Southey*, vol. 6 (London: Longman, Orme, Brown, Green, & Longmans, 1838), 220.

4. For Krepps (or Kreft) and his association with the Wilbrahams, see above L. 140, n. 5. From the context, Nina appears to be a horse or donkey.

5. The Rev. Frederick Apthorpe and his wife Susan (L. 140, n. 9). They had three daughters: Susan, who would marry 29 December 1837 the Rev. J. Fereday (fl. 1814–37), curate of Aston Abbotts, Bucks. (*GM*, NS 7 (1837): 201; *Alumni Oxon.*); Harriet (d. 11 Feb. 1877), who would marry 26 June 1849 as his second wife the Rev. Richard Pretyman (1793–1866), Precentor of Lincoln Cathedral (*GM*, NS 32 (1849): 199; Burke, *LG; Alumni Cantab.*); and Caroline (d. 22 Feb. 1899), who would marry on 13 September 1843 William Watts (1821–53) of Hanslope Park, Bucks., and as his second wife on 17 January 1856, Reginald Robert Walpole (1817–54), grand-nephew of the 1st Earl of Orford (*GM*, NS 20 (1843): 538; Burke, *LG;* Burke). Crabb Robinson thought "the Miss A's look like sensible girls tho' they have made enemies by girlish levity" (HCR, 27 June 1831, Travel Journals).

6. Probably Anne Evelyn (1791–1871), the youngest daughter of George Evelyn Boscawen (1758–1808), 3rd Viscount Falmouth (1782), who had married on 3 October 1810 George Warrender (1782–1849), 4th Bt. (1799). However, the Dowager Lady Warrender was also still alive, widow of Patrick Warrender (1731–99), 3rd Bt. (1772); she would die on 8 May 1838, aged seventy-nine (Cokayne; Burke).

7. Probably Lord George William Russell (1790–1846), second son of John, 6th Duke of Bedford. A Col. in the army (1830), later Maj.-Gen. (1841), he was attached in July 1831 to the mission of Sir Robert Adair to Belgium, the opening of a diplomatic career. His wife (m. 21 June 1817), Elizabeth Anne née Rawdon (1793–1874), gave birth to a

son at Florence on 20 February 1829 (*DNB;* Burke; Thorne; Gibbs under Ampthill; Giorgiana Blakiston, *Woburn and the Russells* (London: Constable, 1980), 209–11).

8. Unidentified.

9. The influential Venetian painter, Giorgio da Castelfranco, "Giorgione" (c. 1477–1510).

10. Agnolo di Cosimo di Mariano (1503–72), "Il Bronzino," a Florentine court painter, is sometimes mistakenly called Agnolo Allori, confusing his family name with that of his pupil, Alessandro Allori (1535–1607). A three-quarter length portrait of *Giovanni delle Bande Nere* has been mistakenly attributed to Bronzino, but he is also credited with a miniature, showing Giovanni in profile, wearing armor, which hangs in the Uffizi Gallery, Florence (Arthur McComb, *Agnolo Bronzino* (Cambridge, Mass: Harvard University Press, 1928), 98, 124–25; Karla Langedijk, *The Portraits of the Medici,* vol. 2 (Firenze: Studio per edizioni Scelte, 1983), 1027).

11. Giovanni de' Medici (originally named Ludovico) (1498–1526), a noted soldier of the younger branch of the Medici family. He was called "delle Bande Nere" for the black banners carried by his troops after the death of Pope Leo X in 1521 (Col. G. F. Young, *The Medici,* 3rd ed. (1912; rpt., London: John Murray, 1930), 2: 200, 213–27).

12. *Anna Bullen* (1692) was John Banks's play based on the life of Henry VIII's second wife, but Sarah Harriet is probably referring to the opera on the same subject, *Anna Bolena.* The music for the libretto of Felice Romani (1788–1865) was composed by Gaetano Donizetti (1797–1848), who became famous when the opera opened at Milan in 1830 (*New Grove*).

13. Karoline Unger (1803–77), the Austrian contralto, who had enjoyed a successful career in Italy since 1825 (ibid.).

14. Probably Giovanni Davide (1790–1864), the Italian tenor, whose voice was showing signs of decay (ibid.).

15. Gilbert-Louis Duprez (1806–96), the French tenor, who was developing his voice and building his career in Italy before returning to France in 1837 (ibid.).

16. The Barretts were on the point of leaving Rome for Pisa from which Charlotte wrote on 17 May 1832 after a rapid and easy journey. Their doctor in Pisa declared that Hetty was "wonderfully better" than when she had left for Rome six months before. However, their physician at the Baths of Lucca, to which they repaired for the summer in late June, did not agree and found it necessary to bleed her (CFBt & JBt & HnBt to HBt, 16–17 May [1832], Barrett, Eg. 3702A, ff. 78–79v; CFBt & JBt to HBt, 30 June–6 July [1832], Berg).

17. Alexander Pope, *An Essay on Man,* Epistle 4, ll. 15–16.

18. The first line of Thomas Percy's poem entitled "A Song. by T. P***cy" which appeared in Robert Dodsley's *A Collection of Poems . . . by several hands,* vol. 6 (London, 1758), 233–34. Set to music by the Irish composer (Charles) Thomas Carter (c. 1740–1804), it was sung at Vauxhall in 1773 and became very popular (*DNB; New Grove*). When and by whom the first line was changed to the Scotticized version quoted here is the subject of controversy (*GM,* NS 27, Pt. 1 (1847): 376–77, 481–82; Alice C. C. Gaussen, *Percy: Prelate and Poet* (London: Smith & Elder, 1908), 18–21; S. J. Adair FitzGerald, *Stories of Famous Songs* (Philadelphia: J. B. Lippincott, 1910), 2: 92–95).

143. With Carlotta Certellini and Giovanni Battista Niccolini to Henry Crabb Robinson

Florence, 4 July [1832]
A.L.S., Dr. Williams'
Address: H. C. Robinson Esqr / 2 Plowden's Buildings / Temple / London
Postmarks: A NOON / 8 [?] / 1832
Endorsed: 4 July 1832 / Niccolini
[*First page consists of an A.L.S. Carlotta Certellini to HCR.*][1]

July 4th

My dear Friend

I received with thanks your kind little stinking (con rispetto!) note. Every thing that enters Italy now from whatever quarter is fumigated to a poisonous excess. I have nothing to say, and therefore am glad these lines will cost you nothing but the trouble of reading. Scarcely any alteration has occurred in my mode of life since we parted. My opposite neighbours, M^r and Mrs Layard, are almost the only English persons I have formed any intimacy with, and they are a host—Always kind, and hospitable, and unceremonious. I long however for home, and shall seize the first promising opportunity of returning; but am willing to wait till I can join some respectable companion or companions.—Thanks for your little account of Richmond. If he publishes,[2] I am certain you will be made a prominent figure in his book.—Perhaps even little i may be alluded to, for he will practice but small discretion on such matters. I care not however—

I must now bid you farewell to leave room to Sig^r Niccolini. Adieu my dear friend—Yours very truly S. H. Burney

[*Third page consists of an A.L.S. Giovanni Battista Niccolini to HCR.*]

1. Perhaps a reply to Robinson's letter of 20 February 1832 to Mme Certellini, this triple missive was received on 10 August 1832 (HCR, 20 Feb., 10 Aug. 1832, Diaries).

2. The Rev. James Cook Richmond, Robinson's travel companion (L. 126, n. 15), who, it seems, was planning to publish an account of his experiences. The only travel book he is known to have published, however, was *A Visit to Iona* (1849).

144. To Anna (Wilbraham) Grosvenor

[Florence, 16–]30 August 1832
A.L.S., Berg
Address: M[rs] Grosvenor / <Grosvenor Square> / <London> / Inghilterra
readdressed to: Warring Lodge / Loughton Essex
Postmarks: FIRENZE
T P / Mount St [OS]
10 NOON 10 / 14 SP / 1832
FPO / SE 13 / 1832

My poor dear Anna, how truly concerned I was to hear of what you call your little, "mishap"![1]—If one could but contrive that some of those who have more bambini than they can well feed, might be permitted to make over their superfluous number to those who have more food than mouths, what a good thing (apparently) it would be. In reality, however, there can be no doubt, that the matter, as it is now regulated, is in fact <the best> better ordered than we in our wisdom could have imagined; so comfort yourself, dearest, and try to persuade yourself, that if you had had a baby you would most likely have spoilt it (being famous, as you well know, for spoiling every pet you have ever had) and have become answerable for making it so disagreeable that nobody but yourself would have cared for it,—except dear Sister Emma, who, for your sake, would have gone on loving it all the better for not being loved by others.—And now, dearest, a word about my letters. I am more than content, I am well pleased that your Sisters, if they think it worth while, should read them; and eke your General when they come in his way, & he has nothing better to do: none of you give me any soggestione; ma, per l'amor del Cielo, do not send them (at least, indiscriminately) to Sister d'Arblay![2] She keeps me more in awe than all the world besides; and many an absurdity I might not hesitate to write to you, I would not send to her, or have placed under her eyes on any account. Good, and kind, and affectionate as she is, she must be allowed to be (as your old Shoemaker used to say) "rather partikler, Ma'am"—So none of your Lettres Circulaires in that direction, dearest. Leave me to write direct to herself such matter as I may hope will suit her; and keep all my profligacy snug amongst yourselves.—

Perhaps for want of better subjects, you will let me retail to you a little Florence gossip, had at second or third hand, however, and very likely more than half false. Mr Trelawney, of course you know, has published a book[3]—I have not seen it, but I think said book contains a part of his own Memoires, <but> no doubt with sundry rather necessary reticences—like the Mems: of the Margravine,[4] and of Madme de Genlis,[5] full of gaps, because, do you see, hiding half adorns the whole. He (Trelawney) spends most of his time at Lady Warrender's. By the way, poor Bati has left her after ten months service, and is now out of place, yet fatter than ever. The Locks are at the Baths of Lucca,[6] getting more and more accomplished, but, I am afraid getting no lovers.—We have had, and it still continues, fiercely hot weather, which begun late, but to make amends, has lasted above six weeks, during which the Thermometre has never been lower than 82, and often at 84 & 85. I am very tired of it, and of hearing so much about the Verb Sudare, which, in either the past, present, or future tense is for ever in the mouths of these worthy Italians. I meant to have furnished you, as I said, with store of Florence gossip: but I forget what it was about, though some time back I recollect to have heard some nonsense of the kind which I thought might have amused you. Catalani[7] you remember has a Villa some three or four miles off. It is now so hot there, even at night, that she lately ordered matrasses to be laid upon the lawn, and she and her daughter have gone forth and spread themselves upon them, as you would Rose-leaves for a pot-pouri, and basked in the moonbeams, Fairy fashion. They were asked whether they were not afraid of the bestie that might crawl upon them? but they said no, for the grass was so completely dried up and colourless, they could see the minutest insect. Besides, as a gentleman observed, two priests who attended them were sufficient to guard them from all other bestie!—

This letter was begun at least a fortnight ago, but till now, August 30th it has been so hot, I had no heart to go on with it, or to do any thing but lye on a Sopha (a deuced hard one!) and read. I have just finished Trelawney's Adventures of a Younger Brother.[8] It is a book that excites whilst reading, and leaves behind it, many painful feelings. A true radical spirit runs throughout it;—a contempt of all establishments, social, political, or religious;—a mad ferocity of disposition that causes the narrative to be filled with details of atrocious murders, so minutely described that ones flesh creeps upon ones bones whilst reading. Yet—to give even the devil his due, he has succeeded in drawing a female character of surpassing loveliness, purity, and tender faithfulness. He makes her an Arab however, that European women may take no pride to themselves from the favorable description he gives of her.—Had she been one <of> belonging to our Western portion of the globe, he would have made her out a demon incarnate. Marchettini called upon me yesterday. He grows fat, is the Babo of two (ugly) children, makes, I believe and hope, a good husband; but is prosy, and the day being hot, sat by me, finding the room cool, nearly two hours, and held forth with marvellous fluency and an evident desire to be admired for his eloquence and wisdom. I admired nothing so much as the <end of the> back of his coat, for so long a visitation had tired me to death.—Gozzini,[9] he says, is well and flourishing.—Florence' latest news are that Fossombroni[10] was married last week to a Widow lady who has two sons of whom he has long been very fond. Either <they were> to her or to them he was Godfather, I cannot quite make out which, and it is supposed he will greatly enrich them, but without injustice to his kindred whom he is wealthy enough to do much for notwithstanding his marriage.—It is not certain that I may not go to Rome again this winter. Some friends of mine talk of doing so, and propose to me to travel with them; & the Barretts will be there. Julia is now at Castelamare with Ly Car. Morrison and the Genl[11] who have taken a great fancy to her. Henrietta is gaining ground at Lucca Baths.[12]—Adieu dearest Anna. I saw Krefts very lately, who is well, and anxious to hear that none of you have experienced any alarm from the Cholera.[13] I am sorry to send you so unamusing a letter—ma, che volete?—Come si fa? Where can I get the materials, leading such a retired life?—Love to the two EE s.[14]—Adieu once more.—Yours ever S. H. B.—

1. Anna Grosvenor's letter does not survive, but the context suggests she had informed Sarah of a miscarriage. She had married the year before at the age of forty-one (L. 140, n. 1).

2. Mrs. Grosvenor and Mme d'Arblay had been sharing their news of Sarah in Italy. After receiving SHB's letter of 8 August 1831, Fanny wrote to Mrs. Grosvenor to inform her of its contents (*JL*, 12: L. 1418). Similarly, Mrs. Grosvenor forwarded SHB's letter of 9 May 1832, which Mme d'Arblay misplaced but eventually sent back, quoting some of its passages (*JL*, 12: L. 1420). Sarah Harriet had learned to her alarm of this circulation of her private letters.

3. Edward John Trelawney (1792–1881) published anonymously the *Adventures of a Younger Son* (1831).

4. Elizabeth (1750–1828), the daughter of Augustus, 4th Earl of Berkeley, had married first on 30 May 1767 William Craven (1738–91), 6th Baron Craven (1769). Separated from her husband in 1783, she was known as the Margravine before her husband's death enabled her to marry, on 13 October 1791, Christian Karl Alexander Friedrich (1736–1806), Margrave of Brandenburg, Anspach and Bareith. Her *Memoirs of the Margravine of Anspach* was published by Henry Colburn in 1826 (*DNB;* Gibbs; Walpole, 28: 247, n. 50).

5. The comtesse de Genlis, whose *Mémoires* Sarah Harriet had read on their appearance in 1825 and called them "paltry stuff" (L. 109 and n. 18).

6. Through Sarah Harriet, the Lockes had met the Barretts at the Baths of Lucca. Mrs. Barrett described the "3 grown up daughters, very fond of drawing . . . [*who*] call for Julia to drive with them before breakfast to some fine point of view which she likes

to sketch as well as they" (CFBt & HnBt to HBt, 7 Aug. [1831], CFBt to HBt, 30 June–6 July [1832], Berg).

7. Angelica Catalani, the Italian soprano, whose performances Sarah had enjoyed during her heyday in London (L. 57 and n. 1).

8. Sarah's title is slightly inaccurate; see n. 3 above.

9. Unidentified.

10. Count Vittorio Fossombroni (1754–1844), prime minister of Tuscany since 1815.

11. Lady Caroline King (d. 3 Mar. 1845), daughter of Robert King (1754–99), 2nd Earl of Kingston (1797), had married 28 April 1800 Gen. Edward Morrison (1760–1843) (Burke; Lodge; *GM*, NS 23 (1845): 448; *JL*, 12: 746, n. 12). A friend of the Barretts in Rome, Lady Caroline was extremely hospitable to Julia during her stay, helping her to look for lodgings, inviting her to dinner parties, arranging for her music lessons and lending her a horse to ride. In mid-August 1832, Julia went to visit the Morrisons at Castelamare, where she was benefiting from "the delightful air & sea breezes," going on "donkey walks" and taking excursions to Naples, Vesuvius and Pompeii. At the end of seven weeks, she would accompany her hostess back to Rome (CFBt to CBFB, 21 Oct. [1831], 19 Jan.–4 Feb. [1832], Berg; CFBt to HBt, 23 Feb. [1832], 13–20 Aug. [1832], 24 Aug. [1832], Berg; CFBt to HBt, 6–7 Apr. [1832], Barrett, Eg. 3702A, ff. 70–71v; CFBt & JBt to HBt, 30 June–6 July [1832], Berg; CFBt to JBt, 8 Oct. [1832], Barrett, Eg. 3702A, ff. 209–10v).

12. Mrs. Barrett gave somewhat mixed reports from Lucca about Hetty's health: "Hetty goes out more than she did last year—she has taken the air every evening this week, either on horseback or in a portantina—but she cannot walk so much, I think." Some of her daughter's weakened condition she blamed on Hetty herself: "I never can get her to walk at all, now. . . . she lies in bed till twelve oclock which is very relaxing and unwholesome . . . I grieve at all these bad habits but cannot persuade her to break through them. she thinks herself much weaker than she was, but these ways help to make her so" (CFBt to HBt, 13–20 Aug. [1832], 24 Aug. [1832], Berg). Hetty was just six months away from her death (see below L. 146).

13. Cholera reached England in October 1831, the first official victim dying on 26 October at Sunderland, co. Durham. The disease spread rapidly through the north and reached London in February 1832 (Longmate, 27, 83, 86 and passim).

14. Anna's two unmarried sisters, Emma and Elizabeth Wilbraham (L. 27, nn. 4, 5).

145. To Anna (Wilbraham) Grosvenor

Florence, 14 December [1832][1]
A.L.S., Berg
Address: Mrs Grosvenor / <Grosvenor Square> / <London> / Inghilterra
readdressed to: Warring Lodge / Loughton Essex
Postmarks: FIRENZE
[T P] / M[ount St O]S
[7] Night 7 / 27 [DE] / 1832
FPO / DE 27 / 1832

Florence, 14th December 1833.

I have just finished a long letter to my poor Sister d'Arblay;—I say my poor sister, because in addition to all our family losses, she has had the misfortune to lose her oldest and dearest friend; Mrs Lock.[2]—Are you, my dearest, like me with regard to letter writing? I always find that ce n'est que le premier pas qui coute;[3] when I have finished one, it becomes more easy to begin another. But, my vast good friend, what a difference between the quantity contained in one of my letters, and one of yours!—Of the quality we will say nothing: but it is certain that one of my pages would in your open writing, & widely-separated-lines, spread out into three. This is bad—reform, reform it altogether, for the little tastes you give me, only serve to make me wish for more. The way you should manage, to avoid fatigue is to write half a page at a time—then lay by, and another day write half a page more—and so on, till the pudding is as full of plums as ever it will hold—I hate to see them, as the children say, "barking at one another."—Madam, I have to inform you, that I have just put the finishing stroke to a beautiful Story-book, in one reasonably-thick volume; title, "the Renunciation", heroine's name, tout bonnement, Emily;[4]—a little in it, but not much, about Italy, become now rather a hackeneyed subject. It is a marvel of a book, and as you may well believe, having it from such good authority—first hand, as one may say—singularly, clever, pithy, and agreeable. By the way, have you read Mr Morier's Hohrab, or the Hostage?[5] And if you have, do you (as I hope) like it? And if you have not, can you tell whether others like it? I was charmed with it here in manuscript, when he kindly lent it me. Besides, I delight in Mr Morier as a man, as well as an author.—My Sister, I find has published a life of my father; I tremble lest she should have buttered him too thickly! This she may have done from genuine enthusiasm and warmth of heart;

but the world will cavil and laugh, and make no allowance for filial affection, and characteristic exaggeration of language. Write to me sincerely what you may happen to hear about it, unless it shall be any thing too sarcastic & severe.[6]—Well—here I am still at Florence, a little bit tired of it, but entirely from my own fault. My niece Mrs John Payne spent a week here with her husband in their way to Rome, & pressed me cordially to accompany them thither; but it was November, & they travelled (an' be hanged to them!) in an abominable open carriage, and I thought my aged carcass would not stand such a mode of crossing the mountains in such a season; so I let them go without me—and lo! it so fell out, that the weather all at once became very mild, and unwindy, and un-foggy, and they had a very agreeable journey.[7] But how could I foresee that?—When, at the same period of the year, I went to Rome, nothing could exceed the chill and wretchedness of the journey, though travelling in a snug close carriage.—Generally speaking, I am a great friend to modern fashions, & venture to flatter myself I have nothing of the grumpy old woman about me, always making injurious comparisons between the days of my youth, & the present:—but there is one mode, now in universal prevalence that I utterly abominate, loath, & detest—viz: that of burying oneself under a suffocating quantity of heavy cloaks & coats in order to sit in an open carriage inhaling all the varieties of damp, bleak, raw, and often, unwholesome atmosphere of a winter day!—É pazzia, Signora mia—è pazzia; the Italians themselves think so, and shudder at the idea.—By hook, or by crook, please Heaven I live, I mean to get home next year. I long to see you all; and after a reasonable stay amongst you, have some thoughts of setting up my tent either at Brighton or Bath. At the latter, I should be near Maria Bourdois & Sophy, both of whom I like & love; at the former, I should have a more frequent chance of seeing old friends, many people resorting to Brighton, who despise poor old Bath.—This important hesitation between the two B's, I shall defer coming to any decision about till my return; and proud ought that B to be to whom another B (Burney) is added!—Is that a pun? or only an ingenious nameless Tom foolery?—Do you remember a certain large vulgar family of little people called Nicholson?[8] Well, this morning, one of the female descendants has sent me a piece of bride-cake, and a visiting ticket from herself and her husband, said tickets tied nattily together with a piece of white ribbon in a true lover's knot. And what think you is her new name? Why, "Mrs J. G. Gutch"[9] an' please you.—I should not know Mrs J. G. Cutch if I met her in my dish, never but once having darkened their doors, and that only to <oblige> please my friend Mrs Layard, who was obliged, she thought, to call upon them, & persuaded me it was a pleasant walk, and would do me good, and was my duty also, they having divers times darkened not only my door, but my countenance by unnecessary and unwelcome visits. There is another offset of the same race about to be married. What illustrious name she may assume to match Mrs Gutch, I do not know. One husband is an M.D. & the other, a Surgeon; and vulgar old Nic chuckles at the idea of getting medical advice, or surgical operations performed in his family gratis. His offsets paint in oils, my dear creature—and they presume to think they have copied the Flora, the Fornarina, the Sybil &c—but I do assure you, *such* wretched, horrid daubs I never saw! They are framed richly, & the foolish father has built an additional room as a Gallery to contain them. The only thing worth looking at, is a small portrait of himself, so frightfully like, it makes one scream. Every defect is exaggerated, & he is made ten times uglier and more vulgar than the reality (c'est beacoup dire) and with a humour in his face;—yet, the beast of a thing is extravagantly like. But enough of these Nics; I am afraid you will think, enough, and too much. A lady called upon me lately, whom the Italian maid announced by the name of la Signora Mischini; I said it was a mistake, as I knew no such person, & desired to be denied. Soon after, she returned, telling me the lady was gone, and had left her compliments, and a visiting ticket. I looked at it—& read; "Miss Skeene"[10]—metamorphosed into Mischini. The Apthorpe's are gone. They winter at Rome, then to Naples, and home by sea. He has been his own enemy here, without knowing it for a long while: but as soon as he did, he left off going to the Casino, and never played but with intimate friends, and for small sums. I assure you he is clever, at least learned, and agreeable, and sweet-tempered, but too easily led by the nose, & blind to the failings of his family. The girls are really accomplished; the eldest sings beautifully, & paints both in oils & miniature in a way that surprised me, and without deception, for I saw her at work in the gallery, & watched her a long time, & convinced myself she knew what she was about, & did her own work her own self. They were in Germany last summer, and brought home Such lithographs! O Annie, if you could but see the perfection to which those Tedeschi have brought that art, you would bless yourself! The most exquisite mezzo-tinto could not excel them; and they are so cheap, that every body here regretted that the Apthorpes had not brought more of them to sell amongst his friends. Our new Clergyman is a Mr Hutton,[11] a young man exceedingly well spoken of. He does not begin till after Christmas. In the interval, a nice old man (name forgotten) performs the duty much to my liking: but he is a valatudinarian & cannot continue.

Krepps, poor dear, has not been quite so well as usual. He has had swelled faces, and pains in the stomach, & feverets—but is better, though thinner.—He is a good creature, & I like him to come and see me after dinner when I am idle, but not in the morning, because his breeches have bird mire on them, & he can never get away, & interrupts all my doings. Your communications respecting Lady C. M.[12] have been confided, under the Rose, to my Niece Mrs Payne, and I refer to her the task of doing what she thinks best in the affair, conjointly with her husband. Julia is now with her Mother. There is no danger for next year, as Lady C. is going home the coming Spring. To be sure I see few people,—but amongst those few is it not singular that no one should ever have breathed a word against her—I do not however, alas the day, question the justice of your apprehensions: but perhaps, as some of her Sisters have been stanch naught, part of their evil reputation may have attached itself somewhat undeservedly to her character.[13] At all events she is charitable to the poor, & kind hearted & friendly to the sick & sorrowful. My Sister d'Arblay writes kindly and gratefully of your attentions to her.—Give my hearty love to your Sisters—And take a large packet for yourself, & if he can swallow it, give a light dose to your General, & believe me ever your most truly affectionate

S. H. B.

Of course, dearest, you will take good care not to send this to my sister; remember what I have confidentially said of my apprehensions concerning the Life of my father.—To your sisters, it is another thing.—Write soon, but write much, a little at a time. I have a nice old French lover—a Chevalier Flechier, a descendant of the celebrated Preacher Flechier.[14] He comes also in the evening with pitched brigs.—

1. SHB dated her letter (erroneously) 1833; it is postmarked 1832, the last winter she would spend in Florence (see below).

2. On 6 November 1832, Frederica Augusta Locke (née Schaub) had died at the age of eighty-two, remembering her "beloved friend" Mme d'Arblay for £100 in her will (*JL*, 12: 756, n. 2, 765–66, n. 4).

3. The famous "bon mot" of Marie de Vichy-Chamrond, marquise du Deffand (1697–1780), on the legendary walk of the decapitated St. Denis. The anecdote is given in the *Letters of the Marquise du Deffand to the Hon. Horace Walpole*, 1: 157, a work mentioned in SHB's letter of 20 January 1812 above. See also Walpole, 3: 305.

4. Sarah Harriet would take the manuscript of *The Renunciation* back to England with her where it would eventually be published as the first tale in *The Romance of Private Life* (1839), possibly after revision (see further LL. 155, 166). The heroine of the published tale, named Agnes, journeys alone through France to Rome by vetturino, as did the author herself.

5. *Zohrab the Hostage* (1832), a work by Sarah Harriet's friend, James Justinian Morier (L. 122, n. 5).

6. Mme d'Arblay's *Memoirs of Doctor Burney* was published in November 1832; for the reviewers' initial response, see *JL*, 12: 765, n. 1. [J. H. Leigh Hunt] complained

mildly of the style in the *New Monthly Magazine* 37 (1833): 48–59, but [John Wilson Croker] in the *Quarterly Review* 49 (1833): 97–125, condemned the whole work strongly: "We would willingly have declined the task of reviewing this book. As a literary work we have not a word to say in its favour." He deplores the fact that Mme d'Arblay has suppressed the *Memoirs* left by Charles Burney and substituted her own version as "the *writer* of a work essentially her own, and not the *editor* of her father's recollections of his life." For two recent views which agree with this assessment, see Lonsdale, Ch. 11; Miriam Benkovitz, "Dr. Burney's Memoirs," *Review of English Studies*, NS 10 (1959): 257–68. The early fragments that escaped Mme d'Arblay's censorship have recently been published as *Memoirs of Dr. Charles Burney, 1726–1769*, ed. Slava Klima, Garry Bowers, and Kerry S. Grant (Lincoln: University of Nebraska Press, 1988); Mme d'Arblay's editorial role is discussed in the introduction.

7. James's daughter Sarah and her husband John Payne; after the death of her mother in the spring of 1832, the Paynes spent most of their time abroad (*JL*, 12: 755, n. 2, 772, n. 4). They reached Rome by 23 November 1832, not apparently without some discomfort: "the Paynes say they had a very penible journey from Florence tho' they came post. the wind & fatigue in mounting the Radicofani mountain were terrible & they think we did best to come by sea" (CFBt to HBt, 23 Nov. [1832], Barrett, Eg. 3702A, ff. 82–83v).

8. A Nicholson family was in Florence 1830–31, according to Crabb Robinson's journal; see next note (HCR, 4, 18, 23 Sept., 6 Oct. 1830, 17, 29 June, 14, 25 July 1831, Travel Journals).

9. Elizabeth Frances Nicholson (c. 1812–69) married at Florence on 12 December 1832 John Wheeley Gough Gutch (1809–62), only son of John Mathew Gutch (1776–1861), journalist and newspaper editor (*DNB*). Educated as a surgeon at Bristol, and a member of the Royal College of Surgeons (22 April 1831), the younger Gutch set up practice at Florence, where he is listed in 1833 and 1835, but apparently returned to England before 1838. His son, John Frederick Lavender Gutch, baptized at Florence 5 December 1833, would die in childhood (*GM*, NS 9 (1838): 557; 3rd ser. 11 (1861): 682–86; 3rd ser. 13 (1862): 112–13; *List of the Members of the Royal College of Surgeons in London* (1822–45); Pedigree of Gutch, Document Collection, Society of Genealogists).

10. Possibly Helen Skene, the sister of James Skene (1775–1864) (*DNB*), of Rubieslaw, Aberdeen, the friend of Scott. Said to be the model for the disagreeable Miss Pratt in Susan Ferrier's *The Inheritance*, she was certainly in Italy in March 1832 when she saw Scott at Naples (Johnson, 2: 1239; Burke, *DLG;* Burke, *Commoners*).

11. Possibly Charles Henry Hutton (c. 1795–1862) of Magdalen College, Oxford, D.D. (1843), who held the British chaplaincies at Geneva and Caen for many years (*Alumni. Oxon.; GM*, NS 12 (1862): 647–48).

12. Lady C[aroline] M[orrison], with whom Julia Barrett had spent several weeks of the summer at Castelamare. Lady Caroline had taken Julia to Rome and helped her to find and prepare a house for her mother and sister. Mrs. Barrett was extremely grateful to Lady Caroline, of whose impending departure she could only express regret "that we shall lose the kindest friend we have here" (CFBt to JBt, 14 Sept. [1832], Barrett, Eg. 3702A, ff. 200–201v). While benefiting daily from Lady Caroline's help, Mrs. Barrett may well have resented her aunt's intimation of injurious gossip about her friend.

Sarah Harriet herself would later attribute to her own untimely interference a breach with her favorite niece that would last for years (L. 159; see Introduction).

13. Lady Caroline, with her two elder sisters (daughters of the Earl of Kingston), had been placed in 1787 under the care of Mary Wollstonecraft (1759–97); the governess was dismissed a year later, ostensibly for having undue influence over her charges, particularly the eldest, Margaret (1772–1835), who adopted republican and atheist principles. Lady Margaret King married in 1791 Stephen Moore (1770–1822), 2nd Earl Mountcashell (1790), but left him for another man, George William Tighe (1776–1837), in 1805. They lived together as man and wife under the names "Mr. and Mrs. Mason" and had two illegitimate children before the death of the Earl in 1822 allowed them to legitimize their union (on 6 March 1826) (Burke; Gibbs; Claire Tomalin, *The Life and Death of Mary Wollstonecraft* (London: Wiedenfeld and Nicolson, 1974), 54–55, 60–65; Kenneth Neill Cameron and Donald H. Reiman, eds., *Shelley and His Circle, 1773–1822*, vol. 8 (Cambridge, Mass.: Harvard University Press, 1986), 908–15; Newman Ivey White, *Shelley* (1940; rpt., New York: Octagon Books, 1972), 2: 108–10. For her biography, see Edward C. McAleer, *The Sensitive Plant* (Chapel Hill: University of North Carolina Press, 1958).

The younger sister, Mary Elizabeth (c. 1779–1819), created a scandal in 1797 when she eloped with Col. Fitzgerald, a married man (also an illegitimate half-brother of her mother), by whom she was pregnant. Col. Fitzgerald was killed by her father and brother, a murder for which they were tried but acquitted, the former by his peers in the Irish House of Lords (18 May 1798), the latter at the Cork Assizes (11 Apr. 1798). Lady Mary King later married in 1805 a Gloucestershire gentleman, George Galbraith Meares (c. 1784–1849) (*GM*, 67, Pt. 2 (1797): 1063; 68, Pt. 1 (1798): 346; 89, Pt. 1 (1819): 587; NS 31 (1849): 557; Tomalin, 237–38, 250; *Times*, 23 May 1798; an eyewitness description of the trial is in Sir Jonah Barrington, *Personal Sketches of his own Times*, 2nd ed. (London: Henry Colburn and Richard Bentley, 1830), 1: 198–204; for an account sympathetic to the lovers, see *Memoirs of the Comtesse de Boigne, 1781–1814*, vol. 1, ed. M. Charles Nicoullaud (New York: Charles Scribner's Sons, 1907), 140–47).

14. Apparently a descendant of Valentin-Esprit Fléchier (1632–1710), a famous preacher who was elected to the Académie Française (1673) for his oratory.

---

146. To Emma Wilbraham

[Florence, 9–]11 February [1833]
A.L.S., Berg
Address: Miss Wilbraham / 54 Upper Brook Street / Grosvenor Square / London / Inghilterra
Postmarks: FIRENZE
FPO / FE25 / 1833

Ah, poor dear Sister Emma!—how sorry I am for your knee!—And how chearfully you write about it;—I cannot tell you how touched I was by such serenity, such real and meritorious resignation: I know it is what we ought all—and always, to feel, under every appointed dispensation: but it is often very difficult. Without being hypocrites, we sometimes flatter ourselves that we should be, or that we are very patient, when, in fact, we are only very melancholy, and mistake despondency for submission, & sadness for piety. When the goodness of Heaven enables us to bow our head, not only without sullenness, but with a loving though a suffering spirit—that seems to me the true frame of mind to be desired.—But I will preach no longer; you need it not, I am rejoiced to find; & perhaps I have been more tempted to do so for my own advantage than for your edification. It may often do us good to draw up a little code of duty, and I fear we can generally do it much more impartially when it is <drawn> called forth by reflecting on the dispensations of others, than when suggested by our own trials.—

I have spent, Sister Emma, not the most unhappy, positively—but the most uninteresting and stupid winter that in the whole course of my long life I ever remember to have passed. The only intimate friends I had here, M^{r} & Mrs Layard, went off to Rome early in November.—A few morning visitors, & a few invitations to evening parties (which I did not accept) have been all that I have since known of human society. I have two dicky-birds to talk to and make pets of at odd moments; and I dine with my two Italian hostesses, & prose for about an hour after the meal is over. But I give up joining their evening circle. I cannot follow the general conversation of an Italian party; and unless they are readily understood, & the force & the fun and the malice of what they say is clearly caught, their society is intolerable. Their harsh and loud voices—their rapid ennunciation, & vehement jestures—their flashing eyes and inexhaustible grimaces, make them resemble maniacs, and, I am ashamed to say, irritate my nerves to such a degree, that it would do me great good to <help> see them all tossed in a blanket.—You, who only saw these people when they stood upon their pps, & their qqs with the Signorine Inglese, and received you only as visitors, can have not the remotest conception of what they are when at home, & at their ease with old friends, and perfectly at liberty to say and to do whatever they list. Then comes "the tug of war."[1] They can do nothing with gentleness and placidity. They have lately, that is for the last half year, taken to play (but not for money) at cards, and four or five of the set are thus employed for a couple of hours every evening. Could you—as I do—sit in a neighbouring room, and hear the apparent fury, the outrageous uproar—the screams, the reproaches, the torrents of vociferation that terminate every deal, you would think that none but mad folks broken loose from confinement could be engaged in these tremendous contests. But it is all a part of the game; the persons thus ranting and roaring are, in fact, as good friends all the time as we should be chatting round a Commerce-Table. They do not know that they are "splitting the ears"[2] of the by-standers; they are not vulgar, uneducated people, they are not cavilling for pence,—they are—Italians! Amongst them, this violence è l'uso, è naturale, and merely indicates that they are enjoying themselves, con spirito.—To me it seems a frightful remnant of barbarity, mixed up with the undisciplined impetuosity common in southern regions.—

Thank you, Sister Emma, for your account of my Sister's book. On the whole, there seems to be in it much more to approve then to censure. I am well pleased for her own sake to recollect having often heard her say she never read Reviews. The Literary Gazette I am told, has treated her with little indulgence,[3] & perhaps so have others. It would do her no good now to see such things, and might in despight of her imagined philosophy, do her much harm.—Sister Emma—I have lived here, reading only French or Italian, till I actually forget how to spell my own language!—You will be sorry to hear that Captn Walker has had a very severe and alarming illness. I have heard nothing of him lately, and trust he is better.[4] We have a new Clergyman,[5] a young man extremely well spoken of, and liked. I have not heard him yet, for the weather has been so intensely cold, & the winds so sharp, that I dared not venture the loss of any part of my pretty little nose by venturing to cross the bridge.—The mal di petto has been very prevalent, and terribly fatal; though I must confess it was not the apprehension of suffering by that which kept me at home; for my chest has hitherto been the freest from complaint of any part of my personage. Kreft (for 'tis thus on his printed card he spells his euphonious name) is quite recovered, and paid me lately one of his usual visits, giving me good measure, well pressed down.[6] But for that fault of staying so long, and prosing so monotonously, he would be perfect. Judge whether I murmur without cause, when I tell you the literal fact, that on one occasion he came at ½ 5, or, say six,—(but the maids swear, it was ½ 5) and staid till . . . twelve at night!—I had serious apprehensions that it was not merely bird-lime that stuck to his brigs,[7] and made him so immoveable, but that he and his chair had grown to each other, and were become inseparable. Conceive my alarm!—Moreover, Sister Emma, I quaked a little for my reputation!—So, since this adventure (which it took me two or three days to recover from, so unutterably fatigued did it leave me) I gave directions to have him admitted "una volta si, una volta no", an order readily and laughingly obeyed.—I have another heavy-sterned visitor, unlike

Krefts in all but the length of his stay. It is an old Venetian Abate, very gentleman-like, & a connoisseur and speculator in fine pictures. He comes with labour and sorrow up my sixty-four steps, bows with the courtesy of la vielle cour, mumbles something with a Venetian accent extremely difficult to understand; arranges himself to his satisfaction on his seat, and then gives me all the trouble, for an hour and half, or two hours, of finding subjects to talk of. Each of these, he answers succinctly, makes no reflection, no comment,—and when his little "sicuro," "lo credo," "é vero," has been uttered, relapses into silence, and leaves me to dig affresh for something further to say. I'll tell you what at last has occurred to me as a resource. I take in the Genoa Gazette, and tant bien que mal, I read it to him, and he seems well pleased, and so am I, because I always hope to be doing myself good by pronouncing Italian aloud.—The Apthorpes are at Rome, & return to England in the Spring. I think I told you I was beginning to know and to like them. They love dress & shew, it is true, but they are really accomplished and industrious, in the morning, however giddy and gay at night; and the father is well-read, full of anecdote, sweet-tempered, & the kindest family-man I ever met with. How different people often are in reality to what they appear. I have not seen the Locks this age. Would you like, Ma'am, to know what I have been doing all alone and at home this winter?—I have, 'an please you, for the 2^d^ time in my life read M^de^ de Sévigné, 9 vols.[8]—Histoire de la Revolution, par Thiers, 10. vols.[9]—Botta's Storia d'Italia, continued from Guicciardini;[10] there are ten vols: I have only read 6 yet. Memoires de l'Abbé Morellet,[11] very entertaining. Memories de M^de^ Dubarry,[12] very naughty, but very amusing, & she the best-natured of the vicious, envious, spightful Court—and sundry other vols, dotted about, & lent me by one body or other.—I hope you are edified, Sister Emma.—

Monday, 11th February.—Since writing the former part of my letter which I had laid by for a day or two expecting to see Krefts again and hear from him whether the Marchesa Pepe had received Miss Eliza's letter, I have had news from Rome of the most afflicting kind. My poor Charlotte Barrett has lost her dear girl, her so loved and so long tenderly nursed Henrietta. I cannot tell you how this news has grieved me. Mrs Payne communicated to me the sad intelligence. The blow has been unexpected notwithstanding the poor girl's long illness,—only two days before she died, her dear Mother said she had several times seen her much worse, and evidently flattered herself she would get over it.—She expired on Thursday last, the seventh,—and when Charlotte has leisure to sit down and mourn,—how dessolate, how bereaved she will feel after the incessant occupation & watchfulness and anxiety of the three last years, resulting from her alternate hopes and fears on the subject of this darling child.[13]—But let me relieve you from this painful theme.—Tell your Sister her letter I am sorry to say has not been delivered—but the Marchesa lately saw Krefts, and expressed her obligation to Miss Eliza for her intention, and desired her love & thanks. Krefts has taken charge of the Sepia which I trust will soon be safely received.—He wishes me to remind you of your Italian Marble tables—To exhort you to look after them, as they are things which just now are of the highest value in this country, and are well worth taking care of every where.—Adieu my dearest Miss Emma—You have my warmest good wishes for the speedy recovery of your poor knee. My best love to your Sisters, & believe me truly yours

S. H. B.

1. Nathaniel Lee, *The Rival Queens* (1677): "When Greeks joyn'd Greeks, then was the tug of War" (IV, ii, 138).

2. Possibly from Hamlet's invective against actors who would "tear a passion to tatters, to very rags, to split the ears of the groundlings" (*Hamlet*, III, ii, 10–11).

3. The *Literary Gazette* was at first noncommittal, but later decidedly negative, the reviewer objecting to Mme d'Arblay's grandiloquent style, and finding that "the manner of relating the facts is as faulty as the narrative is tedious" (no. 826 (17 Nov. 1832), 726–27; no. 828 (1 Dec. 1832), 756–58).

4. Capt. Charles Montagu Walker (L. 132, n. 9) was to die at Florence 9 July 1833 (*GM*, 103, Pt. 2 (1833): 369–70).

5. Mr. Hutton (L. 145).

6. "Give, and it shall be given unto you; good measure, pressed down, and shaken together" (Luke 6:38).

7. Possibly an expression of Charles Burney's, which he used for another of his daughters: "Dr Burney says you carry Bird Lime in your Brains—for every Thing that lights there, sticks" wrote Mrs. Thrale to Frances Burney in 1781 (HLT to FB, 11 [Jan. 1781], Berg).

8. *The Letters of Madame de Sévigné to her daughter and her friends* were published in nine volumes in 1811, translated from the French edition of 1806. Sarah had previously read the work in the original (L. 60).

9. Louis-Adolphe Thiers (1797–1877), *Histoire de la Révolution française*, 10 vols. (Paris, 1823–27).

10. Carlo Botta (1766–1837), *Storia d'Italia, continuata da quella del Guicciardini*, published in ten volumes in 1832. Botta's history starts in 1534, with the death of Pope Clement VII, the point at which *La Historia d'Italia* (1561–64) of Francesco Guicciardini (1483–1540) concludes.

11. André Morellet (1727–1819), *Mémoires* (1821).

12. Jeanne (née Bécu), comtesse du Barry (b. 1743), the mistress of Louis XV, was guillotined in 1793. Any memoirs which Sarah Harriet read were spurious, perhaps the *Mémoires de Madame la comtesse du Barri* [by Baron E. L. de la Mothe-Houdancourt, afterwards La Mothe-Langon] (1829).

13. On Thursday, 31 January 1833, Henrietta Hester Barrett died at Rome at the age of twenty-one. Mrs. Barrett wrote to inform her husband of "the intelligence which is breaking my own heart," of the kindness of the Paynes in making all the funeral arrangements, and of her friend, Lady Caroline Morrison, who "has been like a mother to both my girls." The Morrisons would generously take Charlotte and Julia Barrett back to England with them, paying their costs on the road; they would set out from Rome on 8 April 1833 (CFBt to HBt, 1 Feb. [1833], 6 Feb. [1833], 18 May [1833], Berg; 11 Mar. 1833, 5 Apr. [1833], 25 Apr. [1833], 3 May [1833], Barrett, Eg. 3702A, ff. 84–91v).

Sarah Harriet herself would leave Italy in six months' time, probably with the Paynes, who had offered to take her home with them (*JL*, 12: 787); the £50 paid to Mr. Payne from her account at Coutts on 29 October 1833 possibly reimburses the expenses of the journey, and suggests the approximate date of her arrival in England. She was certainly back by 13 November 1833, when Crabb Robinson called on her at her London hotel: "I found her the same chearful and friendly person she was abroad" (HCR, 13 Nov. 1833, Diaries). Mme d'Arblay, who noted Mr. Robinson's visit "the moment he heard of her arrival," found her half-sister to be "returned all life & spirit—looking younger & brighter & better, in all ways, than when she went abroad" (*JL*, 12: 807).

---

147. To Anna (Wilbraham) Grosvenor

22 Henrietta Street, Bath, 26 March 1834
A.L.S., Berg
Address: M[rs] Grosvenor / <Grosvenor Square> / <London>
readdressed to: Upper Hare Park / Newmarket
Postmarks: BATH / MA27 / 1834 / B
C / MR 28 / 1834
[*?*] / 28MR28 / 1834

March 26 1834
22 Henrietta Street, Bath[1]

By way of being young and giddy, my dearest Anna, I have lost or mislaid, or curled my grey hair, by mistake, with your last letter; so, instead of an answer to, or an observation upon any thing you have said, this precious sheet must be filled entirely with nonsense from the store-house of my own brain. Where shall I begin?—O, I know. I'll tell you a little about the ways and doings of my Bath Boarding-House. You know nothing about such bright places; listen therefore.—The house is in a wide handsome street, and open at one end to the hills & fields. It is kept delightfully clean. The drawing-room is a tolerable size, and

22 Henrietta Street, Bath, where Sarah Harriet lived from 1834 to 1841. (Fotek)

would be well furnished, had it arm chairs, and one or two small work tables. My bed room at the back of the house looks out upon fields, & distant Villas and Cottages, & is chearful & quiet. I have a fire at night, and—(marvellous at Bath) the chimney does not habitually smoak.—I breakfast by myself after I am up in my own room, their ½ eight, or nine o'clock hours, not suiting my fancy.—Besides self, there are four other (female) Boarders. Mrs Thompson,[2] the wife of a Merchant she has quarrelled with, and who lives in London, whilst she resides at Bath, where she has a daughter married, and eke a son, both with lots of children, and no room for Grandmamma: but she goes to see them often, & seems upon good terms, especially with her son's wife. She is a sensible, & lively woman, not much informed, but altogether, rather above par, and when she is out, I miss her, and am glad to see her come back again. Our next fair lady is a Miss Bedford, an Old Maid born, bred, and predestined. She is silly, medling, cackling, tatling, fidgetty, well-meaning, but I really think, half witted. A younger Boarder, a Miss Purefoy, the gay damsel of the party, says poor Beddy has had a narrow escape of being an idiot; & alas! there has been many an assertion made with less truth. The fourth, & tho' last not least of our inmates, is a Miss Elizabeth Sweetapple, an' please you—a tall, sallow, but not ill-looking young person, with fine teeth, large as those of a horse, & a nervous twitch of the under lip when she speaks that causes her to exhibit her rows of ivory like a dog when it snarles. But I must do her the justice to say, she is no snarler in any other way. She is very religious; attends all the Missionary Meetings; takes notes of the different heads of every Sermon she hears; goes to see poor people in the Hospital, or at their own Cottages; renounces Plays, Balls, & gay colours—is not censorious—is not starched, & has never provoked me but by saying she did not like Shakespear! Yet, when "Much ado about Nothing" was acted here,[3] & spoken of in her presence, it came out that she did not know who had written, & had never read it!—Dear Shakespear! Is he to be thus condemned unheard and unknown?—Well, but to go on with my account: we dine, much to my annoyance, & that of Miss Purefoy (a merry Irish girl, with a large Bath acquaintance) at the unreasonable hour of <u>four</u>; just when people are calling, or one wants to return visits oneself. Mrs Camplin,[4] our Hostess, sits at the head of the table in her own parlour, & carves, and one of her daughters[5] at the bottom. The dinners are excellent, but rather too substantial for females, & too rich for any thing but Aldermen—Tea at <u>seven</u>, with hot buttered cakes, & bread buttered as thick as the bread itself. O, and there is, at one o'clock, a meat luncheon besides for those that like it, in the back parlour: but you will believe, I have never troubled it. No supper, unless you are unwell, and ask for gruel, sago, &c. At ½ ten or eleven, all go to their rooms, except the Purefoy, who is out almost every night amongst cousins, and aunts, and Mrs This, or Miss That "The sweetest creatures in the world."—Well—how do you like us? Come and see. We have leave to use the aforsaid back parlour to receive any friends we may wish to ask to tea.

I have lately had a very entertaining letter from Annabel[6] dated Naples. She has been very gay, & has learnt to ride fearlessly on horseback with Nina Cotton & Ld Combermere,[7] & dances with one of the King's brothers,[8] who tries to speak English, but makes a mess of it. Harriet has got safely home again, with her father, & I owe her a letter, as I do almost every body else who ever writes to me—but not our dear Mrs Gregor, for I wrote to her to-day. I purpose, if possible, joining her in May at Cheltenham, & after staying there some little time, going to London for a short trip on a mere matter of business however and to see my Sister d'Arblay.[9]—Adieu my dear friend. Tell your dear Sisters, that they shall hear from me before long, & that I thank them for their letters—but I trust an answer to one will be considered as an answer to both—

Pray present my best compliments to your General, and believe me ever most truly your affectionate

S. H. Burney

1. This is the first letter that survives after Sarah Harriet's return from Italy (L. 146, n. 13). On first arriving home c. October 1833, she apparently visited Henrietta Crewe, and soon went with her to Bath. In February 1834, Mme d'Arblay predicted that Sarah Harriet would "settle at Bath—but I do not think permanently. She will tire of its monotonous composure" (*JL*, 12: 807, 816, 822).

Across Pulteney Bridge, 22 Henrietta Street runs off Laura Place, facing what was then undeveloped land to the east.

2. Mrs. Thompson, like the rest of the boarders named below, has not been identified. A thorough search of directories, parish registers, monumental inscriptions, and death certificates for Bath has turned up several people with the same names as Sarah's fellow inmates but no evidence to link them to 22 Henrietta Street in 1834. The transience of the Bath boardinghouse population is indicated by the fact that the census taken seven years later shows none of the same boarders living there—with the exception of Sarah Harriet herself (1841 Census, Bathwick).

3. Shakespeare's *Much Ado about Nothing* had been revived at the Theatre-Royal, Bath, the previous year, with the first performance given 20 April 1833 (*Bath and Cheltenham Gazette*, 20 April 1833).

4. Anna Maria Camplin (c. 1773–1852), the widow of Thomas Camplin (d. 29 May 1811), an insurance broker of Bristol and granddaughter of Sir Edward Bayntun-Rolt (c. 1710–1800), Bt. (1762), of Spye Park, Wiltshire. By profession a "schoolmistress" (according to the 1841 census), she was listed in the Bath Directory (1822) at 12 Bath Street with her daughters, as "teachers of the pianoforte harp and singing." From 1829 to 1849, she ran a "boarding-house for ladies" or "Ladies' Seminary" at 22 Henrietta

Street. The Land Tax Assessments for the parish of Bathwick show Mrs. Camplin paying the rates at 22 Henrietta Street from 1825 on (*GM*, 81, Pt. 1 (1811): 676; NS 37 (1852): 427; Burke, *Extinct;* Bath Directories (1819–49); 1841 Census, Bathwick; Burials, Land Tax Assessments, Rate Books, St. Mary, Bathwick, County Record Office, Taunton, Somerset).

5. Mrs. Camplin had two unmarried daughters, Amelia (c. 1804–49) and Emma (c. 1811–51), both of whom would be buried at St. Mary's, Bathwick (parish register, St. Mary, Bathwick; *GM*, NS 31 (1849): 554; *JL*, 12: 832, n. 7, 833, n. 3).

6. Annabella Crewe, Sarah's former pupil.

7. Sir Stapleton Cotton, 1st Viscount Combermere (L. 134, n. 4), and his eldest daughter, Caroline Frances (1815–93), "who had been presented at Court, and was an acknowledged reigning beauty in the London world." In September 1833, he took his daughter to Italy, where they wintered at Rome and Naples, "the King, at the latter place, giving a grand review . . . in honour of Lord Combermere" (*Memoirs . . . Combermere*, 2: 240; Lodge; Burke).

8. Ferdinand II (1810–59), King of the Two Sicilies since 1830, had five younger brothers.

9. Mme d'Arblay announced SHB's forthcoming journey to London: "S[arah] Harriet is still at Bath, &—I believe—is meditating a residence there: but she is coming first to London, & is going to visit Mrs. Gregor at Cheltenham, as the latter told me on Thursday" (*JL*, 12: 824).

---

148. [To Charlotte (Burney) (Francis) Broome][1]

22 Henrietta Street, Bath, 12 June 1834
A.L. incomplete, Barrett, Eg. 3700A, f. 148–v

June 12th 1834
22 Henrietta Street
Bath

My dearest Sister

Never suspect <u>me</u> of being exacting on the subject of letter-writing. In good truth, nobody has less right to be so. It is an employment that of all others goes against me most—particularly the first setting about it. Having once begun, I can toddle on pretty tidyly—but <u>le</u> <u>premier</u> <u>pas</u>—Oh, it is misery!—

Thanks, ten thousand, for your kind solicitude about me.[2]—I have had so many tumbles back (returns of fever) that even now, I feel half afraid to think myself better, or, at least, to think the present better means to last. But hoping it does, I must allow that the pain in my side is gradually subsiding; that I cough far less, & have regained strength enough to find my way once into the drawing room, & to feel disposed to renew the experiment. The weather however at present forbids it, being now very damp & chill; so I amuse myself as I best can, with work & books in my own room, on my own comfortable Sofa; & yesterday, I ventured for my dinner, to eat a bit of flounder. Hitherto, I have fed only upon panada, & asparagus, or some other light vegetable. I am housed with excellent people. My medical man has entitled himself to my utmost confidence; I may say, friendship.—He has managed my old frame most judiciously, & been a mental as well as bodily comfort to me.—It has also been a solace to me to have my three Nieces[3] so near at hand. They have been very kind, & poor dear Maria is in despair because I am allowed so few things, that she cannot be sending me the little delicacies usually permitted to invalids.—

My Sister d'Arblay has written to me twice, poor dear, since she first heard of my illness, and in her last very kind letter, made me the same offer of a loan of money in case I wanted it, that you, my darling, have so generously repeated. Be assured, that if I was under any embarrassment, either you or she should be applied to, and that without either shame or hesitation: but I trust, I shall get through this business without being driven to deprive either of you of what you might be doing good with in some other quarter; and as long as I can make my own little income serve, I shall be glad.[4] Unluckily, I answered our dear Sister[5] without seeing the proposal I allude to, wch was written in a small hand round the edge of the paper, & so many little odd scraps—lines & half lines were inserted in different places, that it was only on a second or third reading, I saw what she had said on the money subject. I must write again soon, and set the matter to rights. If you have occasion to address her shortly, say a good word for me. And now, my very dear Sister, Heaven bless you; the rest of my paper I shall give to our Charlotte. [*The text ends at the bottom of the page; no other sheet survives.*]

1. The letter to "My dearest Sister" is most likely addressed to Charlotte Broome, since SHB's other surviving half-sister, Mme d'Arblay, is spoken of in the third person (see below).

2. Sarah Harriet was suffering in the spring of 1834 from "a frightful illness, of a pleurisy" (*JL*, 12: 831).

3. Maria Bourdois, Sophia Elizabeth, and Amelia Burney, the three surviving daughters of Esther Burney, all lived at Bath (*JL*, 12: 831, n. 6).

4. Sarah Harriet was receiving an annual income of £98.17.5 on various investments; she had already spent £150 that year (Coutts ledgers).

5. Mme d'Arblay's letter and Sarah's reply are both missing, but in a letter postmarked 12 June 1834, Fanny reports: "I had a Letter from that poor sufferer 2 days ago—far, far from what we could wish! She has not yet left her room—& moves scarcely but from

Bed to Sofa . . . the 3 nieces she has there are very attentive to her . . . & her Hostess, & Hostess's Daughters & servants are indefatigably her attendants & comforts: & she is entirely confident in her medical aid" (*JL*, 12: 833).

149. To Anna (Wilbraham) Grosvenor

22 Henrietta Street, Bath, 23 January [1835]
A.L.S., Berg
Address: Mrs Grosvenor / <Hare Park> / <Newmarket> / <Cambridgeshire>
readdressed to: Lower Grosvenor St / Grosvenor Sq / London
Postmarks: Newmarket / Penny Post
[BAT]H / [J]A 24 / 1835
NEWMARKET / JA27 / 1835
F / 28JA28 / 1835

January 23^{d} Henrietta Street
N° 22

My dearest Anna (for Anna—my Anna—you must always be, married or not married)

It is worth while to grumble, when the faults we grumble at, are so prettily repaired. You have sent me a letter with a date, and with lines and words that have no need to shout at one another as if lost in a wood. It is really a comfort when we are spared the necessity of saying "I cannot make head or tail of this letter; I do not know where it was written from, nor to what spot its answer must be addressed; nor how long it is since it was endited,—and <short as it is,> little as it contains, that little is all confusion".—Such, dear Anna, have too often been my secret complaints against you; and now I can compliment you on doing better, I have no scruple in confessing my former murmurings.—

It may seem hard that I should require what I am so circumstanced as to be unable to repay—Viz: a chatty, entertaining letter. My illness of last Spring has left certain beaux restes, such as cough, stuffage of the head, huskiness, &c, which oblige me to give up going out entirely. No mountain comes to the mouse, of course; so that till lately I neither saw nor heard any thing more amusing than the few widows and old Maids who are my fellow-boarders. But now, I am rewarded. Harriet Crewe is once more in England, and moreover, she is an inmate with me; sleeps in the next room, dines at the same table, and teas (as Mrs Erswell[1] used to say) with the same drawing-room party. She has been induced for the present, at least, to renounce her plan of becoming a Carmelite; but her mind had been much agitated, & she was grown nervous, <she> and wanted change both of air and society; & a journey to England was therefore agreed upon, and readily sanctioned by her father, who, whatever he may be in other respects, has always been kind and indulgent to her.—She is much at Prior Park, with Bishop Baines,[2]—but this house is her home, and I see more of her than under any other arrangement I could have hoped to do.—She is much liked & admired for her manners and good-nature by every body under the roof. Old James Greville[3] (do you know him? He that every body calls Uncle Jem) is likewise at Bath. He has taken it into his head (don't be scandalized) that he should like me to live with him, an' please you! That is to say, for six months in the year, when he is in town: but in the belle saison, when he goes down to Peesmore, his Living, he would beg to make his bow in return for my curts'y, till the London season came round again. I have begged to decline the agreeable offer—which, after all, is not quite so ridiculous in its object, as may at first sight appear. He fancied I might be able to read to him, when disengaged of an evening. But my recent attack of the chest has rendered that impossible. I get hoarse and short-breathed in five minutes. So, I hope, there is an end of the matter. Remember, Dear, for the credit of my reputation, that my worthy old pretender is upon the stroke of eighty,[4] if not past.—

You talk of reading "a very old book": Boswell's Tour to the Hebrides.[5] Why that's a chickn compared to my present reading. I am reduced to a perusal of my own little library, and am solacing myself with Plutarch's Lives, and Robertson's History of Charles V.[6] and vary my sport occasionally with an Historical Play of Shakespear, or a good Sunday Book.—

I wish I had recollected, when I last wrote to my Sister, to tell her that her name had been so highly honoured by the horticulterists. I hope your "d'Arblay Rose"[7] will prosper, and prove handsome. Pray, do you know a Mrs Bolton, wife of a Doctor of that Ilk?[8] She is reported to be very handsome, immoderately clever, an Astrologer, even, that draws out, or draws up (which should I say?) Nativities; and is, besides, poetry-mad, & has conceived a mad fancy for Alex d'Arblay. She is now at Dover,[9] deprived for the present, of the use of her <long> limbs, but certainly not of her tongue, which goes nineteen to the dozen. She is carried on an inclined plane to peoples houses of an evening, & has struck up an acquaintance with Lady Combermere, where Harriet Crewe saw her. She is very entertaining, & has something of the look of a handsome Witch. Lady Combermere calls her The Sybil.—Alex is gone to pay her a visit at Dover, and, under all the disadvantages of previous praise, has been introduced to Lady C: who, I dare say was disappointed, & perhaps dislikes him.—

I am charged by Miss Crewe to insert her best compliments to you. She has just escaped from a pent-up airing with Uncle Jem in his little Chariot, & on coming back, looked as white as a sheet, & felt half sick. Pray present me to the remembrance of the General, & believe me ever dearest Annie Your truely

& faithfully attached

S. H. Burney.

1. Elizabeth Erswell, the wife of the Master Butler at Chelsea Hospital, and formerly Sarah Harriet's landlady (L. 77, n. 1; L. 79).

2. Peter Augustine Baines (1786–1843), a Roman Catholic Bishop (1823), had purchased Ralph Allen's manor house, Prior Park, in 1829, establishing there a theological college, which would remain open until 1856 (*DNB;* John Haddon, *Portrait of Bath* (London: Robert Hale, 1982), 156–57).

3. The younger brother of Lady Crewe, the Rev. James Greville (1753–1836), Rector of Peasemore, Berks. (1816) (Burke, Lodge under Warwick; *Alumni Cantab.; GM,* NS 5 (1836): 559). Ten years previously, he had made SHB some kind of offer that she refused, an incident expunged from Mme d'Arblay's letters; SHB "has finally denied Mr. J. Greville. I am really sorry. But she had no reasons very rational" (*JL,* 12: 574). It is not impossible that this was an offer of marriage; the explanation offered by FBA's editor (n. 4), that he was inviting her at that time to be his companion and reader during the London season, seems unlikely, since she had recently taken up a responsible and lucrative post as governess for Lord Crewe's grandchildren (L. 104, n. 1). See further LL. 150, 151.

4. James Greville would be turning eighty-two on his next birthday, 27 June 1835 (Burke under Warwick; *Alumni Cantab.*).

SHB's use of the word "pretender" is of interest, since "un pretendant" in French can mean "suitor." It is probably Greville whom Mme d'Arblay calls "a very favourite *Friend* within reach" of Sarah Harriet at Bath in June 1834, and not (as her editor would have it) Harriet Crewe, a recent arrival in January 1835 (*JL,* 12: 833, n. 4).

5. James Boswell (1740–95), *The Journal of a Tour to the Hebrides with Samuel Johnson, LL.D.* (1785).

6. William Robertson (1721–93), *The History of the Reign of the Emperor Charles V* (1769).

7. A peach and white rose, named for Mme d'Arblay, was grown at Tunbridge Wells in 1835 (*The International Check-list of Roses* (Harrisburg, Pa.: McFarland, 1969), 249).

8. At the centre of a literary circle at Dover, Clarissa Marion (née Verbeke) (c. 1804–39), the wife of George Buckley Bolton (c. 1797–1847), a surgeon. She was the former mistress of Disraeli, whom she tried to interest on behalf of her new protégé. Alexander d'Arblay eventually tried to extricate himself from too close an intimacy (*JL,* 12: 752, n. 1, 852, n. 3, 865, n. 2; Robert Blake, *Disraeli* (London: Eyre & Spottiswoode, 1966), 75–77).

9. In a letter postmarked 26 January 1835, Mme d'Arblay mentions that "Alex is just returned from Dover—all alive," but later worries that while he is in "high health & spirits" after his socializing, he may have injured his health with late nights (*JL*, 12: 852, 855).

150. To Henry Crabb Robinson

22 Henrietta Street, Bath, 18 February–30 March 1835
A.L.S., Dr. Williams'
Published: Morley
Address: H. C. Robinson Esqr / 2 Plowden's Buildings / London
Endorsed: Feb: 18th 1835 / reced / June from Miss Nash / Miss Burney

Feby 18th 1835
22 Henrietta
Street, Bath

My dear Friend

How shall I thank you for the opportunity with which you have so kindly furnished me, of becoming acquainted with the animated, intelligent, well-informed and entertaining Misses Nash?[1] One of them (the most hardy of the two)[2] has done me the favour to spend an evening with me; and a short time since, I sat by their fire-side one morning, I know not how many hours "by Shrewsbury Clock,"[3] chatting of this and that, and so highly gratified by their spirit and good-sense, that I came away, at last, half disposed to be out of humour with every other female I have conversed with since I came to Bath—my own Nieces excepted, who, as being, in some measure, part and parcel of myself, I thought entitled to a portion of the same indulgence I should wish for in my own case.

I shall say nothing to you of the heavy rap of the knuckles my health has undergone since we met.[4] You are one of the favoured mortals who know of illness only the name, & can have no spontaneous sympathy with the sick—none but what your good heart obliges you to think you <u>ought</u> to have;—and I do not wish, poor thing, to put it to such a trial. Besides—I am better now, though but a poor creature still.—And, this said, you shall hear no more of that matter. I will, instead talk to you of a journey to town which I meditate undertaking towards the middle or latter end of May. I want to see my Sister d'Arblay, and certain other old friends, and I had purposed applying to my Niece, Mrs P. (Payne,) for a little house room during my London sojourn. But, behold! My charms, either bodily or mental, or both, have captivated the fancy of a gay gallant, aged only eighty—a Rev^d^ (James) J. Greville, Uncle to Miss Crewe—who has a snug bachelor's house in Pimlico, and has so set his heart upon having me under his roof, that when I, at first, declined the invitation, he looked so mortified—so like an unhappy Strephon,[5] that, finally, my tender womanish heart was softened, and I promised him three weeks or a month of my engaging company. This has revived him, and he left Bath ten days since, the happiest of expectant lovers.—Meanwhile, of all the birds in the air, who do you think is actually boarding with me in my present residence, and subscribing to all the ways and doings of a Bath Boarding-House?—Why, Miss Crewe herself, the one you dined with at Mr King's.[6] Since that time, she has been residing again with her father, near Liege: but longing, and sighing for the pleasure of becoming a Carmelite Nun, an' please you!—Something or other, however,—I cannot well make out what—has put her off from this very judicious plan for the present; yet, so excited had been her spirits, and so shaken her health both of body and mind, that it was thought desirable for her to spend a few months in her own country, and amidst persons and scenes that might take off her thoughts from what had so long exclusively engrossed them. To Bath then she came a little before Christmas, partly attracted, perhaps, by me, and still more, by a certain Catholic Bishop Bains, residing at Prior Park, and her great friend. And a good friend too, for he is wholly averse to her becoming a Nun; and, moreover, as she has been advised here by a Medical man to observe a more nourishing diet, he (the Bishop) has given her a dispensation, whereby she may abstain from killing herself by fasting rigourously throughout the approaching Lent.—

I return your Italian Volumes, my dear friend, with many thanks, owning honestly, that I have never looked into them; for the thread of my interest in Botta's History having been interrupted by my leaving Florence,[7] I could not for the life of me connect it again; and I got hold of other books—read no Italian for ages—and, at last, pounced one fine day upon a good, clear edition of Ariosto, and have been and am reading him with even more delight than when he first fell into my hands.[8] Here and there, he is a bad boy, and as the book is my own, & I do not like indecency, I cut out whole pages that annoy me, & burn them before the Author's face, which stands at the beginning of the first volume, and I hope feels properly ashamed. Next to Ariosto, by way of something new, I treat myself now and then with a play of one Wm Shakespear, and I am reading Robertson's Charles V^th^ which comes in well after that part of

Botta's History at which I left off—viz: just about the time of the Council of Trent.[9] And, as I love modern reading, I was glad to find myself possessed of a very tidy edition of a Biographical work you may perhaps have heard tell of—Plutarch's Lives. If you should ever meet with it, I think I might venture to say you would not dislike it.—

I am with good and worthy people, who took much care of me when I was ill—and I like Bath better than Lonnon, as you cockneys call it—and, except once more to revisit the dear, interesting Rome, I never desire to see Italy again in all my born days. Of Florence I had much too much. Adieu, dear friend.

(Yours ever truly,) S. H. Burney.

I wish you would enquire for me, some beau matin, early in June, at N° 16, Pimlico.—

March 30th My plans are altered since writing the above. I have given up all thoughts of London, & accepted an invite into Dorsetshire.

1. Probably Elizabeth and Esther Nash, the daughters of William Nash (fl. 1745–1825), a solicitor at Royston, Herts., and an active member of the nonconformist community. The family were close friends of Henry Crabb Robinson, who had received "a call from Miss Nash and Miss Esther Nash" on 11 January 1835, perhaps on their way to Bath (see HCR, *Reminiscences*, 1: 35–36, 355–56; 2: 63, 107–8, 229 and passim; HCR, 22 Jan., 6 Feb. 1832, 11 Jan. 1835 and passim, Diaries; *New Law List* (1812–24)).

2. Probably Esther Nash, who delivered the letter in person on 4 June 1835 (see endorsement) to Crabb Robinson, who commented, "Miss B: writes with her usual vivacity and seems vastly pleased with the Nashes—but has been very ill. She is certainly growing old very fast according to Hester Nash." On 6 June he "called on Miss Nash—heard of Miss Burney" (HCR, 4, 6 June 1835, Diaries).

3. A proverbial expression used in Shakespeare's *1 Henry IV*, V, iv, 145.

4. Possibly in November 1833 when Robinson had seen her in London on her return from Italy (L. 146, n. 13).

5. I.e., a rustic lover, from the shepherd in Sir Philip Sidney's *Arcadia*.

6. On 17 November 1833, Crabb Robinson records in his diary leaving a card at "Mr. King's, my old acquaintance," whom he had "met on the stairs of Miss Burney's hotel." He dined at Mr. King's on 19 November where he met the Hon. Miss Crewe and Miss Burney, had "a genteel dinner and an agreeable afternoon," and noted that Mr. King's son as well as Henrietta Crewe had converted to Catholicism (HCR, 17, 19 Nov. 1833, Diaries).

7. Sarah was reading Carlo Botta's *Storia d'Italia* during her last winter in Florence (L. 146).

8. Ludovico Ariosto, the poet and playwright of the Italian renaissance, whose work Sarah had included in the catalogue of her reading on 3 November 1805 (L. 30 above).

9. The Council of Trent (1545–63) occurs during the first quarter of Botta's *Storia d'Italia;* in SHB's letter of February 1833 (L. 146), she had claimed to be more than halfway through the work.

151. To Frances (Burney) d'Arblay

22 Henrietta Street, Bath, 30 March 1835
A.L.S., Berg
Address: Madame d'Arblay / 1. Half Moon Street / Piccadilly / London
Postmarks: 8 MORN 8 / AP 13 / 1835
G / AP11 / 1835

March 30th 1835
22 Henrietta Street

My dearest Sister

Some ladies I am acquainted with having offered to convey a letter for me to town, I avail myself of the opportunity just to ask you how you do?—just to tell you I am pretty well I thank you;—just to say, I have seen poor dear Richard of Rympton[1] who came over for a few days to consult some medical man, and went back better than he came, though still looking sadly thin & aged. The fact is, that some how or other, we certainly do not look younger as we live longer! And what is still mighty apt to surprise me, is <the discovery> that persons whom I formerly knew, and considered as little boys & girls hardly worth looking down upon, are now become grey-beards—and seem hardly younger than I once remember to have seen their fathers.

Uncle Jim—I beg his pardon, Mr James Greville—extracted a cold consent from me about a fortnight before he left Bath, to pay him a visit in town this Spring for just three weeks, or, at the very utmost, one month; at the end of which, I told him what is very true, that I was engaged to go to Rympton in Dorsetshire, and could not possibly prolong my abode with him. He acceded to my terms, & went off well satisfied.—But behold! the longer I reflected upon the unlucky engagement, the more I hated the idea of it;—the first thing in a morning it came across my imagination with a painful twinge; the last thing at night it sat heavy on my soul; and all day long it recurred to me with antipathy and disgust. So at last, I said to myself "Why should I undergo this needless, and self-inflicted punishment? Who will thank me for doing a thing I so much loath?—Who shall I materially benefit by thus tormenting myself?"—To these enquiries I received no other answer than this: "Sarah, my dear, you are a goose to deliberate so long about the matter. Nobody wants you to do a thing you have so thoroughly set your heart against; so give it up with a good grace; write a handsome grateful letter of apology to the worthy old gentleman, & let there be an end of the whole business."—I took the advice of my internal monitor, and have received in return a very kind and civil letter from Uncle Jim—I beg his pardon—Mr James Greville,—& a reluctant but final acceptance of my resignation of the undefinable office he had proposed to me in his establishment.—And moreover, I informed him that Miss Lloyd,[2] an old crony of his, was in town on a visit—and perhaps he may tender the post to her; and she would suit him much better than I should. My only regret is, that I shall lose the pleasure of seeing you this Spring: but, considering my engagement to Richard of more than a year's standing, and considering my not very entire recovery (for I still cough, and am utterly deprived of both taste & smell) I think that two journeys—one to London, & the other into Dorsetshire, with all the packing & trouble incident <to> upon both, would have been too much for me.[3] Let me therefore solace myself with the hope of being able when I am stronger, to make amends to myself for what I am now losing.

My friend Miss Crewe, though no longer under the same roof with me, is still in the neighbourhood, at Prior Park, where she will remain till after Easter, and then set out on her return to her father. She has submitted to the homeliness of our style of living in this house, very heroically, (so she ought, you will say, since she had been able to make up her mind to become a Carmelite Nun) and her society, you will easily believe, has been a very gratifying treat to me. But her conversion severs us a good deal in spite of ourselves. We no longer like the same books,—we no longer can associate with the same persons,—our religious feelings, our places of worship are no longer the same,—our very diet must differ, & we must always be upon our guard, lest we should say any thing that could hurt the feelings of the other in speaking of their different modes of worship. With a born & bred R. Catholic, I never felt under all these restraints: but your new converts are always on the qui vive, and poor Harriet is particularly susceptible on such topics. She was so even in her protestant days, and thought it almost prophane to say a Church was ugly, or a Sermon dull, though the one might be in the most barbarous taste, & the other only fit to set you asleep.

Do you know, my dear Sister, that I shall leave off calling Mrs Maltby[4] the Beer-woman, for the two last times I have seen her, she has been really pleasant and agreeable!—Could I ever have believed it?—

Maria and Sophy have been deeply grieved by the death of dear excellent Mrs Sandford.[5] Poor Cousin Edward! He has written such a sweet letter to Maria; it is all simplicity, all genuine, gentle, but profound and heart-felt sorrow. Just such a letter as his mild, and unaffected, but feeling character, would lead one to expect.

And now dearest Sister, with love to Alex, let me conclude by signing
myself your ever affectionate S. H. Burney.—

1. Sarah Harriet's nephew, Richard Allen Burney, Rector of Rimpton (1802) and curate of Brightwell, Berks. (1815), where he lived until 1831, when the appointment of a new Rector caused him to vacate the Brightwell rectory and move back to Rimpton. He had less than a year to live, dying on 29 March 1836, aged sixty-three ("Worcester Mem.," 61–62, 91–92, 97; L. 85, n. 6; *JL*, 12: 891, n. 7).

2. Unidentified.

3. Mme d'Arblay, somewhat preoccupied with her son's engagement (see below L. 153, n. 2), accepted the change of plan quietly: "S. Harriet has remitted her London project" (*JL*, 12: 871).

4. Harriet Maltby (c. 1763–1852), a well-known resident of Bath (at 22 Royal Crescent) and friend of Frances d'Arblay (*JL*, 9: 81, n. 8; *GM*, NS 39 (1853): 219; Bath directories (1805–52)).

5. Rebecca (née Burney) Sandford (L. 85, n. 14), the sister of Esther's husband, Charles Rousseau Burney, had died 5 March 1835, aged seventy-seven ("Worcester Mem.," 97; *JL*, 12: 891, n. 7).

---

152. To Anna (Wilbraham) Grosvenor

22 Henrietta Street, Bath, 28 May [1835]
A.L.S., Berg
Address: Mrs Grosvenor / Hare Park / Newmarket / Cambridgeshire
Postmarks: F / 29MY29 / 1835
BATH / MY28 / 18[35]

22 Henrietta Street
May 28th

My dearest Anna will forgive me for not availing myself of her truly kind proposal of becoming acquainted with her excellent friends the Miss Sothebys[1] by means of the letter she inclosed to me. But being now on the eve of going from Bath into Dorsetshire for some weeks, and very much taken up with dancing attendance upon the Bath Waters twice a day (for I am strongly, and <u>professionally</u> advised to try them); and moreover, obliged to give all the time I can spare to a relation now here with her daughter for a little frolic, I think it hardly worth while to tap a new acquaintance I shall have so little leisure to drink freely or comfortably from,—and may never be thrown in the way of again.—If, however, there is any thing in your letter to them, independently of me, which you wish them to see, let me know it as soon as you can, & it shall be dispatched to them. Only, as you gave me my option about sending it, I thought I might defer the measure till I heard from you; since, were I to see them, and to like them (which I am sure I should) it would merely be making me regret the improbability of seeing them again.—

I wish all you kind friends would learn to consider my residence at Bath as a matter of expediency rather than of absolute choice.—The place is pretty, no doubt, but hitherto I have certainly not found it very intellectual. However, appearances are improving even in that respect, & I am beginning to find out that there are heads with brains in them, even here—I do not mean, here, in this Boarding House, but in Bath itself. But when I get into my new apartment with a gentle, rational, & friendly associate; and, if it please God, enjoy health enough to keep up an intercourse with a few agreeable persons I have at length been fortunate enough to light upon, I shall do very well—quite as well, and better than I deserve. Meanwhile, I am living here for almost half the money it would cost me to live much less respectably in London.[2] If I want it, I can have good medical attendance;—if able and willing to go out, I can have <an> easy and cheap conveyances—I have relations here that I love,—and in London, as you well know, I have not a resting place for the sole of my foot, of a hair's breadth diameter. It must always be visits, or lodgings. Now, visits cannot be turned into homes; and lodgings, if occupied without a companion, and paid dearly for into the bargain, are—der tivel!—

I have given you a dish of egotism, my dearest, which you will not desire to have often repeated; and if you behave well, and agree to the truth of all I have said, I will engage to spare you such another dose for a long time.

Our amiable and friendly Mrs Gregor[3] holds out a faint hope to me that I may have the very great pleasure of seeing her in Bath next winter. How many there are I should be delighted to prescribe the Waters to, or to recommend our mild air to, or to find out some other way of inticing hither! Mrs Gregor finds her Surry residence too bleak for winter;—I dare say, with a little consideration you might make the same discovery. Try, my dearest;—or else, put it into the General's head, whenever he has any little ailment, that the Bath Waters would be a sovereign remedy for it.—

I am glad we agree in liking old books.—As I cannot easily get at new ones, I mean to persuade myself that they are nothing worth compared to the good old Robertsons, and Plutarchs, and Miltons, and Shakespears, and Youngs &c, &c. My few friends with brains as above mentioned, lend me now and then a modern publication which I am condescending enough to peruse. Amongst others, I have had Keith on the Evidences of Prophecy put into my hands, and a most masterly and striking performance it is. Totally dissimilar from Newton on the Prophecies, an excellent book, but not in any degree equal in force or in ability to the work in question, which has already gone through thirteen editions.[4]

Pray, if your sister Emma is still with you, give my kindest love to her. Methinks I can see her trotting about from field to lane, & from lane to field, looking for primroses, and enjoying "all rural sights and rural sounds",[5] and caring for none of the fine London doings that are, I suppose, now going on. I know few persons whose tastes in many respects would suit better with mine. She has more courage than I have to encounter Bulls and other country startlers, but she does not love a Garden, or a Shrubbery better than I do,—or a quiet evening with a book,—or a snug morning with a pencil,—or an exemption from uninteresting visitors.—

How dreadful your account of the shower of stones in Sicily!—Do you not suppose they proceeded from Etna?—It is sad to think how that lovely Italy is often devast[*at*]ed by elemental calamities. Earthquakes, tremendous storms, Volcanic eruptions—and besides all these, infested by scorpions, vipers, & bestie of various descriptions, all either venomous, or alarming from their size and hideousness.—I saw at Luca Baths Such a Spider! Even the Italian Maid was afraid of it! And it was motionless upon the white wall of my bed-room.—Mrs Barrett with some difficulty made away with it.[6] But she was accustomed to all sorts of nasty reptiles, for poor Henrietta liked to collect them. Adieu dearest Annie—ever thine S. H. Burney.

Do you know what a funny shape your letter was? Something like a Dutch tile in a Swiss stove.—

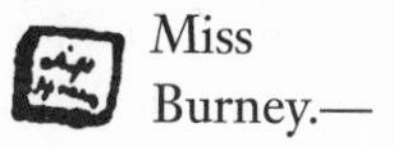
Miss
Burney.—

1. Maria Elizabeth and Harriet Louisa Sotheby, sisters to Capt. Charles Sotheby (L. 134, n. 15) and daughters of the author, William Sotheby. Sarah had actually met these friends of the Wilbrahams years before in their father's home (L. 79, nn. 6, 8).

2. Sarah's account at Coutts shows a debit of only £50 for 1835, from an annual income of approximately £100.

3. Jane Gregor, Sarah Harriet's former employer (L. 97, n. 2).

4. Alexander Keith (1791–1880), who would later join the Free Church secession from the Church of Scotland; his *Evidence of the Truth of the Christian Religion, derived from the literal fulfilment of Prophecy* (1828) became a classic (*DNB*). His work contrasts with that of careerist Thomas Newton (1704–82), Bishop of Bristol (*DNB*), *Disserta-*

tions on the Prophecies, which have remarkably been fulfilled, and at this time are fulfilling in the world (1754–58). Both works ran through numerous editions.

5. William Cowper, *The Task* (1785), Bk. 1, l. 181.

6. The summer that Charlotte Barrett and Sarah Harriet Burney spent together at the Baths of Lucca, Charlotte wrote to her husband, "I killed a black scorpion last night on the wall of our stairs—an inch & half long. the first I have seen in our house" (CFBt to HBt, 7–8 Aug. [1830], Berg).

153. To Frances (Burney) d'Arblay

13 Vineyards, Bath, 31 August 1835
A.L.S., Berg
Address: Madame d'Arblay / 1 Half Moon Street / Piccadilly / London
Postmarks: F / SE 1 / 1835
BATH / AU31 / 1835 / D

Aug^st^ 31st 1835
13 Vineyards, Bath

My dearest Sister

I hear from various quarters such very pleasing accounts of Alex' Promessa Sposa,[1] that I am quite anxious to become acquainted with her.[2] Harriet Crewe who has not long been gone from Prior Park, talked to me a good deal about her when we last met, and I then learnt <through her> the exact nature of her connection with the Greville family, which before I did not very clearly understand. She described to me Miss Smith's personal appearance; mentioned the high degree of favour she stands in with lady Lambert;[3] said that Brook Greville had always spoken of her as a most excellent girl, & further assured me that there could be no doubt she would become a very general favorite in our family. These were pleasant things to hear, and I thought you would not be unwilling to participate in the gratification they afforded me.

There is a worthy man about the world, a Mr Huttner, for whom our dear father had a great regard, and who also holds a high place in my good opinion, who has lately written to me to say that after reading your Memoirs of Dr Burney, he was induced to remit to you some Letters he had received from my father,[4] in consequence of finding you meant to follow up the Life with the Correspondence of Dr Burney.[5] He has since bethought himself that in those letters are contained certain unguarded expressions respecting some individuals concerning whom my father, on Mr Huttner's account, was inclined to entertain a good deal of displeasure. I fancy he alludes to what may have been said of the Staunton family, in which, as you may perhaps remember, he Mr. Huttner, was engaged as Tutor, & accompanied the present Baronet in that capacity to China, in the suite of Ld Macartney.—The Stauntons shewed themselves neither liberal nor friendly, when Mr Huttner was parted with, & it may be in consequence of his knowledge of their shabbiness that my father spoke of them so slightingly.[6] At all events, my dearest Sister, Mr Huttner being unwilling to trouble you with a letter, entreated me the first time I wrote, to request that if you make any use of the letters he sent you, you will have the goodness to omit any passages in them that may appear too personal or severe.—

Having executed the commission with which I was entrusted, I have now leisure to tell you that our Nieces, Maria & Sophy, are pretty well (for them, s'entend) Amelia is still at Rimpton. For myself, I have only a very foolish story to tell, of an experiment I ought to have known better than to have tried.—I took it in my head to join forces with a Lady I was to live with in a private lodging, and to become very fond of, and to be as happy with as the day was long. But it does not do.—It was a mad venture, made upon the mere knowledge of her being respectably connected,—of her having gentle & civil manners, and some little knowledge of the world in consequence of having lived fourteen or fifteen months on the Continent.—I was so tired of people who never had any thing to talk about but Bristol, that I longed for a wider range of subjects. Alas!—I soon found that my new associate could furnish me with no such thing. She is illiterate, naturally common-place, is too high for a servant, & too dull & tiresome for a companion. Bref: I mean to draw my neck out of the collar; & without quarrel or squabble, have intimated to her that at the end of the Quarter for which I engaged these lodgings, I shall return to my <old> former, and pretty apartment at Mrs Camplin's.[7] There, at least, I am not tied down always to sit vis-à-vis the same stupid body. I can have a fire in my own room, & without offence to any one, can retire whenever I like. Besides, in a house whose guests are so often shifting, there is at least a chance that some soul or other may arrive from whom a little agreeability may [*be*] extracted. Nous verrons.

Have you read Bourrienne's Memoirs? Sick as I thought myself of Buonaparte and all that related to his tremendous though short-lived success (I always consider him as a permitted scourge), Bourrienne's book caught fast hold of me, & I was really sorry when I had finished it. Yet, I could only get it in English: but the translation is not very bad.[8]—I wish I could hear oftener of your health, and general proceedings. Are you doing any thing about The Correspondence? I am often asked.—Miss Bowles,[9] a clever friend of mine, & a very pleasing authoress, wrote to me in raptures of "Madame d'Arblay's most interesting & entertaining Biography."—She adds "Princesses Augusta & Sophia[10] told my relation, Lady Neale,[11] they were delighted with all M^de^ d'Arblay wrote of Windsor, &c, than which nothing could be more graphically true".—If it was not for a sensible agreeable letter now & then, I might be tempted to think all the world had become ignorant, dull, & vulgar.—Such an idea is very bad, for there is danger of its leading me to consider myself as a beautiful pearl cast away before swine.[12] I hope I shall be more humble—and indeed, I would be willing to put up with the folks being vulgar, if they would but produce a little mother-wit, or good sterling sense. Adieu my dearest Sister. Give my love to Alex, to Fanny Raper & Co. & believe me ever most truly & affectionately yours

S. H. Burney.

1. *I Promessi Sposi* was the title of the famous novel of Alessandro Manzoni (1785–1873), published in three volumes in 1825–26.

2. Alexander d'Arblay had written to his mother in April 1835 to announce his engagement to Mary Ann Smith of Croom's Hill, Greenwich. Mme d'Arblay met her prospective daughter-in-law c. 10 July and was enthusiastic in her praises (*JL*, 12: 864 and n. 1, 873).

3. Anna Maria Foley (c. 1801–57) had married 7 May 1821 Henry John Lambert (1792–1858), 5th Bt. (1803). She was related to Brook Greville, Lady Crewe's nephew, by marriage. Her husband's mother, Sophia née Whyte (d. 21 Mar. 1839), widowed in 1803, had married in 1805 Brooke Greville's father, Lt.-Col. Henry Francis Greville (L. 113, n. 7) (Burke; *GM*, 3rd ser. 2 (1857): 499, 501).

4. Johann Christian Hüttner (L. 43, n. 1), whom Charles Burney had helped find employment. Sarah Harriet had sometimes taken her father's letters from dictation, or even written in her own name to Hüttner on his affairs (see above LL. 43, 44, 46, 49, 50). Hüttner wrote on 18 January 1833 to Mme d'Arblay, offering her "a whole bundle" of Dr. Burney's letters for the projected edition of correspondence (see next note), and giving her at the same time an account of his own career and acquaintance with her father (JCH to FBA, 18 Jan. 1833, Osborn).

5. After her father's death in 1814, Mme d'Arblay began to sort through his papers intending to publish his correspondence, a work that she continued intermittently until she discovered in 1828 that the copyright act would prevent her publishing without the writers' permission. In her *Memoirs of Doctor Burney* (1832), she announced her intention to print an additional volume of his own letters, and requested their return (*HFB*, 446–55; *JL*, 11: 184–93; 12: 705–6, 784, n. 16).

6. Mr. Hüttner acted as tutor to Sir George Staunton and accompanied him on Lord Macartney's embassy to China in 1792 (L. 43, n. 1). When he left this family, although "still enjoying the . . . uninterrupted great goodwill & friendship" of his former pupil (JCH to FBA, 18 Jan. 1833, Osborn), he received no help in his efforts to maintain

himself, an oversight condemned strongly by Charles Burney: "I thought, indeed, Sir Geo. Staunton treated you harshly, and after so long a voyage in a state of slavery, neither doing anything for you himself, nor procuring you any remuneration from others, was disgraceful to the pompous & consequential Knight" (CB to JCH, 6 Mar. 1807, Berg). Hüttner may well have feared the publication of "unguarded expressions" such as these.

7. For a description of life at Mrs. Camplin's boardinghouse where Sarah Harriet had lived for more than a year, see above L. 147.

8. Louis-Antoine Fauvelet de Bourrienne (1769–1834), *Mémoires* (1829); of several English translations to date, the one by John S. Memes, *Memoirs of Napoleon Bonaparte* (1831), comes closest to the title given here.

9. Caroline Anne Bowles, a minor author and longtime friend of Sarah Harriet Burney (L. 54, n. 2).

10. Two daughters of King George III, the Princesses Augusta Sophia (1768–1840), and Sophia (1777–1848), whom Mme d'Arblay had known as Second Keeper of the Queen's Robes (1786–91) and with whom she still kept in contact (see *JL*, 12: passim).

11. Grace Elizabeth Neale, the wife of Sir Harry (Burrard) Neale, 2nd Bt. (L. 68, n. 15), who was cousin to Miss Bowles's mother, Anne (née Burrard) (L. 54, n. 2).

12. Matthew 7:6.

---

154. To Frances (Burney) d'Arblay

22 Henrietta Street, Bath, 8 December 1835
A.L.S., Berg
Address: Madame d'Arblay / 1. Half Moon Street / Piccadilly / London

22 Henrietta Street
Decr 8th 1835

My dearest Sister

I cannot allow dear Cousin Edward to leave Bath without scribbling a little "How do you?" to you. He brings a not very good account of you, I am sorry to say—yet, I cannot but hope that the cold by which you were suffering[1] has ere now given way to this fine mild (albeit wintry) season. You will be pleased to hear that I now and then get a comfortably-long letter from my brother Stephen,[2] who, at eighty, writes as clear & delicate a hand as a girl of eighteen; and, upon the whole, expresses himself chearfully & contentedly. My kind friend, M[rs] Gregor, holds out a hope to me of visiting Bath in the Spring; but only as a bird of passage to some other place. However, it would be a great pleasure to me to see her even for a few hours.—Cousin Edward is as active, as attentive to every body but himself, and as inveterately amiable & good-natured as ever; and I think he is looking extremely well, though rather too thin. His nieces, in general, do not take after him in that respect. Of Amelia might be said what Mr Graham (of Chelsea College) so comically observed of his eldest daughter[3]—"It begins to take a pretty considerable time to walk round her." Maria also is quite as plump as in reason could be wished. There is only poor Sophy and I who figure amongst the lean kine.—

I know you will be pleased to hear, that the Bath waters which I drank in the summer for five weeks, have, I think, done me considerable good. At present I am quite at my best, and trust I shall do very well for the winter if I keep quiet. The two worst enemies I have are Night air, and East winds. The first, it rests with myself to avoid; the second finds me out even within doors, but may be kept at bay by good fires, and warm cloathing.

I think I told you in a former letter, that I had tried the plan of living in a lodging with a Lady I was to become very fond of.[4] I had better have begun by being fond of her before hand! The experiment failed, & I was glad to come back to my pleasant bed-room, & the use of a drawing-room I am never accountable to any body for not sitting in when I don't like it. Besides, I have got rid of the odious trouble of marketting, and thinking what I shall have for dinner, and how my morcels of meat shall be dressed. Here, I know nothing of the matter till I sit down to table; & I always find some one plain dish upon which I can make a wholesome meal.—We have lately had for a month, two American ladies (sisters) in the house. One of them was a Yankee Bas Bleu; had read a great deal, been spending two or three years in Italy, lived a winter at Paris—knew every body by name—talked perpetually against narrow minds—professed to love England and the English—despised <u>twaddles</u> & <u>twaddlers</u>—and withall was so fatiguing a person, that had I had another month of her, I should have died no other death. It is impossible to convey to you any idea of her interminable torrent of talk! She croaked in a hoarse, husky voice for hours at a time; spoke bad English, or, at least, badly accented & pronounced; betrayed a deep-rooted jealousy of this country, & a susceptibility on the subject of her own that there was <tranquilizing> no appeazing.—<u>Bref</u>—I have not been more relieved for a long while, than when she went away.

I trust, your meditated excursion to Brighton, will not be entirely prevented by the severe cold you were labouring under when Cousin Edward last saw you.[5] If you <u>should</u> put your intended journey into execution, pray give my kindest love to our dear Sister Broome, and to Charlotte & Barrett & Julia—And meanwhile believe me ever, my dearest Sister your most truly affectionate

S. H. B.

Love to the approaching Benedict.[6]—

1. In early October 1835, Mme d'Arblay "was siezed with a rheumatic cold that quite tortured my poor remnant teeth, my Ear, & my head—almost to screaming from mass of suffering." The symptoms, which amounted to a "bodily agony," are described in excruciating detail in a letter of 12 October 1835. Early in November, she was still complaining of "the obstinacy of a violent cold" (*JL*, 12: 876, 881).

2. Sarah's half-brother, Stephen Allen, Vicar of St. Margaret's, King's Lynn, Norfolk, and Rector of Haslingfield, Cambs., was eighty years old (L. 28, n. 8).

3. Richard Robert Graham, the Apothecary at Chelsea Hospital (L. 78, n. 4), and his wife Anne had four daughters baptized in the chapel, the eldest of whom was Henrietta, on 3 June 1770 (chapel register, Royal Hospital Chelsea).

4. SHB's plan of moving to a "new apartment with a gentle, rational, & friendly associate," mentioned optimistically in her letter of 28 May 1835, had already proved disappointing by the time she wrote on 31 August 1835 (LL. 152, 153).

5. Mme d'Arblay's severe cold deprived her of the pleasure of her planned excursion to visit Charlotte Broome, who had settled at Brighton near her daughter Charlotte Barrett; in mid-December 1835, the visit was still being "hoped for" (*JL*, 12: 874 and n. 1, 876–77, 884).

6. "Benedick, the married man" from Shakespeare's *Much Ado About Nothing*, I, i, 250, would be Alexander d'Arblay, engaged to Mary Ann Smith since April (L. 153, n. 2). The wedding, however, was not imminent; Alex was resigning his living at Camden Chapel, St. Pancras, under pressure from his parishioners and was apparently suffering from depression (*JL*, 12: 872, n. 2, 884–86, 888–89 and n. 7).

---

155. To Frances (Burney) d'Arblay

22 Henrietta Street, Bath, 24 January 1836
A.L.S., Berg
Address: Madame d'Arblay / 1. Half Moon Street / Piccadilly / London
Postmarks: BATH / JA25 / 1836 / B
F / 26JA26 / 1836

January 24th
1836.
22 Henrietta Street
Bath.

My dearest Sister

I can let slip no private opportunity of getting a Scrib conveyed to you, and a brother of Mrs Bertie[1] who is here on a short visit, has offered to take charge of any despatch I may chuse to entrust him with. Mrs Bertie, you are to know, is one of my pleasantest friends here. I first became acquainted with her at

Rome; then met her at the Baths of Lucca; then saw her again at Florence; and finally, we have fallen into society together once more here at Bath. She is by many degrees above par as an associate, compared with the general average of those I see here: but I am a hermit, & go into no evening company; and, to say the truth, not much into morning company at this time of year, being always more anxious, when able to get out, for air and exercise, than for making calls. When any new body asks to know me, I am gracious, and let myself be visited; and then, in due time, I return that civility—but seldom shew my face at their door a second time. You see, I have adopted the convenient French advice: mettez-vous là; and the poor, good-natured, idle Tom-Nodies submit to it, and never seem affronted—but keep on, calling—& calling—and never a call do they get from me!—

Since I took up the pen, I have received, my dearest Sister, your most magnificently long, & most incomparably agreeable letter. Why—such a treat ought, <to> and is justly entitled, to be repaid by at least five or six of my very best epistles.[2]—I only regret that you should even make the mere attempt when your eyes are at their weakest.[3] Be assured, I write not for the lucre of gain; & as long as I hear from others that you are tidily well, I acquit you of any repayment, beyond a brief note, now and then, "like angels visits, few & far between".[4]—

I cannot express to you the consolation afforded me by your account of the disposition poor dear Martin was in the last time you conversed with him.[5] To speak frankly, I had my misgivings on that subject; and I will own, that I even ventured to write a short letter of kind exhortation to him, which, however, for fear of agitating and doing him harm, I enclosed to that excellent creature John Payne, to give to Martin, or to hold back, as he might judge best. I trust that God, in his mercy, has touched his heart. A more humane, generous, and affectionate nature than his has always been, I never hardly knew. The misfortune is, that carried away by a mania in favour of talents and cleverness, he gave himself up to infidel associates; and I dreaded lest he should have sucked in any of their poison. All I can add is, that he deserves to be a Christian!

It is but too true that poor Mr James Greville, when you wrote, was in a dying state—and now, the good old man is gone.[6] I never heard of a more pious, patient, and blessed end than his. They all loved him in the house where he lodged; the very Maid, a mere drudge of all work, sat up with him unknown to her Mistress, many nights, & worked as hard as she could in the day to avoid being suspected. The poor, they say, will miss him sadly—and his public acts of charity have been munificent. He quite recently subscribed fifty pounds for the Irish

Protestant Clergy. In short, among the few here who knew him, he has left none but sincere & affectionate mourners. It now gives me pleasure to reflect that though I pay so few visits, I had made more exertion to go and see him this winter, than almost any body else.

My Miss C. liked all she saw of your Miss S.[7] very much: but they have had no communication <but> except by occasional meetings at some third person's house, during a morning visit, or a formal dinner-party. I rejoice, however, that you on further acquaintance, continue to like her greatly. Pray prepare her to like me. When people are worth a return, I am exceedingly fond of being liked. But either I grow difficult, or I live much out of the way of attaching objects—for, between ourselves, there are few whom I care either to be liked by, or feel able to like myself.

It warmed my heart to hear that the truly good Mr Raper has succeeded to a higher place in the War Office.[8] He has fagged steadily and hardly for it these many years, & nothing could ever be more justly obtained. It was Sarah Payne who gave me this piece of pleasant information, to sweeten the so much less gratifying intelligence she had to communicate respecting poor Martin.

Now—about my long-dormant M.S.[9] I have never looked at it since I came from Florence, & I have but a very so so-ish opinion of it. I there read it aloud to my friends M^{r} & Mrs Layard, and their two boys. (Boys are as good by way of tests, as Moliere's old woman).[10] The first third of the work went off triumphantly. The boys listened with bright, eager eyes, and open mouths; the father and mother gave quiet signs of being pleased; and when the evening ended, I went home, who but I? quite delighted. The next reading, for which my young auditors were all impatience, was considerably flatter. I might have supposed the boys entered with less interest into the story when it stood somewhat still to give opportunity for describing characters, & carrying on conversation. But this unction I could not lay to my soul, because, if the truth must be spoken, I myself thought it grew insipid, & would willingly have foreborne reading on to the end. This I could not well do, without its appearing the consequence of being picqued at their want of admiration. So, I "dragged my slow length along,"[11] and drew a long breath, as if relieved from a weary task, when the welcome word finis arrived. Having this impression of the work, with what heart can I turn to it again? I will not burn it, poor harmless thing! for it will never do any <harms> evil, though it may never do much good. But the toil of copying, or rather, of remodelling it, makes me shiver when I think of it.—What is said of Italy, is next to nothing,—the subject is worn thread-bear, & I hardly touched upon it. So, should the poor recluse ever see the light (not that of the Kitchen-chimney, s'entend) she will cut just as good a figure at one time as at another. Basta così.

My good lady, whom I fancied, as you say, I was to be so fond of, has to my great joy, found a situation for which she is much better suited than for that of a tête à tête associate with my (perhaps) fastiduous little self. She is gone to be Superintendant, or Housekeeper to an elderly Batchelor in S. Wales, who has two Sisters living very near him, who promise to be kind to her, and who appear highly respectable & amiable persons. I saw them, & liked their lady-like manners, & I hope the arrangement will succeed.

Now where shall I find room to sign myself my dearest Sister's most sincerely affectionate

S. H. B.

Best of all loves to Sister Broome.[12]—

1. Catherine Jane, widow of the Hon. Willoughby Bertie, whose sad life is recounted in L. 128, n. 19.

2. Probably a reference to Mme d'Arblay's frequent plea to her correspondents to repay her own letters two and three times over (see above L. 111, n. 9).

3. At eighty-three, Mme d'Arblay complained of weakness in the eyes, exacerbated by long hours spent reading manuscripts. However, in the autumn she wondered, "how much of my ill sight is in my nerves—&, consequently, my spirits" (*JL*, 12: 875).

4. Thomas Campbell, *The Pleasures of Hope* (1799), Pt. 2, l. 378.

5. Martin Burney, James's son, who was still causing anxiety to his family (see L. 63, n. 12). He had been the subject of concerned messages between Sarah Harriet and Mme d'Arblay, with Henry Crabb Robinson as the occasional source of Sarah's information (*JL*, 12: 795, n. 6, 808–9).

6. The Rev. James Greville (L. 149, n. 3) died at Bath on 23 January 1836 (*GM*, NS 5 (1836): 559).

7. Probably Miss C[rewe] and Miss S[mith], Alexander d'Arblay's fiancée. Harriet Crewe's account of the esteem in which Mary Ann Smith was held among the Greville family was passed on to Mme d'Arblay in SHB's letter of 31 August 1835 (L. 153) above.

8. Charles Chamier Raper, the husband of Sarah's niece Frances (L. 35, n. 12). Employed in the war office for over forty years, he was promoted to Chief Clerk, an appointment which was announced in March (*The Extraordinary Black Book* (London: Effingham Wilson, 1831), 476; *GM*, NS 5 (1836): 304; NS 18 (1842): 217).

9. Probably *The Renunciation*, which Sarah Harriet had been working on in Florence for two years and "put the finishing stroke to" in December 1832 (LL. 136, n. 4, 139, 145). The last chapters are set in Italy.

10. Molière's servant to whom, according to tradition, he would first read his plays to gauge their theatrical success. See further Pierre Bonvallet, *Molière de tous les jours* (Paris: Le Pré aux Clercs, 1985), 245–49.

11. Alexander Pope, *An Essay on Criticism* (1711), l. 357.

12. Charlotte Broome, who was apparently visiting London, an intention she had announced in December 1835 (*JL*, 12: 884).

156. To Anna (Wilbraham) Grosvenor

22 Henrietta Street, Bath, 23 February 1837
A.L.S., Berg
Address: Mrs Grosvenor / <Hare Park> / <Newmarket> / <Cambridgeshire>
readdressed to: Duke of Graftons / Wakefield Lodge / Stoney Stratford
Postmarks: Newmarket / Penny Post
[BAT]H / [?]23 / [1]837 / D
F / 24FE24 / 1837
NEW[MARK]ET / FE [?] / 1837
E / 27FE27 / 1837

22 Henrietta Street, Bath
Feb. 23^{d} 1837

My dearest Annie

It was like yourself to write to me on seeing the afflicting announcement in the Newspapers of poor dear Alexander's death.[1] It came upon me like a clap of thunder. But I will not talk of myself, for what is any thing I can have felt compared to what my pitiable Sister has endured?—I am told that, God be praised, she has been (after the first tremendous burst of grief) almost supernaturally supported, & is now tolerably composed. A Lady to whom Alex was engaged, and with whom he was very soon to have been married, acted towards her the part of a real daughter—shut herself up with her, & devoted her whole time to her,[2] affording her perhaps more consolation from the circumstance of the connexion that was to have taken place, & which drew them nearer together, than she could have derived from any other of her friends.—I have at length effected the painful task of addressing a letter of condolence to her: but never did I undertake similar exertion with more nervousness. I have myself been dangerously ill, & am now only gradually recovering after a confinement of eleven weeks, full half of which were spent in bed. My complaint was a violent inflamation in the windpipe, & a proportionable degree of fever. My affectionate Harriet Crewe forsook her pretty residence at Prior Park, engaged a room here, & gave me the comfort of her society during the whole of my worst week. She used to be by my bed side by five o'clock in the morning to enquire what sort of night I had passed,—in short, all that the kindest daughter could have done, she gently & unparadingly performed, & never left me except to go down to meals. Poor dear, she has since had an attack of Influenza, sharp, but I am happy to say, short.—I cannot but feel proud as well as grateful for the permanent friendship I have had the good fortune to experience from my pups—Yourself, dearest, included.

Poor Harriet has been deeply afflicted by the death (so sudden too) of her friend Lady Combermere. Whatever her failings might be, she was a most engaging creature. The letters her daughter Nina has addressed to Harriet are the most unaffectedly touching & sweet I ever read. She doaded on her Mother, and with the tenderest exultation records that her last words almost were, "Tell Nina my latest thoughts have been of her."—Her death was easy; she knew her danger, & was perfectly resigned; spoke of Lord Combermere with kindness, and was in charity with all men.[3]

What a nauseous dessous des cartes has been exhibited for the edification of the public in the recent Trial of Lord de Roos!—Master Brook, too, (Shallow Brook as he has been called) cuts but a so so-ish kind of a figure. Think of his bringing upon himself such severity of language as was made use of respecting him by Lord Denham: "The barefaced effrontery of M[r] Brook Greville", &c. Why this was very little better than telling him he had lost caste, & was no gentleman. Altogether, there was a pretty pack of them. I am sorry de Roos is such a scamp, for I spent three days in the house with him at Crewe Hall, & thought I had never seen a more agreeable, well-bred & well-informed man, and though I knew he was a libertine, I never dreamt that he had not even the common feelings, or rather, principles, of meum & teum honesty.[4]

Now, dearest, for want of other subject-matter, and Bath is not prolific (particularly its sick rooms) in entertainment, I'll tell you a story. There is, at no great distance from St. Helena, a small rocky Island, called Tristan d'Acunha, supposed to be an exhausted volcano. My fair Niece, Julia Barrett, recently married, and sailing with her husband towards the Cape of Good Hope, on her way to Madras,[5] heard from their Captain the following particulars.[6] During the reign of Buonaparte a small garison was stationed on this uninhabited rock, but at the close of the war, vessels were sent out to fetch them home. Eight of the soldiers, headed by a Corporal named Glass,[7] refused to quit the Island, and have now resided upon it three & twenty years. I suppose they had wives with them, for at this moment there are a heap of young people & children around them. They have built Cabins, planted gardens, sown corn—& have 50 head of Cattle, 100 sheep, a little corn, 12 acres of potatoes, & plenty of apples, pears &c. Glass, an old man now, is obeyed and respected as the patriarch of the little community. He teaches the children, & says they can read their Bible "very pretty." He and two others dined on board Julia's Indiaman.

When asked what they wanted most, they begged for nails, as the wind, they said, often loosened the roofs of their wooden dwellings. The Whalers who occasionally pass near their shore, have been very liberal to them, & have given them a beautiful boat, a large supply of canvass, of which the men make clothes, & sundry other useful articles. Their <u>ladies</u>, the men told the passengers in the Indiamen, like finer dresses, & would be glad of any cast-off garments the company might send them. So, all the apparel that could be spared was scrambled together, & dispatched to the fair reclusses when their husbands, fathers, or brothers, rowed back in their pretty boat to their rock. They seem perfectly detached from the world, cared very little what was doing in Europe, said they were quite contented & happy, had no quarrels, & never heard a cross word, except when the women now and then fell out. Glass reads the Church Service every Sunday to his companions, and from an odd volume of Blair, a Sermon.[8]—Now, do you not like these primitive creatures? Adieu, dearest. Give my best love to your Sisters,

& believe me ever yours S. H. B

1. Mme d'Arblay's only child, Alexander Charles Louis Piochard d'Arblay, died 19 January 1837 at the age of forty-two. Through the interest of a family friend, the Rev. George Owen Cambridge, he had been appointed minister of the Chapel of St. Etheldreda, Ely Place, Holburn, preaching there for the first time on 27 November 1836. He apparently contracted influenza in December in the cold damp air of the newly reopened church (*JL*, 12: 907–8 and n. 8, 910, n. 4, 911, n. 1; *HFB*, 481; *Alumni Cantab.*).

2. Mary Ann Smith, Alex's fiancée of almost two years' standing, according to Mme d'Arblay's account, "beseeches nay implo[res] to live with me pic nic in a settled domicile betw[een] us," insisting that she had "*promised* him [Alex] in the event of the Union—which was to make me her first—though he must <have> been her Chief charge upon Earth!" Miss Smith would stay with Mme d'Arblay intermittently until 1838 when she would live with her permanently (*JL*, 12: 913, 917, n. 3).

3. Lady Combermere (L. 134, n. 4), separated from her husband, but "devotedly attached" to her children, died quite suddenly at Dover 25 January 1837. "At the last, she generously absolved him [*her husband*] from all blame or unkindness throughout their union, and lamented the years of happiness lost to both, by their unfortunate misunderstanding" (*Memoirs . . . Combermere*, 2: 227, 243).

The eldest daughter, "Nina," Caroline Frances (L. 147, n. 7), was soon to marry on 23 August 1837 Arthur Wills Blundell Sandys Trumbull Windsor Hill (1812–68), styled Earl of Hillsborough until 1845 when he would succeed as 4th Marquess of Downshire (Burke; Gibbs; *GM*, NS 8 (1837): 418).

4. On 10–11 February 1837, a case for libel was heard in the Court of King's Bench before the Lord Chief Justice, Thomas Denman (1779–1854) (*DNB*), of Lord de Ros versus Cumming, "for the publication of a false and malicious libel, in which he is charged with having been guilty of fraudulent and false play at cards at Graham's club and else-

where." The case attracted much attention, was attended by fashionable society and given full coverage in the *Times*, 11, 13 Feb. 1837.

To support the defendant (who "pleaded that the publication is true"), evidence was brought to show that Henry William Fitzgerald de Ros (1793–1839), 22nd Baron de Ros (1831) (Burke; Gibbs), was guilty of marking the cards and of using a sleight-of-hand trick called *sauter la coupe* when dealing.

The counsel for the plaintiff, Lord de Ros, expounded on "the character and reputation of a gentleman illustrious for his descent, and equally distinguished for his private virtues." He attempted to discredit the character of the witnesses: the manager of the club, his waiters, and those who could be shown to live off the proceeds of gaming. He tried to suggest the whole was a plot, laid by professional gamblers, to discredit a superior player and win for themselves a more secure livelihood.

Foremost among these was Brook Greville (L. 113, n. 7), a nephew of Lady Crewe's, whom Sarah had known during her sojourn with the family as governess. Ostensibly a friend of Lord de Ros, he continued to associate and play with him, while collecting evidence and examining witnesses against him. Moreover, it was shown that he was (in the words of the judge) "a very wholesale and successful gambler." The remarks here attributed to Lord Denman were not reported in the *Times*, but he did, in his charge to the jury, instruct them to evaluate his character: "And here, gentlemen, you are to consider whether Mr. Brooke Greville is that most infamous and malignant of mankind," a man who would deliberately plot to defame the character of a friend. Apparently the jury decided not, as they returned a verdict "in less than a quarter of an hour" for the defendant.

Sarah's sense of moral outrage was not unusual; according to one of the witnesses in the trial, "a hideous picture of gambling was exhibited, much that appeared to betoken vicious habits, laxity of moral principle, coldness of honorable sentiment, and the disposition of the great mass of society was to visit with promiscuous censure all the actors in this odious drama, perhaps with too undistinguishing condemnation" (*The Greville Memoirs, 1814–1860*, ed. Lytton Strachey and Roger Fulford (London: Macmillan, 1938), 3: 352).

5. Charlotte Barrett's only remaining daughter, Julia Charlotte, aged twenty-eight, had married at Brighton on 2 August 1836 James Thomas (d. 6 Jan. 1840), a widower. Of the Madras Civil Service, he had left India in 1833 and returned with his bride soon after the wedding, sailing from Portsmouth in August 1836 and stopping at Madeira and the Cape. He was then appointed Acting Deputy Accountant General (21 April 1837), and Judge and Criminal Judge of Rajahmundry (5 July 1837) (*JL*, 12: 895, n. 4, 899, n. 1; Dodwell and Miles, comps., *Alphabetical List of the Honourable East India Company's Madras Civil Servants, from the year 1780, to the year 1839* (London: Longman, Orme, Brown, 1839)).

Mrs. Barrett was not favorably disposed to the match, believing that her daughter was "throwing herself away on a very poor sly fellow," who "has not been open & candid at first in the statement of his circumstances & prospects." One cause of concern may have been the distance her daughter would travel away from her, and her fear that "the fatigue of the Voyage & Climate may carry her off, poor thing, after a very short time." However, she could not deny that "Julia continues to like this poor fellow," and realized that "we had better keep friends & make the best of him—otherwise perhaps he will not let Julia write to us—nor keep his promise of sending her home in 5 years" (CFBt to CBFB, 6 June [1836], 8 June [1836], [14 June 1836], Barrett, Eg. 3702A, ff. 139–44v).

6. This account resembles closely that of Julia's in her anonymously published *Letters from Madras, during the years 1836–1839* (London: John Murray, 1843), 21–24.

7. William Glass (c. 1790–1853) was known as "Governor Glass" on the island of Tristan da Cunha in the South Atlantic Ocean, and would die there 24 November 1853 at the age of sixty-three (*GM*, NS 41 (1854): 553). "I was curious to know whether old Glass was master, and whether the others minded him; but he said no one was master . . . that they have no laws nor rules, and are all very happy together." Glass, however, acted as schoolmaster and chaplain (ibid., 23).

8. Hugh Blair (1718–1800), divine (*DNB*), whose five volumes of *Sermons* (1777–1801) were extraordinarily popular in their day. According to Julia's account: "They had only Blair's Sermons, which they have read every Sunday for the last ten years, ever since they have had them; but the old man said, very innocently, 'We do not understand them yet: I suppose they are too good for us'" (*Letters from Madras*, 23).

157. To Frances (Burney) d'Arblay

22 Henrietta Street, Bath, 24 March [1837]
A.L.S., Berg
Address: Madame d'Arblay / 1 Half Moon Street / Piccadilly / London
Postmarks: BATH / MA25 / 1837 / B
F / 27MR27 / 1837
Annotated by FBA: × <u>Sarah</u> <u>Harriet</u>

March 24th Bath
22 Henrietta Street.
Deep Snow.

How are you, my poor dear Sister?[1]—Get some one (if you admit such) who is of our kindred, to give me a little account of you. I ask nothing direct from yourself, well knowing how painful to your eyes is the exertion of writing. But I should be an unnatural wretch indeed not to pine for intelligence concerning you. In some circuitous method therefore, let me, I beseech you have tidings of you. <u>Bid</u> them write, expressly for that purpose!

I have the kindest enquiries concerning you addressed to me by my excellent Brother Allen. There is much warmth & sympathy of heart in that good man, now, turned eighty.

M[rs] Maltby called upon me when I was too ill to see her, but left a thousand kind messages—and particularly urged, that when I was able to write to you, I should say every thing for her that was most condoling and most affectionate. She was certainly very fond of the dear creature who is gone, & one of his most enthusiastically sincere admirers.[2]

I wish I could give your kind heart the comfort of hearing I was well. But such is still far from being the case. I am yet attended by my Medical adviser, & only leave my bed for my Sofa. When fever once gets access to me, it clings with a tenacity very difficult to remove.

From a sick chamber, and with more than usual want of Spirits, it is not easy to suggest matter for a long letter. Our Nieces come and see me when they can, that is, Sophy and Amelia. But <they have> the latter has been very ill, tho' better now; & the distance between Sophy's residence and mine (She & Maria are now in Ainsley's Belvedere) prevents her coming so often as might be wished. As for poor Maria, she has never once stirred out the whole winter.

My sweet Harriet Crewe, when I was at the worst, took a room here for a week, & devoted her whole time to me. I cannot tell you what a comfort such a gentle & tender friend, at such a moment, was to me! Heaven bless and reward her.

The poor dear Richard Burneys have <u>all</u> been very ill,[3] but except the Mother, are now recovered. She is tormented by an itching irritation of the skin more pungent than can be described. Her Doctor says it is not uncommon after the illness she has had. But every one feels for himself, however general a complaint may be.

This is merely written to supplicate you to make somebody write to me about <u>yourself</u>. I have anxious enquiries after you from my friend M[rs] Grosvenor. Heaven preserve & strengthen you, dearest Sister—

Yours ever faithfully S. H. Burney

When you have any communication with our Sister Broome, pray give my tenderest love to her. And remember me, if you can, to Fanny Raper, Minette, Martin, Sarah Payne, & our excellent Cousin Edward. How this weather must pinch him! I have a fellow feeling.

1. Mme d'Arblay, deeply grieving over the loss of her only child wrote in mid-March, "My Heart is of lead—when alone—I only break from it by exertion drawn out by friendship. . . . Oh blest dearest Alex! for you am I thus tormented! when for you all this busy concern would have been my revival & my joy!" (*JL*, 12: 916–17).

2. Harriet Maltby (L. 151, n. 4), with whom Mme d'Arblay had been friendly during her residence in Bath, was sister-in-law to Sir George Pretyman Tomline (1750–1827), Bishop of Lincoln and Dean of St. Paul's (1787–1820) and Bishop of Winchester

(1820–27) (*DNB; Alumni Cantab.; JL*, 9: 98, n. 3). She had tried to use her influence with this prelate on behalf of Alexander d'Arblay to further his career in the church (*JL*, 9: 283, 438; 11: 410 and passim).

3. Richard Allen Burney and his wife Elizabeth had four children: Henry (1814–93), Clara (1818–59), Cecilia Mary (1823–39), and Emma (1826–post 1901) (*JL*, 1: lxix; 11: 196, n. 23; *GM*, NS 12 (1839): 99; 3rd ser. 6 (1859): 658).

158. [To Frances (Burney) d'Arblay]

22 Henrietta Street, Bath, 13 June 1837
A.L.S., Berg

13th June 1837
22 Henrietta Street

My poor dear—very dear Sister!—I waited to hear from my Banker in London before I answered your most kind first letter, in order to know how my account with him stood, that I might not unnecessarily trespass upon your generosity.—I am glad to say there are in his hands the means of settling all my little debts, & something of an overplus handsomer than I expected. So I can go on without being put to any difficulty, & have only to thank you, (which I do from my heart), for your liberal intentions.[1]

How will you, poor dear soul, get through the fatigue of a removal?—Such an enterprize is always harrassing: but ten times worse in sickness & sorrow,[2]—You have my best wishes towards accomplishing it with tolerable ease.—

I <had> have written to you a letter to be conveyed by Maria Bourdois—It will be a little stale when it reaches you, for she is not setting off so soon as I thought she would: but you will allow for its dullness. Perhaps when she delivers it, I may be at Malvern, whither, if God grants me strength, I purpose repairing before long with one of my Nieces, Clara, dear Richard's eldest daughter. Adieu my kind, beloved Sister—Ever gratefully, most

gratefully yours S. H. Burney.

1. After paying a bill of £50 on 10 June 1837, Sarah had a balance of £155.10.5 in her account at Coutts. It is possible, however, that Mme d'Arblay was the source of £21.7.9 received in her account on 30 June 1837. On 28 July, SHB found it necessary to withdraw £30.

2. Mme d'Arblay, still stricken with grief over the loss of her son (with "bewildered spirits & broken heart"), managed to move nonetheless by 15 August 1837 from 1 Half Moon Street to 15 Mount Street (*JL*, 12: 924, n. 4, 926, n. 1).

---

159. To Anna (Wilbraham) Grosvenor

22 Henrietta Street, Bath, 15–21 January 1838
A.L.S., Berg
Address: M[rs] Grosvenor / <Hare Park> / <Newmarket>
readdressed to: Poast Office / Stamford
Postmarks: F / 23JA2[3] / 1838
BATH / JA22 / 1838 / B
NEWMARKET / JA 24 / 1838
Newmarket / Penny Post

15 January 1838. 22 Henrietta Street
Bath.

My dearest M[rs] Grosvenor—or, <u>do</u> let me say "dearest Anna"

Thanks for your nice letter. I was quite longing to hear from you. Your charming extract has met with a warm admirer in a Lady now boarding under this roof: a Miss Rumsey, the most sensible and agreeable person we have ever had amongst us. Her father was a Physician in high practice in Berkshire,[1] & of course, a scientific man; <u>she</u> is not a scientific woman, but has great respect for those who are, & loves and has been accustomed to clever and accomplished society. You would like her much for her gentleness, her virtuous principles, her unaffectedness, & kindness of manners, & I verily believe, of heart. It will half break mine when she goes away, which there can be no doubt will happen early in the Summer: but I will not renounce the hope that if I live I may see her again next winter.—I yesterday had a letter from Miss Urquhart[2] (now styling herself M[rs] Elinor Urquhart, as I put upon my cards, M[rs] S. H. Burney—see what we spinsters are brought to!) She wrote at M[rs] Gregor's request to enquire after me, that dear soul being much indisposed, from a bilious attack, though in a fair way, her sister says, of amendment. I heartily hope it is so. They spent all last winter at Paris, as you probably know.—And where do you think, Dear, I spent mine? In bed, and latterly <in> on my bed-room sofa, from 9th December, till latter end of April!—It has given me such a surfeit of bed and bed-room, that whereas I used to breakfast upstairs, I am now generally the first in the breakfast parlour at nine o'clock, and when the weather was warmer, was often up before seven. Now, I rise by eight, for I cannot feel clean and brushed and all that under an hour. My illness was inflamation in the windpipe, one of the most dangerous complaints to which we can be liable. Imagine what my state must have been, when, besides leeches round my throat, I was bled twice in one day, and altogether, five times within a week; and starved beside,—in short reduced to the weakness of an infant. As soon as I was capable of undertaking a journey, I took one of my great Nieces with me, an intelligent lively girl between 18 & 19,[3] and went off, first to Cheltenham for a fortnight; then to Great Malvern a month, then to Leamington another fortnight, & lastly to Cheltenham again, where I thought myself strong enough to try the waters, & found they agreed with me perfectly. I returned to Bath in September, engaged a larger room with a warmer aspect than I used to have, <here,> and God be thanked! have never been laid up since.—But my purse has been sadly tried,—what with Doctors, medecines, a Nurse ten weeks at a guinea a week exclusive of what I paid for her board—then my journeys, & little additional expences for Clara, my young companion, & wheel chairs, & Leamington delightful low Phaetons &c, &c. I tell you all this, to account for publishing again.[4] I luckily had one little work quite ready, written at Florence, and another about one third finished. I took courage, & completed it after my return, & the two (making three volumes) are now in the hands of Colburn.[5] The produce will set me clear, & somewhat over; and on the strength of it, I have invited Clara to come & spend a month with me. She does not live at Bath—but having been here before, she has many friends who will be glad to take her out with them, & I hope will amply supply to her my place, since I have entirely given up going out in the evening: Nay—at present I do not even stir in the morning, for the cold is intense. In one room of this house—to be sure it is an atic—the thermometer this morning (Monday 15th) was down at 32!—

I rejoice in the pleasant account of your three nieces.[6] I am now a great, great Aunt, Julia Barrett that was, now Mrs Thomas, has been safely brought to bed at some place 400 [*miles*] from Madras.[7] Mrs Barrett is grown very plump, & I suppose looking all the better for it:—but I have not seen her since we were together at the Baths of Lucca. I fear she never cordially forgave me for expressing distrust of Lady Caroline M——, & cautioning her respecting that person. At all events, the intercourse went on, comme si de rien n'ètoit—and she & Julia came back to England with said Lady C. M.[8]—After all, I begin to think, the reports were unfounded, for I have never heard any thing to her disadvantage since I returned home, even from people who have been abroad. It is very horrid that such things should be rumoured, and the original setters-a-going of these black assertions really deserve the Tread Mill. You and I only spoke on the subject <to> by way of warning;—and what you had insinuated, was confirmed to me by M^{de} le Brun, the mother of a young Paintress at Florence,[9] who had lived some time under the roof <of> with Lady C. M.—I wonder whether she goes into society here. Can you tell?—

I want you, dearest, when you have read this dull trash, to get a frank[10] & send it on to your Sisters. I have exhausted all my letter writing materials by enditing the stuff you have now been reading, and I know your Sisters will be kind enough to excuse my cracking my empty scull by an attempt to compose another of these humdrums.—By the way—Kreift tho' a good creature, is terribly prosy,[11] & I do not envy his wife. He might have written just such a dull letter as this.—

21st January. A thaw—a quiet thaw, without which, they tell me, we should not have had a scrap of vegetable to munch with our meat. I am reading 6th Vol. of Lockhart's Sir Walter, as interesting or more so than any of its precursors. It delighted me to find he (Sir Walter) thought so highly of my prime favorite Miss Austen—he read her "Pride & Prejudice" three times.[12] I have read it as bumper toasts are given—three times three!—Adieu my very dear—

S. H. B.

1. Possibly James Rumsey (c. 1754–1824) of Amersham, Bucks. (a neighbouring county to Berkshire), whose last surviving daughter, Anne, would die at Reading in 1852. Miss Rumsey might also be related (perhaps as sister) to Dr. James Rumsey (1778–1856) of Amersham, Bucks., and his younger brother, Nathaniel (d. 3 Feb. 1845), M.D. (1837), who practiced first at Beaconsfield, Bucks. and then Remenhall Hill, Berkshire (Sir d'Arcy Power, ed., *Plarr's Lives of the Fellows of the Royal College of Surgeons of England*, rev. ed., 2 vols. (Bristol: Royal College of Surgeons, 1930); *GM*, 94, Pt. 1 (1824): 284; NS 37 (1852): 430; NS 22 (1845): 331; NS 45 (1856): 437).

2. Eleanor Urquhart (L. 99, n. 2), the maiden sister of Sarah's former employer, Jane Gregor.

3. Clara, Richard Allen Burney's eldest daughter (LL. 157, n. 3; 158).

4. Sarah had expended £180 in 1837, well beyond her annual income of £100; however, since her return from Italy in 1833, she had been carrying a balance of at least £150 into each fiscal year, and the previous year was no exception.

5. Sarah Harriet's two tales, *The Renunciation*, finished in Florence in December 1832

(L. 145), and *The Hermitage*, would be published in three volumes by Henry Colburn as *The Romance of Private Life* in 1839 (see further LL. 160, 166).

6. Childless herself, Anna Grosvenor took an interest in her three nieces, Julia, Emily, and Louisa, the daughters of her brother William Wilbraham, who had died in 1824. The girls had also recently lost their mother, Julia Fanny (née Montolieu), who died 23 June 1836, ten years after her second marriage to Lt-Gen. Sir Henry Frederick Bouverie (L. 119, n. 4).

7. Julia (Barrett) Thomas's first child, Henrietta Anne, was born 8 June and baptized 26 July 1837 in St. George's Cathedral in Madras (baptismal certificate, Barrett, Eg. 3708, ff. 27–28v).

8. Lady Caroline Morrison (L. 144, n. 11) had been extremely kind to Charlotte Barrett at Rome, and brought her back to England after the death of her daughter, Henrietta. Anna Wilbraham had sent some "communications" about the lady's character to Sarah Harriet at Florence, who had passed them on (L. 145). For Mrs. Barrett's possible resentment of the gossip, her undiminished intimacy with and warm gratitude to Lady Caroline, see L. 145, n. 12; L. 146, n. 13; Introduction.

A curious denouement to this once close friendship is presented in an enraged letter from Lady Caroline to Mrs. Barrett three years after their journey home together:

> Madam
>
> Having this morning heard of your Daughter's marriage I will no longer delay my intention of addressing you. This is not a letter of congratulation, for I am well aware there is no cause for such, but I consider it a duty I owe to myself to demand some explanation of the extraordinary & most unjustifiable conduct, in which your Daughter has persevered towards me during the last twelve months. The zealous affection & unremitted kindness she experienced from me for a period of nearly four years, have been requited by her with falsehood, deceit & the basest ingratitude. . . . I can not conclude without expressing my sincere & profound regret, that a friendship . . . should thus have terminated & I can only repeat the assertion I have made to others, the fault has not been on my side. (Lady Caroline Morrison to CFBt, 11 Aug. 1836, Berg)

Whatever the result of this falling-out with Lady Caroline, Charlotte's estrangement from her Aunt Sarah would end with a warm exchange of letters after her mother's decease and a long holiday together shortly before SHB's death (see below LL. 164, 180).

9. Marie-Louise-Élisabeth Le Brun and her daughter (L. 133, n. 2).

10. Anna could obtain a frank from her brother, George Wilbraham (L. 112, n. 12), who, as M.P. for South Cheshire (1832–41) (Stenton), would have franking privileges. On another occasion, Sarah would send her letter directly to the brother so that Anna would not have to pay (L. 165).

11. Kreft, probably a servant of the Wilbrahams at Florence, had paid Sarah Harriet long and voluble visits during her stay there (L. 140, n. 5; L. 146).

12. John Gibson Lockhart (1794–1854), Scott's son-in-law, whose *Memoirs of the Life of Sir Walter Scott* was published in seven volumes in 1837–38. Sarah is probably referring to Scott's famous remarks of 14 March 1826 on reading "for the third time at least, Miss Austen's very finely written novel of Pride and Prejudice. That young lady had a

talent for describing the involvements, and feelings, and characters of ordinary life, which is to me the most wonderful I ever met with. The Big Bow-wow strain I can do myself like any now going; but the exquisite touch, which renders ordinary commonplace things and characters interesting, from the truth of the description and the sentiment, is denied to me" (John Gibson Lockhart, *Memoirs of the Life of Sir Walter Scott*, 2nd ed. (Edinburgh: Robert Cadell, 1839), 8: 292–93).

160. To Henry Crabb Robinson

22 Henrietta Street, Bath, 20 April 1838
A.L.S., Dr. Williams'
Published: Morley
Address: H. C. Robinson, Esq[r] / Plowden Buildgs / Temple
Endorsed: 20th April 1838 / Miss Burney / Lambs Memoirs

April 20th 1838
22 Henrietta Street

Shall I say, "Dear M[r] Robinson?"—No, I won't,—I'll say "Shabby M[r] Robinson!"—Did you not, when you last wrote, say you thought of coming to Bath at Christmas? And the deuce a bit have you ever done any such thing![1]—I am quite ashamed of you; for had <I not> there not been prepared for you as nice a seasonable frost and snow as heart could desire, with plenty of wind, to say nothing of fogs, and occasional little short-lived thaws, just suited to render the streets nice and slippery and muddy, and every thing that could agreeably remind you that it was mid-winter? What more could you wish? I know, of old, that you do not mind dirty ways—<that cold>, that "fair or foul, or rain, or shine", is all pretty much the same thing to you, provided you are not plagued with any grumbling female, hanging upon your arm, and reproaching you for picking out for her the nastiest ways that can be found, "through bog, through briar",[2]—through stinks (poor dear old Rome for that!) & through every sort of impurity.—These you might have enjoyed here, without the draw-back of the grumbling female; & I am very much disappointed at your not having come to try whether our filthy Streets, or your London ones, approach the nearest to the glorious <porvaria> nastiness of the Eternal City.

Your agreeable—most agreeable friend Miss Nash, has twice favoured me with a visit.[3] The last was paid to-day, & she came accompanied by Miss Kent,[4] whom I like better than I feared I should, having been sadly apprehensive she would reckon me one of the Wicked,[5] and set me down as a person of too much levity, & would almost scare me by her grave and solemn looks. But I find her courteous, & amiable, & disposed I believe to tolerate those she cannot mend.— I have requested her to call again, and obtained her permission to defer returning her visits till I am better able to venture out.—

I think you must remember Dr Nott at Rome & Florence.[6] He is now here, in very indifferent health, and become a perfect misanthrope, hating the whole current of public affairs, and those who direct them, & fortelling nothing but horrors. I cannot say they wear a very pleasing aspect: but I try hard to think as little as I can about them—and at all events, to hope the best.

That arch-rogue Colburn!—How think you he is serving me? After accepting the manuscript, & engaging me to delay its publication till March, & then only to receive payment by instalments,—bills at three months date—he now chuses to put off the whole business till October? This is intolerable.—My long illness of last year, and journeys for change of air, and engaging a larger and dearer room, because its aspect is warmer, have impoverished me, & I really should be quite glad of the money. I am truly sorry ever to have renewed my intercourse with him. In former times, he was civil, humble, & better still—a prompt paymaster: he is now either grown rich & niggardly, or he is threatened with insolvency, for it seems as hard to draw money from him, as to induce him to let go his hold of any poor victim he has once got within his clutches. I have asked him, more than once, to surrender the MS. which I would put into the hands of some less over-stocked Publisher: but he always evades that request, & has now dawdled on, till he may tell me with some truth that the publication coming forth so near the time of the Coronation,[7] will have no chance of being bought or read, every body's mind being engrossed by the gaiety of the impending shew: but whose fault is that? Why did he not put the little work to press as soon as he received it?

Pardon me for bothering you with this statement: but as you had been good enough to apply to him for me, I thought you would take an interest in hearing how the affair was going on.[8]

Materials for an agreeable letter, I have alas! none. All I can say at all likely to give you any pleasure is, that I read poor dear Charles Lamb's Memoirs and Letters with the utmost delight; & not the less so for seeing such continual allusions to one "H. C. Robinson". Do you know such a person? And my dear Brother James too, and kind-hearted Martin[9]—these reminiscences were very pleasant to me. But of Lamb himself—what an affectionate disposition—what originality, what true wit, & what a singular, and I must say, melancholy combination of the truest & warmest piety, with the most extraordinary & irreverent profaneness. I cannot understand the union of two such opposites: but I believe there have been many other instances of it. Amongst fools who may take up the work, the oaths and the levity might do harm, & therefore I regret their insertion: but those who knew him, can only regret, & love him notwithstanding. As for me, I have no merit in not being irreverent, for I Dare Not.

Dr Nott has lent me a Work that I find very interesting, & which comes well after reading Wilkinson's Manners & Customs of the Ancient Egyptians;—It is, Lane's Manners & Customs of the Modern Egyptians:[10] both works are full of Wood cuts in illust[*r*]ation of the subjects they describe, and in Wilkinson's work I found an Ancient Egyptian Car, & a wooden pillow hollowed out for the head, which I immediately remembered having seen at Professor Roselini's Egyptian Museum at Florence.[11] You know the Tuscan Government sent out a deputation of learned men to collect relics of antiquity, & curious objects in that memorable country.—

Pray, are you a Phrenaeologist, or Cranaeologist (which is it)? Your friend Miss Nash is quite a convert. For me, I own I have not studied the subject, & know only enough to make me fear it is somewhat calculated to encourage in young people a system of materialism. Those whose opinions are fixed have nothing to apprehend, & may derive great amusement from the ingenuity of the doctrine, though less, I should think, than from Lavater's system of physiognomeny.[12]—Of that, even I can make a little sense, for surely the passions may be traced by their effects upon the countenance, & a good countenance is so legible, it hardly ever deceives us. So adieu, my dear friend, believe me ever truly Yours S. H. Burney.

Should you see young Layard to whom you have been so friendly,[13] I wish you would ask him to request his Mother when he writes to her, to forward to me here a Case of Books & Drawings that came from Florence with those of our regretted & beloved Mr Layard,[14] & at the same time to present to her my kindest regards—I know not her direction or w^d have written myself.—

1. Henry Crabb Robinson had written to SHB on 17 November 1837, informing her of his intention to spend Christmas at Bath, but instead he traveled to Brighton on 25 December to spend Christmas with his brother's family (HCR, 17 Nov., 23–31 Dec. 1837, Diaries).

2. "I'll follow you: I'll lead you about a round, / Through bog, through bush, through brake, through brier," William Shakespeare, *A Midsummer Night's Dream*, III, i, 101–2.

3. Probably Esther Nash (L. 150, nn. 1, 2), who paid a visit to Sarah Harriet shortly before traveling to London where she would call "unexpectedly" on Henry Crabb Robinson (HCR, 25 Apr. 1838, Diaries).

4. Probably a daughter of William Kent (c. 1775–1840), who lived on Bathwick Hill

(*GM*, NS 13 (1840): 445). He appears at the same address in the Land Tax Assessments for Bath 1823–32 (Taunton, Somerset Record Office), and is assessed in the Rate Book for the Parish of Bathwick (1830) at a slightly higher rate than his neighbours. He is listed in Bath directories (1830–37) as "William Kent gent." Kent was a close friend of Robinson's (see e.g. HCR, 23–31 Mar. 1840, Diaries), whom he names as executor in his will (dated 7 Feb. 1834, proved 20 June 1840, PRO/PROB/11/1929/429).

Of William Kent's three daughters, Caroline (d. post 1870) had already married on 3 September 1828 John Cottle Spender (d. post 1862), a Bath surgeon (parish register, St. Mary, Bathwick; Bath directories, 1829–70; *GM*, 3rd ser. 13 (1862): 628). Eliza Isaac or her younger sister Emma might be the Miss Kent who called on Sarah Harriet; Miss Eliza Kent would marry, on 20 April 1841, a widower and cloth-manufacturer, Henry Rutt (marriage certificate, GRO). Miss Emma Kent would remain a spinster, and is listed in the Post Office Bath Directory (1870–71) living with her sister Mrs. Spender on Bathwick Hill.

5. Shakespeare, *1 Henry IV*, I, ii, 94, also quoted in L. 57 above.

6. The invalid, George Frederick Nott (L. 128, n. 17).

7. On 28 June 1838, Queen Victoria was crowned at Westminster Abbey.

8. On 14 November 1837, Henry Crabb Robinson had "called at Colburn's to make an offer of Miss Burney's new novel at her request. I did not see the great man—but a person in his confidence. . . . He took my message to Colbourne and brought a favourable answer—He will write to Miss Burney—I was so pleased with so easy an execution of a troublesome commission." A few days later he had written to SHB, telling her what he had done (HCR, 14, 17 Nov. 1837, Diaries).

The Romance of Private Life by Miss Burney (L. 159, n. 5) would be published by Henry Colburn in 1839, first announced in the *Times* as "Just ready" on 13 September 1839, and advertised throughout the fall and winter. However, the author's bank account at Coutts suggests she was paid for her work in 1838, since after 1 January 1839 she did not find it necessary to withdraw any funds to cover her usual expenses.

9. Sir Thomas Noon Talfourd (1795–1854) (*DNB*), *The Letters of Charles Lamb, with a Sketch of his Life*, 2 vols. (London: Edward Moxon, 1837). James and Martin Burney are named in the circle of friends at Lamb's Wednesday whist evenings (see e.g., 1: 312) and Henry Crabb Robinson receives honorable mention as well (1: 330).

10. Edward William Lane (1801–76), the Arabic scholar (*DNB*), portrayed contemporary life in his *An account of the manners and customs of the Modern Egyptians* (1836), whereas Sir John Gardner Wilkinson (1797–1875), explorer and Egyptologist (*DNB*), dealt with the *Manners and Customs of the Ancient Egyptians* (1837–41). The first three volumes of this latter work had appeared in 1837.

11. Ippolito Rosellini (1800–43), an Italian archaeologist, who visited Egypt in 1828–29 in company with the French scholar Jean-François Champollion (1790–1832). The results of his excavations (statues, sarcophagi, papyri, musical instruments, etc.) were in the newly founded Egyptian museum in Florence, which Robinson and SHB had visited together on 5 October 1830 (HCR, 5 Oct. 1830, Travel Journals).

12. Johann Kaspar Lavater (1741–1801), whose *Physiognomische Fragmente zur Beförderung der Menschenkenntnis und Menschenliebe* (1775–78) established his reputation throughout Europe.

13. Henry Austen Layard (1817–94), G.C.B. (1878), later diplomat and politician

(Stenton; *Alumni Oxon.;* Shaw, 1: 210). He would leave England in July 1839 to travel overland to Ceylon but was diverted by the task of excavating Assyrian ruins, of which his account, *Nineveh and its Remains* (1849), created a sensation.

Crabb Robinson, who had befriended the young man, was considered a questionable influence by some of Layard's family, who thought the "very wayward and unsettled" Henry needed steadying. At their request, HCR did try to dissuade the youth from leaving the practice of law (HCR, 21 Mar., 15 Apr. 1838, Diaries; Waterfield, 22). However, years later, when Layard's fame was established, Robinson would pride himself on having encouraged "this high-spirited lad. . . . His uncle accused me of misleading him. I believe I did set his mind in motion, and excited in him tastes and a curiosity which now will not be a matter of reproach, seeing that the issue has already been so remarkable" (HCR, *Reminiscences*, 3: 398).

14. Henry Austen's father, Henry Peter John Layard, died in 1834 of congestion of the lungs at the age of fifty-one (Waterfield, 21). He and his wife, Marianne, had lived near Sarah Harriet in Florence and welcomed her hospitably into their home (L. 138, n. 9; L. 142 and passim).

161. To Frances (Burney) d'Arblay

[22 Henrietta Street, Bath, 28 February 1839]
A.L.S., Berg
Address: Madame d'Arblay / 29 Grosvenor Street. / Grosvenor Square / London
Postmarks: BATH / FE28 / 1839 / D
F / 1 MR 1 / 1839

Before I thank you, my poor dear Sister, which, believe me, I do from my heart,—I must lament all the trouble, & the fuss of writing you have had <on> in relation to this affair.—I know the labour & sorrow it costs you, & that nothing but your benevolent anxiety on the subject of this money business, could have drawn from you so rapid a succession even of letter-kins. Accept, once more, my sincere thanks; and assure yourself that had it not been for the wretched expences my ill health entails upon me, I would not have suffered you to deprive yourself of so large a portion of your by no means superabundant wealth.[1]

I like your idea of hunting out mottoes from dear Johnny—His Dictionary,—Shakespear's Plays—& my own old Common-Place books, give me the fairest chance of hitting upon apropos bits.[2]—

Amelia is well, and about to change her residence from New King Street to some other Street in the same neighbourhood.[3] She proposed a partnership with me, but it would not do. It is all very well now & then, but always such perdrix would be a little too much of a good thing. I have one excellent fellow-boarder here, the kindest, & most indefatigable of nurses when I am poorly,—the most friendly & warm-hearted companion when I am better—in short, a really dear & kind creature. Such a one I shall not easily light upon again. I know it will give you pleasure to hear this; & so, leaving you with this bit of sugar in your mouth, I remain my dearest Sister,

Your ever grateful & affectionate
S. H. Burney.

My love & thanks to Henry[4] when you see him. Gen[l] & M[rs] Loveday[5] have both called upon me, but alas! I could not see them, being more than usually unwell.

1. Apparently, Mme d'Arblay had sent Sarah Harriet £50 to lessen the burden of her "ill health." In a letter to Sarah Harriet, postmarked 21 February 1839, she announced: "The affair is at length finished. . . . They acknowledged your name at Coutts & received the fifty." FBA's editor notes that £50 was paid from Mme d'Arblay's account on 27 February 1839 to Col. Henry Burney (*JL*, 12: 961–62 and n. 2); the same day £50 was deposited in SHB's account by Col. Burney (Coutts ledgers).

However, the editor's suggestion in the same note that SHB was "facing the costs of a long and expensive illness necessitating curative travels to Cheltenham, Great Malvern, and Leamington" is misleading. As is clear from the letter cited (L. 159 above), Sarah Harriet traveled to these restorative spas in the summer of 1837 to recover from an illness of the previous winter and returned to Bath in September 1837 fully recovered.

There is nothing in SHB's bank account at Coutts to suggest that any debts would still be outstanding eighteen months later. In fact, 1838 was a particularly healthy year financially, and Sarah was able, perhaps through the sale of her fiction (L. 160, n. 8), to pass from 1 January 1838 to 7 May 1839, without making a single withdrawal from her savings. Unless her sister's gift to defray medical expenses was very long delayed, it must have been for a later and different illness.

2. In the same letter, Mme d'Arblay advised her: "If you have not heard of or tried the plan I will tell you a short cut for getting mottos—Beg—Borrow—or the other thing Dr Johnsons Dictionary" (*JL*, 12: 962). Her advice came a bit late, as the manuscript for *The Romance of Private Life* had been submitted to Colburn more than a year before (L. 160). Almost half of the mottoes came from Shakespeare and others from Dryden, Cowper, Beaumont and Fletcher, Spenser, Tasso, La Fontaine, and Voltaire.

3. Esther Burney's youngest daughter, Amelia, had been living at 19 New King Street, Bath (*JL*, 12: 831, n. 6).

4. Henry Burney, second son of Sarah's brother, Richard Thomas Burney, was in England on leave from a successful diplomatic and military career in India. Having joined

the East India Company in 1807, he rose to the rank of Lt.-Col. (17 Jan. 1834) in the Bengal Army. In 1825, he was sent as Political Agent to the Siamese States, and in 1829 as Resident to the Court of Ava, Burma; some documents relating to the former mission were published as *The Burney Papers*, 15 vols. (Bangkok, 1910–14). He would return to India in 1842, but had not long to live; granted furlough on 17 January 1845, he would die on board ship (4 Mar. 1845) on his way back to England (Hodson; *GM*, NS 24 (1845): 102; Firminger, 247; *JL*, 12: 841, n. 4). Col. Burney's life is the subject of Daniel G. E. Hall, *Henry Burney: A Political Biography* (London: Oxford University Press, 1974).

5. Lambert Richard Loveday (c. 1762–1843), who had joined the East India Company (1778), attained the rank of Col. in the Bengal Army (4 June 1813) and eventually became Lt.-Gen. (1837). On 20 August 1804 he had married on St. Helena, Anne Louise D'Esterre (c. 1784–1867). They lived at Grosvenor Place, Bath (*Army List* (1778–1839); *Alphabetical List . . . Indian Army;* Hodson; *GM*, NS 22 (1844): 91; *Bath Chronicle*, 5 Dec. 1867).

162. To Anna (Wilbraham) Grosvenor

22 Henrietta Street, Bath, 22 March 1839
A.L.S., Berg
Address: M[rs] Grosvenor / Hare Park / Newmarket

I take it most kindly, my dearest Anna, your bestowing time and thought on your absent little friend. Would I had the means of repaying you by <the> sending you in return an amusing letter: but I lead the life of a Hermit; and even if I went out more, and saw more folks, would my Bath gossip afford any entertainment to a London correspondent? Bath has entirely lost its rank as a resort for persons of real fashion. There is much dissipation going on, but it is amongst the <youngest> youngsters of second, third & even fourth-rate station. The quieter people are all elderly invalids,—not temporary Bath water-drinkers, such as one heard or read of in times past,—Lord Chesterfield,[1] for instance, and wits & witlings coming hither to meet one another, & to be in the fashion: but the present race of antiques, are permanent residents; & there <u>may</u> be clever people amongst them: but I cannot say that their fame has reached my secluded ears. The only body with any soul in it, that I am able to keep up an occasional intercourse with (by letter, <u>s'entend</u>) is Miss Bowles, whom you may perhaps have heard, is about to marry her old friend of twenty years standing, M[r] Southey. It is a match that gives me sincere pleasure. His children are all grown up; his wife has been dead more than two years, & was deranged for a very long time previous to her death, and Miss Bowles & Southey agree so perfectly in all their pursuits, & know each others disposition so thoroughly, by having often resided under the same roof for weeks & months when Mrs Southey was living, that the prospect of their future comfort & happiness is the most promising possible.[2]

My Sister d'Arblay makes most grateful & affectionate mention of you in her "few & far-between"[3] letters. I am quite glad you get on together so sociably, & truly rejoiced at your success in getting a snug nitch in her heart.—Poor thing! She has gone through sorrows that in anticipation she herself, and we all should have thought, must have demolished her.[4] You say truly, my Anna, that the loss of my Sister Broome was a heavy blow to me![5] I loved her warmly & fondly,—perhaps, the best of any of my family; & though whilst living here hopeless of seeing her again, the certainty now that I never can do so, often weighs heavy at my heart.

And so, dearest, you have been enacting the Woman of Business! "La femme comme il y en à peu."[6] Well—I honour you for it, & heartily congratulate you upon having now got through such worrying labour. Hang the race-horses, and jokies, and corn & hay bills!—Ma, che volete?—Men will have these inconvenient fancies, & perhaps, might have worse: the bottle, for instance. How should you like a lord and master who tippled? Or who was a glutton, & eke an epicure, for the two often go together. Faugh!

The account you give of your Nieces is charming.[7] How I should like to see the pretty creatures! They may be sources of a little trouble and anxiety to your sister Emma; but I am sure she is all the happier for having them to take charge of, & for knowing herself useful, & seeing herself repaid by their love & gratitude.—

Whatever good you may have heard of my nephew Henry (Col. Burney) is less than he deserves.[8] We had neither met nor written to each other during one and thirty years;[9] yet, scarcely had he landed, before I received from him so affectionate & cordial a letter, that it filled my eyes with tears, & my heart with gratitude. He complains, dear fellow, of what appears to his warm feelings, coldness and distance in his connexions here: but does not remember that to many of them he was almost a personal stranger:—and probably our cooler climate may influence our manners, and tend to make them less demonstrative than <in the open porous (every pore)> in a hot country where every pore is open, and I suppose also every heart for company!—His dear little wife,[10] seems to me the kindest & most pleasing of plain little women. She is full of accomplishments, yet as simple & unaffected as possible.—I like her hugely.

My sister d'Arblay has gratified her much by offering to be Godmother to her new-born bull child[.] (In China a boy baby is called a bull baby, a girl a cow baby).—The infant is to be Christened Alexander d'Arblay. She Mrs Burney, has gone on merrily producing subjects to the Queen; five boys and two girls;[11] and the eldest son at Oxford,[12] where he has lately gained credit by some English verses on Content: My Sister told Henry that the first verses she ever attempted were on the same subject.[13] An odd coincidence. Yours, dearest, were on the decease of "Mister Pea". Do you remember the scrap of an Elegy you wrote on the occasion, and which I am afraid I was so ill-natured as to snigger at? I wish I could remember any of it,—I know you meant to be very pathetic, & now that I am grown more tolerant, I dare say I should neither snigger nor sneer. The truth is, poetry admits of no medium—it ought to be good, or,

"Like that of Mr Dyer
"Should be put behind the fire".[14]—

And now, my Anna, farewel. When you see or write to your sister pray say for me a thousand kind things, and meanwhile, believe me faithfully and truly, your devoted & affectionate old Tut:—

S. H. Burney.

I have taken Brevet Rank, & am now Mrs S. Burney, an' please you. Best respects to the General.

March 22^d 1839
22 Henrietta Street

1. Philip Dormer Stanhope (1694–1773), 4th Earl of Chesterfield (*DNB*), politician and wit, whose *Letters* (1774) to his son tried to inculcate the good manners of elegant society and the art of pleasing.

2. On 4 June 1839, Caroline Anne Bowles (L. 54, n. 2) was to marry her long-standing friend, Robert Southey, whose first wife Edith (née Fricker) had died in November 1837, her last years clouded by madness. The youngest of Southey's four surviving children was twenty (*DNB;* Jack Simmons, *Southey* (London: Collins, 1945), 202–3; see also *The Correspondence of Robert Southey with Caroline Bowles*, ed. Edward Dowden (London: Longmans, Green, 1881)).

3. "Like angel-visits, few, and far between!" Sarah had quoted the line from Thomas Campbell, *The Pleasures of Hope*, Pt. 2, l. 378, in her letter of 24 January 1836 (L. 155) above.

4. Mme d'Arblay at eighty-six had survived all of her siblings, her husband, and her son. The death of the last of her sisters and her chief support, Charlotte Broome, on 12 September 1838 was a "crushing" blow, and her editor notes that "with this loss FBA's correspondence all but ceases" (*JL*, 12: 958, n. 1, 1008).

5. The death of Charlotte Broome seems to have opened up the channels of corre-

spondence again between Sarah Harriet Burney and Charlotte Barrett (see L. 164 below), whose grief for her mother was "of all the sorrows I have felt . . . the deepest" (CFBt to Matilda Aufrère, 15 Nov. [1838], Berg). On 9 March 1839, Mrs. Barrett arranged to pay £20 into Sarah's account (Coutts ledgers) "which my dearest Mother desired should be yours. . . . this little remembrance was not bequeathed as a legacy in the Will, but merely mentioned to me as a token of love she would like to set apart for you—She knew that such an injunction would be equally sacred" (CFBt to SHB, 4 May [Apr. 1839], Barrett, Eg. 3702A, ff. 157–60v).

6. The title of one of the *Contes Moraux* of Jean-François Marmontel (1723–99), first published in 1761; Charles Burney owned a copy of the Paris edition of 1765.

7. The daughters of the late Capt. William Wilbraham (L. 159, n. 6).

8. Opinions were unanimous in favor of Col. Henry Burney: "Your excellent Nephew, Colonel Burney, is as great a favourite with dear Aunt d'Arblay as he is with every one who knows him. He was particularly kind & useful in all the difficulties of her removal, settling with Landlords, &c" (CFBt to SHB, 4 May [Apr. 1839], Barrett, Eg. 3702A, ff. 157–60v). Mme d'Arblay, writing to Sarah Harriet, called him "our Favorite" and named him as executor in her will (*JL*, 12: 961, 979).

9. Sarah had known her nephew Col. Henry Burney as a boy when, with his elder brother Richard, he was sent to school in England 1804–7 (L. 28, n. 10; L. 76, n. 2).

10. Col. Burney had married on 30 June 1818 at Prince of Wales Island, Janet Bannerman (c. 1797–1865), the niece of Col. John Alexander Bannerman, Governor of the island (marriage certificate, India Office Library; *GM*, 88, Pt. 2 (1818): 630; 3rd ser. 19 (1865), 398).

11. Of some thirteen children born to Mrs. Burney in India, six had survived: Henry Bannerman (b. 30 June 1819); Janet Phillips (b. 1 Oct. 1820); Susan Allen (b. 12 May 1823); Charles James (b. Nov. 1833); Richard Thomas (b. 2 May 1835); Frederick William (b. March 1837). The latest addition to the family, named after Mme d'Arblay's son (lately deceased), was Alexander d'Arblay Burney, born 8 March 1839 (Ecclesiastical Returns, Bengal, India Office Library; *Alumni Cantab.*).

12. The eldest son, Henry Bannerman Burney, aged nineteen, had matriculated at Oriel College, Oxford, on 7 December 1837; he would take a B.A. (1841) and an M.A. (1845), and pursue a clerical career (*Alumni Oxon.*).

13. The young Fanny Burney's verses on "Content" are printed in *EJL*, 1: 328.

14. An epigram, attributed to John Reid, M.D. (1776–1822) (*DNB*), by Crabb Robinson, who records the following version:

> The world all say, my gentle Dyer,
> Thy odes do very much want fire.
> Repair the fault, my gentle Dyer,
> And throw thy odes into the fire.
> (HCR, *Reminiscences*, 1: 62)

The poetry in question is that of Lamb's eccentric friend, George Dyer (1755–1841) (*DNB*), who published among other works *Poems, consisting of Odes and Elegies* (1792). See E. V. Lucas, *The Life of Charles Lamb*, 6th ed. (London: Methuen, 1914), 144–67; Winifred F. Courtney, *Young Charles Lamb, 1775–1802* (London: Macmillan, 1982), 203–9.

163. To Henry Crabb Robinson

22 Henrietta Street, Bath, 3 April [1839]
A.L.S., Dr. Williams'
Published: Morley
Address: H. C. Robinson Esqr / 2 Plowdens Buildings / Temple
Endorsed: 3^{d} April 1839 / Miss Burney.

I must say, my dear friend, tho' with thanks for your kind letter, that you are an unconscionable person to call upon me so coolly for an expeditious answer. Lord love you! where am I, the old Hermitess of Henrietta Street, to find materials for a letter to a London gentleman, who goes gadding about from dawn to dewy eve,[1] knows every body, hears every thing, and out of one evening's gossip (beg pardon for so denominating it) could furnish more matter for a full sheet of foolscap than I could scramble together in a twelvemonth. Know you not that I live with seven or eight womenkind, Spinsters and widows, as full of prejudices as they are empty of general knowledge of the world? Kind-hearted worthy persons, some of them, but bigoted to their own narrow view of life; absolutely unacquainted with any literature beyond a Novel or a good book—ignorant of all languages except their own; horrified at what they fancy themselves to know of foreign customs—sure they could not eat this—convinced they would rather die than submit to that—in short, so happily disposed to think whatever belongs to their own country superior to any thing to be met with elsewhere, that they are not only content to be Englishwomen, but absolutely delighted to be Bathites—persons who have never been beyond Clifton, or perhaps Weston super-mer.—Now, from such associates, what can I glean for you? And at present, (indeed, since last October) I have never put my nose out of doors, or seen more than one or two old friends, who come and chat with me now and then, regardless of my receiving them in my bed room, whence I never descend till evening, when I drink tea in the drawing-room, & afterwards roll my arm-chair to a corner near the fire, & by the light of my own private candle sit & read till bed time. If I remain near the table at which my sister Tabbies sit & work, they are so apt to talk altogether, that I, being quite deaf of one ear, and very dunny of the other, find it all confusion, and can make out nothing that is said distinctly. And—dear me!—if I could . . . ma, basta così. You say I am fastiduous, so I will add no more. Only remember who I was fastiduous about: that weariful woman, Mrs Spence,[2] whom you insisted upon my knowing, that I might learn from her how bad were all the Italian maid-servants, and how trifling were the plagues of Egypt compared to the plagues by which she had been beset.—I'll tell you what, my dear Mr Robinson, you have so much uncalled-for patience and indulgence in behalf of these desparate sort of bores, that I almost wonder how you can relish superior society when you fall into it.—"Il faut" says Madame de Sevignè, "savoir supporter la mauvaise compagnie, mais bien ce garder de la trouver bonne."[3]—By mauvaise compagnie, I presume she does not mean scamps & pick-pockets, but dull, and narrow-minded dolts. Now, I own, such sort of folks annoy me, and to say the truth, I should think a funny, witty, animated scamp worth a thousand of them, as acquaintances, s'entend,—I don't mean as friends.

One of the few pleasant persons I now and then hear from, is Miss Bowles, very speedily to become Mrs Southey. I delight in that match. Never could two persons have determined upon matrimony with a fairer chance of happiness. Their pursuits are congenial—their characters well known to each other from having often been inmates for months together, and that, for upwards of twenty years; Southey's children are all married and out of the way of plaguing or being plagued by a mother-in-law; in short, except her giving up her Hampshire residence, beautifully situated near the New Forest, to go and live amongst rocks and lakes and picturesque barrenness,[4]—except that, all the rest is charming.

Well, now, I have covered a large surface of innocent spotless paper, and if you should ask me what I have said, I should find it very difficult to answer you.—O, stop; about Miss Kent[5]—I sent her a very civil message lately by one of my fellow-boarders, who meets her at some charity school, or other good place, & who is to tell her in my name that if she will do me the favour to call, I shall be very happy to see her. Now this I did before the Paynes arrived, and brought me your letter; so do not think me quite so negligent of any Cousin or friend of yours as I may have appeared.

So my dear friend, farewel, and believe me ever your obliged

and faithful

S. H. Burney.

No Miss Nash[6] this year. What has become of her? I like her much, and regret her not coming.

April 3^d^ (colder than Christmas)
22 Henrietta Street.—

1. John Milton, *Paradise Lost* (1667), Bk. 1, l. 742–43: "from morn / To noon he fell, from noon to dewy eve."

2. Elizabeth Spence, the wife of William Spence, the entomologist, acquaintances of Crabb Robinson in Florence (L. 133, n. 15).

3. This particular remark of Mme de Sévigné's has not been found, but in her letters to her daughter, she more than once expresses the paradox: "comme nous trouvions qu'une mauvaise compagnie était bien meilleure qu'une bonne, qui vous laisse affligée quand elle part, au lieu que l'autre vous refraîchit le sang et vous fait respirer de joie!" (31 May [1680]). However, later she seems to caution her daughter against adopting seriously this somewhat cynical attitude: "quand vous me dites que vous vous accomodez mieux de la mauvaise que de rien, et que vous voulez que votre château soit plein, je ne vous connais plus" (25 Dec. [1689]) (Sévigné, *Correspondance*, 2: 954; 3: 787–88).

4. Robert Southey did in fact have an unmarried daughter, Katherine, with whom his new wife was to experience friction; Caroline Bowles gave up Buckland Cottage in the New Forest, her parental home, to join her husband at Greta Hall (*DNB;* Simmons, 204).

5. For the Misses Kent of Bath, members of the nonconformist community, see L. 160, n. 4.

6. Miss Esther Nash, longtime friend of Henry Crabb Robinson (L. 150, nn. 1, 2).

---

164. To Charlotte (Francis) Barrett

22 Henrietta Street, Bath, 17 April 1839
A.L.S., Barrett, Eg. 3705, ff. 51–52v
Address: Mr Barrett / 6 Burlington Street / Brig[h]ton
Postmarks: T P / [?] Baker [?]
10 FN 10 / AP22 / 1839
22AP22 / 1839

You can say nothing, dear Charlotte, however kind and affectionate, of your sweet Mother, in which I do not most sincerely and warmly sympathize. I loved her to my very heart. Every time I saw her, she seemed to me to have become more gentle, more amiable, more attaching than she was before. How you must miss her! The very care she required, in her delicate and weak state, would tend to endear her still more to you. Nothing leaves a sadder gap than the loss of one whom we have watched over, and nursed.[1]—You have, I well know, religious principles that enable you to submit humbly to the privations you have undergone: but, it is not forbidden us to feel; and with reverence be it spoken, even our Blessed Saviour mourned for his friends, & wept with all the tenderness of a compassionate human heart, at sight of sorrow.

I have lately received an extraordinary visit, which awakened in me a mixture of sadness and pleasure. A gentleman, a Mr Ogle, a Clergyman, who when I knew him, was still too young for Deacon's orders, but was intended for the Church, lived above eighteen months in the next Apartment to ours at Chelsea College, where his dear father had been invited by the owner of the rooms to occupy them whilst old Mr Keate[2] was preparing him to undergo an operation for the stone. It was perf[ectly] successful, though he had then attained the age of sixty-eight. He lived twenty years after it, & never experienced any renewal of the complaint till within a few days of his death. Even then, he did not complain, but his face <shewed> betrayed that he was suffering. The son very much won my heart by the assiduous attention he shewed his father during the whole long period of his confinement after the operation. He almost lived at his bed side, and for many weeks I saw no more of him than if he had been in the moon. At other times, as there was then a great scarcity of young ladies in the College, and an equal scarcity of young gentlemen, we met daily, either to walk, to read, or to chat & to laugh together. All this was perfectly undesigning; though the elderly matrons and maids threw out innumerable hints of its being a regular flirtation; & when he went away with his family, condoled with me most pathetically. But the loss was no greater to me than would have been that of a female companion, & I heard all their insinuations with <no tel> provoking composure. He heard from a lady who knows us both, that I was living at Bath, & begged leave to call upon me. O what a picture did he present of the powerful effects of Time! We had not met for five & forty years; I should not have known him any where; his very voice is changed[3] . . . Now, as to me, he as good as declared, I was better looking <now> as an old woman, than I had ever been as a young one: and I can well believe him. I never had any bloom. My nose was often red; my teeth were early injured,—and except fine hair, I had not a single beauty to lose.

The Paynes have been lately spending ten days here. They [went] with Mr Rickman[4] during the week of the Parliamentary recess to see their poor old friend Mr Manning,[5] who is sadly broken down, after a paralytic stroke, but untouched in faculties.—I saw Sarah and John every day whilst they staid, & their sight & talk did me good. Poor old Dr Nott[6] is also in Bath, I believe; at least he <u>was</u> here some time ago. Last Spring he called upon me, sour as verjuice against the world and all its inhabitants, beginning at the present Ministry, and foretelling nothing but horrors accumulate.—

O, yes, I have been to Mr Jay's Chapel,[7] & like him and his preaching extremely: but not his extemporary prayers. He is in high repute with every body who values benevolence and piety, and his Congragation has presented to him a neat little close carriage, something of the Fly kind, drawn by one horse to take him and his wife to Chapel, or on any other good errand he may chuse. Mr Methuen, I understand is at Corsham,[8] either amongst the Baptists or the Independents.

Miss Crewe I see frequently,[9] and find her as affectionate & kind as ever. During the height of my last illness, when appearances were very alarming, she engaged a room here for a week; sent for her night things, & staid with me till all dangerous appearances had subsided. I have seen her, in the depth of winter, at my bed-side at four o'clock in the morning, in her nightcap & night cloaths, anxious to know how I had rested,—in short, shewing all the solicitude of a loving daughter.

Talking of daughters—I hope you will soon hear from your Julia,[10] & have such accounts as your heart could wish. Pray remember me very kindly to Barrett [*1–2 words*] [po]or dear Dick![11] How I should like to see him again—

[And s]o, dear Charlotte, adieu. I don't know when I have written so long a [l]etter. I grow very lazy about such matters, & never liked the job much.—Pray give my best respects to Mr & Mrs Cambridge,[12] & believe me ever truly yours

S. H: Burney.
I have taken brevet rank, & am
Mrs S. Burney now.

April 17th 1839
22 Henrietta Street.

1. Charlotte Barrett wrote to Sarah Harriet of Mrs. Broome's death: "Alas hers is a loss that no time will soften, and I feel it every day—nearly every hour" (CFBt to SHB, 4 May [April 1839], Barrett, Eg. 3702A, ff. 157–60v). Mrs. Barrett had cared for her mother in her old age, as Sarah Harriet had done for both mother and father (see letters of CFBt 1833–39 as listed in *Catalogue;* above passim).

2. Thomas Keate, Surgeon to Chelsea Hospital (L. 19, n. 5), would be called "old Mr. Keate" to distinguish him from his nephew and apprentice, Robert Keate (L. 80, n. 7).

3. Probably the Rev. Joseph Blake Ogle (c. 1770–1849), who had taken his B.A. from Cambridge in 1794 (which was indeed forty-five years previously); the following year he was ordained and appointed Vicar of Somerford-Keynes, Wiltshire (*Alumni Cantab.*). He crossed paths with the Burneys when appointed briefly (4 Dec. 1801) to a curacy at Dorking which Richard Allen Burney was hoping to secure (*JL*, 5: 70, n. 4). He would die at Beckford Cottage, Bathwick, Bath, on 19 March 1849, to be interred at Bath Abbey a week later (*GM*, NS 31 (1849): 549; death certificate, GRO; parish register, Bath Abbey).

His father, Chaloner Ogle of Southampton, Hampshire, died in 1814, at the advanced age of eighty-nine, exactly twenty years after SHB's first acquaintance with him (*GM*, 84, Pt. 2 (1814): 87).

4. John Rickman (1771–1840), a Parliamentary official and statistician, who had belonged to Lamb's circle of friends and briefly employed Martin Burney (*DNB;* Manwaring, 292).

5. Thomas Manning, the Oriental traveller and friend of Charles Lamb (L. 135, n. 2), who had returned to England in 1829 and retired to a cottage in Kent. In 1838, after suffering a paralytic stroke, he removed to Bath for the last two years of his life (*GM*, NS 14 (1840): 97–99; *DNB*).

6. Dr. Nott, "in very indifferent health, and become a perfect misanthrope," was mentioned in L. 160 above.

7. William Jay (1769–1853), a dissenting minister and popular preacher, was pastor of the Argyle Independent Chapel at Bath from 1791 until the end of his life (*DNB*). In her letter, Charlotte had asked about Mr. Jay, "now quite an old man—he was very eloquent & awakening when I knew & heard him 25 years ago—or more:—& they say his preaching is as fine as ever. Do you hear him occasionally?" (CFBt to SHB, 4 May [April 1839], Barrett, Eg. 3702A, ff. 157–60v).

8. The Rev. John Andrew Methuen (L. 131, n. 1), formerly Charlotte Barrett's spiritual adviser, was Vicar of Corsham, Wiltshire, where the family seat was located (Burke).

9. Charlotte had asked politely after Miss Crewe: "I hope Miss Crewe is well—& that no bad weather has prevented your meeting often" (CFBt to SHB, 4 May [April 1839], Barrett, Eg. 3702A, ff. 157–60v).

10. In her letter to her aunt, Charlotte expressed anxiety about her daughter Julia in India, who "was to be confined again in January, and we are anxiously expecting tidings from her husband" (ibid.). On 3 February 1839, Julia Thomas gave birth to James Cambridge, who was baptized at Rajahmundry 16 March 1839 (baptismal certificate, Barrett, Eg. 3708, ff. 29–30v).

11. In the same letter (n. 9), Charlotte mentioned her eldest son: "Dick is now with us, busy about a Hebrew work which is likely to be useful if he ever finishes it." Despite weak eyesight, Richard Barrett took his B.A. at Cambridge in 1835, was elected Fellow 1834–59 and named Tyrwhitt Hebrew Scholar in 1838 (*Alumni Cantab.*).

12. Mrs. Barrett's good friends, the Archdeacon Cambridge and his wife Cornelia (L. 60, n. 24).

165. To Anna (Wilbraham) Grosvenor

22 Henrietta Street, Bath, 4 June 1839
A.L.S., Berg
Address: Mrs Grosvenor / Grosvenor Square

My dearest Anna

It grieves me to the heart to hear so alarming an account of your favorite little Niece. I sincerely hope that before this reaches you, she will be out of danger, & that your anxiety will be exchanged for gladness. Your account of the affectionate solicitude of the Governess gave me great pleasure. Gouvys, you see, may be good sort of people after all.—We have just lost a young Neice to whom Mrs Bourdois, in particular, was warmly attached, & whom she had intended to adopt. She was between sixteen and seventeen, & as amiable a creature as the Cecilia Burney (her namesake) whom you knew & liked.[1] But it is not the young who die that I pity—it is their survivors.

I wonder what the General meant by calling your kind cadeau shabby. I think it remarkably neat & pretty, & love it dearly as a keepsake from the good-natured giver.

The day it was brought by the Miss Sothebys,[2] I was out in a wheel chair (an indulgence I allow myself whenever health & weather permit it) and I unfortunately missed the pleasure of seeing them. I had only begun my hour's wheeling, as they call it here, about a week; for since October last, my blunt-pointed nose had not been once out of doors. I hope your friends may do me the favor to call some other day. They left word they would. I should most gladly return their visit, but for the difficulty I experience in going upstairs. It is not merely shortness of breath, but positive pain I suffer; and, of course, that makes me very unwilling to go into any body's house where such misery may be felt, and may occasion surprise and alarm to those who are not used to see me in that state

I know not how long you may be in town: but at all events I will inclose this to your brother,[3] for I am sure it is not worth paying even the new postage for: i,e. one penny. By the way, is that much-talked-of design passed into a law yet?[4] Or will it ever so pass? For my own part, I think it will only bring upon me more reproaches for not being so regular a correspondent as I ought. However, it may in many cases of real importance, be a very good thing, particularly to poor mothers separated from their children, & anxious to hear oftener from them than they could formerly afford even to wish.

My poor, dear Anna—Think of your having conferences to hold with Lawyers!—I do pity you, with all my heart: for except arithmetic, there is nothing on earth I am so dunny-pated about as legal forms, & all sorts and sizes of Law business.

When you have time & spirits for it, pray read "Sketches by Boz" with Cruikshank's designs.[5] Except ones daily Scripture reading, I like no books that do not make me laugh, provided the laugh is not provoked by any thing bordering upon indecency.—A little innocent vulgarity or even coarseness, I do not mind, if accompanied with wit & humour. Dickens has edited a delightful Life of poor dear Grimaldi.[6] Have you seen Benson Earl Hill's "Recollections of an Artillery Officer"?[7] I was much amused by it.

And now, dearest, having emptied my very small budget, I have only to assure you of my faithful love, & sincere gratitude—And with a thousand affectionate remembrances to your sisters, to sign myself yours ever

S. H. Burney

June 4th 1839
22 Henrietta Street

1. Cecilia Mary, the second daughter of Richard Allen Burney, died at Dorset on 27 May 1839, aged sixteen (L. 157, n. 3; *GM*, NS 12 (1839): 99). She had been named after Richard's sister, Cecilia Charlotte Esther, who had died in 1821 (L. 103, n. 2).

2. Probably Maria Elizabeth and Harriet Louisa Sotheby, friends of Anna Grosvenor, who had arranged for their introduction to Sarah Harriet (L. 152 and n. 1).

3. George Wilbraham (L. 112, n. 12), who had franking privileges as M.P., lived at 56 Upper Seymour Street near Grosvenor Square (Stenton).

4. The new system of prepaid and uniform penny postage would commence in England on 10 January 1840.

5. [Charles Dickens (1812–70)], *Sketches by "Boz"* (1836) was illustrated by George Cruikshank (1792–1878) (*DNB*).

6. *Memoirs of Joseph Grimaldi*, edited by "Boz" [i.e., Charles Dickens] (1838).

7. Benson Earle Hill, *Recollections of an Artillery Officer including scenes and adventures in Ireland, America, Flanders and France* (1836).

166. To Henry Crabb Robinson

22 Henrietta Street, Bath, 26 February 1840
A.L.S., Dr. Williams'
Published: Morley
Address: H. C. Robinson Esqr / 33 Russell Square / London
Postmarks: D / PAID / 28FE28 / 1840
BATH / FE24 / [1]840 / C
Endorsed: 26th Feb: 1840 / Miss Burney / Ans^{d} 6th March
[*with a summary of his reply*]

Feby 26th 1840
22 Henrietta Street

My dear friend

Your most kind & welcome letter[1] should not have remained so long unanswered, had I not been a good deal indisposed for some time after I received it, & then, when getting better, such bitter cold weather set in, that I could not bring myself to move off the hearth rug, & there was no putting ones writing table in so comfortable a situation without some danger of its catching fire.

I am charmed with your good nature about my little booky.[2] It is only those who read but few of these fictions, that <pay> think any more about them when they have <done reading> finished them. The common run of Novel readers, skim their eyes lightly over them, close the last volume, and send for something else. If you ask them a month later whether they have read such a work, they hardly remember, but suppose they have—adding, "I really read so many, that one drives <the other> another out of my head."—You, and a few more, who read better things habitually, are the only satisfactory persons for a writer of fiction to have any dealings with.

Pray do you now and then read modern Biography? I have been highly enter[*t*]ained, & even interested by the Memoirs of Mathews, edited & mostly written by his wife.[3] Well, and another lively amusing book of the same class is the Life of Grimaldi, by Dickens. Both Mathews & Grimaldi, though considered as Buffoons, were full of good feeling, & excellent private characters.[4] I arose from the perusal of each work, with respect & love for both men; and since the publication of Crabb's Memoirs,[5] and Campbell's Life of Mrs Siddons,[6] I have read no Biography I like half so well.

Miss Kent[7] has kindly called twice. The first time, I was keeping my bed for a bad cold, and the second time, I had a medical man with me. But it does not matter much, for I know I am not good enough to suit her; she is gentle & pleasing, yet I never know what to talk to her about. Pray excuse my saying this. It is from no prejudice against, or dislike of the Lady: but solely from a consciousness that she must think me an old worldly-minded person, who would have been the last creature in the world she would have sought out, had it not been to please you. Meanwhile, believe me in all truth, I would give much to be sincerely like her.

Grieved, grieved, indeed I am at the melancholy account you give of that noble creature Southey! And his charming wife, how I feel for her! She is my particular friend, & I was the unconscious means of her first becoming acquainted with Southey. They have now been in habits of intercourse, & in continual communication of each others works and thoughts for many years. She wrote to me just before her marriage, speaking chearfully of her resignation of <the> her pretty house & garden near Lymington, which she was about to part with, & of her future prospects on being removed to a new home. And all this—what has it led to, but misery?—Yet, as a devoted friend, giving up her whole time to him, how great a blessing she will [*be*] to one in so helpless & pitiable a state.—I have often wondered, since her marriage, at not having heard from her; I did not know her proper direction, or I would have written to her. But perhaps it may be as well I did not compel from her a reluctant account of her husband's situation. The first suspicion & the gradual confirmation of what was coming upon him must have been dreadful to her! Poor, poor creatures! I hardly know which to pity most.[8]

I have just received a long gossiping letter from Sarah Payne, dated from Via Belsiana, 71. A. Roma. She passed through Florence, & saw Niccolini, & the Ladies, and Angela is returned to them, her ugly old husband being dead. She misses the Finches very much, and many other English folks of former years. Poor Columba was no where to be found or heard of,[9] & Sarah is sadly afraid she was one of the many thousand carried off by the Cholara.—The streets & general cleanliness of Rome is much improved since that awful scourge overtook them. But it far surpassed in the number of its victims any thing I had the least idea of.[10]

Yes, my dear friend, the annuities you speak of, have been left to Martin & me by my kind sister,[11] and I rejoice at poor Martin's I hope as much as at my own. But I wanted not such a proof of her considerate affection, to love her memory, and to bewail the sad loss in her last years of her only child.—

And now, my dear friend, I want some of you wiseacres to tell me a little about public affairs. Newspapers make my eyes ache, and are besides full of lies; and exclusive of these, I hear nothing but from a parcel of ignorant, prejudiced, & petulant women, who know no more of the matter than I do. I hate female politicians. But I want to know a lot of such things as you could tell me. For instance, what taxes it is supposed will be levied,[12] and what may be the good of the penny postage?[13] It did not relieve the poor, & I much fear something will be substit[*ut*]ed that will burthen them. And will the present Ministry keep their ground much longer? And what can be done about the Chartists?[14]

If life, health & spirits permit <it>, I hope to pay London a visit early in the summer. A dear Nephew of mine, Col. Henry Burney, urges me to pay him & his pleasant wee wifekin a visit,[15] & nothing would give me more satisfaction than to be able to do so. You may then hope for the honour of a visit in your new residence,[16] & a noble chat we will have. As for my reputation being sullied, you impertinent gentleman! do not flatter yourself; I shall be safe as thunder—what you may be, is not for me to say.—

Have not seen Miss Nash[17] these two years. Why does she not come to Bath as usual? Adieu, dear old crony—Yours ever with true regard

S. H. Burney

1. Robinson noted in his diary on 5 February 1840 that he "wrote to Miss Burney after long delay." He received this "chearful and very pleasant letter" in reply on 28 February and wrote again on 6 March (HCR, 5, 28 Feb., 6 Mar. 1840, Diaries).

2. *The Romance of Private Life* (1839) (L. 160, n. 8). Henry Crabb Robinson read the first tale, *The Renunciation*, on 17 October 1839 and found it "an interesting story" although "left incomplete"; on 15 November he was "diverted" by the second, *The Hermitage*, but found the denouement "ill contrived" and the plot "barely enough for a single vol." Nevertheless, on 5 February 1840 he wrote to tell Miss Burney "my opinion of her two tales wch I could honestly give being favourable" (HCR, 17 Oct. 15 Nov. 1839, 5 Feb. 1840, Diaries).

Perhaps Robinson was pleased to bestow even qualified praise, as he had definitely not enjoyed her *Country Neighbours*, concluding, "I shall hardly venture on another novel by Miss B:" as she was "very inferior to her sister" (HCR, 12, 14 Dec. 1831, Diaries). The reviewer in the *Athenaeum*, no. 625 (19 Oct. 1839): 793, agreed with the unfavourable comparison of the two novelists, finding the younger sister was "quite as talkative, but by no means so well worth listening to." The plot devices of *The Renunciation* he considered unrealistic and conventional, but concluded, "the volumes contain no harm." Largely ignored by other reviews, the work was praised in the *New Monthly Magazine*, 2nd ser. 57 (1839): 276–77, as a "capital production in its way, and claims the very first rank in the class to which it belongs"; this periodical, however, was published by Colburn himself.

3. [Anne] Mathews, *Memoirs of Charles Mathews, Comedian* (1838–39).

4. Sarah mentioned reading Dickens's *Memoirs of Joseph Grimaldi* in her letter of 4

June 1839 above; Charles Mathews (1776–1835) was a famous comic actor and mimic and Joseph Grimaldi (1779–1837), a pantomimist (*DNB*).

5. A life of George Crabbe (1754–1832) (*DNB*) by his son [George Crabbe] was published as vol. 1 of *The Poetical Works of the Rev. George Crabbe* (1834).

6. Thomas Campbell (1777–1844), *Life of Mrs. Siddons* (1834).

7. Miss Kent, Robinson's nonconformist friend, who had paid her first visit to Sarah Harriet on 20 April 1838 (L. 160).

8. Very soon after his second marriage to Caroline Bowles in June of 1839 (L. 162, n. 2), Robert Southey's mind and health began to fail; by November it was common knowledge that his mental powers were gone, and by July 1840 he was unable to recognize his friends (Simmons, 203–6).

Robinson responded to SHB's comments on 6 March 1840, "advising her to write to Mrs. Southey." Apparently she would do so and share the contents of her reply with Robinson: "she read me a delightful letter from Mrs. Southey giving an account of Southey's condition. It is not so very distressing for the present suffering, but only because it seems to be hopeless." Several months later, however, he was inclined to doubt the sincerity of her account (HCR, 6, 27 Mar., 28 Dec. 1840, Diaries).

In fact, he would take a different view of the situation after spending Christmas of 1840 with the Wordsworths, who took the part of Southey's daughter, Kate, against her stepmother. (The acrimonious "Statement of Kate Southey, about the affairs connected with her Father's second marriage," in the Victoria University Library, Toronto, was drawn up at Wordsworth's suggestion.) On 26 January 1841, Wordsworth wrote to Robinson a long account of his own role in the Southey family quarrel, a letter that Robinson read to various friends. His zealous partisanship is recorded in his diary: "This day was spent entirely in other people's affairs and the greater part of it in the Southey family occupied my attention. . . . I wrote in the afternoon to Dora W: and informed her of all I had done." It is perhaps significant that his interest in the subject diminishes greatly after the marriage of Dora Wordsworth (HCR, 19 Feb. 1841, Dec. 1840–June 1841 passim, Diaries; *Letters . . . Wordsworth*, ed. Hill, 7: 169–75).

9. Sarah Payne, who had been in Italy for the previous three months at least (CFBt to HBt, 7 Dec. [1839], Barrett, Eg. 3702A, ff. 98–99v), was giving Sarah news of her old acquaintance there: her former landladies, Madame Certellini and her sister, and the poet Niccolini of Florence (L. 128, n. 6; L. 129, n. 4); Robert Finch and his wife, Maria, of Rome, who were both now dead (L. 120, nn. 2, 4); and Columba, Sarah's former maid at Rome (L. 139). Angela is unidentified, but sounds like a former servant at 4131 Via della Vigna Nuova.

10. England fared better than other countries during the cholera epidemic, which ended c. 1837. One citizen in 131 died in Great Britain, which compared favourably with 1 in 20 in Russia, 1 in 30 in Austria and 1 in 32 in Poland (Longmate, 142).

11. Frances (Burney) d'Arblay had died on 6 January 1840; in her will, dated 6 March 1839 and proved 17 February 1840, she bequeathed to her "dear half-sister Sarah Harriet Burney during her natural life and to commence immediately after my decease the sum of two hundred pounds per annum . . . to be paid quarterly and the first payment to be made three months after my death"; she also left an annuity of £100 to her nephew Martin Burney. After their deaths, this property would revert to her residuary legatee, Richard Barrett (Mrs. Barrett's eldest son), who would meanwhile receive interest on

the residue (*JL*, 12: 976–81). Robinson heard the news "to my great pleasure" on 5 February 1840 and wrote to Miss Burney the same day: "I congratulated her in the affluence she has acquired thro' her sister's will." Later he would hear the particulars from Mrs. Barrett and concluded, "Mad d'Arblay seems to have made a wise & benevolent will" (HCR, 5 Feb., 10 Nov. 1840, Diaries).

Mme d'Arblay may have overestimated the income produced by her estate, judging by the executors' payments into SHB's account over the next four years. Instead of £800, she would receive only £655, and the quarterly payments more than once fell £10 short of the expected £50 (Coutts ledgers). Dick Barrett's share, too, fell below the annuity of £100 originally estimated by his mother; when Robinson spoke to Mrs. Barrett ten months after Mme d'Arblay's death, she told him Dick was receiving "only about £40 per annum" (CFBt to HBt, 6 Jan. 1840, Berg; HCR, 10 Nov. 1840, Diaries).

12. In order to prevent a deficit in 1841, the Whig ministry of William Lamb (1779–1848), 2nd Viscount Melbourne (1828), proposed budgetary measures to reduce the deficit: a drastic reduction in the duty on foreign sugar, a readjustment of the timber duties and a fixed duty on corn. Leading the opposition, Sir Robert Peel (1788–1850), 2nd Bt. (1830), introduced a resolution of no confidence in the ministry, which passed by one vote on 5 June 1841. After a general election, the government was immediately defeated on an amendment to the address and resigned (30 Aug. 1841), leaving Peel to form a new Tory administration. See further Donald Southgate, *The Passing of the Whigs, 1832–1886* (London: Macmillan, 1962), 112–34.

13. The reforms by Rowland Hill (1795–1879) (*DNB*) to establish a cheaper, more equitable and efficient postal system had much public support; see Frank Staff, *The Penny Post, 1680–1918* (London: Lutterworth Press, 1964), 76–95.

14. Chartism, the working-class movement in England that subscribed to the six points of the People's Charter of May 1838: universal manhood suffrage, annual parliaments, vote by ballot, equal electoral districts, the abolition of property qualifications for M.P.s, and payment of M.P.s. The Charter was the common basis for widespread agitation between the spring of 1837 and January 1840, including a National Convention held in February 1839 to prepare a petition to present to Parliament. In the winter of 1839–40, an armed insurrection at Newport, Wales, and attempted risings elsewhere led to mass arrests and the imprisonment of many activists, leaving the movement in disarray. See further F. C. Mather, *Public Order in the Age of the Chartists* (Manchester: Manchester University Press, 1959).

15. In early December 1839, Charlotte Barrett had heard that "Aunt Sally is coming to pass a month" with Col. Henry Burney and his wife, Janet, at 26 Hamilton Terrace, St. John's Wood Road (CFBt to HBt, 7 Dec. [1839], Barrett, Eg. 3702A, ff. 98–99v; *JL*, 12: 957, n. 1).

16. Robinson had moved four months previously to 33 Russell Square (see above). In his diary, he describes rather dismally his arrival at his new rooms on 14 October 1839 where all was in "sad confusion," but a week later he was "already quite reconciled to the change . . . [*which*] cannot but be agreeable" (HCR, 14, 20 Oct. 1839, Diaries).

17. Misses Elizabeth and Esther Nash (L. 150, n. 1) were living in a boardinghouse on Bedford Place near Russell Square in London, where H. C. Robinson would visit them on 29 March (HCR, 29 Mar. 1840, Diaries).

167. To Anna (Wilbraham) Grosvenor

[22 Henrietta Street, Bath], 8 June 1840
A.L.S., Berg

June 8th 1840
Whit. Monday

Dearest Anna

I have alas! quite given up all thoughts of a London Journey. Those abominable Rail-roads were no temptation to my cowardly nerves, and moreover I am become quite as hard of hearing as the old woman who would not go a shearing;[1] and I have no breath to walk about, & it tires me mortally to faire l'agréable for more than a quarter of an hour—so, all things considered, I thought it would be best for every body as well as myself to determine against being frisky, seeing as how, I should have been a dead weight upon their hands; & quiet being now what I like best, & am alone fit for. Every age has its pleasures[2] and comforts, & I do assure you, that an infirm Elder like myself, has no enjoyment more gratifying than tranquillity. I should have liked extremely to have seen you all,—but quite in my own way—without trouble, or packing, or bustle of any kind, & not for too long at a time; for the intense earnestness with which my deafness compels me to listen when talked to, quite exhausts me.

I am glad this tedious account of myself will cost you nothing but the trouble of reading it; but I do think the enormous reduction of postage a most foolish experiment. It was a tax that scarcely at all affected the poor, & for the rich it might have been a little lowered for popularity-sake,—but the rating it at a penny all over the Kingdom, will it is feared cause such a deficiency in the Revenue,[3] that some other tax which will fall hard upon the people will necessarily become its substitute. How do you like my Exchequer wisdom?

Is your Sister Eliza arrived? I suppose in about half a year you will let me know. However, if she is actually with you, give my kindest love to her.

My present plan for the summer, is to pay my annual visit to Cheltenham, which has always done me good, and is quite as rural as I am now capable of enjoying. I like the morning Band at the Monpelier Spa,[4] and the morning exhibitions, and Concerts,[5] & all the Cockney doings[6]—and I endeavour to get a lodging in the Promenade, that I may see the folks, pedestrians, equestrians, carriageites &c—One of my Nieces I take with me, & shall hire a good pianoforte, & make her play to me, & subscribe to a well-stocked library, & I trust, get on very tidily.

Adieu my dearest Anna—Give my best respects to the General, & believe me ever your most affectionate old friend

S. H. Burney.

I have taken Brevet rank, & am
Mrs Burney at your service

1. Old woman, old woman, shall we go a-shearing?
Speak a little louder, sir, I'm very thick of hearing.
Old woman, old woman, shall I love you dearly?
Thank you very kindly, sir, now I hear you clearly.
(Iona Opie and Peter Opie, eds., *The Oxford Dictionary of Nursery Rhymes* (Oxford: Clarendon Press, 1951), 429)

2. Nicolas Boileau-Despréaux, *L'Art poétique* (1674), Chant 3, l. 374.

3. The new system of penny postage would create a temporary deficit in the Post Office for a decade after its introduction; not until 1851 would the gross revenue, and in 1854 the net revenue, reach the levels of the year preceding the reform (1839) (Howard Robinson, 322–23).

4. "There are few scenes more animated and inspiring than the Montpellier promenade, on a fine summer morning, between eight and ten o'clock [*with*] the presence of the lovely, the titled, and the fashionable, as they parade up and down the grand walk to the sound of music" (Henry Davies, *The Stranger's Guide through Cheltenham*, 3rd ed. (Cheltenham: H. Davies, [1842]), 79).

5. The Montpellier Evening Musical Promenades were held in the summer on the grand walk or in the gardens. A band of 17 performers played a prearranged program from 7 to 9:30 P.M.: "as the shadows of twilight gather round the scene, the Rotunda and promenade room, as well as the grand walk, are brilliantly lighted up." The concerts were well attended, and particularly fashionable on Saturday evenings (Davies, 105–6).

6. Among other "doings" in Cheltenham were drinking of the waters at various spas, strolling in the gardens, attending the summer balls in the Rotunda or the winter balls in the assembly rooms, watching the public races (an annual two-day event), and playing cards (Davies, 103–21).

168. To Anna (Wilbraham) Grosvenor

[Bath Hotel], Clifton, [post 16 July–]10 August [1840][1]
A.L.S., Berg

My dear kind Nannypanny

I am at Clifton an' please you, for vulgarly as I love the vulgar gape-seed to be had at Cheltenham, I have been too much pulled down by a sort of Influenza (at least an epidemic) which has left me so weak that I was afraid to undertake a journey of only half a day. Instead of that, I got here in two hours, & it being broilingly sun-shiny, was quite heated and fatigued enough. I have a kind, attentive friend with me, & the best nurse possible; & to save myself trouble, have taken rooms & am boarded at the Bath Hotel, whence I can see over the Downs, & inhale good air, the only sort of tonic I dare meddle with.

How very much I like your little history of Captain Stopford & your niece Julia.[2]—A marriage of affection, & yet not entirely unprovided with the conveniencies of life, is a delightful thing to hear of. I hate starving love—

One of the hardships attending my invalidism I most lament, is that of getting my mouth and throat so parched, after conversing any time, that I am almost unable to speak without taking a sip of water, or holding a fruit lozenge in my mouth. And many times in the day, I have to gargle, <& refresh myself> with vinegar & water. Besides the inconvenience, I am not quite so deaf as Uncle Roger,[3] but very near it.

Monday, Augst 10th Your dear kind letter from Brighton & London, is just arrived. What I had written above, <is> was in answer to your former letter from Hare Park, July 16th—How glad I am you had a peep at our dear Gregoriana. If her little face is reduced what must it now appear? It never exceeded the circumference of a breakfast tea-cup. Mine is dwindled down to a most modest octagon. I can neither call it round, nor oval; octagon is the only word. and its colour, a pale orange, sometimes varigated with green—lips of a dirty white, dried & chapped—O, Nanny, Nanny dear—I shall never again wonder that a ci-devant Beauty mourns for and grumbles at her departed loveliness, since I, who never had any loveliness, yet now cannot forbear hating the sight of the effects of age & ill-health upon my sallow countenance.

Thank you for your details respecting Mrs Bradford & her family, & her relics,—and above all, for the little quotation from charming Miss Edgworth's letter. Do you—have you the pleasure of knowing Miss Edgworth?[4] I really envy you, for she has always been one whom I have thought & said I could undertake a long pilgrimage to make acquaintance with.—I have not yet read Princess Dashkaw's Memoirs: but you may be sure that after such an account of their editor[5]—and after the amusement you derived from them, as well as Miss Edgworth, I shall leave no stone unturned in order to get at them.

Two of my Nieces are here in lodgings very near me; one, a lively, entertaining, kind-hearted creature, pleasant to look at, as well as to hear—the other, a heavy, well-meaning, absent, helpless body,—& their names are Mrs John Payne, & Miss Amelia Burney. Mrs Payne, was my brother James' Sarah Burney—& she is now as much a favorite with others almost, as she was formerly with him.—

And now, dearest, farewell—Thanks for all your kind remembrances of me—& love most faithful from my very heart of hearts

S. H. Burney

1. The letter has been dated by Sarah's trip to Clifton (see next letter), and the Wilbraham-Stopford marriage (n. 2). The perpetual calendar confirms this conjecture, as 10 August was indeed a Monday in 1840.

2. Mrs. Grosvenor's niece, Julia Maria Wilbraham (fl. 1829–45) (L. 119, n. 4), married at Malta on 6 August 1840 Lt. Edward Stopford (1809–95) of the Royal Navy, who would be advanced to the rank of Commander 20 July 1841. Her husband belonged to a distinguished family: grandson of James Stopford (1731–1810), 2nd Earl of Courtown (1770); nephew of Admiral Sir Robert Stopford (1768–1847), Governor of Greenwich Hospital (1841) (*DNB*); and son of the Rev. Richard Bruce Stopford (1774–1844), Chaplain to the Queen and Canon of Windsor (O'Byrne; Burke, Gibbs under Courtown; *GM*, NS 14 (1840): 423).

3. Anna's paternal uncle, Roger Wilbraham (L. 112, n. 11), who had died in 1829 at the age of eighty-six.

4. Maria Edgeworth, whom Sarah Harriet considered to be "the pride of English female writers" (L. 75).

5. *Memoirs of the Princess Dashchkaw, Lady of Honour to Catherine II . . . Written by Herself*, ed. Mrs. W. Bradford, 2 vols. (London: Henry Colburn, 1840). The introduction by Martha (née Wilmot) Bradford (1775–1873) explains that when she was in Russia from 1803 to 1808, she had urged the Princess Catherina Romanovna Vorontsova Dashkova (1744–1810) to write about her life and her role in the coup of 1762 that brought Catherine II to the throne.

169. [To Henry Crabb Robinson]

[Bath Hotel, Clifton], 29 August 1840
A.L.S., Dr. Williams'
Endorsed: 29th Augt. 1840 / Miss Burney / The books

Augst 29th 1840.

Many thanks, my kind friend, for the excellent little pamphlet you sent me by Mr Payne. I have now perused it, word for word, to within two or three pages of the end, and can no longer resist giving myself the pleasure of telling you how much I have been gratified by it.—I never could endure the "Life" compiled by those miscalculating sons,[1] who, as it appears, either from bad taste, or from a greedy desire to make a large book in order to obtain a large bit of money, published such unpublishable extracts from their poor Father's secret Diary; & who, but for Mr Wilberforce's known talents & wit, would have misled the world into believing him a maudlin, supersticious, childish fanatic. I remember, in one extract, he reproaches himself for having been too entertaining at some dinner party, & in sundry other instances, absurdities equally preposterous are presented to miscellaneous readers, who, in cool blood, are left to groan over, or to laugh at being betrayed into peeping so unceremoniously behind the curtain. What Mr Wilberforce wrote down for his own admonition, is all very well; & he was, I make no doubt, seriously in earnest: but what had <u>we</u> to do with the knowledge of these secret scruples?—Throughout the whole book, however, (not more than one third of which I was able to wade through) there runs a paltryness of spirit, in the sons a would-be sanctity, the least edifying I ever met with,—so that your naughty little rubs at them,[2] warmed the very cockles of my heart. I was particularly amused with the following, "I can only challenge the Messrs Wilberforce to produce a single word which insinuates disesteem for their father, or esteem for themselves."[3] Eh Viva! Well—but their nasty answer to Miss Cartwright![4] And hers such a lady-like, rational, temperate remonstrance: it is really insufferable. I have no words to express my contempt and dislike of their little-mindedness, & thorough want of feeling.

This rigmarole of mine, I take it for granted, will not find you in town;[5] and during weather of such surpassing beauty, I should be sorry to think it would.—I am still at Clifton: but purpose if I continue pretty well, removing to Cheltenham next week.—The Paynes are at Salt Hill, & talk of a trip to the Isle of Wight.

I have not seen Mr Landor since you brought him to Henrietta Street:[6] but what I regret far more, is the loss of poor dear Mr Manning;[7] & to all his friends, what a sad gap in society will the death of Mr Rickman[8] occasion. I often repeat to myself Johnson's lines:

"Year follows year, decay pursues decay,
"Still drops from life some withering charm away".[9]

And now, dear friend, good by, & believe me ever your sincerely attached
S. H. Burney.

1. Robert Isaac and Samuel Wilberforce, *The Life of William Wilberforce*, 5 vols. (London: John Murray, 1838).

2. Henry Crabb Robinson had evidently sent the latest publication in a controversy in which he was involved, defending his friend, Thomas Clarkson (1760–1846), the abolitionist (*DNB*). The authors of *The Life of William Wilberforce* had attacked Clarkson for exaggerating his own role in the anti-slavery movement and for accepting remuneration (1: 140–41 and n.; 2: 52–55), a charge repeated in the *Edinburgh Review*, 67 (1838): 142–80 (see 158–59).

Clarkson responded in *Strictures on a Life of William Wilberforce* (London: Longman, Orme, Brown, Green & Longmans, 1838), with a defense organized and supplemented by Robinson so effectively that the *Edinburgh Review* 68 (1838): 188–90, printed an apology. The sons, however, replied in the Preface to *The Correspondence of William Wilberforce*, ed. Robert Isaac and Samuel Wilberforce, 2 vols. (London: John Murray, 1840), disclaiming any hostility toward Clarkson but criticizing harshly the editor of the *Strictures* (xix, n.).

In answer to these remarks, Robinson published an *Exposure of Misrepresentations contained in the preface to the Correspondence of William Wilberforce* (London: Edward Moxon, 1840) under his own name. His vigorous and somewhat legalistic arguments were generally considered to be demolishing, and the offensive material about Clarkson was omitted in the second edition of the *Life* (1843). For an overview of the dispute, see Edith J. Morley, *The Life and Times of Henry Crabb Robinson* (London: J. M. Dent, [1935]), 110–15, and John Milton Baker, *Henry Crabb Robinson of Bury, Jena,* The Times, *and Russell Square* (London: George Allen & Unwin, 1937), 226–35.

Robinson's diary records his doubts about the success of his pamphlet before its publication in mid-August, and his pleasure in Miss Burney's praise of his work, received on 1 September 1840 (HCR, 16, 20 June, 4, 11, 14 Aug., 1 Sept. 1840, Diaries).

3. HCR, *Exposure*, 51.

4. Frances Dorothy Cartwright (1780–1863), the niece and biographer of John Cartwright (1740–1824), another abolitionist (*DNB*). She resented a remark attributed to her uncle in the *Life* (1: 245) which she felt misrepresented his character and religious views. She wrote a letter of mild protest to Robert Wilberforce who replied somewhat contemptuously, expressing disapproval of Major Cartwright's beliefs. This correspondence, published in the *Morning Chronicle* in September 1838, was cited by Robinson as another example of the sons' unjust and unnecessary slander of Wilber-

force's associates, and their lack of generosity in refusing to apologize. He also suggests that the religious and political prejudice evinced in the reply may account for the sons' behaviour (HCR, *Exposure*, 84–87).

5. Robinson was in fact in London when he received SHB's letter on 1 September 1840 but would leave on a six-week trip to Germany five days later (HCR, 1 Sept., 6 Sept.–22 Oct. 1840, Diaries).

6. On 26 March 1840, during Robinson's visit to Bath, he had brought his friend Walter Savage Landor to visit Miss Burney; all three had previously met in Florence (L. 135, n. 13). Landor had since separated from his wife (1835) and returned to England, moving to Bath in 1837 (Super, 252–59, 284). Robinson hoped that Landor might repeat the call "for I perceive that he after all wants occupations and objects of interest," but concluded that it was unlikely, since "it is the beauty of early youth that attracts him" (HCR, 27 Mar. 1840, Diaries; *HCR on Books*, 2: 581–82).

7. Thomas Manning, the Oriental traveler and friend of Lamb, who had recently retired to Bath (L. 135, n. 2; L. 164, n. 5). On 26 March 1840, Miss Burney had proposed to her visitors, Robinson and Landor (n. 6 above), to visit Manning; they found him "quite the invalide" (HCR, 27 Mar. 1840, Diaries). On 2 May 1840, Manning died of apoplexy at Bath and was buried in the Abbey Churchyard (*DNB*).

8. John Rickman, the "Census-taker," was a friend of Sarah's relations, the Paynes (L. 164). When he died on 11 August 1840, the House of Commons passed a resolution in praise of his work (*DNB;* Claude A. Prance, *Companion to Charles Lamb: A Guide to People and Places, 1760–1847* (London: Mansell, 1983)).

9. Samuel Johnson, *The Vanity of Human Wishes*, ll. 305–6. The lines are somewhat misquoted: "Year chases Year, Decay pursues Decay, / Still drops some Joy from with-'ring Life away."

---

170. To Anna (Wilbraham) Grosvenor

Belgrave House, Cheltenham, 30 January–6 February [1842][1]
A.L.S., Berg

Jany 30th Belgrave House
Cheltenham

My dearest Anna—for I cannot accustom myself to the formality of calling you, "Mrs Grosvenor"—So, my dearest Anna it must be, and I know that you will allow, or, at least, forgive it.—

Here I am, you see, at Cheltenham, and here I have been ever since June, tho' at first in lodgings, with a Nursy kind of Maid, & too unwell to undertake the trouble of submitting to the ways of a Boarding-House—the dressing for dinner—the late hours—and the number of strange faces. However, I got better under the hands of Dr Gibney,[2] who attended me with great judgment, & encouraged my trying to enter into society; and moreover, I found a lodging with only Nursy for companion, very dull; and so at the end of a month I came to this house; a very chearfully situated one,[3] with several kind, & amiable persons in it—and here I have been ever since, nicking poor old gone-by Bath, where I grubbed on for so many years, from sheer irresolution, and where I was so often ill, and had no inmates save old females like myself,—and nothing to look at but blackened stone buildings containing lodgers, the gayest amongst which was a grey parrot, who now and then whistled, but still oftener screamed. How I bore the thing so long, I am now surprised. Here, both gentlemen and ladies are received, and one of the former, has been in the house as long as I have, & is a great pet of mine. He was originally in the Navy, but broke a blood vessel, & was forced to give up the Service, & go abroad. He has been every where,—was absent nine years—got quite well, & was called home by the death of his sister's husband, one of whose Executors he was appointed. That sister lives here, with two daughters & a son, the prettiest school-boy you ever saw. They do not reside under this roof, but close by, & my pet doats upon the boy, & brings him here to dinner as often as his holidays, or half holidays will permit.—

Feb^r^ 6th

Well, dear—this was begun a week ago, and then I was interrupted, and had not the grace to go on with it till now.—So let me make up for lost time, by telling you what I am sure you will be glad of for my sake: Our dear kind friend, Mrs Gregor is here. She has a house nearly opposite, & stays till April. On first coming, she boarded in this establishment for a week, having her own private drawing-room: but gradually she made her appearance amongst the others, & played her rubber in the evening, & seemed to like a little society; & was most thoroughly liked and appreciated by them all. Elinor obtained a competent share of approval: but—somehow—she is always second best to <u>me</u>, at least.—I have had another treat. A long evening chatty visit from Harriet Crewe, who slept at the Plough[4] one night, in her way to Cheshire on a visit to her brother.[5] She went Rail-road fashion.[6] I suppose, Marm', <u>you</u> are a favourer of Trains and Rails. I hate them most cordially, & have high authority for so doing, since, it is asserted that our little Queen has never yet ventured upon any of them.[7]—I must tell you what delightful invalid vehicles have been established here. There are now three of them. A little Chariot, with side doors, & full sized windows, & curtain spring blinds, & lambs-wool rugs, is set upon three low wheels, like a Bath Chair, and drawn by one man with perfect ease, & costing no more than a common open Chair.[8] Thus, susceptible as I am of cold, I have been enabled to take a little airing almost every day, & no one here can enjoy this novelty more heartily than I do.—

Have you seen the Journal & letters of my dear Sister?[9] & Charlotte Barrett's pretty Introduction. I earnestly hope the work will be liked; and I think it stands a very fair chance, so many celebrated people will be brought forward.—This is a very tolerable place for getting books (English s'entend)[10] but my copy is a present, & will have a fine gauntlet to run, I promise it.—

Now, Darling, I have said all my say—Mrs Gregor does not know of my writing, or she would, I am sure, send her warmest regards, for she is very fond of you, and, in truth, so is, dearest Anna, your faithful & grateful

S. H. Burney.

Remember me most affectionately to your Sisters,—(Sisters-in-law, not included).[11]—

1. The letter is conjecturally dated to 1842 by Sarah's recent move to Cheltenham where she has been "ever since June," probably June 1841, since she was in Clifton in August of 1840 (see LL. 168, 169). Other circumstances, such as the house rented by Mrs. Gregor until April and the Cheltenham chariots, are both mentioned again in her letter of 1 February 1842 (see below L. 171). The recent publication of the *Diary and Letters of Madame d'Arblay* (1842) adds confirmation.

2. William Gibney (c. 1795–post 1854), a native of Ireland who had graduated M.D. from the University of Edinburgh in 1813, and served in the medical services of the British Army from 1813 to 1818 when he retired on half-pay. By 1826, he had set up practice in Cheltenham where he appears as Physician to the Hospital in the directory for 1843. Dr. Gibney was listed at 9 Rodney Terrace in both the 1841 and 1851 censuses, and was still living at Cheltenham in 1854 (Col. A. Peterkin and Col. William Johnson, comps., *List of Graduates . . . Edinburgh; Commissioned Officers in the Medical Services of the British Army, 1660–1960* (London: Wellcome Historical Medical Library, 1968), 1: 243; Cadet Papers, India Office Library; *GM*, NS 30 (1848): 110; NS 41 (1854): 521).

3. Belgrave House, run by Catherine Haydon and Ann Shaw, was one of the principal boardinghouses in Cheltenham. It was located in a "conspicuous position" on the Promenade, at the corner of Imperial Square: "The healthful and pleasant situation of this house will be a great recommendation to its use, and the internal accommodations are on the best scale, affording all the comforts of 'home,' with the ready and convenient egress into the bustle of fashionable life" (*George Rowe's Illustrated Cheltenham Guide* (1845; rpt., Gloucester: Alan Sutton, 1981), 19).

4. There was an inn called "The Plough" in Cheltenham as early as 1559, which may be the same as the one listed in the *Cheltenham Annuaire and Directory* (1843) as a "Principal Hotel" in High Street. *Bailey's New Handbook for Cheltenham* (1847) describes it as a "well-known and old established Hotel, and coaching-house . . . [*to which*] stabling of great extent are attached" (44–45; also see Gwen Hart, *A History of Cheltenham*, 2nd ed. (Gloucester: Alan Sutton, 1981), 16, 65).

5. Harriet's brother, Hungerford Crewe, 3rd Baron Crewe (L. 110, n. 3), lived at Crewe Hall.

6. The Birmingham-Gloucester railway line was completed in 1841, with a station located "about a mile and a half from the centre of High Street"; six trains passed each way every day. Alternatively, passengers could connect to the Great Western Union Railway at Swindon, by a coach which left Cheltenham two hours before each train (Davies, 189–92; *Cheltenham Annuaire and Directory* (1843), 101).

7. On 13 June 1842, Queen Victoria and Prince Albert would make their first railway journey in a specially designed car on the Great Western line from Slough, near Windsor, to Paddington Station, where "she was received with the most deafening demonstrations of loyalty and affection we have ever experienced" (*Times*, 14 June 1842). Queen Victoria was reportedly charmed with the experience, but Prince Albert found the speed somewhat disconcerting (Helmut Gernsheim and Alison Gernsheim, *Queen Victoria* (London: Longmans, 1959), 45).

8. *Bailey's New Handbook for Cheltenham* (1847) lists ten Sedan and Wheel-chair Stands in the town, but three were located very near Sarah Harriet's boardinghouse—on Imperial Square, on Montpellier Street, and at the Queen's Hotel. The fares for sedan chairs, fly carriages (drawn by men) and wheel chairs were all the same—sixpence per quarter mile (*Cheltenham Annuaire and Directory* (1843)).

9. Mme d'Arblay had bequeathed "the whole of my own immense Mass of Manuscripts collected from my fifteenth year . . . consisting of Letters Diaries Journals Dramas Compositions in prose and in rhyme" to her niece Charlotte Barrett "with full and free permission according to her unbiassed taste and judgment to keep or destroy them"—or to publish (according to a written memorandum) for her own and her eldest son's profit (*JL*, 12: 980, 973). The first five (of seven) volumes of the *Diary and Letters of Madame d'Arblay*, ed. by her niece [i.e., Charlotte Barrett], were published by Henry Colburn in 1842. In an "Introductory Memoir," Mrs. Barrett discusses her aunt's early life, bringing the reader up to the point at which the Journal begins, the publication of *Evelina*, trusting that "it cannot be derogatory to her beloved memory to make known her inmost thoughts" which reveal her upright character and can only redound to her credit.

10. According to the *Stranger's Guide through Cheltenham*, there were several public circulating libraries in 1843. Lee's Royal Library in High Street, the first established, "looks out into a pleasant shrubbery at the back." The Montpellier Library adjoining the Rotunda was "much resorted to during the summer season," while Williams's English and Foreign Library, forming part of the assembly rooms, had "a most extensive collection of works in every branch of English literature, history, biography, voyages and travels, novels, romances, &c. &c. . . . [and] a variety of the most popular productions of the continental press." Nearest to Sarah Harriet's boardinghouse was Lovesy's Library, opposite the Imperial Hotel, which specialized in theological works. The terms of subscription to these establishments ranged from two to five guineas per year (Davies, 138–41; *George Rowe's*, 15).

11. Lady Anne Wilbraham (L. 109, n. 17), the wife of Anna's brother, George.

171. [To Charlotte (Francis) Barrett]

Belgrave House, [Cheltenham], 1 February 1842
A.L.S., Barrett, Eg. 3705, ff. 53–54v

Belgrave House
Feby 1st 1842.

No, my dearest, I did not "quake from top to toe" when my first volume was published—and reason good—it was sent forth anonymously.[1] Thank you very much for the Copy you destine for me; I am only sorry old Colburn was not desired to direct it to me here & send it by the Coach. However, I will write to Maria Bourdois, begging her to let one of her "female Maids" take it to the Coach-Office, & see it booked.

I have no doubt that in the scrupulosity of your heart, you have eschewed all probability of giving the slightest uneasiness to any human being.[2] It would have been wrong to withhold from general knowledge my dear Sister's thoughts and feelings, so honourable to herself as I am sure they must be: so, pray do not reproach yourself on that account. My father, when waiting anxiously for her appearance the day he expected her to arrive from France, walked about the room, murmuring to himself—"My Honest Fanny!"[3] And I thought that one of the most delightful exclamations I had ever heard.

My kind Mrs Gregor has taken a house very near this till April. We have both had colds, & have been unable to meet as often as we wished,—but I hope as the weather mends, we shall mend. Meanwhile, they have little chariots here set upon three wheels, drawn by one man, like a Bath Chair, but with doors & windows, & warm rugs at the bottom, just like a grown up carriage, & when I do venture out, it is in one of these. There are now three of them, but the man I employ was the first to set one up, & a more comfortable vehicle never was devised. He charges no more than for a common open Chair.

We are not many now in the house, but we agree remarkably well, and play a little Whist, an' please you, almost every evening,—but only for six pence a rubber; & our <best man> one gentleman, tho' the best player, loses his six-pence as often as any of us.

I rejoyce to hear, dear Col. Henry got safely to Gibraltar. There have been such heavy gales, that I was in a fright for him.—He and his Jessy are treasures to each other, & to all who know them.

My best love to Barrett—I am very sorry his cough continues to plague him.

Remember me most kindly to Julia, whose babies[4] I should so like to see—And do not let Dick forget his old Aunty—And now, dearest, farewel, ever affectionately yours

S. H. B.

I am <u>afeared</u> Eliza[5] is still rather pompous—It is an old failing.—

1. Sarah Harriet had published her first novel, *Clarentine*, anonymously at the age of twenty-four (L. 13, n. 2).

2. In a missing letter, Charlotte Barrett seems to have expressed uneasiness at the publication of the *Diary and Letters of Madame d'Arblay*, and offered Sarah Harriet a complimentary copy. Charlotte had mentioned her editorial work to Crabb Robinson boasting that "the Burney family are already the most literary (she said the most authorial) in the country" (HCR, 16 Nov. 1841, Diaries).

Reaction in the reviews was mixed: appreciation for the vivid portrayal of the manners and society of an earlier era was tempered with criticism of its egotistical character. See e.g., *Athenaeum*, no. 756 (23 April 1842): 355–58 and further L. 173, n. 3; L. 178, nn. 1, 5, 6.

3. Probably in July 1812, when Sarah Harriet and her father expected Fanny's arrival at Chelsea after ten years' exile in France (see above L. 67). The anecdote is repeated in *Memoirs*, 3: 401.

4. Julia (Barrett) Thomas, whose husband James Thomas had died at Madras on 6 January 1840; she returned with her two children to England (*GM*, NS 13 (1840): 669).

5. Probably Elizabeth Wilbraham (L. 27, n. 5) (sister to Sarah's former pupil) who also knew Charlotte Barrett.

---

172. To [Gaetano Polidori][1]

Belgrave House, Cheltenham, 24 February [1842–43][2]
A.L.S., Sophia Smith

Belgrave House
Cheltenham
Feby 24th

My dear old Friend

Is it not singular that after so long a discontinuance of our former intercourse, I should have been prompted to address you once more by the very unexpected circumstance of making acquaintance with your son Henry[3]—him

<that> who altho' my Godson, I had never seen since the day of his Christening whilst still an infant in his Mother's arms?—I like him very much, and have derived great pleasure from the opportunity thus afforded me of obtaining answers to the many, many questions I had to ask him, concerning yourself, your wife, and, in short, your whole family.—

Now, perhaps, you may like to hear a little about my own proceedings since we met. I have been a wanderer, my dear friend, first in various parts of England, and then to Swizerland, whence, after some months, I crossed the Simplon, & repaired to beautiful Florence. There I staid half a year, & proceeded next to Rome in which I spent four or five months, delighted with every thing both Antique & Modern. When the warm weather begun, I went back to Florence, in which I spent four years, diversified only by short summer excursions to the Baths of Lucca. Part of the first year I passed in Italy, I was staying with our old friends the Misses Wilbraham. You probably know that Anna is now Mrs Grosvenor, having married General Grosvenor, who, though much older than her,[4] makes her very happy, and is so sweet tempered and amiable that it would be difficult to meet with any woman who would be otherwise than sincerely attached to him.—I see her now but seldom: but we correspond pretty frequently, & she is as steady in her regard as with so good a disposition might have been anticipated.

You may like to hear of another old friend of yours—Miss James—she is living with her two sisters in the prettiest part of Bath,[5]—is grown plump, looks very well, is as chearful and agreeable as formerly, and, I trust, a little less romantic.—

Basta così—I have exhausted all my little stock of matter likely to amuse you; & have now only to request a little favour of you. It is, that you would either commission a friend, or undertake yourself to procure me a copy of Carey's Dante, Italian on one side, & English on the other. I only want the Inferno.[6] The work, I know, is out of print, but it might I should suppose be met with second-hand, or lying perdue in some odd corner amongst the Bookinists, or such like.—Now, dear friend, as you are not (any more than myself) <u>very</u> young, I conjure you not to give yourself more trouble about the little commission than you can undertake without fatiguing or worrying yourself.—And so adieu. Pray present my best compliments to Mrs Polidori, who is, I am truly sorry to hear, so confirmed an invalid,[7] & believe me ever most sincerely

Yours

S. H. Burney.

I chattered Italian at Florence like a Magpie, and they all declared my pronunciation excellent. <u>That</u> I owe to you.

1. The letter is apparently addressed to Gaetano Polidori, Sarah's former Italian master (L. 30, n. 27), to whose wife SHB presents respects (see below). In 1843, he was living at 15 Park Village East, Regents Park (Rossetti, 2: 10).

2. The letter is dated conjecturally to 1842 or 1843, the two winters Sarah Harriet spent at Cheltenham after her return from Italy.

3. Polidori's seventh child, Henry Francis (1807–85), who changed his name to Polydore, was living in Cheltenham toward the end of his life (Rossetti, 1: 31; 2: 7, 340).

4. Anna (née Wilbraham), Sarah's former pupil, had married Gen. Thomas Grosvenor, twenty-six years her senior (L. 140, n. 1).

5. Miss James had also taken lessons from Polidori, who introduced her to Miss Burney (L. 34). In 1841 at Bath, Crabb Robinson met a Miss James, "an agreeable lady" who was an acquaintance of SHB (HCR, 29 Apr. 1841, Diaries). Bath directories list Misses James at 8 Lansdowne Place West in 1846, 1849, and 1852, but they were not at that address for either the 1841 or 1851 census.

6. The Rev. Henry Francis Cary (1772–1844) (*DNB*), translator of *The Inferno of Dante Alighiere* (London: James Carpenter, 1805–6). The Italian text was reprinted on the left, with an English translation in blank verse on the right.

7. Polidori's wife, Anna Maria (née Pierce) (L. 30, n. 29), suffered from an "internal complaint, and she never left her bedroom, and not often her bed," although she would live into her eighties (Rossetti, 1: 30–31).

---

173. [To Anna (Wilbraham) Grosvenor]

Belgrave House, Cheltenham, 18 May [1842][1]
A.L.S., Berg

May 18th
Belgrave House, East
Promenade, Cheltenham.

Only think, dearest, of its being considered by you as a treat to see my old face!—I promise you it would be a delightful one to me to see your "no-particular-age" one.—But—I have left Bath, I believe, permanently. So often have I been ill there, that I grew to loath it; and I certainly have been better, and have found this place more chearful, and in many respects more agreeable than poor old Bath has appeared to me for many years.—Oh, that you could but come through Cheltenham either going or coming from Plymouth!! But that, I fear, is impracticable.—Our dear Mrs Gregor, has been living opposite to me the whole winter, & only left yesterday, on her way into Cornwell. She talks of returning here next winter. My old friend, Emma Keate,[2] also lives at this place, &

sundry others, who, tho' not equally long known, are very dear & very kind to me. Could we but meet, I have lots of things to say to you, & double lots to enquire about, & to hear from you.—

Am charmed to find "The Diary" is approved by the General. The third vol: I think must be universally interesting—the first, to own the truth, contained too much about the <first> early appearance of Evelina, to please me.[3]—But it went down well with many people, & has caused a fresh demand for Evelina & Cecilia[4] at every Library in Cheltenham.—

Adieu, my own Anna;—It is hard to be obliged to renounce the happiness of seeing you: but you must make me amends by letting me hear from you oftener, & meanwhile believing me ever your warmest & most gratefully affectionate old friend

S. H. Burney.

Kindest remembrances to your Sisters.—

1. The letter is tentatively dated to 1842 by the place of writing, Cheltenham, and the recent publication of the first volumes of the *Diary and Letters of Madame d'Arblay.*

2. Emma Keate, whom Sarah had known over forty years before at Chelsea Hospital (L. 19, n. 5; L. 60). In 1842, a Miss Emma Keate was living in Cheltenham at 8 Lansdown Parade, while in 1847 she was listed at 14 Montpellier Spa buildings, from which she had moved before the 1851 census (*Pigot's Directory* (1842); Hunt & Co.'s *City of Gloucester and Cheltenham Directory & Court Guide* (1847)).

3. The egotism remarked by critics of the *Diary and Letters of Madame d'Arblay* was a source of embarrassment to the family. Crabb Robinson reports a conversation with Sarah Payne who was "very sensitive" on the subject and considered the publication to be "very injurious. . . . Mrs. Payne sensibly remarks that this is the great reproach to Mad d'Arblay that she should record nothing but the conversation that respected herself, be it praise or blame—and that nothing else even of Johnson's or Burke's conversation made any impression on her. It is not possible that they said nothing worth remembering, yet she seems to have remembered nothing" (HCR, 23 May 1842, Diaries). See further L. 175.

4. The first two (and most popular) novels of [Fanny Burney, later d'Arblay], *Evelina* (1778) and *Cecilia* (1782).

174. To Charlotte (Francis) Barrett

[Belgrave House], Cheltenham, 12 October [1842][1]
A.L.S. with typescript, Barrett, Eg. 3705, ff. 55–60

Wednesday
Octr 12th Cheltenham

How little did I imagine, my dear Charlotte, that you were now in England—and how very sincerely I lament the cause that has brought you so unexpectedly back. Let me at least hope that the worst is now over, and that you are fairly on the high road to convalescence.—As for me, I own to a few of the accompaniments of old age—such as troops of little ailments, in addition to the <one> that irreparable and unaccommodating one, y'clept seventy!—

At last, dear Charlotte, I understand all about the portrait of dear Mons. d'Arblay![2]—Its coming from you, never entered my head, thinking as I had reason to do, that you were abroad. Old King Cole I was pretty certain would never have done any thing half so handsome & good-natured;[3] so, at last, I laid it all upon Cousin Edward's shoulders, concluding that as he had condescended to copy other drawings of Mr Wm Lock's, he had likewise copied this, perhaps long ago, and at last bethought himself of the pleasure it might give me to become possessed of it. So, what did my I, but write to thank him for that same?—And what does he, but get Sophy[4] to write me word, the drawing was none of his doing, nor any <thing> of his sending. His eyes were weak, so that was the reason he did not write himself. Well, on hearing how innocent he was in this matter, I was quite in a wood, from which finding it impossible to extricate myself without help, I sat down quietly to await the arrival of some assisting hand,—and behold! it has arrived at last from the very quarter whence I least expected it, your supposed absence being considered.—Now that the discovery is made, let me, my dear Char, thank you cordially for so kind a gift, & at the same time, tell you how very much I admire the very <u>original</u> appearance of the clever <u>copy</u>.

Now tell my poor dear Barrett, that the best place he could possibly go to winter at, would be Guernsey.[5] I am told wonders of its soft & balmy air; of its excellent provisions, its almost incredible cheapness, its respectable English society, and its general beauty of scenery, as well as comfortable look of fertility.—All this, & much more, I have heard asserted by persons who have experienced the truth of every word I have written,—and I really do wish my dear

Barrett would try how far this description may be relied upon. One thing he would be sure to avoid,—the cutting East winds of Feb^{y} & March.

Yes, I liked the two young Burney girls very much, pretty little Ellen particularly. The Mother,[6] as you say, is better worth the rope that might hang her than heretofore: but, after all, she is no great shakes. Charles himself, I really think, one might almost learn to care for if one could but believe he cared for any thing but self & his immediate Co.

Do you ever see Richard & Caroline Burney?[7] They are in town, at N° 1. Cunningham Place. Of all the changes & metamorphosis I ever remember, I know of none greater than that of this funny pair. They are become positively sociable, at least I found them so during a week they spent at Leamington whilst I was there in the summer. And now they write to me, an' please you, pretty often—and he has sent me a dozen & half of Constantia wine which he brought from the Cape, and Game twice, & in short all manner of good-natured generosities; and that after 16 or 18 years non-intercourse of any kind. By the way, do you think a few bottles of Constantia would be a good cordial for my friend Barrett now & then? No wine is good for me, nor do I dare touch this or any other unless it be powerfully watered; and really it is a shame & a scandal to put water to Constantia. Tell Barrett it w^{d} give me the greatest pleasure to send him some, & for you too, my poor Charlotte, whose general debility it might tend to relieve,—& if you do not help me to make away with it, here it will be slumbering in its little hamper, till it falls into the hands of my executor.[8] So, have no scruples about it: but only just write me word how I had best send it, & I shall be delighted.

And now, dearest, good by,
Believe me ever affectionately yours

S. H. Burney

Love to Dicky & Judy.—

1. The letter is conjecturally dated to 1842 by the coinciding circumstances of SHB's living at Cheltenham, turning seventy, and heading her letter Wednesday, 12 October.

2. Probably a copy of the crayon drawing of Alexandre Piochard d'Arblay by the family friend, William Locke Jr., an amateur artist (printed opposite *JL*, 2: x). Although "dear to my Soul!" (*JL*, 11: 55), it is not mentioned specifically in Mme d'Arblay's will, but it may have come to Charlotte with the manuscripts, or to Dick Barrett as residuary legatee (*JL*, 12: 976–81).

3. Probably Charles Parr Burney, who also inherited some manuscripts (those of Dr. Burney) from Mme d'Arblay (*JL*, 12: 980). He also seems to have inherited the ambivalence which Sarah felt towards his father, Charles Burney Jr. (L. 84, n. 9).

4. Sophia and her sister Maria were living at 19 Wimpole Street in London; their uncle Edward lived nearby at 25 Clipstone (*JL*, 12: 943, n. 3).

5. Henry Barrett, thirty years older than his wife, was eighty-six.

6. Probably the two youngest daughters of Charles Parr Burney, Susan Sabrina (1818–74) and Ellen Hodgson (1820–1911). Their mother was Frances Bentley (née Young) (L. 76, n. 6; *JL*, 1: lxxii).

7. Sarah's nephew, Richard Burney (1790–1845), elder brother to Col. Henry Burney (L. 28, n. 10; L. 76, n. 2), had also joined the East India Co. in 1807, risen to Capt. (1824) in the Bengal Army and resigned (1825). He apparently acquired some wealth in India and returned to England on furlough 1817–22, taking a B.A. at Cambridge (1822). He was accompanied by some brothers and sisters, one of whom, Jane Caroline (1802–71), had been chaperoned by Esther Burney. All returned to India, but Richard came back to England in 1838 and was living with his sister at Cunningham Place, St. John's Wood, London. Jane Caroline Burney would ultimately inherit Sarah Harriet's property (Hodson; *Alumni Cantab.*; *JL*, 11: 16 and n. 11, 302, 316, 336–37; Appendix 1).

8. Sarah Harriet had made her will the previous month, dated 21 September 1842 (see Appendix 1), although Crabb Robinson had found her "looking over her will" a year and a half before (in April 1841) when he also thought she looked "thinner and older than before, but not less lively and agreeable" (HCR, 21, 25, 29 Apr. 1841, Diaries).

---

175. [To Henry Crabb Robinson]

[Belgrave House, Cheltenham], 9 December 1842
A.L.S., Dr. Williams'
Published: Morley
Endorsed: Miss Burney / Ans^{d} 3^{d} Mar 1843 *and* 9th Decr 1842 / Miss Burney / Ans^{d} 3^{d} March / The youngest Sister / of Mad dArblay / A very amiable & / also a clever person—
The pages are numbered.

Decr 9th 1842

My dear Friend

You really <u>are</u> a good boy, and deserve the heartiest thanks for the most entertaining, friendly & welcome letter I have received for many a long day. Your whole account of poor crazy Richmond[1] kept me upon the broad grin, & forced open my grey eyes to their fullest stretch whilst reading it. How well, & how concisely you have described him as "a compound of fanatical zeal, wrong headedness, and excessive vanity." Were I to try for a twelve month, I could say nothing that would characterize him better.—I am happy to add, that if he ever wrote to me, his letter never reached me. He must have been a sad bore to you, poor soul—but, after all, what was the bother you went through compared to the annoyance inflicted upon Milman?[2] "Think of that, Master Brook!"[3] think of having an Epic of Richmond's to read!—I really flatter myself it would have given me much less concern to lose 40 or 50£ by him (tho' not overburthened with cash) than to be compelled to read his, soi-disant poetry.—

You want to know what I think of the "Diary". I will tell you fairly & impartially.—After wading with pain and sorrow through the tautology and vanity of the first volume, I began to be amused by the second, and every succeeding volume has, to my thinking, encreased in power to interest & entertain.[4] That there is still considerable vanity I cannot deny. In her life, she bottled it all up, & looked and generally spoke with the most refined modesty, & seemed ready to drop if ever her works were alluded to. But what was kept back, and scarcely suspected in society, wanting a safety valve, found its way to her private journal. Thence, had Mrs Barrett been judicious, she would have trundled it out, by half quires, and even whole quires at a time.[5]—Great amends are occasionally made, by the unaffected high principle, the trust-worthy sense of honour in regard to what related to Madme Piozzi after she fell in love with Piozzi,[6] <and> also during the whole time of the King's illness,[7] <and> when the state of affairs in the Royal family would have furnished such delightful gossip: but all that, she forebore touching upon, & I do say that very few in her place would have had equal discretion. I hope you think Croker over-did his criticism of the early volumes.[8] It was coarsely & ill-temperedly done; and had it only been on account of her sex, and her unoffending and unenvious character, he should have treated her with less impertinence.

Do I know any thing about indigestion?[9] Lord help your silly head!—Am I not at this very time obliged to dine at two o'clock when all my comates dine at ½ 5?—Am I not afraid of the least bit of butter? Of pie-crust, of half the good things that come to table?—Do I dare touch malt liquor?—in short do I not endeavour to live by rule, & even then am I not often as head-achy & as little well as heart could wish?

One fine day about a month ago, into the drawing-room walked a young man rather short but with a good face & upright figure, who proved to be Arthur Layard, 9th Regiment; <who> he was with a friend here for a few days, & gave me great pleasure by remembering & calling upon me. I am not sure you know him, he not having been long returned from India.—His smile is a little like his father's, & that alone would be enough to warm my heart towards him.—Henry & Frederic I never knew, & of Edgar[10] I remember nothing but the clear, rich midnight blue of his beautiful eyes.

I am too old now to live by myself. My eye-sight will not always hold out for a whole day's reading, & when evening comes, I want a little society without being at the trouble of going out for it. This want is supplied where I now am, & not merely by womenkind (as at Bath) but by male as well as female boarders. I must own, a mere peticoat party is rarely worth putting one foot before the other for. There are exceptions no doubt; & could one get hold of some of the agreeable women I have heard you speak of, or from whose letters I have known you read little bits, then I should think females as valuable companions as men. But the fact is, many of the individuals in these Boarding-Houses, are, like myself, old Maids, who would have married if any body had asked them, but whose attractions were not sufficient to procure an offer. Of course they are not rich, else they would have been gladly snapt up, faults & all. But, when not <surprised> touchy, and ill-tempered, they are not seldom <are> eminently trivial, inquisitive, and empty-headed. Hap hazard men at such places, are usually in search of health. They may be vulgar, and they may be illiterate, but at all events, they can bring home some news from the Library,—and they know nothing about caps, & bonnets, & female bargains. Some of the gentlemen who have been here were really men of education, & of extensive general knowledge—but, alas! such have not been the majority. Of Irish folks the place is a perfect colony[11]—We have now but a small party, three of whom are from the Emerald Isle; Mr O'Flanagan[12] being at their head. I don't know whether I have spent [*spelt*] his name right: but it is one that has caught my fancy mightily; it sounds so like a name in a Comedy or Farce.

I could write volumes more in this chit-chat way: but I have other letters to answer, and am rather a slow hand at this sort of work. However, if you will stir up my idleness with another such amusing missive as your last, I promise to give you the best Rowland in my power for your Oliver[13]—So, farewel, & believe me truly & sincerely your affectionate S. H. Burney

1. Henry Crabb Robinson's traveling companion, now the Rev. James Cook Richmond (L. 126, n. 15), arrived in England 16 December 1841 with plans to become a missionary, perhaps on the strength of having served in that capacity in Maine and Illinois 1834–35 (*Appletons' Cyclopaedia*). Despite the warmth of their parting in Italy (L. 134, n. 14) twelve years previously, Robinson anticipated the visit of the young American with trepidation, did not invite him to stay, introduced him to nobody, and eventually forbade his calling more than once a week. He found the American encroaching and disapproved strongly of his missionary scheme. He also lent him money (£72 in total), which was repaid in full. When he heard of Richmond's departure for America (5 Mar. 1842), he exclaimed, "Oh be joyful! I am then got rid of a sad nuisance not likely to return again." He immediately reflected, however, that "his tale supplies an

amusing subject for a colloquial narrative" and recorded an evening party (20 Apr. 1842) when he related it "which amused them all." On 7 December 1842, he "sat down and wrote a long letter to Miss Burney giving an account of Richmond. This kept me there late." He was pleased by her reply, which he thought "a very pleasant letter. . . . I am glad I wrote her" (HCR, 9 Dec. 1841–7 Mar. 1842, passim; HCR, 20 Apr., 7, 12 Dec. 1842, Diaries).

2. Crabb Robinson's friend, Henry Hart Milman (1791–1868), an author of poetic dramas and a historian, who was professor of poetry at Oxford (1821–31) and Dean of St. Paul's (1849) (*DNB; Alumni Cantab.*; HCR, *Reminiscences*, 3: 147, 405 and passim). Richmond had brought with him a letter of introduction to Milman (HCR, 16 Dec. 1841, Diaries) and apparently some poetry to show him. The American would publish several poetic works including *College life* ([1845]), *The country schoolmaster in love* (1845), and *Metacomet: a poem, of the North American Indians* (1851). He also indulged in polemic under the pseudonym "Admonish Crime."

3. A Burney catchphrase (see *EJL*, 1: 81 and n. 3) from Shakespeare's *The Merry Wives of Windsor*, III, v, 113.

4. The first volume of the *Diary and Letters of Madame d'Arblay* records at length complimentary remarks about her first novel; the second volume includes the Streatham years and Fanny's first introduction to the King; and the third begins with her court appointment.

5. Robinson had been consulted by Mrs. Barrett in August 1842 "about the propriety of making omissions in a new edition" of the *Diary and Letters*. Approached again in November, he "had no other suggestion to make to her than that she should correct minute faults of style, the book being full of the most outrageous faults of language—obsolete words & affectations, quite ridiculous. For these she was more than judiciously thankful, & means to correct some of the more flagrant" (HCR, 7 Aug., 14 Nov. 1842, Diaries).

6. Hester Lynch (née Salusbury) Thrale (1741–1821), a close friend of Frances Burney, fell in love after her husband's death with the music master, Gabriel Mario Piozzi (1740–1809). Fanny opposed the match (as did initially Mrs. Thrale's daughters, their trustees and London society), and their friendship was broken upon the marriage 23 July 1784. Almost nothing of this was published in the *Diary;* for a fuller account, see *HFB*, 169–83.

7. As Second Keeper of the Robes (1786–91) to Queen Charlotte, Fanny had excellent opportunities for observation during the crisis of King George III's illness (1788–89). She was reticent even to her closest correspondents about the state of his health and the situation of the court, although not about a potential romance of her own that was developing in these extraordinary circumstances. Until the full text of the journals and letters of her court years is published, the material may be read in manuscript in the collections listed in the *Catalogue*, 99–123.

8. [John Wilson Croker] in the *Quarterly Review* 70 (1842): 243–87, ruthlessly exposed "Miss Burney's vanity and absurdity," attacked the egotism and exaggeration which he felt distorted her writing, and even accused the editor, Charlotte Barrett, of "treachery" in publishing an account of private conversations and society. He devoted very little space at the end of his review to her description of the royal family, which he found the least objectionable part of the first three volumes.

Robinson was "far from agreeing in the most contemptuous review in the Quarterly which declares it to be the worst book of the kind ever written and that Mad: d'Arblay was insincere and altogether an ordinary and very offensive person." He would soon be gratified to read a "capital review of Mad: d'Arblay by Macaulay in which he deservedly lashes Croker for his malignity and meanness" (HCR, 20 Aug. 1842, 23 Jan. 1843, Diaries; see further, L. 178).

9. On the day he wrote to SHB, Robinson noted in his diary some trouble with his digestion and his avoidance of milk (HCR, 7 Dec. 1842, Diaries).

10. Arthur John Layard, a young man of twenty-two, who had been in the service four years and would rise to the rank of Captain before his death at age thirty-five (*GM*, NS 44 (1855): 441). Crabb Robinson also met him about this time and commented, "he is like his brother, [Henry]" (HCR, 5 Mar. 1843, Diaries).

Sarah had known Arthur as a boy in Florence with his parents, Henry Peter John and Marianne Layard (L. 138, n. 9; L. 142). His younger brother, Edgar, had been with him but not the elder two, Henry Austen (L. 160, n. 13), and Frederick Layard, who were at school in England (L. 139, n. 8).

11. Perhaps because at least one of the hostesses, Catherine Haydon, was an Irishwoman. On the night of the 1851 census there would be thirteen boarders and eight servants enumerated in the Belgrave Boarding House; five of the boarders and two of the servants were Irish.

12. Mr. O'Flanagan, whose surname is among the hundred most common surnames in Ireland, has not been traced (Edmond MacLysaght, *Irish Families* (Dublin: Hodges, Figgis, 1957)).

13. Referring to the prolonged and evenly matched battle between two of Charlemagne's knights, "to give a Roland for an Oliver" means to give as good as one gets. The expression was used by various writers including Walter Scott, *The Antiquary* (1816), Ch. 35, and in fact passed into the language (*OED*).

---

176. To Anna (Wilbraham) Grosvenor

[Belgrave House, Cheltenham], [c. January]–2 February [1843][1]
A.L.S., Berg

I have seldom, dear Annie, read a letter with greater gladness than your last. No one, I am very sure, will make, (in the first place), a more just use of the property in question, nor, (in the second), a more charitable one. Long may you live, dearest friend, to prove the truth of this assertion,—and meanwhile, accept my most cordial congratulations.

O, Annie—they are gone now, but we have had such a charming Scotch family boarding here lately, that I cannot describe to you how I learnt to love them.

Their names Thurburn. They have a beautiful place, a sort of Castle, in full sight of the Grampions, of which the daughter shewed me a sketch.[2]—They have moreover, a young Abyssinian, or Nubian servant, purchased from motives of compassion when ten years old by a brother of Mr Thurburn[3] who saw him in the Slave Market at Cairo, and sent him to Scotland as a present to his sister-in-law. He is now 17. She has had him thoroughly instructed, Christened & confirmed. He keeps his original name of Selim, and wears, on week days, the dress of his country (a very becoming one, I assure you) and, on Sundays, a livery Jacket & trowsers. A better creature—more honest, affectionate, and true, I have seldom heard of. He sings scotch ballads like a nightingale, & we have had him frequently in the drawing-room for the sake of hearing him. He has no mauvaise honte, and no conceit,—but sings because his sweet mistress tells him to do so.—His hand writing is that of a gentleman, & he spells as well as you or I. When Mr Thurburn is indisposed, which is not seldom, poor soul! Selim sits by his bed-side & reads to him. He waits at table incomparaably [*incomparably*],—and as far as he has been taught, does every thing well.—As for Mrs Thurburn I have no words to express my liking for her. She is the gentlest, the most unselfish, the most quietly well-informed, & the most interesting both in looks and manner of any person I have for a long time been so fortunate as to encounter: but, alas! she is gone.

Feb^r^ 2^d^

Dearest Annie—I have not been very well lately, & this letter has been forgotten to be finished, for which I am truly ashamed. I begun it the very day your welcome tidings arrived, & after it was nearly finished had to prepare for a drive in a friend's carriage—came home, cold & miserable—was obliged to doctor myself next day, and till I just now opened my letter-case, never recollected that it contained what I had so fully meant to send to you, and had sat down to write with so much glee[4]—

Forgive my neglect, dearest, & believe me ever most truly your grateful & affectionate

S. H. Burney

1. The letter is tentatively dated 1843 by the handwriting, the tone and the situation (living in a mixed boardinghouse), which belong to the last few years of Sarah's life at Cheltenham. As she was writing another letter to Mrs. Grosvenor between 30 January and 6 February 1842 (L. 170) and she would die early in 1844, the intervening year seems the most likely.

2. The only seat of a Thorburn family filling this description in 1843 was that of the Rev. Joseph Thorburn (1799–1854), who occupied the Forglen Manse near Turriff, Banff, Scotland. Ordained in 1829, he became the minister of Forglen in 1831, but joined

the Free Church in 1843. He married on 15 November 1831 Catherine (d. 26 Aug. 1874), younger daughter of Alexander Brown, Lord Provost of Aberdeen. Their only daughter, Catherine (b. 27 June 1834), was then eight (James Findlay, *Directory to Gentlemen's Seats, Villages, &c. in Scotland* (Edinburgh, W. P. Kennedy, [1843]; Hew Scott, *Fasti Ecclesiae Scoticanae*, 2nd ed., vol. 6 (Edinburgh: Oliver and Boyd, 1926), 252–53).

3. Possibly Alexander Thorburn (c. 1796–1864), who lived in Alexandria, Egypt, but left before 1862 and died in Dinan, France (*GM*, 3rd ser. 12 (1862): 220; 3rd ser. 17 (1864): 258).

4. Having passed the age of seventy, Sarah Harriet shows a weakening of memory that is demonstrated in other ways, such as more frequent slips of grammar and spelling.

---

177. [To Henry Crabb Robinson]

[Belgrave House], Cheltenham, 4 March 1843
A.L.S., Dr. Williams'
Published: Morley
Endorsed: Miss Burney / ab^{t} the expence of a journey / to Italy

March 4th 1843
Cheltenham

My dear friend—Let me plunge at once into the very heart of the small matter of business you have written to me about.[1] All I remember <about> concerning my fourteen-year-old journey, is this. I left London in one of Emery's clumsy coaches, which set out from some office in Regent Street. Emery is a well known proprietor of Coaches, usually residing at Lausanne, <who> whence he sends his voitures to any part of the world, under the direction of a decent, respectable Conducteur, to whom, at the end of the journey, you make a present, more or less, according as he may have been civil & attentive. The main expence of the distance from London to Lausanne, amounted as well as I can remember, to £18. That includes every thing.—You pay nothing on the road,—beds, meals &c, &c, every thing is ordered & defrayed for you.—Your baggage is past through the Custom-House by the Conducteur, to whom you deliver your keys, & who stands by during the examination of your trunks, whilst you are refreshing yourself at the Inn or Hotel where you are to sleep. I never undertook a journey in the prosecution of which I was so perfectly un-annoyed by trouble of any kind. To be sure, you must get up early: but that I do not mind—and, moreover, direct that the things, Carpet bag, for instance, you want every night, may be put at the top of the luggage: but that understood, you have nothing more to bother yourself or the Conducteur about.

There, friend, I have told you all I can remember. My further proceedings from Lausanne to Florence, & thence to Rome were carried on in much the same manner,—only with Italian drivers, with wretched Italian horses, and most tremendously hard seats!

Yes, dear—do come amongst us for the week you talk of. We always have some inmate worth either knowing, or laughing at; and the place itself is really very chearful for those who have outlived romantic pastorality. Such, I freely confess, is decidedly my case,—and Cheltenham, with its gaily-dressed visitors sauntering about, its shewy shops, its Musical Band at the Pump-room, its dashing equipages, and Scarlet-coated hunting gentry, amuses me almost as much as an ever-shifting magic lanthorn.[2]

Emery's Office, or that of some other Voiturier, might, I should think, be heard of at the Swiss Hotel in Leicester Square;[3] & there are Swiss Eating-Houses in that neighbourhood, where he might be known.—Try.

We have neither Bigots, nor careless infidels in our party: but a sober, rational set, seeking to do their duty; & saying less than they do, particularly in the way of alms-giving. Coals, & good nourishing Soups, are dispensed by means of tickets that are subscribed for; and the receivers seem very glad of the relief they afford.—We are not apt to enter into controversy, albeit we have a Catholic Boarder, who might, if she chose, set herself up mighty high. She is the widow of Judge Day, the friend of Grattan,[4] and of all the leading men in Ireland in Grattan's time. Of course, his name and fame cannot be unknown to you.

The Paynes are now at Rome—Sarah is a good correspondant, & a very entertaining one. I have lately heard from her, and written her a long answer, of such stuff as I could conjure up.

I am sorry for what you tell me of the prohibition imposed poor Southey's daughter;[5] let me hope it was more by the physician's order than by the stepmothers unauthorized command. But—at any rate, it has been a most disastrous connection,—and I know not who can help wishing it had never taken place.—

Farewell dear friend—Spit a note at me whenever you can find time or goodwill. The "Inheritance" is excellent, & perhaps, Miss Ferrier's best[6]—at least, it has left the best taste in my mouth: but I quite, & always did, prefer Miss Austen. Yours faithfully

S. H. Burney.

1. Crabb Robinson had apparently written to Sarah Harriet, inquiring about her journey to Italy in 1829. On receiving this reply, he sent it on to a female correspondent, "not that it will be of any use whatever as a guide to you because it does little more than shew you how cheaply persons may travel whose circumstances and position in society require & enable them to travel as Miss Burney did." However, he assured his correspondent that he wouldn't place her in "that class" (HCR to Miss Fenwick, 6 Mar. 1843, Dr. Williams' Library).

2. Cheltenham had grown steadily since the discovery of a mineral spring led to the opening of the first Montpellier Pump Room in 1809 (replaced by J. B. Papworth's elegant Rotunda in 1825). Several new spas were established, and a building boom began as the population increased tenfold from 1800 to 1841 (Gwen Hart, 161–76; Davies, 16–26). A contemporary describes the day's amusements which began early when "a gay and fashionable assemblage, arrayed in elegant morning costume" would assemble to drink the waters "to the delightful harmony of the fine bands. . . . This lively scene lasts nearly three hours. At length the music concludes with the national anthem. This is the signal for a general move homeward. . . . As the day advances, the libraries and reading rooms are gradually filled with subscribers . . . the clubs and the billiard rooms are also frequented: and at a later period, the principal streets and fashionable drives are enlivened by groups of accomplished and elegant equestrians of both sexes" (S. Y. Griffith, *Griffith's History of Cheltenham and its vicinity*, 3rd ed. (London: Longman, Hurst, 1838), 20–21).

3. Possibly the well-known Sablonière Hotel, located on the east side of Leicester Square (No. 30), part of which was formerly William Hogarth's house. The d'Arblays had stayed there on their way to and from France (Wheatley, 2: 383; 3: 196–97; *JL*, 7: 485, n. 2 and passim). Emery is not listed in the London directories, although apparently his coaches left from Regent Street near Leicester Square.

4. Henry Grattan (1746–1820), Irish patriot and orator, and Robert Day (b. c. 1744). A fellow student of Trinity College, Dublin (B.A. 1766; LL.B. and LL.D. 1780), Day later shared Grattan's chambers at the Middle Temple, was called to the Irish Bar in 1774, and ultimately became a Judge. He remained a lifelong friend and supporter of Grattan (George Dames Burtchaell and Thomas Ulick Sadleir, eds., *Alumni Dublinenses*, rev. ed., 2 vols. (Dublin: Alex. Thom., 1935); Henry Grattan, *Memoir of the Life and Times of the Rt. Hon. Henry Grattan* (London: Henry Colburn, 1839), 1: 117–19).

5. Robinson had heard from the Wordsworths in 1840–41 that Mrs. Southey did not allow Southey's daughter, Kate, "to attend on her father" nor to visit him more than once a week (HCR, 28 Dec. 1840, 3, 16 Feb. 1841, Diaries). In early February 1843, Robert Southey had an apoplectic seizure and would die on 21 March. His death, however, did not end the differences in the family, which overshadowed the funeral (Simmons, 204–6).

6. The second novel of [Susan Edmonstone Ferrier (1782–1854)], the Scottish novelist, *The Inheritance*, first appeared in 1824. In 1841, Ferrier sold the copyright of her novels to the publisher Richard Bentley, who brought out a corrected edition (*DNB*). Robinson had finished reading it on 7 February 1843 and thought it "full of talent—hardly equal to Miss Austen however, nor even Miss Edgeworth" (HCR, 7 Feb. 1843, Diaries).

178. To Anna (Wilbraham) Grosvenor

[Belgrave House, Cheltenham], 9 March 1843
A.L.S., Berg

March 9th 1843

I am desired, dearest Annie, to return Mr Macauley's letter[1] to you—and see how obedient I am.—Charlotte Barrett sent it to me; & I think it was either from her, or Fanny Raper from whom I heard how kindly active you had been in canvassing for Dr Kingston.[2] You are a good soul!

"I thought so once, and now
I know it!"[3]

I am sorry, methinks, that two of my Nieces should have married young Physicians. The slowness with which men get on in that profession is proverbial. Poor dear Julia, Mrs Barrett's Julia, I mean, has given up her widow's pension, to make this improvident match; for Dr Maitland[4] I am told, was her first love. Alas, I am past the age of admiring such romantic constancy. However, her children by Mr Thomas, are, I believe, well provided for; so that reconciles me a good deal to what I should else be sadly tempted to consider as a folly.

I think I said in one of my recent scrawls all I had to say concerning Mr Macauley's Review: every part of which I like mainly, except his severe mention of the Royal Family, and his unnecessary critique of my Sister's Life of Dr Burney.[5] Surely Croker had cut that up quite bitterly enough;[6]—I cannot see why it need have been brought forward again.

Whether you are at Brighton, or, wherever you may be, I suppose it may be best to direct this to your London House. So, dearest, having nothing more to communicate save love and good wishes to yourself and Sisters, believe me ever faithfully and gratefully

Your
S. H. Burney

1. Thomas Babington Macaulay (1800–59) had apparently been asked by Charlotte Barrett to respond to Croker's attack on the *Memoirs of Doctor Burney* but declined (in a letter dated 21 November 1839), perhaps because he believed it "deserved its doom" (see n. 6 below; *JL*, 12: 796, n. 7; *HFB*, 458–62). In her instructions to her executors, Mme d'Arblay said she "w[d] have gladly accepted my vindication from his hand" (*JL*, 12: 976). After Croker's equally virulent criticism of the *Diary and Letters* (L. 175, n. 8), a similar request may have been made to which Macaulay replied on 28 October 1842 that "I cannot engage to write as an advocate, that I must speak my mind freely, and that I must notice, I hope without asperity or malevolence, the faults as well as the merits of Madame D'Arblay" (cited in *JL*, 12: 968–69, n. 5). This may be the letter that was sent to Sarah Harriet. In the end, Macaulay's review of the *Diary and Letters* would give a fairly sympathetic assessment of Mme d'Arblay's work (n. 5 below).

2. Frances Raper's only child, Catherine Minette, had married c. June 1832 Peter Nugent Kingston (1805–82), the nephew of Henry Barrett (*JL*, 12: 803, n. 2; L. 45, n. 1). Having taken his M.D. degree at Edinburgh in 1831, he was appointed to Westminster Hospital in 1843 (G. H. Brown, comp., *Lives of the Fellows of the Royal College of Physicians of London, 1826–1925*, vol. 4 of Munk's Roll (London: Printed for the College, 1955)). Charlotte Barrett, it seems, petitioned those of her friends who might be able to advance the career of the young doctor (see CFBt to Cornelia Cambridge, [n.d.], Berg).

3. The lines composed by John Gay (1685–1732) for his epitaph, "Life is a Jest, and all Things show it; / I thought so once, but now I know it," were placed upon his monument in Poets' Corner, Westminster Abbey.

4. Two years a widow, Julia (Barrett) Thomas married on 5 November 1842 Charles Maitland (c. 1815–66), who had graduated M.D. from Edinburgh in 1838. However in 1848, aged thirty-three, he would matriculate at Oxford and take his B.A. (1852) (*GM*, NS 19 (1843): 86; 3rd ser. 16 (1864): 403; *List of Graduates . . . Edinburgh*; *Alumni Oxon.*; *JL*, 1: lxxii–lxxiii).

5. Macaulay did review the *Diary and Letters of Madame d'Arblay* in the *Edinburgh Review* 76 (1843): 523–70, giving a general overview of her life and work; he defends her against Croker's charge of vanity and mocks him for his ungentlemanly conduct—"to twit a lady with having concealed her age" (537). However, he agrees with Croker in deploring her later style and perceives a progressive deterioration in her writing that he attributes in part to the pernicious influence of Johnson. A thorough Whig, he views the court appointment with abhorrence as abject slavery. Finally, noting that her characters display exaggerated "humours" qualities, he is "forced to refuse to Madame D'Arblay a place in the highest rank of art" (562–63).

6. In his review of Madame d'Arblay's *Memoirs of Doctor Burney* in the *Quarterly Review* 49 (1833): 97–125, John Wilson Croker had ridiculed her style and mocked her vanity (L. 145, n. 6). Macaulay too condemned the *Memoirs* unequivocally, written in "the worst style that has ever been known among men. . . . They are very bad; but they are so, as it seems to us, not from a decay of power, but from a total perversion of power" (524, 564).

179. To Charlotte (Francis) Barrett

Suffolk House, Cheltenham, 16[–17]July [1843][1]
A.L.S., Barrett, Eg. 3705, ff. 49–50v

July 16th
Suffolk House
Cheltenham.

Here am I, dearest Charlotte, at Cheltenham and not at Cheltenham—that is to say, I am at its outskirts, on a visit for change of air, preparatory to going further afield, if able, when the weather takes up, and becomes more genial, which, to say the truth, now appears to be its intention. I came here to my dear Mrs Gregor for a week, and I have been with her a month all but three days! Hers is a large, detatched house, with a delightful garden, & the first change certainly was favorable to me. I have had sundry little ailments however since, such as often belong, I suppose, to three score years and ten, & which neither air, nor any thing else can remove in this world.—Such as I am, however, very gladly would I accompany you to Malvern if you can put up with a companion deaf, weak, short-breathed, & incapable of walking her own length up any sort of rise. I grunt as little as I can, however, and am always ashamed of myself when I grunt at all: for, thanks to God, I suffer no severe pain (which so many do) and, generally speaking, I have good nights.

Basta così.

I have never had thoughts of inviting any of the young Burney fry, for I really am no longer a fit companion for such like folks,—and being unable to ramble about with them out of doors, or to make myself very entertaining to them at home, I should probably either have taken my Maid with [*me*], and gone alone, or have given up Malvern altogether. But now your letter has given me a fillip, & if you really think it will not be bad for your spirits to be with an old helpless cretur such as I am become, I am perfectly agreeable to agree to your scheme, whenever you chuse to put it in execution. You leave it to my determination whether to meet me at Malvern, or come to Cheltenham & go there with me. I prefer the last. You could either have my Maid's tidy little bed in my room for a night, or a bed in a separate room; for the Belgrave Boarding House is not very full just now.—My visit here will now be over in a very few days. Mrs Gregor, poor dear, has caught a violent rheumatic cold, & at present only gets up to go into a warm bath, & have her bed made, when she steps into it again, and it is imperative to keep her as quiet as possible. She is somewhat better to-day, & when I see her restored to more ease and comfort, I shall take my leave.—

With regard to your Maid, mine will be proud to assist you in any way she can: but do as you like. A lodging, I think, may suit us best, in which the people of the house, or their servant will chuse to do our little cooking; and that being the case, I think two ladies maids will be more than we should know how to find employment for. As it is, I let mine do as little for me as I can; for except I am ill, I hate to be toddled after & waited upon, altho' I feel the comfort of knowing I can have help if I want it.

I am very glad Julia is so well again. Give my kind love to her, & believe me ever dearest Charlotte, your affectionate old Aunty

S. H. Burney

You will let me know what time will suit you best for our trip. Any time will do for me after this week,—to-day is Monday.

1. The letter has been conjecturally dated to 1843 by SHB's trip to Malvern from Cheltenham with Mrs. Barrett (see below L. 180). The Monday of the postscript would probably be Monday 17 July 1843.

180. [To Henry Crabb Robinson]

7 Victoria Terrace, Leamington, 17 September 1843
A.L.S., Dr. Williams'
Published: Morley
Endorsed: Septr 1843 / Miss Burney / Youngest Sister of / Mad: Darblay / she died 1844 / at Cheltenham / a clever & very / amiable person / H. C. R.

Septr 17th 1843
7. Victoria Terrace
Leamington

My dear Friend

I have been upon the tramp ever since the 8th of August, and who do you think with? Why, with my kind and agreeable Niece, Mrs Barrett. She came to see me at the Belgrave Boarding-House Cheltenham, & after a week spent there, proceeded with me to Malvern. The "Water Doctors" have made that place so popular, that no sort of lodging was to be had, either good or bad: so, we staid one week at an Hotel, (the Bellevue) beautifully situated, but a trifle or so dearer than we found convenient; and therefore removed from thence to this handsome, quiet town, where my Niece, having been unwell-ish for some time, has consulted Dr Jephson,[1] who, certainly, has done her good, but though he sees her only once a week (which shews, I think, that he does not keep her for mere greediness) is unwilling to let her go, till <his medecines> he sees that his medecines have taken, & are taking their intended effect. Such being the case, I am unwilling to leave her here by herself, first, because we share the expence of lodging & housekeeping, and next, because I love her, and enjoy the opportunity of having so much of her society.—It grieves me however to think that I may, by prolonging my stay here, lose the pleasure of seeing you at Cheltenham; for I cannot possibly tell to a certainty how much longer we may be kept. I should suppose that another week or ten days may set us free, & I now begin seriously to wish it may be so.

You ask after my health. It has been (for me) very well behaved ever since May.—Shall I write to you a dull little line (the ditto of this) when I get back to Belgrave-House, East Promenade, Cheltenham? Or, shall you be "travelling, travelling all the world o'er?"[2] & therefore out of the way of receiving it?[3]

Mrs Barrett desires her best regards, and I have no more to say than this: read Lady Vavasour's "Last Tour, and First Work, or a visit to the Baths of Wildbad, & Rippoldsau".[4]—It is only one Volume, & is very entertaining and often clever, & lively, with considerable general information. Campbell's Editorship of the "Life of Frederick the Great"[5] has also amused me much—So now, dear friend, good by, & may we meet ere long in comfort & health—Ever faithfully yours

S. H. Burney

How do your flirtations go on with Lady Blessington?[6]

1. Probably a member of a distinguished Leamington family, the surgeon Henry Jepson (1797–1887), F.R.C.S. (1853), who studied at Guy's and St. Thomas's Hospitals. A Henry Jephson was licensed as an apothecary at Leamington Spa on 17 May 1823 and married at Leamington Priors on 21 February 1824 Anne Eliza Geldart (*A List of Persons who have obtained Certificates . . . as Apothecaries* (London: Gilbert and Rivington, 1840); *Plarr's Lives of the . . . Surgeons;* IGI).

2. Probably recalling her father Charles Burney's "recital of the favourite couplets which the good nurse Ball most frequently sang to him at her spinning wheel; and which he especially loved to chaunt, in imitating her longdrawn face, and the dolorous tones of her drawling sadness:

Good bye, my dear neighbours! My heart it is sore,
For I must go travelling all the world o'er.
And if I should chance to come home very rich,
My friends and relations will make of me mich;
But if I should chance to come home very poor,
My friends and relations will turn me out of door,
After I have been travelling, travelling, travelling, all the world o'er.
(*Memoirs*, 1: 5)

3. On 15 September 1843, Henry Crabb Robinson had written to SHB to inquire if there were a room in her boardinghouse at Cheltenham "intending at all events to spend a week with her." After receiving her reply, he wrote, "the Cheltenham magnet is withdrawn—Miss Burney is at Leamington." However, he would call at the Belgrave House, Cheltenham on 25 September 1843 on his way to Hereford, but found she was still away. On 13 February 1844, he would write "a longish letter to Miss Burney relating the circumstances of my journey to Hereford . . . so that I could not return by way of Cheltenham and giving her an account of my occupations." This letter would arrive too late, making him regret his procrastination; see below (HCR, 15 Sept., 8 Oct. 1843, 13, 18 Feb, 1844, Diaries; *The Correspondence of Henry Crabb Robinson with the Wordsworth Circle (1808–1866)*, ed. Edith J. Morley (Oxford: Clarendon Press, 1927), 1: 523–29).

4. Lady Anne Vavasour (d. 7 June 1845), *My Last Tour and First Work; or, a Visit to the Baths of Wildbad and Rippoldsau* (1842).

5. [Frederick Shoberl (1775–1853)], *Frederick the Great, his Court and Times*, ed. Thomas Campbell (London, 1842–43).

6. Marguerite (née Power) Farmer (1789–1849) married as his second wife on 16 February 1818 Charles John Gardiner (1782–1829), 2nd Viscount Mountjoy (1798), created Earl of Blessington (1816). Author of *Conversations with Lord Byron* (1834) and *The Idler in Italy* (1839–40), she was a fashionable hostess in London society. Robinson was first introduced to her on 28 September 1832 by W. S. Landor (Gibbs; *DNB; Lady Blessington at Naples*, ed. Edith Clay (London: Hamish Hamilton, 1979), 151–59; HCR, *Reminiscences*, 3: 12).

181. [To Anna (Wilbraham) Grosvenor]

[7 Victoria Terrace], Leamington, 29 September–5 October 1843
A.L.S., Berg

Leamington
Septr 29th 1843

My ever kind & dear Anna

When you think me graceless enough to call you "faithless," you do me especial wrong, for of you, dearest, it might almost be said, that she

. . . . amongst the faithless
Alone was faithful found."[1]

And still I have another crow to pick with you. You say your letter must appear dull to me because "it is only full of me and mine." Now, that is exactly the stuffing my turkey. <would> likes the best. It would not care a pin for messed-up rareties made out of other peoples adventures and affairs. What I wanted was exactly what you have given me—an account of your own whereabouts, and howabouts.—I heartily rejoice to hear your dear General is so much better, & that Dr Holland[2] (of whom I think so highly) is his medical adviser. With quiet, and a careful regimen, dearest Anna, you may have the comfort of seeing him quite himself again—and most earnestly do I wish it may be so.

Your niece Emily's marriage I saw in the Paper, & could not imagine where another Captn Stopford[3] had started from; nay, I was almost tempted to think there was some mistake. The marriage, as you describe the bridegroom, is likely to turn out a very happy one,—nothing will contribute to it more than his being, as you say, of a fine temper. That is worth all other outward advantages—and so, dearest, you have found it, & are well entitled to speak avec connoisance de cause.

Since I last wrote, I have had the pleasure of a long inmate-ing with my Niece Charlotte Barrett. She came to me in the first place for a week or ten days <to> at my Boarding House, at Cheltenham. Thence we went to Malvern: but the cold-water doctors have so filled that place, that no lodging was to be had, either good, bad, or indifferent. We waited one week at an Hotel, hoping some of the Watered folks would go away: but others followed in such double quick time, that we gave the thing up for a bad job: paid our week's sojourn at the Hotel, and marched off to Leamington. Here Charlotte, whose general health, and eyes, particularly, have caused her much unwellness for some time past, has consulted Dr Jephson, who certainly has improved her strength & done her considerable good: but the poor strained eyes have not proportionally profitted by his advice, & when she passes through town in her way to Brighton, she means, I know, to see & to consult Dr Holland. So be very careful, dear Anna, not to say any thing to him about her having applied to Jephson.—We purpose leaving this place on Tuesday next Octr 3d

Well—here is October the 5th—We did leave Leamington on the 3d and it was with many a heartache I parted from my kind Charlotte. She is now for a few days in London, near Dr & Mrs Kingston, & Mrs Raper who lives with them.[4] I am at my old quarters, which I thought well enough of till I had been upwards of two months with my Niece, talking over old family jokes and nonsense, & reviving long suspended relationship intercourse I now feel quite forlorn. And yet, there are some valuable folks around me. None more so than kind Mrs Gregor who has (perhaps I told you before) taken a house in this place for a year. She is now however, in town whither she went on business, & has been detained by illness. Her sister, also, has been very seriously unwell, and poor Tranick[5] (do you remember her)? has almost sunk under the fatigue of sitting up with her. These are sad warnings to us three, for there is very little difference between their ages and mine.

Now I will quit these dreary subjects, and tell you of a few nice books for you to read & like—The 1st Vol. of Campbell's Life of Frederic the Great. The others I did not enjoy so much. They are chiefly about the seven year's war: but there are parts even of that, which interested me very much.—Then "Stevenson's Central South America."[6] That is not the full title, but I forget exactly how the book is called.—I suppose you know the Life of Lord Howe.[7] I was delighted with it; and it is only in one volume. There, if you chuse to try any of the above, I think I have cut you out work enough to last a good while. Harriet Crewe, who, like yourself, has been <my> "faithful found" to me, came to Leamington & spent a cozey evening with me the day previous to my departure. She is now on a visit at Newbold, Lord Somerville's place near Leamington. Lady Somerville was a Miss Hayman,[8] niece to the witty Miss Hayman, who once upon a time was in the Household of The Princess of Wales,[9] but I know not in what capacity. Harriet Crewe and Fanny Hayman were girls together, & still keep up their intimacy, tho' one is the Mother of six children & the other has turned Roman Catholic. How little did they think at their outset in life, that their paths would be so different! I will say this for Harriet, that however she may have estranged herself from our Church, she has never estranged her heart from us. Lady Somerville has given her a white cornelian seal with a Cat deeply intagliod[10] (is there such a word?) upon it, in allusion to her having become <the Catholic> a Cat—holic!—Poor Hal can only squeeze out a faint smile thereat, but it has not made her angry, albeit she hated Cats long before this trying joke was past upon her.

And now dearest Annie, farewell. May all the good I wish you be showered upon your head! And may you ever believe me your most truly grateful & affectionate

S. H. Burney

1. "So spake the Seraph Abdiel faithful found, / Among the faithless, faithful only hee," John Milton, *Paradise Lost* (1667), Bk. 5, ll. 893–94.

2. Dr. Henry Holland (L. 113, n. 3), the fashionable London physician who had treated Sarah Harriet in 1828. He also tended Mme d'Arblay and was remembered in her will for a ring of mourning (*JL*, 12: 963, 981).

3. Emily Anna Wilbraham (c. 1820–62), second daughter of Anna's brother William (L. 119, n. 4), had married 31 August 1843 Capt. Robert Fanshawe Stopford (1811–91), later Rear-Admiral. He was son of Admiral Sir Robert Stopford and cousin to Edward Stopford who had married Emily's elder sister three years previously (L. 168, n. 2) (*GM*, NS 20 (1843): 537; 3rd ser. 13 (1862): 653; Burke under Courtown; O'Byrne).

4. Charlotte's cousin, Frances Raper, evidently lived with her daughter, Catherine Minette, and her son-in-law, Dr. Peter Nugent Kingston (L. 178, n. 2).

5. Mrs. Tranick (or Trannick as in L. 103) has not been identified but seems to have been an upper servant of Mrs. Gregor's.

6. W. B. Stevenson (fl. 1803–25) (*DNB*), *A Historical and Descriptive Narrative of Twenty Years' Residence in South America* (1825).

7. Sir John Barrow, Bt. (1764–1848) (*DNB*), *The Life of Richard Earl Howe, K.G., Admiral of the Fleet, and General of Marines* (1838).

8. Frances Louisa (c. 1804–85), the only daughter of John Hayman, had married 3 September 1833 Kenelm Somerville (1787–1864), 17th Baron Somerville (1842), whose seat was Newbold Comyn in Warwickshire (Burke; Gibbs; *GM*, 3rd ser. 17 (1864): 670).

9. Ann Hayman had served as subgoverness to Princess Charlotte and later Keeper of the Privy Purse to the Princess of Wales, and was given a pension on the civil list of £266 in 1823 (Thea Holme, *Caroline* (London: Hamish Hamilton, 1979), 55–58; *The Extraordinary Black Book*, 451).

10. Engraved with a pattern or design (*OED*).

182. To Charlotte (Francis) Barrett

Belgrave House, [Cheltenham], 13 October 1843
A.L.S., Barrett, Eg. 3705, f. 61–v

Octr 13th 1843
Belgrave House

Do not be frightened, dearest Char:—I by no means intend always to answer you by return of Post: but I have had given me such a mountain of Queen's heads,[1] that I got quite impatient to send them off, for fear of mistaking them for rubish, & putting them behind the fire. They were collected for some other body, who has now cried out Basta così, and then I was asked whether I knew any body who would accept them; so, I thought you might still be such a body, and thereupon determined to favour you with them.—

I heard from Miss Parr[2] to-day; She speaks highly of her Physician; says "he is very kind & feeling, but gives me little hope of a speedy recovery, tho' he is still very sanguine with respect to my ultimate recovery, but my being in such an exceedingly weak state, will make it very tedious." Poor soul! I heartily pity her.

You dearest of kind Charlottes! How I thank and love you for thinking of my pretty little miniature Squirrels! Only imagine your fancying Dormice were White mice. Of these latter, I never kept any: but I believe their odour is none of the sweetist, & I have no ambition to make their acquaintance.—Harriet Crewe writes word, that Dr Jephson thought her better, gave her prescriptions to last a month, & charged her to persevere in his diet for months. "I hope" she says "my health, please God, may be really improved by this regimen, and shall feel grateful indeed once more to taste of health."—You remember he ordered her meat twice a day, & a glass of wine at each meal. How different to his treatment of poor little you!—

Give Grandmamma's Aunt's love to the dear unseen little Etta & Jemmy,[3] [*2–3? words*] I want my promised kettle holde[r.] Was it he or Etta who was to send [it. There is] nobody here you know: but some [Ir]ish people enough, only too few for the [*1–2? words*]. By the way Madame de St. Martin[4] is still Boarding here, & likely to remain.

I must try to call upon Miss St. Clair, for I am very anxious to know how Col. St. Clair[5] has prospered with his Water Doctors.

O, I must tell you, as a sort of pendant to the story of Dr Jephson a story of

Dr Gibney,[6] but of skill more than liberality,—or, at least, liberality of a different sort. Having been formerly an army surgeon, he is sometimes called in upon surgical cases. A gentleman sent for him who was desparately ill, & he attended him for some time: but the case was so serious, that tho' no operation was required, Gibney advised procuring the highest surgical advice from London. Accordingly, either Sir Benjamin Brodie,[7] or some other great man was sent for, and on his arrival said, there was nothing left for him to do,—Dr Gibney had acted just as he should have done himself, and utterly declined making any alteration in the patient's treatment.—I am afraid the poor fellow died: but that I am not quite sure of. At all events, it was handsome in Gibney to distrust his own skill, & to recommend further assistance—especially as the sick man was rich & could afford paying the Londoner's expences.

Now, once more, adieu, dearest; I have gossipped in true Old Maid character, and you can't deny it. Give my affectionate love to dear Fanny. I am sorry poor Julia has been suffering from Influenza, remember me kindly to her, & believe me ever Your sincerely loving Aunt

S. H. Burney.

Thank Dicky for so kindly consenting to fetch the old Lady when disposed for a frolic. Oh that I could see you all, & be amongst you once more!!—But as for living alone in a London lodging—no.—A Boarding-House, or a comfortable private family might do, if willing to be moderately paid. Brighton I cou[ld] only inhabit for a month or so, as your vis[itor d]ear—but to live there with never a tree to [loo]k at, & a roaring Sea at night, & blinding s[un] by [d]ay—No, no.—

[*Written sideways inside a square drawn on the first page presumably intended to enclose the stamps.*] I thought to send the Queen's Mountain in this one half sheet—but I cannot make it do,—so now let me say farewell, dearest Charlotte, to whom I must hurl back the word kind, for you were lots kinder to me in putting up with my deafness, & hoarse husky unreading-able voice, than I could be to you. I miss & regret you every hour.

1. Postage stamps (*OED*).

2. Jane Parr, who witnessed SHB's will on 21 September 1842 (see Appendix 1), was staying at the Belgrave Boarding House, Cheltenham, on the night of the 1851 census when she was listed as a thirty-two-year-old annuitant from London.

3. Charlotte Barrett's two grandchildren, Henrietta Anne Thomas, six years old, and James Cambridge Thomas, who was four (L. 159, n. 7; L. 164, n. 10).

4. Unidentified.

5. Probably Col. Thomas Staunton St. Clair (c. 1787–1847), C.B. (1815), K.H. (1833), a veteran of the Peninsular War, who would attain the rank of Maj.-Gen. (1846). He

had married 5 April 1817 Caroline, the elder sister of Charlotte's friend, Emma Woodbridge of Richmond (L. 89, n. 7). Miss St. Clair might be his blind sister, Augusta (d. 4 Feb. 1848), also a friend of Mrs. Barrett's, who apparently lived with her brother, or another unmarried sister, Louisa Matilda (d. 2 Dec. 1858) (*Army List* (1810–41); Shaw, 1: 468; Burke, *LG; GM*, 87, Pt. 1 (1817): 370, 466; NS 28 (1847): 639–40; GM, NS 29 (1848): 325; *GM*, 3rd ser. 6 (1859): 104; CFBt to HBt, 28–30 Apr. [1831], Berg).

However, Thomas also had an elder brother, James Pattison St. Clair (1780–1867), Lt-Col. in the Royal Artillery (1827), who had served in the West Indies and North America. Twice married, he had a large family and lived at the family seat of Staverton Court, Glos. (Burke, *LG; GM*, 4th ser. 3 (1867): 261; *Army List* (1810)).

6. Dr. William Gibney (L. 170, n. 2) had attended Sarah on her arrival at Cheltenham.

7. Sir Benjamin Collins Brodie (L. 113, n. 2), the eminent surgeon, who had treated SHB in London in 1828.

---

183. To Charlotte (Francis) Barrett

[Belgrave House, Cheltenham], 19 December 1843
A.L.S., Berg

Tuesday Decr 19th
1843

Thanks my most dear Charlotte for so very kindly and quickly giving me tidings of poor dear Julia's safe accouchment[1]—and thanks also, (tho' minor) for the beautiful Kettle-holder. Tell darling little Grandmamma's grand-daughter, that tho' the work was not quite all done by her, it was, I am sure, from no want of good will, and I love it very much for having had it <u>from</u> her, even without its being <u>by</u> her. It is really quite an ornament to my fire side, where it now hangs upon a new nail, and looks as if it could sing.—

Poor Miss Parr is not yet returned, and I hear from her friend Miss Austen[2] hardly expects to be back quite so soon as by her last letter to me, I had been induced to hope. Poor, poor soul! I grieve for her.

I think that in one of my trumpery joking letters, I mentioned a Boarder here, a Mrs Unitt, who would at least do for two and a half. She was very fat, & unwieldy, owned to 73, and was rich. A Mr Watts, also a Boarder, many years younger, and in his second widower/ship, unsuspected by me, certainly, and by some of the others, I believe, persuaded her to get up one fine morning by seven o'clock and walk off with him to Mr Close's Church[3] to be married at the eight o'clock hour for such doings.[4] She, that never used to rise till ten or eleven, & always breakfasted in bed—think what Dan Cupid urged her to undertake! I really feel a little alarmed for myself;—Dear me, I hope, now I am an heiress,[5] I shall not be tempted to do the like!—

The happy pair immediately went into lodgings, & she has not been seen since. He has called twice, & left his card for me, but I was in my room & did not go out to him. They have also send [*sent*] to me and one other lady here, bridal cards tied with silver cord, & enclosed in a laced edged envellope, sealed with white wax!—Ha, ha, ha—

Mrs Gregor is better, but has had a sad attack of Influenza, & a pulse up at 100. Lady Pepys[6] has also a severe cold, & such maladies are here sadly prevalent. May you & yours escape, is the hearty wish [*of*] your most affectionate Aunty

S. H. Burney

Best & cordial love to Fanny—I am most glad she is with you, and often, often think of you, & now more than ever because I have got a Trumpet, an' please you;

Harriet sends her dutiful respects, & was much pleased and very proud to be remembered. I have never had occasion to speak to her since that memorable remonstrance.

1. Julia (Thomas) Maitland had given birth to the only child of her second marriage, Julia Caroline Maitland (1843–90), who would eventually marry in 1861 the Rev. David Wauchope (1825–1911) (Barrett family tree, Barrett, Eg. 3707, ff. 269–70v; *Catalogue*, xiii).

2. Possibly Elizabeth Smith Austen, the daughter of Robert Austen (d. 3 Nov. 1797) of Shalford House, Surrey, who would die at Cheltenham on 14 February 1845 (Burke, *LG;* Burke, *DLG; GM*, NS 23 (1845): 451).

3. Francis Close (1797–1882), D.D. (1856), curate of the parish church of St. Mary, Cheltenham (1824–26), and perpetual curate there from 1826 to 1856, when he became Dean of Carlisle. In his thirty years' ministry at Cheltenham, he attracted large congregations with his evangelical preaching and encouraged the establishment of new churches and schools. A memorial in the south side of the chancel of the church commemorates its most famous and influential incumbent (*DNB; Alumni Cantab.;* Canon G. W. Hart, *Parish Church of St. Mary, Cheltenham* (1983), 13).

4. On 8 December 1843 in the parish church of St. Mary, Cheltenham, John Watts, an Irish widower, married Rebecca (née Stone) Unett, the daughter of John Stone. The groom may be the John Watts of Cheltenham who died the following year at Genoa on 17 November 1844, aged seventy-four; Rebecca Watts died suddenly on 19 April 1846 at Broadwood Hall, Salop, a property that had been in the Unett family (marriage certificate, GRO; *GM*, NS 21 (1844): 222; NS 25 (1846): 667; Burke, *DLG*).

5. In 1840, SHB had been left an annuity of £200 by her half-sister, Frances (Burney) d'Arblay (L. 166, n. 11).

6. Deborah (c. 1764–1848), the daughter of Dr. Anthony Askew (1722–74) (*DNB*), had married on 29 June 1813 as his second wife Sir Lucas Pepys (1741–1830), M.D., who was created a baronet (1784). She would die 21 June 1848 at Cheltenham (Burke under Cottenham; *GM*, NS 30 (1848): 220).

APPENDIX I

Will of Sarah Harriet Burney

Sarah Harriet Burney, "gentlewoman," died on 8 February 1844 (aged seventy-one) of "natural decay" at Belgrave House, Promenade, Cheltenham. Present at her death was Anne Shaw, keeper of the boardinghouse, who signed the death certificate (GRO). She "appears to have died suddenly and without pain," according to Henry Crabb Robinson, who notes his sadness at the loss: "I sincerely respected her and feel I have lost a friend in her." He also regretted "very much having lost the opportunity of hearing from her again by delaying writing to her for so long a time" and annotated the last letter he had received from her: "Septr 1843 / Miss Burney / Youngest Sister of / Mad: Darblay / she died 1844 / at Cheltenham / a clever & very / amiable person / H. C. R."[1]

The funeral was held on 15 February 1844 at the parish church of St. Mary, Cheltenham, and the remains deposited in the New Burial Ground.[2] The gravestone has since disappeared, according to Mr. J. A. Rawes, compiler of *Memorial Inscriptions of Cheltenham*, vol. 1 (1983), in which he deplores the clearing of the old cemetery without proper recording of the memorial inscriptions.

Her passing was noticed in the newspapers and the *Gentleman's Magazine*, which published an obituary of the "youngest and last surviving dau. of the late Dr. Burney, of Chelsea College. She was well known as the authoress of 'Clarentine,' 'The Shipwreck,' 'Country Neighbours,' &c."[3]

The Will of Sarah Harriet Burney

PRO/PROB/10/6242, dated 21 Sept. 1842, proved 15 June 1844

I Sarah Harriet Burney, Spinster, now residing in the Parish of Cheltenham, Gloucestershire, do declare this to be my last Will & Testament: I hereby appoint my Nephew, John Thomas Payne, to be my sole Executor & Trustee, and bequeath to Mrs Ann Hart Cooper, the sum of two hundred pounds. My books, wherever they may be deposited, I leave amongst my relations to be divided by them as they themselves may agree. My

French watch, I leave to my great niece Clara Burney, with my few rings & trinkets. My large Indian Shawl, I leave to my Niece Fanny Raper, or her daughter, Mrs Kingston. My book of chalk drawings done at Florence, I bequeath to my dear & faithful friend the Honble Henrietta Hungerford Crewe.

Further, whatever money I may have in the funds, or in my Banker's hands at my decease, or whatever other pecuniary property I may die possessed of, I leave <trusting> the same in trust to my afore-mentioned Nephew, John Thomas Payne, to be applied as follows; the interest of half the said property to be paid half yearly to my Nephew Martin Charles Burney during his life; and at his demise, the principal to be made over in perpetuity to my Niece, Jane Caroline Burney, she having, meanwhile, received the interest of half of the whole amount, the other half of which having been paid to Martin Charles Burney.

As witness my hand & seal this 21st Septr 1842
Sarah Harriet Burney—

Joseph Taylor
Mary Elizth Bowdler
Jane Parr

The will was proved in the Prerogative Court of Canterbury 15 June 1844. Joseph Taylor appeared personally to establish that a word in the text was obliterated before the will was signed and witnessed. The estate was sworn at less than £6,000 by the sole executor, John Payne.

SHB's account at Coutts had a balance of £336.12.3 at the time of her death and shows holdings of £5731.1s. total, comprising £1,991.19s. invested at 3½ percent, a £500 Exchange Bill and £3239.2s. in Consols. From this, £1202.1.10 was paid out in various sums during the year following her death; before the account was closed, £63.0.2 was paid to each of her beneficiaries.

1. L. 180; HCR, 18 Feb. 1844, Diaries.

2. Parish register, Cheltenham.

3. *Gloucester Journal*, 17 Feb. 1844; *Bath and Cheltenham Gazette*, 21 Feb. 1844; *GM*, NS 21 (1844): 442.

APPENDIX 2

Poetry Addressed to or Written by Sarah Harriet Burney

Sonnet
To Miss Burney, on her Character of Blanch in
"Country Neighbours," a Tale

Bright spirits have arisen to grace the BURNEY name,
And some in letters, some in tasteful arts,
In learning some have borne distinguished parts;
Or sought through science of sweet sounds their fame:
And foremost *she*, renowned for many a tale
Of faithful love perplexed, and of that good
Old man, who, as CAMILLA's guardian, stood
In obstinate virtue clad like coat of mail.
Nor dost thou, SARAH, with unequal pace
Her steps pursue. The pure romantic vein
No gentler creature ever knew to feign
Than thy fine Blanch, young with an elder grace,
In all respects without rebuke or blame,
Answering the antique freshness of her name.

(*Morning Chronicle*, 13 July 1820; rpt., *The Works of Charles and Mary Lamb*, ed. E. V. Lucas (London, 1903; rpt., New York: AMS Press, 1968), 5: 82-83.)

Sonnet to Imagination
in answer to that to Indifference. 1793

Parent of Genius! at thy shrine I bend;
Awake Imagination! honor'd name!
Propitious to thy votary's prayer attend
And rouse to emulation, & to Fame!

Whoe'er thou art, the blessing dost deplore
Recall thy senses, cease all groundless Fear:
Imagination can past joys restore
The present heighten & the future clear.

The wakeful, sad, & tedious hours of night
Beguil'd by her, how transient seem & few:
If, fade our visions with returning light
The morrow comes & decks the scene anew.
Oh! gay imagination! still be mine,
Real misery soften—& false hopes refine!
Sarah Harriet B.

(On p. 108 of a bound volume of MS verses, "Lines on or by the Burney Family," Osborn; for the discovery and transcription, I am indebted to Professor Lars Troide).

Selected List of Sources

This list of published sources excludes for the most part those given in the Short Titles and Abbreviations list, as well as various directories and registers, annual lists, catalogues, newspapers, and contemporary reviews.

Addison, William. *English Spas.* London: B. T. Batsford, 1951.

Ariosto, Ludovico. *Orlando furioso.* Translated by Sir John Harington. Edited by Robert McNulty. Oxford: Oxford University Press, 1972.

[Austen, Jane]. *Jane Austen's Letters to Her Sister Cassandra and Others.* Edited by R. W. Chapman. 2 vols. Oxford: Clarendon Press, 1932.

Baker, John Milton. *Henry Crabb Robinson of Bury, Jena,* The Times, *and Russell Square.* London: George Allen & Unwin, 1937.

Bannerman, W. Bruce, ed. *The Registers of St. Helen's, Bishopsgate, London.* London, 1904.

Bargellini, Piero. *La città di Firenze.* [Firenze]: Benechi, 1979.

Barrington, Sir Jonah. *Personal Sketches of his own Times.* 2nd ed. 2 vols. London: Henry Colburn and Richard Bentley, 1830.

Barthélemy, Abbé [Jean-Jacques]. *Travels of Anacharsis the Younger in Greece.* [Translated by William Beaumont.] 4 vols. London: G. G. and J. Robinson, 1796.

Beard, Geoffrey, and Christopher Gilbert, eds. *Dictionary of English Furniture Makers, 1660–1840.* London: Furniture History Society, 1986.

Belchem, J. C. "Henry Hunt and the Evolution of the Mass Platform." *English Historical Review* 93 (1978): 739–73.

Benkovitz, Miriam. "Dr. Burney's Memoirs." *Review of English Studies* NS 10 (1959): 257–68.

Bentley, Richard. *A Dissertation upon the Epistles of Phalaris.* London: Printed by J. H. for Henry Mortlock, 1699.

Besant, Walter. *London North of the Thames.* London: Adam & Charles Black, 1911.

Bibliotheca Sanctorum. Vol. 11. [Roma]: Istituto Giovanni XXIII nella Pontificia Universita lateranense, 1968.

Bingham, Madeleine. *Masks and Façades: Sir John Vanbrugh the Man in His Setting.* London: George Allen & Unwin, 1974.

Bishop, Marchand. "Lamb's Mr. M: The First Englishman in Lhasa." *Cornhill Magazine,* no. 1046 (Winter 1965–66): 96–112.

Blake, Robert. *Disraeli.* London: Eyre & Spottiswoode, 1966.

Blakiston, Giorgiana. *Woburn and the Russells.* London: Constable, 1980.

Blessington, Countess of. *The Idler in Italy.* 2nd ed. 2 vols. London: Henry Colburn, 1839.

[———]. *Lady Blessington at Naples.* Edited by Edith Clay. London: Hamish Hamilton, 1979.

Block, Andrew. *The English Novel, 1740–1850: A Catalogue Including Prose Romances, Short Stories, and Translations of Foreign Fiction.* London: Dawsons, 1961.

Blunt, Anthony. *The Paintings of Nicolas Poussin: A Critical Catalogue.* London: Phaidon, 1966.

[Boigne, Charlotte Louise, comtesse de]. *Memoirs of the Comtesse de Boigne, 1781–1814.* Edited by M. Charles Nicoullaud. Vol 1. New York: Charles Scribner's Sons, 1907.

Bonvallet, Pierre. *Molière de tous les jours.* Paris: Le Pré aux Clercs, 1985.

Borough of Twickenham Local History Society. *Twickenham, 1660–1900: People and Places.* Twickenham: Twickenham Local History Society, 1981.

Boswell, James. *The Life of Johnson.* Edited by George Birkbeck Hill. 2nd ed., revised by L. F. Powell. 6 vols. Oxford: Clarendon Press, 1934–50.

Botta, Carlo. *Storia d'Italia continuata da quella del Guicciardini sino al 1789.* 8 vols. Torino: Cugini Pomba e Compagnia, 1852.

Brinkerhoff, Dericksen Morgan. *Hellenistic Statues of Aphrodite: Studies in the History of Their Stylistic Development.* New York: Garland, 1978.

Brown, G. H., comp. *Lives of the Fellows of the Royal College of Physicians of London, 1826–1925.* Vol. 4 of Munk's Roll. London: Printed for the College, 1955.

Bryant, Arthur. *The Great Duke or the Invincible General.* London: Collins, 1971.

Buckingham, George Villiers, Duke of. *The Rehearsal.* Edited by Montague Summers. Stratford-upon-Avon: Shakespeare Head Press, 1914.

Burke, Sir Bernard. *A Genealogical and Heraldic History of the Landed Gentry of Ireland.* Edited by Ashworth P. Burke. 10th ed. London: Harrison & Sons, 1904.

Burnet, Gilbert. *Bishop Burnet's History of his own Time.* Edited by M. J. Routh. 6 vols. Oxford: Clarendon Press, 1823.

Burney, Charles. *A General History of Music from the Earliest Ages to the Present Period.* 4 vols. London: Printed for the Author, 1776–89.

———. *Memoirs of the life and writings of the Abate Metastasio.* 3 vols. London: G. G. and J. Robinson, 1796.

Burney, Frances, later d'Arblay. *Camilla or a Picture of Youth.* Edited by Edward A. Bloom and Lillian D. Bloom. London: Oxford University Press, 1972.

———. *Cecilia, or Memoirs of an Heiress.* Edited by Peter Sabor and Margaret Anne Doody. Oxford: Oxford University Press, 1988.

[———]. *Diary and Letters of Madame d'Arblay.* Edited by Charlotte Barrett. 7 vols. London: Henry Colburn, 1842–46.

———. *Evelina or the History of a Young Lady's Entrance into the World.* Edited by Edward A. Bloom. London: Oxford University Press, 1968.

———. *The Wanderer, or Female difficulties.* 5 vols. London: Longman, Hurst, Rees, Orme, and Brown, 1814.

Burney, Henry. *The Burney Papers.* 15 vols. Bangkok, 1910–14.

Burney, James. *A Chronological History of the Discoveries in the South Sea or Pacific Ocean.* 5 vols. London: G. & W. Nicol, 1803–17.

———. *A Memoir on the Voyage of d'Entrecasteaux, in search of La Pérouse.* London: Printed for the Author, 1820.

[Burney, Sarah Harriet]. *Clarentine. A Novel.* 3 vols. London: G. G. and J. Robinson, 1796.

[———]. *Geraldine Fauconberg.* 3 vols. London: G. Wilkie and J. Robinson, 1808.
———. *The Romance of Private Life.* 3 vols. London: Henry Colburn, 1839.
———. *Tales of Fancy.* 3 vols. London: Henry Colburn, 1816–20.
———. *Traits of Nature.* 5 vols. London: Henry Colburn, 1812.
Burtchaell, George Dames, and Thomas Ulick Sadleir, eds. *Alumni Dublinenses: A Register of the Students, Graduates, Professors and Provosts of Trinity College in the University of Dublin (1593–1860).* Rev. ed. 2 vols. Dublin: Alex. Thom., 1935.
Butler, Marilyn. "Edgeworth, Maria." *A Dictionary of British and American Women Writers, 1660–1800.* Edited by Janet Todd. Totowa, N.J.: Rowman & Allenheld, 1985.
———. *Maria Edgeworth: A Literary Biography.* Oxford: Clarendon Press, 1972.
Byron, George Gordon, Lord. *Byron: Poetical Works.* Edited by Frederick Page. 3rd ed., edited by John Jump. London: Oxford University Press, 1970.
Cameron, Kenneth Neill, and Donald H. Reiman, eds. *Shelley and His Circle, 1773–1822.* 8 vols. Cambridge, Mass.: Harvard University Press, 1961–86.
Campbell, Thomas. *The Pleasures of Hope.* 4th ed. Glasgow: University Press, 1800.
———. *The Pleasures of Hope.* 5th ed. Edinburgh: Mundell & Sons, 1801.
Carter, Harold B. *Sir Joseph Banks.* London: British Museum (Natural History), 1988.
Cervantes, Miguel de. *The Adventures of Don Quixote de la Mancha.* Translated by Tobias Smollett. Introduction by Carlos Fuentes. London: André Deutsch, 1968.
Chaplin, Peter H. *The Thames from Source to Tideway.* Weybridge, Surrey: Whittet Books, 1982.
[Chilcott, John]. *Chilcott's Descriptive History of Bristol.* 3rd ed. Bristol: J. Chilcott, 1835.
Clark, Richard, ed. *An Account of the National Anthem Entitled God Save the King!* London: W. Wright, 1822.
Clarkson, Thomas. *Strictures on a Life of William Wilberforce.* [Edited by Henry Crabb Robinson.] London: Longman, Orme, Brown, Green & Longmans, 1838.
Clifford, James L. *Hester Lynch Piozzi (Mrs. Thrale).* 2nd ed. Oxford: Clarendon Press, 1952.
Coleridge, Ernest Hartley. *The Life of Thomas Coutts Banker.* 2 vols. London: John Lane, 1920.
Collins, William. *The Works of William Collins.* Edited by Richard Wendorf and Charles Ryskamp. Oxford: Clarendon Press, 1979.
[Combermere, Sir Stapleton Cotton, Viscount]. *Memoirs and Correspondence of Field-Marshal Viscount Combermere.* Edited by Mary, Viscountess Combermere [and W. W. Knollys]. 2 vols. London: Hurst and Blackett, 1866.
The Commissioned Sea-Officers of the Royal Navy 1660–1815, TS. Society of Genealogists, London.
Cook, B. F. *The Elgin Marbles.* London: British Museum Publications, 1984.
Cottin, Marie "Sophie." *Élisabeth, ou les Exilés de Sibérie.* Paris: J. B. Garnery, 1820.
Courtney, Winifred F. "New Light on the Lambs and the Burneys." *Charles Lamb Bulletin,* NS, no. 57 (January 1987): 19–27.
———. *Young Charles Lamb, 1775–1802.* London: Macmillan, 1982.
Cowper, William. *Cowper: Poetical Works.* 4th ed. Edited by H. S. Milford. London: Oxford University Press, 1967.
———. *The Poems of William Cowper.* Vol. 1. Edited by John D. Baird and Charles Ryskamp. Oxford: Clarendon Press, 1980.

———. *The Task.* Vol. 2 of *Poems.* 1785. Reprint, Ilkley, Yorkshire: Scolar Press, 1973.

Craveri, Benedetta. *Madame du Deffand e il suo mondo.* Milano: Adelphi, 1982.

Crown, Patricia Dahlman. *Drawings by E. F. Burney in the Huntington Collection.* San Marino, Calif.: Huntington Library, 1982.

———. "Edward F. Burney: An Historical Study in English Romantic Art." Ph.D. diss. University of California at Los Angeles, 1977.

Cucentrentoli, Giorgio. *Gli ultimi Granduchi di Toscana.* Bologna: La perseveranza, 1975.

Cuzin, Jean-Pierre. *Raphaël: Vie et oeuvre.* Fribourg, Switzerland: Office du Livre, 1983.

Dante Alighieri. *The Inferno of Dante Alighiere.* Translated by the Rev. Henry Francis Cary. 2 vols. London: James Carpenter, 1805–6.

[Darwin, Emma]. *Emma Darwin: A Century of Family Letters, 1792–1896.* Edited by Henrietta Litchfield. 2 vols. London: John Murray, 1915.

[Dashkova, Catherina Romanovna Vorsontsova, Princess]. *Memoirs of the Princess Dashchkaw, Lady of Honour to Catherine II . . . Written by Herself.* Edited by Mrs. W. Bradford. 2 vols. London: Henry Colburn, 1840.

Davidson, J. W. *Peter Dillon of Vanikoro: Chevalier of the South Seas.* Melbourne: Oxford University Press, 1975.

Davies, E. T., and Sidney Northcote, eds. *The National Songs of Wales.* London: Boosey & Hawkes, 1959.

Davies, Henry. *The Stranger's Guide through Cheltenham.* 3rd ed. Cheltenham: H. Davies, [1842].

Davis, Bertram H. *A Proof of Eminence: The Life of Sir John Hawkins.* Bloomington: Indiana University Press, 1973.

Davy, Sir Humphry. *Consolations in Travel, or the Last Days of a Philosopher.* [Edited by John Davy.] London: John Murray, 1830.

Debrett's Baronetage of England. 5th ed. 2 vols. London, 1824.

Denham, John. *The Poetical Works of John Denham.* 2nd ed. Edited by Theodore Howard Banks. London: Archon Books, 1969.

Devonshire, Duchess of. *The House: A Portrait of Chatsworth.* London: Macmillan, 1982.

Dodwell and Miles, comps. *Alphabetical List of the Honourable East India Company's Bengal Civil Servants, from the year 1780, to the year 1838.* London: Longman, Orme, Brown, 1839.

———. *Alphabetical List of the Honourable East India Company's Madras Civil Servants, from the year 1780, to the year 1839.* London: Longman, Orme, Brown, 1839.

———. *Alphabetical List of the Officers of the Indian Army.* London: Longman, Orme, Brown, 1838.

———. *Alphabetical List of the Officers of the Madras Army.* London: Longman, Orme, Brown, 1838.

Doody, Margaret Anne. *Frances Burney: The Life in the Works.* New Brunswick, N.J.: Rutgers University Press, 1988.

[du Deffand, Marie, marquise]. *Letters of the Marquise du Deffand to the Hon. Horace Walpole.* [Edited by Mary Berry.] 4 vols. London: Longman, Hurst, Rees, and Orme, 1810.

[Edgeworth, Richard Lovell, and Maria Edgeworth]. *Memoirs of Richard Lovell Edgeworth, Esq.* 2 vols. London: R. Hunter, 1820.

Elwes, Dudley George Cary. *A History of the Castles, Mansions, and Manors of Western Sussex.* London: Longmans, 1876.

Elwin, Malcolm. *Landor: A Replevin.* London: Macdonald, 1958.

Encyclopaedia Britannica. 3 vols. Edinburgh: A. Bell and C. Macfarquhar, 1771.

Entwisle, E. A. "Eighteenth-Century London Paperstainers: The Eckhardt Brothers of Chelsea." *Connoisseur* 143 (March 1959): 74–77.

Eustace, Rev. John Chetwode. *Classical Tour through Italy.* 6th ed. 4 vols. London: J. Mawman, 1821.

Evans, Ivor H., ed. *Brewer's Dictionary of Phrase and Fable.* Rev. ed. London: Cassell, 1981.

Evans, John. *Richmond and its Vicinity.* Richmond: James Darrill, [1825].

A Famous Bookstore. Paris: Galignani Library, 1970.

Farington, Joseph. *The Farington Diary.* Edited by James Greig. 8 vols. London: Hutchinson & Co., 1922–24; New York: George H. Doran Co., 1925–28.

[Ferrier, Susan]. *The Inheritance.* 3 vols. Edinburgh: W. Blackwood, 1824.

Finberg, H. P. R. *The Gloucestershire Landscape.* Rev. ed. London: Hodder & Stoughton, 1975.

Findlay, James. *Directory to Gentlemen's Seats, Villages, &c. in Scotland.* Edinburgh: W. P. Kennedy, [1843].

Firminger, Walter K. "Madame d'Arblay and Calcutta." *Bengal Past and Present* 9 (1914): 244–49.

FitzGerald, S. J. Adair. *Stories of Famous Songs.* Philadelphia: J. B. Lippincott, 1910.

Forsyth, Joseph. *Remarks on Antiquities, Arts, and Letters, during an excursion in Italy, in the Years 1802 and 1803.* 4th ed. London: John Murray, 1835.

Foskett, Daphne. *A Dictionary of British Miniature Painters.* 2 vols. London: Faber & Faber, 1972.

Fulford, Roger. *The Trial of Queen Caroline.* London: B. T. Batsford, 1967.

Furneaux, Robin. *William Wilberforce.* London: Hamish Hamilton, 1974.

Garrick, David. *The Poetical Works of David Garrick.* 2 vols. London, 1785. Reprint, New York: Benjamin Blom, 1968.

Gaussen, Alice C. C. *Percy: Prelate and Poet.* London: Smith & Elder, 1908.

Gay, John. *Fables.* 2 vols. 1727, 1738. Reprint, Menston, England: Scolar Press, 1969.

Genlis, Stéphanie-Félicité Brûlart, comtesse de. *Alphonsine, ou la tendresse maternelle.* 3 vols. Paris: H. Nicolle, 1806.

George Rowe's Illustrated Cheltenham Guide. 1845. Reprint, Gloucester: Alan Sutton, 1981.

Gernsheim, Helmut, and Alison Gernsheim. *Queen Victoria: A Biography in Word and Picture.* London: Longmans, 1959.

Gilson, David. *A Bibliography of Jane Austen.* Oxford: Clarendon Press, 1982.

Gloucestershire Notes and Queries 3 (1887).

Gomme, Andor, Michael Jenner, and Bryan Little. *Bristol: An Architectural History.* London: Lund Humphries, 1979.

Goodwin, Albert. *The Friends of Liberty: The English Democratic Movements in the Age of the French Revolution.* London: Hutchinson, 1979.

Grattan, Henry. *Memoirs of the Life and Times of the Rt. Hon. Henry Grattan.* 2 vols. London: Henry Colburn, 1839.

Grau, Joseph A. *Fanny Burney: An Annotated Bibliography.* New York: Garland, 1981.

Graves, Algernon. *The Royal Academy of Arts.* 8 vols. London, 1905–6. Reprint, New York: Burt Franklin, 1972.

[Graves, Richard, ed.]. *The Festoon: A Collection of Epigrams, Ancient and Modern.* London: Robinson and Roberts, 1766.

Gray, Thomas. *The Complete Poems of Thomas Gray.* Edited by H. W. Starr and J. R. Hendrickson. Oxford: Clarendon Press, 1966.

[Greville, Charles Cavendish Fulke]. *The Greville Memoirs, 1814–1860.* Edited by Giles Lytton Strachey and Roger Fulford. 8 vols. London: Macmillan, 1938.

Griffith, S. Y. *Griffith's History of Cheltenham and its vicinity.* 3rd ed. London: Longman, Hurst, 1838.

del Guerra, Giorgio. *Pisa attraverso i secoli.* [Pisa]: Giardini, [1967].

Gundry, W. G. C., comp. *Index of the Name Gundry,* TS. Society of Genealogists, London, 1929.

Gunnis, Rupert. *Dictionary of British Sculptors, 1660–1851.* Rev. ed. London: Abbey Library, [1968].

Gwynn, Denis. *Daniel O'Connell: The Irish Liberator.* Rev. ed. Oxford: B. H. Blackwell, 1947.

Haddon, John. *Portrait of Bath.* London: Robert Hale, 1982.

Haldane, Charlotte. *Madame de Maintenon: Uncrowned Queen of France.* London: Constable, 1970.

Hall, Daniel G. E. *Henry Burney: A Political Biography.* London: Oxford University Press, 1974.

Halperin, John. *The Life of Jane Austen.* Baltimore, Md.: Johns Hopkins University Press, 1984.

Hamlin, Talbot. *Benjamin Henry Latrobe.* New York: Oxford University Press, 1955.

Hammelmann, H. A. "Edward Burney's Drawings." *Country Life,* 6 June 1968, 1504–6.

Harris, B. E., ed. *A History of the County of Chester.* 3 vols. London: Institute of Historical Research, 1979–87.

Hart, Canon G. W. *Parish Church of St. Mary, Cheltenham.* Cheltenham, 1983.

Hart, Gwen. *A History of Cheltenham.* 2nd ed. Gloucester: Alan Sutton, 1981.

Hasted, Edward. *The History and Topographical Survey of the County of Kent.* 2nd ed. 12 vols., 1797–1801. Reprint, Canterbury: E. P. Publishing, 1972.

Hazlitt, William. *Notes of a Journey through France and Italy.* London: Hunt and Clarke, 1826.

Hinchliffe, Rev. Edward. *Barthomley: In Letters from a Former Rector to his Eldest Son.* 2 vols. London: Longman, Brown, Green, and Longmans, 1856.

Hinde, Wendy. *George Canning.* London: Collins, 1973.

Hitchens, Christopher. *The Elgin Marbles.* London: Chatto & Windus, 1987.

[Hoare, Sir Richard Colt]. *The Journeys of Sir Richard Colt Hoare through Wales and England, 1793–1810.* Edited by M. W. Thompson. Gloucester: Alan Sutton, 1983.

Holme, Thea. *Caroline: A Biography of Caroline of Brunswick.* London: Hamish Hamilton, 1979.

The Holy Bible. Authorized King James Version. London: Collins' Clear-type Press, 1939.

Hunt, Leigh. *Lord Byron and some of his contemporaries; with recollections of the author's life, and of his visit to Italy.* London: Henry Colburn, 1828.

Hussey, Christopher. "Italian Light on English Walls." *Country Life,* 17 February 1934, 161–64.

Hutchings, W. W. *London Town Past & Present.* 4 vols. London: Cassell, 1900.
Hutton, William Holden. *Burford Papers, Being Letters of Samuel Crisp to his Sister at Burford; and other Studies of a Century (1745–1845).* London: Archibald Constable, 1905.
The International Check-list of Roses. Harrisburg, Pa.: McFarland, 1969.
Irwin, David. *John Flaxman, 1755–1826.* London: Studio Vista, 1979.
Jackson, B. D. "The Dates of Rees's Cyclopaedia." *Journal of Botany* 34 (1896): 307–11.
Jackson, J. R. de J. *Annals of English Verse 1770–1835: A Preliminary Survey of the Volumes Published.* New York: Garland, 1985.
Johnson, R. Brimley. *Fanny Burney and the Burneys.* London: Stanley Paul, 1926.
Johnson, Samuel. *A Dictionary of the English Language.* 9th ed. 2 vols. London, 1806.
———. *The History of Rasselas, Prince of Abissinia.* Edited by D. J. Enright. London: Penguin, 1984.
[———]. *The Letters of Samuel Johnson with Mrs. Thrale's Genuine Letters to Him.* Edited by R. W. Chapman. 3 vols. Oxford: Clarendon Press, 1952.
———. *The Poems of Samuel Johnson,* 2nd ed. Edited by David Nichol Smith and Edward L. McAdam. Oxford: Clarendon Press, 1974.
———. *The Works of Samuel Johnson.* 12 vols. London: Nichols & Son, 1816.
Jones, Charles Percy. *History of Lymington.* Lymington: Charles King, 1930.
Kaye, John William. *The Life and Correspondence of Major-General Sir John Malcolm.* 2 vols. London: Smith Elder, 1856.
King, Edward. *Old Times Re-visited in the Borough and Parish of Lymington.* 2nd ed. 1900. Reprint, Winchester: Barry Shurlock, 1976.
Klepac, Richard L. *Mr. Mathews at Home.* London: Society for Theatre Research, 1979.
Klopstock, Friedrich Gottlieb. *The Messiah.* Translated by Joseph Collyer. 2 vols. Boston: John West, 1811.
Koss, Stephen. *The Nineteenth Century.* Vol. 1 of *The Rise and Fall of the Political Press in Britain.* London: Hamish Hamilton, 1981.
L'Accademia di belle arti di Firenze. Firenze: Accademia di belle arti di Firenze, 1984.
La Fontaine, Jean de. *Fables choisies mises en vers.* Edited by Ferdinand Gohin. 2 vols. Paris: Société les Belles Lettres, 1934.
[Lamb, Charles]. *The Letters of Charles Lamb, with a Sketch of his Life.* Edited by Thomas Noon Talfourd. 2 vols. London: Edward Moxon, 1837.
[Lamb, Charles, and Mary Lamb]. *The Letters of Charles and Mary Anne Lamb.* Edited by Edwin W. Marrs Jr. 3 vols. Ithaca: Cornell University Press, 1975–78.
[———]. *The Works of Charles and Mary Lamb.* Edited by E. V. Lucas. 5 vols. London, 1903. Reprint, New York: AMS Press, 1968.
Lambert, B. *The History and Survey of London and Its Environs.* 4 vols. London: T. Hughes, 1806.
Langedijk, Karla. *The Portraits of the Medici Fifteenth-Eighteenth Centuries.* 2 vols. Firenze: Studio per edizioni Scelte, 1981–83.
La Rochefoucauld, François, duc de. *Réflexions ou sentences et maximes morales.* Edited by Jean Lafond. Paris: Gallimard, 1976.
[Latrobe, Charles Joseph]. *Letters of Charles Joseph La Trobe.* Edited by L. J. Blake. Melbourne, Australia: Government of Victoria, 1975.
Lee, Nathaniel. *The Rival Queens.* 1677. Reprint, Menston, England: Scolar Press, [1971].

Lewis, J. Perry. *List of Inscriptions on Tombstones and Monuments in Ceylon.* Columbo: H. C. Cottle Government Printer Ceylon, 1913.

Lillywhite, Bryant. *London Coffee Houses.* London: George Allen & Unwin, 1963.

List of Graduates in Medicine in the University of Edinburgh from 1765 to 1866. Edinburgh: Neill, 1867.

A List of Persons who have obtained Certificates of their Fitness and Qualification to practice as Apothecaries from August 1, 1815 to July 31, 1840. London: Gilbert and Rivington, 1840.

List of the Fellows and Members of the Royal College of Surgeons of England. London: R. Carpenter, 1822.

Lockhart, John Gibson. *Memoirs of the Life of Sir Walter Scott.* 2nd ed. 10 vols. Edinburgh: Robert Cadell, 1839.

London County Council. *Survey of London.* Edited by C. R. Ashbee et al. London: London County Council, 1900– .

Vol. 4. *The Parish of Chelsea.* Pt. 2. By Walter H. Godfrey. 1913.

Vol. 24. *King's Cross Neighbourhood: The Parish of St. Pancras.* Pt. 4. By Walter H. Godfrey and W. McB. Marcham. 1952.

Vol. 25. *St. George's Fields: The Parishes of St. George the Martyr, Southwark and St. Mary, Newington.* By Ida Darlington. 1955.

Vol. 37. *Northern Kensington.* 1973.

Long, Basil S. *British Miniaturists.* London: Holland Press, 1929.

Longmate, Norman. *King Cholera: The Biography of a Disease.* London: Hamish Hamilton, 1966.

Lonsdale, Roger. "Dr. Burney, 'Joel Collier,' and Sabrina." In *Evidence in Literary Scholarship: Essays in Memory of James Marshall Osborn,* edited by René Wellek and Alvaro Ribeiro. Oxford: Clarendon Press, 1979.

Lucas, E. V. *The Life of Charles Lamb.* 6th ed. London: Methuen, 1914.

Lysons, Daniel, and Samuel Lysons. *Magna Britannia; being a concise topographical account of the several counties of Great Britain.* 6 vols. London: T. Cadell and W. Davies, 1806–22.

MacLysaght, Edmond. *Irish Families: Their Names, Arms and Origins.* Dublin: Hodges, Figgis, 1957.

[Maitland, Julia Charlotte]. *Letters from Madras, during the years 1836–1839.* London: John Murray, 1843.

Mallalieu, H. L. *The Dictionary of British Watercolour Artists up to 1920.* 2nd ed. Woodbridge, Suffolk: Antique Collectors' Club, 1986.

Mankowitz, Wolf. *Wedgwood.* 2nd ed. London: Spring Books, 1966.

Mann, Phyllis G. "The Marriage of Martin Charles Burney." *Charles Lamb Society Bulletin,* no. 139 (November 1957): 175–76.

———. "A New Gloss for 'The Wedding.'" *Charles Lamb Society Bulletin,* no. 170 (March 1963): 402–3.

Manvell, Roger. *Sarah Siddons: Portrait of an Actress.* New York: G. P. Putnam's Sons, 1971.

Marchand, Jean, ed. *A Frenchman in England 1784: Being the* Mélanges sur l'Angleterre *of François de la Rochefoucauld.* Translated by S. C. Roberts. Cambridge: Cambridge University Press, 1933.

Mather, F. C. *Public Order in the Age of the Chartists.* Manchester, England: Manchester University Press, 1959.

Mathews, [Anne]. *Memoirs of Charles Mathews, Comedian.* London: Richard Bentley, 1838–39.

Mathews, Henry. *The Diary of an Invalid being the Journal of a Tour in pursuit of health in Portugal Italy Switzerland and France in the years 1817 1818 and 1819.* London: John Murray, 1820.

Mavor, Elizabeth. *The Ladies of Llangollen: A Study in Romantic Friendship.* London: Michael Joseph, 1971.

Maxted, Ian. *The London Book Trades 1775–1800: A Preliminary Checklist of Members.* Folkestone, Kent: Dawson, 1977.

McAleer, Edward C. *The Sensitive Plant: A Life of Lady Mount Cashell.* Chapel Hill: University of North Carolina Press, 1958.

McComb, Arthur. *Agnolo Bronzino: His Life and Works.* Cambridge, Mass: Harvard University Press, 1928.

Melchior-Bonnet, Bernardine. *Jérôme Bonaparte ou l'envers de l'épopée.* [Paris]: Librairie Académique Perrin, 1979.

Milton, John. *Paradise Lost.* 1667. Reprint, Menston, England: Scolar Press, 1968.

———. *Paradise Regain'd.* London: Printed for the Author, 1671.

Mitford, William. *The History of Greece.* 3rd ed. 6 vols. London: T. Cadell and W. Davies, 1795–97.

Molière. *Le Tartuffe ou l'Imposteur.* Edited by Jean-Pierre Collinet. Paris: Livre de Poche, 1985.

Moore, Donald. "The Discovery of the Welsh Landscape." In *Wales in the Eighteenth Century,* edited by Donald Moore. Swansea: Christopher Davies, 1976.

More, Hannah. *Practical Piety.* 2 vols. London: T. Cadell and W. Davies, 1811.

Morgan, Lady. *L'Italie.* 4 vols. Paris: Chez Pierre Dufort, 1821.

Morgan, Prys. *The Eighteenth Century Renaissance.* Dyfed, Wales: Christopher Davies, 1981.

Morley, Edith J. *The Life and Times of Henry Crabb Robinson.* London: J. M. Dent, [1935].

Morris, Rev. F. O., ed. *A Series of Picturesque Views of Seats of the Noblemen and Gentlemen of Great Britain and Ireland.* 6 vols. London: William Mackenzie, n.d.

Musgrave, Clifford. *Royal Pavilion: An Episode in the Romantic.* London: Leonard Hill, 1959.

Nangle, Benjamin Christie. *The Monthly Review Second Series, 1790–1815: Indexes of Contributors and Articles.* Oxford: Clarendon Press, 1955.

[Nares, Edward]. *Think's-I-to-Myself. A serio-ludicro, tragico-comico tale, written by Think's-I-to-Myself Who?* 2 vols. London: Sherwood, Neely, and Jones, 1811.

[———]. *Think's-I-to-Myself. A serio-ludicro, tragico-comico tale, written by Think's-I-to-Myself Who?* 3rd ed. 2 vols. London: Sherwood, Neely, and Jones, 1811.

Nitchie, Elizabeth. *The Reverend Colonel Finch.* New York: Columbia University Press, 1940.

Notes & Queries, 1st ser., 5 (1852): 402.

O'Byrne, William R. *A Naval Biographical Dictionary.* London: John Murray, 1849.
Opie, Amelia. "Memoir." In *Lectures on Painting,* by John Opie. London: Longman, Hurst, Rees and Orme, 1809.
Opie, Iona, and Peter Opie, eds. *The Oxford Dictionary of Nursery Rhymes.* Oxford: Clarendon Press, 1951.
Partridge, Eric. *A Dictionary of Slang and Unconventional English.* 7th ed. New York: Macmillan, 1970.
Patterson, A. Temple. *Hampshire and the Isle of Wight.* London: B. T. Batsford, 1976.
Pedigree of Gutch, Document Collection. Society of Genealogists, London.
Pepper, D. Stephen. *Guido Reni: A Complete Catalogue of His Works with an Introductory Text.* Oxford: Phaidon, 1984.
[Pepys, Samuel]. *Memoirs of Samuel Pepys.* Edited by Richard Lord Braybrooke. 2 vols. London: H. Colburn, 1825.
Percy, Thomas. "A Song. by T. P***cy." *A Collection of Poems. . . by several hands.* Vol. 6. London: R. and J. Dodsley, 1758.
[———, ed.] *Reliques of Ancient English Poetry.* 3 vols. London: J. Dodsley, 1765.
Pescio, Claudio. *Complete Guide for Visiting Pitti Palace.* Firenze: Il Turismo, 1981.
———. *Complete Guide for Visiting the Uffizi.* Firenze: Il Turismo, 1979.
Peterkin, Col. Alfred, and Col. William Johnson, comps. *Commissioned Officers in the Medical Services of the British Army, 1660–1960.* 2 vols. London: Wellcome Historical Medical Library, 1968.
Pettman, Mary, ed. *National Portrait Gallery: Complete Illustrated Catalogue, 1856–1979.* New York: St. Martin's Press, 1981.
Pignotti, Lorenzo. *Storia della Toscana sino al principato.* 12 vols. Firenze: Presso Gaetano Ducci, 1826.
Pinsseau, Pierre. *L'Étrange Destinée du Chevalier d'Éon (1728–1810).* 2nd ed. Paris: Raymond Clavreuil, 1945.
Piozzi, Hester Lynch (Thrale). *Anecdotes of the late Samuel Johnson, LL.D., during the last twenty years of his life.* London: T. Cadell, 1786.
———. *Observations and Reflections made in the course of a journey through France, Italy, and Germany.* 2 vols. London: A. Strahan and T. Cadell, 1789.
———. *Thraliana: The Diary of Mrs. Hester Lynch Thrale (Later Mrs. Piozzi), 1776–1809.* Edited by Katharine C. Balderston. 2nd ed. 2 vols. Oxford: Clarendon Press, 1951.
Pollock, John. *Wilberforce.* London: Constable, 1977.
Pope, Alexander. *The Poems of Alexander Pope.* Edited by John Butt. New Haven: Yale University Press, 1963.
Power, Sir d'Arcy, ed. *Plarr's Lives of the Fellows of the Royal College of Surgeons of England.* Rev. ed. 2 vols. Bristol: Royal College of Surgeons, 1930.
Prance, Claude A. *Companion to Charles Lamb: A Guide to People and Places, 1760–1847.* London: Mansell, 1983.
Price, F. G. Hilton. *A Handbook of London Bankers.* Rev. ed. London: Leadenhall Press, 1890–91.
Prior, Sir James. *Life of Edmond Malone.* London: Smith & Elder, 1860.
Raikes, Thomas. *A Portion of the Journal kept by Thomas Raikes, esq. from 1831 to 1847.* Rev. ed. 2 vols. London: Longman, Brown, Green, Longmans & Roberts, 1858.
[Raper, Frances]. *Laura Valcheret: a tale for adolescence.* London: Henry Colburn, 1814.

[———]. *Observations on Works of Fiction in General, and particularly those for Childhood and Adolescence.* London: Henry Colburn, 1813.

Ravenscroft, Edward. *"The Careless Lovers" and "The Canterbury Guests": A Critical Old-Spelling Edition.* Edited by Edmund S. Henry. New York: Garland, 1987.

Rees, Abraham, et al. *The Cyclopaedia; or, Universal Dictionary of Arts, Sciences, and Literature.* 39 vols. London: Longman, Hurst, Rees, Orme and Brown, 1802–19.

The Register at Buxton, TS. Transcribed by F. A. Forster and D. W. Woodheard. Society of Genealogists, London.

Rene-Martin, Linda. "Wilberforce's Sandgate Summers." *Country Life*, 29 May 1975, 1402–3.

"Retrospective Review." *Hiscoke's Richmond Notes* (March 1963): 4–7.

Richardson, Joanna. *George IV: A Portrait.* London: Sidgwick & Jackson, 1966.

Roberts, Henry D. *A History of the Royal Pavilion Brighton.* London: Country Life, 1939.

[Robinson, Henry Crabb]. *The Correspondence of Henry Crabb Robinson with the Wordsworth Circle (1808–1866).* Edited by Edith J. Morley. 2 vols. Oxford: Clarendon Press, 1927.

———. *Exposure of Misrepresentations contained in the preface to the Correspondence of William Wilberforce.* London: Edward Moxon, 1840.

[———]. *Henry Crabb Robinson on Books and Their Writers.* Edited by Edith J. Morley. 3 vols. London: J. M. Dent & Sons, 1938.

Robinson, Howard. *The British Post Office: A History.* Princeton: Princeton University Press, 1948.

Robinson, John Martin. *The Wyatts: An Architectural Dynasty.* Oxford: Oxford University Press, 1979.

Rooke, Col. H. W., comp. "Pedigree of the Descendants of Giles Rooke," *Genealogist*, NS 37 (January 1921). Reprint, Exeter: William Pollard, n.d.

Rossetti, William Michael. *Dante Gabriel Rossetti: His Family Letters.* 2 vols. London: Ellis and Elvey, 1895.

Royal Commission on Ancient and Historical Monuments in Wales. *Domestic Architecture from the Reformation to the Industrial Revolution.* Pt. 1: *The Greater Houses.* Vol. 4 of *An Inventory of the Ancient Monuments in Glamorgan.* Cardiff: HMSO, 1981.

Rumford, Benjamin, Count of. *Essays, Political, Economical, and Philosophical.* 4 vols. London: T. Cadell Jun. & W. Davies, 1796–1812.

Ryder, T. A. *Portrait of Gloucestershire.* London: Robert Hale, 1966.

Sadleir, Michael. *Nineteenth-Century Fiction: A Bibliographic Record Based on His Own Collection.* 2 vols. London: Constable, 1951.

Safarik, Eduard A., and Giorgio Torselli. *La Galleria Doria Pamphilj a Roma.* Roma: Fratelli Palombi, 1982.

de Salis, Jean-R. *Sismondi, 1773–1842: La Vie et l'oeuvre d'un Cosmopolite Philosophe.* Paris: Librairie Ancienne, 1932.

Salzman, L. F., ed. *The Victoria History of the County of Sussex.* Vol. 3. London: University of London Institute of Historical Research, 1935.

[Santo-Domingo, Count J. H. de]. *Tablettes romaines; contenant des faits, des anecdotes et des observations sur les moeurs, les usages, les cérémonies, le gouvernement de Rome.* Paris: Chez les marchands de nouveautés, 1824.

Scholes, Percy A. *"God Save the King!": Its History and Its Romance.* London: Oxford University Press, 1942.

———. *God Save the Queen! The History and Romance of the World's First National Anthem.* London: Oxford University Press, 1954.

———. *The Life and Activities of Sir John Hawkins: Musician, Magistrate and Friend of Johnson.* London: Oxford University Press, 1953.

Scott, Hew. *Fasti Ecclesiae Scoticanae; The Succession of Ministers in the Church of Scotland from the Reformation.* 2nd ed. 7 vols. Edinburgh: Oliver and Boyd, 1915–28.

Scott, Sir Walter. *The Abbot.* London: J. M. Dent, 1969.

[———]. *The Antiquary.* 3 vols. Edinburgh: Constable, 1816.

———. *Guy Mannering; or, the Astrologer.* Edited by A. D. Innes. 1910. Reprint, Oxford: Clarendon Press, 1926.

———. *The Lord of the Isles; a Poem.* 3rd ed. Edinburgh: James Ballantyne, 1815.

Sergeant, Philip W. *The Burlesque Napoleon.* London: T. Werner Laurie, 1905.

Sévigné, Marie, marquise de. *Correspondance.* Edited by Roger Duchêne. 3 vols. Paris: Gallimard, 1972–78.

Shakespeare, William. *The Complete Works.* Edited by Stanley Wells and Gary Taylor. Oxford: Clarendon Press, 1986.

[Shelley, Mary (Wollstonecraft)]. *The Journals of Mary Shelley, 1814–1844.* Edited by Paula R. Feldman and Diana Scott-Kilvert. 2 vols. Oxford: Clarendon Press, 1987.

[———]. *The Letters of Mary Wollstonecraft Shelley.* Edited by Betty T. Bennett. 3 vols. Baltimore: Johns Hopkins University Press, 1980–88.

Sherbo, Arthur. *Christopher Smart: Scholar of the University.* East Lansing: Michigan State University Press, 1967.

Sherwig, John M. *Guineas and Gunpowder: British Foreign Aid in the Wars with France, 1793–1815.* Cambridge, Mass.: Harvard University Press, 1969.

Shorter, Alfred H. *Paper Mills and Paper Makers in England, 1495–1800.* Hilversum, Holland: Paper Publications Society, 1957.

Sidney, Sir Philip. *Arcadia.* 2 vols. London, 1598. Reprint, Delmar, N.Y.: Scholars' Facsimiles & Reprints, 1983–84.

Simmons, Jack. *Southey.* London: Collins, 1945.

Simpson, D. H. *The Twickenham of Laetitia Hawkins, 1760–1835.* Twickenham: Twickenham Local History Society, 1978.

Smith, Brian S. *A History of Malvern.* Gloucester: Alan Sutton & the Malvern Bookshop, 1978.

Smith, Henry Stooks. *The Parliaments of England from 1715 to 1847.* Edited by F. W. S. Craig. 2nd ed. Chichester: Political Reference Publications, 1973.

South, Robert. *Twelve Sermons Preached upon Several Occasions.* 5th ed. Vols. 1 and 2. London: Jonah Bowyer, 1722.

[Southey, Robert]. *The Correspondence of Robert Southey with Caroline Bowles.* Edited by Edward Dowden. London: Longmans, Green, 1881.

———. *The Poetical Works of Robert Southey.* 10 vols. London: Longman, Orme, Brown, Green, & Longmans, 1838.

Southgate, Donald. *The Passing of the Whigs, 1832–1886.* London: Macmillan, 1962.

[Souza-Botelho, Adélaïde-Marie-Émilie, comtesse de Flahaut, later marquise de]. *Eugénie et Mathilde, ou Mémoires de la famille du comte de Revel.* 3 vols. London: L. Deconchy, 1811.

Spiller, Robert E. *Fenimore Cooper: Critic of His Times.* New York: Minton, Balch, 1931.

Staël-Holstein, Anne-Louise-Germaine, baronne de. *Corinne ou l'Italie.* 3 vols. Londres: M. Peltier, 1807.

———. *De l'Allemagne.* Edited by Simone Balayé. 2 vols. Paris: Garnier-Flammarion, 1968.

———. *Zulma, et trois nouvelles.* London: Colburn, 1813.

Staff, Frank. *The Penny Post, 1680–1918.* London: Lutterworth Press, 1964.

Stanley, Arthur Penrhyn. *Historical Memorials of Westminster Abbey.* London: John Murray, 1868.

Stapylton, H. E. C. *The Eton School Lists from 1791 to 1877.* Eton: R. Ingalton Drake, 1885.

St. Clair, William. *Lord Elgin and the Marbles.* London: Oxford University Press, 1967.

Super, R. H. *Walter Savage Landor: A Biography.* New York: New York University Press, 1954.

Talfourd, Thomas Noon. *The Letters of Charles Lamb, with a Sketch of his Life.* 2 vols. London: Edward Moxon, 1837.

Tasso, Torquato. *Aminta.* Edited by Bruno Maier. Milano: Biblioteca Universale Rizzoli, 1976.

Taylor, A. J. *Conway Castle and Town Walls.* 1957. Reprint, London: HMSO, 1966.

Timbs, John. *Club Life of London.* 2 vols. London: Richard Bentley, 1866.

———. *Curiosities of London.* 2nd ed. London: Virtue, 1867.

Todd, Janet, ed. *A Dictionary of British and American Women Writers, 1660–1800.* Totowa, N.J.: Rowman & Allenheld, 1985.

Tomalin, Claire. *The Life and Death of Mary Wollstonecraft.* London: Wiedenfeld and Nicolson, 1974.

Tooke, John Horne. *ΕΠΕΑ ΠΤΕΡΟΕΝΤΑ, or the Diversions of Purley.* 2nd ed. 2 vols. 1798–1805. Reprint, Menston, England: Scolar Press, 1968.

Vanvitelli, Luigi, Jr. *Vita di Luigi Vanvitelli.* Napoletana: Società Editrice, 1975.

Vincent, E. R. P. "Robert Finch and Enrico Mayer." *Modern Language Review* 29 (1934): 150–55.

[Wade, John, ed.]. *The Extraordinary Black Book.* London: Effingham Wilson, 1831.

Waterfield, Gordon. *Layard of Nineveh.* London: John Murray, 1963.

Waterhouse, Ellis. *The Dictionary of British Eighteenth-Century Painters in Oils and Crayons.* Woodbridge, Suffolk: Antique Collectors' Club, 1981.

Watson, Eric R., ed. *The Trial of Thurtell and Hunt.* Edinburgh: William Hodge, 1920.

Watson, F. J. B. "Canova and the English." *Architectural Review* 122 (1957): 403–6.

Weinreb, Ben, and Christopher Hibbert, eds. *The London Encyclopaedia.* London: Macmillan, 1983.

[Westmorland, John Fane, 11th Earl of.] *Correspondence of Lord Burghersh afterwards Eleventh Earl of Westmorland, 1808–1840.* Edited by Rachel Weigall. London: John Murray, 1912.

Wheatley, Henry B. *London Past and Present: Its History, Associations, and Traditions.* 3 vols. London: John Murray, 1891.

White, Henry Adelbert. *Sir Walter Scott's Novels on the Stage.* New Haven: Yale University Press, 1927.

White, Newman Ivey. *Shelley.* 2 vols. 1940. Reprint, New York: Octagon Books, 1972.

Wilberforce, Robert Isaac, and Samuel Wilberforce. *The Life of William Wilberforce.* 5 vols. London: John Murray, 1838.

———. *The Life of William Wilberforce.* 2nd ed. 5 vols. London: John Murray, 1843.

———, eds. Preface to *The Correspondence of William Wilberforce.* 2 vols. London: John Murray, 1840.

[Williams, T. W., ed.]. *Lean's Collectanea.* 4 vols. Bristol: J. W. Arrowsmith, 1902–4.

Wilson, James Grant, and John Fiske, eds. *Appletons' Cyclopaedia of American Biography.* 7 vols. New York: D. Appleton, 1887–1900.

[Wordsworth, William, and Dorothy Wordsworth]. *The Letters of William and Dorothy Wordsworth.* 2nd ed. Edited by Alan G. Hill. Vols. 6 and 7. Oxford: Clarendon Press, 1982, 1988.

Wroth, Warwick. *The London Pleasure Gardens of the Eighteenth Century.* 1896. Reprint, London: Macmillan, 1979.

Young, Edward. *The Complete Works, Poetry and Prose.* Edited by James Nichols. 2 vols. London, 1854. Reprint, Hildesheim: Georg Olms Verlagsbuchhandlung, 1968.

Young, Col. G. F. *The Medici.* 3rd ed. 2 vols. 1912. Reprint, London: John Murray, 1930.

Ziegler, Philip. *King William IV.* London: Collins, 1971.

Index

This is an index to people and places appearing in the text and notes. Members of the British aristocracy are found under their family names with cross-references from titles. French and European aristocrats appear under the name or title by which they are best known. Women are indexed under the name by which they are known in these letters; if their marital status changes midway, they appear under the later name, with cross-references from earlier ones. Works of art or literature, whose titles are abbreviated, usually appear under the author, editor, composer, or artist. Letters written by SHB are listed by letter number, rather than page number, and appear in bold type.